# TAKING SPORT SERIOUSLY

D1429657

# TAKING SPORT SERIOUSLY
## Social Issues in Canadian Sport
### THIRD EDITION

**Edited by:**
## PETER DONNELLY
**University of Toronto**

**THOMPSON EDUCATIONAL PUBLISHING, INC.**
**Toronto, Ontario**

Copyright © 2011 Thompson Educational Publishing, Inc.

All rights reserved. No part of this publication may be reproduced or transmitted in any form or by any means (electronic or mechanical, including photocopy and recording), or stored in any information storage and retrieval system, without permission in writing from the publisher. Requests for permission to make copies of any part of the work should be directed to the publisher or, in the case of material reproduced here from elsewhere, to the original copyright holder. Care has been taken to trace ownership of copyright material contained in this text. The publisher welcomes any information that will enable it to rectify any erroneous reference or credit.

Information on how to obtain copies of this book is available at:

| | |
|---|---|
| Website: | http://www.thompsonbooks.com |
| E-mail: | publisher@thompsonbooks.com |
| Telephone: | (416) 766–2763 |
| Fax: | (416) 766–0398 |

**Library and Archives Canada Cataloguing in Publication**

Taking sport seriously : social issues in Canadian sport / edited by
Peter Donnelly. -- 3rd ed.

Includes bibliographical references.
ISBN 978-1-55077-206-7

1. Sports--Social aspects--Canada.  I. Donnelly, Peter

GV585.T34 2010          306.4'830971          C2010-906289-2


| | |
|---|---|
| Production Editor: | Katy Bartlett |
| Cover Design: | Tibor Choleva |
| Proofreaders: | Caley Baker and Nina Paris |
| Cover Illustration: | Terry Ananny |

**Photo Credits**: pg viii photo: Image Copyright Nicholas Moore, 2010 Used under license from Shutterstock, Inc. • pg 54 photo: ©iStockphoto.com/Joshua Hodge Photography • pg 91 photo: Image Copyright Don Tran, 2010 Used under license from Shutterstock, Inc. • pg 92 photo: Image Copyright Jeff Schultes, 2010 Used under license from Shutterstock, Inc. • pg 131 photo: ©iStockphoto.com/Brandon Laufenberg • pg 132 photo: Image Copyright Tomas Del Amo, 2010 Used under license from Shutterstock, Inc. • pg 184 photo: Image Copyright ronstik, 2010 Used under license from Shutterstock, Inc. • pg 215 photo: ©iStockphoto.com/creativedoxfoto • pg 216 photo: Image Copyright Foodpics, 2010 Used under license from Shutterstock, Inc. • pg 235 photo: ©iStockphoto.com/Stephan Levesque • pg 236 photo: Mtrommer/GetStock.com • pg 298 photo: ©iStockphoto.com/Christopher Futcher • pg 317 photo: ©iStockphoto.com/Andrew Penner • pg 318 photo: Image Copyright Lucian Coman, 2010 Used under license from Shutterstock, Inc. • pg 338 photo: Image Copyright kitti, 2010 Used under license from Shutterstock, Inc.

Every reasonable effort has been made to acquire permission for copyright materials used in this book and to acknowledge such permissions accurately. Any errors or omissions called to the publisher's attention will be corrected in future printings.

We acknowledge the support of the Government of Canada through the Book Publishing Industry Development Program for our publishing activities.

Printed in Canada. 1 2 3 4 5      14 13 12 11 10

# Table of Contents

# Foreword

This book calls on readers to "take sport seriously," not as a competitive enterprise, but as an object of study. Not only has sport become increasingly important in its own right—as evidenced in part by how many times in recent years sports news has found its way into the hard news sections of the media—but sport also has the capacity to provide insight into other aspects of society such as the economy, politics, education, the family, and attitudes towards violence and other forms of deviance. In turn, knowledge about those other aspects of society provides insight into our understanding of sport in Canadian society.

It is some ten years since the second edition of *Taking Sport Seriously* was published. During that time it has been used widely in Canada, both as a supplementary text for courses on sport in Canadian society and, in some cases, as a primary text.

So much has happened in Canadian sport in the last ten years that I have only kept one article from the second edition, the eponymous "Taking Sports Seriously" by Elliott Gorn and Michael Oriard. Thus, there are eighty-five new articles in this edition, all published since 2000.

This edition of the book has also been substantially reorganized. *Taking Sport Seriously* was always intended as a supplementary text, with readings that were meant to give Canadian cases and current examples at a time when most of the available textbooks used in Canada were written for students in the United States. However, since the last edition of *Taking Sport Seriously* was published there is now one edited textbook with chapters written by various Canadian authors, and one adaptation of the bestselling American textbook, *Sports in Society: Issues and Controversies* (written by Jay Coakley and adapted for use in Canada by me).

Since my adaptation of Coakley's book for Canada has become widely used, and a third edition is now in preparation, the intent of *Taking Sport Seriously* has changed from providing Canadian cases and current examples that support an American textbook, to actually providing specific supplementary examples and current material that support Canadian textbooks. (This does not preclude those who wish to continue to use *Taking Sport Seriously* as a stand-alone textbook.) This edition has been organized so that the sections, wherever possible, follow the same sequence as chapters in *Sports in Society*.

The organization of *Taking Sport Seriously* differs from *Sports in Society* in two ways. First, there are no sections in *Taking Sport Seriously* that correspond to the theory and history chapters in *Sports in Society*. Instead there is a section entitled "Disability and Sports" (Section 13), which reflects the growth of disability sport, the growth of scholarly interest in disability sport, and the increasing attention paid to disability sport throughout recent editions of *Sports in Society*. Otherwise, *Taking Sport Seriously* is organized in the same way as *Sports in Society*: it opens with an introductory section, followed by sections on socialization, children's sport, deviance, and violence. The section on violence in sports, with all of its connections to masculinity, provides a natural segue into the next three sections on social relations, beginning with gender and sexuality, and followed by race/ethnicity, and social class. The following four sections on social institutions and sport cover economy, media, politics, and education. The book concludes with the aforementioned section on disability and sports, followed by a section on the future and sports.

The book continues to take a critical approach to Canadian sport. Such critique acknowledges the significance of sport, and indicates that sport is being taken seriously. While there is much that is good about sport in Canada, there are also many problems ranging from the significant and increasing inequalities of opportunities to participate (as evidenced by the sharply declining rates of participation in sport) to the harassment, abuse, and excessive rates of injury experienced by some participants. Most of the authors and, I suspect, most of the readers of this book see enormous value in participation in sport, and take great delight in watching talented athletes perform to the best of their abilities. However, the authors refuse to see sport as a sacred cow; their critiques are not of sport itself, but of the evident problems in sport. Furthermore, their critiques are intended to help us to learn from the best practices and values in sport in order to make sport more accessible, less abusive, and more enjoyable for all.

I hope that readers of this edition will find it as useful as previous editions. While I continue to try to reflect Canada's regional diversity in the selected readings, I renew my call to readers to contact me if they come across, or write, interesting and insightful articles about sport in Canada that are published in non-academic sources in the Maritimes, Québec, the Prairies, the North, and Western Canada, as they may make useful additions to future editions of *Taking Sport Seriously*.

**References**

- Coakley, J. and P. Donnelly. 2009. *Sports in Society: Issues and Controversies* (2nd Canadian edition). Toronto: McGraw-Hill Ryerson.

## Acknowledgments

No project of this type is accomplished without a great deal of help. I would like to thank Keith Thompson for his continued faith in this book, and for his ongoing efforts to disseminate knowledge about sport and physical education in Canada. Various editors have worked on this edition, but Katy Bartlett's work in gaining permissions and helping to organize the work deserves special recognition. She managed to hold on almost long enough to put the project to bed before the birth of her daughter, Chloe. Thanks to all colleagues and friends who drew my attention to articles, many of which have been used; and especially to those who wrote original pieces and/or adapted their work for use here; and thanks to all of the authors who graciously gave permission for their work to be reprinted here. Finally, thanks again to my wife, Louise, whose forbearance once again in living with boxes and boxes of clippings is greatly appreciated.

# Section 1

## Significance of Sports

Elliott Gorn and Michael Oriard's "Taking Sports Seriously" is one of two articles in this collection that originate in the United States, and is the only carry-over from the second edition of *Taking Sport Seriously*. It was written some fifteen years ago, and the examples given are American and quite dated. However, the authors' argument in favour of a cultural studies approach to studying sport is still relevant, and critical cultural studies has now become the predominant approach in the academic study of sport.

Sport is also becoming increasingly recognized in the larger field of cultural studies in North America. Gorn and Oriard begin and end their article with reference to C. L. R. James, whose book *Beyond a Boundary* (1963) is widely considered to be a foundational text in the field of sport studies. James' comment, "What do they know of cricket who only cricket know?" is a powerful reminder of the relationship between sport and society, and the fact that it is impossible to fully understand sport without a deep knowledge of the social, political, historical, and geographical contexts in which it is being played. In other words, it is a profound statement about the significance of sport.

Critique is an acknowledgement that sport is significant, and that we are taking it seriously enough to want to reflect critically on practices in sport and consider how to improve them. The Declaration on Expectations for Fairness in Sport (also known as "The London Declaration") is included here because it provides a profound statement

of the values and significance of Canadian sport. The declaration was created by the Federal and Provincial/Territorial Sports Ministers at their meeting in London, Ontario, in August, 2001. The meeting was a part of the deliberations that led to the new Canadian Sport Policy (2002), and it includes important statements such as: "Governments are dedicated to providing *the opportunity for **all** Canadians*, whatever their location, their sex or gender or their level of ability or interest to experience the joy of sport and to share in its bounty" (emphasis added). It is worth comparing the set of expectations outlined in this document with your own current experience of Canadian sport. How many of these expectations have been enacted? If Ministers make these important statements, it is our responsibility to ensure that they follow through, that they provide the resources and legislation necessary to implement the Canadian Sport Policy and to realize the "expectations for fairness."

When sport studies scholars use a critical cultural studies approach they do not criticize "sport"—sport is far too nebulous and diverse for that. Rather, they criticize certain aspects of sport. Even "The London Declaration" provided a critique of aspects of sport; it was only necessary for the Ministers to outline the "expectations for fairness" because so many aspects of sport are "unfair." Thus, it is possible to criticize the institutions, structures, and ideologies around sport while still celebrating the hard work, dedication, and achievements of athletes. Varda Burstyn makes this point in "The

Politics of Globalization, Ideology, Gender, and Olympic Sport." She combines history, politics, the media, economics, class, gender, and theory in an introduction to the critical study of sport (using the Olympics as an example/case study).

This section ends with a thoughtful and disturbing article about Canadian sport by a scholar who has not previously focused on sport, Irvin Studin. "Excellence in Sport and Other Circuses" speaks some hard truths about professional and high performance sport in Canada (pointing out, for example, that there is only one legitimately Canadian senior professional sport league, the Canadian Football League, compared to six in Australia; and pointing to Canadian inadequacies in international sport). Studin grounds those critiques in Canadian history, geography, and Constitutional politics. The solutions he offers are also controversial, and provide rich material for discussion.

**Additional Suggested Readings and References**

- McFarlane, J. 2010. "Hockeyland." *The Walrus*, June.
- Black, S. 2007. "The Mirror and the Hammer." *Canadian Dimension*, November/December.
- Blatchford, C. 2004. "Hockey Reminds Us that Life Goes On." *The Globe and Mail*, December 31.
- Dennis, P. 2006. "War is Hell, Hockey is Not." *The Globe and Mail*, March 16.
- Dryden, K. 2004. "The Game of Our Lives: Reflections on Money, Fans and the Future of Sports." *Maisonneuve* 7.
- White, C. 2006. "You Win Some, You Lose Some." *The Globe and Mail*, September 9.

# 1. Taking Sports Seriously
## By Elliot J. Gorn and Michael Oriard

*Studying sport as a part of cultural studies*

■ ■ ■ ■ ■ ■

The West Indian scholar C. L. R. James's 1963 work, *Beyond a Boundary*, is a remarkable book of history and memory. It is about the game of cricket. More, it is about the West Indies, poverty, being black, and colonialism. Cricket is James's microscope, and through it he magnifies whole areas of life and thought. He presents cricket as both sport and metaphor, the property of colonizers and colonized, in which struggles over culture, power, hegemony, and resistance are played out. Many scholars consider *Beyond a Boundary* to be the most profound and moving book ever written about sports.

So we were greatly interested when we received a brochure for a conference at New York University last month entitled "Beyond the Boundary." The conference was held in conjunction with the Whitney Museum of American Art, whose show "Black Male: Representations of Masculinity in Contemporary American Art" had included some images of blacks engaged in sports. A conference on black masculinity, borrowing its title from James's book, looked promising for scholars in American studies who, like us, have tried to take the study of athletics seriously. Yet as we looked at the program more closely, we found that it did not include a single session or paper concerning sports.

Of course, scholars can choose to discuss whatever they want to. But how is it possible to understand American culture, particularly African-American culture, and ignore the role played by sports?

We see all around us team logos, images of athletes, and expensive clothing endorsed by famous athletes. Michael Jordan's is perhaps the most recognized face in the world, just as Muhammad Ali's was a generation ago. Nor is there a lack of experts who might participate in scholarly discussions of sports. Harry Edwards, a professor of sociology at Berkeley, opened up the academic study of blacks in sports twenty-five years ago. His chief concern was the exploitation of black athletes by the sports establishment. He has been succeeded by other distinguished writers—including Gerald Early, a literary scholar at Washington University, and Jeffrey Sammons, a historian at New York University—who have broadened the inquiry into many other aspects of the relationship between race and sports.

Despite the obvious importance of sports in American life, only a small number of American academics have made a specialty of analyzing the relationship between athletics and culture, and their work remains ghettoized. Historians, sociologists, psychologists, anthropologists, and even philosophers and literary scholars have established subspecialties on sports, but their work hovers at the margins of their disciplines.

Moreover, the booming field of cultural studies seems oblivious to the work done on athletics. This is ironic, because cultural studies—the interdisciplinary analysis of history, cultural expression, and power—is exactly where the study of sports is most needed. Where is there a cultural activity more freighted with constructions of masculinity than football, more deeply inscribed with race than boxing, more tied in the public mind to the hopes and hopelessness of inner-city youth than basketball? Gender, race, and power are central theoretical and methodological concerns of cultural studies.

Despite the continuing discussion in American studies of "the body" (of how human beings conceive of themselves physically), athletes' bodies remain curiously off limits. Yet power and eroticism meet most conspicuously in the athletic body—Florence Griffith-Joyner's, Greg Louganis's, or Michael Jordan's.

Is "the body" as conceived in cultural studies a rhetorical construction, while the bodies of athletes are too palpably real? Are we, as intellectuals, just uncomfortable with physicality, because our own bailiwick is the life of the mind? Could it be that professors are creatures of words while the language of athletics is fundamentally non-verbal? Or are we simply playing out the long-standing faculty antagonism to the distorted priorities of universities with multi-million-dollar athletics programs?

Furthermore, although critical scholarship about television's place in American life is an important part of cultural studies, amazingly little of that scholarship is concerned with televised sports. Yet the mass media have always depended on athletics to reach large audiences, from the invention of the sports pages in the first large-circulation metropolitan newspapers in the 1880s and 1890s, to the first World Series radio broadcasts in the early 1920s, to the baseball and football games and boxing matches telecast at the beginning of the television age. Today, international broadcasts via satellite, cable superstations, and pay-per-view television all thrive on sporting events. Sports have been the cash cow of the increasingly pervasive (some would say invasive) entertainment media.

In an age that (properly) embraces multiculturalism, athletics represent both our diversity and our common culture. It is almost a cliché to mention that sports are the lingua franca of men talking across divisions of class and race. Sports also reveal just how interdependent particular subcultures, and the larger consumer culture, can be. Think, for example, of the symbiotic ties between inner-city playground basketball and the National Basketball Association championships.

Sports keep bringing us back to the ever-shifting relationship between commercialized mass culture (the Olympics come immediately to mind) and subcultures of difference (the Gay Games, for example).

Sports also are clearly about gender, although, until recently, this often has been overlooked. Certainly athletics have shaped American masculinity. One hundred years ago, in an essay called "The American Boy," Theodore Roosevelt, exhorted young men to follow the same principles:

in life as in football: "Hit the line hard; don't foul and don't shirk, but hit the line hard."

For women, organized sports became available as feminism grew and they gained access to higher education and other areas from which they had previously been excluded. Even as Roosevelt wrote his essay, women at Vassar, Smith, Mount Holyoke, and Wellesley Colleges were playing baseball—not softball, baseball. By the turn of the century, a particularly aggressive form of basketball had become a source of pride and passion at women's colleges and on countless playgrounds. We are just beginning to ask what such facts say about definitions of feminism and femininity.

The general banishment of sports from cultural studies is not merely an omission of an important expressive form; leaving out sports distorts our view of culture. Sports present unique challenges to theories about cultural power and personal freedom, which cultural-studies scholars discuss using such categories as "representation," "commodification," "hegemony," and "subversion." One of the challenges is that sports differ from movies, novels, music, and television shows, all of which scholars view as wholly "constructed." Sports, however, are essentially "unscripted." They are real contests, in which many people have participated, at least at an amateur level.

This makes sports different from the other forms of entertainment, which are packaged by their creators. Knowledgeable fans can understand the games on their own terms and ignore the silly prattle of the "colour" commentators. Baseball officials cannot script a "Cinderella season" on demand. What sports "means" to their vast audiences cannot be ordained by either owners or media pundits.

The great virtue of cultural studies has been to take seriously the idea of "otherness," a concept that, in part, relates to how a group defines itself by the images that it creates of outsiders. But otherness is a slippery term. To many scholars—whose values are cosmopolitan, whose politics are progressive, and whose incomes are upper middle class—the "other" is not necessarily the same as for most Americans. Young, verbally dexterous, and entrepreneurial rappers—modern-day rebels against a narrow-minded and prissy culture—may be far less alien to hip, young intellectuals than the gifted and disciplined athlete. "Otherness," for scholars, may reside even more in the polyester-clad fan who drinks with his buddies and roots for the home team, or in the middle-aged woman out bowling in her weekly league game. What, in the eyes of many in the academy, could be more unhip, uncool, "other" than American working-class pleasures?

Some scholars have suggested that, after Martin Luther King, Jr., Jackie Robinson may well have been the most influential black American of the past fifty years. Not everyone would agree with this proposition, but it is plausible, and it speaks volumes about American culture that the artistry, grace, fierce will, and embattled restraint of a baseball player could become a symbol of courage and strength to so many people. There is no getting around it: For African-Americans, sports have been a fount of creativity, of art, of genius. Sports have also been a source of respect for black Americans among people of all races. Any list of the most culturally influential African-Americans of the twentieth century would have to include Robinson, as well as Jesse Owens, Joe Louis, Jack Johnson, Wilma Rudolph, and Muhammad Ali.

C. L .R. James was so convinced of the importance of sports that he declared cricket and soccer to be "the greatest cultural influences in nineteenth-century Britain." Although a bit hyperbolic, James's point is well taken. That athletics have remained so far beyond the boundary of most intellectual discourse is beyond belief. As James so brilliantly demonstrated, the study of sport can take us to the very heart of critical issues in the study of culture and society.

◄◄ **Source:** Elliot J. Gorn is a professor of history and American studies at Miami University, Ohio. Michael Oriard is professor of English at Oregon State University. This article was originally published in *The Chronicle of Higher Education*, March 24, 1995. A32. Reproduced with permission.

## Expectations for Fairness in Sport

### A Declaration Enacted by the Federal-Provincial/Territorial Sport Ministers—August 10, 2001

**2.**

### Preamble

Whereas sport enriches the lives of Canadians in a multitude of ways: in their roles as participants, spectators, coaches, and volunteers;

And Whereas, sport offers opportunities for the personal, moral, and value-centred development of children and young people;

And Whereas, ethically-based and safe sport promote an active lifestyle, self-esteem, healthy bodies, lifelong learning, and strong team spirit;

And Whereas, sport is an arena for the development and realization of human excellence;

And Whereas, sport helps to build a civil society by forging healthy and cooperative communities;

Now therefore, the Canadian Ministers of Sport, meeting at their 2001 Conference, August 10, 2001 in London, Ontario, in conjunction with the eighteenth Canada Summer Games, agree to place new emphasis on reinforcing the ethical foundation of sport in Canada by recognizing the following fundamental ethical principles as applicable to Canadian sport:

### Sport is history ...

Sport in Canada is a vital part of history, reflecting a proud tradition of athletic achievements.

### Sport is experience ...

Sport is encountered in a variety of ways, as athletes, coaches, officials, parents and supporters, volunteers, leaders, scientists, medical personnel, sponsors, artists, media, fans, sponsors, and as spectators. Encounters in and through sport enrich lives and the wide variety of sporting traditions flavour the experience of Canadians.

### Sport is for fun ...

At the very heart of sport is a commitment to fun. Sport can bring joy, it can make the spirit soar, and it can enrich lives. Governments are dedicated to providing the opportunity for all Canadians, whatever their location, their sex or gender, or their level of ability or interest to experience the joy of sport and to share in its bounty.

### Sport is for character ...

But sport is also more than just fun. Sport tests and builds character; sport allows the opportunity for children and young people to build the values of teamwork, dedication, and commitment.

Sport requires honesty and fair play. Sport builds courage, testing the willingness to try, to fail, and to try again. Governments are pledged to creating a sport environment untainted by cheating, violence, and other unethical practices. Their goal is a sport environment that allows children and young people to develop as athletes, as people, and as citizens and to pursue their commitment throughout their life.

### Sport is for health ...

Sports are physical and mental games. Sports build healthy bodies as well as good character. Frequent, high-quality physical activity through sport leaves a legacy of health that can last a lifetime. Governments are committed to ensuring safe conditions for the practice of sport and to promoting physical and mental health through sport.

### Sport is for excellence ...

Sport is one of the areas of human activity that allows the quest for excellence. Great sport performances enrich and expand our humanity, pushing beyond the every day, to open new horizons and new ways of experiencing the human condition. But truly excellent sport must be fair sport to be celebrated and supported.

## Sport is for community ...

Sport builds communities. In every corner of this country young people, their parents and coaches, volunteers, sponsors, and supporters are brought together by sport. Sport builds communities as people come together for sport on the fields, on the diamonds, inside the arenas, to leave as more than neighbours, but also as friends. Governments are committed to enriching our neighbourhoods, and developing civil society through sport.

In furtherance of these principles, the ministers agree to advance them through the engagement of all stakeholders in sport in a concerted and coordinated series of actions.

And further, the ministers acknowledge that it is important to reflect these principles in the behaviour of all the participants in sport in accordance with some common, shared norms of conduct. To achieve this goal, the ministers agree to issue this declaration, which articulates a set of expectations for fairness in sport, and to urge all stakeholders in sport to take all necessary steps to ensure that these expectations are satisfied.

And further, the ministers agree to make this declaration widely known and to direct their officials to design, in consultation with the sport community, the terms of reference for a process that will lead to the development and implementation of a Canadian Strategy on Ethical Conduct in Sport.

## Expectations for Fairness in Sport

■■■■■■

The Federal and Provincial/Territorial Sport Ministers believe that Canadians share a vision that ethics and ethical behaviour are integral to sport. The ministers endorse this vision, which requires that:

### Principle

1. There be a firm and public commitment to the principle that lasting and meaningful athletic performance can only be achieved through fair means.

### Participants

2. Participants in sport and physical activity will do so in a manner that adheres to the highest ethical principles.

### Reciprocity

3. Those who participate in sport will receive from their fellow athletes, coaches and officials, and parents/guardians, and spectators, fairness and ethical treatment in a safe and welcoming sport environment, free of harassment and abuse.

### Barriers

4. Their sport system will help to advance the widest array of athletic goals of all participants, with or without disability, without discrimination and in spite of barriers based on personal circumstances.

### Spectators

5. Spectators to sport events can witness the activities without being subjected to abuse, interference, or violence from others.

### Coaches

6. Coaches will be appropriately valued by their athletes, and their athletes' parents/guardians and supporters, that they will receive fair treatment and respect for their valuable contribution to sport, and that they will be free of harassment and threats of violence under any circumstance.

### Officials

7. Sport officials will not be interfered with in the execution of their duties and will be respected for their decisions by athletes, coaches, parents/guardians, and spectators.

### Volunteers

8. Sport volunteers will be respected and recognized for their efforts to make sport participation possible and rewarding for athletes of all ages.

### Parents/Guardians

9. Parents/guardians are assured that their children participating in sport will receive fair treatment from coaches, volunteers, and spectators.

### Dispute Resolution

10. The sport system will provide just treatment in cases of disputes in sport and that there are proper and accessible mechanisms that are available in a timely manner to resolve disputed issues through due process.

### Behaviour

11. Athletes, coaches, and team officials representing Canada in the international sport arena will conduct themselves, in both victory and defeat, in a manner that brings pride to all.

### Transparency

12. Sport organizations in receipt of public funding, will be fully accountable for the use of such resources and will be transparent and democratic in their organizational life.

**◄◄ Source:** Expectations for Fairness in Sport, http://pch.gc.ca/ pgm/sc/pubs/london-eng.cfm, Canadian Heritage, 2001. Reproduced with the permission of the Minister of Public Works and Government Services Canada, 2010. This declaration was enacted by the Federal-Provincial/Territorial Sport Ministers at their 2001 Conference, August 10, 2001 in London, Ontario.

# The Politics of Globalization, Ideology, Gender, and Olympic Sport
## By Varda Burstyn

**3.**

## ■■■ Introduction

To contextualize the perspectives through which Olympic sport may be regarded, it is important to consider academic venues and those outside the academy such as radio, magazines, periodicals, film, or government and public interest organizations. What these have in common is that each is a site where bodies and politics meet—a site of "biopower," in the term coined by Michel Foucault. Thus, in science and medicine, one might consider artificially assisted reproduction, genetics, biotechnology, and population health; in art and culture, pornography and the cultural and political treatment of gender and sexuality come to mind. Indeed, such facets of biopower have been under-analyzed and underestimated in the study, if not the practice, of politics.

Scholars share interests in understanding the myriad ways that sport directly and indirectly shapes personal experiences, gender styles, and gender arrangements. But studies should also consider how the culture of sport affects other political choices as well, notably in economic paradigms, state formation, and public policy, and to what extent sport culture can be described as a political agent in its own right. Because the Olympics are such an important part of the culture of sport, and because, of all the various sports associations and sport subcultures, the Olympic movement and the IOC Games have most frequently been politicized at the level of the nation-state and contending political ideologies, they are an important subject of observation for one with such interests, particularly since the 1960s.

Even after considering the politics of the Olympic Games, one must still be moved and impressed by the performances of individual athletes—their struggles and their achievements. However, this is not to lend support to the Olympic structure of sport, or the economies, culture, and values it represents and promotes. One may be critical of the IOC Games for many reasons, only a few of which will be explored in this paper. In particular, this paper reflects on the question of the politicization of the Olympics first by nation-states, then by transnational corporations; and on the ideological implications of their thorough-going commercialization. These developments in the economic order will then be linked to developments in the gender order—via sport—to address some important questions of political ideology and philosophy.

## ■ ■ ■ Background

Today, the Olympics are a powerful sector within the larger sport nexus. By "sport nexus" I mean the constellation of institutions built around the sport-media complex, but extending out to form a part of the transnational industrial corporate economy, governments, and the institutions of civil society (notably educational and recreational systems). From a political/ideological point of view, one may identity four important stages to the evolution of the IOC Games, and to their relationship to politics on the one hand, and the evolving sport nexus on the other:

- The foundation years (1896–1914), when the basic structures and credos of Pierre de Coubertin's IOC were established, and supporters in various nation states were recruited

- The inter-war years (1918–1939) when the educational and cultural goals of de Coubertin and amateur sport flourished alongside substantial, distinct working class and women's Olympic movements

- The integrationist cold-war period (1945–1980) when nation-states and empires, both American and Soviet, appropriated the symbolic value of the Olympics and Olympic athletics

- The corporate period (1980 to the present), when the corporate culture appropriated the symbolic value of nationalism via Olympic sport

In the first two periods of IOC history, the de Coubertin Games were for and about the international elite—that is, the elites of nation-states. Though rhetorically about brotherhood and a meritocratic democracy, in reality, their organization excluded working-class and women athletes. Working-class people early in the twentieth century in Europe were more likely to be part of sport associations that were linked to trade unions and socialist parties (social democratic and communist), and to focus their attention on their international contests—also Olympiads. Kidd reports that participation in working-class sports associations included large numbers of working men and—far ahead of the de Coubertin Games—women as well. In worker's games in Vienna in 1931, there were over seventy-five thousand participants, of whom roughly twenty-five thousand were women.[2] Between 1920 and 1936, socialist and communist organizations conducted four international sets of Olympic games, before southern and central European fascism swept them away. French, British, and American women athletes of the affluent classes organized a series of women's Olympics in the 1920s and 1930s as a form of pressure on the IOC to include women's events—which it eventually did.[3]

The philosophical differences guiding the IOC, worker's, and women's "Olympic" practices were rooted in the respective values of those who sponsored them. Broadly speaking, the ideals of both workers and women's sports associations and their practices were more inclusive, egalitarian, and participatory than those of the record-driven de Coubertin Games. But the 1930s was a bad decade for women's organizing and for socialism. Feminism was in deep decline, and the Women's Olympics floundered. The socialist sport movement was annihilated in the 1930s and 1940s first through the rise of fascism and the armed suppression of left-wing political culture, then through World War II, then through the triumph of Stalinist bureaucratization in the Soviet Union. The Soviet state joined the IOC after the war, and made its stunning debut in Helsinki in 1952, where the Cold War in sport was launched.

From then until 1990, the Olympic Games were intensely politicized—and their performances intensified in the name of politics—at numerous levels, thanks to how both Soviet and Western regimes understood the ideological role of sport: as an exemplar of the virtues of socio-economic systems and as a point of unification for the disaffected within those systems. The rise of Third World anti-colonial struggles and nation-building, and the growth, in both North America and Europe, of feminism and movements for minority rights, were also expressed in myriad struggles on the Olympic stage. In Mexico in 1968, violent demonstrations surrounded the Games, and black American athletes used the podium for a dissident political statement—the Black Power salute. In 1972, the Palestinian terrorist group Black September massacred Israeli athletes and were in turn massacred by German authorities. In 1976, the city of Montreal was an armed camp, and the Games served the police as a pretext to harass and disperse a number of leading Québecois political figures.

However, in the last fifteen years, as a result of the collapse of the Soviet Union and Eastern European Communist Party regimes, the rise of globalization and neo-liberalism in the 1980s and 1990s, and the complete corporate commercialization and symbolic appropriation of Olympism, the Olympics became purely a showcase for the ideology of transnational capitalism. In 1992, in Barcelona, Nelson Mandela appeared, and used the Games to signal the emergence of the new South Africa. But since then, in terms of ideological contestation, all has been quiet on the Olympic front. Today, a different kind of politics reigns.

Early in the development of the sport nexus, associations between professional teams and entrepreneurial capitalists—stadium owners, team owners, etc.—established a commercial valence to professional sport. With early associations between sports entrepreneurs and local politicians, such teams took on strong civic meanings and identifications, but not national and international ones. The Olympics, however, held out a space that was relatively free of commercialization for a long time (until the late 1960s), and purported to support a different model of sport—"amateur" sport—in which the intrinsic benefits of athleticism were approvingly meant to outweigh the instrumental values of commercialization. Commercial values were seen to skew the athletic experience for athletes themselves, to unbalance the ideal of active physicality as part of a full life. Whatever the hypocrisies of this ideal—and they were legion—among the IOC and national Olympic organizations, at the level of athletic clubs and popular perception, it spoke to a recognition of the prerequisites for well-being, and was identified with in positive ways. This charismatic wholesomeness, combined with the fraternal rhetoric and international nature of the IOC project itself, made Olympic athletics much more open to overt political usage (identification) on the national and international levels.

## ■■■ The Corporate Takeover

If cold war competition, anti-colonial, and anti-racist struggles marched across the Olympic stage from the 1950s to the 1980s in the 1990s we have witnessed the full appropriation of patriotism and national sentiment by the transnational corporate order via sport, particularly the Olympics, thanks to the qualitative new relationships of corporate capitalism to Olympic athletes and athletics. Prior to the mid-1970s the relationship of the commercial sector to Olympic sport was still basically patronage at arm's length—if not in terms of stadium construction and international sponsorships, then at least at the level of local clubs and associations.

In the 1960s, when athletes competed at track and field meets, they won watches and silver cups. If they were lucky, they might also receive some free shoes and blankets from Adidas or Puma, the two leading shoe manufacturers of the time.

But all that started to change in the 1970s. By then, Western governments had convinced themselves that competing at the Olympic Games was important to international status. Through government subsidies (in Canada and Europe) and through a system of sports scholarships (in the United States), a cadre of highly trained but impoverished athletes was developed, competing in the name of their respective nation-states. At the same time, in keeping with their expansive relationships with teams sports and the sport media in the 1970s and 1980s, a number of major corporations turned to Olympic sport and began to demand measurable returns for the funds they directed toward it. Once philanthropic patrons looking for prestige or moral credit, now they became investors who were seeking "value" (profits), and they began to shape sport more directly for their own purposes.

The endorsement contract between an athlete and a firm whose product he or she would promote was a central pillar of the commercial turn by media and sponsors to Olympic sport. This athlete had long been economically vulnerable, exceedingly hard working, and thoroughly fixated on his or her goal. However, with the death of amateurism, by the 1980s if he or she became the one-in-a-hundred who would succeed in getting a major corporate sponsorship, he or (less often) she could now become a millionaire.[4] In exchange, the corporation—Adidas, or Coca-Cola, or Kodak, or Visa—could further extend its marketing reach. To enhance the spectacle that made this contract so lucrative, sponsors sought alliances with the IOC and National Olympic Committees on the one hand, and the mass media on the other. The introduction of media capital into the Olympic pot was so large during the 1980s and 1990s that it conferred virtual shareholder status on the major networks involved.[5] NBC's late 1995 deal of $2.3 billion for Olympic coverage until 2008 makes it as important a player in the Olympic economy as any other single player, and much more important than most. It also places all NBC journalists in the role of publicists, not reporters. *Sports Illustrated*, who paid $40 million to sponsor the Atlanta Games, placed its writers in the same structural position.

The most important function of sport from the point of view of investing broadcasters and advertisers is audience creation. The ability to bring together young and adult males of means— the prime advertising audience, and what might be referred to as 'the masculinity market'— makes sports outstanding programming, and the Olympics the number one sponsorship event on the planet. This status is the result of strategies pursued since the 1970s by the IOC, and more recently under the pro-corporate leadership of Juan Antonio Samaranch. Today, the contemporary Olympic constellation within the sport nexus as a whole comprises a full range of mature transnational capitalisms, fully engaged in, and committed to the spectacle of elite sport.

The Los Angeles Olympics in 1984 marked a new stage in the corporate metamorphosis of the Olympics that had begun, sub rosa, in the 1960s and 1970s.[6] These were the first full-fledged corporate Games, and they demonstrated a new, brassy, wide-open role, no longer covert, for corporate capitalism right at their physical heart. Before 1984, no one would ever have dreamed of suggesting a Mars Bar Olympic pool, or that training facilities should be supported by, and named for, McDonald's. In the old code of amateurism, such hybrids would have been abominable. But the L.A. Games came to be known as the 'McLympics' because they brought these new associations out in the open, and put the corporations, along with the IOC, in the Olympic driver's seat.

By 1992 in Barcelona, despite that city's anarcho-syndicalist traditions and Mandela's appearance, the integration of national Olympic and commercial forms had proceeded even further.[7] It was evident in the Barcelona Bausch and Lomb

Olympic Village and the American Visa Relay Team.[8] Where the nation-state had been the dominant term of Olympic competition in the past, represented by the Olympic athlete, now the corporation achieved equal representational status. One Coca-Cola commercial featured a blond, handsome, Slavic athlete who leaves behind his (undisclosed) war-torn totalitarian backwater and treks over mountains and valleys, seeking and finally reaching the democratic metropolis of Barcelona. The city, the West, the Olympic Games, and the bottle of Coke are all visually associated, and his reverent voice-over speaks of the "freedom" he has found.[9]

Speaking of Nike endorser Michael Jordan's refusal to wear a U.S. team uniform at the Games, Frank Deford wrote that "Jordan essentially chose Nike over country, publicly protesting having to wear the U.S. Olympic uniform just because it was made by the evil Reebokian Empire."[10] In this case in Barcelona, the corporation's importance surpassed that of the nation-state within the Olympic framework. In early September 1998, television commercials were broadcast for an event taking place in Morocco, called 'The Eco-challenge.' This international event appeared to combine Olympic and extreme sports. With slogans such as Team AT&T Canada, once again the hype was patriotic and athletic, and collapsed the national into the corporate. (We also see an example of how corporate propaganda neutralizes dissent by seizing oppositional and transformative notions—in this case 'ecology'—to promote their opposites. There was nothing ecological about this sport event, as the visuals of spandex-covered individuals hammering spikes into desert cliffs and ascending en mass make clear in an instant. This event is a challenge to the ecology not a challenge to be ecological—but the verbal signage confuses this fundamental fact.)

The intimate association between athletes and the products they advertise, sought by corporate advertisers in the service of merging commercial and national themes, has been expressed in a style of television advertising that has virtually swallowed up the athletics. This style intercuts sporting events with sponsored messages that mimic the "look" of sport actuality. The seams between sport "verité" and "advertising," already tight in the 1970s simply disappeared in the 1980s and 1990s. In the summer of 1996, leading up to the Atlanta Games, *Time* magazine ran a promotional advertising series of photographic essays by well-known sport photographer Bud Greenspan, that were virtually indistinguishable from the "journalism" surrounding them. This new visual conflation expressed a new economic association—one in which corporate sponsors have become the real paymasters of Olympism.

As actors who represented overt political agendas disappear from the Olympic stage, those who represent the pure ideology of the corporate order step forward. Today Olympic sport is a celebration of competition itself, and its accomplice, winning. The dramas of Atlanta and Nagano were all personal—either individual rivalries (Donovan Bailey and Michael Johnson, Tara Lipinski and Oksana Baiul) and/or athletes' struggles with injuries (Kerri Strug, Elvis Stojko). Televised, these dramas were relentlessly intercut with personal portraits, and with commercials that combined the close-ups of the portraits with the athletic footage of the events. The Russian and Eastern European athletes told of abandoning their countries for the United States, to make more money. Everyone who was anyone was sponsored by an equipment, or finance, or juice company, or all three.

With the riches of the performance contract, however, came a series of terrible pressures on athletes in Olympic sport—pressures that truly subverted many of the positive goals for which the Olympics had stood. The best known of these is probably the pressure to employ harmful performance-enhancing drugs. The media make disapproving sounds whenever some poor athlete is caught, and usually that is the end of the matter. (The one notable exception being the long, traumatic inquiry after Ben Johnson's 1988 performance in Seoul).[11] Periodically studies are released by academics and *Sports Illustrated* claiming the problem has worsened, but declaring it unstoppable for scientific and economic reasons. This basic indifference is a clear sign that the use of such substances is not a problem that will be addressed seriously or systematically within Olympic and other professional sport. The athletes are punished while the real guilty parties go free and the systemic causes remain in place.

What is perhaps worse than the shameful periodic scapegoating of individual athletes is that we never debate publicly the values that drive this abusive drug culture. These values are embedded in the zero-sum contests glamourized in IOC Olympism. The message is that only winners who win gold count—to the marketing departments of the sponsoring corporations. In the contemporary Olympic economy, and in its discourse, two values dominate. Capitalist competition is evident, though incorrectly valued. The other—masculinism—is still largely invisible, but equally powerful from an ideological perspective.

## ■ ■ ■ Winners and Losers: Neo-Liberalism and the Ideology of Competition

The rise of neo-liberal economics and neo-conservative politics in many of the most important industrial countries, and the transnational corporatization of the Olympics, have gone hand in hand. From Britain's Margaret Thatcher (ideologue and trailblazer), through the United State's Ronald Reagan, to our very own Brian Mulroney, generally large 'C' Conservatives first implemented the domestic and international fiscal and state policies demanded by neo-liberal economics. Hence, especially in the United States, but also in Canada and the United Kingdom, these policies were often cloaked in a neo-conservative rhetoric that invoked the sanctity of the individual and the traditional, father-headed family. Rhetoric aside, the objective import of these policies can

now be measured. Judged by what has been accomplished, these policies have effected:

- The transfer of wealth from the less affluent to the more affluent: economic stratification has concentrated wealth into ever fewer hands, in all countries where such policies have obtained[12]

- The erosion of the powers of the nation-state and its ability to regulate ("set barriers") to transnational capital

Both these objectives have been pursued through similar strategies: divesting and privatizing public resources, enterprises and services; expanding the coercive apparatus of the state (prisons, police, military); restricting representative forums (through private concentration of the mass media); and divesting the state of key regulatory functions—including with respect to labour and employment, the environment, health, and education—that have to do, directly and indirectly, with restrictions on the flow of private capital.

The idea of competitiveness (accompanied by "higher productivity" and "belt-tightening") has been at the core of neo-liberal politics, the rhetorical raison d'être of its policies, the holy grail that, once attained, will somehow magically grant a return to former wealth. In reality, in its name, living standards have fallen for the majority of people, mass unemployment has taken place, degradation of the environment has been hastened, and the gains of thirty years of feminism and environmentalism, and many more decades of trade unionism have been eroded. The transnational corporate order has sought to naturalize the idea that the unregulated market is all, and that competition is its life blood. If enough people accept this idea, it will be possible to continue dissolving all of the constraints on private capital represented by national, social, and environmental state functions, laws, and structures brought into being by prosocial movements in the past. This is the process at the centre of what is referred to as "globalization."

Sport plays a central role, if not the central role, in modeling and celebrating competitiveness in our culture. Sport is where competition is celebrated for its own sake, where the ideology of winners and losers is ritually confirmed and spectacularly celebrated. Sports' heroic idols no longer aspire to be like Muhammad Ali or John Carlos, but to follow in the footsteps of Charles Barkely or Michael Jordan. Jordan gets more in advertising fees than the combined payroll of Nike's southeast Asian factory workers making "his" shoes—about $30 million dollars. With the super-rich, corporate-promoting athlete as a model for the black underclass, for other minorities that identify with U.S. blacks, and for young boys in general, there is little need to worry about dissent, let alone revolution. No-one working to be like Jordan is going to rock the political boat. (Jordan declined to support a progressive black candidate running against Senator Jesse Helms because, in his words, "Republicans wear shoes too.") Since its commercialization, Olympic sport now joins with other professional sports in creating compliance among young athletes in sustaining a system in which only a fraction of them can win. Those who do become iconic, thanks to sports journalism, advertising, and celebrity culture. They embody and symbolize the competitive and ultimately elitist performance principle of capitalism throughout the culture.

Contemporary sport is a sacrificial system and, like our socio-economic system, it sacrifices the many for the few. In addition, it sacrifices the bodies of successful athletes for the spectacle itself. The acceptance of sacrificial ideology as a core belief—though it is never named as such—is part of the ideology of competitiveness, for the reflex to demand why such sacrifices are necessary and to develop alternatives is effectively suppressed. At the same time, its heroics are mobilized to promote consumerism as a way of life that must be pursued, defended, and extended, even as the global environmental crisis shows us that it is a doomed socio-economic order.[13] In this sense,

the commercialization of sport has a (de)politicizing effect on professional athletes, and on those who identify with them—it encourages them to accommodate themselves to present socio-economic arrangements.

To note the obvious, perhaps, movements such as neo-liberalism and neo-conservatism tend to support cultural practices that promote the values inherent in their economic and political enterprises. They will gravitate to cultural practices that partake of, and symbolize, competition and domination, and emphasize active consumerism and passive citizenship. Neo-liberals and neo-cons love sport. Secular neo-liberals are extremely enthusiastic about sport: Bush, Reagan, Ford, and Nixon, to name the last four Republican presidents, were football crazy. But John F. Kennedy was an enthusiast, and Bill Clinton is a fan too. Sport has become the leading trope used in the discourses of patriotism, aggressive business practice, sexual performance, and war. Indeed, to further explore this, it is necessary to shift focus from the structures and ideologies of corporate capitalism in relation to sport and politics, to those of patriarchy or, preferably, masculinism.

## ■ ■ ■ Sport, Masculinism, and Globalization

Enthusiasm for the ideological power of sport is also a feature of the theocratic right and is used as a way to speak to, recruit, and motivate men in their affiliated men's movements. The example of Promise Keepers is most eloquent. This Christian men's movement has involved more than 20 million men in its rallies and activities in the last three years, and has an annual budget of more than $60 million. It was founded by a university football coach and launched from the university basketball court in Denver, Colorado. Its whole rhetoric is based on "combat and sport" and these are mobilized to help rebuild a battered sense of masculinity and construct an ideal of manhood based on the notion that men must "lead in families and in the community, and that men have been unmanned by feminists and homosexuals."[14] Indeed, in its role as masculine and masculinist culture, sport is a very important unifying factor between the secular and religious right, as well as across classes, ethnicities, and nations.

Since the 1970s and the rise of second-wave feminism, women in significant numbers have taken on sports that were previously the exclusive domain of men. Women athletes now compete in hockey, basketball, track and field, as well as in body building and boxing. While they are still far from equal participants, the principle of their equal right to participation has largely been established in Olympic rhetoric, and there has been a steady progression towards their integration. We may count this a major step forward for gender equality. On the other hand, we have seen nothing like a mass incursion by men into sports such as figure skating or gymnastics (sports that provide a more expressive gestural repertoire for men) or into non-sport physical disciplines such as dance. Thus women's inclusion in sport has changed the ratio of men to women in what was once a male preserve. But, at least to date, it has not changed its core culture, its rituals, or its values. These remain masculinist, with sports that involve zero-sum contests "at the extremes of the male body," to paraphrase Messner's words. Hence, even if women become integrated into sport in its present forms and institutions, these would continue to have masculinist cultural and political implications in the broader society.

By far, the most important of these implications are the ways that ideas of athleticized masculine heroics colour ideas of government, social policy, and state formation. A culture that worships competition, domination, might-equals-right, winner-take-all, or hypermasculine qualities in its mass physical culture, will easily come to see the functions of the state that represent the socialization of women's and communal labour—work concerned with health, education, and social well-being, and that requires cooperation—as soft, unnecessary, dispensable, as fat that can be trimmed. By

contrast, expenditure on prisons, the military, and police will be seen as heroic, serious, hard, lean, competitive, and important. Within such a culture, measures to fund preventive programs will be seen as too expensive; but money will be found to house hundreds of thousands of young offenders in the North American prison-industrial complex. In 1995, the amount the United States spent on prisons exceeded that spent on universities for the first time in its history. Canada lags behind in the neo-liberal political revolution, with its emphasis on the macho state, though it is quickly trying to catch up in Ontario at least.

The owners of sport teams and facilities, and their counterparts in other sport-related industries, present the public subsidy of sport infrastructure—which runs to the billions of dollars each year in North America—as a legitimate expense in the public interest. At the same time, through their support to neo-conservative governments and neo-liberal economic policies, they are complicit in withdrawing public subsidies not only from health, welfare, and education but also from publicly supported cultural enterprises (such as PBS and the National Endowment for the Arts in the United States, and the CBC and the Canada Council for the Arts in Canada).[15] In Cleveland in 1995, for example, the city government managed to find $540 million for stadium construction after laying off four hundred staff members (including two hundred teachers) from its school system. In effect, the city opted to subsidize the enterprises of masculinist culture, rather than decent public education.

The right/left distinctions between neo-liberal and neo-conservative ideas of government (with their support to the coercive state apparatus) on the one hand, and liberal and social democratic ideas of government (with their support to redistributive measures that secure the well-being of society as a whole) on the other, are usually ascribed to identifications rooted in economic positions and interests—capitalist or petit-bourgeois versus working class and socialist, for example. In addition to these identifications, those properly related to position and interests in the gender order are also powerfully at work. The ideas and the morality of neo-liberalism and neo-conservatism have been informed by the relations of gender-class and the values of masculinism, as well as by those of economic class.

Morality in this instance refers to a set of values transmitted through socialization of the young, rewards to the successful, codification in law, and celebration in collective ritual. The dominant morality of the United States, like other moralities that have emerged from imperialist nations, is schizoid. On the one hand, much is made in political rhetoric of democracy, egalitarianism, peace, and national well-being. Every politician, regardless of affiliation, purports to speak in the name of these values. In sport discourse, these ideas are reflected in the ethos of good sportsmanship and inclusive participation. We may call these the prosocial values. At the same time, in the elitist and coercive values endorsed and kept alive by various institutions of masculinist culture (with sport in the lead), an alternative, indeed opposite, morality that validates force is affirmed. What may be referred to as "coercive entitlement," this system supports values that are anti-democratic, elitist, and bellicose or anti-social values.

Because of its power in childhood and young adulthood, the culture of sport helps to establish the values of coercive entitlement in emotional impulses and core identifications laid down early in life. When, later, adults who have absorbed the lessons of its socialization are confronted with political choices, these impulses and identifications may become more decisive in forming their views than the findings of social science about the value of public services, or impassioned appeals for socio-economic equality.

## ■ ■ ■ Conclusion

With great respect intended to the many accomplished scholars and dedicated sport reformers who are part of the Olympic movement, Olympic sport should not be regarded as a vehicle to advance either the physical well-being of the majority of Canadians, or the political well-being of democratic societies. Hence, Toronto's Olympic bid should be opposed. In late August, Premier Lucien Bouchard turned down a request for subsidy to the Montreal Expos, and declared that neither cash subsidies nor tax breaks would be extended to professional sport any longer, given the pressing needs of health and education. As suggested by Stephen Brunt of *The Globe and Mail*, and Dave Perkins of the *Toronto Star*, Olympic mega-projects (or other sport mega-projects) do not represent effective strategies for urban development. They do not have a track record of improving municipal economies or—most important—of helping to make active physicality more accessible to ordinary people.

According to the Surgeon-General of the United States, approximately 15% of U.S. adults engage regularly in vigorous physical activity during leisure time. Approximately 22% of adults engage regularly in moderate physical activity. Walking, yard work, and gardening are, for example, by far the most popular of any physical activities. Still, this leaves the majority of Americans—over 60%—without much exercise, certainly much less than the amount recommended by bodies such as The President's Council on Fitness and Sport and the Centers for Disease Control. Approximately 25% of U.S. adults are not active at all. Among young people (age twelve to twenty-one) only half are vigorously active on a regular basis. The patterns of activity and inactivity follow the patterns of privilege and disadvantage: "inactivity is more common among affluent than non-affluent; more common among women than men, more common among African-American and Hispanic adults than whites; and more common among older rather than younger persons."[16]

Patterns for physical activity and inactivity in Canada show similar contours. According to the 1995 Physical Activity Monitor, only two in five Canadian adults are active enough to benefit their cardiovascular health.[17] Statistics Canada contends that only 17% of Canadians exercise regularly in their leisure time.[18] Of active Canadians, the majority are only moderately active, and favour non-sport activities such as walking (74%), gardening, home exercise, social dancing, swimming, cycling, skating, baseball, bowling, jogging, weight training, and golf (in descending order of popularity). Gradual increases in population activity levels in the moderate-exercise category have been registered since 1981 in "unstructured, low cost activities that can often be done outside facilities," reflecting a greater understanding of the importance of exercise in the population as a whole. But vigorous activity levels by about one-fifth of the population, overlapping with competitive sport participation, have not increased.

The barriers to sport participation in Canada, as in the United States, are correlated to gender, socio-economic status, and age: affluent Canadians exercise more often than non-affluent Canadians; men exercise more than women; white persons more than people of colour; young people exercise more than adults. Indeed, as *The Monitor* noted: "The three resources or services that rank the highest in helping Canadians to be active are infrastructure supports: access to safe streets and public places, affordable facilities, services and programs, and paths, trails, and green spaces."[19] The Olympic Games do nothing to advance these supports, and often drains funds away from them.

Advocates of high-performance sport often maintain that there should be a seamless continuum between popular recreation and Olympic sport. However, in practice, by supporting high-performance and professional sport, our public authorities have starved popular sport, and other popular fitness and health related physical activities that have nothing to do with sport. In Canada, where the federal government funds elite (Olympic) athletes directly and supports these and team sports indirectly (through public university funding, business and tax concessions, and stadium subsidization), this trend can be plotted.[20]

Hence, what is suggested here are policies that both expand the place of physical culture within our lives (vital to our individual and physical well-being), and work to diminish the centrality of high-performance sport in that culture, by offering many other ways for people to be active, and creating the real social supports that make it possible for the majority of people to be healthfully active.[21] In our educational and recreation systems, we need to broaden physical culture beyond sport to include dance, eastern disciplines, non-competitive games, and other, emergent physical activities. If we inculcate and valorize the anti-social values of contemporary sport culture, we should not be surprised to see those values replicated in the political arena. Acknowledging the power of physicality and ritual, if we want to use our physical culture to develop capacities for citizenship, we need to use it to teach different lessons and affirm different values.

Such a perspective is built around five principles, all of which have many strategic and tactical applications, depending on context and objectives. These are:

1. Diminish the selective brutalization of males inside and outside of sport. Put an end to the ways that sport, in the name of masculinity, creates systemic maltreatment of young males, including emotional, physical, and sexual abuse. This does not mean that physical culture should not include elements of risk or danger; rather that such elements be bound by and related to pro-social values and goals, equalized between the genders, and achieved in non-abusive ways.

2. Encourage girls and women to be vigorously active and to learn physical disciplines that do not promote anorexia. This will help to diminish the disempowering impact of the way that sport and gender culture more generally treat women's athleticism, and encourage subjectivity in women.[22]

3. Change the "sacrificial" nature of sport for both sexes. Performance standards that involve

harm to the physical, emotional, and mental well-being of athletes of both sexes send at least three anti-social messages: First, that we value gladiator-like contests, whether of brutal inter-male violence or the more refined self-administered violence of individual Olympic sports. Second, that such violence, and hence other kinds of economic and social violence, is legitimate and rewarding. Third, that self-harm in the service of conforming to physical and social standards is important for success in life.

4. Shift the emphasis from aggressive and competitive to cooperative and expressive games and disciplines. We need to develop a game culture of mutual benefit and personal realization through physical activity, not one of "mutually exclusive goal attainment" or "zero-sum" competition.

5. Pursue lively physicality for the majority. The governments of the United States and Canada have admirable goals and objectives for the fitness and health of their populations. But unless the resources are devoted to creating accessible services and facilities, and to providing the social supports necessary to make access meaningful, all ideas of democratizing physical culture will remain just that—ideas without any hold in reality.

These directions, if pursued, would take us a long distance from the present sport culture and economy of the Olympic Games. All of humanity is challenged today with the epochal task of devising greater means of cooperation—not competition; and with working to achieve peace and environmental balance, not war and the ecological destruction wrought by unregulated industry and resource extraction. Given the importance ascribed to the enculturating and socializing power of sport—and given many of the progressive ideas that Olympic sport has represented in the past—it is hoped that those within it will find ways to become a more progressive force in the future.

## Notes

1. See Varda Burstyn, *The Rites of Men: Manhood, Politics and the Culture of Sport*. University of Toronto Press (Spring, 1999).

2. See Bruce Kidd, *The Struggle for Canadian Sport*. University of Toronto Press (1996), 150–156.

3. See Paula Welch and D. Margaret Costa "A century of Olympic competition," in D. Margaret Costa and Sharon Guthrie, *Women and Sport: Interdisciplinary Perspectives*. Human Kinetics, Urbana-Champaign (1994), 123–138.

4. Men get many more endorsements than women. Male athletes with a "bad" image (e.g., NBA star Charles Barkley), get lots of endorsements, but only "good" women (read compliant in body styles and vocabularies of traditional femininity) like Nancy Kerrigan and Mary Lou Retton have any real chance at scoring the Olympic gold. Apparently black women athletes—who by racist definition seem incapable of achieving the "sugar-and-spice" image—have gotten even fewer endorsements than white women; although now that women's professional basketball has been launched, and Venus Williams has emerged in tennis, we may see some change in this. In 1994, Debi Thomas, an African-American skater who competed in Calgary and Albertville, told PBS news (MacNeil-Lehrer Hour, February 1994) that she had received virtually no offers. Even Jackie Joyner Kersee, arguably the finest woman athlete in the world at the time, had received no major offers. Kristi Yamaguchi, on the other hand, the winning American figure skater, did extremely well as "America's Sweetheart."

5. Fees for television rights to the Olympics payable to the IOC have been enormously profitable in the corporate period. In 1984, the IOC charged ABC what seemed an outrageous $175 million for the rights to the Los Angeles Games. The sport world, including the sport media, was horrified. Yet despite a dire prediction in 1986 by *Sports Illustrated* that television would begin to lose interest in covering the Olympics, NBC paid $300 million for Seoul in 1988, $401 million for Barcelona in 1992, and $465 million for the rights to the Atlanta Olympics in 1996. Finally, we have NBC's $2.3 billion. "The implications for the other networks are potentially devastating from a programming standpoint ... In 1996, the Super Bowl, the baseball All-Star Game, the NBA Finals as well as the Atlanta Olympics will all be on NBC, as well as the U.S. Open golf tournament, Wimbledon, The French Open tournament, and the Breeder's Cup. Never before will so many top sport events have been gathered in one place," Sally Jenkins, "Peacock Power," *Sports Illustrated*, (December 25, 1995).

6. See Vyv Simpson and Andrew Jennings, *The Lords of the Rings: Power Money and Drugs in the Modern Olympics* (Toronto 1992).

7. For a commentary on the ironies of the Barcelona Games, as well as on some of the ways Barcelona used the games to improve—rather than destroy—poor and working class

neighbourhoods, see Vincente Navarro, "The Olympic's untold stories," *In These Times* (September 2–15, 1992).

8. For a lament on the corporatization of the Barcelona games, see Frank Deford, "Bring Back the Communists!," *Newsweek* (August 10, 1992), 23. For a lament on the reduction of the Lillehammer Winter Olympics to the sordid Nancy Kerrigan/Tonya Harding story, see Lewis Cole, "Going for the green," *The Nation* (March 28, 1994), 426–428.

9. "Before, we had to win for the government, for politics, for communism. The freedom we now have can lead us to making very good money for ourselves. Now we can reap what we sow. Now, if I win, I become a famous person, I become a rich person. All athletes respond to this motivation." Russian swimmer Yevgeny Sadovyi, in William Oscar Johnson and Jeff Lilley, "Swimmers for sale," *Sports Illustrated* (August 10, 1992) 46.

10. See Frank Deford, "Running Man," *Vanity Fair* (August 1993), 54.

11. See Varda Burstyn, "The Sporting Life," *Saturday Night*, (March 1990), 44–49, Angela Taylor-Issajenko (as told to Martin O'Malley and Karen O'Reilly), *Running Risks*, Toronto (1990), and John M. Hoberman and Charles E. Yesalis, "The history of synthetic testosterone," *Scientific American*, (February 1995) 76–81.

12. See Chris Mulhill, "Poverty is the worlds greatest killer," *Guardian Weekly* (May 7, 1995). See also "Poor and overweight," Associated Press, *The Globe and Mail* (December 5, 1995) and Robert Evans, Morris Barer, and Theodore Marmor, *Why Are Some People Healthy and Others Not? The Determinants of the Health of the Population* (New York, 1994).

13. A current ad for Gatorade is exemplary of how specific communications for trivial products convey these meta-messages. Athletes shot in black and white action and close-up photography (signifying importance, seriousness) are enhanced by neon coloured sweat or tears, the same colour as the bottle of Gatorade the athlete is brandishing. "Is it in you?" the authoritative male voice-over demands, alluding at once to the performance principle and the commodity. "Life is sport. Drink it up," he commands over the final shot.

14. Joe Conason, Alfred Ross and Lee Cokorinos, "The promise keepers are coming: The third wave of the religious right," *The Nation* 263, No.10 (October 7, 1996), 11–18, William Martin, *With God on Our Side; The Rise of the Religious Right in America*, (New York, 1996), 349–353, and Joan Breckenridge and Gay Abbate, "Movement issues 'wakeup call' to Canadian men," *The Globe and Mail* (September 25, 1995).

15. Regarding the politics of the NEA and broader Left/Right cultural conflicts, see William Martin, *With God on our Side: The Rise of the Religious Right in America* (New York 1996), Richard Bolton (ed.), *Culture Wars*, (New York, 1992), and Robert Hughes, *Culture of Complaint: The Fraying of America* (New York, 1993). Regarding the politics of public broadcasting, see James Ledbetter, *Made Possible by...: The Death of Public Broadcasting in the United States*, (London, Verso, 1997), Willard D. Rowland, Jr. and Michael Tracey, "Worldwide challenges to public broadcasting" *Journal of Communication*, 40 (2) (Spring) 1990, and Edward S. Herman and Robert W. McChesney *The Global Media: The New Missionaries of Global Capitalism*, (London, 1997). Regarding the crisis of public broadcasting in Canada, see Wayne Skene, *Fade to Black: A Requiem for the CBC*, (Vancouver/Toronto, 1997).

16. These and other statistics in this paragraph from *Physical Activity and Health: A Report of the Surgeon-General*, U.S. Department of Health and Human Services, Washington D.C. (July, 1996) Chapter 5.

17. See *1997 Physical Activity Monitor*, The Candian Fitness and Lifestyle Research Institute, Ottawa, 1995.

18. See *National Population Health Survey Overview 1994–95*, Statistics Canada, Ottawa, 1997, 12.

19. See *1997 Physical Activity Monitor*, The Candian Fitness and Lifestyle Research Institute, Ottawa, 1997.

20. See Jean Harvey, "Sport policy and the welfare state," *Sociology of Sport Journal* 5 (1988), 313–329. On the ideological value of the ideology of excellence, see Bruce Kidd, "Canada and the ideology of excellence," in Pasquale Galasso, ed. *The Philosophy of Sport and Physical Activity*, (Toronto, 1988), 11–31.

21. "Women's double or triple workdays constitute one of the primary barriers to taking up a sport or physical activity as a leisure pursuit. For example, for women whose workdays include paid employment, child care and domestic work, part-time study and volunteer work ...the idea of entitlement to leisure may seem laughable." Helen Jefferson Lenskyj, "What's sport got to do with it?" *Canadian Woman Studies*, 5, no. 4 (Fall 1995), 6–10.

22. "... [C]hildhood sports teach boys to use their bodies in skilled, forceful ways while providing them a detailed and accurate knowledge of their physical capacities, and limits. Boys learn how to develop force (through leverage, coordination, and follow-through) and to transmit this power through their limbs or through extensions, like balls, bats and golf clubs. In contrast ... the movement patterns of most girls are characterized by their partiality, by their failure to take ... advantage ... of the torque that is generated when the entire body is mobilized in a throw, a swing, or a tackle." David Whitson, "The Embodiment of Gender: Discipline, Domination and Empowerment," in Susan Birrell and Cheryl L. Cole, eds. *Women, Sport and Culture*, (Urbana- Champaign, IL, 1994), 354.

◀◀ **Source:** This article was originally published in the *Proceedings of the Fourth International Symposium for Olympic Research, 2001*. Reprinted with permission.

# Excellence in Sport and Other Circuses
## By Irvin Studin

**4.**

*As Canada prepares for the 2010 Winter Olympics in Vancouver, Irvin Studin reflects on the two key, systemic challenges that have impeded sustained Canadian excellence in sport—challenges that are true for nearly all Canadian institutions (sporting and other). The first is the difficulty of building east to west (and north); the second, the national incapacity to project outwards—that is, beyond Canadian borders. Studin traces the origins of these challenges to Canada's constitutional structure, explains their consequences for Canada's sporting institutions and proposes policy remedies—most notably, the cross-country professionalization of sports training and development (from early ages) and the creation of bona fide national, professional sports leagues in a variety of team sports.*

■■■■■■

As the 2010 Vancouver Olympics fast approach, it is worth considering that, since Confederation, Canada's national institutions—among them, Parliament, the country's schools and universities, and, yes, even Canadian sport—have had to continuously wrestle with two capital challenges: first, how to build from east to west, or west to east (and north, of course), across the country's vast geography; and second, how, if at all, to project beyond Canada's borders. Both challenges are explained, if not anticipated, in the oft-neglected second recital (paragraph) of the preamble to the *Constitution Act, 1867*, which reads that the Canadian federation would "conduce to the welfare of the provinces and promote the interests of the British Empire."

The first challenge is quite evident. That Canada should "conduce to the welfare of the provinces" speaks to an existential challenge that is known to all big federations—the United States, Russia, India—with heterogeneous populations and important regional (or "provincial") dynamics: that is, the struggle against powerful and often chaotic centrifugal forces in order to build coherent, pan-country institutions that unite or bind, with varying intensity, citizens in common identity, culture, and indeed collective ambition.

The second challenge—that of projecting internationally—is less intuitive. A country's institutions may carry peculiar extraterritorial weight by dint of that country's geopolitical importance or the sheer political or cultural attractiveness of those same institutions—that is, their susceptibility to conscious or unconscious emulation by other countries. Or, in a very related sense, a country may be able to project international influence or prestige by means of strategy—that is, the conscientious development and alignment of national means or assets and the national will for the precise purposes of such international projection. Countries like the United Kingdom, France, Russia, and the United States, among others, have all at one time or another in their histories been such countries—geopolitically important, politically and culturally attractive (to different sets of countries) and, to be sure, highly strategic. That Canada, for its part, was made to "promote the interests of the British Empire" speaks, however, to the plain fact that Canada was never made, constitutionally speaking, to be able to project any independent weight whatever beyond its immediate borders—that is, but for the mediation of Great Britain. And, notwithstanding the verity that the Canadian state has since acquired all the formal trappings of constitutional independence, that it was at its genesis bereft of geopolitical heft, political-cultural prestige, and strategic capacity is a brute fact that has patently conditioned the essential "intra-border" gravity of its institutions to this day.

Canadian sport, as mentioned, is just such an institution. To be clear, one could just as easily choose Canadian high culture or the purer arts (the visual arts, music, theatre, dance) as a representative institution—just in case the invocation of sport begets the common instinctual retort: What about the arts? But we choose sport not only because it is an institution to which precious little serious policy commentary is devoted in Canada, but also because it, far more than, say, the sciences, institutions of learning, and formal institutions of governance, is an extreme example of the said two cardinal challenges at play. With very few exceptions, Canada has been exceedingly hard pressed to build bona fide, "thick" institutions of sport across the totality of its populated territory. The cognate difficulty of projecting Canadian sport beyond Canadian borders is far more plain to the casual observer: in general terms, Canada has also been hard pressed to achieve substantial and sustained sporting success on the international stage—at the Olympics, in world championships and in other major, global sporting competitions.

Let us start with the first challenge. Apart from the Canadian Football League, Canada has not a single proper elite sports league. In none of the world's principal team sports—hockey, soccer, basketball, baseball, volleyball, rugby, field hockey, handball, lacrosse, cricket—has Canada a single bona fide senior, professional league that bridges the country. Even in its national and most popular sport, hockey, aside from the superb country-wide network of provincial and regional leagues at the junior level (the Canadian Hockey League), and notwithstanding sporadic efforts here and there to secure new Canadian franchises in the National Hockey League, there are only six Canadian teams of a total thirty in a professional league largely administered, at the strategic level, from the United States. (There are only three Canadian teams of a total twenty-nine teams in the sub-ordinate, American-run "farm league.") Canadian "representation," as it were, is even more paltry in the other team sports: one putatively Canadian team (putative because of the virtual absence of Canadian players) in each of the major American basketball and baseball leagues (and two teams in a largely American lacrosse league). An embryonic aspiration to similar such representation or participation in the National Football League grows slowly but surely.

To the reasonable outsider or foreign observer, all this would seem patently bizarre. For there is hardly a country in the world—small or large, insular or even bestridden by a much larger neighbour—that does not at least have a countrywide league in its national sport or sports. Scotland, at about one-tenth the population of England, has its own national soccer league—and an excellent one at that. (Indeed, Scotland has two national soccer leagues—two divisions, if you will.) Ukraine and Belarus, politically and culturally outflanked by Russia, each have serious soccer leagues. (Russia, a large, complex federation like Canada, of course, also has a very serious soccer league—with several divisions—among many other elite sports leagues.) Finland and Sweden each have serious hockey leagues—as well as soccer leagues, of course. Australia, another physically large—albeit slightly less complex—federation, has some six national sports leagues. Granted, there are different species of national sporting associations and national tournaments in Canada, but the near total absence of national leagues (to be sure, for men and women alike), far from being of negligible moment, means, in perhaps the simplest terms, that individual Canadians and Canadian cities, towns and communities are deprived of one of the chief vectors from which other countries around the world profit to create a meaningful national cultural agora—a common cultural activity outside of politics through which the passions of the citizenry are channelled. Canada's national or east-west "cultural discourse," as it were, is greatly impoverished for this absence. In nearly all of the sports, and for nearly all Canadian cities and towns, there is manifestly no hometown team for which to cheer, no sincere intercity or inter-town sporting rivalries to animate the national spirits, and no common national (team) championship and trophy for which to strive—and to celebrate. In turn, from the perspective of the Canadian athlete, there is, in virtually all cases, no national league in which to ply one's craft, no local Canadian team for which to play, no hometown fans to entertain. Indeed, every talented, young Canadian basketball, soccer, or volleyball player—male or female—is by his or her mid-teens invariably confronted with the brute reality that, outside of participation on the national or Olympic team (a subject to which we shortly turn), the prospects for high-level *épanouissement* in one's sport are close to nil. University sport is an option (in both Canada and the United States), as is, for the most exceptional, recruitment to an American or European professional league. (The majority of the National Hockey League's players evidently remain Canadian.) Failing these, however, there is the far more travelled path of recreational sport or, *in extremis*, outright abandonment of the sport in question.

With the conspicuous exception of hockey, Canada's capacity to export sporting excellence internationally—that is, to prevail with regularity (and indeed with deliberate design) in international competition—has also historically been, and unquestionably remains, pedestrian. This is true of individual and team sports in both the summer and winter seasons, although the national record of international achievement in the summer sports is evidently far poorer than that in the winter sports. Granted, Olympic gold medals, world championships and number-one rankings will be won here and there, and, on occasion, a sporting genius like Donovan Bailey or Rick Nash will be produced, but by and large the national policy approach to sport is substantially invested in what one might call "heroic amateurism": an international hero or two issues from the national fabric, but because the national sporting culture is decidedly amateur,

such heroes will be exceedingly improbable, triumphing largely by virtue of their own striving, and very seldom as a direct result of a Canadian policy infrastructure that targets, intends and aligns national assets for sustained, predictable international winning.

This state of Canadian athletic achievement on the world scene is, as mentioned, anticipated in the constitutional makeup of the Canadian state. Where it exists, domestic—*à la limite*, continental—sport is, as a general rule, privileged over international competition, and, in turn, the handful of Canadian "heroic amateurs" who do prevail abroad, in individual or team sport, are—living as they do outside of the "national" sports discourse—misunderstood, underappreciated, and often scarcely known. Even in hockey, the deep Canadian success of which we take up later in this piece, achievement in the "national" league (the National Hockey League) is, again, as a general rule, more prized than in the world championships and, until quite recently, the Olympic Games. (Let us recall that, before the 2002 men's Olympic hockey gold, Canada had not won a single men's hockey gold medal since 1952. And prior to the 1990s, Canada had not won a single men's world hockey championship since 1961.) The participation of Canada's best players—typically in the NHL—in top international tournaments is to this day never fully assured, and, given the choice between competing in the Stanley Cup playoffs and the world championships for Team Canada, it is nearly always the former that is given preference. Even when the world hockey championships were held on Canadian soil—most recently in Quebec City in 2008, where Canada finished second to Russia—the irony that Sidney Crosby, arguably at present Canada's best hockey player, was playing for the Stanley Cup with the Pittsburgh Penguins in lieu of representing his country among the nations was lost on the entire Canadian sports commentariat.

By contrast, in Europe, most starkly, but indeed on virtually every other continent, international competition decisively trumps domestic championships. Tensions between club and country are certainly not unknown, but it is generally considered countercultural for an athlete to play—voluntarily or through contractual obligation—for a local club at the expense of the national team in major international tournaments. Indeed, it is expressly prohibited by many national and international sporting bodies. One would therefore be extremely hard pressed to find, say, a Ronaldo, a Ronaldinho or, formerly, a Zidane or a Maradona—failing to represent his country in the soccer World Cup because of competing club or local commitments. Quite the contrary: victory in the World Cup is privileged at nearly all costs to more provincial seductions, and the prestige of national success is the decisive imperative.

In individual sports—tennis, track and field, gymnastics, cycling, swimming, skiing, speedskating—with rare exceptions, Canadian athletes are hardly world-beaters. In the main, they are the products of a national culture and different (federal, provincial, even municipal) policy frameworks—well short of a proper sports "system"—that view sport as an uncontroversial subset of health or recreational policy. Athletic participation rates are privileged, as are various social indicators relating to individual "well-being"—all barometers that fundamentally militate against regular international sporting excellence. The "system" is, as a consequence, and in the main, desperately reliant on the raw talent (of which there is no empirical evidence of any peculiar shortage), sacrifice, and indeed heroics of individual Canadian athletes. Different governments, private concerns, and foundations will, to be sure, inject money here and there in support of these athletes, but such monies, while proffered with only good intentions, are typically unconnected to any sophisticated and credible strategy for sustained international success. In short, there is no proper national "system" or policy bulwark in place to ensure a high probability of winning for Canadian sportsmen and sportswomen.

Of course, in policy terms, Canadian sport (like general culture, contrary to the strong claims to the contrary from Quebec) is of mixed constitutional competence; both the federal government and the provinces have legitimate jurisdiction over it. In the famous Anti-Inflation Reference of 1975, Justice Beetz stated that subject matters of excessive diffuseness, such as inflation (or, say, the environment or indeed culture and sport), may not be constitutionally ascribed to a single level of government. In practical terms, however, it follows that, for sport policy, as with many of these mixed-jurisdiction files, in the absence of robust, federal involvement (or "institution building"), the centrifugal pull of the provinces—or the powerful jurisdictional gravity of what is constitutionally called "property and civil rights"—is significant. In other words, the property and civil rights gravity of the provinces overwhelms the federal gravity of interprovincial and international concerns.

More precisely, if the federal government fails to properly drive national policy in this area on a sustained basis, in recognition of the aforementioned two cardinal Canadian institutional dynamics, then Canadian sport becomes a function of a variegated cocktail of provincial (and municipal) health and recreation, education, and cultural programs, as well as provincial amateur sport programs—and, of course, of the said amateur heroism of the athletes themselves. At best, the federal government will intervene muscularly with one or two provinces, as in the context of a one-off major event, such as the 2010 Vancouver Olympics, to inject a degree of stimulus into the national sports infrastructure. In the alternative, the federal government will involve itself in crafting sport policy, but only to a limited degree, and this based on a policy diagnostic and a remedial paradigm rooted in erroneous or facile presumptions about what makes for strong national institutions of sport (discussed immediately below) or excellence in sport (as with the above-mentioned idea—no less than an empirical absurdity—that world champions somehow organically emerge from an otherwise healthy, active population).

It stands to reason that east-west national sporting institutions in Canada, like any of Canada's strongest national institutions, can arise only from proper building supported by conscientious strategy. Indeed, it is only through sophisticated national planning and appropriate alignment of the national means in support of strategic ends that bona fide pan-Canadian structures can be created. In the event, the strategic end of creating national sports leagues (as perhaps the most evident form of a national sporting institution), notwithstanding presumptions about Canada's "smallness" or its *sui generis* market integration with the United States, requires federal policy leadership.

This policy leadership would recognize both the functional import of such leagues in driving national culture—as in other countries—and, just as vitally, the centrality of the federal role in the building of institutions where purely commercial considerations and provincial dynamics alone are clearly inadequate for the job. In other words, while it is reasonably uncontroversial that private concerns would have to provide a substantial share of the investment for different teams in each of the leagues, and while the provincial and indeed municipal levels of government would need to support or incentivize such investment (for provincial and local ends, of course), it would seem equally uncontroversial that all this activity should occur in the context of a national policy framework driven by the federal government. (Appropriate federal-provincial division of labour and cooperation would necessarily form part of this national policy framework.) And the framework, to repeat, would be not for the oft-caricatured purposes of creating wealthy professional athletes or "white elephant" stadiums, but rather for building viable, pan-Canadian sports leagues (institutions) that bind the country's vast segments in common pastime, and, just as signally, provide an outlet for Canadian athletes to perform their craft at a high level, and in Canada.

The link between such national leagues and the export of Canadian sporting excellence is non-negligible—at least in respect of the team sports. Whether each league is of the highest world standard is of far less consequence than the essential fact that the league provides a Canadian base for the professional development of a critical mass of high-level Canadian athletes who either directly populate Canada's various national teams or, in some cases, feed top-tier Canadians to more elite leagues in other countries—as in, say, soccer or baseball—whence Canadian national teams are in turn formed. The presumption, however, that elite foreign leagues alone, without the support of domestic leagues, are in and of themselves adequate for the purposes of building strong national sports programs is empirically erroneous. For the record suggests, broadly speaking, that the pool of athletes that countries outsource to other countries (foreign leagues) for purposes of national team development is insufficiently deep to sustain an elite national program over a material period of time. Where an elite foreign league, such as the English Premiership (soccer), the National Basketball Association, or Major League Baseball exists, a Canadian league, assuming it comes, *ab initio*, with a lower standard of play, should, in policy terms, therefore be seen as a necessary complement for purposes of building internationally excellent national teams. However, the absence of such a fundamental complement, by extension of this logic, almost unexceptionally condemns Canadian national programs to mediocrity. (And, manifestly, this is the current state of affairs.)

For both individual and team sports, another key paradigmatic shift in our national policy treatment would be to professionalize the very development of elite athletes. This shift would be tantamount to a concession that simply investing, *grosso modo*, in athletes once they have already reached the age of senior competition (say, over eighteen years of age)—and this principally to subsidize only their training regime at a fairly modest clip—is a cosmetic, unscientific formula that works at fundamental cross-purposes with any serious national aspiration for international sporting success. For just as the doctor or lawyer issues from many, many years of formal schooling (some twelve or thirteen years before university, followed by seven or eight years in university, and more in certain cases), the elite athlete is the product of a long value chain of training or formation. And to the extent that we strategically interest ourselves in the development of this athlete only in the later, downstream stages of this chain, we necessarily defer to the said paradigm of the "heroic amateur." We hope that a random pot-pourri of factors will yield elite specimens—age-eligible for competition, at which we may throw dollars—but we do precious little to precipitate or guarantee such an outcome.

All of this is patently at odds with the approaches of a good number of countries (Australia, Germany, Russia, China, among them)—all more successful than Canada, generally speaking, in international sporting competition—that have recognized that proper athletic development, as with the cultivation of the musical virtuosos, is no matter for the amateur. International competitiveness requires the establishment of bona fide national institutes of sport. (The famous Australian Institute of Sport, or the AIS, is perhaps our best model in this regard.) These institutes should be populated by properly remunerated elite coaches, trainers, and sports scientists recruited from around the world; after all, if Canada is to become strong in a sport like soccer, it must lever international talent, just as other countries would look to Canada to improve their hockey bona fides. They should have world-class sports facilities and infrastructures. And, most importantly, their mandate should be to select, at reasonably early ages (depending on the sport in question), the most promising Canadian athletes from around the country for sustained, serious, "professionalized" development. These select athletes would evidently have robust academic curricula that they would have to follow in concert with their athletic preparation, but the essential point is that their athletic curricula, much like the academic, would be regulated by government—strategically with the aim of creating world-class athletes in multiple sports.

Campuses of the institutes of sport would be stood up across Canada—with each campus focussing on a handful of sports, according to local comparative advantage. Scholarships would be offered to selected athletic candidates, and high standards of performance (athletic and academic) would be expected of recruits. Athletes could attend local campuses or move to out-of-province campuses to train in a particular sport. Granted, a good number of these recruits could, over time, prove to be unsuccessful in their chosen sport, in which case the proper goal would be for each individual athlete to emerge from the program as a literate, lettered, productive citizen. (We note the concept of the citizen-athlete.) However, a good number of these athletes may well emerge as successful international athletes (in some cases, true world-beaters)—no accidents at all, but the products of a sophisticated, world-class, Canadian strategy or system of athletic development; in itself, a proper national institution.

◀◀ **Source:** Irvin Studin, formerly of the Privy Council Office, is assistant professor and academic director at the School of Public Policy and Governance, University of Toronto. This article was originally published in *Policy Options* (December/January 09/10). Republished with permission of the IRPP (www.irpp.org).

# Section 2

## Socialization and Sports

Socialization "is a process of learning and social development, which occurs as we interact with one another and become acquainted with the social world in which we live" (Coakley and Donnelly, p. 80). With reference to sport, socialization often refers to two related processes: the first is the process of individual development as a human being, often referred to in sport as "character building;" the second is the process of becoming involved in sport, becoming an athlete.

The first two articles in this section deal with the idea of sport and character. "Olympic Dreams and Fairy Tales" was published shortly before the Beijing Olympics. Author Doug Brown asks: "Why do so many of our Olympic-bound athletes make me cringe whenever they respond to inquiries from the media on current international events?" Brown questions why so many of Canada's Olympic athletes appear ready to give up their own rights to free speech and to protest the issues surrounding the Olympics (such as the denial of human rights to so many Chinese people, and the gag order from Olympic officials) in order to preserve their opportunity to go to an Olympic Games. Brown's article challenges the notion that sport is character building, and suggests that Canadian Olympic athletes are encouraged to be immature.

Such immaturity may be even further engrained in professional athletes to the point where it has even been suggested that sport does not build character, but instead *eliminates* character. Ed Smith, a former member of the England cricket team and now an editorial writer for *The Times*, made the following comments with reference to the Tiger Woods infidelity scandal:

> The sport industry delights in celebrating the elimination of weakness. Denying being human has become professionalism's raison d'etre. Coaches prefer willing cogs in a wheel, sponsors want shiny faces on billboards, governing bodies seek stars without opinions. And if the agents and coaches can't quite eliminate what's left of your personality, there are always the sport psychologists to finish the job. We have come full circle.
>
> *Once sport was a means of building character; now it seeks to eliminate character.*
>
> *Professional sport is stuck in a dangerous state of arrested development where it demands that grown adults indefinitely retain the egotistical narrow-mindedness of teenagers* (emphasis added).

Despard, cited below, also questions the character-building qualities of sport. She points out that athletes who compete with injuries, or take the kind of risks associated with concussion and permanent disability (that are becoming increasingly common at the highest levels of sport) may not be appropriate role models for children. Later in this collection (Sections 6 and 7), an additional form of socialization is noted in terms of the way in which sport may be used as a "school" for particular forms of masculinity. No one ever suggests the alternative, i.e., that sport is a school of femininity; but it is still widely considered that sport is a way for boys to learn to become men—incorporating a particularly narrow view of what it means to be a "man."

Jay Coakley's "Sport and Character Development Among Adolescents" provides a comprehensive examination of what we know (quite a lot, and certainly enough to make policy decisions about sport programs if we wish to have a positive effect on the character development of young people) and what we don't know about sport and character building. "The London Declaration" (Section 1), "The Panathlon Declaration," "The *Hockey Act*," and the manifesto "On Kids and Sports" (Section 3) all remind us that there is a great deal wrong with children's sports. They are also a reminder that we know what to do about the problems. To the extent that the problems are related to character development in sport, Coakley shows that there is a substantial body of research evidence to support "doing the right thing."

The series of articles by Cheney and the article by Berg are intended as reminders that the process of socialization into sport and the process of becoming an athlete at various stages of a sports career often involve other people.

Peter Cheney's series "Hockey Dad's Diary" chronicles his experiences while his son plays for an AA Atom team. Seven of the articles from the series are included here; the additional articles are cited below. The series examines a ten-year-old boy's socialization into this higher level of hockey from a father's perspective, and it is clear to see that the father is being socialized into this environment just as much as the son. It is a reminder that parents with children involved in organized sports also become socialized into the role of "sports parent."

Wendy Berg was married to a professional hockey player, and her article about the NHL trade deadline is a reminder that, although we only hear about the players who are traded, wives and children may be even more affected by the decisions made by a professional team. They too are socialized into their roles in sport.

The section concludes with a reminder that socialization into sport also takes place outside of formal, organized settings, and that we learn and know a great deal about how to *play* sports. Daniel Sanger's article, "5, 6, Pickup Sticks" deals with open air, pickup hockey in Montreal. He describes the complex rules of these informal games—rules that are adaptable to the particular circumstances of a game, rules that are not written down anywhere, and which are enforced by the players and not by a referee. It is interesting that these rules are characteristic of informal children's games, and serve exactly the same purpose in pickup hockey: increasing action, increasing personal involvement, creating close scores, and maintaining friendships (Coakley and Donnelly, pp. 138-139).

**Additional Suggested Readings and References**

- Cheney, P. 2002. "Parents Obsessed with Results Take Fun out of Game." *The Globe and Mail*, November 8. This article was not part of "Hockey Dad's Diary," but shortly preceded it, and certainly laid some of the groundwork.
- Cheney, P. 2002. "Ugly Hockey Parent Syndrome Rears its Head." *The Globe and Mail*, December 28.
- Cheney, P. 2003. "Harsh Reality Can't Derail NHL Dream." *The Globe and Mail*, January 11.
- Cheney, P. 2003. "Bantam Hockey a Joy to Behold." *The Globe and Mail*, March 15.
- Coakley, J. and P. Donnelly. 2009. *Sports in Society: Issues and Controversies* (2nd Canadian edition). Toronto: McGraw-Hill Ryerson.
- Despard, E. 2006. "Role models? Think again." *The Globe and Mail*, February 28.
- Smith, E. 2009. "Tiger Must Grow Up—And His Fans Must Let Him." *The Times*, December 3.
- Trevisan, M. 2007. "No Gain in Letting Your Kid Play Through Pain." *The Globe and Mail*, June 5.

# Olympic Dreams and Fairy Tales

## By Douglas Brown

**5.**

*How will Canada's Olympians acquit themselves in Beijing?*

■ ■ ■ ■ ■ ■

On April 6, 2008, Canada's biggest Olympic trials wrapped up at a swimming pool in Montreal. This was the final competition for swimmers hoping to take the next logical step in their sporting careers. As for many other Canadian athletes, competing at the Olympic Games is equivalent to climbing Mount Everest. It is simply the biggest show on earth. Like mountaineers, Olympic athletes can be tongue-tied when trying to justify their pursuits. Why do you climb the mountain? Because it's there. Why do you want to go to the Olympic Games? Because they are there.

This is the reasoning that the International Olympic Committee and its franchises such as the Canadian Olympic Committee depend upon for their self-preservation, and it is the reasoning they hope Canadian athletes and Canadian sport fans will draw on when asked to justify participation in Beijing. While debates over political protests and potential boycotts are prominent in the news, the logic seems to be working. Collectively, Canadian athletes, their administrators, the CBC, and the wider Canadian public all seem prepared for this year's pursuit of Olympic dreams.

A recent special edition of CBC's *Sports Weekend* was a classic illustration of this outlook, combining all the essential ingredients of a message that cultural theorist Richard Gruneau would identify as "stupid realism"—one part news coverage, two parts melodrama, and a dash of travelogue, blended with promotional hype, nationalist excess, and kitschy sentimentalism. When the coverage did address the broader social and political context of the Beijing Olympics, prominent athletes and their coaches did not represent themselves well. Those of the present generation, as well as those affected by the 1980 Moscow boycott, made the same hollow claims: boycotts destroy the dreams of innocent athletes and deprive the next generation of young Canadians of their role models.

Why do so many of our Olympic-bound athletes make me cringe whenever they respond to inquiries from the media on current international events? Because I believe it is not an Olympic dream they are pursuing, but a fairy tale. Dreams can be forgotten or can turn into nightmares, while fairy tales endure as entertainment for children or those adults with childlike imaginations. Heroes and heroines live happily ever after in fantastic other-worlds without complex social concepts such as the collective good and transnational diplomacy. Fairy-tale characters are not burdened by taxes, passports, education, or jobs. And like fairy-tale characters, many Canadian athletes do not expect to endure such burdens of the world beyond their world. Does this have to be the case?

I should make it clear that I have participated in high-level sport throughout my life. As a university professor in a faculty of kinesiology, I try to position myself as an advocate for athletes. Indeed, many of my students are elite athletes aspiring to compete at the Olympics. That said, I am distressed when they stumble so awkwardly in the media. I am beyond distressed when they fail to defend their basic human rights and bend without resistance to the institutions that claim to represent their better interests.

International human rights activists have targeted the Beijing Olympics as a logical site for political protest against the Chinese government's oppressive policies and actions, and as a chance to challenge the world's perception of China as a legitimate player in global society. This is not a plot line that IOC heavyweights want to address, preferring their fairy-tale script. But how do you write a script for a pantomime? Mario Vazquez Rana, president of the Association of National Olympic Committees, threatens athletes who might engage in political protests at Beijing with the possibility of serious sanctions. Canadian IOC member Richard Pound suggested that Canadian athletes should be silent or stay home if they cannot resolve their moral issues over China. It appears that the IOC has learned a thing or two from its Chinese hosts. They are willing to disregard the fundamental human rights of athletes to ensure that the 2008 Olympics—and their precariously thin ideological veneer—are neither cracked nor stained. Of course this is not the first time the IOC has threatened athletes into a state of submission. In 2000, athletes heading to Sydney were expected to waive their rights for independent dispute resolution in the event that they were presumed to be drug cheats.

When sport leaders such as Rana engage in these bullying tactics, Olympic athletes need to regain their voice—taking the example of two-time silver medalist Elvis Stojko, who recently argued that Canadian athletes should "make a stand" for human rights, and that if he were competing in Beijing he would think twice about attending. I agree with many of the athletes that boycotts are not necessarily the most effective form of protest. But ignoring the very real situation you are venturing into and allowing yourself to be muted by a self-serving sport administrator is not acceptable. Many Canadian athletes associated with Olympic sports seem perfectly happy to be silenced. Even more distressingly, they seem to regard this sanction as welcome permission to remain self-absorbed and dependant on sport administrators who claim to have their best interests at heart, while presenting themselves to Canadian society as hapless victims of an irrational force that will

destroy their chance for Olympic glory. When responding to journalists, they represent themselves with mindless rhetoric and a lazy reliance on tired, stock arguments.

Canadian Olympians need to realize the misconceptions associated with their argument that a life singularly devoted to making an Olympic team is a life of sacrifice, and that sacrifices of education, careers, and family should be recognized and rewarded by society. These are lifestyle choices, nothing more—the same types of choices that all adults make without expecting public sympathy and support. Instead, I would encourage Canadian athletes to think about how they themselves have been sacrificed by institutions like the IOC, the COC, and the Beijing Olympic Games Organizing Committee.

Athletes trust and obey these organizations; they exchange their right to free speech and their right to democratic protest for the opportunity to compete at an Olympic Games. Their trust and obedience to the administrative bodies is based on a belief that the Olympic Games experience is worth more than being muted and socially disenfranchised during the months leading up to, and the period of, the Olympic Games.

For example, the IOC and the Beijing hosts promised athletes the best competitive environment, facilities, and competitions. For elite athletes, seeking optimal competition environments at a peak moment in one's career is a logical expectation. However, for swimmers and many other athletes who have grown accustomed to competing in evening finals over the duration of their careers, the optimal competition environment has been traded by the IOC to TV networks seeking the largest possible audiences during prime time in the United States, not China. As a consequence, these elite athletes will be expected to deliver their peak performances first thing in the morning. Athletes travelling to Beijing because they wanted to reach their full potential need to recognize that they have already been sacrificed by the organization they trust for television advertising profits.

From a different perspective, athletes are willing to exchange their fundamental human rights for the opportunity to return home as Olympians. The result, they believe, will be more doors opened for them after the games. Fundamentally there is nothing wrong with the logic of cultural capitalism. However, the cultural capital of an Olympian is relative—dependent not just on the athlete's success at the games, but also on the prominence of their sport, the relative success of other Canadian athletes at the games, the natural charisma of the athlete, and, ultimately, the ability of the athlete to make a productive contribution to whatever field of endeavour he or she seeks once doors are opened. There is also a longevity factor to keep in mind. How long after retirement can an Olympian remain relevant?

But all these arguments pale in comparison with the human rights issues that lie at the core of the current debate. The Olympic movement has retained its prestige in part because the potential of sporting humanism and peaceful internationalism continues to resonate with sportspeople and fans. This prestige is also tied to the historical roots of the Olympic movement and the social and political intentions of its founders. Still, athletes who are willing to disengage from the current debate on human rights and still expect to emerge clothed in this prestige must be exposed as frauds. After all, the idea of an Olympian role model who refuses to speak up for the fundamental principles of positive social change is simply anachronistic.

Gag orders from IOC officials such as Rana and Pound are a sacrifice of real Olympians in an effort to preserve the honour of the Chinese hosts. If such threats are acted on, then the IOC will have effectively negated the potential for legitimate Olympian role models to emerge in Beijing. Athletes who choose to address the very real political context that is shaping their competitive careers will instead be set up as anti-heroes.

It is important to remember that precedents exist for prominent Olympians not to turn their backs on the world beyond Olympic fairy tales.

The 1994 Olympic Winter Games in Lillehammer featured two prominent athletes. The great Norwegian speed skater Johann Olav Koss dominated those games. In addition to his dominance in the athletic arena, he emerged a champion of athlete activism while remaining a darling of the IOC. He did so to bring awareness to the critical issues of child poverty in war-torn Eritrea by announcing that he would donate his prize money to the cause. Strategically, he drew on history and the sentimentality that the Olympics still manage to evoke. Some might regard Koss's campaign as simply fundraising, but it was also a bold assertion that the Olympics are an extremely effective venue for highlighting social and political concerns. At the same Olympics, figure skater Katerina Witt also made an innovative political statement. Witt and a number of other skaters had fought for reinstatement in the Olympic movement following successful professional careers. In itself, this was a bold rejection of the archaic amateur codes that dominated Olympic sport. But as part of her comeback, Witt dedicated her skating performance to the people of war-torn Sarajevo. While this was simple gesture (if somewhat kitschy), it was timely, potent, and effective.

Given the IOC's need to control all aspects of the Olympic performance, how did Koss and Witt get away with such blatant acts of political and social activism? Both drew on powerful cultural capital as mature, well-spoken, and good-looking gold medalists. They also knew something of Olympic history and respected the humanitarian ideology that is part of the Olympic tradition. But, ultimately, the power of Koss and Witt came from their curiosity about the world beyond their training programs and competitive goals. Rather than separating their athlete identities from their humanitarian identities, they let them converge in ways they knew how to control.

Canadian athletes could learn much from Koss and Witt and the precedents they created. They can no longer pretend that their Olympic world is separate from the world of global trade agreements, child poverty, terrorism, and corrupt, dictatorial regimes. They can no longer turn away from the disruption and violence that followed the global torch relay. Nor can they face journalists and continue to claim that they are simply elite international athletes and that the Olympic Games are just a sport competition. They are Canadian athletes who travel the world with Canadian passports. They need to stop referring to the years of training that will go unrewarded if there is boycott. And athletes who did not go to the Olympic Games in Moscow in 1980 have to stop referring to "what could have been." They need to think about how they represent themselves. They need to think carefully about the words they choose and the arguments they formulate.

I want Canadian athletes to be politicians and social activists. It is time that Canadian athletes owned the Olympics Games. If athletes had asserted themselves in 2001, Beijing would not be hosting the Olympics in 2008. Politicized athletes would have had the common sense to recognize that Beijing was too risky, with too many uncontrollable variables. These politicized athletes would have helped ensure the choice of a host city within a politically and economically stable nation. They would have chosen a city that was internationally respected and uncontroversial. These politicized athletes would have made selfish decisions that I wholeheartedly support. They would have made logical decisions to guarantee that their athletic careers would climax at an Olympic Games. To make these self-serving decisions, these athletes would have engaged with current events. They would have understood the financial relationships between corporate sponsors, television, and international non-governmental organizations.

But that is what could have been. Canadian athletes now need to change their rhetoric and their attitudes. They cannot allow the IOC and the COC to tell them to be silent; nor can they distance themselves from controversy. If some Canadian athletes sincerely believe that they have no obligation to react to the international controversies of the Beijing Olympics, then I don't want to see them representing this country. Maybe the Canadian government should take away their passports to give them an opportunity to argue for the honouring of their own human rights. The COC might also consider new qualifying criteria for Canadian Olympians: the achievement of all-round, athletic-qualifying standards, the successful completion of an Olympic Games history course, and, most importantly, the elimination of the word "sacrifice" from their vocabulary.

◀◀ **Source**: Douglas Brown is an associate professor of sport history at the University of Calgary. This article was first published in the *Literary Review of Canada*, June 2008. Reprinted with permission.

## 6. Sport and Character Development Among Adolescents
### By Jay Coakley

*Invited presentation given to the Sunny Sport of Hundreds of Millions of Chinese Students at the 2007 China Forum on the Physical Health of Chinese Children and Youth*

*Beijing, China June 1–2, 2007*

■ ■ ■ ■ ■ ■

For nearly sixty years, researchers in North America and Europe have examined the validity of the belief that "sport builds character."[1] Most research on this issue involves comparisons of the traits, attitudes, and actions of those who regularly play organized sports and those who don't play them. These comparisons have produced inconsistent findings due, in part, to two methodological problems. First, researchers have used different definitions and measures of character in their studies,[2] and second, they have mistakenly assumed that all young people who play sports have the same experiences, and that all organized sports provide experiences that are unavailable to young people who do not play them.[3] Therefore, current research does not support a general statement about the impact of sport participation on character development among adolescents, but it does provide other useful information about the character-building potential of sports in the lives of young people.[4]

### ■ ■ ■ Researchers Have Used Many Different Definitions of "Character" When Studying Sports

In Europe and North America, most definitions of character refer to a person's moral qualities as expressed through their attitudes and actions. In general terms, a person with good character moderates and controls self while acting fairly and ethically in everyday relationships. When studying sport, most researchers assume that character refers to moral or ethical strength, but when they collect data they use widely varying operational definitions to measure character.[5] Even when researchers define character in terms of moral development and moral decision-making, they use different operational measures depending on the theory of moral development that guides data collection and analysis.

The patterns that emerge in this research are not clear, but they raise the possibility that participating in sports during adolescence can be negatively associated with moral reasoning abilities and actions on the playing field. An exception to this pattern exists when a sport program explicitly emphasizes moral development as a goal and

is organized to teach moral lessons in connection with sport participation.[6]

Research also suggests that young people who play competitive sports for a long time are more likely than their peers to accept rule violations and certain aggressive and potentially injurious actions as acceptable in sports. However, most adolescent athletes learn to distinguish between sports and other spheres of life when it comes to definitions of moral action.[7]

In general, when compared to their peers who do not play sports, adolescent athletes appear to have more utilitarian approaches to ethics and moral decision-making. This is especially true for boys when compared to girls, for athletes in contact sports when compared to athletes in non-contact sports, and for athletes who have played organized, competitive sports for many years compared to those who have played for a short time.

These findings show that conventional norms are set aside in sports and that athletes often use an "egocentric morality" in which competitive success assumes dominant importance. Therefore, young people who regularly play organized, competitive sports see the rules of their sports as important but they are willing to break them for strategic purposes.[8] Scholars debate what this means in terms of the character developing potential of sport participation.

### ■ ■ ■ Sports Offer Diverse Developmental Possibilities

The second issue that has created contradictory findings in studies of sport participation and character development is that researchers overlook one or more of the following facts about sports, sport participation, and sport participants.

First, sports offer many different experiences to adolescents because programs and teams are organized in vastly different ways. Given diverse experiences among athletes, it is unrealistic to seek a single conclusion about sport participation and character development.

Second, adolescents who choose or are selected to play sports often have different character traits than peers who are not interested in sports or are not selected onto teams by coaches. For example, coaches perceive certain traits as necessary for success and evaluate young people favorably when they possess these traits prior to participation. This makes it difficult to determine if people with certain traits are selected into sports or if certain traits are developed while playing sports.

Third, the meanings that adolescents give to sport experiences vary from one person to the next, even when they play in the same programs and on the same teams. Therefore, the possibilities for character development vary widely as young people interpret sport experiences and apply them to their lives in different ways. Interpretations and applications vary with perspectives that are influenced by gender, race, ethnicity, social class, sexuality, level of (dis)ability, family and peer relationships, and past experiences, among other factors.

Fourth, the meanings that adolescents give to sport experiences often change as they mature and view themselves in new ways. Therefore, young people revise their evaluation of past experiences as they develop new ideas and values; furthermore, as their sense of self changes, they may revise their interpretations of how sport participation has contributed to their character.

Fifth, character development occurs through the relationships and social interaction that accompany sport participation. Therefore, the impact of participation depends on the social context in which participation occurs; the physical act of merely playing sports is not what influences character.

Sixth, the character development that may occur during sport participation may also occur in other activities. Therefore, adolescents who do not play sports can develop the same traits as their peers who play sports.

When these factors are not taken into account by scholars who study sports it becomes difficult to draw conclusions about the impact of sport participation on character development. However, despite the methodological problems raised by these oversights, it is possible to draw useful conclusions about sport participation in the lives of adolescents.

## ■ ■ ■ Current Knowledge About Sports and Character Development Among Adolescents

A careful review of research indicates that sport participation is most likely to have positive consequences for character development when it does one or more of the following things:[9]

1. extends a young person's knowledge about realities beyond sports

2. facilitates new interests and identities apart from playing sports and being an athlete

3. involves young people in new relationships that are not connected with sports or organized around their identity as an athlete

4. provides explicit information about the ways that sport experiences teach skills that are transferable to non-sport situations

5. provides opportunities to develop and display competence that is observed by people who become mentors and advocates for a young person

In general terms, this means that playing sports is most likely to have positive consequences for development when it expands and diversifies normal, developmental opportunities. On the other hand, when it narrows and constricts normal developmental opportunities, it is likely to have negative consequences. Therefore, neither positive nor negative character traits are automatically or systematically developed in sports.

This conclusion does not mean that sports and sport participation are irrelevant in the lives of adolescents. We know that sport-related discourses, images, experiences, knowledge, identities, and relationships are vivid and powerful in many regions of the world today. However, the influence of sports cannot be summarized in terms of a single or dominant pattern, nor can it be separated from the ways that young people define sports and integrate them into their lives. This knowledge helps us make additional conclusions about sports and character development. These conclusions include the following:

- Sport experiences are diverse because sports are defined and organized in diverse ways.[10] Competitive sports, for example, are generally organized to emphasize power, performance, and a quest for competitive success, whereas recreational sports are organized to emphasize participation, pleasure, and cooperative connections between people. Similarly, there are organizational and experiential differences between adventure sports, informal sports, alternative sports, extreme sports, folk sports, artistic sports, and so on. Playing sports may be accompanied by commitment and deeply felt emotions, but different sports played under diverse conditions offer very different developmental possibilities.[11]

- Sports do not cause specific developmental outcomes; instead, they serve as sites for experiences that have the potential to influence the lives of young people. Research shows that the developmental consequences of sport participation vary with the meanings that young people give to the sports they play and the experiences they have while playing them. Those meanings vary with the characteristics, perspectives, and identities of young people, combined with the social relationships associated with their participation, the prevailing values and ideologies that exist in the culture in which participation occurs, and the relationships between the organization of sports and the structure of the larger society.[12]

- The meanings that young people give to sport participation are influenced by prevailing ideas and beliefs about age, gender, race and ethnicity, social class, sexuality, and (dis)ability, among other factors. Those meanings often change over time as young people mature and see themselves and their relationship with the world around them in new ways.[13]

- Young people make decisions to become involved in sports, stay involved, and terminate involvement, and these decisions are influenced by gender, race and ethnicity, social class, past experiences in sports, access to participation opportunities, material and social support for participation, perceived skills and perceived chances to achieve success, and the perceived relevance of sport participation to developing autonomy and becoming an adult.[14]

- The long-term developmental potential of sport participation in the lives of young people depends on the extent to which sport programs are combined with critically informed strategies to change the forces that produce social, political, and economic dislocation in the communities where young people live. Therefore, positive developmental outcomes are most likely when the young people who play sports feel that they are physically safe, personally valued, morally and economically supported, personally and politically empowered, and connected with a social network of people who can advocate their interests.[15] All of these things make young people hopeful about their future, which supports the process of character development.

- Elite sport programs, such as the interscholastic and intercollegiate sport programs that exist in U.S. schools may discourage general sport participation if the elite programs are given first priority for funding and the allocation of resources in schools and communities. When young people detect favoritism in the ways they are treated in connection with the provision of sport participation opportunities, they may even resist participation in elite sports to register their opposition to the funding and status priorities set by school authorities.[16]

### ■■■ What We Don't Know About Sports and Development Among Adolescents

Knowledge about sport participation and character development in the lives of young people can be extended with more research, especially research that studies the experiences of adolescents over a long period of time. Unfortunately, the unquestioned belief that "sport builds character" has partially undermined support for this research and led many people to resist research that critically examines sport and may lead to findings that contradict their belief.

The topics that are most in need of research are the following:

- What factors influence young people as they make sport participation choices, give meaning to sports and sport participation, and connect sport experiences with family, peer relations, education, work, occupational aspirations and opportunities, economic decisions, and media consumption?

- How are the developmental outcomes of sport participation influenced by particular meanings that young people give to sports in their lives?

- What are the conditions under which marginalized segments of the population, such as adolescents with physical and intellectual disabilities, and from particular social and geographical backgrounds feel welcome and valued as sport participants?

- How are long- and short-term sport participation patterns among adolescents influenced by highly publicized national and international sports and sport events?

- How are sport-participation decisions influenced by the discourses and vocabularies that young people use as they talk about sports and sport participation?

- What is the relationship between elite, competitive sports and the cultures of play and informal games that support other types of sport participation among young people? For example, under what conditions do organized, competitive sports undermine the spontaneity, playfulness, and relationship skills needed to sustain a wide range of physical activities that foster fitness and social connections among young people?

- To what extent and under what conditions does specialization in a single sport restrict the experiences of adolescents in ways that compromise character development?

- What are the prevailing definitions of "character" and "development" that people use in connection with sport participation, and how do those definitions influence the organization of sports and the types of experiences that young people have when they play sports?

### ■■■ The Policy Implications of Current Knowledge

Current knowledge about sports and development provides a useful starting point for recommendations about sport policies that affect adolescents. Important recommendations include the following:

- Encourage young people to participate in diverse types of sports so that experiences, relationships, and identities are expanded in ways that prepare them for adulthood in a changing world. For example, sports organized around an obedience model have different developmental implications than sports organized around a responsibility model. The former model emphasizes surveillance and conformity to rules determined by coaches and team administrators, whereas the latter emphasizes autonomy and allowing athletes to make decisions about training and team strategies. This difference is important because athletes may not see their experiences as being developmentally meaningful when they are closely monitored and regulated and primarily the result of forced conformity and obedience.[17]

- Use the informal games of young people as a guide for designing sport programs that are seen as exciting and fun. For example, when North American adolescents organize their own games and sports they give priority to (1) action, (2) personal involvement in the action, (3) controlled competition and challenges, and (4) the reaffirmation of friendships. Therefore, organized sports possessing these elements are likely to be seen as attractive by young people.

- Use resources to maintain the culture of play and games that exists in local communities, so that it is not replaced by the culture of organized, competitive sports. The developmental implications of sports become increasingly limited when a young person's experiences are exclusively focused on sport performance and competitive success and are not characterized by the joy and creativity that characterize more playful sport forms.[18]

- Emphasize inclusion in sport programs so that the social worlds created around sports do not cause potential participants to feel unwelcome. Sport participation patterns often reflect and reproduce existing social divisions in society. Therefore, participation can be increased when sports are organized to help young people transcend those divisions. Similarly, it is important to provide equitable participation opportunities across all social classes and other social categories so that certain sports are not seen by young people as representing class-based interests or other divisions that subvert participation.

- Widespread sport participation is most likely to prevail under conditions where priorities support publicly funded programs over private, commercial sport programs; recreational sport programs over performance-oriented programs; and a "sport for all" philosophy over a philosophy that emphasizes the production of highly skilled and specialized athletes. When elite adult sports are used as the primary models for sports among adolescents, participation will eventually decline as most young people discover that they cannot meet elite expectations for performance.

In conclusion, we have much to learn about the relationship between sports and character development among adolescents. However, we do know enough to make informed decisions about sport policies and programs on both national and local levels. As policies are considered, it is important to remember that all sports do not provide the same developmental opportunities and that the developmental implications of sport participation are significantly influenced by the ways that young people give meaning to sports and integrate them into their lives.

## Notes

1. Sage, G. 1998. Does Sport Affect Character Development in Athletes? *Journal of Physical Education, Recreation and Dance* 69(1): 1–18.

2. Shields, D. L. L. and B.J. L. Bredemeier. 1995. *Character Development and Physical Activity*. Champaign, IL: Human Kinetics.

3. Stoll, S.K. and J.M. Beller. 2000. Do Sports Build Character? In J. R. Gerdy, ed., *Sports in School: The Future of an Institution*. New York, NY: Teachers College Press. 18–30.

4. Stoll, S.K. and J.M. Beller. 1998. Can Character be Measured? *Journal of Physical Education, Recreation and Dance* 69(1): 19–24.

5. McCormack, J.B. and L. Chalip. 1988. Sport as Socialization: A Critique of Methodological Premises. *The Social Science Journal* 25, 1: 83–92.

6. Miracle, A.W. and C.R. Rees. 1994. *Lessons of the Locker Room: The Myth of School Sports*. Amherst, NY: Prometheus Books.

7. Operational definitions of character and moral strength have included many different traits including courage, fortitude, discipline, hard work, tenacity, assertiveness, competitiveness, confidence, humility, graciousness, self-reliance, a focus on task accomplishment, commitment to success, cooperation, concern for others, altruism, and willingness to share, among others.

8. Ewing, M.E. et al. 2002. The Role of Sports in Youth Development. In M. Gatz, M. A. Messner, and S. J. Ball-Rokeach, eds., *Paradoxes of Youth and Sport*. Albany, NY: State University of New York Press. 31–48.

9. Martinek, T.J. and T. Shilling. 2003. Developing Compassionate Leadership in Underserved Youth. *Journal of Physical Education, Recreation, and Dance* 74(5): 33–39.

10. Trulson, M.E. 1986. Martial Arts Training: A Novel "Cure" for Juvenile Delinquency. *Human Relations* 39(12): 1131–1140.

11. Bredemeier, B. and D. Shields. 1984. Divergence in Moral Reasoning About Sport and Everyday Life. *Sociology of Sport Journal* 1(4): 348–357.

12. Beller, J. M. and S. K. Stoll. 1995. Moral Reasoning of High School Athletes and General Students: An Empirical Study Versus Personal Testimony. *Journal of Pediatric Exercise Science* 7: 352–363.

13. Coakley, J. 2007. *Sports in Society: Issues and Controversies.* New York, NY: McGraw-Hill; chapter 4.

14. Coakley, J. 1983. Play, Games and Sports: Developmental Implications for Young People. In J. C. Harris and R. J. Park, eds. *Play, Games and Sports in Cultural Contexts.* Champaign, IL: Human Kinetics. 431–450.

15. Adler, P.A., and P. Adler. 1998. *Peer Power: Preadolescent Culture and Identity.* New Brunswick, NJ: Rutgers University Press.

16. Coakley, J. 1996. Socialization Through Sports. In O. Bar-Or, ed. *The Child and Adolescent Athlete.* Vol. 6 of the *Encyclopaedia of Sports Medicine, a publication of the IOC Medical Commission.* London: Blackwell Science. 353–363.

17. Miller, K.E. et al. 1998. Athletic Participation and Sexual Behavior in Adolescents: The Different World of Boys and Girls. *Journal of Health and Social Behavior.* 39: 108-123.

18. Coakley, J. and A. White. 1992. Making Decisions: Gender and Sport Participation Among British Adolescents. *Sociology of Sport Journal.* 9(1): 20–35.

◀◀ **Source:** Jay Coakley is professor Emeritus of sociology. University of Colorado at Colorado Springs. Reprinted with permission.

# 7. Hockey Dad's Diary

## By Peter Cheney

*Globe and Mail reporter Peter Cheney is chronicling his ten-year-old son's season in the Greater Toronto Hockey League, where boys and girls leave behind the carefree game of childhood to enter a new, competitive world.*

■■■■■■

November 30, 2002

### ■■■ Penguins Come Riding to Willie's Rescue

**W**hen the coach of the Toronto Penguins called, it might as well have been the governor on the phone, calling to tell the guards that they could turn off the electric chair.

For more than a week, a black mood had hung over our once-happy hockey home—our ten-year-old son had tried out for the top team in his AA atom division and been rejected.

For Willie, hockey had never involved anything but pure, sporting joy. In house league, he had been handed a trophy every season, win or lose. They covered the top of his dresser like little Oscars. But the days of automatic success and acceptance were over—Willie had been dropped into the meat grinder of rep hockey, where feelings mean nothing next to results.

The call from the Penguins coach broke the gloom. Willie had made it onto a real AA team. Getting picked by the Penguins also involved a certain personal vindication. One of Willie's friends, who had been on the Penguins the year before, had been predicting failure all winter. Over and over, he told Willie that he had no chance of making AA.

The friend advised Willie to try out for a select team, the next step up from house league. But Willie wanted to try for AA, several rungs up the competitive hockey ladder. Going out for the Knights had been a case of aiming extra high, like an amateur guitarist who decides to break into rock music by auditioning for the Rolling Stones.

As I had seen it, Willie had nothing to lose by going for the Knights. But he did. The rejection had clearly hurt. Just hours before the Penguin tryout, Willie had started crying. He announced that he wasn't going. My wife snapped instantly into action.

"Yes you are," she replied. "You've been talking about this all winter, and you're going. You're not quitting now. If you don't make it, it doesn't matter. But you're going to try."

The drive to the rink was tense. Willie was clearly worried that he faced yet another humiliation. I knew that my wife was right to order him back on the horse, but I still agonized. After five years of watching Willie's joyous, carefree play in house league, I wondered what he was getting into—should we call this whole thing off, and spend the winter skiing downhill, the sport I had grown up with and still loved?

Frankly, I saw skiing as a far more beautiful sport than hockey, which was played by toothless guys with scars. I associated hockey with Don Cherry rants, stinking locker rooms, and bench-clearing brawls. Skiing took you out into nature instead of jamming you into a refrigerated building where sleep-deprived parents ate from vending machines and dreamed, against all odds, of the day when their little Johnny would appear on *Hockey Night in Canada.*

In skiing, you weren't up against anybody. In hockey, competition hung in the air like Zyklon gas. And in all my years of skiing, I had never seen two dads in mullet cuts punching each other's lights out.

But I also had to admit my six years of watching Willie at the rink, and learning the game through him, had gradually opened my eyes. I began to see the beauty behind hockey's sometimes-ugly face. And even if you never made the NHL, an understanding of hockey could come in handy in unexpected ways. If you understood hockey, you understood your fellow Canadians.

There was a practical element as well. The game had spun off an unimaginable industry that fed everyone from commentators to equipment manufacturers to ticket scalpers. Someone had invented a machine that washed smelly hockey equipment. Someone else published a guide to all the arenas in Toronto—an item that has become a bible for rink parents. At a dinner party, I met a software engineer who marketed CD's filled with information about individual players as a kind of high-tech hockey card.

I didn't know where hockey would lead my son. All I knew was that he loved it. He played it everywhere he went. When darkness fell, he would still be in the alley taking shots. After dinner, he moved to the basement, to practise with the miniature plastic nets I'd bought him at Canadian Tire.

For Willie, hockey was The Game. So of course he had to go to the tryout. A few hours later, Willie was on the ice, his mood improved by the simple fact of being on skates again. I wanted him to succeed. Could he do it? It felt like the big time. The Penguins rink was a deluxe affair, with weight rooms and an elevated viewing lounge that had wingback chairs, a pool table, and a wet bar. Each dressing room was named after an NHL legend—Willie changed in the Boom-Boom Geoffrion room.

On the ice, he looked better than he had with the Knights. He wasn't the best, but he wasn't the worst, either. He got the puck and kept it. An hour later, he was done, and happy. The coach began making his way around to the parents at ice side. He asked us if Willie would come to another practice session.

Two weeks later, we were back. Willie played beautifully, tapping into the reserves of joy and skill that had carried him through house league. The call came on my cellphone as we headed home. Willie was on the team. And then it hit me—so were we.

December 14, 2002

## ■■■ Hockey Families Need Deep, Deep Pockets

Along with all my other deluded ideas about the game, I thought of hockey as a poor man's sport. Then my son Willie made it to the AA Penguins and that notion was quickly shattered. Being the parent of a ten-year-old minor hockey player, I learned, is like running a marathon while having your bank account siphoned.

By November, my wife and I had travelled to so many rinks that they blurred together into a single memory of dank change rooms, overcooked hotdogs, and circling Zambonis. Our bank balance was sinking. We had entered a parallel universe of dawn practices, vending-machine dinners, and childhood dreams, all of it fuelled by an unending flow of cash.

It started with the bill for being on the team—$2,500. That figure was announced at a summer welcoming party held at the home of one of the Penguin parents, which happened to be set in one of Toronto's most deluxe neighbourhoods. The house was a cavernous Edwardian manse, with rolling green lawns, a housekeeping staff, and a pool cabana big enough to live in.

The team manager, who drove a silver BMW, gathered the parents at poolside to go over the budget and tell us what the individual tab would be. We'd been warned that it would be high—at least $1,500, probably more. When the $2,500 figure was announced, my wife and I sagged.

We exchanged panicked glances with our two closest friends, whose son was also joining the Penguins. Moneywise, they'd had a couple of difficult years, and they feared that they were approaching the financial equivalent of what submariners call "crush depth." They had decided to sell their house, only to find that the market was slumping. Now they faced the Penguins bill, which meant a further descent into their line of credit.

My wife and I had a fair line of credit going ourselves. But there was no turning back. Our son's dream of the hockey big time was coming true. Now we had to pay for it. The Penguin team fees would cover ice time, uniforms, matching team tracksuits, hats, backpacks, and hockey bags, plus weekly power-skating sessions and a professional trainer. But that was just the beginning.

At our first game, we were stopped at the door and told that we would have to pay an admission fee of $3 each—and our son would have to pay, too. I soon found out that this policy was in place at every arena. By the end of the season, we will probably have paid about $400 to the rinks—a figure that does not include the money we drop on hotdogs, Gatorade, popcorn, and hot chocolate.

Then there was equipment. Mercifully, most of Willie's gear still fit him, and his helmet was the right colour—black. If it hadn't been, we would have to buy another. But we still needed a custom-fitted Penguin mouth guard ($70) and new skates—his old ones were too small. At the hockey store, I was told that a AA player needed quality blades. The salesman showed me the lowest-priced skates that he could recommend. They cost $200.

"When you're on the ice four, five times a week, the cheap ones don't hold up," he said. "Don't waste your money."

The real financial hit came in late November, when we headed to Pittsburgh for a tournament. The parents voted to rent a bus, so we could all drive down together. We ate together, stayed in the same hotel, and got up each day at 5 a.m. to ride to the arena.

We went to a Pittsburgh Penguin game, hung out in the hospitality suite, and talked hockey. The boys got to meet Mario Lemieux and Martin Straka. Four days later, we came away with enough memories to last a lifetime. On the way back to Toronto, the team manager gave each of us our bill. Including the hotel, ours came to $1,450.

I began to wonder if we were out of our league, financially speaking. I called my friend Rob, who has three sons, two of them in the GTHL. He told me he spends at least $7,500 a year. On top of that, he's on the hook for fundraising—for the past several years, I have received a steady stream of invitations from him to team dinners, raffles, and chocolate-bar sales.

"You're lucky," he said. "All you guys have to do is write a cheque."

It is now mid-December. Already, my wife and I have spent the equivalent of a year's tuition at a good Canadian university. My friend Dave, who raised three daughters and never paid for so much as a hockey stick in his life, finds it hard to believe. "That's a lot of cash," he observed. "It's nuts."

Once, I would have agreed. Now, I consider what we've received in exchange. Willie has learned new skills. He has a nifty Penguins hockey bag, home and away jerseys with his name on the shoulders. More importantly, he has a sense of commitment and discipline that I did not possess at the age of ten. Each day, he does his homework immediately after school, so he can make it to the rink. Even though he is on the ice four to five times a week, his marks have actually improved.

On Saturdays, he gets up at 5:30 a.m. for practice. He works out on the ice, then runs on a treadmill and does plyometrics (a series of movements that forces your muscles to contract, stretch, and then immediately contract again). I have never heard a complaint. For him, this is the price of being a Penguin. My wife and I, like all the other hockey parents, pay as well. Some can easily afford it. Others sacrifice. Either way, the game goes on.

■ ■ ■ ■ ■

January 25, 2003

### ■ ■ ■ Feud Threatens to Tear Apart Team

*Although parents always say the game is "all about the kids," few seem content to sit still if their youngsters are losing*

■ ■ ■ ■ ■

In hot rodding, there is a term for a car that looks good but doesn't win races: all show and no go. This month, we were starting to wonder whether Willie's hockey team was that kind of machine. The Penguins were one of the sharpest-looking squads of ten-year-olds in the league, but they were ninth in a fourteen-team league.

With the end of the regular season looming, and a playoff spot looking increasingly doubtful, the Penguins' future has become the subject of endless discussion—not to say scheming—among the parents. Since I had never played hockey, I had only a vague notion of the philosophy and politics that run through the national game. Now I'm getting a crash course.

Although parents conceal their competitiveness behind a mantra that is summed up in the stock phrase "it's all about the kids," few will sit still if their team is on a losing string. In hockey, losing opens the door to the forces of change. And so it is with the Penguins, where we are now engaged in a battle for control of the team and what it should be.

Two camps have emerged among the parents. One believes in keeping the team together. The other wants to rip apart the team and recruit new players to make it stronger.

The first inkling of change was a rumour that began circulating about the beginning of the new year. One of our friends called to tell us that one of the dads on the team, whose son is a star player, wanted to take over as coach and subject the team to a ruthless culling.

"The word is that he wants to keep four players," she said. "Everyone else is gone."

I was shocked. When Willie made the Penguins last summer, I thought that was the end of the competition, at least until it was time for him to try out for AAA. Now I realized that hockey is an endless tryout.

Things came to a head at a recent parents meeting where we learned that the rumour about the dad taking over was true. Our current coach, whom we admire for his calmness and skill, will be leaving to devote more time to his family. Two fathers on the team wanted to take over as coach—and both wanted to clean house.

If that happened, I didn't know whether Willie would make the team again. Nor would there be guaranteed positions for his friends Jake and Ellery, whose parents live close to us and share the driving. If the team was rebuilt through tryouts and eliminations, our little world would be destroyed—no more drives to the rink with John and Yvonne. No more hot chocolate with our friend Susan. And Willie could find himself a boy without a team.

A number of the parents, including my wife and I, wanted no part of this new, Darwinian world. To us, it was more important that the boys stay together, that they remain friends and that they grow up a team, win or lose. The team manager was on our side. He announced that he would leave if the team didn't commit to keeping all the players.

Others believed it was naive and misguided not to pursue a philosophy of unfettered competition. "They have to compete," one dad said. "That's just the way it is. Nobody gets any promises."

I began to wonder: would guaranteeing every boy a position make a worse team or a better one? On the one hand, it makes sense to get the best players you can by holding tryouts. But I noticed that the best team in the division, the mighty North York Knights, had stayed together for several seasons.

Watching the Knights had shown me the value of teamwork. The Knights are as tightly choreographed as James Brown's band—each player is a cog in a machine that moves the puck up the ice with lethal efficiency.

Player for player, some of the Penguins are the Knights' equal. Take Alex, for example, a forward whose father is one of the Penguins' would-be coaches. Alex is probably the single most skilled player on the Penguins, a ten-year-old virtuoso who can skate and stickhandle with stunning agility.

His only failing is that he doesn't like to pass. This trait is understandable when you see how much better Alex is than most other players. Why give the puck to someone who can't do as good a job with it as you can?

If Alex's dad takes over as coach, he would be guaranteed a position for two reasons: his matchless skills and connection with management. But who would be his teammates? Many of the boys he has played with this year would be gone, to be replaced with others discovered through scouting and tryouts.

At this moment, everything is up in the air. The two dads who want to coach have been asked to submit proposals. A third coach is being wooed by a group of parents who want to keep the current team together.

I think we should keep the team together. The Penguins may be ninth, but they're getting better all the time. Willie is finally learning how to pivot. Alex is passing more and more. Jake, who started playing several years later than the other boys, has caught up. Ellery has become a powerful defenceman.

This is all good. But can the ninth-place Penguins go on to become a dynasty? I don't know. But I have cast my lot with the forces of continuity. Win or lose, I want the Penguins to remain intact. I'm no hockey expert. But I believe that staying together is the most important lesson of all.

■ ■ ■ ■ ■ ■

February 8, 2003

## ■ ■ ■ Coaching Soap Opera Forgets Kids' Welfare

*Unnecessary intrigue of process caters to Scotty Bowman pretenders*

■ ■ ■ ■ ■ ■

By last week, I'd heard minor hockey's catch phrase, "it's all about the kids," a few times too many, and I had slipped it into a mental file of lines that say one thing, but really mean another. It's similar to a salesman who realizes you won't be buying a car from him saying, "have a nice day."

When this past Monday night rolled around, I was in no mood to hear that it was "all about the kids" yet again. It was time for our latest meeting, which was to choose the next coach of the AA atom Penguins.

I had been amazed at the complication of the process, which involved weeks of rumours, counter-rumours, cellphone calls, lobbying, campaigning, a certain amount of mudslinging, and a series of meetings in which it became clear that getting the parents of all fifteen boys to agree would be about as likely as achieving peace in the Middle East.

I wanted it over with. Now we were gathered once again in a windowed lounge that overlooked the rink at the Canadian Ice Academy, where our ten-year-old sons were skating happily through a practice, oblivious to the politics and double dealing taking place on the other side of the glass.

The meeting was supposed to be a formality. Three days before, we had finally come to an agreement about who the new coach would be. The choice, which was nearly unanimous, was my friend John, who had thrown his hat in the ring at the last minute. To me, his win was a happy surprise. But the meeting had ended on a strange note. Instead of calling John and the other candidates in to announce the decision, we had been asked to keep the results secret until after the boys had played two crucial weekend games.

Frankly, I considered the chances of the decision remaining secret extremely slim, but I went along with it. When John asked me how the meeting went, I replied with the lie we had concocted to cover the situation. "It went fine," I said. "We had a good discussion, and we're going to vote on Monday night."

For three days, I couldn't tell my friend that he had won. And then came this past Monday's meeting. It became clear that the secret had leaked out, at least in certain quarters. The manager announced that one of the other candidates, whose son was the Penguin's top scorer, was leaving the team. So was another dad. A third father was on the fence, but clearly leaning toward a move. I began to wonder exactly what was going on.

I assumed that the manager was about to call John and the other remaining coach into the room to tell them the choice had been made. But that's not what happened. Instead, the father who was sitting on the fence began reiterating his concerns about the team, and began talking about who we could bring in as coach.

I was staggered. I thought the deal was done, only to learn that the three-day news blackout over John's win had been used to start yet another round of backroom negotiations for the coaching job.

Others began to object, pointing out that a decision had already been reached. One of the fathers leading the move to continue the search began a critique of the Penguins this year. In his view, the boys hadn't progressed. He wanted more discipline and sharper drills. He said he thought the Penguins weren't really even a AA team.

"What I'm seeing out there is house league," he announced. I had heard this opinion, and many more, at previous meetings. As I was learning, being on a hockey team can be like travelling on a bus where everyone wants to drive. Since I have virtually no knowledge of the game, I am forced to make all my decisions on the basis of common sense, not technical expertise. My common sense was telling me that the direction of this meeting wasn't good.

The father finally wrapped up his lengthy critique with the dreaded line. "Look, it's all about the kids," he concluded.

I finally spoke up. I told him that I didn't think it was about the kids at all. I thought it was about parents living out their own middle-aged hockey fantasies through their ten-year-old sons. As I saw it, some of these dads wanted to be Scotty Bowman, creating a mighty hockey dynasty through their vision and skill.

I agreed that the Penguins should have performed better this season. They were now tenth out of fifteen teams in their division. It seemed to me that they probably could have been fifth or so. But I didn't want to spend any more time haggling over a decision that should have been made weeks before. I thought John was a good choice. I believed that he would reinvigorate the team and serve as an excellent role model. Even if he wasn't perfect, it was far better than no choice at all.

The year before, ten out of fifteen families had left the team amidst a continuing struggle over leadership and direction. In minor hockey, I was learning, this kind of anarchy was common. It happened to team after team. Our dispute was actually going rather well. No fathers had ended up in a fist fight.

But now we were mired in the same tiresome dealmaking that had sucked up the past month or so.

I prayed inwardly for it all to end. And then, miraculously, it did. Several of the other parents spoke. They were reasonable people. What they said made sense. Ten minutes later, it was decided that John would be told that he was the new coach.

A couple of the parents looked unhappy. But most looked relieved. Half an hour later, we were all in the van, heading home. Willie was in the back seat with his friends. A few minutes later, he spoke up.

"How did the meeting go, Dad?"

"Great," I told him.

■■■■■■

April 19, 2003

## ■■■ Owner's Demands Cause Anxiety in Hockey War Environment

After months of turmoil and politicking that had shown us the dark side of minor hockey, the Penguins' troubled house seemed to be in order at last. The great coaching debate, which had divided the team, had ended with the appointment of John O'Hara, one of the other hockey dads.

John's selection had been like the election of a new leader in a country torn apart by war. There were wounds to heal, and problems to be fixed, but we were moving forward. The 2002–2003 season had ended on a bit of a downer—the Penguins had missed the playoffs and wound up in eleventh place out of fifteen teams. Under John, we hoped to crack the top five. In any case, my wife and I were happy, and so was our son Willie.

Then came the phone call.

It was John. The Penguins, he announced, had been taken over and he was out as coach. There would be a weekend meeting where the new owner would outline his plans. That Sunday, we made our way to an arena in Scarborough. A black Porsche was parked outside.

As our ten-year-old boys took to the ice, we gathered in a room filled with stacking chairs and a table at the front that gave it the look of a Second World War briefing room. The new owner, it turned out, was Stu Hyman. I'd heard of him before. It would be hard not to. In the world of minor hockey, Hyman has a reputation that could be compared to that of Napoleon Bonaparte's in the field of European politics.

Like Napoleon, Hyman has conquered the world around him. He is a wealthy man who has five boys and an obsessive interest in the game of hockey. I'd heard countless stories about Hyman and the teams he had created for his sons. These teams were not for the destitute, or for the weak of heart. One had an annual budget of $200,000—nearly five times what we had spent on the Penguins during the past season. I was told that Hyman had once tried to hold tryouts during school time, to weed out the less-committed parents and players.

After all I'd heard, I expected a cross between Harold Ballard and Saddam Hussein. But, in person, Hyman seemed nothing like an evil dictator.

Instead, he seemed like a pleasant, average guy, someone you might run into at at Canadian Tire. He was dressed in a baggy T-shirt and worn running shoes, and talked in a style that suggested reason. But as he spoke, I realized that nothing would be the same for us again.

Hyman's plan was to convert the Penguins into the top team in the AA atom division. He outlined the new program like a general detailing an invasion. He had hired one of the best coaches in the country. The team would practise at least twice as much as before. We would play and practise year-round, with a six-week break in the summer. Before school started in the fall, the boys would attend a two-week camp to polish their skills.

There would be new uniforms, new discipline—and a new budget. Hyman spoke of "making a Mercedes," and said there would be a significant fee increase. How significant? That would be worked out later. I sagged inwardly. The Penguins already had the highest fees in the GTHL—last season, my wife and I paid $2,500 for Willie to be on the team.

I wondered what we would be in for now. There were no figures as yet, but it would clearly be steep. Hyman softened the blow by telling us that we should talk to him if we couldn't afford it, and said he was prepared to subsidize some families under the right circumstances. I wondered what those circumstances would be. Did you have to be the unemployed parent of the next Wayne Gretzky?

The next question was whether our sons would be welcomed onto the new, improved Penguins, or whether they would be blown out to make room for more skilled players. On that score, there

was no clear answer. Hyman said he wanted us all back, but cautioned that the coach would have the final say.

There would be a few practices where the coach could evaluate Willie and his friends. Then there would be a tryout, where the Penguins would look at new prospects. Who knew what would happen?

My wife and I realized that we had reached a fork in the road. Hyman was upping the ante, in every sense of the word. There would be more pressure. There would be more practices. There would be more skills development. And there would be a bigger bill.

We could choose that, or we could go to another team, assuming we could find one. Hyman was presenting an opportunity to be part of something unique. He wanted to take our sons on a journey to hockey excellence—or was that extravagance? He wanted the Penguins to grab for the brass ring.

We didn't know what the tab would be, or who Hyman was prepared to subsidize. Could we cry poor? My wife and I had jobs, a house (semi-detached, badly in need of renovation), and a minivan (dented, in need of new tires.) Was I supposed to sell something to pay for my ten-year-old son's hockey? Were we condemning him to hockey mediocrity because we weren't ready to move into a garret?

As we headed home, thoughts ran through my head. Once again, our boy's hockey career had sucked us into a vortex of decision-making and angst. We had some big choices to make. Could we run in the same pack as hockey-obsessed millionaires? Would the team split up? Could we find another one?

I could see that the Penguin team I had known was gone. That team was a Chevrolet, or maybe a Honda. Now we were being offered a Mercedes. It might be a great ride. But what would happen when the payments were due? And could we really see ourselves in a Mercedes?

■ ■ ■ ■ ■ ■

April 29, 2003

### ■■■ Time Had Come to Make the Big Decision—To Stay or Leave

We had been promised that things would change with the Penguins, and at the first practice with the new coach, it was clear that they had. My wife and I watched in wonder. We'd never seen Willie and his ten-year-old teammates perform like this before.

The drills ran with machine-like precision, and the boys seemed infused with new energy. The AA atom Penguins had been transformed from a Chevrolet into a Porsche. There was no slacking. Our sons were skating as if their lives depended on it. And in a way, they did. Under the Penguins' new management, everyone would have to earn a place on the team again.

The takeover of Penguins had abruptly altered our lives. New owner Stuart Hyman had arrived on the scene like General Tommy Franks in Iraq— the old order was gone, instantly replaced by a new regime. The new coach was only part of the equation. The amount of ice time would be more than doubled, and the team would operate forty-six weeks a year. There would be new uniforms, matching home-and-away helmets, and brand new Penguin hockey bags, even though the old ones looked just fine to me.

That raised the question that was on all our minds. How much would we have to pay? The Penguins budget, we were told, would be increased from $45,000 to about $135,000. We all did some mental math, trying to figure out what our share would be. Hyman had said that he would subsidize part of the cost, but we could see that we were in for a shock. We felt like condemned prisoners waiting for news about our sentence. Would it be flaying or burning at the stake?

Two weeks later, we got the news. The bill would be $5,000. We were numb. Could we come up with the money? Would we cripple our son's hockey career if we didn't keep him on the Penguins with the new coach? Maybe we could sell our minivan to raise the money—except we needed it to carry all the hockey equipment.

Cost wasn't the only problem. There was the matter of whether the boys could make the team. We thought it might be great for Willie and his friends to stay on the Penguins and experience the thrill of the transformation. But would they be allowed to stay? Competition was now the order of the day.

Hyman had already brought in a couple of new players to skate with the team. One of them, in particular, recalibrated the skill level entirely. The rest of the Penguins, including Willie, essentially served as pylons for him to skate around. The tryouts would bring a further flood of talent.

Getting cut would hurt. But there was a practical matter to be considered. Willie had joined the Penguins with two friends whose parents carpooled with us, spreading the burden of the five-times-a-week journey to rinks all over the city. If they didn't get on the same team, we would find ourselves in commuter hell.

Of the three friends, Willie probably had the best shot of making the team, given that he had been the team's second-highest scorer. What if he made it and his friends didn't? Should our old gang of friends split up? What should come first, our social arrangements or unbridled competition?

We hoped that somehow, they'd all make it back onto the team. By the second practice with the new coach, the boys were tired. The pace was tough, and he allowed no respites. Sometimes, the coach would whack them on the back with the flat of his stick blade, like a jockey flogging a thoroughbred. He wanted them to be winners, and he wasn't afraid to push them.

As this went on, we knew our sons were being appraised. Then came the word. After the third practice, we would be told who would have a spot on the team. It felt like we were living on a reality TV set. Who would be offered a rose? Who would get booted off the island?

The night of the third practice was tough. We drove to the rink with our friends, knowing that it might be our last ride together as teammates. On the ice, the boys looked like they were running out of gas. As they changed into their street clothes, the manager said he would call us later that night with the news.

We went back to our house for a glass of wine. One glass turned to three. The phone rang. It was the manager. Willie was in. His friends were out.

The questions we had been pondering were no longer theoretical. We had to choose. Did we want Willie to be on a team that cut his friends and cost $5,000? Would the Penguins go from eleventh place to the top three? Could we handle forty-six weeks of hockey a year? Did we want him with a coach who could make him a better player but hit him with a stick?

The next day, we sent an email to the manager. We were out. The money was only part of it. We thought it was wrong for the team to up the ante so sharply in the name of competition. No other team would spend so much, or practise so much. What message would this approach send to our son?

The Penguins were going to go for the brass ring. There was nothing wrong with that. But there would be other teams trying to do the same thing without spending so much money or driving the kids so hard. That was the way we'd have to go.

It was done. We were no longer Penguins. The next morning, Willie walked to school wearing his team jacket, which had his number stenciled on the sleeve. I remembered the pride he had felt when he first got that jacket after making the Penguins.

For him, making it onto a AA hockey squad had been like a dream come true. Now it was over, and he needed a new team.

■ ■ ■ ■ ■ ■

May 3, 2003

## ■ ■ ■ Mad Scramble to Place Boys on a New Team

Once we decided to walk away from the Penguins, we were a family without a team. And so we began our descent into the hell of spring hockey tryouts in Canada's biggest city.

For the family of a ten-year-old boy looking for a AA squad, April really is the cruelest month. The weeks passed in a haze of late-night drives, drive-through meals, and desperate phone calls. The clock was ticking. We were caught up in a city-wide game of musical chairs, trying to find a team that would take Willie and his two buddies before all the rosters were filled.

We spent our nights and weekends going to what are known as "birthday skates," thinly-disguised tryouts that give coaches a chance to look at new players—and collect up to $20 from their parents each time. Some teams ran five or six.

We started our search with some of the top teams in the league, in the deluded hope that one of them would take Willie, Jake, and Ellery as a package. We were soon forced to lower our sights.

Before long, we were looking at the league's middle and bottom feeders.

The sessions have now blurred together, but I still recall one where the boys performed for a coach who had a mullet cut and an approach that seemed to combine the worst qualities of Don Cherry and Simon Legree. He hammered his stick on the ice and yelled "Come on kid! Skate!"

We ate french fries at the rink snack bar that night and got home late. Our teenage daughter was long asleep. We checked our emails, hoping that there would be some encouraging messages from coaches. There weren't. For weeks on end, we had been on a hockey mission—we went to rinks, networked with parents, checked the GTHL website, and called coaches. So far, it had been to no avail.

When Willie played house league hockey, all we had to do was write a modest cheque and show up at the rink. Double A was a different universe. Everything about it was bigger, faster, and harder. Willie loved it. And overall, my wife and I did, too. The cost, commitment, and politics had been a little tough, but there had been a lot of fun along the way.

Now, the takeover of the Penguins had thrown us for a loop. We knew that leaving the Penguins had been the right choice. We didn't want to be on a team that went for the brass ring by spending three times as much money as anyone else and keeping our boys on the ice forty-six weeks a year.

But the true difficulty of marketing all three boys to a new team was beginning to sink in. We were constantly talking to coaches, trying to sell them on the merits of Willie, Jake, and Ellery. Our friend Yvonne had taken to calling it "pimping the kids." Despite all our efforts, there were still no takers.

And so on we went, Palestinians wandering through a great hockey desert. Various prospects loomed, only to disappear like mirages. It was rumoured that a team in the suburbs needed at least ten players. After we checked, we saw why that might be—they'd finished the season dead last. A friend told us that he knew about a A team that might take our boys. Single A? Willie had scored more than twenty goals in AA. Why move him down?

As the final tryouts approached, we realized that we had to come up with a plan. We began listing all the teams we were considering. In a single weekend, there would be dozens of tryouts. I entered the critical ones in my PalmPilot—the calendar page started to look like the radar screen of a major airport, filled with conflicting times and locations.

We had to make choices, and one team stood out in our minds—the Leaside Flames. They had placed a respectable sixth in the league, and had a reputation for putting the kids first. Of all the team officials we had met at the tryouts, Flames coach Nigel Etherington was the only one who had taken the time to meet each player and their parents, and to outline his approach and philosophy.

The team took the summer off, and the fees were reasonable: The Flames were going to try for the top, but they would do it within limits imposed by the schedules and finances of normal families. Through our rapidly expanding hockey network, we made further inquiries about the Flames. All the reports were positive.

The die was cast. We wanted our boys to be Flames. Now we'd see if they could be. The team was looking for two new forwards (Willie and Jake?) and one defenceman (Ellery?) But we knew it wouldn't be easy. There would be stiff competition for every position.

That Saturday, we went to the Flames' first tryout. The boys had been instructed to play like there was no tomorrow. My wife was a nervous wreck. Every time one of our boys fell or lost a wind sprint, she cringed. As usual, Willie looked less than stellar during the drills. He has always excelled in a game situation, but his jets rarely ignite in practice. My wife could barely stand to watch. She wanted the boys to get on the team together, and she saw the chances slipping away.

"It's out of our hands," I told her. An hour and a half later, it was over. We prepared ourselves for rejection. As the boys changed, Etherington came up to the stands.

"We're offering Willie a position," he said.

I was stunned.

I asked him about Ellery and Jake. Etherington said there was still a slim chance for Ellery, based on the final configuration of the defence, but Jake was out of the running—he was a forward, and Willie and another boy were being offered the two available positions.

Etherington needed an answer within five minutes. The parents of the next candidate in line were waiting to hear their son's fate, and the clock was ticking down toward another tryout.

Thoughts careened through our heads. Jake's mom didn't have a car. If we chose the Flames, how would she get to the rink? What about us? Could we handle five practices and games a week without our friends to share the load?

The seconds were passing. We had to give the coach an answer. We said yes. The search was over.

Willie was a Leaside Flame. The rest would have to get sorted out later.

◀◀ **Source**: Peter Cheney is a staff writer for *The Globe and Mail*. This series was originally published in *The Globe and Mail* between November 2002 and May 2003. Reprinted with permission.

## NHL Trade Deadline: The Blueline Blues
### By Wendy Berg

**8.**

*While the upheaval of a trade is hard on a hockey player, the stress might even be harder for his wife and family— both before and after*

■ ■ ■ ■ ■ ■

Two days ago, March 13, is the day hockey fans listen and watch reports in loud, crowded sports bars, hoping their favourite player doesn't get traded and waiting to see if their predictions transpire.

It is the last day that National Hockey League teams are permitted to move or acquire players until the end of the season.

I spent many trade deadline days at home alone listening in fear and hoping that I would not hear the name of the only player I really cared about.

When my husband, Bill Berg, played professional hockey, I sometimes felt like I was just along for the ride.

The problem was this: he wasn't even driving the car. The day of the trade deadline heightened my feelings of powerlessness.

Hockey season was a long ride and we just watched and waited to see where it would lead. Deadline day was a pivotal fork in the road. If not traded, our days would be bright: a Sunday afternoon drive with no more turns until the end of the year.

If traded, we were sure to spin out of control.

When I listen to reports of the deadline looming, I no longer worry about Bill packing up and leaving us behind. I don't walk down the aisle of the grocery store worrying about overstocking the fridge before the possibility of a move.

We were never traded at the deadline, but we were traded. I use the word "we" because Bill's course of action was set. His flights were arranged and all he had to do was kiss us goodbye before he walked out the door. My immediate future after a trade was always questionable. I had to pack more clothes to send to Bill, put the house up for sale, close bank accounts, prepare the kids' things, and try to maintain my composure. I seemed to incur more work than he did. The trade deadline, being so close to the end of the season, complicates the situation. It increases all the unknowns.

Each deadline day, I sat next to the radio listening for updates, fearing that I would hear Bill's name. Many of our friends learned of their trades this way. Reporters at times seem to know more about hockey players' lives than the players themselves. The phone and the radio were the only items in the room that were of necessity to us those days.

We asked our friends not to call us on the trade deadline so that we could avoid heart palpitations each time we heard the phone ring. Of course family still called: "Have you heard anything?" We didn't have call display yet.

We also learned never to call a player on deadline day. Bill and I listened to reports with sweaty palms the year I was pregnant with our daughter. She was due in a month. Leaving a pregnant wife behind could possibly be the worst trade-deadline scenario.

We did not hear Bill's name that day, but our good friend was traded. Bill immediately called to wish him well. It seemed like a nice gesture, until we realized he had not yet been notified and so of course he assumed Bill was pulling a cruel joke.

Decisions of great magnitude are thrust upon hockey players and the families must bear the brunt of the player's fast-paced career.

A wife or partner with no children may be slightly more mobile than a wife with babies or preschoolers and so may choose to move to the new city and live in a hotel room.

A mom may choose to move back to their hometown where they have family support rather than moving to the new city.

A wife with children in school is the most limited. She usually waits out the school year before arrangements are made. Wives can put their lives on hold. Children grow and exist beyond the home and beyond the hockey career.

The player will most likely remain in a hotel room until the end of the season, unless it is certain the team will do well in the playoffs. It is just too late in the season to sign a lease or buy a home.

Families are split by geographical distance and both spouses feel pressure. The player needs to perform well with the new team and the spouse must move a family with little or no assistance.

The first day of separation was always the worst. The only reason I lived in New York was because Bill played hockey. Once he was traded, I had no reason to be there, but I had too many responsibilities to leave. I felt alone and awkward.

I waited for Bill to call and then asked a barrage of questions: Will the new team make the playoffs? How far do you think they will go? How long a plane ride is it? How long a drive? Are the players nice? What about their wives? If I come with the kids can we stay in a hotel suite? Is there a wives' room?

Of course Bill could never answer any of these questions, having been there only a day, but my life was in turmoil. I knew I would never be in complete control of our lives, but I wanted to be able see the direction we were headed. It's hard to move out of the fog when a trade occurs at the deadline.

Now, it is only by coincidence that I listen to the radio the day of the deadline. My heart drops momentarily when I recognize a name, thinking about the upheaval the player and his family will experience—and then I feel relief. I am content: Bill and I are taking turns in the driver's seat and the refrigerator remains full throughout the year.

◀◀ **Source**: Wendy Berg lives near Toronto. This article was originally published in *The Globe and Mail* on March 15, 2001. Reprinted with permission.

# 5, 6, Pickup Sticks
## By Daniel Sanger

**9.**

*Hockey at its best is a cool, clear night, an outdoor rink, and a gaggle of strangers*

■ ■ ■ ■ ■ ■

Winter, the most depleting of seasons, can arrive any number of ways, some disarmingly pleasant. The most enchanting beginning is with a snowflake, then another, drifting down outside the classroom/office/kitchen window just about the time the mid-afternoon doldrums are kicking in. As daylight dwindles, the scattered snowflakes become a full-on storm, with drifts forming, cars spinning and skidding, and a rare euphoria in the air.

Those who didn't catch the morning's forecast, or who just failed to process it, slide and skate their way home in loafers and pumps, grinning at perfect strangers all the way. Meanwhile, those who left the house prepared march triumphantly through a world gone wild, but one from which they'll emerge unscathed thanks to their Sorels and parkas. The kids among us—male or female, child or long past—fire off a few snowballs. We know that, contrary to all logic, the first throws of the year will be the most accurate and that we'll nail, no problem, the stop sign at the corner, the telephone pole across the street, the maple two houses down.

Maybe the snow slacks off by ten or eleven, when it's time to take the dog out or grab some milk for the morning. Maybe it continues deep into the night, leaving a foot or more of beautiful, blinding whiteness for first light. Either way, the world is transformed, softened, and, it seems, warmed up by all the little flakes rubbing against each other as they fell. The grey glum of late autumn is done with, even if all the snow does melt away by the weekend.

That's the storybook start to winter, and, objectively, a very pleasant way for it to announce its arrival. But for people like me, it's the absolute worst way winter can begin.

The best way involves cold—lots of it—and cold alone, no snow, coming down like a hammer and not going anywhere, as soon after Halloween as possible. That means ponds and lakes freeze over like sheets of glass, the municipal parks departments begin getting the outdoor rinks in shape, and, sooner rather than later, it becomes possible to enjoy that most sublime of Canadian activities: open-air, pickup hockey.

Hockey in general has become a lame cliché in Canada. The tall foreheads at the CBC feel the country needs some national healing? Commission a unifying special or, better yet, a series. The prime minister's handlers decide he needs some humanizing? Organize a photo op of him tying up little Chad's skates. Tim Hortons wants to pitch a new soup-and-sandwich combo? Wal-Mart wants to promote a new line of kids wear made in Burmese sweatshops? The Royal Bank wants to justify the billion or so it made in profit last week? Marketing's automatic reflex: wheel out a hockey backdrop.

The game in all its guises is invoked, the more sentimentally the better: street hockey with a tennis ball on Happy Valley Crescent; Fred, Ed, Ted, and the boys and their beer league; the future superstar, age two, ankle-skating around the backyard rink.

At the same time, our practical notion of hockey—the money, time, and mental energy we spend on it—increasingly revolves around the game as played in organized leagues, whether by the pros in the NHL or the atoms of the Kirkland Lake Minor Hockey League: inside an arena, inside cumbersome equipment, most of the players on the bench most of the time, behind which a pacing, anxious coach barks out orders, behind whom one or more idiot fans or parents take it way, way too seriously. The players are said to be playing hockey, but judging by the limited laughter and smiling, there is little play involved. Rather, organized hockey is about following instructions, executing set plays, confronting opponents, scoring, and winning.

Open-air pickup hockey on the other hand, is a game of endless variety, spontaneity, adaptation, and unspoken rituals. With no coaches telling players what to do and no prescribed way to play, it lends itself to an often-beautiful creativity. With no referees and few hard-and-fast rules, it insists upon self-regulation and, in so doing, encourages accommodation and tolerance. Pickup hockey is always unpredictable and almost always instructive, even edifying, in a life-lessons kind of way. And as social interaction, it's unique: virtually no other activity involves strangers gathering in a public place, with no prior organization or commercial exchange, and engaging in a pleasurable pursuit together. Playing.

A typical evening of pickup hockey in Montreal: coming home from work or school, the thought occurs that conditions are ideal. It's not a case of remembering that it's Monday and you and your buddies have ice reserved at 11:05 p.m. at a rink in suburban Boisbriand or Brossard. Instead, you simply note that there's no sign of snow and it's not so bitterly cold that your toes will get frostbitten. So you go home and change your plans—cancel the movie, convince your girlfriend that there'll always be another parent-teacher night (and that, yes, she can, actually, record *Deadwood* for you). Until suppertime, the local rink will be aswarm with the after-school crowd, so you do other chores, perhaps making dinner for the family in order to earn the evening pass. Finally, seven, seven-thirtyish, you slip out and head to the rink, skates on stick, stick over shoulder, puck in pocket.

Even if it's ten blocks away and the rink lights are turned off at ten, you walk—it seems somehow sacrilegious to drive—the snow crunching under your boots. On the way, you pull your stick off your shoulder to fire a small chunk of ice into a snow bank or across the street. As the rink comes into view, you squint to see if there's a game going on. It's impossible to know. One night, you'll be alone, or virtually. The next—same temperature, same high-pressure system making for a similarly perfect, starry winter night—there'll not only be a six-a-side match with three subs per team in full swing, but also a more casual spillover game taking place in the dark on the adjacent, unlighted pleasure-skating rink.

Still, usually, if your timing's right, people will just be beginning to congregate. Some of the faces might be familiar. Maybe the guy you call the Bumblebee because of the way he defies the laws of physics with his split-second stops, starts, and turns. With any luck, the bright-eyed, sweet Laurence—the best woman player to frequent the rink—will show too. You never see enough of her. Then there are the archetypes: as often as not, there will be a really big—as in fat—guy who plays like a cat, all deft passes and slick, minimal manoeuvres and very little actual skating. But one of the best things is that the players will never be the same from one evening to the next.

In the changing room, one or two will be putting on their skates, but there is little chatter—at most a "ça va bien?," a "la glace a l'air bonne," or a "crisse, mes patins sont plus serrés que jamais." Everyone is eager to join the four or five others already on the ice, busy practising their shots, playing hog, or otherwise waiting for a game to begin.

Once the magic number—six if people are particularly impatient, more often eight—has been reached, someone will corral whoever is on the rink to gather at centre ice and throw their sticks into a pile. Then the youngest—universally accepted as the least devious (as well as he to whom menial tasks are assigned)—drops to his knees and gathers the sticks in front of him. Closing his eyes or making a show of looking above or off to the side, he then throws a stick toward one net with his right hand while throwing another toward the other net with his left. In this way, teams are drawn.

If someone is hung up on formalities, there'll be a faceoff. More often, a player on one team will just slide the game puck over to someone on the other team as the signal to start playing. The first minutes tend to be chaotic and confused, as players figure out who exactly their teammates are, who is playing where, and who is worth passing to—all the while skating too hard, too fast because it feels so good to be out on the ice again.

Gradually, the game evens out and hits its stride. Coordinated rushes explode out of own zones as if practised for months. Rink-wide passes land on the blades they were intended for as if sent by FedEx. Shots wend their way through impossible forests of skates and sticks as if pulled by an invisible thread.

Some nights, the nights when the rink is dominated by eighteen- to twenty-five-year-olds blessed with endless cardio and strong hockey skills, it will be almost forbiddingly fast. Other nights, when the mix is, well, more mixed—an eleven-year-old tagging along behind his older brother and his buddies, a few women in figure skates, maybe another not-so-young dad out on evening leave, perhaps a guy who is even older, creaking around for what is clearly the first time in years—it will be, if anything, too slow.

But usually a game will be both fast and slow. In the unwritten code of pickup hockey, democracy is primordial: anyone who shows up gets to play. If a player isn't very good, the game might whir around them at a dizzying speed. But once they pick up a loose puck or are fed a pass, the game will decelerate abruptly. They'll be allowed to skate a little, take a shot, or make a pass themselves. It's a nurturing gesture one wouldn't expect from a group of mostly young men, and it suggests that their own first forays onto the intimidating ice to play with the big kids are still fresh in their memories. And if someone is so unschooled in rink etiquette as to strip the weaker player of the puck as soon as he gets it, that person—typically a thirteen- or fourteen-year-old hotshot—will usually have the puck unceremoniously stripped from him, often by his own teammate, and see it returned to the weaker player.

These accommodations, coupled with constantly changing lineups as new players come and winded players go and trades are made to even out teams in terms of strength and number, mean that nobody takes the score seriously, if they bother keeping track of it at all. It is thus understood that all goals are not equal—players will pass up an easy tap-in and instead try an elegant deke or spinorama, a drop pass, or a tic-tac-toe. In this way, pickup is more about the beauty of hockey than any final result.

And if no one takes the score seriously, no one takes the game too seriously either. This makes the hockey more imaginative and the whole atmosphere at the rink less competitive and more celebratory—of the sport, of winter, of the country, of the culture.

Often, midway through a game, there'll be a pause. No buzzer or whistle will sound, no announcement will be made. It will just happen, after a goal or when the puck has flown out of the rink and whoever shot it is digging through the snow to find it. During such a break, some people will hoist themselves up to sit on the boards while others will stand about steaming in the night air. Some will stare down at the ice or gaze at the lights in the houses and apartments bordering the park. Others will small-talk, strangers an hour ago and strangers in an hour's time but partners in the same enterprise now. The lull allows everyone to catch their breath and affords us a moment's reflection—to worship the game, the night, our lives, and our good fortune in bringing them all together.

All this is not to idealize the game of pickup hockey, at least not unduly. Tempers do flare, blood does get spilled. Unlike organized hockey, however, rarely does the blood follow the anger. When someone loses his temper—about every half-dozen games or so and as the result of a cheap shot or a bad day, or perhaps of being embarrassed once too often by that dipsy-doodling fourteen-year-old who hasn't yet learned how to humiliate in a graceful, self-effacing manner—the responsibility for keeping things under control is everyone's. Usually, through good-natured chiding, the collective admonishes whoever is deemed to be out of line. It's not as if a meeting is held, and the group rarely divides along team lines. Instead, players who have an opinion say their piece, and invariably things work out. There's very occasionally pushing and shoving—testosterone, after all, is abundant—but never, in countless excursions to the rink over three decades, have I witnessed a real fight, let alone a brawl. In my three or four years playing serious organized hockey (during the Broad Street Bullies era), brawls were a regular feature.

The collective also does its thing to ensure that there is no reckless raising of the puck. That, after all, is what usually leads to blood. Even if it flows very rarely, accidents do happen. Several years ago, I made the same guy bleed twice in the same evening. After the second incident, caused by a deflected puck, we got the message and called it a night. The only anger expressed was at having an otherwise perfect night ruined.

In Montreal, the night begins to end when the rink worker walks onto the ice and pushes the nets toward the lamppost to which they will be shackled until the next day. This is usually done contritely. The rink worker, male or female, is often a player, or, if not, a fan, and knows that the game is generally at its best just before closing. The young kids and quarter-milers have gone home, the creakiness and cobwebs have been shaken out, and players have built a rapport, a relationship, solid if fleeting, with their teammates. They'll know to pick on the give-and-go, be ready for the drop pass, cover the net for the defenceman with a taste for rink-long rushes.

The nets gone, most call it a night. Whereas before the game, the change room was an entirely functional place, now it is transformed. Having played together, we're all pals. We talk about the game, tools of the trade, anything that comes to mind.

"Tes Bauers—sont-ils pas pire?" one guy will ask.

"Ils n'sont pas pas pire—ils sont d'la marde," comes the reply.

Eventually, though, the rinkie will want to shut down the shack, and we'll head home, the night clearer, the atmosphere less full of static than two or three hours earlier. By then the big lights will have been switched off. Still, especially if it's late in the season, a hard core will sometimes play on, shadows dashing across the ice, less visible than audible by the skates cutting dryly into the ice, the puck banging against the boards.

Like corn on the cob, pickup hockey has to be gorged on when it's available, because it won't be around long. The season is short and fickle. A thaw, a bit of rain, or a big dump of snow can mess things up for days. If it happens late enough in the season, it might just spell the end of the season. In this way, the need to fill up on pickup grows toward the end of February and the beginning of March, when the ice along the south- and west-facing boards gets rotten and mushy in the day and freezes unevenly at night. Then those of us with the bug are out there as often as possible, neglecting family, work, school if need be, desperate to get our dose before the gravel, asphalt, or grass starts poking through the ice and the long, long, much-too-long off-season begins.

Winter began perfectly in central Canada in both 2002 and 2003. The first year we were living in Toronto—a city which, in my books, cemented its place as a bastion of civility and clear thinking by constructing dozens of refrigerated outdoor rinks in the 1950s and 1960s—thus insulating to a very large degree pickup hockey from the vicissitudes of the weather.

In 2002, however, no refrigeration was necessary: the cold arrived, as if ordered off eBay, the moment November ended. After a day or two, my brother determined that Grenadier Pond would be skateable. So he collected some sticks and a few pucks, pulled the Tacks out of the basement, picked up his two sons after school, phoned me, and we all headed west to High Park. The pond was a perfect mirror, allowing for the most exquisite skating imaginable, even if the ice was no more than seven or eight centimetres thick and creaked and groaned as we glided across it. We weren't entirely imprudent—the kids were there to keep us sensible—and we stuck close to shore, ending the game when the last puck slid too far out to be retrieved. After that, we just skated around looking at the leaves and the little sardine-like fish—smelt I think—frozen in the ice.

The cold kept up that week, and Richard, Malcolm, and Louis hit the pond every day, my stepson, Ariel, and I joining them two or three times. Each outing, the ice was a little thicker and we could venture farther from the shore. By Saturday, the whole pond was skateable, and others had begun to follow our lead. A glorious game of pickup, the kind with kids, adults, and the occasional overexcited golden retriever, broke out about 11 a.m. and continued until dusk. At one point, the Toronto Police Marine Unit (there is such a thing) drove their suv down to the edge of the pond and tried to spoil the fun. Eventually, they admitted they had no authority to kick us off, but Malcolm, rebel that he isn't, refused to keep his skates on.

A week or so later, Toronto's soggy winter weather returned and messed up the pond, but by then the switches had been thrown on the city's refrigerated rinks so the outdoor hockey continued. (Alas, Toronto isn't the pickup mecca that it might be: many of its outdoor rinks are reserved for permit play most evenings. And during those few hours when it is "open hockey," players descend in such numbers that a reasonable game is often impossible.)

By December 2003, we were back in Montreal, and the hammer came down on the second. It was a real cold—mean daily temperature of about -10°C. Even then, without my brother around to

spur me on, it took me almost the entire week to realize that where Toronto has Grenadier Pond and Ottawa the Canal, at the top of Mount Royal, Montreal has Beaver Lake. Finally, after phoning almost everyone I knew, I had drafted enough players and we made the trek up the mountain. Again, it was perfect, at least for a while. Then one of my best friend's plastic Micron skates—he'd had them since we first met in the mid-1980s—literally broke into pieces. Shortly afterward, the first fast-falling flakes of what would be a foot of snow began to descend. That was that.

Still, that winter and the next turned out to be superb seasons of pickup in Montreal, with a minimum of climatic interruptions before spring finally arrived when it's supposed to and not before: in mid- to late March. I had an ever-eager companion in Ariel, and often, when we were feeling like a change of scenery, when our regular rink in Outremont was feeling just a little old and bourgeois, we'd pile our skates and sticks into the Ford Escort (cognizant of the sacrilege) and head northeast or southwest and find a game in Petite-Patrie or Saint-Henri.

One of those years, we set ourselves the challenge of never losing if we ended up playing on the same team together and actually pulled it off (not that anyone was taking it seriously, of course). At thirteen and fourteen years old those winters, Ariel was a long, skinny joy to watch, his play exponentially more creative, more playful, than for his hard-luck school team. And even if pickup didn't come with all the same perks—the team sweaters and bags, the trips to Toronto where the team stayed in a hotel with buffet meals—and even after taking a puck in the face in a game in Saint-Henri (lots of blood, no stitches), Ariel eventually decided to give up organized hockey. The boy has a very cultivated sense of pleasure, and it just became clear to him: if playing hockey is about having fun, pickup has no competition.

◀◀ **Source**: Montreal journalist and author Daniel Sanger would like to die with his skates on ... but not anytime soon. This article was originally published in *The Walrus*, December/January 2007. Reprinted with permission.

# Section 3

## Children and Sports

The previous section on socialization referred to children and youth because that is the major period of socialization in a person's life. However, sports for children and youth have been an ongoing concern in the sociology of sport because adult intervention in and organization of children's sports has created a number of social problems since such involvement began on a large scale in the 1950s and 1960s. As this section shows, problems are ongoing. We have a great deal of experience and research-based knowledge about how to resolve those problems, but the will to act upon that knowledge is clearly not evident and is continually thwarted by the ambitions of some adults.

"The Hockey Act" is a parody written in the form of a formal piece of legislation. This amusing piece reminds us of all of the things we know are a problem with children's organized sports. The Act legislates hockey back into the control of children, for the best interests of children, and for *fun*.

The "Panathlon Declaration on Ethics in Youth Sport" (which also incorporates the "Panathlon Charter on the Rights of the Child in Sport") takes the form of a series of commitments regarding the conduct of organized sports for children. Such important public declarations would not be necessary if the problems in adult-organized sports for children were not widely recognized—if adults had not begun to run children's sports in ways that expressed their own interests rather than the interests of children.

Despite the importance of public pronouncements such as the Panathlon Declaration, there is a failure to actually enforce such commitments made in the best interests of children. International sports federations and international multi-sport organizations such as the International Olympic Committee (IOC) could easily take the lead in enforcement, but they invariably hold back. The IOC Consensus Statement on "Training the Child Athlete" was developed by the IOC Medical Commission, and incorporates many important points that would serve to maintain and improve the health and development of young high performance athletes. However, the whole statement is couched in weak language, suggesting what sport organizations "should" do rather than establishing appropriate regulations with penalties for failing to enforce them.

Children in high-performance sport appear to be the most vulnerable to the problems that result from adult expectations, and from the failure of some adults (some coaches, some parents, many sport administrators, even fans) to recognize that these individuals who are superbly talented athletes are still children. The interests of ambition and success appear to supercede the interests of the child. Hugh Graham tells the story of Tracey Wainman in his article "Ice Storm" (See "Additional Selected Readings and References"), a story that unfortunately is all too typical. Wainman was a superb young figure skater who would go on to be described as "all-washed up" at the age of sixteen. "

'There is a widespread view,' [Debbie] Wilkes wrote in her 1994 book *Ice Time*, 'that the CFSA [Canadian Figure Skating Association] took one of the most talented skaters this country has ever produced and destroyed her'" (Graham, 45). Another disheartening example is that of Elaine Tanner—a remarkably successful young swimmer whose Olympic silver medal was considered to be a failure as she was "supposed to" win gold). [See "Elaine's Story" in "Additional Suggested Readings and References."]

The shameful treatment of child athletes also occurs at lower levels of sport. In her article "Red-Carded," Hayley Mick tells the story of Michael Kinahan, the coach of a soccer team for seven- and eight-year-old girls in Massachusetts—a coach whose controversial actions were actually supported by some of the players' parents. However, his actions pale in comparison to some of our homegrown examples where sex, control, and power have been involved in the relationships between male hockey coaches and their young, male players in two well-known cases. Graham James abused a number of players in the eighties and nineties, including at least two who went on to play in the NHL (Sheldon Kennedy and Theoren Fleury). Christie Blatchford describes a more recent and equally disturbing case in her article, "In Thrall to David Frost." [See also Section 5: Violence in Sports.]

Parents need information, education, and, sometimes, encouragement to do the right thing. The last two articles in this section provide just such an incentive. André Picard points to the Active Healthy Kids Canada annual Report Card in his reminder to parents to "Reshuffle your Priorities and Play with your Kids." And Jay Coakley reminds us once more that we have both research and experience on our side when it comes to organizing sports in the best interests of children. The "DOs" and "DON'Ts" in his "Manifesto on Kids and Sports" represent an important set of principles for those whose children participate in organized sports, and for those who coach them.

**Additional Suggested Readings and References**

- Graham, H. 2006. "Ice Storm." *Toronto Life*, April, pp. 39-45.
- Tanner, E. "Elaine's Story." [http://elainetanner.ca/story.html]

# 10. The *Hockey Act*[1]
## By Thomas G. Keast

The following statute, popularly referred to as the Hockey Act, *received royal assent on September 28, 2022, the fiftieth anniversary of Paul Henderson's game-winning goal for Canada against the Soviet Union with thirty-four seconds left in the eighth and deciding game of the so-called "Summit Series." In his speech from the throne Lieutenant-Governor Stanley Smyl recognized the vigorous debate leading up to the bill's third reading, not all of which was provided by adults as defined in section 1 of the Act.*

The Hockey Act *is aimed at preventing the breaking of the hearts of children who, for a variety of reasons, become separated from the pure joy of the sport of hockey. It is also* an endeavour to address the anarchy that boils around the edges of the game. Its application will be closely monitored by stakeholders in amateur sport for possible extension to other sports such as soccer, field hockey, and marbles.

■ ■ ■ ■ ■ ■

Amateur Sport Appreciation and Management (Minor Hockey) Act

Chapter 4

[Updated to Dec. 7, 2022] Assented to Sept. 28, 2022

**Definitions**

**1** In this Act:

---

[1] The first, and only, prize-winner in the *Advocate* short fiction competition for 2001.

**"Adult"** means, if male, a person who exhibits a composite of the characteristics portrayed by Robert Young in *Father Knows Best*, Fred McMurray in *My Three Sons*, and Bill Cosby in *The Cosby Show* and, if female, a person who exhibits a composite of the characteristics portrayed by Barbara Billingsley in *Leave it to Beaver*, Meredith Baxter Birney in *Family Ties*, Patricia Richardson in *Home Improvement*, and Lady Byng.

**"Arena"** means an indoor or outdoor facility designed for the playing of games.

**"Bag"** means a closable container intended for the temporary storage of a player's equipment.

**"Equipment"** comprises all of the clothing and protective gear worn by a player on the ice with the exception of the stick.

**"Fun,"** for purposes of this Act, is defined as the state of mind of a player, regardless of the player's ability to express verbally or demonstrate in any other fashion that that state of mind exists for him or her, which manifests itself in one or more of the following:

(a) carrying his or her bag into and out of an arena

(b) referring to the coach as "cool" or other equivalent adjective

(c) voluntarily going to bed early because of an early morning practice

(d) smiling while engaged in a conversation about playing hockey

(e) a willingness to attempt backward crossovers

(f) an admission obtained pursuant to Section 2 of this Act

**"Fun tribunal"** means the tribunal established pursuant to Section 3 of this Act.

**"Game"** means a contest of ice hockey or in-line hockey or, when used with reference to road hockey, a contest played by the rules established pursuant to Section 13.

**"Ice hockey"** means a game played in an arena on ice under the rules and regulations made from time to time by the Canadian Hockey Association.

**"In-line hockey"** means a game played in an arena on a hard surface under the rules and regulations made from time to time by the Canadian Hockey Association.

**"Parent"** means a guardian or biological or adoptive mother or father of a player, but not necessarily an adult as defined above.

**"Player"** means any participant in a game of hockey, road hockey, or in-line hockey who is also a minor as defined by the *Age of Majority Act*.

**"Player complainant"** means a player who has answered the question "are you having fun?" negatively or in a manner that may be reasonably construed to be negative such as a single or double shouldered shrug.

**"Road hockey"** means a game played on a highway as defined in the *Highway Act*.

**"Time out"** means a period of time prescribed by regulation made pursuant to this Act during which a parent shall have no contact with any player and shall be used by the parent for growing up, getting a life, or otherwise altering his or her personality to better conform with that of an adult as defined by this Act.

## ■■■ Part 1—Fun and the Game
### Fun

**2** (1) A player may be asked at any time by an adult, or by a parent who is not an adult no more often than once every seventy-two hours, whether he or she is having fun playing hockey.

(2) In the event that the question referred to in subsection (1) is posed by a parent who is not an adult in contravention of subsection (1) the player is not required to answer.

(3) In the event that the question referred to in subsection (1) is posed in accordance with subsection (1) and the answer of the player is negative, or may reasonably be construed to be negative, this answer shall constitute a complaint on the part of the player who shall be deemed a player complainant.

## Fun Tribunal

**3** (1) All complaints arising under Section 2 shall be referred to the fun tribunal for resolution.

(2) The fun tribunal shall be comprised of three players from the player complainant's team including an appointee of the player complainant, a second appointee to be designated by a second player who has been designated by the player complainant to make the designation of the second appointee, and a third player chosen by the first and second appointees.

(3) The fun tribunal shall conduct their deliberations on the merits of a complaint for a period of no less than sixty seconds and no more than one hundred and twenty seconds.

(4) In the event that a complaint of a player complainant is found by the fun tribunal to have merit, the fun tribunal may make recommendations on various aspects of the game of hockey including, but not limited, to the following:

(a) food and beverages to be provided to the player complainant's team

(b) extent and frequency of sleepovers for the player complainant with his or her teammates

(c) the frequency of the provision of new hockey sticks to the player complainant

(d) choice of recorded or live music and level of volume during the transportation referred to in Section 10

(e) timeouts, as defined in Section 1, for the player complainant from parents but not from adults

(5) The determination of the fun tribunal shall be final and its recommendations, with the exception of those arising under subsection 4(a), shall be implemented forthwith by the parents and coaches of the player complainant and his or her teammates.

(6) Notwithstanding subsection (5), any recommendations under subsection 4(a) shall be subject to appeal to the player complainant's physician by the parents of the player complainant which appeal shall be determined by said physician within twenty-four hours.

## ■■■ Part 2—Personnel Management
### Parental Failure Offence

**4** (1) It is an offence for a parent:

(a) not to be an adult, as defined in Section 1 of this Act, at all times in dealing with a player or coach or administrator of a hockey team

(b) to verbally address a referee during a game or within three hours thereafter from a distance of less than one mile

(c) to form an opinion concerning any player or coach or administrator of a hockey team

(d) to be present in an arena while experiencing a pulse rate in excess of one hundred beats per minute.

(2) Any person who is a parent and who commits an offence under subsection (1) is liable to punishment, including grounding as defined in subsection (3), for a period of up to five years.

(3) For purposes of this section, grounding shall mean to deprive of all alcoholic beverages, certain prescribed media privileges including, but not limited to, access to the Internet and reality television, and consumption of calories in excess of a daily maximum prescribed by regulation.

(4) In appropriate circumstances, and in lieu of grounding, a parent may be required to engage in a timeout for the purposes set out in Section 1 of this Act.

(5) In addition to any punishment imposed under subsections (2) or (4) the fun tribunal may, at its sole discretion using the medium of MSN Messenger Service or equivalent communication tool, make known to any persons that a parent has been found not to have been an adult pursuant to the provisions of this Act and has been punished together with the particulars of the punishment imposed.

### Coaching Qualifications

**5** A coach must be an adult but in addition must be able to do the following:

(a) list without notice, when asked, the five most popular snacks and drinks amongst players aged five to sixteen years and their most current rating as reported by Consumer Reports or equivalent publication

(b) describe without notice, when asked, the process for the vulcanization of rubber

(c) state without notice, when asked, the top ten reasons why Don Cherry is not an adult

(d) recite without notice, when asked, the chorus to The Hockey Song by Stompin' Tom Connors

(e) state without notice, when asked, the meaning of the C and the H on the Montreal Canadiens' playing jersey

(f) state without notice, when asked, the top ten reasons why the Toronto Maple Leafs have not won the Stanley Cup since 1967

(g) state without notice, when asked, which skate, left or right, the player is tying in Ken Danby's open edition reproduction print called "Lacing Up"

(h) state accurately the answer to the question referred to in subsection 2(1) for each of the players on his or her team

(i) teach backward crossovers

## Communicating with Coaches

**6** A parent who is not an adult is prohibited from speaking to, gesturing at, or otherwise communicating with a coach.

## Player Comportment

**7** A player must become an adult upon reaching the age of majority as defined by the *Age of Majority Act*.

## ■■■ Part 3—Equipment and Transportation Management

### Equipment Offences

**8** (1) It is an offence for a player or parent to leave equipment in a closed bag for more than seven days or to open a bag or remove any equipment from a bag that has been closed continuously for thirty days or more.

(2) In addition to any penalty imposed pursuant to the provisions of this Act, ownership of any equipment enclosed in a bag for thirty days or more will vest in the Crown in right of the Province of British Columbia and thereafter be deemed to be waste and subject to the provisions of the *Waste Management Act*.

## Equipment Mingling

**9** A bag must not contain the equipment of more than one player unless a certificate has been issued prior to the insertion of a player's equipment into a bag by a member of the College of Physicians and Surgeons of British Columbia certifying that the equipment of the player is safe for mingling with that of another player.

## Arena Transport

**10** (1) Only an adult shall provide transportation for a player or players to and from an arena.

(2) In the event that an adult is unavailable to provide the transportation referred to in subsection (1) a parent who is not an adult may provide the transportation.

(3) In the event that a parent who is not an adult provides the transportation referred to in subsection (1) the parent will remain silent throughout the period of transportation and for fifteen minutes before and after the transportation commences and ends except where required by regulations made pursuant to this act to speak or in the interests of the safety of the players.

## Transport Syntax

**11** No player when being transported by an adult to or from an arena is permitted to use the word "like" more than once in one sentence or like six times during each like leg of the trip.

**12** No parent is required to provide the transportation referred to in Section 10 if any player insists on listening to rap or hip hop music which is performed by any professional athlete unless the aforesaid music has been approved by a panel of adults pursuant to the provisions of the *Popular Music and Tattoo Approval Act*.

# ■■■ Part 4 - Miscellaneous

## Rules of Road Hockey

**13** (1) The rules of road hockey may or may not exist, but in the event that a player alleges that a certain rule exists then that rule as stated by that player is deemed to be a rule of the game.

(2) Notwithstanding subsection (1) it is open to any other player in a game of road hockey to allege that the rule as stated by the first player under subsection (1) does not exist or that the rule is different from that alleged by the first player.

(3) In the event that both events described in subsections (1) and (2) occur in a game of road hockey, then the playing of the game will be suspended while each player states his or her opinion of what the rule is, was, or should be or until there is insufficient daylight to continue the game, whichever occurs first.

(4) The rules of road hockey cannot be changed more often than every ten minutes of a game and can only be changed by the player who is holding the ball or puck in his or her hand at the time of the change.

(5) The provisions of this section render void and of no further effect or application the rules of road hockey established in Canada and known as the Lower or Upper Canada Rules.

## Administration and Regulations

**14** (1) The Lieutenant Governor in Council, if having once been a player, may make regulations referred to in Section 41 of the *Interpretation Act*

(2) Without limiting subsection (1), the Lieutenant Governor in Council, if having once been a player, may make regulations respecting the following matters:

(a) the maximum number of calories per day as part of any grounding of a parent imposed under subsection 4(2) which shall in any event be no fewer than six hundred

(b) when a parent may speak during the transportation referred to in Section 10

(c) the length of timeouts which can be imposed pursuant to subsections 3(4)(e) and 4(4)

## Offence

**15** (1) A person who knowingly fails to become an adult upon reaching the age of majority or who causes another person to so fail commits an offence.

(2) A person who commits an offence under subsection (1) is liable to a fine not exceeding a billion dollars and grounding for no more than infinity plus one years.

## Application of Offence Act

**16** Section 5 of the *Offence Act* does not apply to this Act or to the regulations.

**17** The provisions of subsection 7(1) of the Offence Act with respect to access to a telephone by a person taken into custody who has committed an offence under this Act are limited by this section to contact with an adult as defined in Section 1 of this Act.

## Commencement

**18** This Act comes into force by regulation of the Lieutenant Governor in Council.

◀◀ **Source:** This article originally appeared in The *Advocate*, Vol 60, Part 2 in March 2002. Reprinted with permission from the author.

# Panathlon Declaration on Ethics in Youth Sport

**11.**

*This declaration represents our commitment to go beyond discussion and to establish clear rules of conduct in the pursuit of the positive values in youth sport.*

■ ■ ■ ■ ■

We declare that:

1. We will promote the positive values in youth sport more actively with sustained effort and good planning.

■ In training and competition, we will aim for four major objectives in a balanced way: the development of motor (technical, tactical) competence, a healthy and safe competitive style, a positive self-concept, and good social skills. In this we will be guided by the needs of children.

■ We believe that striving to excel and to win and to experience both success and pleasure, and failure and frustration, are all part and parcel of competitive sport. We will give children the opportunity to cultivate and to integrate (within the structure, the rules, and the limits of the game) this in their performance, and will help them to manage their emotions.

■ We will give special attention to the guidance and education of children according to those models which value ethical and humanistic principles in general, and fair play in sport in particular.

■ We will ensure that children are included in the decision-making about their sport.

2. We will continue our effort to eliminate all forms of discrimination in youth sport.

■ This coheres with the fundamental ethical principle of equality, which requires social justice, and equal distribution of resources.

■ Late developers, the disabled, and less talented children will be offered similar chances to practise sport and be given the same professional attention available to early developers, able-bodied, and more talented children without discrimination by gender, race or culture.

3. We recognize and adopt the fact that sports also can produce negative effects and that preventive and curative measures are needed to protect children.

■ We will maximize the children's psychological and physical health through our efforts to prevent cheating, doping, abuse, and exploitation, and to help children to overcome the possible negative effects of these.

■ We accept that the importance of children's social environment and of the motivational climate is still underestimated. We will therefore develop, adopt, and implement a code of conduct with clearly defined responsibilities for all stakeholders in the network around youth sport: sport governing bodies, sport leaders, parents, educators, trainers, sport managers, administrators, medical doctors, physical therapists, dieticians, psychologists, top athletes, children themselves, etc.

■ We strongly recommend that the establishment of bodies on appropriate levels to govern this code should be seriously considered.

■ We encourage registration and accreditation systems for trainers and coaches.

4. We welcome the support of sponsors and media but believe that this support should be in accordance with the major objectives of youth sport.

■ We welcome sponsorship from organizations and companies only when this does not conflict with the pedagogical process, the ethical basis of sport, and the major objectives of youth sport.

■ We believe that the function of the media is not only to be reactive (i.e., holding the mirror up to the problems of our society) but also to be proactive (i.e., stimulating, educational, and innovative).

5. We therefore formally endorse The Panathlon Charter on the Rights of the Child in Sport. All children have the right:

■ To practise sports

■ To enjoy themselves and to play

■ To live in a healthy environment

■ To be treated with dignity

■ To be trained and coached by competent people

■ To take part in training that is adapted to their age, individual rhythm, and competence

■ To match themselves against children of the same level in a suitable competition

■ To practise sport in safe conditions

■ To rest

■ To have the opportunity to become a champion, or not to be a champion

All this can only be achieved when governments, sports federations, sports agencies, sports-goods industries, media, business, sport scientists, sport managers, trainers, parents, and children endorse this declaration.

◀◀ **Source:** GHENT 24 September, 2004

## 12. Training the Elite Child Athlete
### IOC Consensus Statement

Protecting the health of the athlete is the primary goal of the International Olympic Committee's Medical Commission. One of its main objectives is the promotion of safe practices in the training of the elite child athlete. The elite child athlete is one who has superior athletic talent, undergoes specialized training, receives expert coaching, and is exposed to early competition. Sport provides a positive environment that may enhance the physical growth and psychological development of children. This unique athlete population has distinct social, emotional, and physical needs which vary depending on the athlete's particular stage of maturation. The elite child athlete requires appropriate training, coaching, and competition that ensure a safe and healthy athletic career and promote future well-being. This document reviews the scientific basis of sports training in the child, the special challenges, and unique features of training elite children and provides recommendations to parents, coaches, health-care providers, sports governing bodies, and significant other parties.

### ■■■ Scientific Basis of Training the Elite Child Athlete

Aerobic and anaerobic fitness and muscle strength increase with age, growth, and maturation. Improvement in these variables is asynchronous.

Children experience more marked improvements in anaerobic and strength performance than in aerobic performance during pubescence. Boys' aerobic and anaerobic fitness and muscle strength are higher than those of girls in late pre-pubescence, and the gender difference becomes more pronounced with advancing maturity. Evidence shows that muscle strength and aerobic and anaerobic fitness can be further enhanced with appropriately prescribed training. Regardless of the level of maturity, the relative responses of boys and girls are similar after adjusting for initial fitness.

An effective and safe strength-training program incorporates exercises for the major muscle groups with a balance between agonists and antagonists. The prescription includes a minimum of two to three sessions per week with three sets, at an intensity of between 50%–85% of the one maximal repetition (1RM).

An optimal aerobic training programme incorporates continuous and interval exercises involving large muscle groups. The prescription recommends three to four, forty- to sixty-minute sessions per week at an intensity of 85%–90% of maximum heart rate (HRM).

An appropriate anaerobic training programme incorporates high-intensity interval training of short duration. The prescription includes exercise at an intensity above 90% HRM and of less than thirty seconds duration to take into account children's relatively faster recovery following high-intensity exercise.

A comprehensive psychological programme includes the training of psychological skills such as motivation, self-confidence, emotional control, and concentration. The prescription applies strategies in goal-setting, emotional, cognitive, and behavioural control fostering a positive self-concept in a healthy, motivational climate.

Nutrition provided by a balanced, varied, and sustainable diet makes a positive difference in an elite young athlete's ability to train and compete, and will contribute to optimal lifetime health. Adequate hydration is essential. Nutrition requirements vary as a function of age, gender, pubertal status, event, training regime, and the time of the competitive season. The nutrition prescription includes adequate hydration and individualizes total energy, macro- and micro-nutrient needs, and balance.

With advancing levels of maturity and competitiveness, physiological and psychological training and nutrition should be sport-specific with reference to competitive cycles. Confidential, periodic, and sensitive evaluation of training and nutritional status should include anthropometric measures, sport-specific analyses, and clinical assessment.

## ■ ■ ■ Special Issues in the Elite Child Athlete

Physical activity, of which sport is an important component, is essential for healthy growth and development.

The disparity in the rate of growth between bone and soft tissue places the child athlete at an enhanced risk of overuse injuries particularly at the apophyses, the articular cartilage, and the physes (growth plates). Prolonged, focal pain may signal damage and must always be evaluated in a child.

Overtraining or "burnout" is the result of excessive training loads, psychological stress, poor periodization or inadequate recovery. It may occur in the elite child athlete when the limits of optimal adaptation and performance are exceeded. Clearly, excessive pain should not be a component of the training regimen.

In girls, the pressure to meet unrealistic weight goals often leads to the spectrum of disordered eating, including anorexia and/or bulimia nervosa. These disorders may affect the growth process, influence hormonal function, cause amenorrhoea, low bone-mineral density, and other serious illnesses which can be life-threatening.

There are differences in maturation in pubertal children of the same chronological age that may have unhealthy consequences in sport due to mismatching.

Elite child athletes deserve to train and compete in a suitable environment supported by a variety of age-appropriate, technical, and tactical training methods, rules, equipment, facilities, and competitive formats.

Elite child athletes deserve to train and compete in a pleasurable environment, free from drug misuse and negative adult influences, including harassment and inappropriate pressure from parents, peers, health-care providers, coaches, media, agents, and significant other parties.

### ■ ■ ■ Recommendations for Training the Elite Child Athlete

The recommendations are that:

- More scientific research be done to better identify the parameters of training the elite child athlete, which must be communicated effectively to the coach, athlete, parents, sport governing bodies, and the scientific community

- The International Federations and National Sports Governing Bodies should:
  - Develop illness and injury surveillance programmes
  - Monitor the volume and intensity of training and competition regimens
  - Ensure the quality of coaching and adult leadership
  - Comply with the World Anti-Doping Code
- Parents/guardians develop a strong support system to ensure a balanced lifestyle including proper nutrition, adequate sleep, academic development, psychological well-being, and opportunities for socialization
- Coaches, parents, sports administrators, the media, and other significant parties should limit the amount of training and competitive stress on the elite child athlete.

The entire sports process for the elite child athlete should be pleasurable and fulfilling.

**◀◀ Source:** Reprinted with permission from the IOC Medical Commission.

## 13. Red-Carded
### By Hayley Mick

*A youth soccer coach resigns after telling parents their girls should down protein shakes and be prepared to "kick ass and take names." Was he being funny? Did he go too far? Are we all just too sensitive?*

■ ■ ■ ■ ■ ■

**A** soccer coach for young girls rants that second place is worthless, spilled blood builds character, and girls who "kick ass and take names" become winners in the game of life.

Is he a loose cannon unfit to mentor kids, or a witty satirist commenting on the state of youth sports today?

Michael Kinahan of Scituate, Massachusetts, south of Boston, has been called both since his pre-season manifesto shocked some parents and led to his resignation as coach of a team for seven- and eight-year-olds.

"I believe winning is fun and losing is for losers," Mr. Kinahan wrote in a letter to parents last month. "I expect us to fight for every loose ball and play every shift as if it were the finals of the World Cup."

He went on to say the girls were expected to drink protein shakes, eat red meat, and heckle the referee. He then signed off: "Go Green Death!"—his nickname for the team.

It was all a joke, he said later. "It's just backfired because it's a PC world," says his wife, Mary Kinahan. (Mr. Kinahan declined an interview.)

Indeed, the case has become a lightning rod pitting those who say it is another case of an overzealous adult taking kids' sports too far against others who say parents need to loosen up.

"I think there's a longing for the old days of just being able to pick up and go play," says Chris Park, a board member of the Scituate Soccer Club where Mr. Kinahan has coached for several years.

"And when people see that threatened, they react like this," Mr. Park said.

The letter came to the board members' attention after they received a complaint from parents whose daughters were new to the team. Parents who knew Mr. Kinahan and his "witty" sense of humour did not complain, Mr. Park noted.

The board asked Mr. Kinahan to apologize. When he refused, the board promoted his assistant coach to replace him and Mr. Kinahan quit.

By then, the story—and the letter—had found its way online, igniting fierce debate among parents, coaches, and readers about whether Mr. Kinahan had stepped out of bounds. Many called Mr. Kinahan scary, unfit to coach, and an "A-1 nutjob."

"The email was over the top ... and indicative of the attitude of the coach. He should not be in any leadership role to children at all," posted Sera on the website of *The Patriot Ledger*, the first newspaper to report the story.

But others, including players' parents, defended him by urging critics to get a sense of humour—and asking what's wrong with wanting to win, anyway?

"Okay, let me get this straight. The parents were offended that he wants the girls to be strong-minded, and to be winners in life?" asked one reader.

"One only has to go to a game to see he really does care and motivates the team with a great sense of camaraderie," wrote another, who said his child was coached by Mr. Kinahan last year.

Dan Del Mastro, a high school athletics coach from Toronto and recipient of a national youth coaching award from the Canadian Football League, said the letter plays into a larger issue: Adults—whether it be coaches or parents—are too involved in youth sports.

"These days it seems that everything's regimented," he said. "It's kind of a dying art of the kids getting together and playing on their own, without leagues being in place."

Coach Kinahan's letter, he said, with its accompanying instructions on practice times, fees, and uniforms, would "never have been sent twenty years ago."

Those thoughts are echoed by Ed Arnold of Peterborough, Ontario, who coached eight-year-old hockey players for more than a decade before writing the book *Whose Puck Is It, Anyway?* He argues that fun has been stamped out of kids' games by hypercompetitive adults. "You coach for the children, make sure they have fun [and] learn some fundamentals," he wrote in an email. "Never mind about the parents, they pay the registration fee."

Mr. Park said the board holds no ill will against Mr. Kinahan. "I wouldn't hold back from hiring him again," Mr. Park said. "Not this season, though."

Ms. Kinahan says her husband enjoys coaching and is always encouraging his players to have fun. He quit, she says, because he didn't want any girls to be yanked from the team by angry parents. "He's not ashamed," she said. "He's not going to retract what he said."

And he will still be involved with the team this season: He plans to be on the sidelines, cheering his daughter and her teammates on.

■ ■ ■ ■ ■ ■

### ■ ■ ■ You Make the Call

An excerpt from Michael Kinahan's original email:

*Some say soccer at this age is about fun and I completely agree. However, I believe winning is fun and losing is for losers. Ergo, we will strive for the "W" in each game. While we may not win every game (excuse me, I just got a little nauseated) I expect us to fight for every loose ball and play every shift as if it were the finals of the World Cup.*

*While I spent a good Saturday morning listening to the legal liability BS, which included a thirty-minute dissertation on how we need to baby the kids and especially the refs, I was disgusted. The kids will run, they will fall, get bumps, bruises, and even bleed a little. Big deal, it's good for them (but I do hope the other team is the one bleeding). If the refs can't handle a little criticism, then they should turn in their whistle.*

◀◀ **Source:** Hayley Mick is a staff writer for *The Globe and Mail*. This article originally appeared in *The Globe and Mail* on April 7, 2009. Reprinted with permission.

## 14. In Thrall to David Frost
### By Christie Blatchford

*The former hockey coach was a cruel manipulator of young people*

■ ■ ■ ■ ■ ■

At some point down the road, it is the Canadian justice system—either judge or jury—that will determine if David Frost's conduct with some of the teenagers either in his charge or his sphere of influence, as now is alleged by the Ontario Provincial Police, was criminal.

But there is plenty of evidence long on the public record to conclude that Mr. Frost, a former National Hockey League Players Association-certified agent and coach, is a creepy bully, a clown, and a cruel manipulator of vulnerable young people.

Now thirty-nine, Mr. Frost first came to widespread attention in the spring of 2004, when the FBI arrested his twenty-three-year-old client Mike Danton, then with the St. Louis Blues of the NHL, and charged him in a bizarre and failed murder-for-hire scheme.

It isn't often that one's heart goes out to the guy trying to have someone whacked, but no one who knew both men saw Mr. Danton as anything other than the victim of the sordid piece.

The "plot" was pathetic, undeserving of the label: Mr. Danton, who is now serving the seven-and-a-half-year sentence he received after pleading guilty, used a teenaged girl he had dated briefly as the conduit to hire a complete stranger to kill Mr. Frost, a stranger who turned out to be a local police dispatcher.

But Mr. Danton was transparently desperate to get Mr. Frost out of his life, at one point pleading with the hit man he thought he'd hired to do the job quickly and telling him, "I'm pretty much begging."

After more than a decade in Mr. Frost's thrall, it's no wonder the young man could see only one way out. No fewer than three people who knew both of them told me at the time of Mr. Danton's arrest that if he had hatched the plan, it would mark "the first time in ten years that Mike has thought for himself."

It didn't last long. Mr. Frost inexplicably was able to deluge Mr. Danton with phone calls even when he was in jail, awaiting trial, and it was only a judge's order that belatedly stopped that contact, and soon enough, Mr. Danton was again denouncing his parents (using Mr. Frost's language), sticking by his agent and conveniently pleading guilty, obliterating any chance he, or Mr. Frost, would be required to testify.

Man met boy when Mr. Danton, who was born as Mike Jefferson, was just a ten-year-old and Mr. Frost was just beginning to earn a reputation as a successful but volatile and controlling coach.

Within a few years, Mr. Frost had moved virtually next door to the home where Mr. Danton was then living in the 'M' section of Bramalea, that curious planned subdivision west of Toronto where the streets in each section begin with the same letter of the alphabet, with his parents, Sue and Steve, and his little brother.

By the time Mr. Danton was fourteen, he had sufficiently withdrawn from his family that he was eating alone in the basement and flinching at even a light touch on the arm from his mom or dad. Someone who trained with him just a couple of years later, in junior hockey, noted that by then, Mr. Danton had sufficiently hardened that even during hand-pad work, where players wearing head protection are taught to keep their hands up in a fight, he wouldn't even blink at a blow.

Shortly before he turned sixteen, Mr. Danton moved to Deseronto in Eastern Ontario, the area where most of the charges against Mr. Frost are centred and where he was then coaching the Quinte Hawks. It was then that Mr. Frost, you can be sure with trademark charmlessness, forbade his players' parents from having any contact with their sons but for attending the games and clapping. Mr. Danton's mother remembered she was specifically told not to hug her son in public.

By the time the Jeffersons realized that there was serious trouble brewing in the big chance Mr. Frost appeared to offer his players, it was too late: The son they knew and loved, however imperfectly, was effectively gone.

A player who was a member of the Toronto Young Nationals bantam club, which won the all-Ontario championship in 1995–96 with Mr. Danton on the roster and Mr. Frost as the coach, and who I interviewed after Mr. Danton's arrest, remembered that even by Mr. Frost's vile standards, Mr. Danton and his dad were singled out for particular ridicule. Mr. Frost would refer to Mr. Danton's dad as "a worthless piece of shit" and "an alcoholic" and ask him if he wanted to end up like him, "driving a sandwich-and-coffee truck."

Mr. Frost, of course, did this in front of the entire team.

This player said that every player on the Young Nats team was afraid of Mr. Frost. "He'd pace around the dressing room, while reaming people out, and you'd flinch when he came near you, I'd never felt that before from a coach."

This young man was one of the few, out of dozens of former · players, coaches, and hockey people I interviewed, who was willing to talk about Mr. Frost, albeit anonymously. Even two years ago, only Mr. Danton's poor parents, whom he formally renounced with his name change in 2002, were courageous enough to speak out on the record—or had sufficiently little left to lose that they felt they could.

Even then, when it was pretty plain that the wheels were falling off the David Frost train, people were frightened of him: His penchant for sending threatening lawyers' letters, his vicious profanity, and his menacing physical presence had done the trick. Most parents were afraid to speak to me, for fear their sons, some of whom are still in hockey, would suffer, and players Mr. Frost had coached or represented had nothing to say. Among hockey agents—that select group, which until last year inexplicably included Mr. Frost, certified by the National Hockey League Players Association as fit to negotiate young men's contracts and guard their interests—the silence was particularly galling.

Among the agents who would sternly denounce Mr. Frost off the record, but not utter a word against his methods on it, were some of the most storied names in the national game.

One family I interviewed two years ago told me of a photograph they discovered in their son's belongings; the son was a friend of Mike Danton's. In the picture, Mr. Danton was sitting on a couch between two pretty girls. The expression of shamed humiliation on his face seemed out of place, until these people noticed that the crotch of his blue jeans was ripped fully open, his genitalia exposed.

The family destroyed the photograph, out of consideration for their son's friend, as surely as David Frost, out of self-interest and self-preservation, destroyed Mike Danton.

◀◀ **Source:** Christie Blatchford is a staff writer for *The Globe and Mail*. This article originally appeared in *The Globe and Mail* on August 26, 2006. Reprinted with permission.

## 15. Reshuffle Your Priorities and Play With Your Kids
### By André Picard

The fact that Canada scores a dismal D when it comes to producing active, healthy kids should come as no surprise.

The constant stream of stories about childhood obesity has largely inured us to the notion that we are producing a generation of tubby tots.

Still, the new report card that was released last week by Active Healthy Kids Canada serves as a useful reminder of where we have gone so terribly wrong.

Canadian children—citizens of one of the wealthiest (in every sense of the word) countries on Earth—have succumbed to a dreadful combination of sloth and malnutrition (in the form of too many calories, not too few).

But let's not blame the kids. They are born athletes: squirming little bundles of joy at birth, soon crawling, walking and running—until we beat it out of them.

Children's lives today are highly structured, and most of that structure involves sitting. We sit them in classrooms all day, and then we sit them down again at night to do homework. And, in between, there are occasional breaks for transportation (sitting in the car or bus) and leisure (invariably sitting in front of a TV or a computer screen).

In short, children are overweight and obese, in large part because they have few opportunities to be physically active. We have engineered activity out of their lives and, in the process, engineered chronic illnesses such as heart disease and diabetes into their lives.

Children need to be moderately or vigorously active for at least ninety minutes daily for healthy growth and development, according to Canada's physical activity guidelines.

But only 43% of children meet that minimum standard. Girls are consistently less active than boys and, come adolescence, the gender gap becomes even more pronounced.

More troubling still is that parents are woefully—and perhaps willfully—ignorant of this reality. Close to 90% of parents think their own children are sufficiently active.

"No one ever says their kids are the problem," says Dr. Mark Tremblay, the chair of Active

Healthy Kids Canada. "There's a real disconnect. A lot of parents are in denial."

So let's be clear: It's *not* somebody else's problem.

Children, the inactive, overweight lot that they are, are merely following in their parents footsteps.

Three in every five Canadian adults are overweight or obese. Only one in three adults engages in moderate or vigorous physical activity on a regular basis—the equivalent of a brisk thirty-minute walk daily.

In other words, parents are poor role models.

The most alarming element of the new report card, however, is one that garnered little attention in the media coverage.

Active Healthy Kids Canada revealed that one-third of parents rarely or never play active games or sports with their children. And one-third of children rarely or never engage in unstructured play.

Sure people are busy. Everyone suffers from so-called time poverty.

But if you rarely or never have time to play with your kids, there is something fundamentally wrong with your priorities, and your life. If children can find two hours or more a day to watch TV, but no time to play, there is something terribly wrong with their lifestyle.

Parents today lavish their children with expensive baubles—Game Boys, iPods, snowboards, and so on. Some sign them up for expensive, organized sports but, again, we learn that fewer than half actually attend games or practices.

There is nothing as precious as making a bit of time to play tag, toss a football around, or to embarrass yourself trying to skip double dutch.

Silken Laumann, the former Olympic rower, makes that point eloquently in her delightful new book entitled *Child's Play: Rediscovering the Joy of Play in Our Families and Communities.*

She urges parents to lace up the runners and get out there with their kids. Doing so is a lot more important than catching up on email or unwinding in front of the TV after a hard day at the office.

For their part, Active Healthy Kids Canada makes three principal recommendations in the report card:

- Step away from the screen and replace TV and computer time with physical activity.

- Establish quality, school-based daily physical activity programs.

- Inform Canadian parents and caregivers about the importance of unstructured physical activity and play.

It's not enough to entertain, educate, and medicate our children. We have to let them play. We have to let kids be kids.

When they are, they won't be inactive, and they won't be obese.

◀◀ **Source:** André Picard is a former board member of Active Healthy Kids Canada, but did not play a role in the creation of the report card. This article was originally published in *The Globe and Mail* on June 1, 2006. Reprinted with permission.

# 16. On Kids and Sports: A Manifesto

## By Jay Coakley

**Don't**: Use adult sports as models for organizing youth sports.

**Do**: Encourage children to play informal games, and facilitate informal games by providing children with time, safe spaces, and various indirect forms of guidance.

**Don't**: Use coaches of elite adult teams as models for organizing your own coaching. Bela Karolyi and Bobby Knight may be heroes to many for their ability to keep young athletes totally dependent and dedicated, but they are not good models for how to socialize children when it comes to anything that I would call positive character development.

**Do**: Use child-oriented teaching methods grounded in the realization that children are not little adults, and should not be treated as such.

**Don't**: Use an "Obedience Model" of coaching based on:

- Providing constant and pervasive supervision
- Using established and non-negotiable rules for athletes on and off the field
- The use of sanctions to produce compliance with rules
- Encouraging athletes to look to authority figures for approval
- Emphasizing the consequences of failure to obey and follow rules

**Do**: Use a "Responsibility Model" of coaching based on:

- Providing information for decision-making
- Enabling athletes to develop individual and team rules for on and off field
- Focusing on consequences of decisions and learning from mistakes
- Encouraging athletes to be responsible for their decisions
- Emphasizing an awareness of how decisions impact others and the overall context

**Don't**: Make underage children sign contracts committing themselves to long-term goals. Remember, it takes informed consent to sign a contract, and children cannot give informed consent no matter how talented they are in a sport!

**Do**: Help children take control of their own lives so they will be able to set realistic goals when they are ready to do so.

**Don't**: Use dominance over others as the measure of excellence.

**Do**: Use personal progress in the development of physical competence as an indicator of excellence. The goal should be to create achievement motivation, not the desire to feel compelled to beat others to feel good about self.

**Don't**: Emphasize external rewards as a source of motivation.

**Do**: Emphasize internal rewards associated with participation and competence as a source of motivation. Many young people today have never developed a deep love for the sports they play apart from all the perks that come with them. Such love is grounded in joy combined with a sense of personal achievement.

◀◀ **Source:** Jay Coakley, Ph.D. Fort Collins, Colorado, USA. Reprinted with permission.

# Section 4

## Deviance and Sports

The term "deviance" is problematic in sociology. As Coakley and Donnelly (2009) note, the terms "normal" and "deviant" "are based on the assumption that there is a widespread consensus in society about what is 'normal' ..., and therefore what is non-normative or 'deviant.' If we think of these concepts in terms of who has the *power* to define what is 'normal' and what is 'deviant,' we can see how they raise concerns for critical [sociologists]" (p. 145). Actions defined as normal at one time or in one place may be defined as deviant in another time or another place, and vice versa. For example, "diving" in soccer is considered to be normal in some places and deviant in others; and some municipalities in Canada, at a time when we are concerned about children's inactivity, have banned road hockey—thereby categorizing playing road hockey as deviant.

Although many actions by athletes in both sport and non-sport settings have been defined as deviant, perhaps the most attention in recent years has been paid to the use of prohibited performance-enhancing substances and methods. Therefore, this section focuses on doping—showing that there is no clear definition of doping, and no systematic enforcement of anti-doping policies throughout sports. The recent doping cases in Canadian Interuniversity Sport (CIS) football, especially at the University of Waterloo and other universities in Southern Ontario, are a reminder that policies, definitions, expectations, and enforcement practices all figure into attempts to understand and control performance-enhancing substances in sport. Attempts to control the use of prohibited substances and methods to enhance performance have become more systematic since the establishment of the World Anti-Doping Agency (WADA) (See Pound, 2003), but enforcement is still clearly problematic. Rumours still abound about the "legality" of Lance Armstrong's Tour de France wins and, at the time of writing, congressional hearings are about to start in the United States to try to resolve the matter. And, while the CFL is about to start testing players for the very first time, recent information from the NFL (rumoured to have one of the best anti-doping programs in professional sports) indicates that players know when they are going to be tested—and may, of course, take appropriate measures (Schmidt, 2010). What follows are four different views on doping/performance enhancement.

The Ben Johnson doping case at the 1988 Summer Olympics in Seoul is often mentioned, even in the articles that follow, and it is crucial to everything that has happened since in terms of doping control in Canada. It has been over twenty years since that notorious event, and the details and significance are not well known among young Canadians. Thus, this section starts with a piece about Ben Johnson, written some twelve years after the Seoul Olympics. Stephen Brunt's article, "Unforgiven," reviews the circumstances surrounding Johnson's world record-breaking 100-metre final race, the subsequent announcement of a positive doping test, and the resulting Dubin Inquiry into the incident. In the article, we get to know more about Ben Johnson as an individual, find out what has happened to him since 1988, and meet his mother and a publicity-seeking agent who is supposedly helping him out. This article is intended to put a human face on doping, and Brunt asks some hard questions about why Johnson was apparently a scapegoat when so many others were using performance-enhancing substances, even in his gold medal-winning race.

The normalization of doping noted by Brunt in sports such as professional football, baseball, and wrestling is picked up by Stephen LaRose in his article, "Death or Glory?" LaRose starts with the murder-suicide of Canadian pro wrestler Chris Benoit, and goes on to review drug use in the sport and the extraordinary number of early or untimely deaths among pro wrestlers. This issue is raised again, with regard to CFL players, in Section 14 in an article by Randy Turner.

Dick Pound's article, "Un-Levelling the Playing Field," reminds us of the politics of enforcing dope-testing regimes. He deals with the case of U.S. track and field athletes whose positive tests were not revealed by the U.S. Olympic Committee and the U.S. Track and Field Federation. The Ben Johnson case is mentioned again because Carl Lewis, the athlete who came second in the Seoul final, who was awarded the gold medal originally given to Johnson, and who made a number of public anti-doping pronouncements, had himself tested positive three times some two months before the Seoul Olympics. Lewis' positive tests were covered up by anti-doping authorities in the United States.

Of course, Pound's article is part of his case in support of the establishment of WADA, while the final article in this section, Doug Brown's "The Hypocrisy Game," questions the whole premise of anti-doping. Brown's article is a review of Beamish and Ritchie's 2007 book, *Fastest, Highest, Strongest: A Critique of High-Performance Sport*, and in the subtitle to his article Brown states that "our athletes work like pros and get treated like children." Brown outlines and endorses the position argued by Beamish and Ritchie, focusing on the origins of "performance enhancement" (both "legal" and "illegal"), noting the need to incorporate the health and welfare of athletes into any future policies, and in particular emphasizing the importance of making athletes a part of the policy-making process. Brown relates Beamish and Ritchie's arguments to preparations for the 2010 Vancouver Winter Olympics, and especially the Own the Podium program.

## Additional Suggested Readings and References

- Coakley, J. and P. Donnelly. 2009. *Sports in Society: Issues and Controversies* (2nd Canadian edition). Toronto: McGraw-Hill Ryerson.
- Pound, R. 2003. "Dealing with Performance-Enhancing Drugs in Sport." *Policy Options*, February.
- Robinson, L. 2003. "The Horror of Perfection." *The Globe and Mail*, January 6.
- Schmidt, M. 2010. "Without Surprise, NFL Players Expect the Doping Inquisition." *The Globe and Mail*, August 23.

# 17.

# Unforgiven
## By Stephen Brunt

He seems so much smaller than in memory. Of course, he could never seem that big again, never be the Canadian idol who streaked past the Yankee star Carl Lewis, took a moment to glance back, raised an arm in triumph, and still covered 100 metres faster than anyone ever had. Back then, he was all sinew, all muscle, the whites of his eyes turned yellow from the drugs. A quiet anger always seemed to lurk behind them, even in that moment of triumph. Now, in street clothes, he's no longer superman. There's still the sprinter's gait, belying the bulky thighs, but Ben Johnson otherwise is ordinary, which for better and worse hasn't often been an option since that afternoon in Seoul.

It's not only his physical appearance that's jarring. It's his speech. The stutter—which made it so difficult for him to utter first the denials ("I have never, ever knowingly taken illegal drugs") and then the sad confession ("I know I did wrong")—is nearly absent. That impediment overcome, the man who, as part of his ill-advised defence strategy before the Dubin Inquiry, was cast as too simple even to complete a long-distance phone call may not be a sophisticated thinker, but he is no moron. His words are clipped but clear, and now the anger has found a voice.

"I was fifty, one hundred years ahead of my time," he says. "The whole world knows that Ben Johnson is the best sprinter. But that's not what the media writes, trying to convince the public mind that Ben Johnson didn't even exist.

"Only sports columnists would try and erase Ben Johnson from the books," he says to the sports columnist. "But you can't. You can't erase it. No matter what. Fifty years from now, people are still going to remember."

Just as you can't erase his performance, Johnson himself refuses to fade away, refuses to wait quietly for the world, and especially for Canada, to forgive him. He's forcing the issue. He can talk now. He's not afraid. And he's not particularly sorry.

What that means for us, who rode so high with him and crashed so low, who turned him into a martyr suffering for the sins, of the athletic world, is that the time has come to reconsider. To reflect on what it all meant, and to put the man in context, twelve long, cynic-making years down the road. Can the hero turned villain ever be a hero again?

"I was trying to do something good for my country," he says. "I slip and they all start to point fingers, trying to harm me. When somebody is drowning, you don't push him back in the water. You help him up."

You help him even if he threw himself into the river. Even if, by the rules of the day, he cheated.

In forty-eight hours, Johnson is scheduled to fly to Tripoli, Libya—the pariah state run by Moammar Gadhafi—where he will spend ninety days training the dictator's son, Al Saad, as a soccer player. The last few days have been frantic, with travel arrangements and telephone calls and dealings with the press, for whom this is just more easy quick-joke fodder. A few months ago, he was running against horses in Prince Edward Island. Now he's going to work for one of the world's premier bad guys. Tsk, tsk. How far he's fallen. Why can't he just get on with it, find a job and a life and some dignity in the process?

Not to mention that Johnson also recently tested positive for a third time for using a banned substance. This time, it was a diuretic, which could have masked performance-enhancing substances and which might have been useful if Johnson wasn't banned from competition as a result of his second positive test, in 1993. He acknowledges having taken the drug, but says he was feeling bloated and didn't realize that it would show up in a test.

The Libya scheme was cooked up by his ebullient manager, Morris Chrobotek, who, when Ben isn't talking much, provides more than enough talk for two. "Ben didn't rape anyone," Chrobotek says. "Ben didn't bite anyone's ear off. Ben didn't defraud anyone. Ben just wants food in his mouth, and shelter." There's no denying Chrobotek's persistence, or his commitment to the project—loosely defined as clearing Johnson's name, getting him back into competition before time runs out, and making a few dollars along the way—this last especially important, since Johnson's money is all but gone. The Libya job will bring in $50,000 and Chrobotek isn't even taking a percentage.

Their act has been well established over the three and a half years they've been together, Chrobotek babbling on about conspiracies, Johnson silently taking it all in. These days, though, there's more give and take. Johnson leads the conversation. Chrobotek leaps in less and less—the signal for intervention comes when Johnson stares straight into his eyes.

"I have to make a living," Johnson says of the Libyan trip. "I have to get out of here. I've been in this country for a lot of years, and I'm not making any money here. Back in my glory days, I made $6 million—none of it in this country. I didn't make no money in this country. And so I will go anywhere in the world. I'm not afraid of anywhere. I know the people love me. They read about me, and they see me on TV. They know that I'm a nice person. They give me the opportunity to do something, to help out a great player and improve his ability, so I'm going over.

"When I go anywhere in the world, I feel like I'm at home. People doesn't bug me about what happened. They know the concept, they know the corruption. They don't point fingers at you. [Overseas] they're going to welcome me, because their mind is different. They treat you as a person and also treat you as a celebrity is supposed to be treated."

What exactly happened to that $6 million? The long answer, which Johnson and Chrobotek are happy to allege, is a tale of deceit and exploitation, of agents and government officials who had their hands in the till while the sprinter was raking in money from appearance fees and endorsement deals—though nothing like what he would have brought in had the result at Seoul stood. Whether or not Johnson authorized what they were doing is perhaps beside the point, because, according to Chrobotek, he wasn't sophisticated enough to understand. "The thing is that Ben is easy to set up," he says. "He thinks he's sharp? There's business people out there that can eat him alive."

"Apparently, I was too busy running and travelling all over the world," Johnson adds, "and they were having fun with my money."

After Seoul, Johson says, he had about a million dollars left in the bank. His legal bills for the federal inquiry headed by Mr. Justice Charles Dubin into the use of drugs in amateur sport came to about $100,000. By the time he was reinstated, in 1991, having had no income in the interim, the cupboard was bare. His comeback grossed about $500,000, but that ended in 1993 with his second positive test—for elevated testosterone levels, indicating possible steroid use. He says he didn't have the money to mount a legal challenge, which might have overturned that test, and that he hasn't made much since. He sold his dream house in Newmarket, moved into much smaller quarters in Richmond Hill with his mother and his two sisters, and hoped against hope that someday, somebody might let him run again.

In the meantime, Johnson rises late, never before 11 a.m. He then returns his phone messages—many of them from women, who come and go. He hopes to marry and have children, but at the moment there's no one special. He drives his mother wherever she needs to go—he's renowned for his sense of direction—and trains at York University for four hours each afternoon. Then he comes home and showers, something he does four or five times a day. At night, he watches television—hockey is a passion, as are tapes of Richard Pryor and his favourite television show, *Sanford and Son*, of which he has a complete set. He goes out to clubs, but isn't much. of a dancer. He has few friends. He's a loner.

In the good times, he would think nothing of dropping $2,000 on a pair of shoes. He dressed in Armani and Versace. He loved his Ferrari, but that's been gone for a few years now, since the money ran out.

There have been two moments in Canadian history when sport and culture and passion have come together in a way that helped define the nation. The first was Paul Henderson's series-winning goal against the Soviet Union in 1972. Until then, hockey had been ours and ours alone, the sport that divided Canadians from the rest of the world. Suddenly, we found ourselves down and almost out, outflanked by a mysterious foe who played the familiar game in an entirely different way. Then something else took over: character and heart overcame the sports science of the Evil Empire. When Henderson—bland, white of course, squeaky clean, soon to be born-again—banged in that rebound, we proved that we wanted it more, cared more. It was our game, and in the end we simply had to triumph.

What happened on September 24, 1988, was something else entirely. The 100 metres is the common denominator of global sport. No competition is more elemental. At the Olympic Games, virtually every country that can produce a flag also produces a sprinter who can cover the distance faster than any of his countrymen. When the starter's pistol sounds, the event requires no translation. To win the gold, Johnson had to beat the whole world.

He came from a different Canada than the one that produced Paul Henderson. He was born December 30, 1961, in Falmouth, Jamaica, and became part of the great immigrant wave that hit Canada in the sixties and seventies. He was raised by his mother, in the Lawrence Heights public housing project in Toronto. His father remained back on the island, where he had a good job with the telephone company. Ben Sr. suffered a stroke in 1990, a fatal heart attack in 1991: the family blames his death on the stress brought on by Seoul.

"When I came here, I do two jobs," says Gloria Johnson, in her rich Jamaican lilt. "I work fourteen hours a day to support my family." One of her jobs was in the cafeteria of the Canadian National Institute for the Blind, where she made change for the visually impaired.

Ben never heard Foster Hewitt, but he could run; he'd always been able to run, even back in Falmouth, where he raced other children for pennies and bottle caps. The first time he ran in Canada, as a ninety-three-pound fifteen-year-old who looked much younger, he covered 100 metres in 11.8 seconds, wearing flat shoes, not spikes. Not long afterward, his older brother, Edward, brought him along to a track meet organized by a coach named Percy Duncan. Duncan's protege, Charlie Francis, who would later become Ben's coach, was also there.

Johnson started lifting weights, building his upper body and his legs to sculpted perfection. Duncan helped him devlelop the flying start that made him literally airborne for a couple of feet before his back leg touched down. And later, of course, there was, the chemical enhancement, supervised by the man some called Charlie the Chemist.

The lone Canadian to win the Olympic sprint before Johnson was Percy Williams, in 1928—another time. Our only modern hope in the event, Harry Jerome, had come up lame in the 1960 Olympics, when he was the world-record holder, and then won bronze in 1964 in Tokyo.

By the time Johnson arrived in Seoul, he was already world champion and world-record holder, as well as a surprise bronze medallist at the boycott-marred 1984 Olympics in Los Angeles. But he'd stumbled during the lead-up to the Games, beaten by his great rival, Carl Lewis, and he'd been injured. By and large, Americans had dominated the 100 metres, and Lewis, because of his triumphs at Los Angeles, was widely celebrated (especially in the United States) as the greatest athlete in the world.

The preliminary heats in the Olympics are a cat-and-mouse game. No one wants to give too much away before the one race that matters. And so, before the gun, there was mystery—and Canadians, if they're honest, will tell you there was also a sinking feeling, the sensation that goes with believing second place is the best you can hope for.

Then Johnson ran the perfect race. He exploded from the blocks as no one had before, as no one has since. In the moments when he might have tightened up (as, for instance, Bruny Surin did against Maurice Greene at the 1999 world championships), Johnson instead surged ahead with a confidence, a kind of arrogance Paul Henderson would never have dreamed of. 9.79 seconds. For nearly twenty years, the world record had remained almost static. Johnson had dropped it by more than a tenth of a second. It was as unimaginable as Bob Beamon's miracle long jump in Mexico City in 1968.

"I never really see the race, because my eyes were closed," recalls Gloria Johnson, who sat in the stadium that day. "I never see the race. But I knew he was going to win. I only hear the people calling out for Ben, Ben, Ben. I hear them say, 'He did it!' I opened my eyes, and he was at the finish line. It was beautiful. It was beautiful."

Goodbye Norman Bethune, Shania Twain, Jim Carrey, Céline Dion. In that tape-hitting instant, Ben Johnson became the most famous Canadian of all time. It was the kind of high the country had never experienced, an unequivocal, total victory over everyone else—especially over Lewis and our great neighbours to the South. When Johnson stood for "O Canada," hearts leaped from sea to shining sea. Forget the millennial lists. Forget the polls to determine our country's greatest athlete of the century. Forget Gretzky. It was Ben Johnson.

The only question is what to do with the asterisk.

The day after the race, Gloria Johnson returned to the stadium in Seoul to watch her son's teammate, Mark McKoy, compete in the 110-metre hurdles. Even as the race went off, there was no sign of Ben. Gloria worried. "I started to wonder what happened to him. I never feel good about it."

She tells the story in the living room of the house in Richmond Hill that she shares with Ben and his sisters. It's a typical suburban box, small compared to the monster Johnson had hoped to build, smaller than the one in Newmarket, but comfortable enough. The street outside is treeless, and everything inside seems brand new. In the dining room, the white linen tablecloth is covered with a clear plastic slipcover, as is the oriental rug.

In the living room, there's a gilded bust of King Tut, and on the wall a familiar print, 'Boulevard of Broken Dreams,' a knock-off of an Edward Hopper painting, the original characters replaced by Elvis Presley, James Dean, Humphrey Bogart and Marilyn Monroe.

Mrs. Johnson is petite and pretty and seems young to be Ben's mother. She's a devout Christian who speaks softly and seems nervous at first—this is a rare interview, as she's developed a distrust of and distaste for the press.

Mother and son have always shared a special bond, she explains, forged when Ben was a toddler. In Jamaica, he contracted the Hong Kong flu, which was killing children around the island. "I nursed Ben like he was still a newborn baby,'" she remembers. "I don't let him out of my hands. I just want to keep him close to me. Because I feared if anyone else held him, he might pass away. But close to me, I feel much better. He sleep on my hands.

"'When I took him to the doctor one day in Falmouth, the doctor looked out from where he was mixing his medicine and said to me: 'He doesn't die yet?' I didn't say anything. It didn't sink in. When I come home, that's when it registered. That's when I cried, because the doctor had given up on him. And I decided that there must be a reason he was still here. We cooked pigeons and gave him the broth. That's all the thing he drink day and through the night. And I pray for him. Sometimes my tears were falling down on his face."

Only in the Olympic year, after he had already earned millions of dollars, did Johnson finally persuade his mother to quit her jobs and travel with him. "I know I had to support my family," she says. "I never wanted to leave my job. I kept saying not till next year."

That day in Seoul, the day after his race, Ben never did show up at the stadium. His mother had a disturbing premonition. "When we came back to the hotel after Mark McKoy finished, Ben was in his room. When I saw him through the door, he was standing with one of his feet on a chair. He said to me, 'Mom. Guess what happened.'

"'What happened?'

"'I tested positive.'

"'You what?'

"After he tell me that, I go into my room. Then I went back to him. He was lying down on the bed. He put his hands behind his head. I don't even remember what I said to him. Because the only thing that come to me is like it's a mistake. It will blow over. And I said to him everything is going to be OK. Don't worry. That's all I said to him. But when I came back to my room and I was lying down, there was a feeling that came over me. I thought, it's not going to be so easy."

Yes, he did it. He cheated. He used a banned substance, the steroid stanozolol. He had been using it, and other drugs, for six years. He was part of an athletic subculture in which everyone around him was using. They were taught, if confronted, to deny, deny, deny. It would later be suggested that Johnson didn't really understand, that because of his blind loyalty to his coach, Charlie Francis, and his doctor, Jamie Astaphan, he simply did whatever they asked. But that strained credulity then, and it strains credulity now. He knew what he was doing, and he did it for the same reason so many other athletes use performance-enhancing drugs: they work. Steroids didn't make Ben Johnson fast, per se, but they helped him train harder to build the body that enabled him to run faster than any of the other six billion people on the planet. Whether he could have done it without drugs, we'll never know, though it seems unlikely.

Think back to those first days after Seoul, and through the national ordeal of the Dubin Inquiry. Think how it could have been different. The early denials and explanations—remember the suggestion that the positive test might have been the result of Johnson's drinking sarsaparilla?—were desperate and often ludicrous, but Canadians were willing to listen, and to hope. It has become a myth that the moment the positive test was announced, Johnson was transformed from Canadian Hero to Disgraced Jamaican-Born Sprinter. But almost up

to the moment he took the stand for his Dubin confessional, Canadians were looking for a way to let him off the hook. When he uttered his first, stage-managed words after Seoul—a denial offered to the sports editor of *The Toronto Sun*—there were many who desperately wanted to believe him. Even as he walked into the Dubin hearing room, after everyone else had already spilled the beans, a crowd outside was waving supportive placards and hollering, "We love you, Ben!"

"What the agent was telling me and my lawyer was telling me—and mostly my doctor was telling me—was do not talk to anyone about what's been going on," Johnson says. "Charlie said it, too. Don't speak to anyone."

When he finally did confess, when he cried, when he was scolded by Dubin like a misbehaving child, he had compounded his sins. He was a cheat and he was a liar. He had broken hearts and then prolonged the agony.

"He's the only disgrace?" his mother asks. "Nobody never do nothing? Only Ben Johnson. Only Ben. If they could have, they would have cut him up and thrown him to the wolves."

If he had it to do all over again, Johnson says, he would have refused to appear before Dubin, and he doesn't think he could have been legally compelled. "I denied it until the Dubin Inquiry comes around, and then everybody started pointing fingers, so I had no choice. But if I'd known the laws and the rules, then I wouldn't go."

Off he went into exile, a worldwide punchline, a living example of the corruption of sport—the only one, since no one else of significance got caught. Carl Lewis went home with the world record and the gold medal. Florence Griffith Joyner was celebrated as the greatest female athlete of her generation. Ben had fallen, but it hadn't spoiled the party—not for the International Olympic Committee, not for the International Amateur Athletic Federation, not for television. Just for Canada.

Consider how it might have been. Consider what would have happened if Ben Johnson had stepped off the plane from Korea and said something like this: "I did it. I did it because I wanted to win for Canada. I was told by a lot of people—including a federal cabinet minister—to bring that gold medal home, whatever it took. I'm not the only one who was using something, not the only one in those Olympics, not the only one in that race; I'm sorry. I'm very, very sorry." Canadians are a forgiving lot. We would have gotten over it. When he'd done his penance, we would have welcomed him back. And eventually, less innocent ourselves, we would have understood.

Because Johnson didn't do the right thing, or the smart thing, the road back was that much more difficult. And of course, there was the little matter of testing positive again. After doing his time and earning reinstatement and filling Copps Coliseum in Hamilton for his first comeback race, Johnson climbed all the way back to the 1992 Olympics. But he stumbled out of the blocks in the semi-finals—he blames an all-night session with drug testers, to whom he was trying to provide a satisfactory urine sample, for sapping his energy—and finished dead last in his heat.

"I was just five days away from being the old Ben," he claims. "I was able to run about 9.90 that year, to win the Olympic gold. I was right there." The English sprinter Linford Christie would claim the 100-metre gold in Spain with a time of 9.96—the same Christie who, in 1999, tested positive for a banned substance, had the test thrown out on a technicality and quietly retired.

Running indoors in the winter of 1993, Johnson was tested three times within a week. The first and third tests came back normal. The middle one showed elevated levels of testosterone, a strong suggestion that he was using something again. (Though it seems unlikely for two tests to be clean and one dirty over such a short time, it can happen.)

Johnson and his agent vehemently deny that he was using anything. "If he was taking it," Chrobotek says, "he would have been a hell of a lot faster than he was." But there was certainly motivation—Johnson had been unable to recreate the times he'd run in the past, and faced the prospect of dramatically diminished earning power.

Though he had the option of challenging the test, Johnson declined. He says he had about a half million in the bank at the time, that his lawyer asked for a $100,000 retainer and told him the final tab might be as high as $300,000 and the process might take two years.

"He doesn't want to drag us through what we would have go through in the inquiry," Gloria Johnson says. "It was going to take a long time before it was resolved. So he said he was going to retire. If he feels like that, then you know I will support him."

Could Johnson have beaten the test? Perhaps, by attacking, the process, by tracking his urine samples and uncovering every time they might have been mishandled or exposed to contamination. (Stranger things have happened—ask O. J. Simpson.) It wouldn't have "proved" that he didn't do it, of course, but other positive tests have been overturned on technical grounds without ever getting to he heart of the matter, most famously those of Christie and of American runner Butch Reynolds, who later successfully sued the IAAF.

In choosing not to go forward, Johnson all but acknowledged that his career as a runner was over. But what was he going to do with the rest of his life? It's not the kind of question he likes to consider, never mind answer. "Ben's way of thinking is I'll cross that bridge when I get there," Chrobotek says. "He doesn't like to focus 100 metres away. He's more instantaneous. It's just the way he deals with things."

His mother, who eventually returned to work to help out financially, didn't know what Ben was going to do, either. But her faith led her to believe that somehow everything would be okay in the end.

"I just say things may work out," she says. I just have that belief that somebody's going to come and do what's supposed to be done. That God is going to send somebody to come and take over and help him through."

Ah, but would God really have sent Morris Chrobotek? Only if He has a sense of mischief. Chrobotek is difficult to capture in a few paragraphs, though anyone who spent time in the money-and-cologne Yorkville of the eighties would get the picture. At age fifty-one, in leather pants and collarless shirts and black-on-black, he still has the look.

He was born in Germany in 1948, the son of Polish Jewish parents who emigrated to Israel when Morris was a child. They moved to Toronto in 1959. He struggled in school, he says, largely because he struggled to master English; Hebrew was his first language. Leaving high school at seventeen, he moved to London to learn hair styling at Vidal Sassoon. In 1968, he came back to Toronto to work at the Sassoon salon in Yorkville. He took investment courses, dreamed of being a lawyer—even worked as a researcher for several local lawyers and wrote the Law School Admission Test. Eventually, he drifted into the hotel business, working at the Four Seasons and the Park Plaza, among others. There he came up with the idea for the business he still operates, block-booking rooms for airlines, to be used by their flight crews around the world.

That profession has become a sideline since August 1996, when Chrobotek was introduced to Ben Johnson at Movenpick in Yorkville. The people with Johnson thought that Chrobotek, who had a passion for causes, lost and otherwise, might be able to help. Three years after throwing in the towel, Johnson had decided he wanted to run again—or rather had to, since the money had dried up and there were no prospects.

Following the two most recent positive tests—and the decision not to fight the second one—it seemed a long shot at best that Johnson could convince first Canadian and then international track officials to readmit the most notorious user in sports history. But Chrobotek, who is not easily discouraged (or embarrassed, or humiliated, or silenced) decided after several conversations with Johnson that he liked the odds.

At first, Chrobotek was widely dismissed. His call to the Canadian Centre for Ethics in Sport, which oversees drug testing for Canadian athletes, was met with: "Is this for real, or is this a joke?" Chrobotek got his name in the papers, took to the airwaves, argued Johnson's innocence with whomever would listen. When he was ridiculed, when Johnson was pilloried he took it in stride, having already decided that the press was conspiring against his client.

Chrobotek's biggest—his only—victory came last year, when an arbitrator ruled that Johnson had not received due process in 1993, and ought to be allowed to compete in Canada. It was a limited win, though: the IAAF upheld the lifetime ban, and because any athlete who competed against Johnson would be "contaminated" and barred from international competition, Johnson found himself technically able to run in Canada but unable to compete against anyone.

Chrobotek overcame that little obstacle last summer by having Johnson sprint not against other runners, but against a thoroughbred, a pacer, and a stock car at a charity event in the pouring rain in Charlottetown. For going through with an event widely regarded as humiliating and demeaning (the great sprinter Jesse Owens was also reduced to racing horses late in his running career), Johnson, and especially Chrobotek, took a pounding in the press. Neither expresses even a hint of regret. It was a charity event, Johnson says, to benefit terminally ill children. He received only expense money and he did beat the stock car, which bogged down in the mud. "If I was in good shape, I would do it again," he says, smiling. "I almost beat the horse."

The announcement that Johnson would travel to Libya to train Gadhafi's son, hot on the heels of the third positive test, was greeted with the kind of skepticism and ridicule anyone but Chrobotek might have imagined—especially after Chrobotek, perhaps not entirely seriously, suggested that Johnson might qualify for the Nobel Prize because he was helping people come together through sport. "He only knows sports," Chrobotek says. "I know politics. If somebody helps people come together, they should get a Nobel Prize. I wasn't talking specifically about Libya."

"I don't care what people say," Johnson says. "Some people has been saying things since 1988. I don't care about that. I care about what I believe in and what is right and what I'm supposed to accept in life. And that's final."

**A sportswriter's epiphany, part one.** In Stuttgart, Germany, covering the World Athletics Championships in 1993, and in particular Canadian decathlete Michael Smith, for a book project that was eventually scrubbed. Watching, without much expertise, the distance races for women. Seeing a group of Chinese women runners, unheralded before that meet, all but lapping the greatest runners on the planet, shattering world records, and appearing to do so without even working up much of a sweat. Sitting through a press conference in which the Chinese-to-German-to-English translation made the answers a little difficult to understand, but realizing that the Chinese coach was claiming his runners drank a mixture that included turtle blood, and that this explained their great leap forward. None of those runners tested positive, in Stuttgart or anywhere else, though their results fell off dramatically about the time that testing technologies became more sophisticated.

**A sportswriter's epiphany, part two.** Following the great home-run derby during the summer of 1998, in which both Mark McGwire and Sammy Sosa beat Roger Maris's longstanding record of sixty-one homers in a season. Watching McGwire acknowledge that he'd been using a dietary supplement banned in nearly every sport but baseball, and in the Olympics, because it, had an effect not unlike that of steroids. Hearing McGwire say there was nothing wrong with using

something that helped his training, but didn't help him to hit home runs—just as stanozolol didn't make Ben Johnson fast, per se, but helped him train harder. Getting upset about it in person and in print, and then realizing that the people cheering McGwire each time he hit one out didn't give a damn. And that the viewers of the National Football League, watching 300-pound men who run 40 yards in four and a half seconds didn't care what kind of juice might have permitted such feats.

The sportswriter, who had taken the high moral ground at Seoul, who had written that Johnson cheated and lied about cheating and didn't deserve anyone's sympathy, who believed it was still possible to draw a line between dopers, and non-dopers (or at least still worth trying) was left in a crisis of conscience. Was everybody doing it? Did anyone really care, so long as the show went on? Were the Olympic Games, which had made purity part of the product even if the IOC itself was rotten to the core, really any different than a night at the ballpark?

And if, in this corrupt, doped-up world, athletes seemed to be getting away with it—if not lauded for their chemically aided accomplishments—then what was Ben Johnson? What did it mean to be a cheater and a liar in that context? Why was he the only truly big star to take a fall? How different was he, in the end, than everyone else?

Things are going well in Libya, Chrobotek says. Al Saad Gadhafi may not be much of a soccer player, but he's making progress, and you would imagine they'll find a place for him on the national team. This gig, Chrobotek believes, will lead to all kinds of opportunities for Johnson as a personal trainer to the rich and famous—and eventually to the construction of a training centre, with its own track team.

What Chrobotek is saying less and less, though, is that Johnson will ever compete again. If he isn't reinstated soon, he won't have any chance of getting in shape and qualifying for the Sydney Olympics this fall (the third positive test probably put a damper on that, in any case). And so, with Johnson still in Libya, Chrobotek has set an unofficial deadline: if nothing happens by the spring—and there's no reason to believe anything will—Ben Johnson's track career will be declared officially dead.

At which point his career as a litigant will begin.

"All the torpedoes are aimed," Chrobotek says. "'And we mean busines. They can't get away with this. I'm going to make them live through more misery than they did to Ben Johnson. Now they're going to see the other Morris, the quiet Morris. I'm going to put them through the courts for the rest of their lives." It's a long list: Canadian track officials, both personally and through their associations; the International Olympic Committee; the International Amateur Athletic Federation, which in 2001 will hold its world championships in Edmonton. Lawsuits, Chrobotek says, will be flying. Great scandals and conspiracies will be uncovered. Other dopers will be unmasked, including some of the most famous athletes of our times. The world will come to understand—just as it came to understand that the IOC itself is corrupt—that Ben Johnson was the fall guy, that he suffered for everyone's sins, that while he was playing St. Sebastian, a lot of others who knew exactly what was going on made sure the money kept rolling in. Now, Chrobotek says, they're all going to pay.

Well, maybe. Chrobotek is nothing if not persistent, so it's at least a safe bet that uncomfortable times lie ahead for the sports administrators in this country.

In 1912, Jim Thorpe, who ought to be considered in any account of the century's greatest athletes, won both the decathlon and the pentathlon at the 1912 Olympics in Stockholm. A year later, the Amateur Athletic Union and the American Olympic Committee found him guilty of a violation of the Olympic rules—in 1909 and 1910, he had accepted $15 a week to play baseball games with the Rocky Mount Railroaders of the East Carolina League. He was tainted—he was a professional when he competed against amateurs

in Sweden—and so the International Olympic Committee stripped him of his medals. In the following decades, the IOC (which from 1952 to 1972 was headed by Thorpe's Olympic teammate Avery Brundage) refused to consider repeated requests to restore the medals. Thorpe, who went on to play professional football and baseball, died in 1953.

It wasn't until 1982, when the distinction between professional and amateur sport had been sufficiently blurred, and the old rules seemed sufficiently ridiculous, that the IOC voted to give the medals back (finally moved to do so, it should be noted, not because it was the right thing, but because of a technicality—no written objection to Thorpe's participation in the Olympic Games had been filed during the required thirty-day period back in 1912). Thorpe's family was presented with the medals, not because he was innocent, but because the world had changed.

Imagine a day when the battle against performance-enhancing drugs has been abandoned—because they've been deemed safe, and because detection has become nearly impossible. A day when it has been revealed that, besides the East Germans, who have acknowledged their systematic doping program, all kinds of Olympic medallists were using right back to the 1970s. A day when it's been confirmed that positive tests were suppressed during the Olympic Games at the behest of IOC honchos and the American television networks, who knew that bad news would spoil the show.

Imagine 9.79 back in the record books for 1988. Imagine Ben Johnson, or his descendants, being presented with the gold medal that was taken from him in Seoul. Impossible?

"I believe it will happen," Gloria Johnson says. "I told Ben that in 1988. I don't think back. I think forward. Because there must be a reason why these things happen."

"This is the way people thinks," Ben Johnson says. "Somebody do something good for a nation, and twenty years later, forty years later, that athlete has died before they recognize him. Not when he's alive, because when he's alive they can say this or they can say that. When he's dead, they only say the good things."

◀◀ **Source:** Stephen Brunt is a sports journalist and a leading columnist for *The Globe and Mail*. This article was originally published in *Toronto Life* in March 2000. Reprinted with permission.

# 18. Death Or Glory
## By Stephen LaRose

*Pro wrestling didn't kill Chris Benoit's wife and son but it's not blameless, either*

■■■■■■

World Wrestling Entertainment rarely takes nights off, but July 15—the scheduled date of an ECW/Smackdown event at Regina's Brandt Centre will be an exception.

One of the featured wrestlers on that bill was to have been Chris Benoit, the Montreal-born, Edmonton-raised former WWE World Champion. Benoit hanged himself on June 25, after strangling his forty-three-year-old wife and seven-year-old son in their suburban Atlanta home and leaving Bibles by their bodies.

The WWE says steroids couldn't have led Benoit to do what he did. There was too much evidence of careful, deliberate planning, and no signs of the destruction and extreme violence that characterizes "roid rage." They note that steroids found at the home were prescribed by doctors.

Nevertheless, Benoit's murder-suicide focused attention on the dark side of pro wrestling in general—and Vince McMahon's empire in particular.

Vince McMahon, who had taken over his father's New York City area World Wide Wrestling Federation (as it was known in the 1960s), discovered something in the early 1980s: you attract more fans to a spectacle than a sporting event.

Those people don't care if pro wrestling's a sport or not, or if the outcome is fixed. The more buff and beefcake the wrestlers are, the more stunts they perform, the wilder the audience gets. And there's a near-endless supply of performers.

In the 1980s, McMahon's WWE convinced most state-licensing bodies that pro wrestling wasn't a sport; it was "sports entertainment," abandoning all licensing or outside monitoring of their events.

Meanwhile, by buying out competing wrestling circuits (such as Calgary-based Stampede Wrestling) or driving them into bankruptcy, McMahon's empire can be considered the Wal-Mart of the sports and entertainment business—a business that's driven out its competition and sets its own rules.

While Stu Hart was putting on Stampede Wrestling shows in Alberta and Saskatchewan during the sixties and seventies, Karl Lauer was doing the same in Los Angeles. "During that time, there was a lot more 'mat' wrestling, a huge variety of holds, and there wasn't as much 'flying off the top rope' or 'pile drivers,' " he says.

Those were actually finishing moves: he adds. "We used to say that it was 80% wrestling and 20% showmanship."

"People look at wrestlers as entertainers today. You have to be a good athlete to wrestle 320 times a year in 320 different cities," says Lauer. "He's going to fly 150–170 times a year, and he'll drive to the rest, from a half hour to two hours ... You wonder why these guys get involved with pain pills?"

Pro wrestling today is 80% stunt work and 20% 'mat time.' The human body isn't meant to take the abuse of wrestling moves standard to today's WWE events. Wrestling-related injuries are much more common and much more serious than a generation ago.

"In my time, the worst injury was something like a broken finger or a pulled muscle," Lauer says.

Legally or otherwise, athletes in many sports have used steroids and human growth hormones to recover from serious injuries, such as broken bones, ligament damage and muscle tears. The body naturally makes the compounds in steroids. In most cases, doctors prescribe them for people with a serious medical need.

"My mother had rheumatoid arthritis, and she took steroids," says Greg Oliver, who has written about Canada's pro wrestling scene for more than two decades.

But in concentrations from ten to one thousand times what the body naturally produces, synthetic steroids' effect on the body is akin to taking the governor off an engine and pushing the throttle wide open, he warns.

Many wrestlers may be finding this out the hard way.

"That's why you see a lot of them dying of heart failure," Oliver says. "It's heart failure because their bodies have given out. The way that it's been used in wrestling—to pump up the bodies—hasn't been good for wrestlers' bodies."

Benoit broke his neck in 2002 and took steroids to speed the healing process (that's probably why police found legally prescribed steroids in Benoit's home during their investigation: when people get steroid injections, the body stops making its own testosterone, and never restarts). "Broken necks are like an epidemic in wrestling," says Eric Cohen, who writes about events at prowrestling.about.com.

Wrestlers feel a lot of pressure—from the promoters, from their accountants, and from themselves—to get back in the ring as soon as possible. They don't work, they don't get paid. Wrestlers work as independent contractors—no health plan to speak of, paid a very low base rate, and only make their money if they get more fan support and make more money for the WWE.

"The very nature of the business is to be better than the guy beside him, and draw the money, and therefore be pushed up the card," Oliver says. "It's a very back-stabbing business in a way, because to get above someone else on the card, a wrestler may feel he has to shoot up more, or do these sorts of stunts or get [his] hair cut a different way ... it's all about pushing themselves."

The McMahons are doing well. According to corporate records filed with the U.S. Securities and Exchange Commission, Vince collects $850,000 a year as WWE president. His wife, Linda, collects $500,000 annually as chief executive officer. The couple's two children also hold down vice-president positions.

Vince owns 97 million shares of the WWE, and the family controls 96% of the WWE's shares. On May 11, 2007, the WWE announced a twenty four-cent-a-share dividend. Two days after police found Benoit's body, those shares traded on the New York Stock Exchange at over $15 a share.

Is Vince the bad guy in all of this? Probably not, says Cohen.

"Even if the WWE does the right thing, there are still other wresting promotions, not just in America but also overseas, where wrestlers can go if they fail a drug test. It's an industry problem."

As well, the WWE is making money from wrestling because it's making money for other companies—cable companies who resell the pay-per-view packages, networks that air the shows, companies that supply T-shirts and ball caps, and who make action figures, and the retailers—Toys "R" Us, Wal-Mart—who sell them.

"Vince is a content provider," says Cohen. He can deliver television viewers to advertising companies, and consumers to products ... But if those companies put pressure on McMahon to implement greater safety and drug-testing standards, the WWE would certainly comply," he adds.

Missouri is one of the few American states that didn't decertify pro wrestling, says Lauer, now a cattle rancher in that state, and also a member of the state's combative sports regulating body. McMahon threatened not to hold WWE events in the state again but, Lauer says, that turned out to be an empty threat. "St. Louis has always been a good town for the WWE to do business," says Lauer. "Vince is a good enough businessman to know that."

The fate of wrestlers is much on Lauer's mind: he's also vice-president of the Cauliflower Alley Club, a non-profit organization that's a benevolent club for current and retired wrestlers, with over five thousand members. "Chris Benoit was a member," Lauer says. "Last time I saw him he paid two years' worth of dues."

Outside of that club, and some wrestling fan sites, who thinks of these guys when their careers end? WWE wrestlers, if they're lucky and popular, have a career of about five to seven years before the scriptwriters drain everything that the fans want to see from them. For every wrestler who uses the WWE to mount a second career—Dwayne "The Rock" Johnson to Hollywood movies, Jesse "The Body" Ventura to the Minnesota governor's mansion, Stacey Keibler to *Dancing With The Stars*—hundreds of others scrape by, working security at rock concerts or casinos, or as personal trainers.

Neither the Benoit incident, nor the resulting examination of wrestlers dying early from steroid abuse, will kill the WWE.

"It survived its loss of popularity in the early 1990s, its steroid scandals in 1993 and 1994, the Owen Hart incident, and when its rated-R plotlines went too far for the 'morality police,'" Cohen adds. "Just as the NFL survived Rae Carruth and it'll survive Pacman Jones."

The show always goes on, as it will in the Brandt Centre soon.

■■■■■■

## ■■■ Dead Grapplers Society

'Flyin' Brian Pillman, 35, October 5, 1997. Discovering steroids while a football player, the former Stampede Wrestling and WWE star died in his sleep just before a WWE pay-per-view event in St. Louis. Cause of death was a heart attack stemming from an undetected heart condition.

Louis Mucciolo, "Louis Spicolli," "Bad Radford," 27, February 15, 1998. The one-time WWF jobber died after mixing prescribed anti-depressants with alcohol, and choking on his own vomit at a friend's home in Los Angeles.

Richard Rood, "Ravishing Rick Rude," 40, April 20, 1999. He testified in a 1994 trial that he used anabolic steroids to relieve joint pain and build muscle mass. He died of a heart attack in Alpharetta, Georgia. An autopsy report noted that "mixed medication" had contributed to his death.

Owen Hart, 34, May 23, 1999. Something went wrong with his harness as he descended from the rafters of Kansas City's Kemper Arena during a WWE pay-per-view event. He fell twenty-five metres to the ring, bouncing off the turnbuckle before hitting the mat. His widow reached a reported $18 million out-of-court settlement with the WWE in 2001.

Rodney Anoa'i, "Yokozuna," 34, October 22, 2000. The four hundred-pound-plus former WWE champion died of a massive heart attack in Liverpool just before a match.

Davey Boy Smith, "The British Bulldog," 39, May 18, 2002. The ex-Stampede Wrestling, WCW, and WWE star died in Invermere, British Columbia from heart failure. An autopsy speculated that previous steroid use had led to his death, but reached no conclusions.

Curt Hennig, "Mr. Perfect," 44, February 10, 2003. The one-time WWE and WCW star was found unconscious in a Florida hotel room just before a scheduled bout. The Tampa coroner's office attributed his death to acute cocaine intoxication, while his family maintains steroids and prescribed painkillers also contributed to his death.

Michael Hegstrand, "Road Warrior Hawk," 46, October 19, 2003. An admitted steroid user who suffered from drug and alcohol-related problems, he was diagnosed with a heart condition that halted his wrestling career in 2001. He died of heart failure in Indian Rocks Beach, Florida.

Raymond Traylor, "Big Bossman," 41, September 22, 2004. The one-time WWE stalwart died of a heart attack at his home in Paulding County, Georgia.

Chris "Skip" Candido, 33, April 28, 2005. He broke his fibula and tibia and dislocated his ankle during his first appearance at a Total Nonstop Action Lockdown event on April 24, 2005 in Matewan, New Jersey, and died from complications after surgery.

Eduardo Gory Guerrero Llanes, "Eddie Guerrero," 38, November 13, 2005. After years of battling drug and alcohol addiction, Guerrero was clean and sober for four years when he was found dead in a Minneapolis hotel room. He was scheduled to wrestle at a WWE event that evening. Cause of death was ruled as heart failure.

Marlon Kalkai, "Tiger Khan" 33, June 26, 2006. The Brooklyn-born Khan was a fixture during the 1999–2001 rebirth of Stampede Wrestling. He was found in Los Angeles, dead from heart failure.

Scott Charles Bigelow "Bam Bam Bigelow," 45, January 19, 2007. The former WWE and World Championship Wrestling star was found dead in his Hudson, Florida home. A coroner's report said he had multiple drugs in his system at the time of his death, including lethal levels of cocaine and an anti-anxiety drug. He was also suffering from heart problems.

Michael Lee Alfonso, "Mike Awesome," 42, February 17, 2007. The former Extreme Championship Wrestling World Champion and WWF Hardcore champion committed suicide at his Tampa home.

Shayne Bower, "Biff Wellington," 42, June 24, 2007. Formerly of Stampede Wrestling, Bower also wrestled on the Japanese circuit. He had suffered several strokes and, according to a friend, nearly died last year. He was found dead in his Calgary home. Initial reports said he suffered a heart attack.

◀◀ **Source:** This article was originally published in *Prairie Dog* magazine (July 5–18, 2007) in Regina. Reprinted with permission.

## Un-Levelling the Playing Field
By Richard W. Pound

**19.**

The recent disclosure of documents proving that the United States Olympic Committee (USOC) systematically exonerated scores of athletes guilty of using performance-enhancing drugs has brought into question the moral authority of a national Olympic committee that has always positioned itself as a leader in the fight against doping in sport.

The facts, unfortunately, are all too clear. Much of the media attention has focused on one of the American superstars, Carl Lewis, although he is by no means the only athlete involved. He was, however, the most well-known and is noteworthy for his vocal opposition to drug use and his self-proclaimed personal standard of competing "clean."

In what now appears to be one of life's particular ironies, Lewis was awarded the gold medal in the 100-metre sprint at the 1988 Olympic Games in Seoul, after Canada's Ben Johnson tested positive for anabolic steroid use and was disqualified from the event. This is no apologia for Johnson—he cheated and fully deserved to be disqualified and to forfeit his medal. Lewis, having been beaten soundly in the final, stepped into Johnson's shoes as the new Olympic champion. Wearing that medal around his neck, Lewis publicly criticized Johnson for having resorted to drugs in order to win. Johnson was disgraced and Lewis adroitly polished his own halo.

What Lewis failed to disclose in the process was that, some two months earlier, at the U.S. Olympic trials, he had himself tested positive for performance-enhancing drugs. Not once. Not twice. Three times. The drugs were banned stimulants. There was no error in the analysis of the samples he provided; in each case, the initial analysis was confirmed when the second portion of the sample was analyzed. The drugs were well and truly present in his system. For someone competing in sprints and the long jump, stimulants might well have had an effect on his performance.

These were not just inadvertent uses of cold tablets or something reasonably innocent. These were so-called nutritional supplements with names like Power Surge. Carl Lewis was no fifteen-year-old Romanian gymnast given something by a reckless physician. In 1988, he already had four Olympic gold medals from the previous Summer Games in Los Angeles. He was a multiple world champion, a veteran of international competition, who was fully aware of the rules and warnings regarding performance-enhancing drugs.

The International rules are clear. Doping in sport is governed by strict liability rules. Athletes are responsible for what they ingest or inject, or permit to be ingested or injected, into their bodies. The doping offence is complete once the presence of the substance in the athlete's system has been established, no matter how it got there. The only question then becomes what should be the sanction.

But, in all cases, the result of the event in which the doping occurred has to be nullified. Lewis should have had no results recorded and no possibility of reaching the Olympics. To the discredit of American sport, the American people and the clean athletes who were beaten by the drugged athletes—and thus did not get well-deserved places on the U.S. Olympic team—this did not happen.

The USOC adopted a policy at complete variance with international rules. It routinely exonerated athletes with positive tests on the spurious grounds that the substances had been taken "inadvertently," and mildly warned them against doing it again. The process was so automatic that the letters were mere formalities. On one letter informing an athlete that he had tested positive, there was even a handwritten note saying the sender was obliged to send the letter, but that the athlete would be exonerated.

Whatever adjective might be applied, calling Lewis' drug use inadvertent is little short of a joke. Even had it been a cold tablet, that would not have changed the rule. The only inadvertence is, perhaps, that he has now been caught.

The U.S. Track and Field Federation (USATF), advised of the test results, was required to advise the international federation (the IAAF) in turn. It did not. All knowledge was confined to a small group within the USOC and the USATF.

What distorted system of values was the USOC following? How could it justify hiding positive drug tests from its own public and the athletes who competed fairly? How could it insist that everyone else follow the rules, while breaking those rules over and over?

Drug use in sport is not unlike alcoholism: until the problem is acknowledged, it is not possible to implement an effective cure. America is not the only country with a doping problem in sport. Nor is it the worst; it has never used a state-sponsored, mandatory drug program for its athletes, as did, among others, the former East Germany. There is no country and no sport that is free of the risk of drug use. The same Olympics that celebrated American excellence were a Gethsemane for Canada, with the Ben Johnson scandal. The difference between the two countries is that Canada has acknowledged the failure and become one of the leading nations fighting for drug-free sport. Even Germany, by prosecuting those responsible for former programs, has come to terms with its past.

It is now time for the United States to do the same. There is little possibility of changing results from fifteen years ago, but the USOC has a duty to explain to the American people and to the Olympic world how this travesty was allowed to occur. Is America willing to countenance cheating, to celebrate tainted Olympic performance, in the name of some misguided national pride? If so, it has been masquerading under false colours. If this is not what America stands for, then the USOC should acknowledge publicly that it erred. Its people, its athletes, and the world at large require nothing less.

---

◀◀ **Source:** Richard Pound is an Olympic athlete, past president of the Canadian Olympic Committee and chairman of the World Anti-Doping Agency. This article was originally published in *Maisonneuve* (June, 2003). Reprinted with permission.

# The Hypocrisy Game
## By Douglas Brown

**20.**

*Our athletes work like pros and get treated like children*

■ ■ ■ ■ ■ ■

A Review of: *Fastest, Highest, Strongest: A Critique of High-Performance Sport*. Rob Beamish and Ian Ritchie (Routledge, 2006)

■ ■ ■ ■ ■ ■

Canada has a strange and dubious distinction in the arena of international sport. It is the only country to have hosted the Olympic Games (summer or winter) without winning a single gold medal. Being successful hosts is one thing, being successful athletic participants is quite another. Over the past thirty years, our role at the Olympics has generated considerable public debate over the need—and the methods—to end up on the podium. Drugs are at the heart of this debate, which will only become louder and more urgent as the 2010 Winter Games at Vancouver/Whistler approach.

*Fastest, Highest, Strongest: A Critique of High-Performance Sport* offers an interesting context in which to consider this issue. It is a well-researched book that focuses on the attitudes and ideas that have generated current international policies on the use of performance-enhancing substances. The book challenges the squeaky-clean sport ideals that the International Olympic Committee and national governments like to use to justify their "institutional" stakes in the world of high-performance sport. In other words, authors Rob Beamish and Ian Ritchie ask us to re-examine the relationship between the ideals and the real practices of achieving sporting success. Modern sport is work; it is rational; the best athletes in the world do not play sport—they work at it. The logic that athletes should disregard the advantages of some technologies (drugs, blood doping, DNA therapy) over others (scientifically based rehabilitation regimes, enhanced bio-medical monitoring, and altitude training) seems flawed in this era when no one can genuinely describe the Olympic Games as a beacon of amateur sporting ideals.

A quick survey of Canadian sports history will be helpful here. During the period between the 1976 Olympic Games in Montreal and the 1988 Olympic Winter Games in Calgary, the federal government attempted to improve the rankings of Canadian athletes by centralizing a national sport delivery system in Ottawa that emphasized success at the Olympics.

But in the late 1980s, just when Canadian athletes began asserting international prominence in a few high-profile sports, disaster struck in the form of the Ben Johnson drug scandal at Seoul. Under the influence of the subsequent Dubin Commission, Canadian sports bureaucrats reimagined themselves as international crusaders against drug use in sport. No Olympic Games success was worth the international humiliation of another high-profile positive test.

In 1988, Canada's modest drug-testing program was run by a part-time administrator out of a closet at the Sport Medicine Council of Canada. Today, that has been replaced with a suite of executive offices and a staff of more than thirty. The operation is known as the Canadian Centre for Ethics in Sport and is based in Ottawa. Its 2005–06 operating budget exceeded $5 million. At the international level, Canadian anti-drug zealots have earned themselves a place on the front line in the war against illegal use of performance-enhancing substances in sport. The most visible and controversial Canadian is former IOC vice-president Richard Pound, who is the founding chair of the World Anti-Doping Agency. When it comes to defending the inherent ethical principles of "clean" sport, Pound performs his role with grave (nearly maniacal) commitment.

Now that the Olympic Winter Games are returning to Canada in 2010, with the discomfiting prospect of sustaining Canada's unique reputation as the most winless hosts ever, sport bureaucrats have decided that Canada must "own the podium."

"The Pursuit of Excellence," our ambiguous rallying call for the last three decades, no longer reflects official Canadian attitudes toward international sporting success. In Vancouver/Whistler, Canadian athletes must prove that they are the best in the world. Own the Podium is a sport technical program that is costing $110 million over five years.[1] The objective is simple: Canada will win the most medals at these winter games. Performance enhancement is no longer the dirty concept it was during the post–Ben Johnson era. In fact, it has been developed into the cute little acronym "PET" (performance-enhancement team). To become the best in the world, Canadian Olympians will be assigned PETs leading up to the games. They will also benefit from a program called Top Secret— "an innovative, research program designed to give Canadian athletes 'the edge' in equipment, technology, information, and training."[2] Although Top Secret sounds potentially shady, Canada's official policies on, and sanctions against, doping of all kinds have never been more restrictive. The Own the Podium documents are silent on this loaded question. Canadian athletes remain subject to year-round drug testing (in and out of competition). As a university professor, I have witnessed student athletes being followed around campus by volunteer pee collectors until they deliver an out-of-competition urine sample. Clean athletes remain the overriding "ideal" for Canadian sport bureaucrats and politicians.

Remarkably, Canada's strategy for global sport dominance has been adopted with very little resistance or ethical debate, which makes *Fastest, Highest, Strongest* a welcome addition to the library of volumes on high-performance sport. Beamish and Ritchie critique national sport systems and expose the paradoxes and hypocrisies that the Olympic Games create and sustain.

The authors dissect what most observers and sport participants understand intuitively, but struggle to articulate in any meaningful social or political context: sport is not what it used to be. Nineteenth-century ideals like "the gentleman amateur" and clichés like the "inherent purity of sport" no longer provide a moral and ethical foundation when confronting issues in twenty first-century sport. Furthermore, for more than a century, the Olympic Games and the IOC have been attempting to define and redefine just exactly what constitutes legitimate sport. Beamish and Ritchie highlight that the IOC has never managed to consolidate a single universal world of sport at the Olympic Games; at the height of the Cold War, for example, IOC officials did not fret about the odd mixture of professional athletes from the eastern bloc competing among amateur athletes from western countries. Realistically, international sport has always been a plural enterprise from nation to nation and from athlete to athlete.

Using this sociological and historical framework, Beamish and Ritchie illustrate the artificiality of the moral argument that underpins current policies on doping in sport. The book offers a two-part argument: 1) "any policy prohibiting selected substances by separating 'doping', on the one hand, from 'sport,' on the other, is misguided. The frequently held assumption that the 'essential nature of sport' automatically precludes certain performance-enhancing substances and practices and allows others reinforces the mistaken belief that the 'ethics' of performance enhancement are self-evident"; and 2) "the question policy-makers need to address concerns performance enhancement in its full socio-historical context."

For example, policy-makers must acknowledge that "practices constituting sport today are dominated by instrumental rationality, the quest for victory, the pursuit of the linear record, and the desire/demand to push human athletic performance to its outer limits." Governments and powerful sport organizations (international sport federations and the IOC) have been promoting myths about these questions for more than a century to a sport-consuming public. The authors suggest that elite international sport is scientifically rationalized work where performance enhancement and performance-enhancing technologies play a central

and essential role in the lives of athletes and the careers of coaches and sport bureaucrats.

In the end, Beamish and Ritchie suggest that the current policies of drug proscription and the penalties for being caught may, indeed, create situations that put athletes at an even greater risk of hurting themselves. Their argument is complex, and based on several premises. The first, and most important, premise is that anti-doping legislation is couched in a misplaced paternalism: the notion that sport officials must protect athletes from themselves. Next, the list of banned performance-enhancing substances is far too arbitrary and does not acknowledge profound distinctions between substances that are extremely harmful and substances that are less harmful. In order to minimize the risk of getting caught, athletes are choosing drugs that are more harmful but less detectable than drugs that are relatively benign but more easily detectable.

For example, injected oil-based anabolic-androgenic steroids are less toxic to the liver and kidneys but stay in the system longer and are more easily detected in doping tests. Orally consumed water-based steroids are far more likely to damage the liver and kidneys but clear the system quickly and are, therefore, more difficult to detect in doping tests. The authors warn that some misinformed athletes will make decisions to minimize the risk of getting caught at the expense of their long-term health.

The book concludes that three criteria ought to guide future discourse on performance enhancement in sport. These criteria specify that policies on performance enhancement must confront "real" international sport practices in the twenty-first century, athletes' health and welfare must be a central consideration while it must be accepted that performance enhancement lies at the core of elite sport participation, and athletes must be brought into the policy-making processes of international sport and the Olympic Games.

To give substance and background to their recommendations, the authors concentrate on two major paradigm shifts that have occurred in the world of athletics over the past century: the shift from amateurism to professionalism and the shift in our understanding of the limits and potential of human performance. The first of these shifts was completed in 1974 when the IOC officially revised its rule on amateurism. Ideologically, the concept of the gentleman amateur implied that an athlete's pursuit of performance excellence ought to be mediated by his or her willingness not to try too hard. When Pierre de Coubertin reinvented the Olympic Games for the modern world in 1894, he envisioned a class of athletic aristocrats for whom sport competition was an expression of social unity and harmony. He referred to the experience of *eurythmie*, an aesthetic imperative where the use of excessive force and outward appearances of stress and strain were undesirable. The achievement of this aesthetic was contingent on the notion that real sportsmen pursued sport for sport's sake, not for external rewards.

By the 1970s, however, efforts to maintain the myth of amateurism clashed dramatically with the reality of the lives of Olympic athletes. In spite of the Olympic Games' rhetoric, athletes were training full time, and under sophisticated and rationalized supervision. Once the nineteenth-century amateur ideal was abandoned in 1974, the IOC effectively opened the door for athletes, coaches, sport administrators and politicians to push the concept of performance enhancement as far as necessary. Moreover, Beamish and Ritchie present a solid argument that, from the 1970s to the present, real sport cannot be separated from big money and big-P Politics. As athletes, governments, and the marketplace openly embraced the "pursuit of the linear record," the IOC shifted its moral compass. Working at sport was no longer perceived as a threat to the legitimacy of the IOC and its authority.

A second paradigm shift the authors refer to occurred when physiologists' knowledge turned dramatically from one understanding of the human body to another. In the nineteenth and early twentieth centuries, scientists believed that the first law of thermodynamics explained athletic potential and human performance. This law of physics suggested that humans have finite capacities for work and that achieving peak performance is the product of balancing energy conservation with energy expenditure. By the middle of the twentieth century, European scientists realized that human capacities for work could, in fact, be increased. Beamish and Ritchie call this "a paradigm shift in the ontology of human performance." The fundamental training techniques for achieving athletic performances that exceeded so-called "natural" capacities included "overload" or resistance training and "specificity" training. During roughly the same time period, breakthroughs in biochemistry also presented new theories on augmenting "natural" human capacities with performance-enhancing drugs. This new concept of the body presented scientists and sportspeople with new questions and new challenges. What are the limits of a human's capacity for work? How can technologies be used to enhance human performance? How do the discourses of ethics and morality intersect with the discourses of physiology and biochemistry? And finally, how do these intersecting discourses affect the ideology and practices of modern sport?

Each chapter in the book weaves together events that explain and complicate the moral and ethical issues surrounding the use of drugs in high performance sport. Sometimes all this socio-historical detail can pull the authors off track, but sometimes the detail is fascinating. For example, Chapter Two focuses on the early use of steroids. In the two decades following World War II, international sport and especially competition at the Olympic Games were haunted by the mystery of steroid use. This vague, yet palpable, anxiety was a confluence of rumours that WWII German soldiers had been systematically given steroids to increase their levels of aggression on the battlefield with the arrival of highly successful Soviet athletes on the international sporting scene when the USSR entered the Olympic Games in 1952. Western coaches, athletes, and sport officials speculated that these new powerful Soviet bodies were the product of the same mysterious pharmaceuticals that created the fierce German soldiers of the Wehrmacht.

*Fastest, Highest, Strongest* concludes with a compelling though not especially controversial critique of modern high-performance sport. The authors suggest that critiques should focus on "real" (that is, performance-enhanced) sport, rather than on the ideologies of powerful organizations like the IOC that have consistently denied the "real" political and "real" economic practices that sustain high performance sport in the twenty-first century. They demonstrate conclusively that the logic of banning specific performance-enhancing substances is flawed. And—this is particularly welcome although the authors do not deal with it in detail—they introduce the athlete into the equation as a powerful and necessary agent in policy-making related to sport and the use of drugs and other enhancements.

Which brings us back to the Canadians, preparing for 2008 in Beijing and 2010 in British Columbia. With Own the Podium, Canadian sport bureaucrats have created an ambiguous and disingenuous mandate for Olympic athletes and their coaches. Practically, the "must win" and "can do" spirit of Own the Podium is muted by the reality that Canadian athletes train like professionals within a sport system that treats them like children at best, or repeat offenders at worst. Our sport system operates from a code of ethics that does not adequately address the reality of human performance and technology (pharmaceutical or otherwise) in the twenty-first century.

## Notes

1. C. Priestner Allinger and T. Allinger. 2004. "Own the Podium 2010: Final Report with Recommendations of the Independent Task Force for Winter NSOs and Funding Partners," September 10 <www.olympic.ca/EN/organization/news/2005/files/otp_final.pdf>.

2. Own the Podium 2010. 2006. "Own the Podium 2010 Fact Sheet—August 2006" <www.ownthepodium2010.com/images/stories/OTP%20Resources/media_otp_factsheet_aug_25_06.pdf>.

◀◀ **Source:** Douglas Brown is an associate professor of sport history at the University of Calgary. This article was originally published in the *Literary Review of Canada* in October 2007. Reprinted with permission.

# Section 5

## Violence in Sports

At the time of writing, the World Hockey Summit in Toronto once more has violence (and injury) in the game on its agenda, while the Canadian Medical Association meeting in Niagara Falls has come out against the impending legalization of Mixed Martial Arts (MMA) in several provinces, arguing that physicians cannot endorse any activity where there is a deliberate attempt to injure. Violence may be considered as an aspect of "deviance," but it is so widespread in sports, and has received so much research and media attention in Canada, that not only is it possible to devote a separate section to violence in sports, but also—because of the many forms of violence in sports—to divide that section into two: "Player and Spectator Violence" directly associated with a sports contest; and the "Hazing, Harassment, Bullying, and Abuse" that is often associated with off-the-field actions in sports.

### A: Player and Spectator Violence

In one of the more insightful contributions to a long-standing debate in Canada, Mark Moore argues that "Hockey Doesn't Need Fighting." Moore is well-positioned to make this case; he is a former university and professional player, whose book *Saving the Game* (2006) is a thoughtful contribution to resolving the crisis in the current game. He is also the brother of Steve Moore, a National Hockey League player whose career-ending injury resulted in criminal charges being brought against another

player, Todd Bertuzzi (see "Violence in Sports" later in this section).

John Allemang confronts the issue of injuries produced by violence in hockey more directly in his article "Enough Brain Damage Already." Concerns about fighting and violence have been reinvigorated by new data about the effects of repeated concussions, and by the death of a player (Don Sanderson) as a result of a hockey fight. Allemang's article was written in anticipation of what proved to be an excellent men's hockey tournament at the Vancouver Winter Olympics, and Allemang argues that "if the Olympics can be enlightened about hockey and head shots [and attract huge television audiences into the bargain], so could the NHL."

We frequently hear strongly argued and divergent opinions about the involvement of the law in sports, especially when criminal charges are brought against players. But those arguments are rarely grounded in the actual legal principles that lie behind criminal charges being brought against athletes. Two prominent professional hockey cases in Canada—against Marty McSorley for his hit on Donald Brashear, and against Todd Bertuzzi for his hit on Steve Moore—are the subject of Law Connection's "Violence in Sports." In this article, the actual cases are cited and discussed in the specific context of the laws involved.

Stephen Brunt, the well-known sportswriter and boxing specialist for *The Globe and Mail*, is the ideal person to review the relatively new combat sport of Mixed Martial Arts, especially now that the sport, under the guise of the Ultimate Fighting Championships (UFC), is now permitted in many parts of Canada (it has been legal in Quebec for some time). He provides insights into the physical risks and the successful business model of a sport which is unabashedly violent.

Finally, Kevin Young is one of the few scholars to have studied spectator violence in North America. His article "Five and a Half Myths About North American Sports Crowd Disorder," is now somewhat dated, but is still an important reminder that we are not immune to fan violence in Canada and the United States. Young points out both the similarities and the differences between fan violence in North America and the more often discussed "soccer hooliganism" in Europe.

[Although it is often not stated, it should be noted that all of the articles above deal with men's sports and male violence. The issue of sport and masculinity is examined by Atkinson and Young in Section 6: Gender, Sexuality, and Sports.]

### B: Hazing, Harassment, Bullying, and Abuse

Initiation rights for sport teams, often referred to as hazing, have not gone away despite many universities and leagues in Canada having zero-tolerance regulations. Two incidents in 2005 received a great deal of publicity—one involving the Windsor Spitfires OHL team, and the other involving the McGill University Redmen football team. Daniel Drolet provides a detailed look at hazing in relation to university sport in Canada in "When Rites go Wrong." This article is followed by McGill University's official statement to the football players and the university community "regarding the investigation into a complaint about the football team initiation activities."

Following on from the Blatchford article in Section 3, Erin Anderssen looks at "Coaches Cornered," and provides a detailed look at the constraints on Canadian coaches following the incidents of abusive behaviour by coaches such as Graham James and David Frost. These constraints include police checks, teams initiating "no hugs" rules, and coach-

es refusing to drive athletes home after practices or games. She points out that Canada is ahead of many countries in terms of child protection in sport, but that there is still a great deal to be done.

In some professional sports, certain athletes have a reputation for sexual promiscuity and, evidently, a sense of entitlement. This can lead to problems of both sexual assault and false accusations. Whether it involves the alleged sexual assault by NFL quarterback Ben Roethlisberger; the failure of CFL player Trevis Smith to disclose his HIV positive status to his sexual partners; or the sensationalized rape accusation against NBA player Kobe Bryant, the issues provide real teachable moments. Jackson Katz, a leading U.S. activist on the issue of male violence against women, used the Kobe Bryant case in just that way—providing important context and pointing out the legalities involved in the case. Any discussion of the Bryant case could benefit from Katz's careful outlining of the issues.

Finally, the IOC Medical Commission has worked on the issue of sexual harassment and abuse in sport. They convened an expert panel, which included several Canadians including physician Margo Mountjoy, and Respect in Sport co-founder Sheldon Kennedy. The resulting Consensus Statement entitled "Sexual Harassment and Abuse in Sport" was adopted by the IOC in 2007 and provides important information about sexual harassment and abuse. However, as with other recent IOC Medical Commission documents, the recommendations are weak, suggesting that "all sport organizations **should**" do various things to prevent sexual harassment and abuse rather than using the power of the IOC to insist that participation at the Olympic Games is contingent on "all sport organizations" actually following their recommendations. (See also the recent and long-awaited UNICEF report on child protection in sport in "Additional Suggested Readings and References.")

### Additional Suggested Readings and References

- Cheney, P. 2006. "Online, the Gloves Come Off." *The Globe and Mail*, December 2.
- Kennedy, S. (with J. Grainger). 2006. *Why I Didn't Say Anything: The Sheldon Kennedy Story*. Toronto: Insomniac Press.

- Moore, M. 2006. *Saving the Game: Pro Hockey's Quest to Raise its Game from Crisis to New Heights*. Toronto: McClelland & Stewart.
- Priest, L. 2010. "Changing the Game: Concussions." *The Globe and Mail*, March 9.
- Robinson, L. 2000. "Code of Silence: Hockey's Dark Side." *The Globe and Mail*, April 25.
- Robinson, L. 2008. "Girl Unprotected: Hockey Coach on Trial for Sexual Abuse of Players." *Victoria Times Colonist*, November 5.
- Robinson, L. 2008. "Another Canadian Hockey Scandal." *The Globe and Mail*, December 1.
- Scanlan, L. 2007. " 'Do You Wanna Go?': Hockey Fight in Canada." *The Globe and Mail*, March 29.
- Stothart, P. 2004. "The Trouble with Canada's Game: Goons and Bumper Cars on Ice." *Policy Options*, May.
- UNICEF 2010. *Protecting Children from Violence in Sport: A Review with a Focus on Industrialized Countries*. UNICEF/Innocenti Research Centre, Florence, Italy.

# Section A: Player and Spectator Violence

## Hockey Doesn't Need Fighting
### By Mark Moore

**21.**

Exciting game on Saturday! Except for what happened to Newbury ... If you're a Toronto sports fan, you've probably heard those words a hundred times in the past few days. If you're not familiar with Toronto sports, the Pittsburgh Penguins beat the Maple Leafs 6–5 in overtime, and Ronald Petrovicky knocked out Kris Newbury. If you're not from Canada, this was no boxing match—this fight took place in an NHL hockey game.

Nearly everyone who watched the match enjoyed it. The exciting back-and-forth affair delivered on the hype that has accompanied the "new and improved NHL" led by Sidney Crosby and the young guns from Pittsburgh. Most Toronto fans seemed content with the one point the Leafs earned for their overtime loss, alongside the entertainment they got from a fast-paced, highly skilled game.

But then, there was what happened to Newbury. Taking a hard punch in the fight with Petrovicky, Newbury fell unconscious to the ice, struck his head and temporarily lay motionless. After a delay, he was removed on a stretcher, a sight fans never want to see.

Although the debate over the place of fighting in hockey will no doubt continue, Newbury's injury is a sharp reminder that, while some welcome additions have graced this "new and improved NHL," there are still important issues left untended from the old NHL—especially around the issues of injuries and violence.

Here are ways the NHL can gain ground.

1. Eliminate head checking: Concussion rates in hockey have reached staggering levels in recent years. While head checking was not responsible for Newbury's concussion or several other cases, it does remain a common, easily preventable cause of concussions in

hockey. Any bodycheck with a deliberate high follow-through to the opponent's head or neck should earn the perpetrating player an automatic minimum two-game suspension, to be doubled with each repeat offence by the same offender.

2. Full-time four-on-four: The thrilling end of Saturday's game came in the more open and offence-oriented four-on-four format of NHL overtime. Four-on-four also yields fewer collisions between players—the most common cause of all injuries in hockey. What better way to add extra excitement and alleviate excess injuries than to switch to the four-on-four format full-time?

3. Better equipment: The new uniforms recently announced by the NHL addressed questions of fashion and performance. What, then, of the gladiator gear players today wear underneath those uniforms and carry into collisions with each other? Softer surfaces, streamlined designs, and other sensible equipment adjustments could reduce many needless injuries.

4. Tracking violent penalties: Hockey infractions typically fall into categories of either obstructive acts (holding, hooking, interference, etc.) or violent acts (charging, slashing, cross-checking, fighting, hitting from behind, etc.). The latter are a more serious threat to players' safety. And a relatively small number of players consistently earn a disproportionately high number of such penalties. It's time the consequences were designed to change that. The simplest way is to log all violent fouls, and to have automatic suspensions kick in when players reach successive levels of violent fouls. Tracking likewise by team, suspensions would fall on coaches of consistently violent teams.

5. What about fighting? Fighting has its proponents, or in cases like the Newbury fight, apologists. But here is what Leaf coach Paul Maurice, a former player, said: "It doesn't matter how tough you are or how many punches you've taken. If you get hit in the right spot, you're going down." A few years ago, Phoenix Coyotes general manager Mike Barnett predicted "one of these days, a guy's ... going to land a bomb in the wrong place ... and somebody could die. And then all hell will break loose because everyone will stand back and say 'how did we ever let this happen?'"

Thankfully, it didn't happen to Newbury. But what did happen was enough to make us think about the potential consequences, and how hockey would be if there was no fighting.

---

◀◀ **Source:** Mark Moore is a former professional hockey player and author of *Saving the Game: Pro Hockey's Quest to Raise its Game from Crisis to New Heights.* This article was originally published in *The Globe and Mail* on February 14, 2007. Reprinted with permission.

# 22.

# Enough Brain Damage Already
By John Allemang

*If the Olympics can be enlightened about hockey and head shots, so could the NHL*

■■■■■■

If sport has its origins in combat, if hockey is just a commercialized version of war with better sightlines, then, yes, maybe brain damage is an essential component of our national game.

How else to explain the cult of the concussion that prevails in the National Hockey League? Brutality-loving general managers rule the professional game, and they have consistently refused to banish the head shots that compromise players' lives and livelihood. In the NHL, where celebrated players such as Eric Lindros, Pat Lafontaine, and Keith Primeau have had their careers cut short by attacks to the head, it's still considered acceptable, even desirable, to drive your body armour into an opponent's skull at high speed in order to hasten his post-retirement dementia. Big, hard hits are praised for creating "momentum," hockey's proud euphemism for the energy boost that comes from watching a fast-skating opponent knocked senseless by a blow to the head.

What should be considered a medical travesty and a national disgrace is instead positioned as a point of pride: Canada's game is inherently violent, and only real men need apply. "If you don't want to get hurt, don't play the game," said CBC commentator and former general manager Mike Milbury recently, the kind of know-it-all response that hockey neanderthals like to offer up whenever their blood lust is called into question.

It's not as if the NHL were ignorant about the damage concussions create: The league administers a state-of-the-art policy to diagnose players who have been concussed and assist them in their recovery. This program has served as a model for the National Football League as it tries to make up for its own inattention to brain injuries.

The difference with the NHL is that, while it's prepared to help players after they've been hurt, it doesn't do nearly enough to prevent them from entering that brain-damaged state in the first place—"getting their bell rung," as commentators like to say with sports-fan glee.

Medical professionals unconnected to the NHL have long urged the league to change hockey culture and institute a zero-tolerance policy for head shots. Impossible, say the national game's self-appointed gatekeepers, who have staunchly opposed what Mr. Milbury has called a "pansification" of the sport's exaggerated macho masculinity. Yet, this is exactly the kind of protective protocol that will be followed at the Vancouver Olympics, where the style of play is governed by the enlightened free thinkers of the International Ice Hockey Federation—a Europeanized body long suspected by old-school commentators of trying to devalue hard-nosed hockey.

Does any hockey fan, let alone any medical expert, seriously believe that the calibre of Olympic hockey will suffer because the best players in the world cease to be moving targets for headhunters? Will well-heeled spectators demand their money back because Team Canada's best are unable to create momentum through hits to the head and have to rely, instead, on the ancient arts of skating, passing, shooting, and checks to the body?

Yet, at the same time that the Olympics are delivering undeniable pleasure through hockey's unbeatable combination of speed, skill, and toughness, the NHL brain trust will be preparing for a round of meetings in March designed to sort out good head hits from bad. Like abstruse medieval philosophers, the league's general managers take pride in discerning minute differences between brain-jarring attacks that are a proper part of the game and those that may no longer suit the sensitivities of the times.

### ■ ■ ■ Blame the Pedestrian

A concussion is a concussion, you might well say. Why not listen to the doctors and do everything in your power to look after players' brains—or at the very least treat them as long-term economic assets deserving of stringent protection? Yet, the NHL's decision-makers have long maintained a blame-the-victim strategy that essentially says to its legion of concussed puck handlers: You should have seen it coming.

Or to quote Toronto Maple Leafs general manager Brian Burke, a Harvard Law School graduate, one-time college hockey player, and former vice-president in charge of discipline for the NHL:

"We've always said, if a player puts himself in a vulnerable position, that's his fault." Apply this argument to the real world, and imagine what you'd get—where vulnerability is somehow made to equal culpability, it's open season on momentarily distracted pedestrians for any speeding driver who wants to feel the thrill of a bone-jarring collision.

The only way to be invulnerable in this version of hockey is to take your eyes off the puck or the pass and be constantly on the alert for the disabling bodycheck that is the trademark of the tough-guy NHL—and the pride of many Canadians who have come to believe that the ruggedness of our game is somehow proof of a superior national character.

Mr. Burke is regarded as one of the smartest thinkers in hockey management, perhaps in part because he never went through the mind-numbing apprenticeship that is an NHL playing career. He's been depicted as a moderate on concussion issues because, at a recent general managers' meeting, he actually managed to envision a grey area where some open-ice bodychecks to the head might be less suitable than others—a blindside hit, say, where the checker might ultimately have to share the responsibility.

Yet, this is the amiable, polysyllabic man who, when he was hired to rescue the Leafs from long-term oblivion, stated his deepest hockey desires without a trace of irony or doubt: "We require, as a team, pugnacity, testosterone, truculence, and belligerence."

It may be true that, to survive in the brutal reality of the NHL night after night, those are exactly the kind of qualities that matter most. Players are bigger and faster than they ever were, shoulder pads are lethally plated with brain-damaging armour, the boards and glass are unforgiving points of constant contact, and the smallness of NHL rinks conspires to limit the open ice available to an elusive skater. If easygoing elegance is what you're looking for, head for the Russian league, where larger rinks and a more open-minded understanding of physicality mean there's less of a premium on commando-style belligerence. In Russia, as it happens, hockey culture evolved out of low-contact soccer traditions rather than from the arts of war and, as a result, clever puck movement is still prized over mindless pugnacity.

### ■ ■ ■ Fostering Dementia

But however much the modern NHL style of play is shaped by its working conditions, none of it would necessarily produce job-related brain damage if there weren't an aggressive meanness built into the game at the managerial level—the truculence demanded by Mr. Burke and his peers. When headhunting hockey is broadly embraced as Canada's national game, to the point where the national TV network encourages Mr. Milbury's depansification strategy and lets Don Cherry fuse the game's values with our Afghan military mission, it's worth asking how much this caricature of workplace violence has corrupted the nation's soul.

At the very least, we tolerate, which is to say, cheer on, a sports culture that places a value on fostering early-onset dementia. Neurologists familiar with the game know this is the likely outcome of hockey's hits to the head, and players who have been forced into early retirement, such as Mr. Primeau, reluctantly accept it as the future they face for having earned a good living at the game's highest levels. Few retired hockey players, understandably, have come forward to talk about their cognitive problems, but Mr. Primeau has promised his brain to the Sports Legacy Group, a research centre engaged in a long-term study of concussion-related cognitive damage suffered by athletes.

And if we're willing to accept possible dementia as the price retired hockey stars must pay so we can celebrate the toughness of our national game, what does that say about Canadian values? Lack of empathy for star hockey players surely translates into a lack of fellow feeling for anyone who "should have seen it coming." If you buy that argument, how much easier is it to ignore or tolerate abuse of Afghan prisoners, or allow Omar Khadr to rot in Guantanamo because he wouldn't be there if he didn't deserve to be?

### ■ ■ ■ The Military-Hockey Link

The link may seem far-fetched. And yet our military and political leadership, much like our hockey leadership, prizes aggression and controlled, self-serving violence while disdaining the pansified peacekeeping politeness that represents a different vision of what Canada could be. It's what the fans want, you can almost hear them saying.

As a military policy, it's proving to be damaging. As a political strategy, it now looks very risky. But as a business model for professional hockey, it remains highly attractive, as long as the fans keep cheering the big hits without bothering to imagine the health-care consequences.

The NHL's bosses don't see a point in eradicating the head shot as long as their culture encourages it, and the players have little choice as long as they want to make NHL money. So, in the end, it's up to those who live vicariously through the national game to take ownership of the sport. In this cruel world, it's time to treat professional hockey players not like willing gladiators "butchered," as Byron wrote, "to make a Roman holiday," but as fellow human beings. In the end, not to sound too pansified, it will humanize the rest of us. But as the Olympics will show, it can also make hockey a better, faster, smarter game.

◀◀ **Source:** This article was originally published in *The Globe and Mail* on December 12, 2007. Reprinted with permission.

## The Barbarians are in the Living Room
### By Stephen Brunt

**23.**

Keith Jardine errs in his judgment, and it's obvious to everyone looking on. That's the beauty of the elemental sports, the contests without a cult of technology attached, without elaborate equipment, without designed-to-baffle terminologies and strategies. On some level, anyone can get them, can understand instantly what's going on without enduring a short course on the fine points of the game.

Mr. Jardine has the look, certainly, demanded in the Ultimate Fighting Championships (UFC), the leading purveyor of a sport known generically as Mixed Martial Arts—a shaved head that was covered in a black tuque as he made his walk to the ring at the MGM Grand Garden Arena; a nasty little goatee; an expression of extreme grumpiness; and a magnificent *nom de guerre*—The Dean of Mean.

Forget for the moment that Mr. Jardine holds a degree in human performance and sport from New Mexico Highlands University (you can look it up), that he is a former football player and rugby player, and more gym rat than street thug. In appearance, he is all cartoon menace, as is his opponent, Houston Alexander—African-American, same shaved head, same intimidating countenance, equally ominous nickname (The Assassin), but minus the college degree.

Mr. Jardine is a rising star, Mr. Alexander a near unknown, and so the outcome seems inevitable: When Mr. Jardine lands his first punch, Mr. Alexander wobbles and Mr. Jardine moves in for the kill.

Trouble is, Mr. Alexander was only a little off balance, and trouble is, Mr. Alexander is one skilled and savage guy. He starts punching in return and rocks Mr. Jardine's head backward with an upper-cut to the jaw. Eventually, Mr. Jardine falls to the canvas, but in this sport, there's no eight count, no retreating to a neutral corner, and the referee doesn't intervene immediately.

Mr. Alexander keeps pounding away at Mr. Jardine's head until he is on his knees and finally unconscious. His mouthpiece drops to the canvas just before his face hits, hard and flush and uncomprehending. There's a bit of blood dripping from between his slack, gaping lips. Only then is Mr. Alexander pulled off.

The fourteen thousand fans in attendance, including a sprinkling of minor Hollywood celebrities, love every minute of it. A continent-wide audience is tuning in, in record numbers, through pay-per-view. This night is the coming-out party for the UFC, its first real crack at the mainstream, and as always it delivers bang, and blood, for the buck. Though it still isn't even legal everywhere, there is a growing sense that the product packaged and sold by the UFC has the chance to largely supplant boxing and cross over to mass acceptance.

It's certainly not to everyone's taste. The short bout, over in forty-eight seconds, seems everything that those who see the UFC as the featured event in a Wide World of Dystopian Sports imagine it is: two men, locked in an octagonal cage, stripped to the waist, barefoot, wearing minimal padding across their knuckles, assaulting each other by just about any method they choose until one or the other quits, is knocked or choked unconscious, submits in the face of unendurable pain, or, occasionally, is judged the (invariably bloodied) winner or loser once a bout reaches its time limit.

Ah, the triumph of the baser instincts, the descent of the human species, the coarsening of modern culture, the handiwork of porn and video games and ultraviolent films and equal doses of ecstasy and Red Bull. "I was going to rip his fucking arm off and take it home with me!" one of the fighters shouts after winning a submission victory. Weep for a world that could produce this, and remember what happened to Rome.

But really it's more straightforward and ancient, though perhaps no more benign. The origins of this spectacle predate even the big Cain versus Abel bout. It goes all the way back to the snake in the tree, to the essential capitalist equation. Give the people what they want, even if some of them won't acknowledge those desires, and then make them pay for it.

The human-nature argument: Men will always fight and others will always watch them (women, too, on both counts), the crowd of the curious as predictable as the one that gathers in any school-yard at the first hint of a brawl. The origins of what we consider sport would have involved some form of wrestling or fist fighting, long before anyone thought to kick or throw—or create—a ball.

And beyond that, war games, mano-a-mano duels, often with grave consequences for the loser, were the National Football League of their time. For the spectator, combat sports deliver at the gut level, they provide a primal, anti-intellectual, amoral adrenaline rush as seductive to Joyce Carol Oates as it is to knuckle-draggers. That is us, that has always been us, though through the centuries, through the millennia, right-thinking people have tried their best to stamp the instinct out.

### ■ ■ ■ The Red-Light District

Two forms of fighting sports survived into the twentieth century—boxing, which was first codified a couple of hundred years earlier, but which didn't achieve full legitimacy until the adoption of the Marquess of Queensberry rules in the mid-1800s, providing an illusory framework of reason and order around the violence; and wrestling, which evolved into pure pantomime once a couple of commercial principles were fully understood, i.e., that it was a ticket-selling bonus if you could guarantee dramatic momentum and a slam-bang finish, and that audiences were quite willing to suspend disbelief in order to get it.

During its modern history, boxing has often been made illegal in one jurisdiction or another.

It has been cast as the "red-light district of sports," not just because of the lurking danger (ring deaths, though very rare, will always happen), but because as a largely unregulated bastion of the free market, it was a forum for the ruthless exploitation of its poor, desperate combatants.

But even as tastes changed, even as other sports passed it in importance—soccer, baseball, football, hockey, basketball, auto racing—boxing survived and occasionally thrived. The biggest one-off sporting events of all time, measured in dollars, have always been fights.

In the 1980s and 1990s, there were attempts to grab parts of the boxing and wrestling audience by aiming farther down-market, by staging "tough man" contests where most of the niceties of rules and regulations were eliminated. The problem was the sheer scuzziness of it all, plus the fact that most of those no-holds-barred fighters were technically inept and tended to collapse in exhaustion.

The original Ultimate Fighting Championship, a promotional company that began operation in 1993, provided a slightly more sophisticated take: Eliminate all rules but three (no biting, no eye gouging, and no "fish hooking"—inserting fingers into the nose or mouth); don't bother with weight classes; and then see what might happen if you put a bar bouncer in with a sumo wrestler, or a jujitsu expert with a boxer. And put it not in a ring, but in a cage: Two men enter, only one leaves standing.

When I attended one of those early shows in Buffalo, the fights seemed remarkably crude and pointless, and the audience seemed drawn from a demographic that would have found pro wrestling as challenging as Shakespeare. It's what Senator John McCain, a devoted boxing fan (he once sat ringside at a fight in Phoenix happily wedged between Don King and Mike Tyson), famously labelled "human cockfighting," calling for it to be banned.

By 2001, even pay-per-view providers, who will show just about anything for money, were getting queasy, and the Ultimate Fighting Championship seemed on the fast road to extinction.

The whole shebang was purchased for the relative pittance of $2 million (U.S.) by Las Vegas-based brothers Lorenzo and Frank Fertitta, who had made a considerable fortune running the suburban casino business that their father had started and by investing in Las Vegas real estate. (Lorenzo Fertitta had also served on the Nevada State Athletic Commission, which regulates boxing in the state.)

Their partner was a guy they had met in the gym, a small-time boxing trainer and manager with no formal business background, someone who shared their new-found passion for jujitsu-style fighting: Dana White.

Mr. White was sitting in the stands before the biggest night of his professional life, and his voice was worn down to nearly nothing. He does all of the talking for the sport. (Though Lorenzo Fertitta sits a few rows away, he and his brother remain steadfastly in the background.)

Mr. White seems born to the role of front man: He is a charming, charismatic figure, and of course he has the UFC look—jeans, shaved head, a tight shirt to show off the gym work—along with his ready smile.

In the single corporate entity that effectively controls the entire sport (especially since buying out its only significant competitor, the Japan-based Pride Fighting), Mr. White is much more than just the face of Mixed Martial Arts. He is the president, the matchmaker, the paymaster, the de facto commissioner, the negotiator, the disciplinarian, the uber-boss.

Boxing, the one true free-market bastion in professional sport, has long been dominated by promoters working only in the interest of their own enrichment and willing to cut each other's throats to get there. Here, it's a de facto monopoly, a one-man, one-company show.

"The guys who have run boxing for the last forty years have destroyed it," Mr. White says. "Boxing became all about money, all about greed. They've done nothing to secure the future of their sport.

Nothing. It's been all about how much money I can put in my pocket now."

He, on the other hand, can take the long view—untroubled by competitors, by agents, by a union, by exorbitant athlete wages. (For absorbing those forty-eight seconds of face pounding, Mr. Jardine was paid just $7,000.)

When they first saw a live UFC, in Louisiana, back in what are now considered the dark ages, Mr. White and the Fertittas thought the same thing as everyone else—that it was ugly and primitive and, in that form, doomed. But they also saw something else.

"What was great about [the competitors] was their personalities," Mr. White says. "They were good people and they all have their own different stories.

"You know how [wrestling kingpin] Vince McMahon builds characters in the WWE? You've got Haystacks Calhoun—he's a big country boy? We've got Matt Hughes. He's a real country kid who really does farm. He's real. Chuck Liddell [UFC's biggest star] looks like an axe murderer. He's an accounting major from Cal Poly."

So there was part of the formula: wrestling-style storylines, but with real, unscripted, violent, bloody action in short-attention-span bites. Athletes who didn't have the usual boxing background: African-American or Hispanic, from bad places, fighting as a means of economic survival or to stay out of jail.

UFC fighters were largely middle-class white guys—former college wrestlers and football players who took up martial arts of one sort or another initially to say in shape—so they could easily be marketed to a middle-class white audience.

Kalib Starnes, the only Canadian on the card, is fairly typical. He is thirty-two years old and began studying a Brazilian variant of jujitsu twelve years ago, making his leap to the UFC through the Ultimate Fighter reality series. (He winds up winning an impressive victory over another product of the show, Chris Leben.)

"I fought in the first martial arts shows in B.C.," Starnes says. "They were illegal at the time. We had police helicopters flying over the ring and the fire department coming in and trying to shut down the venues. Like it was a death match. I don't think people really understood that it was a legitimate sport ...

"The fighters enjoy danger as much as somebody who is a skydiver or a downhill skier. There are a lot of dangerous sports and lifestyles that people can take up, but that's what they're into. Sure, it's dangerous, but so is crossing the street."

Mr. White and the Fertittas also understood that in order to cross over to a mass audience, to get out of the tough-man ghetto and reach a more attractive demographic, the UFC would need to go straight—the outlaw, no-holds-barred sport needed rules and more than a whiff of legitimacy.

"You have to turn it into a real sport with real athletes," Mr. White says. "Nobody wants to see crazy, death-sport shit."

To that end, they immediately began emphasizing the skill sets and specialization of their competitors. Then they hired Marc Ratner, who for fourteen years had been the director the Nevada State Athletic Commission, and one of the most respected figures in boxing.

(Back in the "human cockfighting" days, Mr. Ratner actually appeared with Senator McCain on *The Larry King Show* during a debate on ultimate fighting, arguing that the sport-without-rules would never be made legal in his state.)

Mr. Ratner's job was to help draft a set of statutes, and then to begin the long process of persuading various athletic commissions to sanction the UFC. Five weight classes were created, and the original three rules grew to thirty-two (including a prohibition against "putting a finger into any orifice or into any cut or laceration on an opponent," and also against "abusive language" and "timidity").

Mostly, Mr. Ratner had to make the case that, appearances aside, MMA was in fact safer than boxing. Having watched seven boxers die from a ringside seat, he was more than comfortable with that argument. "There are certainly cuts and contusions [in UFC]," he says. "But what I can document [is that] during my whole time as a director, we probably had eighty cards of MMA—about seven hundred individual bouts. There were cuts, contusions, broken toes. The most serious injury we had was a broken arm. That's it."

Boxing features longer bouts, repeated head blows (not just in competition but in training), eight counts that allow fighters to continue after they've been concussed and an ethic in which surrender is the greatest sin. (Consider how Roberto Duran never really lived down his "no mas" performance against Sugar Ray Leonard, when he simply turned his back in mid-fight and walked away.)

By contrast, MMA bouts are stopped quickly once a fighter is knocked out or choked unconscious, with no reprieve. And it's quite acceptable to quit by "tapping out."

That said, everyone involved with the UFC continues to live in fear of a grave injury or death in the octagon, however improbable, knowing that, unlike boxing, the sport wouldn't have enough history to survive the political backlash.

However, Mr. White is confident enough now to sound rather flip on the whole subject of life and death: "At the end of the day, this is a combat sport. Two guys get in there and start hitting each other and anything can happen. Such is life. You'd shit if you knew how many kids die every year playing high-school football. But nobody thinks about it because it's football. You wouldn't believe how many people die playing polo every year. Dying is part of life. It happens."

The final master stroke in the relaunch of the sport was to ride the reality-show wave with *The Ultimate Fighter*, a program on the male-oriented Spike Network, which became a platform for building personalities who could then arrive on the big stage complete with a fully realized backstory. Stars come and go, champions eventually lose, but the TV show, in which Mr. White is prominently featured, provided the UFC with its own farm system combined with an extended infomercial.

With that structure in place, and with boxing on a path of commercial self-destruction, all that was left was letting the darker elements of human nature take their course.

## ■ ■ ■ A Very Profitable Savagery

Chuck "The Iceman" Liddell, the accounting major who looks like an axe murderer, is knocked out in 113 seconds at UFC 71 by Quinton "Rampage" Jackson, surrendering the light heavyweight championship.

Unlike Mr. Jardine, Mr. Liddell at least gets well paid for his pain, cashing a cheque in the neighbourhood of a half-million dollars, plus a percentage of the pay-per-view sales that would take his purse into the seven-figure range. That's the reward for being the sport's biggest breakout personality, the magazine cover boy, the guy who made the cameo appearance on *Entourage*.

In boxing, the humiliating demise of such a star would be disastrous, but in the UFC fighters seem to suffer little as commodities even after they are beaten. Mr. Liddell will be recycled soon enough, Mr. Jackson is already matched with an opponent chosen by Mr. White to maximize the potential box-office appeal, and UFC 72, to be staged in Belfast, Northern Ireland, is just beyond the horizon.

The Las Vegas event has generated more than $4 million at the gate (a sold-out, beer-drinking, frat-boy kind of crowd, almost exclusively Caucasian) and more than a million pay-per-view buys.

More significantly, this week has provided vindication for all of Mr. White's dreams of reaching the mainstream. The UFC graced the covers of both *Sports Illustrated* and *ESPN The Magazine*, the two biggest sports publications in the United States. And the ESPN all-sports network covered the fights, straight, for the first time, the same way they would have covered baseball, football, or basketball.

Forget about the gates: The barbarians are in the living room.

And now, to conquer the rest of the world. The UFC is currently sanctioned in twenty-two U.S. jurisdictions, with Illinois, Michigan, and New York soon to come on board. More events are planned for the United Kingdom, for Canada (Ontario remains a holdout), for continental Europe, for Japan. Five years from now, Mr. White envisions the first truly global pay-per-view event.

Do the math: Multiply a $50 price tag by however many millions of buy-ins you might imagine (the recent Oscar De La Hoya-Floyd Mayweather Jr. boxing event drew a record 2.15 million pay-per-view subscribers in the U.S. alone), and subtract the relative pittance they're paying the fighters.

It's potentially an astounding number, all based on that original premise, on an appeal rooted somewhere deep in our DNA.

"Think about the NFL," Mr. White says. "The NFL can't get arrested in any other country. With [UFC], I don't have to explain anything ... When I take two guys fighting in the octagon, it crosses all barriers, all language barriers, all culture barriers. Everybody gets two guys fighting in the octagon, and they like it. It's something primal inside of us that we like combat sports."

And as for those who don't get it, who don't like it, who conscientiously object?

"Listen, it's not 1973," Mr. White says. "We've got five hundred channels now. I don't like golf. I think golf's the stupidest game in the history of sports. That doesn't mean other people shouldn't watch it. I can change the fucking channel if I don't want to watch golf.

"So, back in the day when there were only four or five channels, I get that you had to be careful what you put on television. Now that there are so many different channels, everybody can have whatever they want."

---

◀◀ **Source:** Stephen Brunt is a sports columnist for *The Globe and Mail*. This article was originally published in *The Globe and Mail* on June 2, 2007. Reprinted with permission.

## 24. Violence in Sports Backgrounder
### Law Connection

There was great interest in the prospect of seeing Todd Bertuzzi in court to defend himself against the criminal assault charges that resulted from the on-ice encounter that injured Steve Moore. Although it is often preferable to settle charges before trial (saving both time and expense), some were disappointed to hear that a trial would no longer be necessary after Bertuzzi's decision to plead guilty to assault.

In this backgrounder to the trial that would never be, we will talk about the criminal law, look at what might have happened if the matter had gone to court, and consider the problem of violence in sport in general. Since Steve Moore recently launched a civil action against Bertuzzi, this backgrounder will also examine the civil case. Then we will look at the question of whether the court is the best place to resolve the issues related to violence in sports.

The first thing you should know is that there are two possible legal responses to violence in sports: criminal prosecution and civil action. The criminal law steps in where the Crown, acting on behalf of state and public interests, determines that the violence that has occurred constitutes a crime. The civil law makes it possible for an injured person to sue the person who caused the injury and, if the court determines that intentional or careless conduct caused the injury, award financial compensation for the damages suffered.

A lot of people think the criminal law has no place in policing violence that occurs on the ice or the field, while others think that criminal law doesn't step in often enough. Lately, the spotlight has been on Vancouver when it comes to that debate, given the trial of Marty McSorley, which took place in 2000, and the charges against Todd Bertuzzi, resulting in his guilty plea in December 2004.

### ■■■ Why Criminal Charges?

In B.C., the decision of whether or not to lay a criminal charge ultimately rests with the Crown, who, in the language of *Law & Order*, "prosecute the offenders" on behalf of Canada. The Crown might be influenced by the police or sometimes by public opinion, but ultimately the decision is the Crown's alone.

In the McSorley case, lots of people were asked why criminal charges were appropriate and the Crown gave this response:

> In our submission, that act is precisely why the law, the criminal law, has a place in the hockey rink. It is why the law refuses to sanction those acts as a matter of public policy. It is particularly significant when that act is carried out in the National Hockey League at the highest level of the game in circumstances that are watched by millions of people for whom the game is important, many of whom play that game at a whole variety of levels.

> That's why the public policy issue justifies the criminal law's involvement, and that's why these rules as to the application of the criminal law are present. Our submission is that this is precisely the kind of case, precisely the fact situation that the criminal law is intended and has a place to deal with. It is way beyond the scope of this game. It is irrelevant. It is an act that is completely irrelevant to the game that is taking place on the ice. Mr. McSorley may have felt that there was a need to deliver a message to his team that we don't quit, but you don't deliver that message by putting another player's health and safety at risk, and that is what happened in this case, we submit, and that is why it is a criminal act. (*R. v. McSorley*, [2000] B.C.J. No. 1993, 2000 BCPC 116 at para. 9.)

One of the arguments that is often raised against bringing criminal charges is that the player has already been punished or disciplined by the applicable league, so criminal sanctions are unnecessary. That argument was raised by the NHL in the McSorley case.

There have been similar sentiments as they concern Todd Bertuzzi.

This idea isn't exclusive to sports cases; putting it in another context may help illustrate why the Crown has viewed discipline by the NHL as insufficient punishment. There are lots of associations that have the ability to discipline their members for actions that may also attract criminal charges. Say, for example, a lawyer stole money from one of his clients. That lawyer would surely be disciplined by the Law Society, which is responsible for overseeing the practice of law, but that lawyer may also be subject to criminal charges for theft. There would be a huge public outcry if that lawyer weren't prosecuted for theft just because he was disciplined by the Law Society. Should it really be different for sports associations? The Crown has an obligation to the public interest, but the NHL has no such obligation.

## ■■■ Why Are Some Hits "Criminal" and Not Others?

Another question that comes up a lot in discussions about violence in sports is why the Crown considers some hits "criminal," but not others. The answer lies in the essence of the criminal charges.

Todd Bertuzzi was charged with assault causing bodily harm; Marty McSorley was charged with assault with a weapon (his hockey stick). As in all criminal charges, the burden is on the Crown to prove each element of the offence beyond a reasonable doubt.

One aspect of each of these charges that the Crown must prove is that the victim did not consent to the hit in question.

Most fans realize and accept that there are going to be some hits in professional hockey; it's part of the game. The players accept it too. But there is a limit on what is deemed acceptable. In legal terms, the question is what hits, what level of violence the players have consented to.

It is up to the judge to determine whether or not the player consented to the hit in question. It's not just a matter of the player who was hit testifying about what he consented to. That testimony is important, but ultimately the question of consent is a legal one that only the judge can answer.

In making that decision in the McSorley case, Mr. Justice Kitchen considered many sources of evidence, including the testimony of both Donald Brashear and Marty McSorley. He also considered the rules of hockey—written and unwritten—as well as how those rules were applied by the referees and the league. Within that context, Justice Kitchen had to determine whether the slash by McSorley on Brashear was, although outside the written rules of the game, nonetheless within the customary norms of professional hockey.

The reason it isn't just up to the recipient of the hit to say what he consented to is that the question is a legal one that requires an examination of all of the circumstances surrounding the incident.

Justice Kitchen looked at videos of the game and heard testimony from coaches, referees, linesmen, and players to determine the atmosphere of game in which the hit took place. And, even if a player testifies that he was okay with the hit, the judge must still take into account public policy considerations. There are some levels of violence that, regardless of the consent of the participants, are criminal because public policy demands that such violence be punished, not condoned. It's up to the judge to determine where that line should be drawn.

## ■■■ The Outcomes

In December 2004, just weeks before the trial was scheduled to begin on January 17, 2005, Bertuzzi entered a guilty plea and presented himself to the court for sentencing. As a condition of his guilty plea, both the Crown and defence lawyers recommended to the judge that Bertuzzi be given a conditional discharge, meaning that if he fulfilled all of the conditions, he would not have a criminal record. In determining whether the recommended sentence was appropriate, the judge considered the circumstances of the hit, and Bertuzzi himself. The judge found that although the hit was beyond the proper scope of the game and Moore was seriously injured by the hit, Bertuzzi was genuinely remorseful, had no previous criminal record, and was otherwise an upstanding member of the community. The judge ordered a conditional discharge, with conditions including regular reporting to a probation officer, and a number of hours of community service. (*R. v. Bertuzzi*, [2004] B.C.J. No. 2692, 2004 BCPC 472.)

After the guilty plea became public, the injured player, Steve Moore, complained that he did not have the opportunity to tell his story in court. He wrote what is called a victim impact statement in which he described how his life has been affected. Although the statement was read out in court, Steve Moore could not be there in person because of the short notice of the sentencing hearing.

Moore's view was that more should be made of the fact that the assault had caused him serious injury.

In the McSorley case, Justice Kitchen found McSorley guilty of the assault and sentenced him to an eighteen-month conditional discharge. The sentence meant he had to keep the peace and be of good behaviour for eighteen months, and not participate in any sporting events where Donald Brashear was on the opposing team. If he met those conditions, he would be left with no criminal record. (*R. v. McSorley*, [2000] B.C.J. No. 1994, 2000 BCPC 117.)

In both the McSorley case and the Bertuzzi case there was considerable debate about the message of the courts regarding violent behaviour in sports, and whether the sentences were appropriate.

### ■ ■ ■ Exercising the Civil Court Option

Steve Moore has, in fact, decided to sue Bertuzzi as well as other members of the Canucks organization, including other players, the coach, manager, and owners. Few were surprised when the civil suit was filed; the surprise was that it was filed in Colorado, not in Vancouver where the hit took place. The lawsuit was filed under Colorado's "Long-Arm Statute," alleging that the hit in Vancouver on March 8, 2004, was the culmination of events that began in Denver on February 16, 2004. Moore claims that as a result of the hit he delivered against Marcus Naslund during the February 16, 2004, Avalanche-Canucks game, Bertuzzi, Brad May, and others in the Canucks organization entered into a conspiracy to injure Moore as retaliation for the hit on Naslund. Since Moore alleges that the Canucks' wrongdoing began in Colorado with the conspiracy to injure him, he is entitled under Colorado law to file his lawsuit there, even though the hit to him occurred in Vancouver.

At a civil trial, Moore will have an opportunity to testify about his recollections of the Bertuzzi hit, the circumstances that led up to it, and the impact it has had on his health and his hockey

career. All the defendants, including Bertuzzi, will also be given an opportunity to speak in their own defence.

While there is no official defence position yet, the defendants may claim that, by participating in the game, Moore consented to being hit. Consent is an important issue in the civil arena, just as it is in the criminal law. Since Steve Moore is the plaintiff, the burden is on him to show that he did not consent to the hit that was leveled against him that day.

Not only must Steve Moore convince a jury that the defendants intentionally or negligently injured him, he must also prove the extent of his injuries. The goal of a civil suit is to put the injured person back in the position he would have been in had the injuries not occurred. One important difference between the Colorado lawsuit and one that could have been filed here is the potential amount of money Steve Moore may receive if he wins. In Canada, damages for "pain and suffering" are capped at around $300,000, an amount which is reserved for the worst injuries. In Colorado, there is no such limit, so it is entirely up to a jury to determine how much Steve Moore is entitled to for "pain and suffering." In general, successful American plaintiffs receive far more money than their Canadian counterparts.

Some worry that a substantial verdict for Steve Moore could have a chilling effect on the way hockey is played, as players and team owners may become acutely aware of the consequences of becoming involved in such a lawsuit. Others question whether, in order to reduce the involvement of the courts, some other avenue may be established for holding players accountable for their actions during games.

### ■ ■ ■ Solutions Outside the Courts

Some commentators suggest that the court, through its response to violence in sports, may be indicating that these matters are best resolved in a different forum and that sports leagues should shoulder more responsibility for controlling the actions of players. If this is the case, the question remains: Will leagues get the message, clarify what is acceptable and what is not, and implement effective methods for dealing with offenders and deterring unacceptable behaviour?

The National Hockey League suspended Bertuzzi indefinitely following the incident, and he missed the final thirteen games of the regular season. The cancellation of the 2004/05 hockey season has made it uncertain when he will be reinstated. There is no question that Bertuzzi has suffered both professionally and financially as a result of his suspension. Is that sufficient punishment for his wrongdoing? In laying criminal charges against him, the Crown indicated that its answer to that question was no. But is it sufficient punishment for other acts of sporting violence in other circumstances?

Further questions arise from the contentious issue of violence in sports. Would a public outcry against violence be a more effective means of educating both players and spectators? Is it necessary or enough to change the sports environment that many feel encourages physical violence? Does is encourage physical violence? Is it the aggressive physical nature of games that attracts a large fan base? Would the fans stay if the violence were gone? There are, of course, many more questions than can be answered here in this forum. What to do about violence in sports—if anything—is surely a debate that will go on in the public consciousness for some time to come. It neither started with Todd Bertuzzi, nor will it end with him.

◀◀ **Source:** This backgrounder was originally published in 2005 on www.LawConnection.ca by the Justice Education Society. It is currently being revised and updated. Reprinted with permission.

# 25. Five and a Half Myths About North American Sports Crowd Disorder
## By Kevin Young

### ■■■ 1. It Doesn't Exist – Part I

Consider the following cases from five of North America's most popular spectator sports:

- Amid scenes of vandalism and mass fighting, police use "pepper guns" to disperse an unruly crowd, killing a college student who is struck in the eye by one of their 'bullets'. (MLB, Boston, 2004).

- Fans pelting the field with thousands of bottles and other missiles prompt both teams and officials to take cover (NFL game, Cleveland, 2001).

- Male and female fans fight and one man attempts to strangle another, resulting in arrests and ejections (U.S. Open golf tournament, Pebble Beach, 2010).

- Following a playoff game thousands of fans gather and fight on a downtown street. Two men in their twenties are stabbed and forty-nine arrests are made. To allow ambulances to reach the stabbing victims, police use tear gas to disperse the crowd (NHL, Edmonton, 2006).

- Fans throw bottles, vandalize over a dozen police cars and buses, start bonfires, and loot a gas station. Over twenty fans are arrested and five police officers are injured (NBA, Los Angeles, 2009).

These episodes are not weekly occurrences, but neither are they rare. Although the research on fan violence in North America has often been impressionistic and the explanations frail (ethnographies of North American fans are virtually non-existent), there is copious evidence to suggest that North American sports crowds have expressed their "aggro" with regularity for many decades. Whether one focuses on melees breaking out at "prize fights" at the turn of the twentieth century, brawling baseball and football fans during the inter-war years, or destructive post-event outbursts throughout the last quarter of the twentieth century and now into the twenty-first, it is clear that North American sports crowd disorder is neither new nor uncommon.

## ■ ■ ■ 2. Its Size and Extent are Crystal Clear

Part of the complexity of explaining fan violence concerns the methodological fact that it is not easy to study or count. As with other aspects of crime and social deviance, while identifying the main behavioural dimensions of the phenomenon is relatively uncomplicated (we know some things about how fan violence is done), detailing its causes and extent is not. This is particularly true in North America where fan violence is not restricted to one sport or level of sport. We do know that alcohol plays a key role.

The majority of incidents of fan-to-fan violence occurring at North American sports involve individuals or small groups of spectators participating in activities such as common assault, drunken and disorderly behaviour, and confrontations with authorities. Less frequently, larger episodes have occurred—these have taken place both inside as well as outside stadia and are often related to post-event "celebrations." Generally speaking, collective episodes of fan fighting, especially involving rival groups, are less common in North America than, for instance, at European soccer matches, although certain teams have become well known for the consistently hostile behaviour of their fans. This has prompted efforts to "retake" stadium sections from chronically violent fans by temporarily closing them.

Conventional ways of counting and reporting crime have, in general, not been applied to North American sport, and teams are often loath to share their records. Thus, limited to sparse team, police, and media reports, which may be biased, inaccurate, or contradictory, and to a modest academic literature at best, the demographics of North American sports crowd disorder remain unclear. However, a thumbnail sketch includes the following. Though there are occasional cases of females involved in fan violence, most offenders predictably tend to be young males, indicating that, as with other forms of physical violence, North American sports crowd disorder is both gendered and normatively a youthful phenomenon. Both casual attendees and season-ticket holders are involved. Very little is known about the social class background of offenders, but since some of the rowdiest crowds on the continent are students (such as U.S. college football crowds), education should not necessarily be viewed as a deterrent. CNN recently referred to college fan violence as a "campus craze" (CNN, 2004), and USA Today estimates that there are between ten and fifteen seriously riotous college episodes annually (MacDonald, 2004). Data from professional teams indicate that the majority of offenders in crowd ejections and other stadium-based disturbances are white, but there is also evidence that race and youth factors have coalesced in fan violence in both Canada and the United States, especially with respect to street gang involvement in post-event conflicts.

## ■ ■ ■ 3. It's Unidimensional

Fan violence in North America is not limited to any one behaviour. A cluster of practices have become familiar to the authorities. These include but are not limited to:

**Missiles:** As any baseball outfielder will confirm, there is substantial evidence that North American fans have participated in missile throwing for many decades. Police sometimes use the term "simple battery" to refer to the action. Players as far back as the 1930s have complained of being struck by cans, bottles, batteries, coins, and other missiles launched from the bleachers. The tradition continues. At a college football game in Colorado in September 1999, student fans threw bottles at police and sprayed them with mace. Missiles retrieved and reported by ground staff at other U.S. college football stadia include batteries, golf balls, and marshmallows weighted with coins and metal. The use of such objects in crowd disorder clearly hints at the preconceived nature of the practice—one hardly arrives at a football game with such objects "accidentally." Objects thrown by fans have also prompted further violence in "indoor" sports. In November 2004, Ron Artest of the NBA's Indiana Pacers led a player-fan brawl that followed the player being pelted with beer and other debris from the stands.

**Weapons:** Couched in the wider concern about the place of weapons in North American, and particularly American, society, there has been much conjecture about their presence at sports events. No systematic research has been carried out, but we do know that, for example, weapons are sometimes smuggled into stadia, and that guns, knives and other weapons have featured prominently in post-event riots. Stabbings in fan fighting episodes are not uncommon. Occasional incidents have been even more troubling. For instance, when searched by security guards, a belligerent fan following golf star Tiger Woods at a 1999 PGA event was found to have a loaded semi-automatic handgun in his waist-pack, and a man posing as part of the official honour guard at a 2010 Michigan-Michigan State football game where 113,000 people had collected was allowed to carry two M16 rifles onto the field before being questioned and removed by police.

**Field Invasion:** Field invasion at North American stadia has most commonly been associated with team victory revelry in playoff and other important games. For example, fans of both collegiate and professional football have been associated with the peculiar convention of goalpost

destruction and even goalpost theft for several decades. As a result, it is not uncommon for goalposts to be smeared with grease, and for playing areas to receive a significant police presence (replete with "attack" dogs, horses, and other protections) at the conclusion of games. One of the ugliest field invasion episodes in recent memory occurred at the University of Wisconsin-Madison in 1993. Organizers watched helplessly, making numerous announcements, as thousands of fans poured onto the playing area. Dozens of fans dismantled the goalposts as injured fans receiving medical attention lay sprawled about them. Over seventy people were injured, six critically. Mounted police horses were needed to enable ambulances to access the playing area. Following a Ball State University football victory in 2001, a similar episode resulted in the goalposts striking and paralyzing a fan.

### ■ ■ ■ 4. It Takes Place at the Game

Perhaps the most predictable and widely publicized form of North American fan disorder is the "post-event riot" (since these incidents can follow team victory or defeat, the broadly adopted term "celebration riot" is misleading). Mass inebriation, fighting, looting, vandalism, arson, vehicle destruction, and physical and sexual assault have occurred during these episodes, especially at college-level sport in the United States.

Cases can be found across the twentieth century, with the period from the 1970s to the 1990s perhaps being worst in terms of frequency, damage toll to persons and property, or arrest rates. The locations of post-event riots following professional sports events include, but are not limited to: New York (1969), Pittsburgh (1971), Philadelphia (1980), Toronto (1983), Detroit (1984, 1990), San Francisco (1985), Chicago (1991, 1992, 1993, 1996, 1997), Dallas (1993, 1994), Montreal (1986, 1993, 2008, 2010), Vancouver (1994), Denver (1998, 1999), Boston (2004, 2007), Edmonton (2006), Calgary (2004), and Los Angeles (2000, 2010). Probably the most catastrophic injury toll related to a post-event riot is eight deaths in Detroit in

1990; in addition to dozens of arrests and injuries related directly to the behaviour of "celebrating" fans, four people were killed by an errant driver. After three consecutive Chicago Bulls NBA World Championships between 1991 and 1993, the cumulative damage reported by Chicago police included 1,700 arrests, over a hundred police cars burned or destroyed, two people shot dead, and approximately $8 million in damages to property. After the defeat of the Vancouver Canucks to the New York Rangers in the 1994 Stanley Cup Final (following a game played in New York), up to seventy thousand people poured into the Vancouver downtown core. Police deployed tear gas to disperse the crowd and fired a fatal rubber bullet. Over two hundred people were injured, fifty people were arrested, and dozens of shops and properties were damaged. Following the L.A. Lakers' 2000 NBA World Championship victory, police battled rioting fans outside the Los Angeles Staples Centre, trapping inside other fans, players, and celebrities for several hours. Twelve people were injured and a further dozen arrested. Similar episodes occurred in Los Angeles in 2010.

The policing and understanding of such episodes are made none the easier by the fact that many participants are known not to have attended the event in question or in fact to be sport spectators at all. For example, several post-event troubles in Chicago and Detroit in the early 1990s displayed evidence of street gang involvement and have led to concerns with so-called "band-wagoning" during these occasions.

## ■ ■ ■ 5. It's Under Control

Anyone who thinks that North American sports crowd disorder is innocuous needs to look no further than the increasingly resolute role played by the authorities, and the number of special "task forces" struck and inquiries undertaken across the continent to review "best practices" and better understand the phenomenon. While their rate of success remains vague, it is clear that sports, legal, municipal, and educational bodies have perceived a need to improve security measures and violence-prevention strategies at sports events. Having treated sports crowds more or less with "kid gloves" until the mid-1970s, sports and security groups have begun to introduce far more stringent measures both in anticipation of, and in response to, crowd disorder.

Concrete changes include more circumspect ticketing procedures, increases in fines for trespassing and field encroachment, a heightened police presence both inside and outside the grounds, the use of hi-tech surveillance systems including new photographic and video technology, screening procedures at the gate, use of police dogs and horses, modifications in alcohol concessions including continent-wide efforts to reduce alcohol-related misconduct, remodelling of stadia including the construction of protective tunnels and "safety zones" for players and officials to safely enter/exit the field, and judicious security planning in anticipation of post-event revelry, such as the assignment of special investigation units. Team-, sport- and level-specific initiatives have sprung up across the continent aimed at creating safer and more respectful fan environments (e.g., the Texas Longhorns "Make Us Proud" and the Canadian Interuniversity Sport codes of conduct, the NCAA Division III "Be Loud, Be Proud, Be Positive" program, and Hockey Canada's "Respect in Sport" program).

Historically, North American authorities have reacted to crowd disorder on essentially local levels. Apart from occasional attempts to have U.S. Congress seriously address the issue of violent sports fans—most of which seem to have been ineffective or stymied—no wide-ranging legislation has been introduced to curb the problem, and state legislators do not seem to have given the problem of sports crowd disorder much thought. But there is some evidence to suggest that this situation is changing. Several state-wide and even national initiatives show this, including programs aimed at repeat offenders and tactics for dealing with dangerous item screening and confiscation (e.g., Centre for Problem-Oriented Policing, 2010).

## ▪▪▪ 5.5. It Doesn't Exist – Part II

Despite the volume and frequency of outbursts during the twentieth century and already into the twenty-first century that range from simple streaking to murder, North American sports crowd disorder has been and remains relatively immune to serious debate and sustained official attention. Simply put, the stigma, stereotypes, and moral panic now long associated with soccer and its often bellicose fans in the United Kingdom and elsewhere have been eluded in North America. Indeed, North American sport has shown a stubborn, if perhaps faltering, resilience in maintaining its "squeaky clean," family-centred, and essentially safe image despite the fact that crowd disorder is well-known to the authorities, shows patterned dimensions, and has clearly changed the configuration of stadia and game-day experiences in a number of sports.

Because invidious comparisons persist, it seems important to emphasise that soccer hooliganism and the miscellaneous North American fan disorders neither represent social problems of the same magnitude nor are one and the same thing. While there are some common sociological threads in crowd disorders on both sides of the Atlantic (such as gender—crowd violence is predominantly a male domain) and while the problem may reflect similar social causes in those contexts (such as socio-economic status, the cultural significance of sport and its related celebratory conventions, and social and psychological conflicts occurring in the wider society), it is also clear that many aspects of sports crowd disorder are culturally specific. This certainly seems true of the North American case

where, to date, there has been no major at-stadium crowd tragedy, no travelling "super crews" or "firms" of hooligan supporters, no paramilitary policing operations punctuating the sporting calendar (inflated policing at North American championship games is more related to the perception of terrorist threats in a post-9/11 world), and no judicial reviews prompting sweeping organizational changes. But comparing the North American picture to its counterpart in other parts of the world is less than helpful if we want to understand the phenomenon objectively and, more importantly, be prepared to tackle it. Relatively speaking, North American sports crowd disorder may not have posed as ominous or consistent a problem as its European counterpart, but there is more than enough evidence to suggest that the view, still tightly held onto in some quarters, that there is no "serious" or "patterned" fan violence in North American sport is severely, and perhaps dangerously, flawed.

### References

- Center for Problem-Oriented Policing. 2010. "Responses to the Problem of Spectator Violence in Stadiums." Retrieved from: http://www.popcenter.org/problems/spectator_violence/3
- CNN Education. 2004. "Rioting: The New Campus Craze," February 26, (www.cnn.com/2004/EDUCATION/02/26/life.rioting.reut/index.html).
- MacDonald, G. J. 2004. "After the Big Game Why is There a Riot Going On?" November 1, (www.usatoday.com/news/health/2004-11-01-riot_x.htm).

◀◀ **Source:** Kevin Young is a professor in the Department of Sociology at the University of Calgary. Included with permission.

# Section B: Hazing, Harassment, Bullying, and Abuse

## When Rites Go Wrong

### By Daniel Drolet

**26.**

*Initiating new members to a team is an age-old rite of passage that's meant to promote team loyalty and build up athletes' confidence. So how have hazing rituals come to this?*

■■■■■■

The photos are candid snapshots of a part of student life most universities and colleges probably wish didn't take place. Among the tamer ones: a women's swim team member with "Do Me Here" written on her bare back and arrows pointing to her buttocks. A shirtless young man from a baseball team having his hair buzzed off while he holds a bottle of what looks like vodka to his lips. A volleyball player blindfolded, tied to a post, dressed in a dress and splattered with some sort of liquid.

The photos, posted on the Internet at badjocks. com, were from sports team hazings in the United States and were included in a presentation to the Canadian Interuniversity Sport (CIS) annual general meeting in Ottawa in June. With the start of a new academic year, and with the memory of incidents at McGill and Simon Fraser universities still fresh, hazing is on the minds of a lot of athletic directors.

Harmless fun? Valuable team-building? That's what teams' initiation rites are supposed to be. But changing technologies, in particular digital cameras and the Internet, mean that more people are finding out about formerly secret rituals—rituals that, according to some researchers, have become more sexualized and more degrading. And changing attitudes mean more initiates are willing to complain about the rituals. The result is that hazing is now largely prohibited, while university sports officials try to find positive ways to build team spirit—ways that don't involve excessive drinking, humiliation, nudity, or broomsticks.

The Simon Fraser swim team was prevented from competing at a championship in March, and the university revised its code of conduct, after it determined that unacceptable behaviour took place at a house party organized by senior team members. Last year, McGill cancelled its football season after an eighteen-year-old rookie said he was sexually assaulted with a broomstick.

"We really don't have a good sense of how prevalent [hazing] is," says Marg McGregor, executive director of CIS. She says she knows of no Canadian statistics on hazing. "Part of that is that people just aren't going to go on record and say it's happening."

The data that exist are from the United States. A 1999 study of initiation rites in U.S. sports teams prepared by Alfred University in Alfred, New York, found that more than three-quarters of the 325,000 university athletes in the United

States had experienced some form of hazing to join a team. Half of those rituals involved alcohol, two-thirds involved humiliation, and one in five involved illegal or violent activities such as kidnappings, beatings, or crime.

## ■■■ Questionable Rites

The study defines hazing as any activity that humiliates, degrades, abuses, or endangers a person wanting to join a group. It notes that "because people's perceptions of hazing vary, it is difficult to delineate positive or acceptable initiation rites from questionable or unacceptable ones." What one student finds funny or acceptable, another will find degrading.

The Alfred University study was part of a presentation to the CIS annual meeting by Joseph de Pencier, director of ethics and anti-doping services at the Canadian Centre for Ethics in Sport. A Canadian who played sports at an American university when he was a student, he says he thinks the two countries are similar enough for American statistics to be relevant to Canada.

Initiating newcomers is deeply ingrained not only in sports, but in various aspects of university life. There are some gripping descriptions of hazing in *Making the Team: Inside the World of Sport Initiations and Hazing*, published in 2004 by Canadian Scholars' Press and edited by Jay Johnson, a PhD candidate at the University of Toronto, and Margery Holman, a professor in the faculty of human kinetics at the University of Windsor.

In an introductory essay in the book, Mr. Johnson and Brian Trota, the producer of a weekly radio sports show in Toronto, write: "historically, tradition in the hazing ritual is important to bring a sense of cultural identity to the youth."

Dan McNally, director of athletics at Acadia University in Wolfville, Nova Scotia, says that initiations are team-driven. While he doesn't see the benefit, a number of players have told him they felt good about initiations that made them feel part of the team. "For me to sit here and say there's

nothing good about it, it's presumptuous," he says. "All the coach does is tell you whether you make the team. Your teammates tell you whether you are part of the team."

The Trota and Johnson article cites a sharp rise in all kinds of hazing on university campuses after the Second World War. But what hazing involves seems to have changed considerably over the last half-century. A description of hazing on U.S. campuses published in October 1956, in the Massachusetts Institute of Technology newspaper *The Tech*, sounds positively quaint:

"Freshmen are generally required to wear a beanie and an identification tag. Then to give the upperclassmen a feeling of superiority, several rules like do not walk on the grass, carry matches for upperclassmen, know the college songs and cheers and be ready to recite them on demand, etc., are imposed upon the freshmen."

Yet, even then people worried that rituals were becoming bolder and more sexualized. The same article refers to incidents at two Canadian universities. Quoting the *Queen's University Journal*, it says freshmen were given a tape measure and told to obtain the vital statistics of co-eds designated by seniors. And it describes a "deskirting" of "freshettes" at the University of British Columbia: "The Society for the Prevention of Cruelty to Freshettes reported that action would be taken against the EUS's [Engineering Undergraduate Society's] treeing four skirtless girls ... They were left ravished and weeping in the EUS offices by the lustful mob."

Marc Lamont Hill, a professor of urban education at Temple University in Philadelphia whose research focuses on the intersections between youth, popular culture, and pedagogy, says there's been a shift over the years in what hazing involves. "Initially, hazing was a practice designed to promote unity and loyalty within a particular organization," he says. "The idea was to break you down and build you up, and in many ways the rituals were symbolic; they weren't abusive. A person may have you doing their laundry for weeks" or rookies might have to carry the baggage of other players.

The rituals were designed to have people humble themselves to ultimately build their self-confidence, and also to have more trust in the organization they were joining, he explains. "But we've become more obsessed with the process than with the product. It becomes more about making someone do what I did, or worse—just for its own sake. Building a strong community is not the goal anymore."

This has led to more degrading hazing ceremonies. "They are going more and more underground, and they are becoming more and more sexualized. You see more homoerotic acts, even among females," says Dr. Lamont Hill.

Curiously, it's technology that allows people to brag digitally about what is supposed to be a secret: that's how photos get posted to the Internet. "It's not just a ritual, it becomes a spectacle," says Dr. Lamont Hill. "Now universities are forced to respond to these things."

These incidents are becoming both public and the subject of complaints, partly because society as a whole is changing. Mr. de Pencier of the Canadian Centre for Ethics in Sport says the Charter of Rights and Freedoms has made people who believe their rights are being violated feel they can take on large institutions. He says the media may also play a role by shining a light on what used to be secret. "Until these things are put under public scrutiny, people don't think about them. The attitude has been: That's the way we have always done things. It's not until you see something on the front page of the Globe or on the Internet that you say, 'That's harmful!'"

### ■■■ Competitive Environment

It's possible that the competitive sports environment may itself damage athletes' sense of responsibility. Sharon Stoll, a University of Idaho professor of physical education, has measured the moral-reasoning skills of more than seventy thousand American student athletes since the 1980s. She says her research shows that athletes have lower moral-reasoning skills than the general student population. Dr. Stoll says she believes the situation is a direct result of the competitive sports environment, where better-than-average players early on develop a sense of entitlement and where competition is often practised in a negative way. A curriculum she's developed, called "Winning with Character" (a four-year intervention program that at least six U.S. colleges have purchased), aims to help players improve their moral reasoning and develop a sense of responsibility through extensive discussion, writing, and feedback.

But once you decide to stop hazing, how do you welcome new members into a group? Even people who are front and centre admit there's no magic solution.

Jay Johnson, co-editor of *Making the Team* (and who's teaching this fall at the University of Windsor), believes it's important to retain the concept of a ritual. "When schools come down with a zero-tolerance policy, it creates a huge void," he says. "I think the ritualistic aspect of the rite of passage is crucial to maintain."

Mr. Johnson also says that sports teams may rebel against hazing alternatives imposed on them by university administrators. One solution is to offer teams a menu of alternatives, or to step back altogether and tell them to develop their own rituals within set limits that don't involve shaving team members, stripping them naked and parading them around.

An option put forward by some universities is community service, which nowadays is often proposed for the broad student community. But Mr. Johnson says community service doesn't work for every team. "Women's teams are a lot more receptive to community service or cooperative games," he says, "whereas the men's teams need challenge or physicality. Things that do work with men's teams are rock climbing, white-water canoeing—something that's challenging."

At McGill, one type of team-building involves getting team members from one sport—say, football—to spend a day with a team from a completely different sport—say, rowing. The footballers learn how to row and at the end of the day have a friendly competition with the rowing team. Captains are encouraged to take the lead in suggesting activities, says Derek Drummond, McGill's interim director of athletics and professor emeritus of architecture.

But positive activities have to be reinforced in other ways to prevent hazing from continuing. "You have to get rid of bad apples who can't adapt," says Mr. Johnson. "And that's from the bottom up—athletes, coaches, athletic directors. They are all complicit in creating this culture."

Ms. McGregor of CIS says that something as simple as selecting team captains can be critical. "All the universities have policies prohibiting hazing. The issue is what happens in those moments when the teams find themselves in a situation. If the captain says 'we're not going to the dark side' then the team will follow."

Ms. McGregor says alumni sometimes pressure teams to keep time-honoured hazing rituals alive, and again it takes a strong captain to resist that pressure.

Corey MacDonald, a fourth-year student in human kinetics, is captain of the University of Ottawa Gee-Gees men's hockey team, and he knows what hazing can be like. "I've been around hockey for quite some time, and hazing has always been there," he says, adding that he encountered it before entering university, and it usually involved alcohol.

The Gee-Gees hockey team might make new members clean up the bus after a road trip, or pick up pucks after practice—but that's as far as it goes, says Mr. MacDonald. "We're not interested in alienating guys by embarrassing them."

However, he acknowledges that there are times a team can come under pressure to do things—either from players who have picked up hazing habits in junior hockey, or from alumni who recall stories from their time on the team. "It's my position as captain to put an end that that kind of mentality," he explains. "If the captain is not going to control that, who is?"

For Ms. McGregor of CIS, hazing is "one of those issues that will always be a work in progress." To assert that hazing can be eliminated is like saying racism can be eliminated, she concludes.

"I don't think there's a finish line there. The potential exists for this to occur. You will always need to be vigilant."

## ■ ■ ■ Codes of Conduct

Most universities have codes regulating student behaviour—either codes of conduct or regulations governing such things as sexual harassment. In some cases there are codes specifically for sports teams, but often the general university policy applies. And in many instances, universities are in the process of revising or updating their codes. The following examples link to the codes of selected universities around the country:

- Simon Fraser University has a Code of Student Conduct—www.sfu.ca/policies/teaching/t10-01.htm—that outlines inappropriate conduct and provides for penalties, ranging from a warning or reprimand to deregistration, forfeiture of awards or financial assistance, and permanent suspension. Registrar Ron Heath says that students signing up for sports have to sign the SFU Clan code for sports teams. Both the sports and the general university codes are in the process of being revised.

- University of Saskatchewan has a policy on discrimination and harassment: www.usask.ca/policies/2_05.htm. A specific code on hazing is still in the works.

- University of Toronto has a Code of Student Conduct, www.utoronto.ca/govcncl/pap/policies/studentc.html, that deals with such things as sexual harassment and more general items such as knowingly endangering health or safety. Sanctions include reprimands, fines, community work, right up to suspension or expulsion.

- University of Ottawa doesn't have a code of student conduct, though it does have a code that applies to students in residence. The university is in the process of preparing a code of conduct for athletes.

- University of New Brunswick has a Student Disciplinary Code (www.unb.ca/current/disciplinary_code/) to regulate misconduct. UNB at Saint John also has a handbook for sports clubs (www.unbsj.ca/athletics/clubs/documents/UNBSJClubsHandbook2005-6.pdf) that states hazing is not tolerated: "A good rule to follow when deciding whether an activity is hazing is this: If you have to ask if what you are doing is hazing, it probably is."

**◀◀ Source:** This article was originally published in *University Affairs* in November 2006. Republished with permission.

■ ■ ■ ■ ■ ■

*The following was a report sent out in 2005 to the McGill Community by Anthony C. Masi, who was the Interim Provost at the time.*

■ ■ ■ ■ ■ ■

McGill University is known as a leader in academic excellence and achievement. Our students come from all around the world, with a desire to expand their horizons through learning and living in an outstanding university environment.

As a university, we have the duty to provide our students with the best academic education in an environment that is free from harassment and comfortable and that promotes the highest standards and values of human behaviour.

Today, we have evidence that we have not lived up to the very highest standards that we at McGill set for ourselves.

An in-depth investigation of a complaint resulted in a report that was submitted to the Principal on Monday. The report concluded that the Redmen Football Team has engaged in activities involving hazing, in clear violation of McGill's existing policies and the Code of Student Conduct and Disciplinary Procedures. Despite these policies, despite the fact that all athletes signed commitments that they would not engage in hazing and, despite warnings from the coach that inappropriate behaviour would not be tolerated, activities were planned and carried out in clear violation of the rules.

During training camp at the beginning of this season, football rookies were subjected to harassment in the form of threats and sporadic intimidation by team veterans. Some of the harassment purposefully foreshadowed the activities that had been planned for Rookie Night (August 27, 2005), to be held after the team dinner. Rookie Night involved, over the course of an evening, serious hazing, including threats and intimidation, by comments and actions and by the use of demeaning, stereotyped epithets. Contrary to some media reports, there is no evidence that anyone was sodomized; however, our investigation shows that the event did involve nudity, degrading positions and behaviours, gagging and touching in inappropriate manners with a broomstick, as well as verbal and physical intimidation of rookies by a large portion of the team.

Hazing is based on the humiliation and disrespect of others. It has no place at McGill. It will not be tolerated in any form. No excuses. No exceptions.

The hazing was organized as a team activity by veteran players and a large majority of team members participated. Consequently, the team as a whole is being held responsible, regardless of varying degrees of blame that may be attributed at the individual level. Separate disciplinary actions are underway to deal with individuals in accordance with university policies and regulations regarding students and staff. These actions are confidential, according to McGill's policies and procedures.

The team and the program will be held responsible, and we will do everything in our power to ensure that similar events never happen again at McGill.

Hazing is a secretive activity. Even with clear anti-hazing policies and guidelines, repeated written and verbal warnings and formal individual commitments from students not to be involved, this incident shows that hazing can occur anywhere. It occurred at McGill. Greater vigilance, a stronger emphasis and investment in positive team-building programs and activities, a greater awareness and responsibility on the part of our coaches, staff, and the players themselves are critical to ensure that this never happens again. That is our clear goal.

We commend the courage of the young man who engaged in exemplary behaviour by coming forward with the complaint that led to the investigation of the incident.

We will respond to the challenge we now face in ways that make McGill an even greater university, deeply respectful of individual dignity.

McGill is announcing the following sanctions:

1. The football program is cancelled for the rest of the playing season.

2. Disciplinary actions against individuals are being taken in accordance with university policies and regulations regarding students and staff. In order to respect due process and the rights and privacy of the individuals, the university will not comment on these actions.

The university is taking immediate actions to strengthen policies and regulations:

3. Revisions are being made to the Student Athlete Code of Ethics to include a zero-tolerance policy for hazing applicable to all sports teams at McGill and to reinforce values such as sportsmanship, respect for individuals, and healthy team spirit as the basis for positive team-building activities.

The university will:

■ Suspend for the playing season any team that engages in hazing.

■ Revoke the athletic awards of any student who engages in hazing.

4. Action is underway to specifically identify hazing as a form of harassment, both in the Proposed Policy on Harassment and Discrimination and in the Code of Student Conduct and Disciplinary Procedure.

5. McGill Athletics will develop a mission statement to include references to our core values such as sportsmanship, respect for individuals, and healthy team spirit.

6. Immediately, the Director of Athletics and the Dean of Students will convene a work group to specify ways in which the new Student Athlete Code of Ethics can be linked to the Code of Student Conduct and Disciplinary Procedures.

7. The Senate Committee on Student Affairs is now asked to draft an appropriate policy on hazing for all student activities at the university including orientations for academic and other non-athletic activities and programs, or recommend revisions to current policies, with the goal of defining the responsibilities of student leaders, deans, directors, and chairs, as well as academic and non-academic members of staff for ensuring that hazing does not occur at McGill and that all students are welcomed into groups by means of positive team-building activities that respect the dignity of individuals, including their right to participate voluntarily without any pressure.

8. The Director of Athletics will appoint an Associate Director (Athlete Affairs) to ensure closer support, supervision, and monitoring of student athletes, and to oversee the implementation of positive team-building measures in all teams and all activities.

The University is taking the following steps to ensure that these policies are enforced and that each member of the community—

students, faculty, and staff—understands that they have a duty and responsibility to prevent hazing and inappropriate behaviour in all our activities:

9. This behaviour of the football team has stained the reputation of the McGill Redmen, McGill Athletics, and the university. Positive actions will be taken to repair that damage. The football team, including staff, will be asked to perform community service for at least two years.

10. Communications to the McGill community about harassment will explicitly address the issue of hazing.

11. The Director of Athletics will immediately undertake to prepare anti-hazing educational plans, to be approved by the Provost, for personnel in Athletics, and for athletes on all sports teams, to be delivered as soon as possible. Members of the Department of Athletics will be made aware of the signs of hazing and must understand its dangers. It will be their responsibility to play an active part in ensuring that the environment in Athletics is indeed free of domination, intimidation, and other forms of hazing.

12. The revised Student Athlete Code of Ethics will be well publicized in accordance with a communication plan, to be prepared by the Director of Athletics with the approval of the Provost, to inform all personnel and athletes of the procedures to be followed by victims or witnesses of hazing. The plan will spell out actions to be taken to assist victims of hazing

or of other violations of the Code of Student Conduct and Disciplinary Procedures and to bring perpetrators of hazing and individuals who fail to report it to the attention of the appropriate university authorities.

13. All coaches will play a role in implementing anti-hazing policies, and will demonstrate the leadership necessary to ensure that the policies are fully endorsed by their staff and fully respected by their athletes, and to ensure that only appropriate team-building activities are used.

14. The Director of Athletics will ensure that issues in Athletics are dealt with in a way that duly reflects the Charter of Students' Rights and the Code of Student Conduct and Disciplinary Procedures, as well as to the revised Student Athlete Code of Ethics.

15. The Director of Athletics will ensure that official publications and websites in Athletics reflect the values of the university and prominently feature the revised Student Athlete Code of Ethics.

16. Staff members throughout the university, particularly those who are likely to come into contact with any hazing activities that may take place in any arena when and where they might occur—e.g., staff in security services, student services, and residences—will be made aware of the signs of hazing and its dangers as well as of their responsibility to respond appropriately if they encounter students engaged in it.

◄◄ **Source:** Professor Anthony C. Masi, Interim Provost.

# 27. Coaches Cornered

## By Erin Anderssen

*Canada's one million coaches have to adjust to new procedures*

■ ■ ■ ■ ■ ■

**W**indsor soccer coach Larry Palazzi makes his rules clear: He does not drive his players home alone. In team meetings or in hotel rooms at tournaments, he makes sure another adult is present—what sports teams call the "two-deep rule." High-fives are okay, but not victory hugs.

If it were pouring rain, with a lone player still waiting for his parents, Mr. Palazzi would let the boy sit in his car while he stood outside, getting soaked. It hasn't happened yet, says the eight-year veteran of coaching boys' soccer, but "there's always an umbrella in my car."

Coaches have to be careful—even when your son plays on the team, your wife is the manager, and you've known most of the parents for years. It's not just for the players, he says, but for the coach, to protect against false allegations. "In today's age, you have to be aware."

For parents and coaches such as Mr. Palazzi, Graham James is a reminder of the need to know what's going on when your kids play sports. Last week, news broke that the disgraced junior-hockey coach had received a pardon three years ago from the National Parole Board for sexual abuse against two young players, even as more of his former team members, including Calgary Flames and New York Rangers veteran Theo Fleury, came forward with new allegations.

The James case may be the most high-profile, but it's one of a list. In December, a Calgary hockey coach was charged with sexually inappro-priate behaviour with a fifteen-year-old player. A Montreal soccer coach faces twenty-five sex-related offences, several of them involving three former players.

In California this month, a lawsuit was filed against USA Swimming alleging that a failure to do background checks had allowed more than thirty coaches across the country to sexually abuse or harass young female swimmers.

There are about one million coaches in Canada, running drills on rinks and soccer pitches, and the vast majority are unpaid volunteers. In that crowd, the few, self-camouflaging child predators are hard to spot—even before considering that many sports organizations are already struggling to find volunteers, both to coach and to monitor the coaches.

The process of selecting coaches often comes down to a short interview and a police background check. Sometimes, but less often, references are followed up.

Sports isn't alone, of course—as a society, after confronting too many cases of long hidden abuse, we have become more careful and specific about the interaction between children and the adults who have power over them. Teachers don't give hugs. Kids aren't left alone with camp counsellors.

Every new case—like every revelation of abuse in the Catholic Church—heightens the sense that we need to keep adults at a safe distance from their young charges.

Coaches aren't watched with the same level of scrutiny as teachers, says Sandra Kirby, a former Olympian and sports researcher at the University of Winnipeg. "We give them a lot more licence. We seem to accept that a coach can take an athlete in his or her vehicle and drive away for a five-day excursion, without someone thinking about the need to supervise the child."

Yet the Graham James case has been game-changing. When National Hockey League player Sheldon Kennedy came forward in 1996 to detail his sexual abuse at the hands of Mr. James, who had been his junior-league coach, he helped to push open the door for athletes to share their own damaging experiences.

The relationship between athletes and coaches often falls into a fuzzy space between parent, friend, and teacher, complicated by the fact that very often the coach controls whether an athlete succeeds or fails, plays on the starting line or sits on the bench.

In 2005, André Guilmette, a prominent Montreal speed-skating coach, was sent to prison for eight months after pleading guilty to sexually touching two teenaged athletes over a two-year period. One of his victims, who had been seventeen when it happened, explained that she had been afraid to come forward for fear of losing her path to the Olympics.

"If I quit him, it was over, I would never go to the Olympics, and that was my biggest dream at the time," she told the *Montreal Gazette*. "I thought my life would be nothing if I didn't go. But staying with him just got worse."

Abuse in sports, particularly involving women, has matched roughly the rates in areas such as schools and workplaces, according to several studies.

Dr. Kirby, who sits on an international task force on the issue, found in one survey that nearly 23% of high-performance athletes, nearly all females, reported having sexual relations with a person with power over them on their team, most often their coach. (Under the age of sixteen, the number was 3.5%.)

The study was released shortly before the 1996 Atlanta Summer Games and just a few weeks before Mr. Kennedy went public with his story.

In the years since, Dr. Kirby says, studies in countries such as the Netherlands and Britain have produced similar results. And she points out that while the actual number of coaches committing abuse may be small, the James case and others show that they can leave a trail of victims.

## ▪▪▪ The Limits of Background Checks

Police checks are recommended by national sports bodies, such as Hockey Canada, and most clubs now require them of volunteers, but they are not mandatory. Last year, Britain took the sweeping step of requiring by law that every adult who works or volunteers with children has to have a police check—a step that has been criticized for being too onerous and expensive for non-profit groups.

The coach recently charged in Calgary had returned to assisting a boys' team only a few weeks earlier, after a criminal check that came back clean and an interview with the team's head coach. (He has now been removed from the position.)

"You can be as diligent as you possibly can," says Perry Cavanaugh, the president of Hockey Calgary, "and unless there's a history, there's not going to be any evidence of a problem."

Mr. Cavanaugh estimated that such police checks would cost Calgary hockey clubs $40,000 a year. "The cost of sport is through the roof as it is," he says, arguing that a better approach is to use the likelihood of a background check as an effective deterrent for would-be abusers to volunteer. (He also advocates stiffer penalties for convicted abusers.)

He says teams should be thoroughly interviewing coaches and checking references. But he concedes, "Sometimes that's a little tough when you've got a candidate list of one."

Ruth MacKenzie, president of Volunteer Canada, also points out that police checks, revealing only convictions, not charges or investigations, can also give a false sense of security. Abusers may go years without ever coming to the attention of the police.

"The one thing I always say that scares people is that Paul Bernardo would have passed a police record check," Ms. MacKenzie says. "It's one part of the screening process. It's not a panacea."

There's also the concern that too much red tape will deter people from volunteering in sports where coaches are already in short supply. "Some people just don't want the hassle," says Terry Brodie, an award-winning hockey coach in Viking, Alberta.

He accepts that police checks are a must these days, but in fifteen years he has seen how careful the atmosphere has become, right down to the words he uses, to safeguard his own safety and reputation. "Ten years ago, I wouldn't have thought a lot about it. Now I do. You have to watch yourself."

John Bales, the chief executive officer of the Coaching Association of Canada, an organization that trains and certifies coaches, says he regularly hears from coaches a sense of disappointment that the sports atmosphere has become more formal, even if they understand why.

"Even congratulating an athlete and giving them a hug after a performance—some of those things are lost," he says. "But it's also the reality … You can't be happily naive."

Canada is actually ahead of other countries on safety for athletes, according to Dr. Kirby, in large part because the likes of Mr. Kennedy and Mr. Fleury have come forward with their stories. There is much more awareness about the risk of abuse among athletes, and coaching clinics stress the issue, she says.

A new national code of conduct, led by the Centre for Ethic and Sports, is being finalized, with the intention that it be adopted by all sport organizations in the country.

Swim Canada, for instance, which screens all its coaches (most of them hired, using only a few volunteers), also prohibits any banned coaches, from any sport, from attending swim meets—giving security a list of their names and photographs (even though almost all the banned coaches in Canada have been punished for doping violations, not abuse).

And, unlike in many other countries, most coaches in Canada, even at the recreational level, have some form of certification.

"Canada is really at the leading edge," Dr. Kirby says. "But does it stop it? Clearly it doesn't."

Sports groups could go even further, she says, by improving their complaint process, an awkward and complicated situation often left to volunteers. An anonymous tip line would help, allowing people to tell someone about their suspicions, rather than leaving it up to the victim to make the difficult first step.

"What we say way too often, when a case does come forward, is that people knew something was wrong," Dr. Kirby says. "The rumour mill in sport is very strong, but we don't actually act on it."

But in the end, she suggests, the most important supervision lies with the parents, who can monitor practices and carefully quiz their children on locker-room antics. Don't leave your child at the rink every practice to get groceries done.

"We say it's a good place to go, a good place to raise your kids. But what we also have to be saying is you need to be with your children. You need to be watching them."

◄◄ **Source:** Erin Anderssen is a feature writer for *The Globe and Mail*. This article was originally published on April 10, 2010. Reprinted with permission.

# When You're Asked About the Kobe Bryant Case 28.

## By Jackson Katz

*Note: The following points are intended to give anti-rape advocates and educators ideas about how to think about and respond to various aspects of the Kobe Bryant rape case.*

■ ■ ■ ■ ■ ■

1) Because of its high-profile nature, the Kobe Bryant rape trial presents a rare teachable moment. There is and will continue to be a deluge of media attention that exploits the salacious aspects of the case: sex, violence, race, and celebrity. But the case also provides the opportunity for anti-rape educators and activists to educate the public about rape. How? Through media interviews, television specials, newspaper articles, and trainings for journalists. Also, by raising the issue in middle school, high school, and college classrooms across the country.

Television coverage in these sorts of cases tends to emphasize the contentious legal issues: defence attorneys and former prosecutors arguing endlessly about rules of evidence, who is or is not an effective witness, etc. We should try to broaden the conversation to talk about the societal context within which rape is so common. Some questions we should raise whenever we get the chance: Why is the rape rate so high in the United States? Why do so many men rape women? If over 99% of rape is perpetrated by men—whether the victims are female or male—why is rape considered a "women's issue"? What is going on with American men—whether we're star athletes or just average guys—that causes so many of us to assault women? Do men who are not rapists contribute to the problem—or to its solution? What role is played by friends, family members, classmates, and teammates?

We should also educate people about connections between rape-supportive attitudes and real acts of rape. Examples of rape-supportive attitudes include saying, as some have in this case, that a woman "should know what to expect" when she goes up to a man's room late at night; defending some men's sexist or degrading comments about women; or laughing uncritically at jokes about rape and other forms of men's violence against women.

2) Kobe Bryant is a wondrous athlete and a phenomenal basketball player. His exploits on the court and his public image off the court have won him millions of fans, presumably most of whom want to believe he is not guilty of anything beyond adultery and incredibly poor judgment. It is important to note that before this incident, many of his fans included women and men in the anti-rape movement, as well as rape survivors.

But people who know a lot about rape—from the perspective of victims as well as the perspective of the criminal justice system—know that false reports of rape are rare. Rarer still is the situation where a victim falsely reports a rape, then sticks to her/his story long enough for a district attorney to file charges and commence the prosecution of a case. It is understandable that Kobe Bryant fans are hoping their hero will be exonerated. But if they have any sense of fairness, these fans have to support a fair trial, and withhold judgment until all of the evidence is presented in a court of law.

3) It is important to emphasize that this case is The People of Colorado vs. Kobe Bryant. It is not a "he said, she said" case, or the entertainment-like "Kobe vs. the Cheerleader." When people say it's a "he said, she said" case, we need to correct them by

pointing out the following: on the morning of July 1, 2003, the alleged victim went to the police and reported that she had been raped by Kobe Bryant the night before. Soon thereafter, Eagle County Sheriff Joe Hoy approached a judge, who signed an arrest warrant. Two weeks later, Eagle County District Attorney Mark Hurlbert, after reviewing the physical and testimonial evidence he had available to him, made the decision to prosecute Kobe Bryant on one charge of felony sexual assault. If people have a problem with the charge, they should address their concerns/complaints to the duly elected and appointed authorities in Colorado. It was, after all, the district attorney who made the decision to prosecute—not the alleged victim.

It is simply not true that this case pits one person's word against another's. Kobe Bryant most assuredly deserves a fair trial on the charge against him. No one would deny him his right to defend himself to the best of his ability in a court of law. But let's be clear. Calling the case a "he said, she said" is part of an attempt by Kobe Bryant's defenders to discredit the alleged victim before a jury has even seen or heard the evidence. It also fits a larger pattern where some men—and women—seek to reduce the serious felony charge of sexual assault to a matter of poor communication or an unhappy sexual encounter. This fundamentally misstates the gravity of what is alleged to have happened, which is an egregious violation of one person's bodily integrity by another.

4) Media commentators and others have been referring to the nineteen-year-old alleged victim as Kobe Bryant's "accuser." This is an inappropriate usage because the term "accuser" subtly but powerfully undermines the credibility of the alleged victim, and furthers the mistaken impression that this is a "he said, she said" case. Imagine if every time people said Bryant's name, they referred to him as "the accused," or "the accused rapist" Kobe Bryant. As Los Angeles Commission on Assaults Against Women Executive Director Patti Giggans and others have maintained, referring to her as the "alleged victim," or the "victim-witness," and him

as "Kobe Bryant," or "the defendant," is a much more fair and even-handed way to describe the principals in this case. Rape crisis advocates have also traditionally used the term "rape survivor" and "victim/survivor" when referring to rape and sexual assault victims.

5) There has been a lot of victim-blaming and victim-bashing on talk radio and in parts of the male sports culture over the past few weeks. But it is not accurate to make blanket statements about the tone of the commentary. In fact, there have been a number of thoughtful pieces written by men—including men of colour—that have explored some of the issues of this case with sensitivity and balance. A couple of examples: Kevin Jackson, the coordinating editor of ESPN.com, wrote a widely circulated piece around July 29 called "Who's the Victim Here?" Jack McCallum wrote a cover story in the July 28 issue of Sports Illustrated called "The Dark Side of a Star."

If you're a woman and want to deflect criticism that you're "biased" or somehow don't understand the "men's perspective" (these are sexist assumptions), you can reference some of these male writers to support your position.

6) Race will continue to be a factor in the popular conversation about this case—whether it's spoken aloud or not. Depending on the strategy chosen by the defence, it might also be a factor in the courtroom. It is important for anti-rape advocates and educators to bring up the racial subtext whenever possible - or at the very least be prepared to discuss it when others raise it. The defendant is an African American man, and the alleged victim a white woman. Our country has a long and sordid history of racism. Rape and racism have been the pretext for untold numbers of lynchings and other racist outbursts on the part of whites. It is important to acknowledge this history and denounce it.

It is especially important to acknowledge the "whiteness" of the environment where the crime allegedly took place—and where the trial is likely to be held—because the defendant is an African American man. You should condemn racism in all its forms. But then you can say that we need to focus on the facts of this case, because justice demands that we do our utmost for the rights of everyone concerned: the victim, the community, and the defendant.

It might be useful to point out that men and women of colour have been among the many thoughtful commentators about the Bryant case in the past few weeks (e.g., Kevin Jackson on ESPN. com). It might also be useful to mention that there have been other high-profile rape trials involving professional athletes where the racial aspects have been different, but some of the sexist arguments have been eerily similar to this case. For example, the Mike Tyson rape trial evoked charges of racism from some quarters—but the victim was also African American. (Tyson was convicted.) In the Mark Chmura rape trial, Chmura, a tight end for the Green Bay Packers, who is white, was charged with raping a seventeen-year-old white girl at a prom party in April 2000. (He was acquitted.) In both of those cases, the victim was described—by people who didn't know her and had never met her—as a "gold digger" out to take advantage of a wealthy man through a false allegation. If you want more info on either of those cases—to show the similarities of the sexism in different racial contexts—go to Google.com or another search engine.

7) There are some national data which suggest that male athletes are more likely than non-athletes to assault women. One oft-cited study of ten large universities and colleges in 1995 found that male student-athletes comprised 3.3% of the male student population, yet accounted for 19% of reported perpetrators of sexual assaults. Clearly, much more study in this area is required. But even if it could be proven conclusively that male athletes are more likely to commit sexual assault than non-athletes, we're still left with the fact that the vast majority of sexual assaults are perpetrated by non-athletes. So while it might be useful to know why some (male) athletes assault women, this knowledge alone wouldn't help us much in trying to

figure out why stockbrokers, teachers, priests, auto mechanics, and Ivy League students also commit rape.

Rapists are mostly non-athletes. They come from every socioeconomic class, racial, and ethnic group. They can be slight of build or big and powerful. The most important characteristic rapists have in common is their gender: approximately 99% of rapists are men.

8) There has been a lot of talk in the past few weeks about women who use false allegations of rape to extort money from professional athletes. Men who make this claim often do so with the slightly self-inflated air of someone who wants you to think they're privy to valuable insider information, like they're members of the club. Some men who travel in elite sports circles claim to know that it's a common practice. But how do they know? Has it ever happened to them, or someone they know? And even then, how do they know that extortion is what actually happened? Presumably, in the rare instances when there is an out-of-court cash settlement between an athlete and a woman who alleges that he raped her, one condition of the settlement is a public gag order. So we don't know if he actually raped her and then bought her silence, or if they had consensual sex as part of her scheme.

One way to respond to people who claim that "false rape accusations for the purpose of extortion are common" is to ask: Can you cite statistics on how prevalent this is? Can you provide the names of women who have done it, or the athletes who've been extorted? If not, then what is the basis for your belief that there is a widespread problem of women falsely accusing men? Rumours?

9) Rape shield laws apply to the type of information that is admissible as evidence in a court of law. Among other things, they prevent defence attorneys from turning a case away from a debate about the merits of the evidence of an alleged crime by the defendant and into a referendum on the alleged victim's prior sexual history. But there are no rape shield laws on the streets, around the water cooler

at work, or in the lounge in a college dormitory. Media commentators are not bound by rape shield laws. In other words, outside of the courtroom, people can say what they want about the alleged victim—and some people have been saying some nasty things about the nineteen-year-old Eagle, Colorado, woman at the centre of this storm.

It is important to remember that one group of people who will be watching this case closely is rape victims. Most never report the crime, in part because they fear the type of vilification (albeit on a much smaller scale) that Bryant's alleged victim is encountering. Many victims never disclose their stories to people around them. (Do you know every detail of the life histories of people around you?) We can support these silent victims—in some cases they are our family members and friends—by speaking up and interrupting trash-talking about Bryant's alleged victim whenever possible. Suggested retorts: "Do you know her?" "How can you say something like that—do you have some sort of inside knowledge of what went on that night?" "How would you feel if it was your sister or your friend who reported a rape?" "It takes a lot of guts for a victim to come forward." But every time one does, it makes it that much harder for the culture of rape to continue.

10) Some have argued that, for high-profile male athletes, the most important lesson of the Kobe Bryant case is: "Don't have sex on the road with women you don't know," (because of how supposedly vulnerable these high-profile men are). This feeds into the inflated fear on the part of some prominent male athletes that there are all sorts of women out seeking to extort money from men by falsely accusing them of sexual assault.

But the most powerful lesson of the Bryant case to high-profile athletes—indeed, all men—is: DON'T EVER FORCE A WOMAN (OR A MAN) TO HAVE SEX WITH YOU. If you don't force yourself on anyone, you are highly unlikely ever to be charged with a crime. If you do have sex with someone against her will—regardless of how many other women might willingly have sex with you—you are committing rape. You may or may not ever be charged with a crime. Contrary to some men's inflated fear of being falsely accused, the vast majority of rapes are never reported. But you'll know in your heart that you've committed a terrible crime, and you'll have to live with yourself. And you do run the risk of facing criminal charges, which will turn your life upside down and potentially threaten everything you've worked so hard to achieve.

◀◀ **Source:** This article was written by Jackson Katz, PhD, and was previously published on his website. Reprinted with permission.

# 29.

# Sexual Harassment and Abuse in Sport
## IOC Consensus Statement

In its role of promoting and protecting the health of the athlete, the IOC Medical Commission recognizes all the rights of athletes, including the right to enjoy a safe and supportive sport environment. It is in such conditions that athletes are most likely to flourish and optimize their sporting performance. Sexual harassment and abuse are violations of human rights, regardless of cultural setting, that damage both individual and organizational health. While it is well known that sport offers significant potential for personal and social benefits, this potential is undermined where such problems occur. Sexual harassment and abuse occur worldwide. In sport, they give rise to suffering for athletes and others, and to legal, financial, and moral liabilities for sport organizations. No sport is immune to these problems which occur at every performance level. Everyone in sport shares the responsibility to identify and prevent sexual harassment and abuse and to develop a culture of dignity, respect, and safety in sport. Sport organizations, in particular, are gatekeepers to safety and should demonstrate strong leadership in identifying and eradicating these practices. A healthy sport system that empowers athletes can contribute to the prevention of sexual harassment and abuse inside and outside sport.

This document summarizes current scientific knowledge about the different forms of sexual harassment and abuse, the risk factors that might alert the sport community to early intervention, and the myths that deflect attention from these problems. It also proposes a set of recommendations for awareness raising, policy development and implementation, education and prevention, and enhancement of good practice.

### ■ ■ ■ Defining the Problem

Sexual harassment and abuse in sport stem from power relations and abuses of power. Sexual harassment refers to behaviour towards an individual or group that involves sexualized verbal, non-verbal, or physical behaviour, whether intended or unintended, legal or illegal, that is based upon an abuse of power and trust and that is considered by the victim or a bystander to be unwanted or coerced. Sexual abuse involves any sexual activity where consent is not or cannot be given. In sport, it often involves manipulation and entrapment of the athlete. Sexual harassment and abuse occur within an organizational culture that facilitates such opportunities. Indeed, they are symptoms of failed leadership in sport. Gender harassment, hazing, and homophobia are all aspects of the sexual harassment and abuse continuum in sport (see Appendix 1). Gender harassment consists of derogatory treatment of one gender or another which is systematic and repeated but not necessarily

sexual. Hazing involves abusive initiation rituals that often have sexual components and in which newcomers are targeted. Homophobia is a form of prejudice and discrimination ranging from passive resentment to active victimization of lesbian, gay, bisexual, and transgendered people.

### ■ ■ ■ Scientific Evidence: Prevalence, Risks, and Consequences

Research indicates that sexual harassment and abuse happen in all sports and at all levels. Prevalence appears to be higher in elite sport. Members of the athlete's entourage who are in positions of power and authority appear to be the primary perpetrators. Peer athletes have also been identified as perpetrators. Males are more often reported as perpetrators than females.

Athletes are silenced by the sexual harassment and abuse process. The risk of sexual harassment and abuse is greater when there is a lack of protection, high perpetrator motivation, and high athlete vulnerability (especially in relation to age and maturation). There is no evidence that the amount of clothing cover or the type of sport are risk factors: these are myths. Research identifies risk situations as the locker room, the playing field, trips away, the coach's home or car, and social events, especially where alcohol is involved. Team initiations or end-of-season celebrations can also involve sexually abusive behaviour against individuals or groups.

Research demonstrates that sexual harassment and abuse in sport seriously and negatively impact on athletes' physical and psychological health. It can result in impaired performance and lead to athlete drop-out. Clinical data indicate that psychosomatic illnesses, anxiety, depression, substance abuse, self harm, and suicide are some of the serious health consequences. Passive attitudes/non-intervention, denial, and/or silence by people in positions of power in sport (particularly bystanders) increases the psychological harm of sexual harassment and abuse. Lack of bystander action also creates the impression for victims that sexually harassing and abusive behaviours are legally and socially acceptable and/or that those in sport are powerless to speak out against it.

### ■■■ Relationships in Sport

Sexual harassment and abuse in sport do not discriminate on the basis of age, gender, race, sexual orientation, or disability. Athletes come from many different cultural and family backgrounds and are the centre of a system of relationships focused on helping them to achieve their sport potential. There is always a power difference in an athlete's relationships with members of their entourage (coaches, scientific and medical staff, administrators etc.). This power difference, if misused, can lead to sexual harassment and abuse and, in particular, to exploitative sexual relationships with athletes.

These relationships require that a significant amount of time be spent together in the emotionally intense environment of competitive sport. This situation has the potential to put the athlete at risk of isolation within a controlling relationship where his/her power and right to make decisions is undermined.

All adults in an athlete's environment must adopt clear guidelines about their roles, responsibilities and appropriate relationship boundaries. It is essential that each member of the entourage, and any other authority figure, stays within the boundaries of a professional relationship with the athlete.

### ■■■ Prevention Strategies

Accepted prevention strategies include policies with associated codes of practice, education and training, complaint and support mechanisms, and monitoring and evaluation systems. Regardless of cultural differences, every sport organization should have these provisions in place.

The policy is a statement of intent that demonstrates a commitment to create a safe and mutually respectful environment. The policy should state what is required in relation to the promotion of rights, well-being, and protection. It allows the organization to generate prompt, impartial, and fair action when a complaint or allegation is made. It further allows it to take disciplinary, penal, and other measures, as appropriate.

Codes of practice describe acceptable standards of behaviour that, when followed, serve to implement the policy. Standards of behaviour set a clear benchmark for what is acceptable and unacceptable. They can help to minimize opportunities for sexual harassment and abuse and unfounded allegations (see Appendix 2).

### ■■■ Recommendations

All sport organizations should:

1. Develop policies and procedures for the prevention of sexual harassment and abuse

2. Monitor the implementation of these policies and procedures

3. Evaluate the impact of these policies in identifying and reducing sexual harassment and abuse

4. Develop an education and training program on sexual harassment and abuse in their sport(s)

5. Promote and exemplify equitable, respectful, and ethical leadership

6. Foster strong partnerships with parents/carers in the prevention of sexual harassment and abuse

7. Promote and support scientific research on these issues

Through sexual harassment and abuse prevention in sport, sport will become a safer, healthier, and more positive environment for all. In case of divergence between the English version of the Consensus Statement and the translated versions, the English version prevails.

# Appendix 1: The Sexual Exploitation Continuum

**SEX DISCRIMINATION**

————————————————————————————————————————→

**SEXUAL & GENDER HARASSMENT**

————————————————————————————————→

**HAZING & SEXUAL ABUSE**

——————————————————————→

**INSTITUTIONAL**........................................................................**PERSONAL**

| "the chilly climate" | "unwanted attention" | "groomed or coerced" |
|---|---|---|
| vertical & horizontal job segregation | written or verbal abuse or threats | exchange of reward or privilege for sexual favours |
| lack of harassment policy and/or officer or reporting channels | sexually oriented comments, jokes, lewd comments or sexual innuendoes, taunts about body, dress, marital situation, or sexuality | groping |
| lack of counselling or mentoring systems | ridiculing of performance | indecent exposure |
| differential pay or rewards or promotion prospects on the basis of sex | sexual or homophobic graffiti | forced sexual activity |
| | practical jokes based on sex | sexual assault |
| poorly/unsafely designed or lit venues | intimidating sexual remarks, propositions, invitations, or familiarity | |
| absence of basic security | domination of meetings, play space, or equipment | physical/sexual violence |
| | condescending or patronizing behaviour undermining self-respect or work performance | rape |
| | physical contact, fondling, pinching, or kissing | incest |
| | vandalism on the basis of sex | |
| | offensive phone calls or photos | |
| | stalking | |
| | bullying based on sex | |

**Source: Adapted from Brackenridge (1997)**

# Appendix 2: Criteria for Sexual Harassment and Abuse Policies and Codes of Practice in a Sport Organization

The policy on sexual harassment and abuse should:

- Identify and address these issues
- Be clear and easily understood
- Involve consultation with athletes
- Be widely communicated through publication and education
- Be approved by the relevant management body (e.g., management Board or executive committee) and incorporated into its constitution and/or regulations
- Apply to all involved in the organization
- Be supported by a comprehensive education and training strategy
- Be reviewed and updated on a regular basis, particularly when there is a major change in the constitutional regulations of the organization or in the law

The policy should:

- State that all members have a right to respect, safety, and protection
- State that the welfare of members is paramount
- Identify who has responsibility for implementing and upholding it
- Specify what constitutes a violation
- Specify the range of consequences for such violations
- Specify procedures for reporting and handling complaints
- Provide details of where to seek advice and support for all parties involved in a complaint
- Specify procedures for maintaining records
- Provide guidance for third-party reporting ("whistleblowing")

There should be codes of practice on sexual abuse and harassment for specific member roles in a sport organization. The code of practice on sexual harassment and abuse should:

- Provide guidance on appropriate/expected standards of behaviour from all members
- Set out clear processes for dealing with unacceptable behaviours, including guidance on disciplinary measures and sanctions

## Resource List—Sexual Harassment and Abuse in Sport

This is not a definitive list but merely indicative of some of the baseline sources on this subject.

- Australian Sports Commission. 2006. *Ethics in Sport—Member Protection*. Available at www.ausport.gov.au/ethics/memprot.asp
- Brackenridge, C. H., A. Pitchford, G. Nutt, and K. Russell. 2007. *Child Welfare in Football: An Exploration of Children's Welfare in the Modern Game*. London: Routledge/Taylor & Francis.
- Brackenridge, C. H. and K. Fasting (eds). 2002. *Sexual Harassment and Abuse in Sport—International Research and Policy Perspectives*. London: Whiting and Birch.
- Brackenridge, C. H. 2001. *Spoilsports: Understanding and Preventing Sexual Exploitation in Sport*. London: Routledge.
- David, P. 2005 *Human Rights in Youth Sport: A Critical Review of Children's Rights in Competitive Sports*. London: Routledge.
- Fasting, K., C. Brackenridge, and J. Sundgot-Borgen. 2003. "Experiences of sexual harassment and abuse among Norwegian elite female athletes and non-athletes." *Research Quarterly for Exercise and Sport*. 74(1):84-97.
- Johnson, J. and M. Holman (eds). 2004. *Making the Team: Inside the World of Sport Initiations and Hazing*. Toronto: Canadian Scholars' Press.
- Kirby, S., L. Greaves, and O. Hanvkivsky. 2000. *The Dome of Silence: Sexual Harassment*

*and Abuse in Sport.* Halifax, Nova Scotia: Fernwood Publishing/London: Zed Books.

■ Outgames. 2006. "Declaration of Montreal on Lesbian, Gay, Bisexual, and Transgender Human Rights." (en.wikipedia.org/wiki/Declaration_of_Montreal).

■ Panathlon International. 2004. "Declaration on Ethics in Youth Sport." (www.panathlon.net).

■ Sport England/NSPCC Child Protection in Sport Unit. 2003. "National Standards for Safeguarding Children in Sport." (www.thecpsu.org.uk).

■ Tofler, I. and T. F. de Geronimo. 2000. *Keeping Your Kids Out Front Without Kicking Them From Behind: How to Manage High-Achieving Athletes, Scholars and Performing Artists.* San Francisco, CA: Jossey-Bass.

■ "WomenSport International Position Statement on Sexual Harassment in Sport." (www.womensportinternational.org).

Resource list compiled by C. Brackenridge and K. Fasting, November 12, 2006.

◀◀ **Source:** Reprinted with permission from the IOC Medical Commission.

# Section 6

## Gender, Sexuality, and Sports

**G**ender is **the** defining organizing principle in sport, of even greater importance than age. While social class considerations are extremely important with regard to participation, athletes are not usually selected on the basis of their social class. However, almost all sports are organized by gender, with separate teams and competitions for boys and girls, men and women. Questions about and challenges to this organizing principle have made gender and sexuality major topics in the sociology of sport, and they are also often prominent issues in the media. Recently we have seen Caster Semenya struggle over the definitions of sex and gender with the International Association of Athletics Federations, the unsuccessful struggle by women ski jumpers to compete at the 2010 Winter Olympics in Vancouver, a challenge by a girls' hockey league in Toronto for more equity in the allocation of ice time, an increasing number of gay male athletes coming out, and ongoing concerns about the relationships between masculinity, violence, and injury.

The first article in this section deals with challenges to gender as a defining principle. In 1987, Justine Blainey was selected to play on a boys' hockey team on the basis of her skills. The Ontario Hockey Association challenged this disruption of its traditional organizing principle in the courts and had Blainey removed from the team. After several years, that decision was reversed in the appeal court, making the Blainey case one of the most prominent in Canada to challenge segregation in

sports on the basis of sex rather than skill. Justine Blainey-Broker revisits her personal experience with that case in her article, "Someone's Gaining on You, Boys," and makes a strong case for equal opportunity. The repercussions of the issue of girls playing on boys' teams are still being felt. Hayley Wickenheiser was denied a place on a men's professional hockey team in Italy before playing for a men's professional team in Finland, while female players such as Annika Sorenstam and Michelle Wie have managed to play in the formerly all-male PGA tournaments. In a recent decision by the Ontario Federation of School Athletic Associations (OFSAA), girls who are able to make the team on the basis of their skill are now permitted to play on boys' teams. (For more on this decision, see the two articles by Hayley Mick in "Additional Suggested Readings and References.")

The next two articles deal even more directly with equity. Guylaine Demers reports on new research related to the "We are Coaches" initiative by the Coaching Association of Canada. The new data show that female coaches never exceed a third of all coaches at each level of coaching certification, and that women's representation on national team coaching staff is significantly lower than that. A quick examination of the coaching staff at any college or university will almost certainly show a similar under-representation of female coaches. (See "Analysis of Male and Female Coaches in Canadian Interuniversity Sports" in "Additional Suggested Readings and References.") Moving from numerical equity to legal equity, Ann Travers examines the lawsuits and appeals surrounding "Vancouver 2010 and Women's Ski Jumping" and the female athletes who fought for a chance to compete at the Vancouver Olympics. Despite the powerful challenge made by the ski jumpers, and the fact that the absence of women violated the Canadian Charter of Rights and Freedoms, the challenge was ultimately unsuccessful as the International Olympic Committee is not bound by the rules of Canada's Charter. Marcus Mazzucco argues that the legal challenge may have had more success if it had been brought to the International Court of Arbitration for Sport (see "Additional Suggested Readings and References"). Similar challenges are likely to be made prior to the forthcoming PanAm Games (Toronto 2015) since there are also men-only events on that competition schedule.

The gender part of this section concludes with a reminder that masculinity is also a part of gender studies. Although violence was discussed in the previous section indirectly in terms of its relationship to masculinity, Mike Atkinson and Kevin Young make that connection much more distinct in their article "Cracking 'The (Male) Code' of Player Violence." This article is a reminder that sports can be a school for a particular type of masculinity (see Section 2, Socialization and Sports).

In addition to much of social life, sport is organized on the basis of an overly simplified two-category gender classification model. This obliges sport to define who is a man and who is a woman, and leads to cases such as the one involving South African middle-distance runner Caster Semenya and an increasing number of cases involving transgendered and transitioning athletes. In 2004, the IOC was obliged to publish the Stockholm Consensus, a statement outlining the conditions under which athletes would be able to compete in events for a sex that was not their birth sex. Rachel Corbett outlines these conditions and gives important background and definitions in her paper, "Transgendered and Transitioned Athletes in the Sport System." (See also "Promising Practices: Working with Transitioned/Transitioning Athletes in Sport" in "Additional Suggested Readings and

References.") Anne McIlroy discusses these issues with regard to Canadian track cyclist Kristen Worley in her article, "I'm a Woman on the Move."

The section concludes with three articles on gay and lesbian athletes. Mark Tewksbury has become one of the leading spokespeople in Canada on the issue of "gay jocks." The Olympic gold-medal-winning swimmer came out in 1998, and organized the Outgames in Montreal in 2006. (It should be noted that participation in the Outgames and the Gay Games is not segregated or limited to gay and lesbian athletes.) James Christie interviewed Tewksbury and reports that "Tewksbury Foresees Bright Future for Gay Jocks." Gordon Laird's article about gay rodeos, "Bucking the System," is a reminder that gay and lesbian sport is widespread; although, since the release of the film *Brokeback Mountain*, perhaps people are not surprised that there are gay cowboys. Discussions about gay and lesbian athletes were prominent after Brendan Burke (son of Toronto Maple Leafs General Manager Brian Burke) came out in 2009. Erin Anderssen and Jeff Blair pick up on these discussions in their article, "Throwing in the Towel on Homophobia," pointing out that homophobia is still widespread in sports, but that there are encouraging signs that it is being challenged more today than in the past.

**Additional Suggested Readings and References**

- AthletesCAN/CAAWS. 2008-09. "Promising Practices: Working with Transitioned/Transitioning Athletes in Sport." (www.athletescan.com/Content/Resources/PromisingPractices.asp?langid=1).
- Atkinson, M. 2011. "Chapter 5: Sporting Masculinities" in *Deconstructing Men and Masculinities*. Toronto: Oxford University Press.
- Canadian Interuniversity Sports. 2005. "Analysis of Male and Female Coaches in Canadian Interuniversity Sports." (www.cisport.ca/e/research/documents/analysisofmensandwomenscoachesinCIS_000.pdf).
- Mazzucco, M. 2010. "The Role of National Courts in Regulating the International Sport System: A Case of *Forum Non Conveniens*?" Paper presented at the Bodies of Knowledge Graduate Research Conference, University of Toronto, May 12–15.
- Mick, H. 2010a. "The Struggle for Girls Who Can Play with the Boys." *The Globe and Mail*, May 8.
- Mick, H. 2010b. "Breaking Down Towering Gender Barriers." *The Globe and Mail*, May 15.

# Someone's Gaining on You, Boys

## By Justine Blainey-Broker

**30.**

*With golfer Suzy Whaley qualifying for the PGA, another woman is closing the jock gender gap, says hockey veteran Justine Blainey-Broker.*

■ ■ ■ ■ ■ ■

In 1987, I was a child crying out in the wilderness: "I can play but may I?" I had earned a place on a boys' team in open tryouts but the Ontario hockey organization wouldn't let me play. A newly trained lawyer, J. Anna Fraser, heard me. Five court cases, and a Supreme Court decision later, I became the first girl to legally hit the ice with the boys. Today I am a doctor of chiropractic and a mother, and every day I yearn for the swish of the ice and the rough and tumble of top-level competitive hockey.

What is this door Anna and I helped open? It is small, accessible to very few women—5'10" and up, superdedicated, supertalented, and thick-skinned enough to withstand the sexist jibes and isolating spotlight sure to follow.

"That one is a girl! Look! Where does she dress?" "Did she sleep with her coach? Does she sleep with her teammates?" "Is she any good? Is she the token female?"

I wonder what Jackie Robinson felt in 1947 when he became the first black in major league baseball—and how he would feel today, fifty-five years later, seeing fully integrated baseball teams where colour is not worth mentioning. Weight, height, batting averages—skills—count. Not colour.

So why is it that sex still counts? Suzy Whaley recently qualified to become the first woman to play in a Professional Golf Association Tour event. Tennis star Venus Williams's serves have been clocked at around 190 kilometres per hour, about the same as Andre Agassi's. And women can match men in long-distance running and swimming marathons. In 1995, Australian champion Shelley Taylor-Smith swam around Manhattan and set the record for both men and women, a feat she repeated in 1998.

In *The Frailty Myth: Women Approaching Physical Equality*, Colette Dowling cites physiological studies that show remarkable similarities between male and female strength, once height and weight are factored in—the same variables that get taken into account when men box, or wrestle, or lift weights.

Female soldiers, female police officers, female athletes have to fight antiquated rules, rigid organizational structures, ridicule, and anger. Hayley Wickenheiser, the Wayne Gretzky of the Canadian Women's Olympic Hockey team, is going to Europe to get competitive play with male hockey players. Go for it, Hayley! But develop a thick skin.

Because you'll have to dress in hallways and bathrooms. You'll find tampons in your water bottle and propositions in your skates. You'll have to be better than most of them to even make the team and you can never let up. Any mistake you make will be pointed out as the place the game was lost—because you are a woman in a man's game.

Fast forward a few years, and what if the best women golfers, or tennis players, or hockey players end up playing with the men? Will that mean that fewer people will watch women's leagues? It should not—if these are the leagues where exciting new players are coming from. But it may.

And what about boys playing on girls' teams?

Until female hockey is equal to male hockey in terms of funding, skills, number of games, ice time, media coverage, a whole host of categories, female hockey will continue to bar males.

Does this offend my egalitarian sensibilities? Not at all. In sport, it is honourable to play up, demeaning to play down. If a lightweight boxer can win the middleweight world championship, he is a hero, but the heavyweight is not allowed to challenge him. In Ontario today, male sport is the arena of more talent, opportunity, funding, and remuneration. To play up is an honour; to play down should be disallowed until female sport has caught up.

Equal opportunity means more funding for female sport. We're not there yet but facilities for women are getting better and better. Equal opportunity means that schools can no longer give 80% of their sport funding to the boys, and arenas have to give part of their precious ice time to female teams. Our high schools should no longer have big boys' gyms and small girls' gyms. And girls should get some of that precious after-school field time previously the sole domain of male teams.

I played several glorious years of top-level women's hockey until, one day, I found myself unexpectedly pregnant and hesitant to tough it out in the corners. Coach Terry Richardson laughed. This was how his wife had retired from elite hockey—pregnancy.

My two-year-old daughter is a tiny, perfect person. We play hockey in the driveway. She loves the game already. Will she be passionate, talented, driven to be the best that she can be? Will she want to play male sport to hone her talents and challenge her horizons? I don't know, but her father and I will cheer her on. For now, she raises her little arms and yells: "She shoots! She scores! *Goal*!" And my heart hears the swish of the ice.

---

◀◀ **Source:** Justine Blainey-Broker, of the Justine Blainey Wellness Centre in Brampton, Ont., took her fight to play on male hockey teams all the way to the Supreme Court of Canada. In 1987, she won. This article was originally published in *The Globe and Mail*, October 7, 2002. Reprinted with permission.

# 31. "We are Coaches": Program Tackles the Under-Representation of Female Coaches

By Guylaine Demers[1]

## ▪▪▪ Introduction

At the 2005 Petro-Canada Sport Leadership sportif conference, the Coaching Association of Canada (CAC) launched its "We are Coaches" initiative. It was the first phase of a three-year program for which the goal was to increase the number of trained female coaches at the community level in order to provide role models and mentors to young participants in sport. In concrete terms, it meant providing National Coaching Certification Program (NCCP) Community Sport training to groups composed of women only.

"We are Coaches" was implemented in three sports in co-operation with their national sport organizations (NSOs): Hockey Canada, the Canadian Soccer Association, and Softball Canada. These sports were selected because of the large number of female participants involved at the community level and the inverse proportion of female coaches. The need to train more female coaches was evident.

The "We are coaches" pilot phase ran from 2006 to 2008, during which time a considerable number of major adjustments were made. This article reflects the changes and enhancements made during that first phase in order to achieve the program's goal.

As the researcher, my first objective was to assess the impact of the recruitment campaign to gain a

| Table 1: Numbers of Certified Coaches, NCCP, October 2007 | | | |
|---|---|---|---|
| | Women # | Men # | Women % |
| NCCP Level 1 | 76,594 | 181,028 | 30 |
| NCCP Level 2 | 22,600 | 43,978 | 34 |
| NCCP Level 3 | 2,830 | 6,927 | 29 |
| NCCP Level 4 | 177 | 669 | 21 |
| NCCP Level 5 | 10 | 81 | 11 |

better understanding of what drives women to take that first step toward becoming a coach. My other objective was to gauge the impact of the training received by the women involved in the program. To this end, I collected feedback and followed up with the participants to find out how many decided to go into coaching after the training.

As well as summarizing the three years, I will describe the reasons for "We are Coaches," report statistically on its performance, and outline the lessons learned and the outlook for the future.

## ■■■ Reasons for the "We are Coaches" Program

### The Numbers Say it All

Canadian statistics confirm that the number of women in coaching has not kept up with the steadily increasing number of young girls participating in sports. In recent years, there has been a dramatic increase in female participation at all levels of sport. Yet the literature shows that, in some sports, the number of female coaches has not grown, and in other sports the number has even decreased, despite the fact that it is now recognized that women bring a unique contribution to coaching.

### National Statistics

Table 1 lists the numbers of female and male coaches certified in the NCCP. The proportion of women has been steady at about 30% up to and including Level 3. It must be remembered that Level 3 certification is required for all those wanting to coach Canada Games athletes. Coaches who wish to join a national team must have Levels 4 and 5, yet the number of female coaches at these levels is quite small.

Currently, nine women are head coaches of national teams, compared to seventeen in 1997. Looking at recent Olympic Games, statistics for female national team coaches are outlined in Table 2.

Statistics for the "We are coaches" sports: hockey, softball, and soccer in 2006 are outlined below:

■ Hockey: 11% of participants were girls or young women, but only 4% of coaches were women. The number of girls playing hockey had doubled over the previous five years (from 2,713 in 1999 to 5,527 in 2005), and the Fédération québécoise de hockey sur glace estimated that the number of female players would continue to grow by about 10% per year in coming years.[2]

■ Soccer: 42% of participants were girls or young women, while the number of female coaches was estimated to be 5%.

■ Softball: An estimated 40% of participants were girls or young women, with only 5% of coaches being women.[3]

### Women in Coaching Program

Aimed specifically at Canadian women coaches, the objective of the Women in Coaching program is to increase the number of coaching opportunities for women at all levels of sport. The program has the support of a number of people and organizations committed to improving the sport environment for women, including nine support activities divided into three categories: financial, training, and information and networking.

Before "We are Coaches," the only service specifically aimed at young female coaches was mentoring through a free, online mentor program.

This program enables young women with little coaching experience to benefit from the support and advice of experienced female coaches. However, the service is available only to female coaches who have, at minimum, received NCCP training. This is where "We are Coaches" comes into play. Specifically targeted are women who have already considered becoming coaches but never tried to make the jump. They have no connection with CAC and are unaware of its services. Through "We are Coaches," CAC fills a gap in the continuum of initiatives put in place for women coaches, initiatives that were not reaching women who were outside the sport system.

### ■ ■ ■ Statistics for "We are Coaches"

Tables 3 and 4 present a quantitative view of the three years of "We are Coaches." A total of 884 women received NCCP Community Sport training in fifty-four communities and eight provinces. Five communities offered training during the first year, a figure that rose to twenty-two in the second year and twenty-seven during the final year.

Six months after each training session, the participants were surveyed to find out how many chose to become coaches. To date, ninety-one responses have been received. This low number is due, among other things, to the fact that some email addresses are no longer valid. A survey of women who took part in training during the third year of the program is nearing completion. We expect that many more will have chosen to go into coaching. It should be noted, however, that from the responses to date, we know that 63% of respondents went into coaching while 11% decided to get involved in their sport in another capacity (as an official, manager, or volunteer). It is possible to state that "We are Coaches" had a major quantitative impact on the recruitment of women for coaching positions.

| Table 2[4] : Coaches at the 1996, 1998, 2000, 2002, 2004, 2006, and 2008 Olympic Games | | | | | | | | | | | |
|---|---|---|---|---|---|---|---|---|---|---|---|
| | Head coach M | Head coach F | Male coach | Female coach | Assistant coach M | Assistant coach F | Total no.: M | Total no.: F | Total: all coaches | Total: F % | Head coach: F % |
| 2008 | 20 | 2 | 55 | 7 | 9 | 2 | 84 | 11 | 95 | 12% | 9% |
| 2006 | 12 | 1 | 46 | 10 | - | - | 58 | 11 | 69 | 16% | 8% |
| 2004 | 14 | 1 | 59 | 7 | - | - | 73 | 8 | 81 | 10% | 7% |
| 2002 | - | - | 45 | 14 | - | - | 45 | 14 | 59 | 24% | - |
| 2000 | - | - | - | - | - | - | - | - | 65 | - | - |
| 1998 | - | - | 36 | 10 | - | - | 36 | 10 | 46 | 22% | - |
| 1996 | - | - | 59 | 11 | - | - | 59 | 11 | 70 | 16% | - |
| Totals | 46 | 4 | 300 | 59 | 9 | 2 | 355 | 65 | 485 | - | - |

## ▪▪▪ Lessons Learned

The lessons learned over the past three years are, in my view, the most valuable aspect of "We are Coaches." Although the main objective was reached—an increase in the number of women trained and involved in the NCCP Community Sport stream—the information collected throughout the program also enables us to interpret the figures and gain an understanding of what motivates women to become coaches.

### Impact of the Promotional Campaign

The promotional material for "We are Coaches," designed specifically to attract mothers to coaching, included posters, brochures, a DVD, and sample press releases. All stakeholders in community sports acknowledge that mothers represent the group most often seen at their children's practices and games. The idea was to recruit them so that they would progress from being spectators to getting involved as leaders and coaches.

During the first year, very few of the women who signed up were aware of the campaign; most learned about it during their training. On a few occasions, I showed the women the campaign DVD along with the promotional brochures and posters. Most of the women had learned about the training itself from a friend's email or through their local sports association.

The women were receptive to the visual component of the campaign content and suggested that aboriginal communities and young women be included in the promotional material. We quickly realized that female athletes nearing the end of their athletic careers were also a target group with considerable potential for entering the coaching stream. We therefore plan to produce new posters depicting female athletes as well as female aboriginal coaches.

### Table 3: Program Numbers – Communities and Participants, by Sport

| Sport | Year 1 | Year 2 | Year 3 |
|---|---|---|---|
| Hockey | 2 communities | 10 communities | 10 communities |
| | 56 participants | 170 participants | 163 participants |
| Softball | 3 communities | 7 communities | 7 communities |
| | 48 participants | 80 participants | 66 participants |
| Soccer | 0 communities | 5 communities | 10 communities |
| | 0 participants | 139 participants | 162 participants |
| Totals | 5 communities | 22 communities | 27 communities |
| | 104 participants | 389 participants | 391 participants |

### Table 4: Program Numbers – Follow-up

| Sport | Participants | Responses received (follow-up) | Women who became coaches | Women who took other responsibilities in their sport |
|---|---|---|---|---|
| Hockey | 389 | 55 | 28 | Occasional assistance (4) Board member, Volunteer (2) Manager, Official |
| Softball | 194 | 29 | 22 | Official |
| Soccer | 301 | 7 | 7 | |
| Totals | 884 | 91 | 57 (63%) | 10 (11%) |

Thus, the first year of the program enabled us, with the aid of the participants, to improve program promotion and to identify better ways to reach our target audience by:

- Promoting the training at women's sporting events such as senior women's tournaments

- Inviting female athletes directly from the sports targeted by this training

- Providing training in conjunction with major women's sport events such as national women's championships

- Inviting a celebrity speaker such as hockey's Melody Davidson to training sessions

- Placing brochures and posters in public sport venues such as arenas

- Distributing brochures to mothers who come to register their children for the targeted sports

- Providing more information in brochures such as dates and locations

- Posting information about training workshops on the websites of sport associations and emailing all members

A number of these suggestions were picked up by the involved NSOs. Hockey Canada, for example, offered some training during major events such as the World Senior Women's Hockey Championship and the National Women's University Hockey Championship, an approach that was quite successful. Softball Canada promoted training sessions at registration days, which provided an opportunity to reach women who are not part of the usual sports networks.

With these comments in hand, CAC developed a handbook for communities wishing to provide training under the "We are Coaches" banner. It describes how to promote the training workshops, how and where to recruit women, reasons for offering women-only training sessions, and steps to follow, including ordering promotional material, the funding application, and the content of the report to be submitted at the end of training. The handbook can be used by all sport organizations wishing to recruit women to coaching positions.

## Why the Project was Successful

The data collected during the training sessions enabled us to identify the main reasons why women chose to take part. The two most frequent responses were that the training was free of charge and that it was specifically for women.

Many women indicated that they doubted their coaching abilities. Thus, they came to the training sessions to find out whether they really liked coaching and whether they felt prepared to take on the role. They did not hesitate to register, because it was free and there was nothing to lose. Most said that they would not have invested money to test their coaching ability.

The women clearly expressed the importance of taking part in training designed only for women. Because there is a low proportion of female coaches in Canada, women have very few models with whom to identify. Most feel inadequate when considering coaching (www.coach.ca/WOMEN/e/journal/july2004). Women-only sessions provide a secure environment where the participants feel comfortable asking any and all questions about coaching without fear of seeming ignorant or incompetent in the eyes of men. That was a key component of the success of "We are Coaches."

Other reasons given included the desire to improve sport-specific technical and tactical sports knowledge, an interest in female sports in general, a love of sport and coaching, a desire to become a role model for girls, a feeling of obligation to give back to the community, and a desire to coach their children.

## ■ ■ ■ Teaching a Group of Women

One of the great lessons we learned, which we had not anticipated, was the uniqueness of training addressed exclusively to women. I realized this first after attending a training session delivered by two women and then a short time later another session given by two men. The sessions were in the same sport but in different communities.

Two key observations emerged. First, when training was led by women, the participants appreciated the friendly atmosphere and the opportunity to network with women. Also noted was the major impact on confidence, with the instructors quickly becoming models of sport leadership, and the ease of communicating with the instructors, with whom the participants readily identified. A relationship of confidence rapidly developed between participants and instructors. I noted that women, when together with other women, may express themselves on topics that are not part of the training but are issues with them, such as young women's eating disorders, body image, and self-esteem. As a result, CAC has begun to create a web space providing additional information on topics of interest to female coaches.

It should be said that the experience also proved to be extremely positive for the female instructors. For many, it was the first time they had taught a group made up only of women, and they appreciated the impact of the role model and networking aspects.

It was not possible to get female instructors for many sessions. In those instances, one or two men delivered the course. When that happened, some participants indicated surprise, at the very least, to find men teaching a course offered only to women. They perceived the message to be ambiguous: "We are Coaches" is promoting women's access to leadership (that is, coaching positions), but we cannot get women to facilitate the training. It was also noted that the male instructors had never handled women-only groups, which made them somewhat uncomfortable. Training literature says that men and women do not always learn the same way. Women, for example, focus on process and need to understand why things are done in a certain way. Men focus more on results and want to know how to get there; how it is done matters little. Thus, when men teach women for the first time, which often happens in the NCCP, there

is a good chance that the context will not facilitate learning by women and will not encourage a climate of confidence. This led CAC to prepare a document intended for all "We are Coaches" facilitators, men and women, on the particular requirements of teaching groups of women how to become coaches. The document will be available for the second phase of the program. Here is its introduction:

> Learning facilitators are where "the rubber hits the road," the point where plans are executed. The success of "We are Coaches" **depends**, to a great extent, on how you do your job. "We are Coaches" focuses on recruiting women to be community coaches. For many women, taking the course you offer is their first step in coaching. Some are unsure about whether they are going to coach. The way you conduct the course can make the margin of difference in their decision.

## ■ ■ ■ What the Future Will Bring

Over 60% of the women reached in the follow-up phase decided to become coaches. A few stated that without the "We are Coaches" training, they would never have considered it. This is a very important message for the future of the program. I believe that the objective of enabling women to get into coaching, even though they had not thought it possible, is certainly being met.

Reasons cited by participants for not going into coaching after taking the "We are Coaches" training were highly varied. Some said it is difficult to carve out a spot in a male-dominated world. They find this intimidating and need support to break down barriers. In fact, one woman volunteered her services two years in a row and was not offered even an assistant position. Others were waiting for their children to reach the minimum age for a sport, at which point they will come in as coaches. In certain cases, it was a matter of circumstances, such as a new job or a move. Interest in coaching is there, but some women are waiting either for new opportunities or for their personal situation to stabilize before committing themselves.

This information is critical for the second phase of the program. The first phase produced an increase in the number of trained female community coaches. The second, while continuing the recruiting aspect and the training, will deal with the follow-up to the training. We want to find out what experiences women have after they became coaches in order to identify the support and assistance they need to stay in their jobs. It is no longer just a matter of training; we must ensure that we provide coaching opportunities and access to support if the women are to have a positive experience and remain active coaches for a long time.

For phase 2 to get off the ground, sport communities must show an interest in "We are Coaches" training. Be proactive, visit the CAC website (www.coach.ca), and be on the lookout for the next call for funding applications for free NCCP Community Sport training as part of the "We are Coaches" campaign.

**Notes**

1. I thank Britany Gordon and Michael Van Dusen for their contributions to the preparation of this article.

2. Government of Quebec (2006). La place des femmes dans le sport au Québec.

3. Estimates reflect the facts that many community-level soccer and softball coaches have no training and that clubs do not require it in many cases. In addition, many clubs have no formal registration procedure for volunteer coaches. The estimates, however, are consistent with the 2006 Quebec study.

4. Information confirmed by the Canadian Olympic Committee.

◀◀ **Source**: Guylaine Demers, PhD, has been a professor at the Department of Physical Education of Université Laval since September 2001. She takes particular interest in issues of women in sport, coach education, and homophobia in sport. Guylaine was a coach for nearly fifteen years and was also a technical director with the Quebec Basketball Federation. This article is reprinted with permission of *The Canadian Journal for Women in Coaching*, where it originally appeared in April 2009.

## 32. Vancouver 2010 and Women's Ski Jumping
### By Ann Travers

Dubbed the "Flying Fifteen," fifteen women ski jumpers from Canada, the United States, and Europe took the Vancouver Organizing Committee for the 2010 Winter Olympic Games (VANOC) to court over the exclusion of a women's ski jumping event (*Sagen v. VANOC*, 2009). Invoking s. 15(1) of the Canadian Charter of Rights and Freedoms, they argued that the exclusion of a ski jumping event for women constitutes gender discrimination and harms their human dignity. While the International Olympic Committee (IOC) is the body responsible for leaving women's ski jumping off the 2010 Olympic Program, the suit was brought against VANOC. VANOC, the plaintiffs argued, was the organization delegated by city, provincial, and federal governments to stage the 2010 Olympic Games and, in this role, was providing unequal benefits to male and female ski jumpers. VANOC's failure to organize a ski jumping event for women at the Games, while doing so for men, the plaintiffs argued, constituted a violation of their rights under the Canadian Charter of Rights and Freedoms.

Ski jumping was included as one of the events at the inaugural Winter Olympics in 1924. Participation then was restricted to men. (Vertinsky Affidavit, Exhibit B, para 20, p. 42). Today, ski jumping and Nordic combined (which includes ski jumping and cross-country skiing) are the only disciplines at the Winter Games that are still restricted to men. The IOC justified its decision to exclude women's ski jumping by characterizing women's ski jumping as a "new event" that has yet to satisfy the criteria for inclusion (2004 Olympic Charter Rule 47(3)). Women ski jumpers and their advocates countered that ski jumping itself is not a new event[1] at all; it is simply an event that women have been excluded from due to sexist discrimination. The ski jumpers took little comfort from the IOC's encouraging remarks about the likelihood of a women's ski jumping event being included at the Sochi (2014) Olympics.

Despite the IOC's unprecedented success in selling its brand across the globe, a brand that links sport with meritocracy and international solidarity through friendly competition, its track record is at odds with multiple dimensions of social justice (Staun and Sparre, 2007). The celebration of masculinity that underlies the Olympic movement is one important example. This masculine bias is neither merely historical nor accidental; it is foundational (Travers, 2008). In an interview with CTV on April 22, 2009, Bruce Kidd of the University of Toronto drew a parallel between the struggle of the ski jumpers and that which women long distance runners faced in the 1980s. Judged by members of the IOC to be "too frail for such a grueling competition," it was not until the Los Angeles Olympics in 1984 that a women's marathon event was included (Lovett, 1997, p. 132).

The case between the women ski jumpers and VANOC was heard by the British Columbia Supreme Court in April 2009. Lawyers for the ski jumpers argued that, because VANOC was either controlled by government and/or carrying out a government program or policy in staging the Olympic Games, it was therefore subject to the equality provisions of the Charter. VANOC defended itself against this legal challenge by arguing that:

- It is the IOC that sets the program and VANOC merely implements it
- The Charter does not apply to VANOC
- There is no gender discrimination involved anyway

The ski jumpers gained a small moral victory when the Justice Fenlon ruled that the Charter did apply to VANOC, and that the exclusion of women's ski jumping was discriminatory, but concluded that because the IOC had exclusive control over the decision, VANOC could not be held to have breached the Charter. The IOC, an international non-governmental entity, is not subject to the constitutional laws of Canada (although certainly subject to the statutory laws).[2] The jumpers appealed to the BC Supreme Court of Appeal and lost again. The appeal court held that the Charter did not apply to VANOC; and went on to note that even if the Charter did apply, s.15(1) of the Charter (the right to equal benefit of law) did not apply in the circumstances since an Olympic event is not "a benefit of the law" conferred by the Canadian government that must be distributed or accessed equally; rather, it is a benefit conferred by the IOC. A last-ditch appeal to the Supreme Court of Canada to hear the case was refused in January, 2010, shortly before the start of the Vancouver Olympics. Women's ski jumping and women ski jumpers were excluded from the 2010 Olympic Program—this, in spite of the fact that, at the time of writing, a woman holds the record on one of the Olympic jumps at Whistler.

The controversy surrounding women's ski jumping is significant for contesting gender injustice and for provoking an interrogation of the gendered subtexts of citizenship. As Carter (2008) emphasizes, sport engages the "politics of passion" where meaning is constructed at the everyday level. When such public controversies emerge, the impact on broader society can end up being quite significant. The organization of sport has long been the focus of activists and scholars motivated by social justice. The ski jumping case reveals one moment in the historical trajectory of the sport nexus where exclusion is contested.

The ski jumping case merits attention because of its powerful symbolic significance relating to the full participation of women as citizens in democratic societies such as Canada. According to VANOC's defence in the ski jumping case,

> Free and democratic societies around the world compete very hard to host the Olympic Games and have done so on the very same terms. Less free and democratic societies are set to become more so when the games are hosted there (114).

The public insistence of the ski jumpers to be treated with dignity equal to their male peers struck a chord in a country that prides itself on being democratic, and that celebrates the Olympics as an expression of that democratic impetus. As critical sports journalist Dave Zirin emphasizes, drawing attention to contradictions between the lofty proclamations of the Olympic Charter (e.g., non-discrimination, the right to participate in sport) and the baseness of Olympic reality is a legitimate and hence powerful basis for social protest (Zirin, Vancouver: January 20, 2010). By demanding that VANOC stage an Olympics free of gender discrimination, the ski jumpers invited an interrogation of the meaning of the Olympics and of sport participation, the meaning of Canadian citizenship, and the meaning of democracy.

Despite VANOC's limited success in various courtrooms, as a result of the exclusion of women's ski jumping, VANOC and the IOC may have lost in the court of public opinion. An editorial cartoon published in *The Globe and Mail* on Wednesday, April 22, 2009—day three of the trial court proceedings—showed what were apparently members of the Taliban cheering as an Olympic official placed a "No Women" notice on the ski jumping sign.

Important languages of contention (Carter, 2008) concerning the relationship between gender inclusion and gender justice surround the meaning of "new event." By assigning women's ski jumping to the category of "new event" (see Note 1), the IOC attempted to sidestep the issue of almost a century of gender discrimination in that sport.

The sexist exclusion that has and does characterize participation in this event remains unrecognized.[3]

## Notes

1. The IOC counters that the terms sport, discipline, and event are gender-specific. Although men's ski jumping was already in the Olympic program, women's ski jumping, a separate "event," would technically be new.

2. Mazzucco (2010) argues that the Court of Arbitration for Sport (CAS) would have been a more appropriate venue for the women ski jumpers to argue their case since, unlike the Canadian courts, the IOC is not exempt from CAS decisions.

3. However, in the most recent amendments to the Olympic Charter, criteria for the inclusion of "new events" were removed. Mazzucco (personal communication) argues that the IOC may be attempting to remedy the discriminatory effects of the criteria by re-drafting its selection rules.

## Acknowledgement

- The author, and the editor, acknowledge the assistance of Marcus Mazzucco in the interpretation of legal decisions.

## References

- Government of Canada. 1982. The Charter of Rights and Freedoms: a Guide for Canadians. Ottawa: Minister of Supply and Services Canada.

- Carter, T. F. 2008. *The Quality of Home Runs: the Passion, Politics, and Language of Cuban Baseball*. Durham: Duke University Press.

- Lovett, C. C. 1997. *Olympic Marathon: A Centennial History of the Games' Most Storied Race*. Westport, CT: Praeger Publishers.

- Mazzucco, M. and H. Findlay. Forthcoming. "Re-thinking the legal regulation of the Olympic Movement: Envisioning a broader role for the Court of Arbitration for Sport." In R. K. Barney et al. (eds.). *Re-thinking Matters Olympic: Proceedings of the 10th International Symposium for Olympic Research*. London, ON: International Centre for Olympic Studies.

- Staun, J. and K. Sparre. 2007. "The Olympic Games As a Force for Social Change." Playthegame.org Knowledge Bank, June 26.

- Travers, A. 2008. "The Sport Nexus and Gender Injustice." *Studies In Social Justice Journal*, 2(1): 79-101.

◀◀ **Source**: Ann Travers is an assistant professor of sociology at Simon Fraser University. This article was included with permission from the author.

# Cracking "The (Male) Code" of Player Violence

## 33.

By Michael Atkinson and Kevin Young

Explanations of player violence in sports such as ice hockey, offered by coaches, league executives, and broadcasters, are framed by a traditional, and some might say "dangerous," code of hyper-masculinity. As part of selling ice hockey as a risk-filled entertainment spectacle worthy of audience celebration (in a North American market saturated with a vast array of other spectator sports) players are asked and taught to consent to regular physical injury and victimization, even in ways that cross the boundaries of acceptable physicality in the game. Ice hockey players become super-male heroes or weaklings, leaders or wimps, aggressors or losers, and quintessential men or sissies depending on their ability to be ruggedly masculine participants and to use violence as a competitive skill. Conforming to the codes of dangerous masculinity can be informally rewarded within teams through salary and contract incentives, praise, and other forms of preferential treatment (Young, 1993; Robidoux, 2001). Fans and media broadcasters draw attention to the toughness and durability of the masculine or violent player and his ability to withstand ongoing abuse on the ice, or for returning to the ice after being "stitched up" or having body parts "frozen" between periods. These players are mythologized, not simply as on-ice heroes, but also as masculine legends in North American sport culture. Gordie Howe, Dave Schultz, Eddie Shack, Maurice Richard, Dave "Tiger" Williams, Bob Baun, John Wensink, Bob Probert, Dave Semenko, and Tie Domi are all icons in the pantheon of gonzo masculinity in ice hockey. In the mass mediation of the game, sanctioned and unsanctioned body checks, fist fights, and injuries are regularly showcased on sport shows—often in segments dedicated to "Plays of the Day," and celebrated by the stereotypically macho TV hosts presenting them.

The real-life consequences of ignoring or contesting the hyper-masculine codes of aggression and violence in ice hockey are made plain from time to time. For example, those who dare to undermine or publicly challenge codes of dangerous masculinity suffer intense social condemnation from their peers or authority agents within the sport. Tim Gmeinweser, a volunteer hockey coach with the Knights of Columbus Sabres (Edmonton), removed his thirteen- and fourteen-year-old players from the ice during a 2003 game against a team from New Sarepta, Alberta. Gmeinweser's team was losing by a score of 7 to 1 during the second period of the game. Several of his players, including his own son, had been injured during the match and he feared for the safety of the rest of his team. Gmeinweser called the boys off the ice and forfeited the contest, and subsequently received a one-year suspension from the Edmonton Minor Hockey Association for his insolence (CBC News, 2003). Charlene Davis, the president of the local hockey association strangely remarked that, "coaches, who are volunteers, can't be made responsible for players' safety" (ibid.). Only a few weeks later, Kent Willert, head coach of the Knights of Columbus Thunder peewee ice hockey team (players aged eleven to twelve), received a one-year suspension from the Edmonton Minor Hockey Association for taking players off the ice for similar safety reasons.

Marty McSorley's (Boston Bruins) notorious slash to the back of Donald Brashear's (Vancouver Canucks) head in 2000, and Todd Bertuzzi's (Vancouver Canucks) sucker punch to the back of Steve Moore's (Colorado Avalanche) head in

2005 are prime examples of how the exaltation of hyper-masculinity at the professional level of the game manifests itself, at times in tragically vicious ways. In each case, the spectacularly violent altercations were justified by the perpetrators as acts of retribution for apparent violations of the unwritten codes of acceptable male violence and "chivalrous thuggery" shared between players (i.e., in the first instance, refusing to fight another "goon"; and in the second, for injuring a star player from the opposing team). But no violent altercation between players as chillingly illustrates the consequences of the performance of dangerous masculinity in hockey as the death of the Ontario Major League Hockey player Don Sanderson. Sanderson died on January 2, 2009, only twenty days after banging his head on the ice at the end of a "run of the mill" hockey fight during a game that pitted his Whitby Dunlops against rival Brantford Blast. His fateful fight began as a mild scuffle with the Brantford Blast player Corey Fulton next to the Dunlops' goal. Toward the end of the fight, Sanderson's helmet slipped off as he stumbled from Fulton's grip and plummeted to the ice. His exposed head crashed against the ice and Sanderson immediately slipped into unconsciousness, and later died in hospital.

A poll reported by Sun Media shortly after Sanderson's death revealed that 59% of respondents felt that fighting should be banned in minor and amateur hockey. Yet National Hockey League commissioner Gary Bettman publicly expressed the league's reluctance to more rigorously police player codes or official rules regulating fighting in the wake of Sanderson's death. Bettman, like other gatekeepers in the world of hockey, is clearly mindful of the risks involved in alienating hockey's remaining "passionate fans" who strongly support fighting and other forms of violence in the game. Canadian sports broadcasting icon and committed defender of fighting in the game, Don Cherry, declared at Don Sanderson's funeral: "I can't believe that some people in the anti-fighting group would take advantage of something like this to

make their point." Author Ross Bernstein, a pro-fighting advocate whose books on hockey violence include *The Code: The Unwritten Rules of Fighting and Retaliation in the NHL*, stated, "the paying customers like it, so it serves a purpose. Plus, if you're doing something dirty [to another player], that's like whacking a guy in the mob. You have to take your medicine, and it's war" (Associated Press, 2009).

Sociologists of sport have offered many answers to questions regarding the causes and effects of hockey violence, the codes of masculinity underwriting them, and multi-institutional reluctance to intervene. Apart from the examples noted above, consider how rituals of dangerous masculinity figure into harsh and punishing hazing rituals in the sport, the sexual abuse and "grooming" of young players (e.g., Sheldon Kennedy, Theoren Fleury, and Mike Danton), or cultures of rape among junior-level players (Robinson, 1998). For as long as sociologists have examined the cultural settings that give rise to, and provide meaning for, sporting practices, specific brands and codes of masculinity have been linked to the performance of a full range of violent behaviours in athletics. Indeed, few other cultural groups, perhaps except for organized crime families and gangs, have been as extensively probed for the link between gender and violence. In reviewing the empirical research on masculinity in sport, and how codes of aggression become second nature for many young male participants, Erving Goffman's (1961) concept of a total institution potentially explains why and how such is the case. Goffman contends that, in most societies, certain groups and settings exist that may operate as all-encompassing socializing agents. Each member is bound by strict codes of behaviour, socializes mainly with other members of the group, and is subject to constant monitoring and ideological training by authority figures and group leaders. In his landmark text, *Asylums*, Goffman (1961, pp. 15-16) identified five conceptual types of total institutions in his classification: i) those established to care for incapable and "harmless" persons (e.g., an orphanage); ii) those established to care for incapable but dangerous persons (e.g., psychiatric institutions); iii) those established to protect the community against what are felt to be risks and endangerments to it (e.g., prisons); iv) those established to pursue some work-like tasks, and justifying themselves only on these instrumental grounds (e.g., the military); and, v) those established as retreats from the world (e.g., monasteries).

Goffman's (1961) fourth and fifth types of total institution reflect helpfully on life within sports, and how crisis-producing codes of violence are generationally taught as normative within particular sport subcultures. The usefulness of Goffman's fourth category is easy to see because learning and playing the role of an ice hockey player is obviously related to work-tasks, pay, and reputation. Although Goffman intended his fifth category to represent an ascetically oriented refuge such as a monastery, it might be argued that sports allow for a certain type of retreat from the banality of modern life. As such, sports organizations like the NHL possess a taken-for-granted license to create, through the showcasing of violence as part of the game, a retreat from the mundane or predictable world of everyday life where acts of physical aggression are normally, and increasingly, prohibited.

A close inspection of ice hockey reveals the power of sports organizations as total institutions. In thinking about how definitions of acceptable, wanted, unwanted, and even criminal violence in the sport of ice hockey are created, hockey insiders and outsiders might seriously consider how ice hockey (and other) sports organizations manufacture and police consent to their ideologies of, and expectations for, traditional hegemonic male violence in the following ways. First, as a total institution, ice hockey creates a culture of insularity regarding violence in the sport (think of the examples noted previously), underpinned by an historical ethos of traditional masculinity and aggression. When this is questioned, those making the "noise" are effectively silenced in one way or another. Second, strategies are deployed within the sport in order to publicly frame violence in the game as unfortunate but exciting, unsanctioned but accepted, and ultimately, risky but tolerable. In this case violence is never completely right, but neither is it ever really that wrong.

In the end, what makes the male culture of violence in the sport so difficult to alter is that players understand and accept how the kudos gained from being dangerously aggressive with their bodies outweighs the personal risks. Being hyper-male within hockey consistently proves to be a privileging cultural status for players: it constructs the normative male identity as one exuding strength, courage, dominance, emotional detachment, and social power and authority in a sport that rarely tolerates weakness (McKay, Messner, and Sabo, 2000). As Burstyn (1999) notes, possessing a stereotypical masculinity in sports like hockey not only is rationalized as integral for winning contests but also is used as a symbol of men's ability to exert social dominance in life more generally. In plain terms, the stark lesson derived from one's acceptance of "the code" of male violence in the game—which is often labeled as a character-building exercise by insiders (Miracle and Rees, 1994)—is that to be the aggressively and even violently masculine man is to be the socially revered man. What is particularly ironic and lamentable, as Burstyn (1999) and Whannel (2002) recognize, is that most men will never attain or maintain such idealized masculine statuses within the total institution of ice hockey. According to Colburn (1985) and Robidoux (2004), this fact is nowhere more socially obvious than it is in ice hockey cultures, where masculinity in its ultra-traditional form is one of the most punishing and elusive gender statuses chased by participants—even to frequently destructive ends.

## References

- Associated Press. 2009. "Players, NHL: League Should Handle It." *Calgary Herald*, March 8.
- Berstein, R. 2006. *The Code: The Unwritten Rules of Fighting and Retaliation in the NHL*. Chicago: Triumph Books.

- Burstyn, V. 1999. *The Rites of Men*. Toronto: The University of Toronto Press.
- CBC News. 2003. "Alberta Hockey Coaches Suspended for Ending Violent Games." Retrieved from www.cbc.ca, January 16.
- Colburn, K. 1985. "Honour, Ritual and Violence in Ice Hockey." *Canadian Journal of Sociology,* 10:153-70
- Goffman, E. 1961. *Asylums*. Chicago, IL: Aldine.
- McKay, J., M. Messner, and D. Sabo. 2000. *Men, Masculinities, and Sport*. Thousand Oaks: Sage.
- Robidoux, M. 2001. *Men at Play: A Working Understanding of Professional Hockey*. Montreal: McGill-Queen's University Press.
- Robinson, L. 1998. *Crossing the Line: Violence and Sexual Assault in Canada's National Sport*. Toronto: McClelland & Stewart.
- Whannel, G. 2002. *Media Sport Stars: Masculinities and Moralities*. London: Routledge.
- Young, K. 1993. "Violence, Risk, and Liability in Male Sports Culture." *Sociology of Sport Journal*, 10 (4): 373–396.

◀◀ **Source**: Michael Atkinson is an associate professor in the Faculty of Physical Education and Health at the University of Toronto. Kevin Young is a professor in the Department of Sociology at the University of Calgary. This article was adapted by the authors from *Deviance and Social Control in Sport* (Human Kinetics, 2008). Included with permission.

# 34. Transgendered and Transitioned Athletes in the Sport System
By Rachel Corbett

## ■■■ Background

This document is based on a presentation "Transgendered and Transitioned Athletes in Our Sport System" made by transitioned female athlete Kristen Worley to staff of Sport Canada and other sport leaders in Ottawa in October 2005. As a result of the interest generated by that presentation, Athletes CAN organized a half-day workshop for sport leaders on the topic "Respecting Differences: Making Sport Inclusive" in January 2006.

Following that second workshop, an interest was expressed in pulling together this information into a short document for mission staff, and in particular medical staff, supporting Canadian teams at upcoming international games.

This document summarizes the content of the October 2005 presentation by Kristen Worley and provides some general background information on gender terms, gender dysphoria, the process of gender transition, the impacts of transition on athletes, issues arising from the IOC's policies relating to gender identity, and some thoughts about Canada moving forward on this subject.

## ■■■ Gender Terms

**Sex** is usually understood to mean the presence of genitalia (phenotype) and the presence of gonads (testes or ovaries), which will determine reproductive function. Usually, sex, gender identity, and gender role are aligned with each other and with the underlying chromosomal patterns of forty-six XX for a female and forty-six XY for a male.

**Gender** or **gender identity** is the psychological identification within the brain as male or female, that is the recognition of oneself and the desire to be regarded by others as fitting into the social categories of boy/man or girl/woman. These social categories generate expectations of gender roles, or how we are expected to behave in society.

**LGBT** is an acronym term used to refer to lesbian, gay, bisexual, and transgendered persons. There are significant differences among these four groups, and particularly between the GLB and the

T portions. Transgender identity, which has to do with gender identity, is distinctly different from gay, lesbian, and bisexual identity, which have to do with sexual orientation. In other words, transgenders are not necessarily gay or lesbian.

**Intersexed,** also called hermaphroditism, is a general term used for a variety of conditions in which a person is born with a reproductive or sexual anatomy that does not fit the typical definitions of female or male. An intersexed person will have both XX and XY chromosomes. One in 1,666 children are born intersexed.

**Androgen insensitivity syndrome (AIS)** is a condition that affects sexual development before birth and during puberty. People with this condition are genetically male, with XY chromosomes, however, as a foetus their bodies are unable to respond to the androgen hormone and as a result they have mostly female characteristics. One in 1,300 children are born with AIS.

**Klinefelter's syndrome** is a condition that typically affects males and involves the body having three chromosomes (XXY). Although anatomically male, at puberty the body matures with female characteristics due to release of estrogen. Young males with this condition develop breasts, do not grow facial hair, gain weight, and may become lethargic. One in 1,000 children are born with Klinefelter's Syndrome.

**Gender dysphoria** describes the intense and continuous discomfort a person feels when their physical sex and gender identity are not aligned. Not all people experiencing gender dysphoria seek treatment. Long before they consider medical treatment, in fact often long before they even realize what is happening within them, most gender dysphoric people will show signs of thinking and behaving in ways more usual to the sex opposite to that of their physical appearance. Because of social pressures, many gender dysphoric people enter a period of denial in their late teens, in which they try to suppress any thoughts or feelings to do with their gender identity. Gender dysphoric people suffer distress and impairment from societal intolerance, discrimination, violence, shame, and denial of personal freedoms that ordinary men and women take for granted. One in 500 children are born with gender dysphoria.

**Transgendered** is an umbrella term used to describe an array of persons whose gender identity does not conform to stereotypical norms of female or male. Twelve percent of all transgendered people pursue transition through complete surgical intervention.

## ■■■ The Transition Process

Persons experiencing gender dysphoria who choose to align their gender role and gender identity are referred to as **transitioned**. A transitioned female is a person who was born male but has become female, while a transitioned male is a person who was born female and has become male.

Transitioned individuals undergo hormonal treatment, surgery and possibly other body modifications so that they may live their lives fully as either a woman or a man. Transition is said to occur in two categories: the physical and psychological transition from one sex to the other, and the social transition with family, friends, education, community, and career.

These are some of the physical changes that occur in the male to female transitioner:

- Effects of hormones vary greatly from person to person, but noticeable effects occur within two to three months, and these are irreversible in as little as six months.
- Development of breasts (will usually be smaller than those of close female relatives)
- Softening of skin tissue
- Redistribution of body and facial fat. Over the long term, fat will migrate away from the waist and be re-deposited at the hips and buttocks, giving a more feminine figure.
- The face will become more feminine, with fuller cheeks and less angularity.

- Body hair growth reduces and body hair may lighten in both texture and colour. However, there is seldom any major effect on facial hair.

- Scalp hair often improves in texture and thickness, and male pattern baldness generally stops progressing.

- Lack of testosterone diminishes drive and motivation, as well as metabolic function and the ability to thermoregulate, all of which adversely impact athletic performance.

- Medically forced premature menopause.

- Due to estrogen administration, the pituitary gland functions continuously at a high level, preparing the body for conception, thus the transitioned female continually experiences the hormonal impact that menstruating women experience only during their periods.

- Many people report sensory and emotional changes: heightened senses of touch and smell are common, along with generally feeling more "emotional."

Female transitioners have unique long-term health concerns arising from the regular administration of estrogen including: weight gain, breast cancer, blood clotting, risk of heart attack and stroke, and depression.

These are some of the physical changes that occur in the female to male transitioner:

- Effects of the testosterone hormones is quite rapid, and thickening of the vocal cords and hair appears in as little as two weeks. A permanent deepening of the voice occurs within four months and is irreversible.

- There is some breast atrophy, but at the early stage of transition it is more common to bind the breasts.

- Menstruation ceases within a few months.

- Permanent clitoral enlargement occurs.

- There will be increased strength and weight gain particularly around the waist and upper body with decreased hip fat.

- Growth of facial and body hair is likely to follow the pattern of hair growth inherent in the family.

- Increased social and sexual interest and arousability may occur, as well as heightened feelings of aggression.

## ■ ■ ■ Transitioned Athletes and Performance

It is widely assumed that transitioned females compete at an advantage over biologically born females, although such a view is not supported by science. There is a growing body of evidence to show that transitioned females compete at a disadvantage to all other female competitors.

Transitioned women do not produce or have the means to produce testosterone during transition and after sex reconstruction surgery. Testosterone is a fundamental hormone in the bodies of both men and women and serves to regulate many body functions. Testosterone enables the body to build muscle; allows muscle recovery during and after physical activity; supports heart and lung development and recovery; supports, regulates, and burns body fat; regulates weight and the immune system; and provides overall drive and energy.

Physically born males have a testosterone level of between sixty-four and ninety-six (based on a standard blood volume scale of one hundred). After age fifty this declines by about 1% per year. Physically born females have testosterone levels of between nine and sixteen, on the same standard blood volume scale of one hundred. When such levels fall below nine, testosterone administration may be prescribed for health reasons. Typically, most high performance female athletes have testosterone levels higher than the range for an average female.

Transitioned women will lose 30 to 40% of overall muscle mass and strength during transition and after transition will have zero testosterone levels. Due to such low levels, transitioned women lose the ability to develop new muscle and have tremendous difficulty sustaining existing muscle no matter the level of output or intensity of training. They also lose the ability to recover quickly during and after exercise. Their bodies lose the ability to burn and lose fat, and even with adequate exercise, weight control becomes a significant concern.

It is now acknowledged that studies linking gender transition and athletic performance are lacking, and that many of these widely held assumptions, supported by the views of the IOC Medical Commission, are not supported by science.

### ■ ■ ■ IOC Policies on Gender

Sex testing was introduced at the 1966 European Athletics Championships in Budapest after allegations that some women competitors were technically male. Initially such testing consisted of a visual examination of athletes while naked, while later procedures were based on hair samples and DNA testing of mouth swabs. These tests attracted much criticism and were considered to be intrusive and discriminatory. Often, such tests would reveal the existence of androgen insensitivity syndrome (AIS) or other atypical gender conditions, resulting in public embarrassment and ridicule for the athlete. Many times these athletes chose to leave the competition, faking an injury, rather than face such public scrutiny. The IOC and major international sport federations continued sex testing until 1999, when it was discontinued.

In May 2004, the IOC published the Stockholm Consensus, a policy statement setting out the conditions under which individuals would be permitted to compete athletically in a sex different from their birth sex. Lacking education and awareness of gender transition issues, the global sport community has widely accepted this document, despite its flaws, as the best available guide for determining the eligibility of transitioned individuals to participate in sport.

The Stockholm Consensus permits athletes to compete in their transitioned sex if they meet several strict conditions, including having had anatomical surgery with external genitalia changes, being able to verify through medical records a course of hormonal treatment of prescribed length, and having been legally recognized as their transitioned sex. As well, all athletes are required to undergo a case-by-case medical evaluation.

In recent months however, the Stockholm Consensus has come under closer scrutiny. The December 2005 issue of *The Lancet* has acknowledged that there are very few studies specific to gender transition and athletic performance, and that the Consensus was arrived at on the basis of a limited number of studies. As noted in this document, there is also a growing body of information to suggest that the competitive advantages that a transitioned female athlete is assumed to have in comparison to a physically born female may not exist, and in fact, that transitioned females are competing at a decisive disadvantage.

There is an emerging concern that the Stockholm Consensus, in its entirety, is not only discriminatory towards individuals who undergo sex reassignment, it also places a significant burden on both the transitioned athlete and the sport organization. Further, the Consensus does not address the concerns of transitioned males, the majority of whom will not undergo anatomical surgery due to its expense and complexity.

### ■ ■ ■ Moving Forward

Recently in Canada, the sports of cycling and waterski/wakeboard have gone through the process of reinstating a transitioned female athlete. From this experience have emerged concerns about the validity of the Stockholm Consensus. Following the Athletes CAN workshop, a small group of leaders within the Canadian sport system has begun work to develop a uniform policy to guide Canadian sport federations dealing with this issue.

It is hoped that Canada might take a leadership role in the global sport community to develop strong, well-informed sport policy to ensure a balanced, educational, and safe approach to integrating transitioned women and men into all levels of sport, nationally and internationally.

◀◀ **Source**: This article is a Gay and Lesbian International Sport Association (GLISA) position paper and is available on the GLISA website (www.glisa.org). Reprinted with permission.

## 35. "I'm a Woman on the Move"
### By Anne McIlroy

Kristen Worley grabs a large pink gym bag out of her car and walks into the women's change room at the Forest City Velodrome.

She emerges in skin-tight racing gear provided by a potential new sponsor and carefully tucks her ponytail into an aerodynamic helmet for her final workout on her home course before the women's national track cycling championships, being held this weekend in Dieppe, New Brunswick. A good showing will give her a shot at qualifying for next year's Olympic Games in Beijing.

At thirty-nine, Ms. Worley is a serious contender; she has a commanding presence among the other cyclists as she travels the London, Ontario, track's steep curves at 50 kilometres an hour. And yet the muscles in her thighs and arms look beefy; they don't have the definition you might expect in someone who grinds through five or six hours a day on a bike.

The cycling skills are a holdover from what she calls her "previous life," but the extra fat is the result of leaving that life behind. In 1996, as a man named Chris, she started taking hormones to begin the process of becoming a woman. Five years later, surgery completed the transition.

"If I were to take my clothes off, you wouldn't know," Ms. Worley insists. "I'm no different than any woman who has had a hysterectomy."

It has been fifty-five years since an ex-GI named George Jorgenson realized his dreams and shocked the world by travelling to Denmark for surgery and returning to the Bronx as Christine Jorgensen. Hard numbers are still difficult to find, but a research paper presented this week at a conference in Chicago suggests that as many as one person in five hundred feels estranged from his or her body. These people are so distanced from their assigned sex that they are desperate to change it.

As a result, parents are more accepting of children who feel this way, and so are schools. Last year, a boy was admitted to a South Florida kindergarten class as a girl. A year earlier, the boy who had been elected to head a Toronto high school's student council came back after the summer holidays as a girl, and officials made sure students and teachers alike were sensitive to the situation.

The trend also has spread to the pantheon of physical perfection: athletics. A growing number of transitioned athletes now compete at an elite level. Professional mountain biker Michelle Dumaresq won the Canadian women's downhill championship last year and Danish golfer Mianne Bagger has earned a berth on the Ladies European Tour.

Like Ms. Worley, both were once men, and there are those who contend that, when it comes to world-class athletics, they simply aren't the same as other women. They challenge the notion that it's fair to have competitors who were born and raised as males pull up to the starting line with women.

At the same time, a growing number of sports experts now counter that argument; in fact, many contend that because of what they've had to do to their bodies, transitioned women are really at a physical disadvantage.

But Ms. Worley insists that the real issue is one of equality for people like her—both in sport and in broader society. She dreams of carrying the Canadian flag into the Olympics' opening ceremonies, of sending a powerful message that people who change gender aren't mentally ill or sexual deviants, that they're normal and can lead healthy, successful lives.

She, for example, is an elite water skier as well as a competitive cyclist, has a successful career as a design engineer, and is in a loving relationship with the woman she married when she was a man. They live in Toronto and hope to start a family.

"I'm a woman on the move," she says as she pulls off the track for a pit stop to make adjustments on her new bike. Sweat drips off her face, carrying flecks of mascara with it.

But is Beijing really in her future?

Sports have been part of Kristen Worley's life for as long as she can remember, an escape from the overpowering anxiety she felt even as a four-year-old, when her parents told her to toughen up or dressed her in blue and grey, not the bright colours she craved.

Born in 1967, she was adopted as a baby into a sport-minded, middle-class family in Mississauga. Little Chris had a sister four years his senior and when he got older he would skip family sailing expeditions so he could stay home and dress up in her clothes, play with her dolls, try her makeup, or relax in her sleigh bed.

Looking back, Ms. Worley says it's too simplistic to describe that she felt like she was trapped in the wrong body. It was more like there was a profound disconnect: She saw herself as a girl, yet to everybody else, she was a boy.

"Your brain is telling you one thing and your body is telling society something else."

Adolescence was difficult. The anxiety got worse and the troubling thoughts were becoming harder to suppress. It took a toll. Chris became anorexic and depressed; he started drinking, hanging out with older kids, and smoking pot.

Every month or so, he would break down and start to shake and cry, but he couldn't tell his mother what the trouble was. He didn't know. He would see the odd reference in magazines or on television to men who became women. "Oh, my god," Ms. Worley remembers thinking. "That is too far out."

He feared that he might be gay. "I don't have a homophobic bone in my body. But I knew in my heart that this was something different." Unable to express such feelings properly, "I suppressed everything."

Enter sports. Already a competitive water skier, Chris took up cross-country running and became friends with a group of top athletes in high school. That led to mountain biking and road racing, which he loved in part because it gave him an excuse to shave his legs. But he was serious about cycling and dreamed of making it to the Olympics.

"Sports saved my life," Ms. Worley says. It provided an outlet, something positive to focus on, a way that Chris could so exhaust himself that he could fall asleep rather than lay awake feeling anxious.

But then, during a road race in London, a crash took twenty riders down, Chris among them, and he broke his pelvis. He was eighteen and thought he would never ride again.

### ■ ■ ■ Lost and Found

The months that followed were painful, both physically and emotionally. Sports had been his life and, without the training regime and the races, he felt lost and left out. Then he reconnected with Alison, an old acquaintance, and recalls that when they started to talk in a bar near Peterborough's Trent University, it was as if everyone else at the table had faded into the background.

When they were married in 1993, Chris still believed that he could conquer what he was feeling. "You think that you can hold it off, that if you do masculine things, it will go away," recalls Ms. Worley, who now believes that Alison had a sense of what might be coming. "I don't think it was a huge surprise to her."

After leaving Trent, Chris had studied graphic design and illustration at the Ontario College of Art in Toronto and then begun to work in animation. While in New York for a business meeting, he had an acute anxiety attack.

"I don't know what happened, but it felt like the bottom floor dropped out of my life," Ms. Worley remembers. "All the years of suppression overcame me physically and that on-off switch was staying on … All those cross-gender thoughts weren't going away."

Chris made it to the airport and sat there sweating, shaking and thinking: "Oh my god, I'm in trouble."

With the assistance of his sister-in-law, he sought medical help, but was horrified by doctors who made him feel like a deviant. He was told that he would have to divorce Alison and should prepare to be rejected by the people he loved.

"I tried to hang myself," Ms. Worley says. "I tried to drown myself—twice."

Eventually, Chris found a physician he was comfortable with and began the transition to womanhood, choosing the name Kristen to make things easier for family and friends.

The couple have stayed together, but Ms. Worley says the change hasn't been easy for Alison. "We've been through a lot of challenges … It is really about the relationship. A lot of people don't seem to understand that. I am very lucky."

No longer in touch with her adoptive family, she now considers her in-laws her mother and father—Worley is their name. She hesitates to discuss her transition but is thrilled with the results and laughs when told no one would suspect she was once a male.

On the other hand, she is wary of rejection and wonders how each person she meets will react to her.

Before that last workout in London (the velodrome is the closest indoor track to Toronto), she met at a nearby Tim Hortons with Paul Gonsalves, a potential sponsor and distributor of Blue Competition bikes. He didn't seem to be aware of her past and she didn't bring it up, but afterward she worried that their deal—a new bike at cost—would fall through if Mr. Gonsalves weren't comfortable with who she really is.

Afterward, Mr. Gonsalves said he knew all along, but didn't want to make Ms. Worley uncomfortable. Some sponsors might think twice, he said, but all he wants to do is "help an athlete accomplish her goals and not allow equipment to be a limiting factor."

During a break later that evening, Ms. Worley tells another cyclist about her past. A former captain of the national junior women's hockey team, Heather Logan is also competing at the cycling championships this weekend.

At first, she was skeptical, she says—not certain that Ms. Worley should be included. Now, "I would want her hormone levels to be checked, but I guess it is fair."

## ■ ■ ■ Jumping with Girls

The only man ever to admit to entering the Olympics as a woman is Hermann (Dora) Ratjen, a German who bound his genitals for the 1936 Berlin Games and placed fourth in the women's high jump. Two decades later, he said the Nazis made him do it.

No transitioned athlete has ever taken part—openly, at least. But in 2004, the International Olympic Committee put in place rules that would allow it. Those rules require a confidential evaluation no earlier than two years after an athlete has undergone surgery to remove either ovaries or testicles. Surgical alterations of genitals also must have been completed by that point. (Women who become men are at an added disadvantage because their reconstruction can cost three times as much, and the results are imperfect.)

Ms. Worley has had to submit her medical records and blood work to four separate panels: the two organizations that oversee cycling and water skiing in Canada and the two that govern international competitions in both sports. (Water skiing is not an Olympic sport, but its federation is pushing to have it included.)

As well, she had to undergo questioning, something she found very difficult. Now lobbying for a more sensitive approach, she describes a conference call she had with officials of Water Ski and Wakeboard Canada as "gross."

"They were all men, and I'm sure they were thinking, 'Why would someone do this to themselves? Why would they cut their penis off?' "

Joseph Quigg, the national team's physician, was in on that call and has since become a strong supporter of Ms. Worley. He prepared for the interview by searching the scientific literature but could find very little about male athletes who had become women and whether they might enjoy a competitive edge.

Before long, he came to the opposite view: that Ms. Worley had a physical drawback because other women produce small amounts of natural testosterone in their ovaries and adrenal glands.

It's a conclusion that Sport Canada, the governing body for athletics, now shares. "There is a growing body of evidence to show that transitioned females actually compete at a disadvantage to all other female competitors," according to a government background document. "Transitioned women do not produce, nor have the means to produce, testosterone – a fundamental hormone for both men and women.

"Testosterone enables the body to build muscle; allows muscle recovery during and after physical activity; supports heart and lung development and recovery; supports, regulates, and burns body fat; regulates weight and the immune system; and provides overall drive and energy."

Last year, organizations such as the Canadian Olympic Committee, Sport Canada, and the Canadian Centre for Ethics in Sport struck a committee to address the ignorance surrounding transitioned athletes.

And Ms. Worley says she has lobbied hard to change the official view, telling the Canadian Academy of Sport Medicine and government bureaucrats how she lost muscle strength and had trouble controlling her weight. "I became an apple," she says.

Crashing fatigue has been another pitfall. She'll be in the front pack in a road race, then suddenly have no energy and fade to the back.

But not everyone feels that all the evidence is in.

Can someone who grew up with lots of testosterone really be at a disadvantage compared with "women who have never had increased levels?" asks Gabriela Tymowski, a sports ethicist at the University of New Brunswick. "Right now, we don't know. We have competing rights—Kristen's right to compete at the highest levels of sport and the rights of other women who have trained … with the female physiology from day one."

Dr. Tymowski says she put the question to students taking her course on ethics in sports and almost all of them felt that someone who used to be a man would have the upper hand. But three years ago, officialdom came to the opposite conclusion.

In 2004, both the cycling and the water-skiing associations restored Ms. Worley's accreditation, this time as a woman. They recommended that the international bodies governing their sports do the same, and those bodies agreed.

The rest is up to her. "I just have to cycle my butt off."

## ■ ■ ■ Olympic Longshot

The practice doesn't finish until 9 p.m., and even then Ms. Worley seems reluctant to get off the bike she is test-driving, the one she hopes will carry her to a berth on the national team in the 3,000-metre pursuit—an event in which two competitors start at opposite sides of the track and try to overtake each other.

But making the qualifying time—3:51:07—is just the start. Under IOC rules, Canada can't send someone to Beijing unless it has a rider in the world's top nine, says Kris Westwood of the Canadian Cycling Association. So, as well as making the national team, Ms. Worley will have to do well at international competitions, so "chances for us qualifying for the Olympics are pretty slim."

But Ms. Worley says she has a shot. "Remember Lori-Anne Muenzer?" she asks, referring to the thiry-eight-year-old Edmonton legal secretary who went from nowhere to gold in Athens.

So she has been training hard (up to six hours a day on the bike, plus weights) – but hasn't interrupted her bid to change how people think.

And change is slowly coming about. Doctors have begun to take a different approach to treating the condition formally known as gender identity disorder, or gender dysphoria.

A number of clinics, including one in Toronto, now give transgender adolescents drugs that delay puberty and stop the development of secondary sexual characteristics, such as breasts. Hormone therapy can begin at as young as sixteen, with sex-reassignment surgery at eighteen.

Ms. Worley wishes she'd had surgery as a teen – and that more doctors were like Herbert Schreier of the Children's Hospital and Research Center in Oakland, California. "We don't use the term 'gender identity disorder,'" Dr. Schreier said in an interview. "We call it 'gender variance.' The disorder comes in the minds of others."

She also is fighting to allow transitioned women athletes to take small amounts of testosterone, which would improve their health but is currently against Olympic anti-doping rules

And she has taken up the cause of Santhi Soundarajan, the Indian runner stripped of her silver medal in the 800 metres at the Asian Games last year after failing a gender test.

Ms. Soundarajan may have androgen insensitivity syndrome, the term for people who are born with male sex chromosomes—XY instead of XX—but develop as females because their bodies don't respond to male hormones.

In a letter to IOC president Jacques Rogge, Ms. Worley argues that Ms. Soundarajan should never have been subjected to gender testing.

Outside athletics, she works with young people and, last summer, when she invited some of them for a day of water skiing, one boy said he had always felt like a broken toy.

That, she says, is the kind of stigma she hopes to erase by speaking out and becoming a role model—by pushing as hard as she can on the track.

"When we think about each other, about men and women, male and female, we are all in the grey," she says. "It is not black and white for any us."

◀◀ **Source**: Anne McIlroy is *The Globe and Mail*'s science reporter. This article was originally published in *The Globe and Mail* on September 8, 2007. Reprinted with permission.

# Tewksbury Foresees Bright Future for Gay Jocks

## 36.

By James Christie

*"I really feel like in the next five years, we're going to see a major shift to where it becomes a non-issue."*

■ ■ ■ ■ ■ ■

Olympic gold-medal swimmer Mark Tewksbury has dealt with a lot more backwash since he left the pool than he did when he was one of the world's premier backstrokers.

Tewksbury, thirty-eight, outed himself as a gay athlete in 1998. He has since done a one-man show about who he is (since he couldn't tell the story as an active athlete), seen sponsors turn away because of his orientation, enjoyed a broadcast and public-speaking career, battled for athlete rights in the face of corruption in the International Olympic Committee, and become the co-chairman of this summer's inaugural Outgames in Montreal.

Check for Tewksbury on the World Wide Web these days, and the swim career is the part of his life that's in the closet. References to the 1992 Olympic record win in Barcelona and being Canada's male athlete of the year are outnumbered by references to Tewksbury's status as a touchstone for gays in sport.

"I had to come out so I could go back in," said Tewksbury, on a cross-Canada tour to launch his new book *Inside Out: Straight Talk from a Gay Jock*. "My own journey has become one of leadership, but it's hard to lead when you can't talk about what you're leading, or about who you really are."

The truth avoided by the sport world is that gay athletes exist in every sport, said Tewksbury, who says in the book that Canada's swim icon Victor Davis, who had a caveman persona, knew Tewksbury had a crush on him. Tewksbury also reveals former Canadian Olympic Association boss, the late Carol Anne Letheren, told him he had a future in the Olympic movement if he would stay in the closet. He also says he was once caught in a threesome in a bathroom cubicle with a male and female swimmer.

It was all part of the fear-based double life gay athletes still lead, Tewksbury said. "I can say for a fact they [gays and lesbians] exist in every one of the major sports, and that's from insider knowledge; and the numbers are much higher than people think in women's team sports.

"It's interesting that gay women and the gay men come at sport from a different perspective, but in the end it remains a culture of silence. For women, if you play sport, you're branded gay; from the male side, if you're gay, you can't play sports. They don't welcome you or even want you. Unfortunately, both sides keep you quiet and in the closet.

"What is truly ironic is that sport asks us to look inside and to be your absolute best at any moment. That's very tough to do when you can't acknowledge what you are."

Tewksbury expects that, for these days, while he is promoting his book and organizing the Outgames, he'll be defined as "the professional gay guy."

But, in the end, he believes that the darkest days for closeted athletes are passing. "I really feel like in the next five years we're going to see a major shift to where it becomes a non-issue," he said. "In January, Athletes Can [the association of Canada's national athletes] brought together most of the stakeholders in Canadian sport to look at different issues of diversity. They touched on racism and homophobia and what transitioned athletes go through. It indicated to me things are really shifting."

There is more acceptance of a gay reality in sport. Montreal's Outgames and this summer's Gay Games in Chicago will have more than twenty thousand participants in total, Tewksbury said.

The Gay Games are a longer-established entity with separate marketing and promotional rights. The July 29 to August 5 Outgames will involve at least twelve thousand people from more than one hundred countries in thirty-five sports and a host of cultural events: music, art, dance, stage, and comedy.

"The Outgames became community-based. We're being supported in Quebec with the sanction of all the official provincial sport governing bodies and, in the case of rowing, the sanction of the international sport federation. We have volunteers and officials from the traditional world of sport.

"That's how things start to happen," Tewksbury said.

There is still a way to travel, however, Tewksbury said. To draw a parallel to the way gay male athletes have coped to date in sport, he said, "Imagine, in the straight world, if you were accepted in the workplace for your contribution, but told you couldn't talk about your wife or your kids, or your favourite places or what you did after work and where you went on vacation. Life becomes one-dimensional. People start living in silos."

He was used to the one-dimensional tag "Mark the swimmer." Then it was "Mark the fag." Then "Mark the advocate."

"The great thing about the book is that it brought all the facets of me together in one place. I'm more at peace than I've ever been," Tewksbury said.

◀◀ **Source**: This article was originally published in *The Globe and Mail* on May 3, 2006. Reprinted with permission.

## 37. Bucking the System
### By Gordon Laird

*This week's Stampede may hog the spotlight, but the more remarkable rodeo in Calgary this summer is the tenth annual Rockies International, Canada's only gay rodeo, where the gender stereotypes that rule the pros are turned upside-down. While Premier Ralph Klein badmouths same-sex marriage, roughriding pink cowboys and cowgirls prove gays and lesbians are right at home on the range.*

■ ■ ■ ■ ■

Out on the rodeo grounds, the livestock is running wild. A steer rises up on its hind legs, a rope trailing from its neck, and takes flight, soaring briefly before crashing down, scattering cowboys left and right. Undaunted, one cowgirl charges forward, grabs the rope and pulls tight, reeling the flailing steer in. Expertly, she takes the horns of the steer and puts it into a headlock.

Then a large man in a tank top and a hula skirt hops on. Clinging to the steer's neck, he rides it bareback across the finish line, falling hard into the dirt.

This is the kind of scene you can take in at Canada's only gay rodeo. In this event, the Wild Drag Race, a cowboy, a cowgirl, and a drag queen match wits with a large steer on a long rope. Nearby, another team is pulled through the dirt as they try to control their animal. A fellow in a prom dress jumps sideways onto the beast before falling, staggering back. The steer trots off into a corner of the arena, where it stands quietly as the team staggers out of the corral, defeated.

Each year, a special group of cowboys crosses the continent—whether from Pasadena or Washington, D.C.—not for the grand spectacle of this week's Calgary Stampede, but for the Canadian Rockies International Rodeo, discreetly held on the outskirts of town. But in its tenth year, this tightly knit amateur event still boasts a majority local contingent. All around are burly cowboys and tall cowgirls who hail from Carstairs, Didsbury, Medicine Hat, Airdrie, or Dewinton.

Some are city folk who grew up in the countryside, and some are still full-time farmers and ranchers. While premier Ralph Klein argues Alberta has no stomach for gay rights, and has vowed to go down fighting before his province joins Ontario and British Columbia in recognizing same-sex marriage, the scene at this rodeo proves that gays and lesbians have been home on the range all along, part of Alberta's bedrock rural constituency.

At registration night on this weekend in late June, it looks like any other amateur rodeo, the kind you'd find in Stavley or Millarville. In hats and boots, contestants line up to enter events, mulling over details and exchanging horse talk. Like any other rodeo, it's a moment of truth—who will ride the broncs and bulls, 800 to 2,000 pounds of twisting, burning roughstock? For many contestants, it's a chance to make good on the bad luck of past years, another kick at the perfect ride or smooth catch.

It's a long way off from the cowboy grandeur of the Calgary Stampede, with its million-plus gate attendance and 500 competitors riding, roping, and racing for $1-million in cash prizes. Out here, 113 men and women ply this modest corral for a few silver beltbuckles, several thousand dollars in pocket money, and the affections of 900 spectators.

Next to me, an out-of-towner named Hamish is putting his name down for just about everything,

save for the bulls and calf roping. Although this is his first rodeo—and he'll be lucky if he can walk straight by the end—he wonders if there will be enough time for costume changes in between events. Faced with the perils of chute dogging, where contestants wrestle a steer three times their size, several other nervous first-timers ask if there's still time to enter the ever-popular goat dressing and steer decorating events.

"Well, of course you can, sister," jokes a volunteer from across the registration table. "This is gay rodeo. You can do whatever you like."

Hamish, who so boldly entered a slew of roughstock events, hails from New Zealand, where gay rodeo is unheard of. He grew up on a sheep station in the high country and often pined for the cowboy life that still thrives across the West. "I came to Canada wanting to rodeo," he says. "This seems like the real thing, you know, not just a show."

This is Canada's hidden West, the gay frontier, where cowgirls ride bulls and cowboys dress up fancy. Community, not prize money, is the focus at this rodeo. There are even a few token straight people, like myself, who attend and participate largely for the friendly mix of cowboy culture and high camp. In some ways, it is a lot like old-time rodeo, echoing the pre-war West, when cowgirls would ride broncs in competition. Except, of course, that these days the rodeo parade queen is a man.

By the time I reach the front of the registration line, my decision is made: I will calf-rope on foot, a modest skill event that's unlikely to cause permanent injury. I hand over my contestant card to Wayne Jakino, renowned rodeo announcer and founding president of the International Gay Rodeo Association. This card contains vital information—my stage name, my past rodeo history, and any personal tidbits that I'd like to share with the audience. Alas, I draw a blank on each one.

Mr. Jakino, a salty Denverite known as the great-granddaddy of the sport, sizes me up in one glance. Smiling, he scrawls "VIRGIN" in big block letters across my card, a label he'll not forget to mention over the PA system tomorrow, as I wait for a calf to bolt across my path.

On rodeo day, a large crowd gathers next to the dirt arena. On one side of the corral stands bleachers, kiosks, and PortaPotties for the public; on the other, the judges' rickety wooden platform, the animals, and the steel chutes that launch riders and bull doggers into the arena.

Contestants, officials, and volunteers continuously mill among the spectators at this two-day event. It's a Canadian polyglot—hairy leather men from Vancouver, lesbian grannies toting grandchildren, straight men who cross-dress to look like Patsy Cline, muscle-bound pretty boys in short-shorts, textbook cowboys in boots and wranglers, and scores of others who simply enjoy rodeo.

"We drove all night for this," says Ray Powder, who's from the Athabasca First Nation just outside Fort McMurray. He and three friends have escaped the confines of Canada's biggest boomtown—and the wake of a troubling gay-on-gay murder trial—to bask in the freedom of this event. The 2002 murder of Richard Sneath, a local teen who was beaten to death on a date with another gay man, underlines the perils of gay life in the hinterland.

"It's hard to build a community and feel safe when people are looking over their shoulder," says Mr. Powder, noting that rodeo has always drawn outsiders—native people, gays, lesbians—despite pressures to keep the status quo. "Even in Fort McMurray, we are 'out,' but we don't go around shouting and chanting that 'We're queer, we're here,' " he says. "I think you get the idea."

One member of the crowd who knows the challenges of country gay life very well is Louis, one of the organizers of the very first Calgary rodeo. Growing up on a farm, he faced the dual pressures of being gay and wanting to do rodeo—a sport that, at least since the 1940s, has been structured on gender-exclusive events. The men's roughstock events, such as bull riding and broncs, are rodeo's premier tickets, with big money and big crowds.

Barrel racing—a women-only event where contestants race horses around barrels in a tricky cloverleaf course—is usually second-tier in billing and prize money.

Gay rodeo, by contrast, allows open entry in all events. "When people hear the word gay, they think it's nothing but camp events," Louis says. "Instead, we've got a lot of roughstock: the women can ride whatever they want, the guys can barrel race and run flags. When I was growing up, I always wanted to barrel race. But we couldn't because it was just a girl's thing."

The very first gay rodeo was held in 1976 in Reno, Nevada, as a fundraiser for local charity. They couldn't find a stock contractor who would work with them, the story goes, so organizer Phil Ragsdale went out and found ten wild cows, ten feral range calves, one pig, and a Shetland pony. When gays led the way in the "urban cowboy" craze of the early 1980s, gay rodeo grew rapidly: By the 1990s, there were nineteen local gay-rodeo associations across North America, including Calgary's well-regarded event, which has been held every year since 1993.

"I went to my first rodeo twelve to fourteen years ago in Phoenix," says Louis, as the barrel racers take the field. "And I thought, 'My god, if they can have a gay rodeo in the States, why can't we bring one up here into Canada's ranchland?' "

Calgary's fledgling rodeo was an underground operation. Basically, people snuck around so that they could ride horses together. "One of our first events was at a riding arena," says Louis. "There were about six of us total—and two of those were my kids." It was held at an undisclosed location for fear of reprisals.

Many people still worry about being identified or targeted. Gay cowboys and lesbian cowgirls aren't always accepted back home or at work. Many contestants will not use their real names or allow photos to be taken. "There was lots of hatred back then. And there's still lots of gay-bashing," says Louis, who withholds his own last name to protect family.

Despite fears that people might sabotage or shut out gay rodeo in Alberta, organizers eventually found themselves a good venue and a reliable stock contractor. It turned out that there were a lot of gays who wanted to rodeo—and more still who wanted to throw the kind of big rainbow party seen in Toronto and Vancouver, with its unapologetic bacchanalian revelry.

There are still plenty of full-on partygoers here, but this is more than just Pride Day with horses and boots. For many gays, rodeo is an important part of their identity. "I grew up on the prairies near Lloydminster," says Louis, who now lives in the city and regularly flies around the continent for work. "We still have a farm there. And over the years, a lot of gays moved to the city because what are you going to do? This is one way of staying with that past."

Gay rodeo's upending of conventions evokes the history of the West before corporate sport, but today's mainstream rodeo remains out of reach for many, especially the women.

"The barriers to competing pro aren't the rules, but an unwillingness to sponsor women," explains Star Artz, an accomplished cowgirl backed by Medicine Hat's Desert Dolls motorcycle club. Even with sponsorship, good amateur competitors often stay amateur. Especially lesbian cowgirls.

Women are often the strongest competitors at the gay rodeo, beating men in everything from bull-riding to speed events, but it's still much harder for them to cross over to the pros. "It's a boys' club," Ms. Artz says, point-blank. "You can talk one of the [pro] cowboys into backing you, but it'll get back to him. He's got to be a person that doesn't give a damn about what the other cowboys say."

Ms. Artz came to chute dogging and steer riding because it was already a strong part of her upbringing, a working-ranch life that she returned to a few years ago. "When I was growing up," she says,

"I got dared by the boys to ride. And I kept on doing it."

Gay rodeo is often regarded as a more pure form than the pro circuit, simply because the competition is about skill and gumption, not gender. "Personally I think it's ridiculous," says one anonymous rider, who also works at the Calgary Stampede. "If you can ride, you should ride. Look at it here, there's guys who can ride barrels better than women can. So let them do it."

If men can ride barrels just as fast as women, and women can beat men on broncs, the last forty years of mainstream rodeo starts to seem like a puzzling anomaly. Just as Alberta's arguments against gay marriage seem likely to fail in the long run, there may well come a time when happily married gays and lesbians cheer on women bull riders and male barrel racers at the Stampede.

At my rodeo event, you can tell all the city boys—we try to throw the lariat like a baseball. There are many of us, hurling around rope loops in the hope that a running calf might step into one as it lands flat on the ground.

There's much applause anyway. I missed my calf, as it ran out of the chute beside me, but I looked like a real cowboy doing it, I'm told—and that, to be perfectly honest, counts for something at a rodeo, gay or straight.

While rodeos used to be run by country folk for country folk, a modern rodeo is really all about the meeting of disparate worlds. The past runs into the future, as it often does in Alberta, and gay rodeo is one of those frontiers where history is ascendant.

Calgarians Keith Purdy and his partner Rick Kennedy made headlines several weeks ago in their bid to have their union legally recognized. Now the couple is enjoying the sun at the rodeo as they wait for their human-rights appeal to go through proper channels, likely ending in a Charter case that could crack open gay marriage in Alberta.

But Mr. Purdy doesn't blame Mr. Klein for his hardline stand against gay marriage. It's predictable, he says, given the internal politics of his cabinet and the vocal-minority influence of the religious right. What's strange is how surprisingly forward Alberta's Conservative government has sometimes been on other same-sex policies, while fighting gay lawsuits tooth and nail.

"They are very progressive with other legislation: Bill 30 spousal benefits, same-sex healthcare," says Mr. Purdy. "But at the same time they're holding back so that they don't appear to their rural voters and rural supporters that they're just giving in and going with the flow."

The irony, as this rodeo so plainly shows, is that gays are rural too. And with the support of diverse groups like EGAL, Amnesty International, and the Alberta Civil Liberties Union, the quest for gay marriage here is starting to look like Preston Manning's crusade against big government: Eliminate protocol, stay grassroots, make things equal. "It's all process, it's all political, it's all red tape," says Mr. Purdy. "Red tape in Alberta, who'd figured?"

Back in the throng of partygoers and drag queens, Louis still can't believe how gay rodeo has grown in ten years. With more contestants than ever before—over 25% more than last year—organizers actually had to order more stock last night to keep everyone in broncs and steers. "Look at the diversity," he says. "We've got one of everything here—doctors, teachers, cowboys. People come from all over to see the West, the gay West."

As the day winds to a close, everyone gets ready for bull riding, the heart of any rodeo. Bulls don't care if you're gay or straight—they just want to get you. The rodeo bull is a predator, no mistake about it. The compulsion to ride these wild things probably goes back to the days when we scratched drawings on cave walls, unsure of our place on nature's food chain.

Standing behind the chutes with the other contestants, I can hear the bulls from the other side of the stockyard: They emerge from the backlot, banging along the steel fencing that runs beneath the rodeo platform and, braying and snorting, shuffle into the narrow chutes single file, where guillotine doors slam behind them and they stand, full of menace and energy, waiting to launch across the arena. At this point, everything changes. The boards underneath your feet rumble, the riders draw back a little, people talk less.

When the bull kicks against the chute, it echoes like a gunshot. Its lumbering mass, upwards of 2,000 pounds, affects a peculiar gravity. It compels riders to rig up and lower themselves into the metal cage of the closed chute where the bull waits, even when all good sense says otherwise.

After a long pause, the rider calls "Pull!" and in a second the gate swings open, followed by a rush of air as the bull accelerates sideways into the arena. The bull kicks high and all four hooves leave the ground. For the next six seconds, the animal rushes forward into a clockwise spin, orbiting along some unknown axis. The rider leans back hard and rocks against the furious pitch of the bull, one hand waving free.

When the horn finally sounds, the bull continues to fight and a pickup horse hovers near. The rodeo clown, known as the Bullfighter, tries to coax the animal out of its spin, drawing it out for the chase. Because there really isn't a graceful way to exit a bullride, the rider simply unravels her roped hand and rolls off backward into the dirt, instinctively covering her head as the bull's rear hooves slice the air above.

Then the only sound is the low roar of the crowd—because Anne-Marie Champagne has just finished the ride of her life. No one else today comes close, not even the men. And it ends, just like that, in a cloud of dirt with a cowgirl limping off the field, and everybody smiling.

◀◀ **Source**: Calgary-based writer Gordon Laird is the author of *Power* (2002) and *Slumming It at the Rodeo: The Cultural Roots of Canada's Right-Wing Revolution* (1998). This article was originally published in *The Globe and Mail* on July 12, 2003. Reprinted with permission.

# Throwing in the Towel on Homophobia

## By Erin Anderssen and Jeff Blair

**38.**

*Recent progress in gay rights doesn't appear to have made it to the locker room. For athletes who feel they must choose between their identity and the love of the game, Brendan Burke's coming out has got the sports world talking—and that's a start.*

■ ■ ■ ■ ■ ■

Brendan Burke's target was the locker room, that traditional space of gay slurs and macho pranks. When the twenty-year-old former goalie revealed his homosexuality to the sports world this week, he knew the fact that his father, Brian Burke, is the general manager of the Toronto Maple Leafs would shape the headlines. But it's the guys on the bench he wants to reach.

"The important thing is that it's started a discussion," he told *The Globe and Mail* in an exclusive interview, "and people realize there could be a gay person next to them in the locker room."

And for many gay athletes—and a growing number of their straight teammates—that's a discussion long overdue in sports, which one Canadian expert called "the last bastion of homophobia." Despite the recent progress made in same-sex rights, gay athletes can't be certain of their welcome, especially in team sports such as hockey and football—it's not a coincidence that there are no openly gay athletes playing professional sports. Many former high school and university athletes describe how they faked being straight, joining in the locker-room banter about "faggots," pretending to pick up girls.

"As a young guy, it's a decision: Do I want to be gay or do I want to be an athlete?" says Jay MacDonald, thirty-one, an alpine skier in high school and former captain of the cross-country team at the University of New Brunswick, who

spent several years flirting with women in front of his fellow runners before revealing he was gay. "I chose to be an athlete."

Many others make the opposite choice: avoiding sports altogether in high school for fear of being found out, returning only as adults to the game they missed.

But there are steady signs of change. Earlier this year in New Brunswick, the Woodstock High School Lady Thunder hockey team united to support two players who had recently told their teammates they were gay. Facing another team, the insults escalated on and off the ice, to the point where the opponents refused to shake hands. "You expect attention," says Sierra Paul, sixteen, now the team captain, who made the decision last December to change her Facebook page to say she likes girls. "But you don't expect hatred. It's a slap in the face out of nowhere."

"They started treating the fact that they were gay like a disease," says sixteen-year-old right-winger Hannah Steeves. "If anybody touched them on the ice, or if we fell on them, they'd be like, 'Get off me, lesbian.' I was sick of it."

A close-knit group of friends in the small town 100 kilometres west of Fredericton, the players began speaking out. Along with the coaches and some parents, they wore anti-homophobia pins, even sharing them with players they met at a tournament who'd faced a similar experience. This fall, the Woodstock players received a provincial human rights award. (The other team, who they won't identify, eventually apologized.)

But Adam Tittley, twenty-four, remembers long years when the gay taunts flew around the locker room and no one spoke up—not even him. A former member of the junior national water polo team, the Montreal native says he used sports to disguise his sexuality and fit in. "In my mind, gay men were not good at sports. If I could swim that much faster, score one more goal, nobody would suspect me."

So he lived undercover, getting a girlfriend, watching quietly when his teammates would bully another player by casting them as gay. "It was mean and cruel, and it was what guys did to each other," Mr. Tittley says. "Everything I did, I did to survive."

But several years ago, he quit water polo. Hiding his identity was weighing on him, and he just didn't love it any more. "No one knew who I really was," says Mr. Tittley, who now rock climbs. "I couldn't stand to be in that environment."

But sometimes, the reaction to finally coming out doesn't match the fear of being found out—Brendan Burke says the emails, telephone calls and postings on his Facebook page have been bereft of negative comments.

When Kelly Granley, twenty-four, a former Junior A hockey player in Red Deer, Alberta, now working as a youth adviser at an Edmonton school board, came out to his teammates in high school, some of the parents had a harder time dealing with the news, refusing to let their sons share a hotel room with him. The players, many of them good friends, accepted him—partly, Mr. Granley believes, because he handled the situation with humour.

"That was a gay play," they'd say. And he'd joke, "Oh, do you mean in a good way?" He doesn't think the trash talk, which came across as homophobic, is the issue—he's done it himself, he says, as part of the game. The problem lies with old-school coaches, Mr. Granley believes, an issue that will correct itself as the next generation takes team management positions.

Trevor Ritchie, a nineteen-year-old student at the University of British Columbia who came out to his junior team in September, got more support than he was expecting: As a surprise, his teammates chose pink for their uniform. "I can't stand pink," he says, laughing. "I don't know what they were thinking. But I appreciate the gesture."

But athletes concede that it's easier to tell their fellow players when they are either at the top of their game—as Mr. MacDonald was—or have already stopped playing, as in Mr. Tittley's case. For both men, the reaction was accepting. But the young high-school athlete, especially a player who's not a star, or lives in a small town, has more pressure to stay quiet.

Canada's high-school atmosphere still sets an anti-gay tone: A new national survey of 3,600 students in twenty school districts, conducted by researchers in Manitoba, found that 70% reported hearing homophobic comments every day—and that's outside the locker room.

Ryan Powell, for instance, who grew up in a small Alberta city, and who kept his sexuality quiet all through high school, stopped playing sports when he was in Grade 6. "I just stepped away from the controversy of being found out," says Mr. Powell, now thirty, who works in the hotel industry in Vancouver. He has picked up soccer again by playing on a gay-friendly team in the city—a trend that has developed rapidly over the past ten years, to include soccer and hockey leagues, and a rugby team called the Muddy York in Toronto.

By coming out, Mr. Burke has helped open the door for other high-level gay athletes to join him, says Roger LeBlanc, a kinesiology professor at the University of Moncton, who studies the issue. But to really change the sports environment, he says, players' associations need to crack down on anti-gay behaviour, and straight athletes need to start speaking up against the homophobic atmosphere in locker rooms.

"People follow by example," says Alyssa McLean, seventeen, assistant captain and the other openly gay player on the Woodstock High School team. Her teammate Ms. Steeves puts it this way: "It's like when you're in high school, and the teacher asks an awkward question, and everyone looks around. And once one person raises their hand, everybody feels free to do it."

◀◀ **Source**: This article was originally published in *The Globe and Mail* on November 27, 2009. Reprinted with permission.

# Section 7

## Race, Ethnicity, and Sports

**A**lthough Canada's multiculturalism policies have helped Canadians from many different racial and ethnic backgrounds to live together, and Canada's multicultural diversity is the envy of many nations who are struggling with issues of racial and ethnic strife, racial and ethnic relations in Canada are by no means perfect. And, despite frequent claims that sport is "colour blind," it is obvious that problems evident in the wider society will also be evident in sports.

The first three articles in this section deal with First Nations people in Canada. John Stackhouse's article, "The Healing Power of Hockey" looks at Native Canadian hockey in The Pas, Manitoba. Despite ongoing examples of racism, and strained relations between Native and non-Native communities following the rape and murder of a young Native woman by non-Native men, Stackhouse shows how hockey helped to restore relations in the community.

In her article, Laura Robinson reminds us that, despite all of the claims of inclusion of First Nations in the lead up to the Vancouver Olympics, "VANOC draws on indigenous symbols but fails to support indigenous athletes." She points out that, of the 331 Canadian athletes that competed at the 2008 summer Olympics in Beijing, the only Native athlete was Monica Pinette, a Métis. There were **no** First Nations athletes on the Canadian team at the 2010 Vancouver Olympics. Robinson's article is a critique of VANOC, but also a more widespread critique of the Canadian sport system.

Laura Robinson's theme of lack of support for First Nations athletes continues in her article "The Loneliness of the Native Athlete." The article is an important reminder that although distinctions are often made based on gender or sexuality, race or ethnicity, and social class, such distinctions are necessarily artificial. "Each of us has a gender, a social class background and a racial/ethnic affiliation; we live our lives in some combination of these three (and other characteristics); and we relate to each other on the basis of ours and theirs" (Donnelly, 1993, page 417). Race/ethnicity and social class come together in Robinson's article in terms of the ability to afford access to sporting sites and facilities. Indeed, "the three resources or services that rank highest in helping Canadians to be active are infrastructure supports: access to safe streets and public places; affordable facilities, services and programs; and paths, trails and green spaces" (*Physical Activity Monitor*, 1997).

In his article, "Where have you gone Jackie Robinson?" Bob Levin looks back at how Jackie Robinson made his professional debut in Canada, playing for the Montreal Royals in 1946 before going on to break the racial barrier in U.S. baseball with the Brooklyn Dodgers. Levin contrasts this with the fact that, in 2003, the *Toronto Star* proclaimed that the Toronto Blue Jays were "the whitest team in baseball" (i.e., had the fewest minority players). Levin also contrasts the philosophies of two baseball general managers—J. P. Ricciardi of the Blue Jays, who claims to be "colour blind" and only focused on hiring white players because they were less expensive and they fitted his system of play; and Omar Minaya of the New York Mets, who actively sought to hire players who would reflect the diverse New York City community, and therefore attract more fans. The article raises an important question of representation—should professional sports teams attempt to represent the communities in which they play? These are precisely the type of representation and distribution issues addressed by Guylaine Demers with regard to gender and coaching in the previous section. Laura Robinson's article "Put Race Back in Racing" also addresses this issue (see "Additional Suggested Readings and References").

Participation in sports has often been a struggle for Muslim and Sikh Canadians when dress codes for sport have conflicted with religious or cultural practices. For Sikhs, referees in sports as diverse as boxing and soccer have attempted to prevent players from wearing the patka or the turban, while Muslim women have encountered the same obstacles with regard to wearing a hijab or attempting to dress modestly (e.g., keeping arms and legs covered). These issues are slowly being resolved in sports, but not easily. Tu Thanh Ha's article, "Muslim Woman Wears her Hijab and a Black Belt with Pride," shows the division in the world of tae kwon do, with one international federation supporting the wearing of the hijab and the other banning it.

Finally, Lindsey Craig asks, "Where are the Minorities?" The number of young Canadian boys playing hockey is static or declining. The reasons include cost, risk of injury and, it has to be said, the whiteness of the sport which, along with other cultural factors, has reduced hockey's appeal among minority and new immigrant communities. The 2010 International Hockey Summit in Toronto specifically addressed ways in which to make the game more appealing to new Canadians and visible minorities.

**Additional Suggested Readings and References**

- Donnelly, P. 1993. "Democratization Revisited: Seven Theses on the Democratization of Sport and Active Leisure." *Loisir et Société / Society and Leisure*, 16(2): 413–434.
- Hicks, B. 2009. "Hard Times Ahead for National Sport." CBC Sports, January 12.
- Jimenez, M. 2009. "Scoring Points with Newer Canadians." *The Globe and Mail*, March 13.
- Mick, H. 2009. "Broadening the Bonspiel." *The Globe and Mail*, November 19.
- Paperny, A.M. 2010. "Youth Hockey Reaches Out to New Canadians." *The Globe and Mail*, April 21.
- The Canadian Fitness and Lifestyle Research Institute. 1997. *Physical Activity Monitor*. CFLRI: Ottawa.
- Reinhart, A. 2009. "Mahriaa Shot, Keeta Goal!" *The Globe and Mail*, April 25.
- Robinson, L. 2000. "Put Race Back in Racing: Do Canada's Mostly White Olympic Coaches Need an Affirmative-Action Program?" *The Globe and Mail*, August 11.
- Wiwa, K. 2002. "Gentleman Jarome." *The Globe and Mail*, February 9.

# 39. The Healing Power of Hockey
## By John Stackhouse

### ■■■ More Than a Game

The final words of "O Canada" as it's sung in Cree are still reverberating in the rafters when the arena's overflow crowd begins hurling the high-pitched invective that every junior hockey team travelling to northern Manitoba has come to dread.

"Hey, loser!" a big man from the Opaskwayak Cree Nation (OCN) shouts at the visiting goalie, Reg Legace, from Winkler in Mennonite country, a seven-hour drive to the south. "Faggot!" adds a man from The Pas, a dreary mill town across the Saskatchewan River from the reserve.

"Pull yourself before it's too late!" yells "Mouse," another Native man who is perched behind the Winkler net and hammering the glass with a puck in a bid to throw Legace off his game. Mouse is also the goal judge.

The verbal deluge seems to work. Less than a minute into game two of the provincial finals, the home team's star forward, Justin Tetrault, a Métis, takes a pass from captain Terence Tootoo, who is Inuit, and blasts it home.

Before Mouse can flash the red goal light, the Gordon Lathlin Memorial Centre is shaking with the sound of air sirens, noise makers, and the woodsy voices of 1,248 people from two communities that once were the most racially divided in Canada. To the sounds of Bachman Turner Overdrive ("You Ain't Seen Nothing Yet") the Crees, Métis, whites, and the odd Inuit embrace in the stands, and on the ice.

For the next two hours, the modest Native-owned arena overlooking The Pas will rock with delirium as the OCN Blizzard trounce the Winkler Flyers and build a commanding lead in their run for a third straight provincial championship—a feat not seen in Manitoba in nearly thirty years.

But in the racially mixed stands, most people know that the Blizzard's sudden dominance is about much more than hockey. In this isolated town and reserve, which straddle the Saskatchewan River 600 kilometres northwest of Winnipeg, the team has built a bridge that people once thought impossible.

It was near the arena site, thirty years ago, that a Cree woman named Helen Betty Osborne was murdered after being sexually assaulted by men from The Pas.

The horrible crime was followed by one of the darkest periods for race relations in modern Canadian history, as the entire population of The Pas joined in a notorious conspiracy of silence.

For an entire decade, townspeople who knew the killers refused to identify them. Finally, one of the attackers, unable to bear his guilt any longer, went to the police.

Only one generation later, the Native-owned Blizzard has used a mixed-race team and integrated home crowd to start a new chapter for both the town and reserve.

"I really believe it was the hockey club that bridged the divide," says Gary Hopper, mayor of The Pas, which is one of the Blizzard's top corporate sponsors. "When the team was announced, people bought season's tickets [he has two] and all of a sudden there was white sitting beside Native, a total mix, and new friendships developing."

Amazingly, he says, "You would be hard pressed to find two communities that get along better."

Although only five years old, the Blizzard has left its mark on the record book, trouncing established clubs from the south game after game. Before the 2001 playoffs, it won fifty of its sixty regular-season games with players from so many communities that its coach calls it "the United Nations of hockey."

It is also one of the struggling Manitoba Junior Hockey League's few financial successes. Not only does the team sell out most home games, its bruising style of hockey packs so many arenas on the road that it has been credited with saving a league that, ironically, once ostracized Cree players.

In wins, pennants, and box-office receipts, the OCN Blizzard may be the most successful new sporting franchise on the Prairies. Which may be the reason people still wonder, when the hugs and high-fives are finished, why Perry Young killed himself.

### ■ ■ ■ The Blizzard Calms a Racial Storm

The story of the Blizzard's lightning success, the harmony it has restored between two communities, and the tragic loss of the best hockey player the reserve has produced in a generation has its source in a river of racial tension that persists despite the Cinderella story on ice.

Born in 1981, a full decade after the Osborne murder, Perry Young grew up on a reserve that knew little of the antagonism or poverty that had shaped its past. Like most of the 1,500 residents, he lived in a subdivision of compact prefab homes, played on the reserve's nine-hole golf course and attended its $9.5-million school.

People on both sides of the river still marvel at the transition. Only a generation ago, they had a situation that was as close as Canada could get to the Deep South. The seven thousand residents of The Pas never crossed the river to the reserve, and the Natives went to town only to shop, drink, or go the movies, where they were expected to sit in a separate section.

The division was about more than segregation; it spoke the unstated but common belief in both communities that the Crees were inferior people. Band councillor Henry Wilson remembers going to watch westerns with his boyhood friends and, even though they had to sit in the Indians-only section, "when we came home, every one of us wanted to be cowboys. No one wanted to be an Indian."

Discomfort turned to antagonism in 1971 after the Helen Betty Osborne killing, which became international news and the subject of a film. Whites still joke about "HBO, The Movie," in which an entire town was presented to the world as conspirators to murder.

But while the killing further divided the communities, more fundamental changes also were under way. Once bold enough to call itself "Chicago of the North," The Pas was in steady decline as its timber-based economy wilted.

Across the river, a more positive change was afoot: OCN was emerging from the Osborne case as one of Manitoba's more forward-looking bands. Money from a land-claim settlement with the federal government was invested in a modern hotel, high school, the hockey arena, and the region's biggest shopping mall, a dream of the late chief Gordon Lathlin, who had tired of having his people ignored by shopkeepers in The Pas.

The new school and rink meant that white and Indian kids rarely saw each other, not even for peewee hockey. Rather than share the ice, Cree teams drove all the way to Thompson (about 400 kilometres) away for tournaments, while The Pas kids went to Winnipeg.

The reserve's new mall proved to be almost as divisive. Local shopkeepers—the ones who had refused to serve Natives—claimed that, with the allure of an IGA grocery store, Saan department store, Tim Hortons, and Shell station, it would siphon off their business. Vandals smashed the mall's windows.

But instead of anyone losing business, retailers on both sides of the river began to see a steady rise in traffic as the mall helped the twin communities to become a shopping magnet for northern Manitoba.

Then the Crees began lobbying for a junior hockey team.

Ever since The Pas had lost its beloved Huskies when the old northern Manitoba league folded in the 1980s, no one from the town had been willing, or able, to provide financing for a new team. The Crees, for once, were in a better position. They had a $50-million-a-year business operation to backstop a new sports franchise, and a game plan to sell junior hockey to the north.

The struggling MJHL was not so sure. Its teams were so leery of making the long bus trips north—to "Indian country," they called it—that they demanded that OCN pay travel costs for visiting teams. The band agreed, and the league responded by waiving its usual waiting period. Instead of two years, OCN was asked to have a team on the ice in four months.

### ■ ■ ■ The Pride of OCN

The arrival of a Junior A franchise on the reserve was about the biggest day of Perry Young's life. He and his brother, Mike, were the stars of their midget team, and eagerly awaited the tryouts. The band council had told everyone that the new team was very much about giving opportunities to local boys like Perry, who was quickly nicknamed "the Pride of OCN."

But the band also believed in success; after all, it had built a small-business empire. It decided to hire the best coach and managers, regardless of race, and soon there was pressure from many reserve residents to recruit players the same way.

"How OCN operates is epitomized by this team," says Jim Smith, one of the Blizzard's founders. "We get the best management we can."

The band put up $100,000 to bring in a coach and a general manager from Saskatchewan. It renovated the dressing rooms and training room to semi-pro standards. And it allowed the new management team to scour Western Canada for the best players available.

Perry Young was among the first cuts. Still, with sixteen Natives on the first year's roster and a physical style of Northern hockey, the Blizzard became known as a Native team. As a result, the players, Native or not, discovered the true feelings of some Prairie people. On road trips, they were jeered as "welfare bums" and "drunks." In one arena, security guards were stationed in the sections where Blizzard fans sat. A now-defunct website claiming to represent the MJHL went so far as to state that OCN home games were always sold out because "they're all on welfare."

Even when the Blizzard shocked the league by making the playoffs in its debut season, the racism did not let up. Phillip Albert, a player from remote Norway House, says an opposing coach once yelled "fucking Indian" at him. His childhood friend, Clifford Scatch, says another coach called him "a brown, buck-toothed Indian," but he says it does not bother him. "Racism, I'm used to it. I've had it my whole life. If I ever hear a remark, I let it blow by."

In time, the Blizzard came to be seen as some kind of ghetto for Native players. Jerry Mosiondz, an assistant coach, noticed that other teams had begun to call, offering to trade their own Native players. "They usually say, 'We think he would fit in there,' " Mosiondz says. "I ask, 'If the boy's a good hockey player, why doesn't he fit in with you?' "

Still, the more the Blizzard won, the less the Crees seemed to care about affirmative action on the ice. When the team, in its third season, set a league record for wins and captured the provincial championship, the fans clamoured for more star players to help reach the national finals. The Cree management agreed, and dropped one of its original goals: a roster that's two-thirds Native.

By last year, the team that once dressed sixteen Native players was down to six, and only one who was local—a Métis boy from The Pas. Coach Kerry Clark (brother of former Toronto Maple Leafs captain Wendel Clark) used his connections across Canada, and a handsome budget from the Crees, to acquire the best players under twenty-one he could find.

By season four, Perry Young, the Pride of OCN, was one of those players. He came to training camp with added strength and speed—and pressure. When he did not get as much ice time as other players, local fans, including his uncle Danny, who was on the team's board of directors, demanded to know why. Clark told the board that Perry routinely arrived late for practice, sometimes still drunk from the night before. Then, a couple of months into the season, Perry simply stopped showing up.

Clark struck his name from the roster, and was called a "racist" to his face at a community meeting. A second man demanded that he resign, but many more people supported him. They liked the championship banners draped over centre ice—it gives their kids something to dream about, they said.

They also like being the centre of Manitoba hockey's attention, and they enjoy driving to distant places such as Winkler and watching their team whip the opposition.

Perhaps most of all, they liked the idea that townspeople now drive to the reserve for entertainment, and pay the Native band for it.

Last year, the arena's concession stand alone contributed almost $50,000 to OCN minor hockey teams, which travelled to Long Island, N.Y., and British Columbia and this winter plans to go to Sweden.

In time, Perry Young faded from view and the team did not hear much about him until the summer of 2000, when his girlfriend had a baby boy. She then kicked him out of their house, telling him to sober up before he could move back. That September, while on a binge, Perry pushed his way into the house, took a carving knife from the kitchen and, in front of his girlfriend and baby, stabbed himself five times in the heart. His mother, Marlene, reached the scene within minutes, but he was already gone.

To this day, she believes that the hockey team bears some responsibility for her son's suicide. She feels that its emphasis on winning has overshadowed the many social problems that Native kids often carry. If Perry drank, it was because he had to carry the expectations of a community, she says.

"They did say local boys break the rules, come late. I've heard people say it about our kids: 'They're drunks. They're lazy. They're no good,' " Marlene says. "Who are they to judge that these [non-Native] Blizzard don't break the rules? They turn around and treat them better than our kids."

So now she refuses to let her eldest son, Mike, try out for the Blizzard (he plays for the Southeast Blades, the province's only other junior Native team), and talks about leaving the community so that her youngest, ten-year-old Garrett, can play elsewhere.

## ▪▪▪ The Subtle Differences

The day after OCN's big win, racism seems to be the last thing on anyone's mind as the Blizzard board a chartered bus bound for Winkler, seven hours south across a dreary table of farmland, frozen lakes and forests still sprinkled with snow. Because its fans have booked every hotel room in the Winkler area, the team will spend the night in Winnipeg. Even so, the coach is in a good mood, joking about what southern Manitoba's Mennonites may do to his team.

"Be careful," he warns the players, who seem more interested in a copy of Playboy. "I hear the Winkler fans will throw Bibles at you."

For the rest of the journey, there is little to do but watch videos, play *Survivor* trivia—and show off. Most of the players remove their shirts to show off their pecs and abs. Other than race, there is not much to distinguish them. They are all sixteen to twenty, and most have dyed their hair blond—but not Steve MacIntyre, a Saskatchewan farm boy, and Ryan Braun, from a remote northern Cree reserve. They have shaved their heads.

The players like to say they stay as one, whether on the ice or in school or at a party. Even the Natives prefer to have billets across the river in The Pas, where houses typically are less crowded than on the reserve.

But there are subtle differences, which the Native players quietly say is why their numbers are so few.

The team's top Native scorer, Jamie Muswagon from Cross Lake, about 300 kilometres northeast of The Pas, says he and the other Cree players like to go hunting and ice fishing together. They don't need a licence, for one thing, and out in the wild, they can talk freely about the isolation that shaped their upbringing in hockey.

Muswagon first left home to play in Brandon, west of Winnipeg, but at sixteen he felt so alienated that he went back to Cross Lake every other weekend. Many Native hockey careers end at the midget level because leaving a close-knit community proves too painful.

The Native players also talk about Perry, but only a little. They agree that he broke the team rules. He missed practices. He drank heavily. Some of them understand why, but that does not mean they want to pay a price on the ice because of it. "Some of our players don't buy into the 'program'—the drinking, the after-hours stuff," says Jim Smith, the team's early backer. "Sometimes the youth, they may have the talent, but not all that it takes to be a hockey player."

But slowly, he believes, the Blizzard's discipline is rubbing off on a younger generation. "They're starting to understand hockey is not just a sport, it's a lifestyle, the development of a human being."

Others are not so sure, not when so many Aboriginal players must struggle growing up on remote and often socially dysfunctional reserves. Even athletes face the same stigmas, says former team manager Derek Fontaine, who played professional hockey. "The thing that pisses me off," he says, "is that, once a Native kid has a couple of beers, he is given that stereotype: he's a boozer."

Fontaine now manages the Southeast Blades, which last season carried fourteen Native players as well as Perry's Young's brother, Mike, but had the worst record in the league. With just seven wins in sixty-four games, the franchise was on the brink of financial collapse.

Talent is not the problem, Fontaine argues. "I say Native kids playing hockey are more gifted than a lot of non-Native kids—they're just naturally gifted. But when it comes to making that next step, the discipline is not there ... There's just too much love." Parents "love their kids to the point where, if the kids do something wrong, they won't correct it," he explains

Last season, the Blades cut a seventeen-year-old player over chronic alcohol and drug abuse. When Fontaine called the young man's grandmother, who was his guardian, she would not believe what he told her.

As the Blizzard bus passes through the first scattered settlements between Manitoba's big lakes,

and another action-thriller video begins, a few players at the back eat potato chips and talk about their own struggles with hockey off the ice.

Braun, a brick-like forward from the hamlet of Wabowden, north of The Pas, had to drive with his father 100 kilometres every day to his midget team's practice and games in Thompson. Most of his friends couldn't count on a parent to make the same trip. Finally, his own parents grew tired of the driving, and paid $400 a month for him to billet with a Thompson family, on top of the $1,300 a year they spent on equipment and arena fees.

Tootoo, the Inuit team captain from the Northwest Territories, faced a greater challenge while learning to play hockey in Rankin Inlet. The town had an arena, but not enough players to form two teams, so everyone played shinny—it was impossible to play a proper game. Tootoo didn't learn a set position until he moved to Thompson when he was sixteen, and a coach once benched him for chasing the puck all over the ice.

He made the transition well enough to lead the league in scoring, but he knows how many people feel. "I kept hearing things like, 'You guys aren't going to make it.' There's a lot of 'downs' in Native communities—drugs, alcohol."

But he does not despair for Aboriginal kids—they just have to be tougher, he says, in body and spirit. He has not forgotten what his father told both him and his brother, Jordan, who plays for the Brandon Wheat Kings: that hockey could be their ticket out of Rankin Inlet.

"I have no respect for those kids who just give up," he says. "I see those guys when I go home for the summer and they're doing nothing. If you give up, you'll be a nobody."

### ■ ■ ■ "There isn't a white way of passing"

The bus reaches Winnipeg by late afternoon, leaving the team enough time to plow through an all-you-can-eat buffet, drive through the red-light district for amusement, and reach their airport hotel by dark. They will head to Winkler, just shy of the U.S. border, the next day.

Until then, coach Clark does not want any more distractions. He fears that his players will buckle under the pressure of Winkler, whose rich soil produces more than an abundance of grain. The farming town is home to a big new Mennonite church, pleasant subdivisions and a sprawling recreation park with its own waterslide. Winkler and The Pas could be in different provinces.

Clark jokes again about the prosperous Mennonites as the bus turns into the hotel, but then turns serious. The game "has nothing to do with race," he says. "It has everything to do with who you are. I look at it as I'm trying to coach hockey, not coach colour. There's only one way to pass a puck. There isn't a white way of passing."

He is an outsider, but this view seems to be gaining acceptance in the two communities his hockey team has brought together. Once angry and segregated, they are carefully seeking out new ways to work together. For example, in summer, OCN dancers demonstrate their prowess at the rodeo put on by Kelsey, the rural municipality that surrounds the reserve and The Pas. Kelsey's residents are mostly non-Native farmers, but they have hired the reserve to provide firefighting services, while the reserve has provided half the funding for a new homeless program in The Pas run by the Anglican church.

Together, the town, reserve, and Kelsey also put together a successful bid for the 2002 Manitoba winter games, and are now lobbying for a bigger regional health centre. Almost without fail, the mayor, the chief, and the reeve show up at each other's events. The chief refers to Hopper as "our mayor," and Hopper gives visitors lapel pins both for his town and OCN.

The cooperation goes beyond public relations. When rural teens mugged some Natives in The Pas and declared themselves to be a gang called "White Power," the heads of the three communities met the kids (who had been tracked down by the RCMP) and their parents to discuss what had happened. No charges were laid. White Power has not been heard from since.

This once-improbable racial unity appears in Winkler when the Blizzard arrive for the game. Half of the spacious new arena, with its orderly stands and well-stocked snack bar, is filled with well-dressed local people. But on the other side, behind the visiting team's bench, there must be seven hundred raucous OCN fans, with their obnoxious air horns and vulgar chants.

Against the crisply painted white stands, their dark and light faces resemble a northern patchwork; their denim jackets and cowboy hats an alien costume in the pristine south; their melding of Cree and English insults a bizarre dialect. By contrast, the most radical offering from the Winkler side comes before the game, with an electric guitar version of "O Canada."

The action begins and Winkler takes the lead, but the Blizzard fans do not let up. "Legace: You're a LOSER!" they shout at the goalie, whose standing-room-only hometown crowd can muster only a few prep-school cheers in return.

"Go white go!" the Winkler crowd shouts, referring to the colour of their players' jerseys, not their skin, as one by one the fleet-footed Flyers are hammered into the boards.

By the third period, the Blizzard's awesome hitting power has filed down the Flyers like a jagged piece of metal. OCN ties the game, and then, a few minutes into overtime, Jamie Muswagon, the star scorer from Cross Lake, puts it away.

The home crowd turns silent and leaves, trying not to notice the many hues on the other side blowing horns and waving OCN banners.

### ■ ■ ■ Home to a Feared Champion

The next evening, Winkler's chance to cheer ends with the opening anthem. The Blizzard score three times in the first eleven minutes. In effect, the series is over, and in the third period, goalie

Reg Legace comes out of the game—to a huge ovation from the OCN delegation.

After just five years in business, the Blizzard have won their third Manitoba title. They go on to lose to Saskatchewan's champions, the Weyburn Red Wings, in the qualifying round for the national championship tournament. But not without a fight. About four hundred OCN fans, including a group that chartered three small airplanes, travelled to southern Saskatchewan for the series, which ended four games to two.

But winning the three consecutive provincial titles, the OCN did what no Manitoba team has done since the 1970s—since before Perry Young was born, since the days when two nations were segregated in The Pas cinema, since the time of Helen Betty Osborne.

Once an easy target for racists, the Cree Nation is now home to a feared champion. They are on top of their province, and want to show it in a new way.

After the season, Kerry Clark quit to take a job in the Western Hockey League. The Blizzard promptly recruited a new coach, Glen Watson, from the WHL and told him to win the championship yet again.

He will have to do so without Terence Tootoo, who has graduated from the junior ranks, turned pro, and gone even farther south to the Roanoke Express of the East Coast Hockey League.

But, remarkably, the Blizzard's Cree stars all turned down offers to move to stronger leagues. They prefer to stay with a Native-owned team, playing on Native land, most likely dreaming of yet another title. It is hardly an impossible dream, considering that this season the team is off to the best start in its history—twenty wins and just one loss going into Friday night's game against the Dauphin Kings.

And the fans had nothing less in mind when they packed the gravel parking lot outside the Lathlin arena for a tailgate party before the season opener. As barbecues crackled, and beer flowed freely, people from The Pas and OCN mingled as if there had never been a divide between them—as if there were no Saskatchewan River, just 100 metres away, separating one community from the other.

The mayor was there, along with the chief, and on the bridge over the river a long line of cars travelling from the town to the reserve, to an arena both call their own.

◄◄ **Source**: This article originally appeared in *The Globe and Mail* on November 7, 2001. Reprinted with permission.

## VANOC Draws on Indigenous Symbols but Fails to Support Indigenous Athletes

By Laura Robinson

**40.**

*In this op ed, first published in the Ottawa Citizen, Laura Robinson comments on the lack of attention paid to the Canadian Aboriginal athletes by the Vancouver Olympic Games organizer, VANOC, despite the extensive use of indigenous symbols in promoting the Vancouver Games.*

■ ■ ■ ■ ■

Modern pentathlete, Monica Pinette, who is Métis, was the lone Aboriginal person on a team of 331 athletes in Beijing. The 2006 Canadian census tells us 1,172,790 people identify as Aboriginal in a population of

32,852,849, which means there should have been at least eleven Aboriginal athletes on the team.

During the weeks I covered the Beijing Games, and the days since I returned to Canada, I have asked a few questions to the Vancouver Organizing Committee for the 2010 Olympics: How will VANOC and the Canadian Olympic Committee ensure that Aboriginal youth have real access to the facilities and programs that become the sport legacy of the Vancouver Games, and how are they working with national sport organizations, like Cross Country Canada, or Alpine Canada to ensure Aboriginal youth are included in their future Olympic plans?

It should be an easy question to answer given the way in which VANOC went Native in their displays in Beijing—or at least symbolically with Inukshuks, glossy photos of totem poles, and a USB plug in the shape of a kayak, filled with all the VANOC info you could want, except what I asked for. VANOC sent me reams more, but they never did answer the questions. Presently there are two successful programs, but only in one of the twenty-one sports in the Winter Olympics: Chill, a snowboarding program brings inner-city youth, many of whom are First Nations, to Cypress Mountain to snowboard, and the First Nations Snowboarding Team (FNST), started by Aaron Marchant, of the Squamish First Nation. The FNST is also backed by Crazy Canuck, Steve Podborski, who urged Marchant to make his dream of seeing First Nations kids careening down hills a reality.

That's it, and not only is there nothing in place to ensure that these kids continue to access facilities and programs once the five-ring days are long over and are no longer needed on posters and websites, there are no plans in the works for any other programs of this magnitude in any other sport. There should be because the FNST has already put three athletes on the B.C. Snowboarding Team and has broadened its program to other communities in the province. Imagine a Canada, as former long-distance runner and Cree professor Janice

Forsyth did, at the North American Indigenous Games this year, where looking for the Indigenous athlete at the Olympics was no longer a guessing game because there were so many?

It's possible. The FNST has received $550,000 over the past four years from the Aboriginal Youth Sport Legacies Fund (AYSLF), a $3-million-dollar, one-time fund that was established through Legacies Now, a B.C.-government-funded non-profit society established so British Columbians can benefit from Olympic "legacies."

Marchant says he also receives support from area hills, equipment and clothing suppliers, top coaches, First Nation communities, the YWCA, and plenty of others for whom First Nations youth matter. "For a lot of our communities it's [elite sport] the furthest thing from their mind. The kids have chipped boards, no gloves, but we have several hundred kids accessing the hill."

And the word is getting out. "I received an email from a seven-year-old girl in Alberta. All she wanted to do was join our program, but it's B.C. only. Alberta, Quebec, Ontario, Manitoba—they need national support. They want this program. It's unfortunate that youth have to move all the way here for a program like this."

Marchant adds that trying to establish the FNST without the funds from the AYSLF "would have been like pushing water uphill."

Aboriginal leaders in sport have been calling for such programs for years, but they don't believe hosting the Olympics should be a funding criteria, and $3 million once around isn't going to do it, especially compared to the billions spent on the Games. If, before executing their very important mission in Beijing, the high-ranking VANOC brass stopped first in the Cowichan Valley for the North American Indigenous Games, they would have seen five thousand Aboriginal youth from above the Arctic Circle to the Mexican border. They would have seen what Marchant has seen, and may have clued in that they must play a large part in that future.

One of the honoured elders at the Games was Cree chief Willie Littlechild. He helped found the games in 1990 in Edmonton, was the first Aboriginal person in Canada to obtain a phys. ed. degree, and did his masters thesis on long-distance runner Tom Longboat the same year he entered law school. Littlechild became an MP in the Mulroney government, and now represents Alberta at the Assembly of First Nations. He is also one of the authors of the Maskwachees Declaration.

The declaration, written eight years ago at the National Recreation Roundtable on Aboriginal/Indigenous Peoples, recognizes "that many social issues including poverty; health concerns such as type II diabetes, heart disease, and fetal alcohol syndrome; rates of incarceration; substance abuse; harassment and racism; and a sedentary lifestyle have contributed to poor health and a low quality of life for many aboriginal/indigenous people."

It states "aboriginal youth are the fastest growing segment of the Canadian population, that there is a lack of priority in allocation of adequate financial and human resources for recreation and sport, that sport's infrastructure is complex, and that there is a need to enhance communication and accountability between aboriginal and non-aboriginal sport and recreation organizations and governments."

Finally it asks for "all governments, non-governmental organizations, communities and individuals in Canada to endorse this declaration."

Many of the signatories of the Maskwachees Declaration were recognized, with Littlechild, in a very old and sacred ceremony by the Cowichan Nation before the Indigenous Games commenced. I watched as Sport Canada types and non-governmental sport reps simply packed their bags and left partway through. Maybe they had a flight to Beijing to catch.

The cost of bringing the VANOC sales pitch to Beijing—one of thousands of junkets—could have paid for plenty of Aboriginal sport programmes. Canada's sport decision-makers are happy to take the kayaks, Inukshuks, and totem poles, but real respect for people and culture, and a deep understanding of the work we all have to do together so Aboriginal youth have the same opportunities as others to fulfill their sporting dreams are still sadly lacking.

---

◄◄ **Source**: Laura Robinson has covered four Olympic Games and four North American Indigenous Games. She coaches the Anishinaabe Nordic Racers at Chippewa of Nawash First Nation. This article originally appeared in *The Ottawa Citizen* on December 18, 2008 and on the Play the Game website (www.playthegame.org). Reprinted with permission from the author.

## Loneliness of the Native Athlete
By Laura Robinson

**41.**

*Thanks to the 1988 Olympics, Calgary has great sports facilities. Too bad they effectively bar some athletes*

■ ■ ■ ■ ■ ■

In his first national athletics championships, Ian Many Fingers, twenty-one, placed sixth in the 3000-metre steeplechase, a gruelling event consisting of running, hurdles, and water jumps.

He says his father, who is a member of the Kainai First Nation and a City of Calgary police officer, "never lost against a criminal." I meet Ian when he is warming up for a race at Foothills Stadium just two weeks after the nationals. "My dad and my uncles always ran on the reserve," he says. "They weren't competitive, they just liked to stay in shape."

Ian's training will culminate at the end of July when he and eight thousand other athletes gather in Winnipeg for the North American Indigenous Games (they'll be joined by an equal number of cultural performers). Hundreds of First Nations visitors are expected, and that's not counting Métis participants, whose numbers will be significant. These games are larger than the Olympics in terms of participants—but not in terms of funding.

In 1997, when Victoria hosted the Indigenous Games, Ottawa contributed $950,000, which was matched by the B.C. government. This year's games are receiving $2.5 million from the feds, which has been matched by the province and topped up with another $1 million from the City of Winnipeg, according to Alex Nelson, a soccer player from Alert Bay, British Columbia, and chair of the North American Indigenous Games Council.

"It's a start," says Mr. Nelson, "but compared to other major games, it really isn't much at all. Look at what they are predicting for Vancouver's 2010 Olympics. When have our people had the money to do winter sports and go to Whistler?" If Vancouver gets the Olympics, he fears, it could raise costs for winter athletes of all kinds.

The federal and provincial governments have each committed $310 million to the Vancouver Olympic Games. This is on the heels of $13 million spent by the three levels of government on the unsuccessful bid for the 2008 Toronto Olympics (that's $8.5 million more than what has been committed to the entire Indigenous Games).

And staging a major games is just one cost associated with sport. "The membership to the Calgary Spartans Track Club is pretty good, and running's a cheap sport," says Ian Many Fingers. "It's $175 a year, but there's another $3,000 per athlete we have to raise through bingos and casinos, and that's not including things like plane tickets. And I spend at least $500 a year on running shoes. My mom and dad are really supportive, but a lot of Aboriginal kids can't get that kind of support."

The Indigenous Games, which take place every three to four years, are the major way the Aboriginal community lends support to up-and-coming athletes. But compared with most, Ian Many Fingers is an exception; he also competes at the club level. Even though Calgary has a large Aboriginal community, and even though the 1988 Olympics left the city with some of the best training facilities for winter and summer athletes, he is the only Calgary athlete competing at the Indigenous Games. Why is that? There certainly is no shortage of Native people in the Calgary area.

Perhaps, given what has happened to that Olympic legacy, this isn't surprising.

Canada Olympic Park is situated on the Trans-Canada Highway, on the west side of Calgary. It contains state-of-the-art winter sports facilities for bobsled, luge, skeleton, ski-jumping, alpine and Nordic skiing, and snowboarding. But its grounds and extensive gym and weight room could be used by summer athletes too. The Ice House, which contains practice areas for luge, skeleton, and bobsled, was just completed to the tune of $4.1 million.

The legacy of the 1988 Games, supposed to be for the people of Canada, is privately owned by the Canadian Olympic Development Association (CODA). To even walk, cycle, or run around Canada Olympic Park, you must pay a $9 entrance fee. It costs more to train at the facilities.

Chris Dornan, a public-affairs spokesman for CODA, rationalizes the fee this way: "The legacy from the 1988 Olympics totalled $75 million. In 1988, the federal government sold the park and facilities to CODA for $1, which gave them half of that $75 million. The Canadian Olympic Association, now the Canadian Olympic Committee, received the other half. We build and maintain these facilities from the interest made on that legacy."

It's possible to understand why a fee is charged to people who want to slide down icy runways in the middle of the summer. The upkeep alone must be costly—although we may want to ask what greater good comes from spending essentially privatized government funds on a handful of toboggans when the health and fitness of Aboriginal children has been so neglected. But why is CODA charging $9 if people want to ride their bicycles or run in the Olympic park?

"Due to the high volume of people and vehicles we decided all people in and out of the park would pay a day fee," says Mr. Dornan. "We want to make sure we know who's in the park. It's for their own safety."

Huh? I rode my bicycle on the road to the ski jump (until the fee gate was erected) precisely because it wasn't busy. This concern over safety is relative to what—letting kids who can't afford the fee ride their bikes on the Trans-Canada? And why is CODA so interested in knowing who is in the park? From what I saw, virtually every athlete was white and the parking lot was filled with minivans and SUVs. How comforting for CODA. But how impenetrable for poorer, Aboriginal youth.

Mr. Dornan argues that Olympic facilities have been "destroyed" in the past because their upkeep was so expensive. If this is true, it's a good reason not to build them. But is it true?

Lillehammer, Norway, hosted the 1994 Winter Olympics. Its facilities are still standing. Nordic and Alpine skiers can take public transit to ski hills and trails. Nordic skiing is free, so is mountain biking, running, and walking—and that includes trails within the Olympic stadium. At the recent Salt Lake City Olympics, Norway, a country of five million people that believes in the philosophy of sport for all, beat Canada in the medal count.

The day I saw Ian Many Fingers run, he ran as if he didn't even touch the ground. He easily won his race at the meet. He says he looks forward to doing it again in Winnipeg. Too bad he and other indigenous athletes have to do it without use of Calgary's Olympic legacy.

◀◀ **Source:** Laura Robinson's latest book is *Black Tights: Women, Sport and Sexuality.* This article was originally published in *The Globe and Mail* on July 12, 2002. Reprinted with permission.

## Where Have You Gone, Jackie Robinson?
By Bob Levin

# 42.

*Even before the barrier-breaking player made his Montreal debut sixty years ago, race and baseball were a volatile mix. Today's Toronto Blue Jays have been criticized for being heavily white. It's just an unintended consequence of the team's strategic choices—but diversity merits attention for its own sake.*

■ ■ ■ ■ ■ ■

In baseball's off-season, when teams deal and fans obsessively discuss, they were speaking of racial matters on sports radio in New York. The guest was Omar Minaya, formerly general manager of the Montreal Expos, now that of the New York Mets. The subject was his acquisition of so many Hispanic ballplayers. Some callers accused him of racism, a charge he adamantly denied.

"To me, it's about signing the best players possible," Mr. Minaya said. "I don't think about the player's race, his colour, his religion, his sexual orientation. I don't get into that stuff."

Sound familiar? It's more or less what J. P. Ricciardi, the Toronto Blue Jays GM, said when the *Toronto Star* pointed out the exact opposite phenomenon in 2003—that the Jays, who once ran a virtual pipeline to Latin America, had become the whitest team in baseball.

"We don't look at players as black and white," Mr. Ricciardi told the newspaper, and fans seemed to agree. In calls and emails and open-line radio rants, many accused the paper of liberalism run amok, saying, in essence: "Who cares about race? Just win baseball games." Or, as Carlos Delgado, now of the Mets, then of the Jays, concluded: "It was probably the stupidest thing I've ever seen."

Race—it's the great igniter. Volatile, complex, intensely personal, freighted with politics and history, it is an issue at once ubiquitous and slightly submerged, surfacing to stir pride and discord. And sports, for all their escapist pleasures, are no refuge.

Lest anyone forget, baseball was a white bastion until Jackie Robinson made his debut with the Montreal Royals sixty years ago, on April 18, 1946. He went on to a decade-long, Hall of Fame run with the Brooklyn Dodgers, enduring unfathomable abuse to break down barriers not only for blacks but for Latinos as well (although a handful of Hispanics had played previously in the majors).

My parents lived in Brooklyn then and went to Ebbets Field often. I grew up on Jackie stories.

Now, about 37% of major-leaguers are Latino, black, or Asian. Sixteen nations sent teams to the first World Baseball Classic last month, the final four consisting of Japan (which won), Cuba, South Korea, and the Dominican Republic—the United States having been conspicuously eliminated.

And still, any mention of "race" not preceded by "pennant" can touch off a media brawl.

Yet, as another baseball season opened this week, the fact remains: Here are two general managers, Mr. Minaya and Mr. Ricciardi, both insisting they're colour-blind, and the Mets broke camp with fifteen members of visible minorities on their twenty-five-man roster (thirteen of them Hispanic), while the Jays have four.

What gives? And why can't we talk about it—calmly, reasonably, and beginning with this proviso: No one is accusing anyone of racism.

Like other enterprises (including newspapers), baseball wrestles with the diversity issue. The league itself, closely monitoring both the field and the front offices, has watched with concern as the number of black players has plunged to 9% from a high of 27% in 1975. Somehow, to young blacks, baseball has lost its allure beside the turbo-charged appeal of basketball and football.

But not to Latinos, who now account for about one-quarter of major-leaguers—and twenty-four of the sixty players originally chosen for last year's All-Star Game.

Enter Mr. Minaya: Dominican-born, New York-raised, baseball's first and only Hispanic GM. While signing players of every shade, Mr. Minaya plainly feels an affinity for Hispanics, and his office has marketed "Los Mets" directly to Spanish-speakers.

The Mets, wrote Jonathan Mahler in a *New York Times Magazine* cover story on the team last summer, are "self-consciously rebuilding and, no less important, rebranding themselves as an international team whose ethnic makeup will reflect the increasingly Hispanic city they represent."

But, as Mr. Mahler notes, the Mets are also built to reflect the style of play Mr. Minaya prefers—athletic and aggressive. "You can't walk your way off the island" goes the saying, and Latin players, at least by reputation, tend to swing freely even at errant pitches.

Which brings us back to Mr. Ricciardi and the Jays.

Mr. Ricciardi isn't partial to free-swingers. His statistics-centred approach eschews undisciplined hitting and embraces high on-base percentage. So he has preferred to draft college boys, whose stats are easily analyzed and whose progress to the majors is often rapid. And most college players are white, as are many of the modestly paid free agents the GM has signed.

Cost-effectiveness is key: For most of his four-plus years in Toronto, Mr. Ricciardi has operated with a suffocatingly tight budget—about $46 million (U.S.) at the end of last year. Compare that with the Mets' $104 million, which has made Mr.

Minaya freer to pursue pricey free agents, many of whom—Pedro Martinez, Carlos Beltran—happen to be Hispanic.

This off-season, when Jays owner Ted Rogers began bankrolling a serious playoff run, Mr. Ricciardi made five prize acquisitions by trade and free agency. Four happen to be white, and one Hispanic.

Whatever the merits of the competing methods in creating winning teams, the result is self-evident in the field of diversity. The only question is whether it matters. The answer, like the assessing of talent, is ultimately subjective.

Does having a largely white baseball squad matter to multicultural Toronto? Not much, it seems, judging from the multi-accented enthusiasm of callers to sports radio.

Unlike New York, Toronto is not heavily Hispanic. The Maple Leafs are all white and the Raptors mostly black, and no one remarks on that. But then, those teams generally reflect the talent pool of their particular sports. The Jays, in baseball, plainly do not.

Does it matter in any larger sense? Here, for the record, is why I believe it should: Diversity is good. It has history on its side. It has intrinsic worth, not at the expense of excellence but in conjunction with it—a difficult trick in some businesses, but surely less so in this increasingly international pastime.

Besides, I just like cheering on athletes of different colours and backgrounds, hearing the chatter of different languages. Sports, like life, isn't just about winning; it's about savouring the ride.

So yes, I miss the more multi-hued Jays of old—the days of Bell, Barfield, and Whitt; of Alomar, Molitor, and Carter. Nothing against any of the current Jays, a talented group generating more baseball buzz than Toronto has heard in years. But to me a racially diverse team is usually a more interesting team, just as a diverse city is a more interesting city. Check out any travel article on Toronto, if you doubt the latter.

"What surprises me," Mr. Minaya said of the racial discussion on radio, "is that in the year 2006 we are even talking about this."

In another way, it might also surprise Jackie Robinson. But, at least here in Canada, maybe we should be talking about it more.

◄◄ **Source:** Toronto journalist Bob Levin is a former writer for *Newsweek* and executive editor of *Maclean's*. This article was originally published in *The Globe and Mail* on April 8, 2006. Reprinted with permission.

## Muslim Woman Wears Her Hijab and a Black Belt with Pride
### By Tu Thanh Ha

**43.**

*Tae kwon do is an ideal sport for devout Muslims, professor believes*

■ ■ ■ ■ ■ ■

When news came that young Muslim girls had been turned away from a tae kwon do competition in Quebec because they wore Islamic head scarves, one of the people upset was the former dean of engineering of the University of Ottawa.

Aside from being an electrical engineer, Tyseer Aboulnasr is a hijab-wearing black belt in tae kwon do, a mother of two who began practising martial arts in her forties.

While she understands that officials at the Fédération de Tae kwondo du Québec are applying their rules to the letter, she feels that they are betraying the sport's spirit of inclusiveness.

"Honestly, when I heard about it, I thought, this is unbelievable," she said yesterday.

Dr. Aboulnasr's embrace of tae kwon do is a rebuke to the traditional image of hijab-wearing Muslim women as people from a cloistered, inward-looking community.

The Egyptian-born fifty-two-year-old is one of the rare women, let alone Muslim women, to have been a dean in such a male-dominated academic field as engineering.

She had never heard of tae kwon do until 1995, when her eight-year-old daughter wanted to learn martial arts after watching *The Next Karate Kid*, starring Hilary Swank.

When Dr. Aboulnasr took her daughter to a tae kwon do school, she noticed that it was an ideal sport for devout Muslim women because it allowed them to be athletic while remaining modestly covered.

"I went into tae kwon do because I saw it as a sport that is very Islamic," she said.

What happened during Sunday's tournament in Longueuil, Quebec, underlines the complex reality of both the world of sports and the world of Canadian Muslims.

The tournament was held under the rules of the Seoul-based World Taekwondo Federation (WTF). WTF rules are unambiguous. Article 4.2 states that "wearing any item on the head other than the head protector shall not be permitted."

However, unlike other sports, tae kwon do does not have a single-world body. The Vienna-based International Taekwon-do Federation (ITF), under which Dr. Aboulnasr has competed, has looser rules that allow "bandaging or strapping" as long as they don't give a competitor an advantage.

In more than a dozen years practising under ITF rules, no one ever questioned whether she should remove her hijab. "It never came up. It is soft. It poses no threats to anybody."

The girls who were banned from competing are between the ages of ten and fourteen and come from the Centre Communautaire Musulman de Montréal, an organization of mostly Lebanese Shia Muslims whose website promotes a religiously orthodox view of the world.

"Wearing the hijab ... liberates women from the trap of Western fashion and maladies," one article on the website says.

One of the girls' coaches, Mahdi Sbeiti, said the tae kwon do program uses the Centre Communautaire's facilities but is not restricted to Muslims and does not feature any religious instruction.

"There's no religion, these are sports classes," he said, noting that the team's other coach is an old-stock, francophone Quebecker.

Jean Faucher, president of the Fédération de Tae kwondo du Québec, has argued that the hijab isn't banned for religious reason but rather in the same way as other non-standard items, such as sweatbands.

But Dr. Aboulnasr said the hijab should be allowed precisely because it is not a mere sweatband but a religious garment, albeit not a dangerous object.

"There is a difference between people wearing things out of conviction and people wearing something for convenience. And if you cannot see the difference between the two, I would say, 'Go back, find out about the spirit of tae kwon do, and apply that.' "

While tae kwon do is a contact sport, there is no grappling on the floor like judo or wrestling, Dr. Aboulnasr said, so it is unlikely a head scarf could throttle a competitor.

Also, blows to the head are forbidden, she noted. "Even when you kick, you're supposed to touch with the tip of the toe to score points."

Mr. Sbeiti said his group has been invited to a meeting in two weeks with the Quebec federation. Meanwhile, he said, they will ask the World Taekwondo Federation to clarify its rules.

◀◀ **Source:** This article was originally published in *The Globe and Mail* on April 17, 2007. Reprinted with permission.

# Where are the Minorities?
## By Lindsey Craig

**44.**

*New Canadians and visible minorities are staying away from Canada's game*

■ ■ ■ ■ ■ ■

Abdalhafiz Nur arrived in Canada nearly twenty years ago from Eritrea, a country bordering Ethiopia and Sudan. He grew up playing soccer, as his father did, and is raising four kids with his wife in Toronto.

His ten-year-old son plays rep soccer year-round. His daughters play sports in school. Nur doesn't know which sport his two-year-old son will try, but he is sure of one thing—none will play hockey.

"Most of the people who come from Africa, they like soccer. When they come to Canada, hockey is expensive. Then there's all the material. Everyone can't afford to buy it," he said. "Hockey, it's very expensive, and aggressive. When I see it, it seems more violent than soccer. They fight."

Nur, forty-four, is a trained lab technician who works as a concierge at a condo. His wife is unemployed. They're just two of many immigrants who aren't registering their kids in Canada's national pastime.

Cost, cultural differences and, for some, a seemingly uninviting atmosphere are keeping immigrants and non-whites from playing Canada's game. Some work is being done across the country to change the trend, but it's a daunting task, and efforts have only just begun.

While Hockey Canada doesn't keep race-based stats, many involved with the sport say few players are of non-white descent, and overall registration numbers are dwindling.

Hockey Canada believes there's a link between the two trends and says new Canadians must be reached for the game to endure.

"We've always just opened our registration doors and people flock in ... But we can't do that anymore," said Glen McCurdie, Hockey Canada's senior director of member services.

"We don't feel we do a good job of marketing to new Canadians whose number one choice may not be ice-related sports, but soccer, cricket, or something else," he said.

It's important to reach visible minorities and new Canadians, McCurdie said, since they comprise a large and growing part of Canadian society. It's something Hockey Canada is only starting to work on.

Canada's visible minority population is growing much faster than its total population, according to Statistics Canada. Between 1996 and 2001, it increased by 25%, but in the same time period, the general population grew by only 4%.

By 2017, roughly 20% of Canada's population could be visible minorities—6.3 million to 8.5 million people—with close to half projected to be South Asian or Chinese.

The numbers are especially important considering recent census figures indicate Canada's pool of youth under-fifteen is shrinking. With a growing number of visible minorities comprising that pool, it will be essential for minor hockey associations to connect with them to keep afloat.

### ■■■ Money Is an Issue

As Nur's situation demonstrates, doing so won't be easy.

The cost for a child to play house league hockey can easily surpass $300. Equipment can cost at least that amount, and that's not including expenses like travel or tournament fees. Hockey at more competitive levels can cost a several thousands of dollars each year.

Lorraine LeClair, executive director of the Multicultural Association of the Greater Moncton Area in New Brunswick, said financial obstacles can be even more paramount for new Canadians.

"There could be a situation where a doctor arrives and made 'X' amount of dollars, but comes here and has accreditation that may not be recognized ... So they're making $20,000 to $40,000 less because they're in survivor mode as opposed to career mode," she said.

"You can see where they wouldn't have the extra funds for extracurriculars. You're worrying more about having a roof over your head and three square meals on your plate," she added, also noting that parents are "less likely to spend $1,500 on equipment for a sport they don't know."

For Marcelina Benites and Richard Benites, who moved from Peru to Victoria in 2004, putting their six-year-old son, Gonzalo, in hockey is impossible to consider.

"We can't do it. We are still settling. We started from zero and we had to spend a lot of money ... The price is too high. We bought a house, we had to pay a high mortgage, it's not easy for us," Marcelina said.

They came to Canada because Richard, an IT professional, was offered a permanent job. But set-up costs put them back and they had to adjust from having two incomes to one. (Marcelina worked in Peru but now stays at home because they can't afford daycare for their three-year-old daughter.)

The couple still manages to register Gonzalo for indoor soccer in the winter and swimming in the summer. Such sports are much easier to afford, Marcelina said, noting she prefers them to hockey because they're not as rough.

"I do think the game is violent," she said. "I watch it on TV and I'm kind of disappointed ... It's the main sport in Canada and I ask myself why is this [behaviour] allowed?"

### ■■■ "She thought it was a dangerous sport"

Perceiving hockey as violent seems to be a common thread among those new to Canada.

Brian Tran, nineteen, who was born in Canada and raised by immigrant parents from Vietnam, said his mom didn't perceive hockey as a positive sport.

"She thought it was a dangerous sport and didn't want me to play ... I ended up in figure skating because it was less aggressive," he said, adding that his parents also put him in soccer and tennis.

But there are other reasons, as well, for new Canadians and visible minorities to turn from the sport.

Anthony Stewart, associate professor of English at Dalhousie University in Halifax, and author of the soon-to-be published book, *You Must be a Basketball Player*, says racism is also an issue in the minor hockey arena.

Stewart was raised in Ottawa by Jamaican parents and didn't want to play hockey because he didn't feel comfortable as a minority in the sport.

"I never played hockey, but just about every boy I knew growing up did. I remember hearing a few harrowing stories about black kids who played. You heard the things they were called and how they were treated," he said.

"Hockey looked very hostile for kids who are different," Stewart said, noting the tensions that also exist between English and French players.

"When you hear white guys badmouthing other white guys, when that started happening, none of that did anything to make me think hockey culture was any more welcoming to me," he said.

He can't say if racial slurs and insults are as prevalent as they once were, but notes, "You hear the stories the Williams sisters [Venus and Serena] tell, and Tiger Woods, the list goes on. It would be naïve to think hockey would somehow be exempt from those sorts of practices. You see it all the time," he said.

"Has it changed? ... Look at the Canadian junior team and [P.K.] Subban. You'd have to ask him ... What I can say with certainty is it's not easy for a variety of reasons to be the only anything in a place where people who look like you aren't normally present," he said.

P.K. Subban is a black defenceman from Toronto who recently made national headlines as one of the Canadian junior team's top players. He's been called a role model to young visible minorities, and CBC News recently asked him about it.

"If I am [a role model] to black kids, that's great. I hope I am. But truly to all kids, I want to inspire all kids," Subban said.

Just how many more Subbans there will be will depend greatly on minor hockey's ability to overcome the reasons why many visible minorities stay away from the sport.

## ■ ■ ■ Pilot Project Underway

Last year, Hockey Canada launched a pilot project, one of which was set-up in Victoria, aimed at encouraging new Canadians to lace up.

For one day, children of immigrant families were provided with free equipment and given skating lessons. At the end of the day, those who wanted to sign-up for a season could do so for $50. They could also keep the equipment they had worn that day.

Despite her reservations about violence hockey, Marcelina wanted her son to have the chance to try it. Gonzalo played the season and liked it so much he wanted to register again.

But to play a second season, the family would have had to pay regular fees, which they couldn't afford.

"It's such a high price for us," Marcelina said.

Such a scenario draws attention to what some are afraid of—temporary solutions.

"It's not something can be done overnight," said John Gardner, president of the Greater Toronto Hockey League.

In effort to connect with new Canadians, Gardner plans to distribute brochures about hockey in different languages in the school system. But he knows that education isn't enough.

"Hockey today, nationally, has to develop new ways to innovate and encourage more kids to get involved in the game," he said.

Scarborough Hockey Association president John Kelloway knows what can happen if such efforts aren't made.

Over the past ten years, the SHA has shrunk from ten thousand players to three thousand.

The organization is down to four house leagues from seven, and the hockey association in Wexford, where Nur's son plays soccer, recently folded completely.

Estimating that less than 5% of the SHA's players are first-generation Canadian, Kelloway said, "Hockey is just becoming too expensive."

---

◀◀ **Source:** This is Part 3 of Our Game's series on the number of kids playing our national game, and why some are opting out. Reprinted with permission from CBC Sports.

# Section 8

## Social Class and Sports

An overwhelming amount of research evidence shows that social class, both on its own and in combination with gender, race/ethnicity, and other social characteristics, is the most important determinant of participation in sport and physical activity in Canada. The more money you have, the higher your occupational status, and/or the higher your level of education (all used separately or in combination to determine a person's social class), the more likely you are to participate in sport and physical activity. The previous section's introduction concluded by pointing out that cost was one of the factors leading to declining participation in hockey. The more money a family has, the more likely its members are to be able to participate in expensive sports such as hockey, making participation a social class issue.

The first article in this section deals directly with the issue of cost. Mary Ormsby examines "Minor Hockey's Increasingly Major Costs," using Toronto as an example, and also looks at some of the subsidies that are available to families that cannot afford to register their children in the sport. It should be noted that costs have increased since this article was written.

Gina Browne makes a powerful case, based on research evidence, that subsidizing participation in sport and recreation for low-income children more than pays for itself in terms of costs saved in other sectors. Browne and her colleagues at McMaster University carried out an extensive four-year study which, in part, provided recreation subsidies and transportation to children in low-income, sole-support families. The study concluded that:

> Age appropriate child care and recreation for children on social assistance results in a 10% greater exit of parents from social assistance in one year, maintains the academic, social and physical competence with baseline behaviour disorder at two and four years, and pays for itself within one year because of reduced use of professional and probationary services and after four years, not only continues to pay for itself but results in one-third the annual per child health and social expenditures when compared to children of parents receiving [for example] employment retraining (p. vii).

Patti Edgar, Paul Egan, and Leah Janzen report on community recreation centres in Winnipeg in their article "It's for the Kids." They found that the centres depend on volunteer labour but, as might be expected, the most volunteers were available at the centres in the highest-income neighbourhoods (where children are more likely to be enrolled in programs), while the fewest volunteers were available at centres in the lowest-income neighbourhoods. Interviews with some of the volunteers provide insight into this situation.

Wendy Frisby and Larena Hoeber also look at community recreation in their study of "Factors Affecting the Uptake of Community Recreation as Health Promotion for Women on Low Incomes." They focus on the relationship between community recreation and public health, and identify factors that are likely to lead to successful recreation programs for underserved populations, as well as factors that are likely to inhibit involvement.

Social mobility is an aspect of social class, and sport is usually considered in terms of its relationship to upward social mobility. For example, winning an athletic scholarship to a university or becoming a professional athlete are achievements that are likely to enhance an individual's education and/or income and therefore increase their social class status. Jim Parcels' study of one quite successful cohort of players in the Ontario Minor Hockey Association (OMHA), "Straight Facts About Making it in Pro Hockey," has been used widely by minor hockey associations in an attempt to provide a reality check for parents with NHL ambitions for their sons. Parcels shows that, even in a relatively successful cohort, the chances of becoming an NHL player are extraordinarily limited. This is a study that's just waiting to be updated, but Parcels' data are still a striking reminder of the limitations of sport as a means of social mobility. When these data are combined with the costs outlined in the first article in this section, it becomes even more apparent that social mobility opportunities are limited.

The section concludes with an excerpt from Dave Bidini's forthcoming book *Home and Away* on the 2008 Homeless World Cup (HWC). The HWC has become part of the growing "International Development Through Sport" movement (see Section 14), and Bidini shows how homeless people, many of whom have experienced downward social mobility or addictions, still have an opportunity to be involved in international sport.

**Additional Suggested Readings and References**

- Bidini, D. 2010. *Home and Away: In Search of Dreams at the Homeless World Cup of Soccer.* Toronto: Greystone Books.
- Bonoguore, T. 2009. "Team Goes for the Gold on Nickels and Dimes." *The Globe and Mail.* April 6.
- Browne, G., et al. 2000. *FINAL REPORT: When the Bough Breaks: Provider-Initiated Comprehensive Care is More Effective and Less Expensive for Sole-Support Parents on Social Assistance—Four-Year Follow-Up.* Hamilton, ON: McMaster University's System Linked Research Unit on Health and Social Services Utilization.
- Grange, M. 2007. "From Jane and Finch to Ivy League." *The Globe and Mail*, June 23.
- Mick, H. 2009. "I'll Take that $600 Swimsuit in Size XXS." *The Globe and Mail*, July 30.
- Reinink, A. 2007. "Closing Recreation Centres Won't Win Over Youth." *Youth Voices* (Canadian Centre for Policy Alternatives, Manitoba), February 1.
- Shaw, C. 2008. "Olympic Profits: The 2010 Games Versus Vancouver's Downtown Eastside." *Briarpatch Magazine*, August.
- White, P. 2008. "Home-Ice Advantage." *The Globe and Mail*, February 15.

# 45. Minor Hockey's Increasingly Major Costs

By Mary Ormsby

Jonathan Custodio is at that perfect, dreamy stage when anything is still possible.

"I'll try to go as far as I can in hockey," said the thirteen-year-old Toronto athlete, playing in his first house-league season. "I'll try to get into the NHL or the OHL."

Sticks, skates, pucks, a smooth sheet of ice—the main ingredients that all Canadian kids mix at this time of year to measure themselves against idols like Sidney Crosby, Martin Brodeur, or Hayley Wickenheiser.

Or do they? More precisely, can they?

While most of us take playing hockey for granted, the grim reality is Canada's national game is so far out of reach for GTA kids like Jonathan, that without financial, logistical, and moral support from hockey organizations, schools, charities, and even strangers, hockey wouldn't be part of their lives.

In the GTA—home to one of the NHL's most fabled franchises and the largest amateur minor hockey league in the world—playing hockey is no longer an inclusive right of passage, but increasingly a luxury item that prevents some kids from ever trying the game.

As the busy Christmas tournament season gets underway, the Greater Toronto Hockey League boasts approximately 40,000 registered players. That seems like an enormous number until it's compared to the 949,945 children under age fourteen in the GTA, according to the latest census results.

Playing at the GTHL's AAA level (which is predominantly male) can cost upwards of $5,000—and that doesn't include equipment. In hockey specialty stores, popular high-end skates are $700, composite sticks top the $200 mark, and helmets are more than $100—there's a quick $1,000 and the kid's not even wearing pants yet.

"We pride ourselves on our sport being very team oriented with all the values that come with our game: Respect, history, tradition, and passion," said NHL goaltender Kevin Weekes, who grew up playing competitive hockey in Toronto. "But at the same time, the pricing is such that our sport is becoming an elitist sport."

In this hockey-rich city, who would have thought charity was needed to bring boys and girls into this game? From house leagues and camps waiving fees, to individuals like Weekes sponsoring and mentoring children, to programs like the city-run, Maple Leaf-supported Hockey in The Neighbourhood (HITN) league, there's a subculture of aid pulsing through the GTA to put kids on ice.

And it's still not enough.

"We try to help where we can to connect kids and hockey," said Ray Williams, a long-time leader of the HITN program that lends equipment and teaches skills to close to three hundred children—with more on a waiting list.

"But we don't even touch the smallest portion of kids who want to play."

Even families that can initially afford hockey may not be able to keep financial pace at the AAA or even AA levels. In addition to hefty registration fees, thousands of dollars more are routinely demanded by teams for extra weekly ice time and increasingly, payment for coaching staffs.

Former Toronto Maple Leaf Peter Zezel, who played AAA minor hockey with the Don Mills Flyers, decries this cheque-book body checking. He is also incensed at parents buying teams or personally bankrolling coaches to guarantee their child a roster spot and potentially bumping a more talented child without the same financial ability.

"We are catering to the kids that are more spoiled in that they come from money—they want this, they want that—and those are the kids that eventually down the line don't make it because they've had everything given to them easy," said Zezel, who has sponsored needy kids to join leagues and attend his skills camps.

"It's the ones that have to work harder, train harder, and don't have the money (who) are hungrier to get (successful) and we're knocking those kids out of the game."

Jonathan, an aspiring blueliner, was one of the lucky ones who found hockey help. At the urging of a school friend, he joined HITN when he was eight years old. Five years later, he wanted more.

So, in September, he and his mother Janice spent more than an hour on the bus and subway to travel from Jane and Steeles to Scarborough's Malvern Community Centre to receive a free, complete set of hockey equipment with fifty other kids. Just as important as the gear (donated through the One Goal hockey industry coalition program), Jonathan also received a spot in a house league near his Downsview home (from a Hockey Canada initiative) allowing him to walk or take the bus to games.

With both parents on disability and unable to work, Janice Custodio said her hockey-mad son couldn't stay in the sport without this type of help.

"With the amount of money we get, it's just enough to pay the bills," she said.

And she's not alone. One-third of Canadian parents with a child under the age of eighteen say they have not been able to enrol their kids in organized sports when they wanted to because it was too expensive, according to a 2005 Ipsos-Reid survey commissioned by Canadian Tire. Compared to baseball's house league and competitive programs (typically $250 to $300 and between $1,000 and $2,000, respectively) and those of soccer (about $200 in house league and $500 for elite play), hockey—with its long list of mandatory equipment—looks more like a mortgage payment than a sports activity.

However, there are other barriers beyond writing cheques.

Speaking in broader terms, former Olympian runner and sports advocate Bruce Kidd said certain activities—and hockey is one—take enormous energy and commitment from adults, who become a "personal manager."

"You not only have to have the time available and the car to get there and the disposable income, but (a parent) can run interference for their kid and that is such a big part of it," said Kidd. "There are jokes in the United States about soccer moms, but that disparaging remark underestimates the enormous skill that these people have and how they're important to whether (a child) makes it in the system or not. It's just huge."

Low-income, single-parent families and new immigrants to Canada may be more at risk to get lost in navigating the overwhelming hockey system here, but it's not always the case, Kidd said. He said while newcomers may find certain sports foreign to them, they will listen to what their children want and try to make it happen.

The Bo family did just that when they immigrated to Canada in March 2006. Originally from the Philippines, Emelita and Lucilo moved to Scarborough "for a better future" for their two sons after spending eleven years in Malaysia.

Assertive and enterprising, Emelita, a stay-at-home mother, and Lucilo, who works in electronics, immediately sought out free local tennis and hockey programs for Matt Lawrence, ten, and Michaelangelo, nine, because they couldn't afford private instruction. The boys joined the HITN program at Malvern last winter and improved so quickly they were granted spaces in the Scarborough Malvern Penguins house league this year.

"Some of their peers quit after the first day after falling so much," said Lucilo, who also watched fearfully as his sons tumbled during their skating debut. "But the boys kept getting back up and they really wanted to keep playing."

To do that, the house league fees of nearly $700 in total for the two boys was waived, and the pair received a set of new equipment—worth about $350 apiece—from the same program that aided Jonathan Custodio. The delight on Michaelangelo's face as he picked up his new stick was evident when he described why he enjoyed hockey.

"When I first came to Canada, I didn't have any friends but now I have lots of friends," he said.

His older brother concurred, adding he's addicted to the game.

"I'm getting better, I'm getting faster and I've made a gajillion friends," Matt Lawrence said.

Still, in order to provide this opportunity to "get fit and to fit in" says Emelita, the Bo family required aid.

"Especially for a family with a low income, without help like this, we wouldn't have been able to join," Emelita said. "Plus, the boys can walk to the arena with their bags, so there's no extra (transportation) cost."

In a minivan culture, taking a player and his bag to practices and games without a minivan is not so simple.

Sam Krishna is a single parent whose son, Daniel, is a goalie. Sam is disabled after undergoing major back surgery, must walk with a cane and cannot work. So, with no van and no car, how did the Parkdale pair get to games?

"Just TTC [Toronto Transit Commission] and a bag with wheels," Sam said, laughing.

It's physically easier now since Daniel is fifteen and can lug the heavy load himself to house league games, though Sam is always there to watch. But the financial burden that kept Daniel from accepting a place on a AAA GTHL team is a constant worry for his dad, who diligently salts what money he can to buy replacement equipment "piece by piece" for his sprouting teenager off his disability cheques and birthday presents of cash from Daniel's grandmother.

"It seems like his equipment only lasts a year," Sam said, sighing.

Even though he's sacrificed much to keep his son in hockey—and had help, too, with free hockey camps and HITN play—Sam's outlook is positive. "There are a lot of people who are doing exactly what I'm doing," he said, adding that his drive comes from providing a healthy experience for Daniel.

"The community I live in, there are pockets of violence in the area and I'm just so fortunate I was able to get him involved in hockey and that he actually likes it," Sam said.

"(Other parents) would have given up a long time ago ... slowly, things are progressing for Daniel and I feel the future is not so grim for him, as far as hockey goes."

Weekes, in contrast, is not so sure.

After playing his entire minor career with the GTHL's AAA Toronto Red Wings, the thirty-two-year-old New Jersey Devils netminder fears that parents will opt for cheaper sporting alternatives rather than drain bank accounts for hockey.

"Our sport is supposedly a game that the common Canadian can enjoy and relate to and is passionate about. I think in order to maintain that, the pricing and the financial structure for minor hockey kids and their parents has to change," he said. "Otherwise, we'll continue to lose traction and kids will pursue other sporting opportunities."

◄◄ **Source:** This article was originally published in the *Toronto Star* on December 8, 2007. Reprinted with permission.

## Making the Case for Youth Recreation Integrated Service Delivery: More Effective and Less Expensive
### By Dr. Gina Browne

**46.**

*This article is based on the talk Gina Browne gave at **Action Speaks Louder**, a forum on youth recreation convened by the Laidlaw Foundation and Ideas That Matter held in Toronto in November, 2002.*

■ ■ ■ ■ ■ ■

### ■ ■ ■ Counting Up the Costs

I'm going to begin with an economic perspective. Health economists like to act like this is really hard to do, but every person who shops for groceries knows that you can't add different kinds of resources together—a banana with an apple with a can of beans. You have to translate

| Table 1: The Annual Per Patient Cost* by Level of Adjustment to Mental Illness | | | |
|---|---|---|---|
| Adjustment | Good | Fair | Poor |
| **Direct Costs** | | | |
| **Health Services** | $$ | $$ | $$ |
| TGH Primary Care Visits | 349 | 699 | 1,266 |
| TGH Specialists | 1,511 | 1,846 | 2,348 |
| Hospital Days | 4,023 | 8,062 | 9,373 |
| Other Emergency Room | 14 | 24 | 35 |
| Other Specialists | 57 | 165 | 390 |
| Health Professionals | 113 | 758 | 1,143 |
| Laboratory Services | 1,548 | 2,121 | 3,219 |
| **Total** | 7,615 | 13,675 | 17,774 |
| **Out-of-Pocket Expenditures** | $$ | $$ | $$ |
| Medications | 446 | 627 | 482 |
| Medical Devices | 12 | 36 | 699 |
| Babysitting | 179 | 341 | 294 |
| Transportation | 171 | 170 | 233 |
| Parking | 65 | 91 | 208 |
| **Total** | 873 | 1,265 | 1,916 |
| **Total Direct Costs** | 8,488 | 14,940 | 19,690 |
| **Indirect Costs** | $$ | $$ | $$ |
| Lost income by patient due to illness | 301 | 3,589 | 3,900 |
| Lost income by others due to patient's illness | 904 | 57 | 293 |
| Lost income due to receiving treatment | 99 | 93 | 0 |
| **Total Indirect Costs** | 1,304 | 3,739 | 4,193 |
| **Grand Total Direct/Indirect Costs** | 9,791 | 18,679 | 23,883 |
| **Cash-Transfer Effect on Illness** | $$ | $$ | $$ |
| Unemployment Insurance | 83 | 346 | 0 |
| Worker's Compensation | 0 | 0 | 0 |
| Government Benefits | 2,117 | 1,168 | 2,718 |
| Private Insurance | 780 | 942 | 4,690 |
| **Total** | 2,980 | 2,4456 | 7,408 |
| *in 1987 Canadian Dollars | | | |

resources into a dollar value and then add up the cost of the groceries. Similarly, in our work, we count up the cost of people using different kinds of resources. There are direct costs such as hospital care, emergency-room care, laboratory services, and social work services. In addition to the direct costs we also have out-of-pocket expenditures that people have to pay which sometimes accrue to government agencies, but most often accrue to the individual. Then we also have indirect costs such

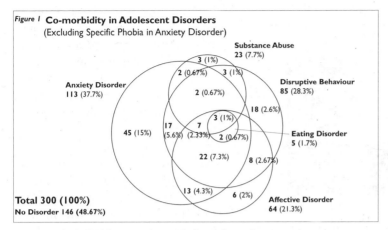

Figure 1  **Co-morbidity in Adolescent Disorders**
(Excluding Specific Phobia in Anxiety Disorder)

as time that children and youth lose from having received care, plus hours off work by their parents. These are the direct and indirect costs. Now the health economists would say, "That's it." However, there's an additional cost called the "cash transfer cost" that happens when people are poor and unemployed. It includes unemployment insurance, worker's compensation, social assistance, and different kinds of cash transfers.

We take all these kinds of services—direct costs, out-of-pocket expenditures, indirect costs, and the cash-transfer effects—and we multiply by the cost for each unit of service. We studied chronically ill people attending the medical outpatient clinics at Toronto General Hospital who were grouped by level of mental health—good, fair, and poor. As mental health declined, patients used more of every kind of service—not only publicly funded health services but also out-of-pocket expenditures. There is a strong linear gradient where each type of cost is higher as a function of declining mental health (**Table 1**). The surprising thing is that this is not at all related to the severity or type of disease but to the level of mental health.

### ■ ■ ■ A Picture of Youth at Risk

Let's now turn to a study we did to determine the prevalence and costs of youth psychiatric disorders in primary care. We randomly sampled three hundred youth between the ages of ten and seventeen. As a family therapist, I know kids engage in a lot of risk behaviour and I was trying to find out what underlies their risk behaviour. We find out that it is highly related to the presence of behavioural or psychiatric disorders such as hyperactivity, emotional disorder, oppositional defiant disorder, and conduct disorder.

The more youth have these disorders, the higher the number and nature of risk behaviour events they engage in. You can see in the Venn diagram the tremendous overlay among these psychiatric disorders (**Figure 1**).

Of the total adolescents in the study, 48.67% had no disorder and the rest, 51%, had one or more psychiatric disorders. Any one of these disorders, such as anxiety disorder, only exists in its pure form in a small number of cases. I remember a physician saying to me, "Gina, I have to have the diagnosis," and I said, "Well, they qualify for three at the same time." "No, we have to have THE diagnosis," as if there is one. These youth have many disorders at the same time.

What's the cost of this to society? (**Table 2**) If there is no disorder, the costs are $331 per child per annum. When there is one or two disorders, the costs are $587 and in adolescents with three to five disorders the cost of treatment is almost $1,500, a five-fold increase. With the increase in risk behaviour, the cost of every service increases: higher use of physician services, higher use of specialists, higher use of the emergency room, higher use of physiotherapy … So you can see every cost goes up as a function of the child's emotional–behavioural–mental health problems.

### ■ ■ ■ A Framework for Evaluation

Now in a decision-making position you have to decide which recreation or arts programs you should provide. How much should you provide?

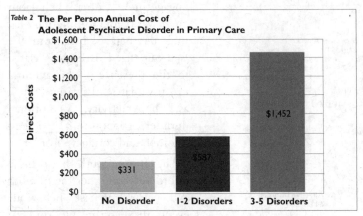

Table 2  **The Per Person Annual Cost of Adolescent Psychiatric Disorder in Primary Care**

At what stage in the developmental process should you provide services? Who should they be provided to? The hyperactive kid or the mother who's exhausted? Who are you taking care of? The answer to these questions is based on ideas of effectiveness and efficiency. People think that's a simple notion with a simple answer—and they're wrong.

There are four types of efficiencies which can be achieved from service delivery (**Figure 2**). It is possible for recreation to improve children's outcomes, keep them the same, or to make them worse. We can achieve these outcomes for more, the same, or less expense. In the triangle you see the four types of efficiencies which improve youth outcomes. In box 1, you improve youth outcomes but it costs more. You could improve youth outcomes and it costs no more (box 4). You can improve youth outcomes and in fact save the system money because you've reduced costs (box 7), or your recreation and other approaches can have the same outcomes but the cost is less expensive (box 8).

Within community care and within health and social care, we operate from different assumptions. We keep adults and youth from progressing in their illness, but we're not funded to promote healthy child development. All the big bucks go to health and social care aimed at deficiencies and diseases but recreation programming is based on resources and resilience. The medical profession works on repair and replacement, while recreational programmers work on restoring self-esteem and capacity. We supplement people's deficiencies, whereas you, as recreational programmers, empower them to have skills that they never believed they could develop. We offer specialized services and you offer a holistic kind of service where you have vulnerable kids hooked up with mainstream children. We offer services on demand, and you offer them on a proactive basis. We work on health care, but your services determine health. In fact, many of us in the health care system think any further investment in health care for children will be of limited help to children.

## ■ ■ ■ Integrated and Proactive Services Versus Self-Directed Services

We now come to a study entitled, "When the Bough Breaks" funded by the Hamilton Community Foundation and the Children's Mental Health Division of Health Canada. This was a collaborative project between the university and the community in the Hamilton/Halton area. We worked with two Commissioners of Social Service and two heads of public health nursing.

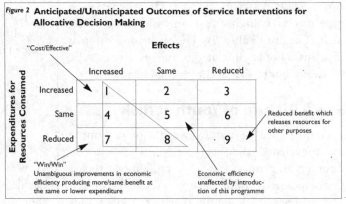

Figure 2  **Anticipated/Unanticipated Outcomes of Service Interventions for Allocative Decision Making**

In addition, the YMCA was a broker organization providing not only recreation to children and youth, but involving twenty-nine other youth-serving organizations. The network of services in Hamilton that grew out of this study is called Youth Serving Network (YSN). We looked at the question whether proactive, comprehensive, and integrated care is better than self-directed care (i.e., letting people on social assistance just fend for themselves).

We approached 1700 single-parent mothers on social assistance and asked them to participate in this study. A total of 765 mothers agreed to participate. We had each social case worker rate the mental health of mothers who refused and those who agreed to participate. We found that the mental health of mothers who did not participate is much worse than the mental health of those that did. So any conclusions about the mental health of these households is a serious underestimation of the magnitude of the problem. We allocated the 765 parents to a randomized trial of five social policies. There was no consent for parents to be allocated to a particular group. They only consented to fill out before and after questionnaires over time. The 1300 children in these households were between the ages of zero and twenty-four.

The parents who received comprehensive care had in-home visits by public health nurses, pro-active employment retraining, subsidized, quality child care, and recreation skills development. The public health nurse went in and helped each mother proactively decide where her challenges were—housing, finances, child care, or her own health. They then tried to figure out what to do about all that. The employment retraining people proactively called and offered job training. The third service was subsidized age-appropriate arts and recreation programs for children. Here, the recreation coordinator proactively visited the mothers and worked to gain entrée to their homes, sometimes over a period of two years. She would then help each mother decide what kind of programming suited her children. Now, this is one thing that children get to choose.

There are four terms a year of recreation programs—fall, winter, spring, and summer.

The recreation coordinator would go four times a year to the household and arrange programming for the children, everything from arts, ballet, and music lessons to sports programs.

If you give a mother and child these three services, is it effective compared to any one approach alone or compared to letting them just fend for themselves? This was the first randomized trial to compare this. There are seven randomized trials in the literature that look at the value of preschool programming, like the Perry Preschool Program, but this is the only one that has compared treatments against each other to see who, with what characteristics, might benefit from which approach.

We also wondered if we could help the mother's mood. 45% to 50% of the mothers suffered from major depressive disorders. If we could help the mother's mood, maybe we could help her capacity to parent (the parental adjustment scale). If we could help her mood and her capacity to parent, maybe her children's behaviour would improve, and maybe their use of all kinds of services would go down. At the time of this study, 1995 to 1999, 50% of welfare clients were single-parent mothers and 45% of these self-support parents had major depressive disorders. Not only were parents overwhelmed, 60.4% had two or more mental health conditions at the same time. 30% of the women lived with pain that limited their activities and 38.8% had two or more health conditions.

To complete the picture, 33% of their children had behavioural disorders, and 61% had children over seven.

The first measure of effectiveness in social policy is acceptability. In the first group—the comprehensive services approach group—we offered all three services (**Table 3**). Nearly 79% of parents who were offered children's services took it up. Public Health services were taken up 66.2% of

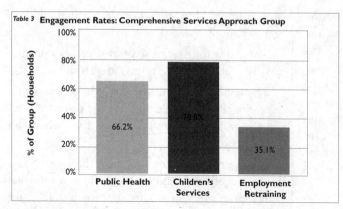

Table 3 Engagement Rates: Comprehensive Services Approach Group

the time, and employment retraining was taken up 35% of the time. If we look at the definition of "engaged," the measure of acceptability is reinforced. In public health, the public health nurse had one home or office visit either in person or over the phone for greater than ten minutes. In employment retraining, one home visit or telephone visit greater than ten minutes was considered engagement. In children's recreation programs, engagement meant at least one child in the family attended one program in that year and attended 80% of the sessions, which were usually thirteen-weeks in length. So what you have to offer is very acceptable and timely for the mother.

Looking at the other groups (**Table 4**), if you only offer one of these services by themselves, then nearly 80% of families would take up the public health services, whereas 38.4% would take up employment retraining. A resounding 73.8% would take up recreation services if offered. In the self-directed group, the fifth group, of course, nothing was offered.

From a second angle, approximately 50% of the parents in each group suffered from major depressive disorders. After two years, we looked at the reduction in the proportion of parents with a depressive disorder receiving each of the five approaches to service. They all declined equally, from approximately 50% down to about 20% (**Table 5**). Had we only measured this as an outcome, we

would have had to conclude that it is very expensive to offer these services if there is no significant difference between the four proactive approaches and the self-directed approach.

Using the methodology I have just described, if you leave families alone, 10% would exit social assistance (this is before the introduction of the Ontario Works program). If you offered any one service, and I've already argued this is more acceptable, the exit from social assistance doubles to 20%. If you offered families full intervention then you can create a 25% exit from social assistance (**Table 6**). Now, that might not seem impressive, but when you multiply these additional exits times the cost of benefits for a welfare family, you get $300,000 saved for every one hundred mothers offered the program. The City of Toronto has twenty-nine thousand single-parent mothers on welfare, so you have some idea of the amount of savings possible within one year. So, the real measure of effectiveness of a proactive approach is the exit from social assistance.

## ■ ■ ■ Recreation Benefits Both Child and Mother

What is the role of recreation in all this? We know from other studies that recreation increases the academic, social, and interpersonal competence of all children with behaviour disorders (the

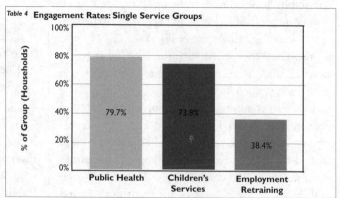

Table 4 Engagement Rates: Single Service Groups

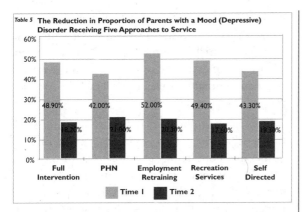

Table 5  **The Reduction in Proportion of Parents with a Mood (Depressive) Disorder Receiving Five Approaches to Service**

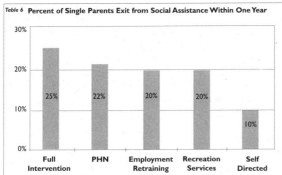

Table 6  **Percent of Single Parents Exit from Social Assistance Within One Year**

Offenbach Measure of Interpersonal Competence). Recreation skills development has an effect regardless of whether you are high or low risk. This is not the same thing as competence. One can be both highly risky and highly competent. What you want to focus on, of course, is competence and not pay so much attention to risk.

Public health services and employment training helped mothers out, however recreation was the only thing that helped the child (and of course, by extension, helped the mother). We had one hyperactive child who was enrolled in nine programs at the same time! If you had that kind of a child, you'd enroll him for everything too! It's not rocket science. It's what recreational programmers all know, but this is the first empirical evidence to document this.

If you add up the total cost for the family's use of all health and social services including recreation (if they got recreation), the cost is $3,389 per family per annum. (**Table 7**) Without recreation

programs the cost of health and social services is $3,809 per family per annum—a $500 difference which would more than pay for a pass for the whole family to the YMCA. There are also the additional savings which we looked at earlier through the doubling of the exits from social assistance.

How did recreation pay for itself? Families receiving recreation used half the physician specialists. Give the kid a coach and he won't use the doctor. It paid for itself by half the use of the Children's Aid Society. You can see that overwhelmed mother with that pain and that kid, she's going to beat him up if you don't get him out of her hair. The use of occupational therapists was down by one-half and the use of physiotherapists by one-third. Give the kid a coach and he won't need the psychologist. There is a 90% reduction in the use of social workers and a 90% reduction in the use of probationary officers. The use of chiropractors and the use of 911 services both went down by one-half.

### ■ ■ ■ What Are the Lessons?

What did we learn? Raising children is a community responsibility and reaching out is better than waiting to be asked. Our single-parent mothers didn't want to call Parks and Recreation in Hamilton because they said, "I'm already overwhelmed and I can't focus and problem solve, and when I call up I have to prove that I'm poor? This is hard." So it was really important to have this proactive recreation coordinator go out and

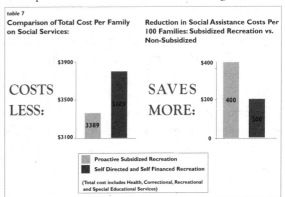

table 7
Comparison of Total Cost Per Family on Social Services: / Reduction in Social Assistance Costs Per 100 Families: Subsidized Recreation vs. Non-Subsidized

set all this up for mothers. It probably was the single most important aspect of the intervention. The recreation coordinator said "We got him on the school team, but he has no shoes." "Get the shoes. Just buy them." And of course, we needed the money to be located in a nonbureaucracy because we didn't want the child to apply for aids and devices in social service just because he needed shoes. The recreation coordinator created a voucher system and gave mothers the money for the transportation. Mothers get the voucher, go up to the mall, get the shoes and they're all happy. What you offer is entitlement. When a public health nurse goes into the home, there's an insinuation that there's a problem. Social support services work best when they are comprehensive, integrated, and customized. If you can't do it all, just do the recreation piece because is so clean, so acceptable.

So, to conclude, one-third of social assistance parents were willing to engage in employment retraining compared to 80% who would engage in recreational services. With a comprehensive service approach, two years later, parents' economic adjustment was improved by 13.6%. How did that happen? Well, you get this demanding kid out of mother's face and get him into a program where quality food, juice, and cookies are offered, then he's not spending her discretionary income on candy bars.

It is no more expensive in total dollars to provide a comprehensive and integrated service approach. What we've shown is that outside investment in a voluntary sector such as recreation, ends up saving publicly-funded health, social, and correctional services. This money can then be reinvested from social services into programming at a local level.

Peel County has implemented this comprehensive approach with recreation, nursing services, and employment retraining. They received $1.3 million from council to implement this program and within one year they had a 33% exit from social assistance, which is better than our study showed. That's a higher exit rate with a more impaired population because it was after the Ontario Works program was implemented.

Eighteen randomized trials show the same thing—that proactive and comprehensive care for vulnerable populations pays for itself in the same year. A win-win situation from every point of view. We've had a lot of impact from our results. I understand that forty-one of forty-seven governments in Ontario are taking the National Child Benefit and putting the money into recreation. Hamilton started with $500,000, then $750,000, and now they're up beyond a million dollars. That's a source of money for communities that can be implemented in a variety of ways.

■ ■ ■ ■ ■ ■

## Recreation/Child Care Pays for Itself by Reductions:

- 1/2 the use of medical specialists
- 1/2 the use of C.A.S. services
- 1/4 the use of occupational therapists
- 1/3 the use of physiotherapists
- 1/2 the use of 911 services
- 1/2 the use of psychologists
- 1/10 the use of social workers
- 1/10 the use of probation officers
- 1/2 the use of chiropractors

◀◀ **Source:** Dr. Gina Browne is a professor of nursing and epidemiology and the Director of the Health and Social Service Utilization Research Unit at McMaster University in Hamilton, Ontario, Canada. This article was reprinted with permission from the author.

## It's for the Kids

### By Patti Edgar, Paul Egan, and Leah Janzen

**47.**

*Volunteers spend countless hours making community centres run*

◼ ◼ ◼ ◼ ◼

They are the lifeblood of Winnipeg's community centres. They serve hot chocolate in the canteen, teach the intricacies of the offside rule in hockey, call bingo numbers, chaperone teen dances, and make sure water bottles are full for the neighbourhood soccer tournament.

They are the hundreds of volunteers who give their time and expertise to keep community clubs in Winnipeg running.

But they're not always easy to come by. A *Free Press* analysis of recreational facilities in three economically diverse Winnipeg neighbourhoods found the wealthier the area, the more likely a community club is to have a glut of parents and others willing to volunteer.

Clubs in low-income areas struggle to find people willing to make that commitment. The issue is compounded by the fact that poorer community clubs often have less parental involvement and almost no ability to do their own fundraising, meaning they have a higher need for the services of volunteers to fill those gaps.

The *Free Press* examination of community clubs in three Winnipeg neighbourhoods has found that clubs in the most impoverished areas have the fewest active volunteers.

Tuxedo Community Centre, located on Southport Boulevard in one of the city's wealthiest areas, reports about 155 active volunteers, while Park City West Community Centre, on Sanford Fleming Road in middle-income Transcona, has 30 active volunteers.

Meanwhile, Ralph Brown Recreation Centre on Andrews Street in the Point Douglas recreation area—a low-income neighbourhood—has only five active volunteers. In fact, all of the community centres in Point Douglas get by with an average of fewer than seventeen active volunteers, while clubs in the most affluent area of Assiniboine South have an average of one hundred and eight volunteers helping out. In middle-income Transcona, community clubs operate with an average of thirty-eight volunteers. Transience in the lower-income areas also means volunteers often move, making the recruitment of new volunteers a constant problem.

The *Free Press* examination of community centres in Winnipeg also found clubs in wealthier areas are more successful at fundraising.

Clubs in Assiniboine South receive an average of $400,000 in revenues—including city funds, grants, and privately raised money. In Transcona, that number drops to $250,000, and in Point Douglas it falls further to $80,000.

Jack Harper, co-ordinator of Recreation Management and Community Development at the University of Manitoba, said people living on low incomes face a variety of challenges that prevent them from getting involved as community volunteers.

He noted many low-income families have only a single parent. Those parents are less likely to have time to devote to volunteering because they are solely responsible for maintaining their households.

According to Harper, residents of low-income neighbourhoods are also more likely to be transient, which means they are less connected to their community and less willing to become volunteers.

Harper said the discrepancies suggest the volunteer-driven model of community centres in place in Winnipeg deserves review. He said the cost of providing programs and maintaining facilities has increased and become more bureaucratic. Volunteers are left doing administrative or custodial work instead of spending their time with the kids.

"In some cases we expect too much from our volunteers," he said. "Often, the reason they got involved is to be engaged in recreational activities with kids. Should they be responsible for maintaining and running the buildings and doing community surveys to find out what residents want? The reason they got involved is to be engaged in recreational activities with kids, but they often end up filling out grant forms."

Harper said some communities might be better served if they established larger, central recreation facilities that would have a larger pool of residents from which to draw participants and volunteers.

Regardless of the socio-economic status of the neighbourhood, community centre volunteers offer to do the work for similar reasons: They love kids, they love their community, and they want to help make it a better place to live. Here's a look at three volunteers in different Winnipeg neighbourhoods.

■■■■■■

Valerie Himkowski, forty-six, has lived in the Point Douglas neighbourhood all her life. In fact, her family first settled in the inner-city enclave in 1898. But she didn't become involved as a volunteer until she had her son, Morgan, thirteen years ago. Now there is almost nothing Himkowski isn't involved in.

"Having my son got me to places where I noticed they needed people," she said while on a break from a volunteer shift at the Norquay Community Centre. "I hadn't thought about it before that."

Today, Himkowski—a married, stay-at-home mother—sits on the Point Douglas residents'

committee and the North End Housing steering committee. She is a regular volunteer at the community centre, even though Morgan no longer uses the facility. She also spent years volunteering at his school and continues to edit *The Point*, the Point Douglas newsletter.

"I've lived here all my life," she said. "I know what's possible, but it takes people." Himkowski said she worries about the future of Norquay. With just four active volunteers and almost zero fundraising ability, the club is always struggling to survive. She helps out because she feels the centre is crucial to the area and knows it won't be there for future generations if she doesn't.

Himkowski realizes that asking people to volunteer—especially in a low-income neighbourhood like Point Douglas—is tough. She said Point Douglas residents are often renters who do not stick around long enough to get involved.

But, she said, volunteering helps build a stable community. If more people volunteered, perhaps they'd put roots down and not be so tempted to move. At Norquay, Himkowski—who estimates she volunteers between four and six hours a week—picks up food for the after-school program from Winnipeg Harvest, decorates the gym for special events, and spins the tunes as DJ at the teen dances.

"I do it because I like kids and I see the need," she said. "I want a good, stable community. By volunteering I hope to set a good example."

Himkowski said areas like Point Douglas, where poverty and transience make it difficult to attract volunteers, should receive some extra support from the city. She said some positions that are typically filled by volunteers should be paid positions. That would fill the need and provide a paycheque and some work experience for local residents.

■■■■■■

When Bruce Tailing was growing up in West Kildonan, his father, Jim, regularly helped out at the community centre and coached Bruce's teams.

For the last ten years, Bruce Tailing has continued that tradition in Transcona, where he and his wife, Mona, have raised three children.

Tailing is a hockey convenor at the East End Community Centre and also volunteers on the centre's board as vice-president of sports.

The centre was abuzz last weekend when it hosted a major Aboriginal hockey tournament.

It has two indoor rinks, one outdoor rink, and one large and one small hall available for rental. Outside, it has two mini soccer fields and a baseball diamond.

Tailing is one of about eighteen active volunteers at the centre, which has the equivalent of five full-time employees and reports total annual revenues of about $466,000.

His daughter Amanda, nineteen, is in college now. But she used to figure skate at the centre. Tailing's sons, Scott, fifteen, and Brent, fourteen, played soccer through the centre and both played AA hockey this winter.

Tailing, who used to coach his sons, shuttles them to practices and games.

"My dad did it and I respect him for it," said Tailing. "You learn a lot. Kids learn to get along with other kids. That's what I had kids for, to teach them values."

Tailing, forty-three, has a middle-income, nine-to-five job in inventory control for Manitoba Hydro. It leaves many of his evenings and weekends free to volunteer at the community centre.

Earlier this month, he used a vacation day to get a Friday off work, which he spent working with club president Don Gale and other volunteers to prepare for the community centre's winter carnival.

"I'm there for the kids. So is Don," Tailing said. "We had no kids involved in that carnival, but we were there."

Mona Tailing, who never misses one of her sons' hockey games, worked at the carnival too, cooking hot dogs for the kids.

The other twelve or thirteen members of the volunteer board and many of their spouses also helped out in some way, Tailing said. "Having a team like that makes everything run smoothly."

After starting as a soccer coach about ten years ago, Tailing also coached hockey at the centre and joined the board about seven years ago. Winter is the busiest time, when his hockey convening and board duties can easily consume more than five hours a week.

"It's a pretty busy lifestyle, let me tell you," Tailing said. "I enjoy it. It passes the winter."

■ ■ ■ ■ ■ ■

Lora Stotts grew up figure skating outdoors at the Fort Garry Community Centre.

When her first son, Chris, turned five and wanted to play hockey, Stotts turned to her neighbourhood community centre in upscale Tuxedo in Assiniboine South. Today, all three of her boys are playing hockey and soccer through the centre. This spring, nine-year-old Tyler is going to join flag football too.

Tuxedo Community Centre is made up of two buildings, one newer and one older, adjacent to a school.

Youth softball, soccer, hockey, baseball, karate, and lacrosse are the mainstays of the centre. There's also a pre-school for 150 children, a small hall, two ball diamonds, a picnic area, a toboggan slide, and two outdoor hockey rinks with change rooms.

Stotts is a stay-at-home mom in Tuxedo who also works the lunch program at her sons' school. During hockey season, there is barely a day in the week when Stotts or her husband aren't driving out to a game or practice.

But she still finds time to volunteer with Tuxedo, managing hockey teams, organizing soccer, and helping out with the craft sale. She's never kept track of how much of her time she's put into the centre, nor has she ever thought of it as a burden or stressful.

"I really enjoy being involved with my kids and my kids' activities," she said. "There's nothing more enjoyable than watching your kids have fun. You're getting to know their friends and watching them achieve the goals they set for themselves in the activities they choose."

There are more than 150 volunteers pitching in at Tuxedo, and the centre pulls in $206,112 in revenue each year before expenses, which eat up most of that cash. After seven years of volunteering, Stotts has made close friends with other parents and plans to stay involved until her boys outgrow the sports. After that, she may join the board.

"There is certainly a great volunteer base," she said.

"We always talk about the wonderful group of parents we have in the sports my kids are involved with."

◀◀ **Source:** This article was originally published in the *Winnipeg Free Press* on March 27, 2005. Reprinted with permission.

# 48. Factors Affecting the Uptake of Community Recreation as Health Promotion for Women on Low Incomes
By Wendy Frisby, Ph.D., and Larena Hoeber, MSc

## ■■■ Abstract

**B**ackground: There have been repeated calls for research on the factors that promote the spread of successful, local, health-promotion initiatives from one community to another. We examined the factors that affected the uptake of an initiative designed in one community to improve the health of women living below the poverty line through increased access to community recreation.

**Methods**: Workshops were held in three other communities, and uptake efforts were tracked for one year through follow-up site visits and telephone interviews with workshop participants.

**Results**: Making the issue a priority, actively involving the women in planning, pooling resources, sharing responsibility through partnerships, and addressing the structural dimensions of poverty were factors that enabled uptake. Factors that inhibited uptake included an emphasis on revenue generation, professionally led planning, inadequate attention to structural barriers, the undervaluing of certain resources, and an over-reliance on one idea champion.

**Conclusion**: A shift in how municipal recreation departments view their role as partners in community health promotion is required if programs are to promote health and be accessible to underserved populations.

■■■■■■

**R**esearchers have long lamented that findings from local health promotion projects, including those that are unsuccessful, are rarely published, creating a void in our knowledge regarding the factors that enhance or inhibit the dissemination of these initiatives from one community to another.[1-3] Understanding these factors is important because a community's capacity to take action is heightened when there is high awareness of both the enabling factors and the potential pitfalls.[1,4,5]

It is particularly important to understand the factors affecting uptake from the perspectives of those who are the intended beneficiaries of locally generated health promotion programs, as these individuals are often marginalized from the knowledge production process.[6,7] Women living in poverty are rarely involved in the planning of community recreation programs or in the analysis of research, even though they are the most likely to experience poor health and the least likely to participate in physical activity and other health-promoting forms of recreation.[8-12] The individualistic approach to health promotion tends to blame those with poor health for not adopting healthy lifestyles, while ignoring how their living conditions and local government policies and practices create barriers to participation.[13,14] Rather than expecting marginalized women to solve their own lifestyle problems or have professional staff do it for them, finding ways of bringing women on low incomes together with those who control local recreation program provision and policy development could lead to creative low-cost programming solutions.[15-18]

Municipal recreation departments in local government are well positioned across Canada to play an active role in health promotion, and these departments typically have mandates to provide a wide variety of services to all members in a community. However, there are few documented examples of how these departments are collaborating with marginalized citizens and other community partners to promote community health. Municipal recreation departments are facing increased economic pressures and, as a consequence, user pay policies are being introduced, making programs increasingly inaccessible to those who live below the poverty line.[19]

The Kamloops Women's Action Project (KWAP) is one example of a collaborative effort that involved a partnership between women on low incomes, a municipal recreation department, a number of community partners, and a research team. The impetus for KWAP arose when women on low incomes identified a lack of access to community recreation as a factor affecting their health and that of their families during informal discussions with a public health nurse. Other partners were then mobilized to address this community health issue. Principles of feminist action research

that legitimized the experiential knowledge of the women, democratized the research process through a collaborative approach, and strove for personal and social transformation guided the project.[20,21] Multi-level outcomes were achieved, including increased participation rates and improvements in self-reported dimensions of physical and mental health, changes in municipal recreation policy, and the formation of new community partnerships.[9,22]

The purpose of this study was to disseminate the "lessons learned" from KWAP to three other communities through a workshop intervention in order to examine the factors that enabled or inhibited the uptake of similar initiatives. While the researchers set the purpose of the study, the participatory and action-oriented principles of feminist-action research guided the workshops and the evaluation component where workshop participant perspectives on uptake efforts were tracked for one year.

## ■ ■ ■ Method

After obtaining ethical approval from the University of British Columbia, a full-day workshop intervention was conducted by original members of the KWAP team (including the lead author) in three communities in British Columbia that had requested additional information. A contact person was recruited in each community to generate interest and to invite women on low incomes, municipal recreation staff, and representatives from a variety of community groups to the workshops (see **Table 1**). One third of the day was spent sharing the lessons learned from KWAP using the Leisure Access Workbook as a guide.[22] Workshop participants spent the rest of the day discussing the relevance of launching similar initiatives in their communities and making initial action plans.

The tracking of uptake efforts entailed two return visits to each community to attend follow-up planning meetings and thirty follow-up telephone interviews with workshop participants who voluntarily agreed to participate in the study. After

| Table 1: Description of Communities and Workshop Participants | Community #1 | Community #2 | Community #3 |
|---|---|---|---|
| Approximate Population (1996 census) | 31,000 | 18,000 | 102,000 |
| % English Speaking (1996 census) | 85.3% | 90.5% | 68.7% |
| Geographic Region in British Columbia | South West | South Central | Lower Mainland |
| Municipal Recreation Annual Budget | $13,481,630 | $3,830,500 | $20,940,196 |
| # Workshop Attendees by Role | | | |
| Women on Low Incomes | 3 (25%) | 18 (75%) | 75 (88%) |
| Municipal Recreation Staff | 2 (17 %) | 1 (4%) | 5 (6%) |
| Other Community Partners (e.g., staff from public health units, family services, women's centre, mental health organizations, schools) | 7 (58%) | 5 (21% | 5 (6%) |
| Total # of Workshop Attendees | 12 (100%) | 24 (100%) | 85 (100%) |

the first return visits, transcripts from the meetings were coded to identify major themes. These were subsequently refined and verified in the telephone interviews and the second return visits when participants were asked to provide updates on action taken and to elaborate on the factors affecting uptake. Fifteen interviews were conducted with women on low incomes, five were with municipal recreation staff, and ten were with other community partners (e.g., staff from public health units, women's centres, family services, mental health organizations, schools).

Approval was obtained from the University of British Columbia and study participants to tape-record the workshops, follow-up meetings, and telephone interviews. Tape recordings and researcher field notes were transcribed, coded, and analyzed with the assistance of the qualitative data analysis software package Atlas.ti.

### ■■■ Results

The enabling and inhibiting factors that were discussed most frequently by workshop participants are identified in **Table 2**. In all three communities, a lack of access to community recreation was deemed to be a relevant community health issue for women on low incomes and this enabling factor served as the stimulus for further action. The women on low incomes saw increased participation as an avenue for connecting with their communities in a positive way, thereby reducing their social isolation and other related health problems (see E-1, **Table 2**). However, there was a difference in how municipal recreation staff balanced the issue of relevance with the economic pressures faced by their departments. In Communities #1 and #3, the health issue took priority and creative new low-cost strategies for increasing access were entertained. As illustrated in **Table 2** (see I-1), there was political pressure to make cost recovery and revenue generation a priority in Community #2 and this became an inhibiting factor because it was used as a rationale for not acting on the new ideas generated.

Actively involving the women on low incomes in planning through a community development approach was identified as a second enabling factor. This approach was evident in Communities #1 and #3 where professionals adopted facilitator rather than expert roles, encouraged shared leadership roles at meetings, and actively engaged the women on low incomes in discussions. The illustrative quote in section E-2 of **Table 2** illustrates the positive impact this approach had on the women. In contrast, in Community #2, a professionally driven approach where municipal recreation staff adopted expert roles was viewed as an inhibiting factor. The women on low incomes quickly became disillusioned in this instance

| Table 2: Factors Affecting Uptake | |
|---|---|
| **Enabling Factors (E-1 to E-5)** | **Inhibiting Factors (I-1 to I-5)** |
| **E-1. Relevance of the issue takes priority.**<br><br>Illustrative quote:<br><br>*Instead of focusing on all my problems alone, this has given me something positive to focus on … something to look forward to. It's what's getting me out of the house in the morning. And it's not just me. Others have the same problems. (Woman on low income, Community #3)* | **I-1. Pressure to generate revenues takes priority.**<br><br>Illustrative quote:<br><br>*We need to have a minimum of eight participants in a program in order to justify the cost of instructors, space, and equipment. We've tried running programs in the past but did not get enough people so it just wasn't worth our while. City council wants us to demonstrate how everything we do contributes to the bottom line so we have to achieve those minimum numbers. (Municipal Recreation Staff, Community #2)* |
| **E-2. Women on low incomes actively participated in planning.**<br><br>Illustrative quote:<br><br>*I've never had anyone care about what I have to say, but the staff people around the table are listening. They know how the system works, who to go to for help, and they care about my situation. (Woman on low income, Community #3)* | **I-2. Professional, staff-directed planning.**<br><br>Illustrative quote:<br><br>*The municipal recreation staff announced at one follow-up meeting that the swimming pool could be made available twice a week in the afternoons for the women and an instructor could be provided for the kids.*<br><br>*However, it was clear that swimming was not something the women on low income wanted to do. They talked about not having the appropriate bathing attire, not having enough money to buy a bathing suit, and not wanting to wear one in public. The staff person did not respond to these concerns and emphasized that a minimum turnout would be required.*<br><br>*She was basically doing what was easiest for her and her department based on the availability of a facility, rather than obtaining input from the women about their preferences. (Researcher field notes, Community #2)* |
| **E-3. Structural dimensions of poverty addressed.**<br><br>Illustrative quote:<br><br>*I've got a two-year-old and I'm trying to go back to school so I can get a decent job to support him. I'm exhausted at the end of the day and I wouldn't make it to these meetings unless child care was provided and [her friend] picked me up and brought me here. (Woman on low income, Community #3)* | **I-3. Structural dimensions of poverty ignored.**<br><br>Illustrative quote:<br><br>*We jumped at a solution too quickly when the municipal recreation department offered free swimming lessons. We did not really consider the women's issues in any depth. (Public Health Nurse, Community #2)* |
| **E-4. Resources are identified and pooled.**<br><br>Illustrative quote:<br><br>*The community partners already have relationships with the women and learning more about their situations helps us make better decisions. We can find creative ways to get free space and keep costs to a minimum. (Municipal Recreation Staff, Community #3)* | **I-4. Some resources are undervalued.**<br><br>Illustrative quote:<br><br>*We were only able to get three women out to our meeting. I'm sure that there are more who are interested, but they are a transient group and are hard to reach. (Municipal Recreation Staff, Community #1)* |
| **E-5. Responsibility for uptake is shared through partnerships.**<br><br>Illustrative quote:<br><br>*The responsibility is not all on my shoulders, so this is not so overwhelming. I've been energized by the interest and support from the other community partners who are involved. (Women's Centre Staff, Community #3)* | **I-5. An over reliance on one idea champion for uptake.**<br><br>Illustrative quote:<br><br>*[Name] was the person who got things started with the initial workshop. But when he left town, everyone else was just too busy to pick up where he left off. (School Principal, Community #1).* |

| Table 3: Response to the Workshop Intervention | | | |
|---|---|---|---|
| | Community #1 | Community #2 | Community #3 |
| **Presence of Enabling Factors** | E-1 | E-2 | E-1, E-2, E-3, E-4, E-5 |
| **Presence of Inhibiting Factors** | I-2, I-3, I-4, I-5 | I-1, I-3, I-4, I-5 | |
| **Response to Workshop Intervention** | Initial plans were made, but were not implemented. | Some plans were initiated outside the municipal recreation department. | Extensive plans were initiated within and outside the municipal recreation department. |

because their situations were not being taken into account and power imbalances were accentuated (see I-2, **Table 2**).

Addressing the structural dimensions of poverty was also identified as an enabling factor. During the workshops, the women described how poor public transportation, inadequate child care, fears of going out in unsafe neighbourhoods, and previous degrading treatment, created major barriers to involvement in community recreation. Community #3 went the furthest in addressing these types of barriers by creating carpools, arranging free child care, and creating telephone trees to provide social support for the women on low incomes (see E-3, **Table 2**). In the other two communities, discussions in follow-up meetings centered primarily on recreation programming and less attention was devoted to structural barriers. This inhibited the ability of the women to actively participate in planning and programs because insufficient attention was given to transportation and childcare (see I-3, **Table 2**).

Identifying and pooling resources was identified as a fourth enabling factor. When women's experiences of living in poverty were combined with the recreation staff and community partners' knowledge of local politics, programs, and policies, a wider range of options were considered and, in Community #3, this helped to create the social capital required for community activation (see E-4, **Table 2**).[23] When this did not occur in Communities #1 and #2, it was viewed as an inhibiting factor because the resources brought by some of the women and community partners were undervalued (see I-4, **Table 2**).

Sharing responsibility for action through partnerships was most evident in Community #3. This was viewed to be an important enabling factor because it reduced stress levels for the women on low incomes who were unable to attend all the meetings and for the community representatives who were increasingly feeling overburdened in their public sector jobs (see E-5, **Table 2**). Contrary to the health promotion literature,[24] relying on one "idea champion" was viewed as the main inhibiting factor that explained why uptake did not occur in Community #1 (see I-5, **Table 2**).

The response to the workshop interventions varied considerably in the three communities and can be attributed to the presence of enabling and inhibiting factors that were identified by participants (see **Table 3**). In Community #1, initial plans were developed but were not subsequently implemented, primarily because the "idea champion" moved to another community. In Community #2, women on low incomes assumed a major leadership role and implemented action plans outside of the existing municipal recreation system because they encountered a number of obstacles with that department's policies and practices. In Community #3, all of the enabling factors were present. Partnerships emerged between a larger and more diverse group of women on low incomes, community representatives, and municipal recreation staff, and more extensive action plans both within and outside existing municipal recreation programs were implemented.

## ■ ■ ■ Discussion

As called for in a recent dissemination research agenda,[1] the results of this study provide insights into the factors that affect uptake when efforts are made to disseminate successful health promotion initiatives from one community to another. While the program offerings of municipal recreation departments show considerable promise as vehicles for community health promotion, existing professional norms and practices can inhibit the uptake of initiatives like KWAP. As other studies have shown, when professionals adopt expert roles, it is unlikely that initiatives involving the active participation of marginalized groups will be adopted.[5,25] A community development approach where the views of marginalized populations and community partners are valued fosters community mobilization through mutual learning, more equitable power relations, and the pooling of resources.[2,3,26-29]

The question remains as to whether municipal recreation staff possess the training and support required to effectively engage in participatory planning with marginalized populations. Addressing the structural dimensions of poverty is critical if the barriers to participation in community health planning and municipal recreation are to be overcome. However, staff are under pressure to generate revenues so business tactics targeting members of the public with disposable incomes are being adopted. Partnering with staff from other community groups with experience in community development and ongoing relationships with women on low incomes provides a starting point for sharing responsibility and working collaboratively on issues of social relevance.

Additional insights into the role of "idea champions" were obtained in this study. While they can play a crucial role in advocating initiatives like KWAP, an over reliance on one "idea champion" can undermine uptake efforts if that person is no longer able to participate.

This study was limited to three communities and uptake factors were tracked for only one year. As a result, it is possible that other enabling factors will permit Communities #1 and #2 to uptake initiatives like KWAP in the future and other inhibiting factors may prevent Community #3 from sustaining the action it has undertaken. Nonetheless, the overall findings suggest that a shift in how municipal recreation departments view their role as partners in community health promotion is required if programs are to promote health and be accessible to underserved populations.

Additional research is required that documents the physical and mental health benefits of participation in community recreation. The examination of leisure access policies across the country, particularly from the perspectives of those on low incomes who are trying to access services, is also warranted.

### Notes

1. Johnson JL, Green LW, Frankish CJ, MacLean DR, Stachenko S. A dissemination research agenda to strengthen health promotion and disease prevention. Can J Public Health1996;87(Suppl.2):S5-S10.

2. Poland BD. Knowledge development and evaluation in, of and for healthy community initiatives. Part I: Guiding principles. Health Prom Int 1996;11:237-47.

3. Poland BD. Knowledge development and evaluation in, of and for healthy community initiatives. Part II: Potential content foci. Health Prom Int 1996;11:341-49.

4. Baker EA, Teaser-Polk C. Measuring community capacity: Where do we go from here? Health Educ Behav 1998;25:279-83.

5. Goodman RM, Speers MA, McLeroy K, Fawcett, S, Kegler K, Parker E, et al. Identifying and defining the dimensions of community capacity to provide a basis for measurement. Health Educ Behav 1998;25:258-78.

6. Reutter L, Neufeld A, Harrison MJ. Public perceptions of the relationship between poverty and health. Can J Public Health 1999;90(1):13-18.

7. Ristock J, Pennell J. Community Research as Empowerment: Feminist Links, Postmodern Interruptions. Toronto: Oxford University Press, 1996.

8. Evans RG, Barber, ML, Marmor TR (Eds.). Why Are Some People Healthy and Others Not? The Determinants of Health of Populations. New York: Aldine de Gruyter, 1996.

9. Frisby W, Crawford S, Dorer T. Reflections on participatory action research: The case of low-income women accessing local physical activity services. J Sport Manage 1997;11:8-28.

10. Hoffman A. Women's access to sport and physical activity. Avante 1995;1:77-92.

11. Reid C, Dyck L, McKay H, Frisby W (Eds.). The Health Benefits of Physical Activity for Girls and Women: A Literature Review and Recommendations for Policy. Vancouver, BC: British Columbia Centre of Excellence in Women's Health, 2000.

12. Reutter L, Neufeld A, Harrison MJ. Nursing research on the health of low-income women. Public Health Nurs 1998;15:109-22.

13. Shiell A, Hawe P. Health promotion, community development and the tyranny of individualism. Health Econ 1996;5:241-47.

14. Lyons R, Langille L. Healthy lifestyle: Strengthening the Effectiveness of Lifestyle Approaches to Improve Health. Ottawa: Health Canada, Population and Health Branch, 2000.

15. Green LW, George MA, Daniel M, Frankish CJ, Herbert CJ, Bowie WR, et al. Study of participatory research in health promotion: Review and recommendations for the development of participatory research in health promotion in Canada.. Vancouver, BC: Institute of Health Promotion Research, 1995.

16. Greenwood DJ, Levin M. Introduction to Action Research: Social Research for Social Change. Thousand Oaks, CA: Sage, 1998.

17. Minkler M, Wallerstein N. Improving health through community organization and building. In: Glanz K, Lewis FM, Rimer B (Eds.), Health Behavior and Health Education Theory, Research, and Practice. 2nd ed. San Francisco: Jossey-Bass; 1996;241-69.

18. Minkler M. Community organizing among the elderly poor in San Francisco's Tenderloin district. In: Minkler M (Ed.), Community Organizing and Community Building for Health. New Brunswick: Rutgers University Press, 1997; 244-60.

19. Thibault L, Kikulis L, Frisby W. Interorganizational linkages as a strategic response to institutional pressures. Managing Leisure 1999;4:125-41.

20. Maguire P. Doing Participatory Research: A Feminist Approach. Amherst, MA: The Center for International Education, University of Massachusetts, 1987.

21. Reid C. Seduction and enlightenment in feminist action research. Feminist Qualitative Research 2000;1/2:169-88.

22. Frisby W, Fenton J. Leisure access: Enhancing opportunities for those living in poverty. Vancouver, BC: BC Health Research Foundation and the BC Centre of Excellence in Women's Health, 1998.

23. Lomas J. Social capital and health: Implications for public health and epidemiology. Soc Sci Med 1998;49:181-88.

24. Orlandi MA. Health promotion technology transfer: Organizational perspectives. Can J Public Health 1996;87(Suppl.2):S28-S33.

25. Botes L, van Rensburg D. Community participation in development: Nine plagues and twelve commandments. Community Dev J 2000;35:41-58.

26. Callaghan M. Feminist community organizing in Canada: Postcards from the edge. In: Wharf B, Clague M (Eds.), Community Organizing: Canadian Experiences. Toronto: Oxford University Press, 1997;181-204.

27. Dominelli L. Women in the community: Feminist principles and organizing in community work. Community Dev J 1995;30:133-43.

28. Fortin J, Groleau G, O'Neill M, Lemieux V, Cardinal L, Racine P. Quebec's health communities projects: The ingredients of success. Health Prom 1992;31:6-10.

29. Israel BA, Schulz AJ, Parker EA, Becker AB. Review of community-based research: Assessing partnership approaches to improve public health. Annu Rev Public Health 1998;19:173-202.

◀◀ **Source:** The authors gratefully acknowledge funding received from the British Columbia Centre of Excellence in Women's Health (BCCEWH). This article was originally published in the *Canadian Journal of Public Health*, Volume 93, No 2 (March/April 2002). Reprinted with permission from the authors.

## Straight Facts About Making it in Pro Hockey

**49.**

By Jim Parcels

*An analysis of "What Hockey Doesn't Have to Offer"*

■ ■ ■ ■ ■ ■

What are the chances of making it in professional hockey? Does it matter where my son plays minor hockey if he has professional or collegiate hockey aspirations?

Those are questions that are asked every year by parents, players, and coaches alike across the minor hockey community.

As an employee of the Ontario Minor Hockey Association (OMHA), I have had the opportunity to work with the largest grassroots hockey organization in the world. It is a position that has allowed me to analyze the minor programs of over three hundred associations in southern Ontario as well as other local programs across the country.

Working the past three years with the OMHA has led me to analyze what parents really think the game is for. Is minor hockey provided as an avenue to the National Hockey League? Is minor hockey designed to develop players who are aspiring to attain a hockey scholarship? Was minor hockey designed to develop skills, community spirit, and teamwork? Is it for the development of individuals' well-being and character? Is it about learning how to win and lose?

I have found in my experience that many parents feel that there is some sort of "pot of gold" at the end of the hockey rainbow that involves a huge signing bonus, a card contract, and their son's action figure on a Sega Genesis video game.

Most parents will tell you it isn't, however, a vocal minority believe there is supposed to be a financial paradise, provided by hockey, at age twenty. Believe me, that paradise just isn't there.

What people within minor hockey never see is the actual cold, hard facts related to "turning pro" or "getting noticed" that get distorted every day by recruiters, managers, and coaches. It happens in both minor and junior hockey.

It amazes me, the stories that I have heard about organizations attempting to acquire the services of minor hockey players, some as young as the age of seven or eight, living in communities one to three hours from those teams. Things such as guaranteed ice time, video games, bicycles, jackets, track suits, and that never-ending term "exposure" that gets parents' heads spinning. Those organizations will tell you anything to get your services, just to fill a roster spot on their team, because there are dozens of other teams out there competing to tell you the same thing.

Recruiters love painting the rosy picture at the "front door" with promises of exposure and elite instruction. What very few people think of is the not-so-rosy picture at the "back door" of the development process for the 99.999% that pass through minor or junior hockey systems without guaranteed financial returns.

As a former employee of two Ontario Hockey League franchises (Peterborough Petes and Guelph Storm) I had a first-hand opportunity to see how the top of the development triangle in this province worked for players.

The OHL is considered the number one breeding ground for junior players aspiring to play professional hockey and rightfully so. The OHL provides an excellent opportunity to combine high-calibre hockey with educational opportunities between the ages of sixteen and twenty. I would strongly recommend any player who has the opportunity to play in the OHL to do so.

In 1989, when I joined the Petes as a twenty-year old trainer, I saw the pictures of Yzerman, Gainey, Redmond, and Jarvis adorning the walls of the dressing room. The Petes are reputed as the number one organization in the world for producing players for the NHL. The first thing I thought was "Wow, all the guys in this dressing room this year are going to the NHL!" Boy, was I wrong.

After two years as trainer for the Petes, I moved onto a marketing position for the Guelph Storm. Over five years I witnessed first-hand approximately 250 players who played or tried out with the two major junior teams. Some players moved on to pro and collegiate careers while others moved into the mainstream workforce. Five years later I got thinking; "How many of those players received some sort of financial return or end result on their investment of fifteen to twenty years into the game of minor and junior hockey?"

Of the thirty-eight players who went through the Petes dressing room in two years, only four ever played in the NHL, and only two are still there on a regular basis today.

That got me thinking: If the odds are that slim for the number-one team in the world for putting players in the NHL, what are the odds for players in the dressing rooms of the Mississauga Senators Atoms, North Bay Athletics Bantams, Waterloo Tigers Minor Peewees, Markham Waxers Novices, or Etobicoke Canucks Bantams?

Hence the reason for my study:

In 1995, when I returned to college, I decided to begin writing a research paper, "The Chances of Making it in Pro Hockey for Ontario Minor Hockey Players." During my research I accessed the various OHL Draft lists, rosters, and pro and college statistics from 1989 through to the 1996 season and found some very sobering facts that all parents, players, and coaches alike should be aware of.

The only accurate way to measure the chances of making the "pros" is to take an actual "birth year" as a sample category. Since hockey's competitive structure is based on the age of players, this is really the only accurate way of taking a sample group.

In my research I utilized the birth year 1975 as a sample. This included all players active in minor and junior hockey in the province between the years 1988–1991. After collecting registration information from the OMHA, Northern Ontario Hockey Association (NOHA), Metro Toronto Hockey League (MTHL), and Hockey Development Centre for Ontario (HDCO), the approximate number of players active in Ontario in 1991 was roughly twenty-two thousand.

That total doesn't include approximately 7,500 players who left the game through attrition from Tyke to Bantam who were also born in 1975. Therefore, there were about thirty thousand players who played minor hockey at one time or another in this province who had 1975 birth dates. That creates a sample group of thirty thousand players, born in 1975, on which this study is based.

For the players born in 1975, the Ontario Hockey League draft was held in 1991 (for underage Bantams born in 1975), and 1992 for the "open" Midget draft year.

Remember, that many NHL scouts considered the 1975 group of players in Ontario the strongest of any crop ever to come out of the province.

In the 1991 and 1992 OHL Drafts, there were 232 Ontario-developed players selected by the sixteen major junior teams (at that time). The following breakdown shows how those original thirty thousand players active "progressed."

Out of those 232 players drafted to the OHL, only 105 ever played one game in the OHL.

Out of those 105 players, only 90 finished their full three to four years of eligibility in the OHL.

Of those twenty-two thousand players, only forty-one played NCAA Division I hockey. Remember too that U.S. scholarships are not the large educational packages that have been offered by NCAA schools in the past.

What should also be noted is that full scholarships to Canadian players are almost non-existent today. The United States is developing hockey players at an incredible rate, and when it comes time to recruit, NCAA schools are offering their packages to American players. The number of Ontario players on scholarship in the United States has dropped 63% in the past ten years.

Scholarships too, are not "full" as many people tend to think. Canadian players are considered "out of state" and regular tuition for a player without scholarship ranges between $25,000–$40,000 US per year. In most cases, Canadian players are on partial scholarships where only 40%–60% of their education costs are covered. That means if you spend four years at an NCAA school, you may return home owing or having paid approximately $50,000–$75,000 US! Very few Canadian players today attain "full rides" to NCAA schools. Most NCAA teams only have seventeen scholarships per team with approximately thirty players on their roster. Something has to give financially for a roster that big.

What is disturbing, however, is out off those forty-one NCAA players, very few graduated from their programs of study when they left university. That begs the question: Why did they pursue an education through hockey if they have a minimal hockey future and no degree? With many hockey scholarships, fifth years are not covered by the university unless players are entering a post-graduate program. So to finish their degree, players would have to dole out between $25,000 and $40,000 to complete the degree at that university. Scholarships are also reviewed after each academic year, therefore if grades, part-time work, and hockey ability are not measuring up to school standards, the scholarship can be withdrawn.

Of the ninety players who finished their OHL careers and the twenty-three who played in the NCAA, only forty-eight were drafted to the NHL, while two signed NHL free agent deals.

This was the best NHL draft result for any birth year in Ontario! It was also the last year the NHL had twelve rounds in their draft. Today there are only nine rounds.

Of those forty-eight drafted players (and three free agent signees), only thirty-four signed contracts with NHL teams. Four signed free agent deals as non-drafted players.

Of those thirty-eight signed, only twenty-three have seen action to date in an NHL game.

Of those twenty-three, only eleven are currently active in the NHL (as of January 1, 1999). The low for the 1975 category active in the NHL was seven earlier in the 1998–99 season.

Of those twenty-three who have played an NHL game to date, research shows that only ten to twelve will earn a second contract with an NHL team. About half of those players earning second contracts will see them finish that second contract with an NHL team. The remainder of the fifty draftees will toil in the minor pros in the IHL, AHL, ECHL, or lower.

Of those thirty thousand players there were approximately eighty 1975 players active in Canadian University (CIAU) programs. Many of those players (about 75%) were former Major Junior (OHL, WHL, QMJHL) players who decided to pursue an education instead of minor pro deals. The others entered CIAU programs through Jr. B./Tier II or minor programs. The graduation rate from those programs by former major junior players from CIAU schools is about 50%–60%. In the cases of many players from major junior, a portion of their tuition (ranging from $1,000–$5,000 per year of service in the league) is paid by their former junior teams. This "education package" is usually reserved for players selected in the first four or five rounds of their junior league draft and are null and void if the player signs any professional hockey contract regardless of its amount.

The following is a breakdown of the average salary and the expected career length at each pro level:

| NATIONAL HOCKEY LEAGUE (NHL) |
| --- |
| Twelve current Ontario "1975" players |
| Average career: 2.4 years |
| Average initial salary: $220,000 |
| Original signing bonuses ranged between $550,000 and $750,000 for those nine players. These players are the lucky ones. |

| TIER TWO MINOR PRO |
| --- |
| AMERICAN HOCKEY LEAGUE (AHL) |
| Thirteen current Ontario "1975" players |
| Average career: 3.5 years |
| Average salary: $40,000 |
| INTERNATIONAL HOCKEY LEAGUE (IHL) |
| Eight current Ontario "1975" players |
| Average career: 3.3 years |
| Average salary $40,000 |

| TIER THREE MINOR PRO |
| --- |
| EAST COAST HOCKEY LEAGUE (ECHL) |
| Twenty-nine current Ontario "1975" players |
| Average career: 3.1 years |
| Average salary: $25,000 |

| TIER FOUR MINOR PRO |
| --- |
| UNITED HOCKEY LEAGUE (UHL) formerly Colonial Hockey League (CoHL) |
| Five current Ontario "1975" players |
| Average career: 1.8 years |
| Average salary: $16,000 |
| CENTRAL HOCKEY LEAGUE (CHL) |
| Eight current Ontario "1975 players |
| Average career: 1.6 years |
| Average salary: $18,000 |
| WESTERN PROFESSIONAL HOCKEY LEAGUE (WPHL) |
| Five current Ontario "1975 players |
| Average career: 1.5 years |
| Average salary $16,000 |
| WEST COAST HOCKEY LEAGUE (WCHL) |
| Two current Ontario "1975" players |
| Average career: 1.6 years |
| Average salary $20,000 |

Well, there you have it. This is the breakdown on a generation of players from Ontario who were in that elite group of players who "made it" and where they are today. Just imagine what the numbers are for some of the "weaker" birth years for Ontario. Some birth years like 1971 and 1968 had only ten to twelve players see action in NHL games. The 1976 birth category has seen only nine skate on NHL ice to date.

Remember that this was the best year the province of Ontario yielded in the past dozen. Other birth years are much less fortunate than the 1975's.

Another factor to consider in pro hockey is the lifestyle. Yes, playing in the NHL for a million a year sounds tempting and attractive, but many will tell you that the years fly by living a lifestyle of airports, busses, hotels, apartments, late pay cheques, contract haggling, games every other night, and the constant threat of trades. Players in the minor pros, however, live on a day-to-day basis, with many fearful of picking up the phone and taking a call from their GM or coach telling them to pack up the family and move on through a trade or waivers.

The average number of times a player gets traded, waived, or signs with another team for a minor pro player is 3.5 times over the course of a five-year career. That number increases once every two years after five years of service. One player that was with the Petes during my tenure in Peterborough played with eighteen minor pro teams in four years! That didn't include the four junior teams he played for in three years in the OHL.

The key development years for a player under an NHL contract is between the ages of twenty and twenty-three. Usually players sign a three to four year contract with an NHL team that will see the player play in the American Hockey League (AHL) or International Hockey League (IHL) during that contract. Only one in ten players drafted will see action in over one hundred NHL games. Keep in mind that the NHL Players Pension does not kick in until four hundred NHL games are played. The study also determined that for every year past the age of twenty, your chances of making the NHL are virtually cut in half in each succeeding season. Remembering too, that there is a draft of new players each year looking to take your job.

What also has to be taken into account in all of this is the fact that these players have "benefited" from the massive pro hockey explosion. Just imagine what the odds were for players in the sixties and seventies when there were more players active in minor hockey programs and fewer pro teams!

So next time you are considering where to play minor hockey for "development and exposure purposes" you can refer to this little gauge to see just where your child fits in. It's not as rosy as the picture painted at tryouts by managers and coaches of "alternative" minor hockey programs.

Where does all this lead us? What is the motivation for parents to go to the lengths they do to get their kid "noticed" in a minor hockey program? Why is it that 60% of Ontario players who currently play in the NHL played in minor hockey programs below the A classification (i.e., BB, C, D, E, etc.) in smaller rural towns?

Don't fall for the sales pitches that are constantly utilized to entice you to make a minor hockey move! Let the game take you as far as it can. Don't gamble your future by concentrating on hockey full time. Make the game part of your life, not a majority of it.

When considering junior hockey, remember to make hockey a priority right alongside education. The Ontario Hockey League has an excellent record of producing pro players *and* students, and many of their clubs work hard at trying to keep those priorities straight.

In closing, I should point out that this story is in no way an attempt to dishearten or demoralize the dreams of children playing minor hockey, because I know there are thousands who "dream the dream" every year. What this study does, however, is rationalize the whole system to educate parents and players about what "hockey doesn't have to offer."

It is neither an attempt to downgrade or diminish the efforts of junior programs in Ontario. It's just an eye-opener for many parents, coaches, managers, and recruiters who have an idea their players are "long shots" but have never researched or been presented with the exact numbers.

Bottom line? Play minor hockey at home with your friends, go to school, and concentrate on a career outside of hockey in addition to playing the game for fun! If you have a chance to play at a higher level in junior, take it, but don't expect it to be a ticket to the National Hockey League and throw out all educational concerns.

Don't sacrifice a normal family lifestyle trying to turn your nine-year-old into a pro. He is up against a lot more in life at that age than having to deal with the pressure his parents put on him to become their possible retirement plan.

The thing that scares me about publishing a story like this is that there will be five thousand parents out there that will read this and truly believe that their kid will buck the odds and be one of the "fortunate" dozen or so players. That's what concerns me the most!

◄◄ **Source:** Jim Parcels first wrote this piece in 1999. At the time he was working for the Ontario Minor Hockey Association.

# 50.

## Down and Out—But Competing for Canada
By Dave Bidini

Hell-bent on generating huge profits and flaunting its spectacles from the Super Bowl to soccer's World Cup, professional sport addresses the times only rarely—and now is not one of those occasions. Despite the global economic slump and the collective belt-tightening imposed upon the fans, the big leagues seem to care about nothing except themselves.

But one international competition exists solely to be socially relevant, and succeeds even though it boasts neither million-dollar star players, nor a vast TV audience. In fact, its athletes are drawn from the world's legion of street people and the games they play aren't broadcast at all.

The Homeless World Cup is a soccer tournament started in 2003 by a Scot named Mel Young as a way of bringing attention to homelessness and world poverty.

Games are played by three forwards and a goalie over two seven-minute halves on a court that measures 22 by 16 metres, and to qualify, team members must have been homeless at some point within the preceding twenty-four months.

Only four teams took part in the first cup, held in Graz, Austria, but six hundred players representing fifty-four nations gathered last month in Melbourne for the seventh.

Canada managed to field a team, but it was no easy task. Team Canada manager Paul Gregory, a social-housing strategist from Peel Region, west of Toronto, and coach Cristian Burcea, a city worker based at the John Innes Recreation Centre in downtown Toronto, drew from athletic programs for the homeless across the country.

Even so, they wound up with barely enough players. The Old Brewery Mission program in Montreal folded a month before the tournament because of waning funds, and the Vancouver chapter failed to file the necessary papers in time to allow the team's goaltender, a political refugee from Mexico named Memo, to make the trip.

But the Calgary Dawgs, run by Kevin Scullion, produced two players: Perry Senko, a businessman who lost his company and marriage in one fell swoop, and a young Moroccan-Canadian shelter-dweller who calls himself Juventus and has spent most of his life wandering in search of home and employment.

The John Innes Centre, where homeless men and women practise twice weekly in an airless old, gym, also provided two players.

Krystal Bell, nineteen, is a former soccer prodigy who ran away from home to live in garages and rooming houses.

Billy (Basile) Pagonis, forty-four, was once a star with the North York Rockets and Toronto Blizzard, but an addiction to opiates resulted in the collapse of his restaurant, loss of his home, estrangement from friends and family and, eventually, rehabilitation at the Centre for Addiction and Mental Health in Toronto.

## Going Cold Turkey at 30,000 Feet

The trip to Melbourne via Los Angeles requires twenty hours of travel. When Mr. Gregory first learned where the 2008 tournament would be held, his mind reeled because journeys much shorter had already proved nearly impossible for members of earlier teams.

In 2007, a player who had paid for his passport by gathering bottles after Toronto's annual gay pride parade decided to use the flight to the

Copenhagen game that year to quit methadone, cold-turkey, revealing his plan only after the plane had taken off.

In another instance, a player who lived rough near the Don River in Toronto and subsisted on whatever food he could scrounge, locked himself in the bathroom after hearing voices in his head. (He turned out to have a more serious case of schizophrenia than the team had realized).

Mr. Gregory helped him work through the ordeal, and he played in the tournament. But upon his return, he made his way back to his tarpaulin home near the river, never to be heard from again.

To cover the cost of the trip, Team Canada relies on small private donations while some teams, such as Ireland and Scotland, are supported by their national football associations. Fifteen African teams were brought to Australia using money raised by cup organizers, while others like the Cambodians, were assisted by relief programs.

The competition opened with a parade down Swanston Street, one of Melbourne's main thoroughfares. On the way to the event's main field in Confederation Square, Diana, a member of Team Belgium, told me that a few weeks earlier she had been spat at and called horrible names while living on the streets of Antwerp. Now, she was walking beneath her country's flag and being high-fived by throngs of Aussies cheering the sporting dispossessed.

Krystal, who keeps a photo in her back pocket of her mother, a prostitute and drug user who died of AIDS when her daughter was just 2, moved back and forth among teams, having her picture taken with the English, the defending-champion Scots, and Team India, which had taken thirty-two hours to reach Oz and then, at the airport in Sydney, lost one of its players, who spoke no English and had never travelled before. Because it had only four players, Team Canada was forced to draw from a squad of local reserves known as the "Street Socceroos" (after Australia's national team) and extras from other countries. Canada's reliance

on locals was even greater after Juventus caught his foot in the pitch's foamy rubber turf a few minutes into Canada's inauspicious opener against Holland, the injury quashing his experience just as it started.

Juventus was replaced by a crudely tattooed Scot named Dove, a former soldier and prize fighter from Port Glasgow who was recovering from a lifetime of abuse. Discharged after killing a Royal Air Force pilot in a bar fight with a single punch, he ended up in the drug trade and addicted to heroin before making four attempts to take his own life. (The last time, his seventeen-year old son caught him in the act.)

In keeping with the Canadians' bad luck, Dove was injured in the first half and forced out of the tournament (later, another sub broke a finger in a game against Ghana).

But by week's end, other teams had dozens of players—many out of shape because of the nature of their lives—shrouded in bandages. Diana's Belgians lost four players to injury, but were awarded the Fighting Spirit citation for not letting setbacks stop them.

Canada defeated Sierra Leone after the loss to Holland, but was beaten badly by Ghana and Russia before triumphing over a young Cambodian team made up of kids who had been born, and still lived in, the dumps of Phnom Penh. They had never left their city, let alone travelled by plane or held a passport, which their organizer, an Irishman named Paraic Grogan, said would win them instant status upon their return.

## Well-Heeled "Homeless" are Shown the Door

En route to Melbourne, Mr. Grogan reached the Phnom Penh airport to discover that local organizers had acquiesced to demands from some wealthy families that their sons be on the team.

"When I arrived, they were there with their families, dressed in fine clothes and everything. I had to disqualify them on the spot. I had to tell them that the Homeless World Cup wasn't for them, and sent them home. Because of this, there are parts of the city I can't visit any more."

In the tournament's second round—teams were seeded according to calibre after the third day—Canada lost in a shootout against East Timor, but defeated Cambodia a second time, which, amazingly, meant that the Canadians would be competing for the trophy given to the winner of the tournament's lowest tier.

About eight thousand spectators gathered for the final day's games (including the lost Indian player from the airport).

This time, Canada's goalie was a rail-thin Vietnamese refugee named Vannie who, Australia's coach told me, had sat in the corner for two weeks before summoning the courage to join the Socceroos.

Vannie was a stick figure in yellow and black who had been diagnosed with a slight mental deficiency. Asked about his life, he refused to talk about Vietnam, and as Team Canada waited to start the championship game against Malawi, he shook with fear and the excitement of what was probably, his coach said, the biggest day of his life.

Vannie had been pressed into duty because another Canadian substitute, an Aussie named Stan, had come down with the flu. After growing up with two alcoholic parents and hitting the streets at fourteen, Stan had spent two years in prison after an altercation with a policeman and was trying to piece his life back together while battling severe depression and a lingering heroin dependency.

Everyone felt badly that Stan was ill—he had proved to be an excellent teammate, roaring at his charges and showing great leadership—and even more so after Perry and Billy spotted the thirty-year-old dry-heaving behind a tree at the college dorms where most of the athletes stayed.

Billy, who had two of his pro teammates overdose in his arms, said, "You don't dry-heave when you get the flu." Stan was going through

withdrawal. He was back on the street before the event ended.

Canada lost 12–5, hamstrung by having only three nationals on the field, most of them ravaged by injury. "I was so sore lying in bed at night that I couldn't bring myself to walk to the washroom," confessed Billy, the old pro.

"Instead, I shouted, 'Look out below!' and peed out the window."

Only Krystal avoided serious injury and by tourney's end; you couldn't bump into another player or coach who hadn't noted her resilience and athleticism. She had scored twenty goals, played nearly every minute of every game, and almost single-handedly carried a threadbare team to a trophy.

This attention culminated in a visit from Steven Coleman, the former Dutch international player who was coaching the Netherlands. After Team Canada's second game against Cambodia, he called over the teenager—who shares a room with her brother and two nephews in Toronto's Regent Park social housing complex—and asked if she would consider going to school in Rotterdam and playing for his university women's team.

"You have a good left foot," he told Krystal, who instantly grew wary—her default mode after years of being cheated and misguided by friends and accomplices. Was the offer for real? Already back working toward her high school diploma, she later decided that, if it pans out, she'll go for it.

On the final night, tournament organizers handed out awards at a closing party. When it was time to announce the top female player, everyone was certain Krystal would win, but the trophy was given to Liberia's Dehkontee Sayon.

The players were perplexed, but the next day learned that the entire Liberian team, save Dehkontee and another player, had claimed political asylum, joining a handful of Zimbabweans, Afghans (whose team had defeated Russia to win the overall tournament), and a Kenyan. In all, fifteen players failed to go home.

When Dehkontee returned to Monrovia without her team, perhaps the trophy would stave off some of the inevitable questions: Why had she returned when they all stayed in Australia, and why hadn't she stopped them?

## Recruiting Vannie Pays Off Handsomely

But the ceremony wasn't over. Finally, the announcer said, "This next trophy perhaps best represents the values of the HWC, and is maybe the most important one handed out tonight."

Then he announced the winner of the trophy for fair play: Canada.

Caught off-guard, the players threw their arms into the air and then stood onstage as coach Cristian thanked the Australian reserves. Most sporting competitions have some teams that were assembled expressly to win—teams that would have scoffed at having Vannie added to the roster moments before their biggest game.

But the Canadians had embraced all of the reserves, suggesting that they were competing for the right reasons and deserved to be cheered by people who, like themselves, had escaped, at least momentarily, the dark parts of their lives.

Or would the escape be more than temporary? Research shows that good things happen to a high percentage of those who take part in the Homeless World Cup. Unlike Stan, vomiting behind the trees, they get clean, reunite with their families, find jobs and decent housing. Perhaps going back to where they had suffered their worst defeats would not be so bad after all.

The next day, six hundred men and women turned and faced a single direction: home.

◀◀ **Source:** Toronto writer Dave Bidini's next book, *Home and Away: The Story of the 2008 Homeless World Cup*, is published by Greystone Books. This article was originally published in *The Globe and Mail* on January 3, 2009. Reprinted with permission.

# Section 9

## Economy and Sports

In previous editions of *Taking Sport Seriously*, the section on economics has been overly focused on professional sports. Fortunately, at a time when those interested in sports have become a little weary of the struggles between millionaires (players) and billionaires (owners), more articles and reports have become available relating to other aspects of the sports economy. Of particular interest are the "hidden economies" of sports— the vast army of volunteer labour that supports sport (about which very little has been written in terms of what it would cost to replace those individuals with paid staff); and the vast, primarily Asian-based army of low-paid labour that makes huge profits for athletic clothing and equipment manufacturers in wealthy nations. Bruce Kidd addresses this issue in "Olympic Sweat," pointing out that just as the IOC would not accept sponsorship from a corporation making tobacco products, they (and National Olympic committees, and international federations, and national sport organizations) should make a similar moral decision with regard to the manufacturers of athletic clothing and equipment, especially with regard to fair wages and working conditions, and the health of the workers who produce the clothing and equipment. The anti-sweatshop campaigns are ongoing (e.g., Clean Clothes Campaign: www.fairolympics. org; Clearing the Hurdles: www.clearingthehurdles.org), along with specific campaigns aimed at specific Olympic Games (e.g., Playfair 2012: www. playfair2012.org.uk).

Charities represent another "hidden economy" with very close connections to sport. Robert Cribb recently blew the whistle on charitable foundations linked to professional sports teams, pointing out how little of the funds raised are actually donated to the causes for which the money was solicited (see "Additional Suggested Reading and References"). Events such as sponsored runs and endurance events are also ubiquitous in charitable fundraising; perhaps the best known of these is the Run for the Cure in support of breast cancer research. While it seems almost sacrilegious to question what is widely considered to be such a good cause, it is invariably a mistake to accept such things at face value. Samantha King raises difficult questions about "the breast cancer industry" in her book, *Pink Ribbons, Inc.* (2006). In an interview, Dr. King ("Pink Ribbons Go Corporate"), explains that people's charitable endeavours have been exploited by corporations for marketing purposes, and that some of those corporations may be selling products made with chemicals that have been linked to breast cancer.

In a neo-liberal climate, where every facet of the public sector is expected to be run like a business, cities have taken to reporting how even sports and recreation have significant economic value. Two such reports were carried out by Caminata Consulting in 2000 and 2002 for the cities of Edmonton and Calgary respectively. The executive summaries from these reports, which make numerous claims about the economic benefits of sport, are included here. The Edmonton report, for example, claims that each dollar the city spent on recreation would generate $22 in value. Such claims should be read with critical and skeptical eyes—if spending on public recreation was so profitable, cities would certainly be spending far more than they are. However, the economic impact studies are frequently carried out in order to justify public spending on sports and recreation, and may be seen as "instruments for political shenanigans," since such "studies are commissioned to legitimize political positions rather than to search for economic truth" (Crompton, 2006, p. 67). Crompton's critical analysis of a number of reports from economic impact studies includes the Edmonton study presented here.

Economic impact studies are also used to justify public spending that is often more politically controversial—on professional sports stadia, and on sporting mega-events such as Olympic and Pan Am Games. Jess Hajer's article ("New Stadium as 'Urban Renewal' Is More Fantasy than Fact") on the planned construction of a new professional football stadium in Winnipeg questions a number of the claims that were made to justify public spending at the time. Developer David Asper planned a $150-million stadium, and was asking for $25 million from the provincial government and $15 million from the federal government, as well as a number of concessions including ownership of the Winnipeg Blue Bombers. In an indication of how quickly matters change when large amounts of public money may become available for a project favoured by both developers and politicians, the new stadium is now planned at the University of Manitoba, with only $10 million up front coming from the developers and $105 million from Manitoba, a provincial government with deficits in the amount of $1.4 billion over the next four years (White, 2010). Excavation for the planned stadium site started in August 2010.

The final costs for the Vancouver 2010 Olympics will not be known for some time, but they are substantially more than the figures included in the bid materials and in the original economic impact studies. Kim Hart-MacNeill and Jasmine Rezaee report a total cost of over $9.2 billion in "Mathletics,"

as well as identifying a number of sponsors who appear to have little to do with sport or health. At the same time, Dawn Paley and Isaac Oommen were reporting the portion of that spending to be paid by the public (through taxes) in their article, "Boosters' Millions: Better Ways than the Olympics to Spend $6.1 Billion." They identify what could be achieved for that amount of money in education, family services, housing, transportation, community welfare, and the arts.

### Additional Suggested Readings and References

- Black, S. 2006. "Why the Canadian Football League is the Sweden of the Sports World." *Canadian Dimension*, September/October.
- Bramham, D. 2009. "Olympics Bill Tops $6 Billion—So Far." *Vancouver Sun*, January 23.
- Bula, F. 2010. "Olympics Cost [City of] Vancouver Nearly $600 Million." *The Globe and Mail*, April 16.
- Cribb, R. 2010. "Star Investigation: The High Cost of Sports Charities." *Toronto Star*, April 24.
- Crompton, J. 2006. "Economic Impact Studies: Instruments for Political Shenanigans." *Journal of Travel Research*, 45(August): 67–82.
- Dembicki, G. 2010. "From Olympic Ideals to Corporate Blitz: A Brief History—How Business Saved the Games by Turning them into a Tightly Controlled, Billion Dollar Advertisement." TheTyee.ca, January 8.
- King, S. 2006. *Pink Ribbons, Inc.: Breast Cancer and the Politics of Philanthropy*. Minneapolis: University of Minnesota Press.
- Klanac, B. 2006. "Huge Costs, Legacy Issues Challenge for 2010 Olympics." *Western News*, October 19.
- McQuaig, L. 2010. "Restraint for Everything but Sports." *Toronto Star*, February 23.
- Landau, S. 2008. "Olympics 2008: Real Gold Winners: Coke, McDonald's, KFC." *Canadian Dimension*, September.
- Milner, B. 2007. "Open Invite for a Sponsor." *The Globe and Mail*, April 24.
- Palmer, J. 2002. "Bread and Circuses: The Local Benefits of Sports and Cultural Businesses." *C.D. Howe Institute Commentary*, No. 161, March.
- Reguly, E. 2002. "The Economics of Pro Sports Can't be Sustained, Period." *The Globe and Mail*, August 29.
- Slack, E. 2002. "Municipal Funding for Recreation." *Ideas that Matter*, 2(2): 15–24.
- Westhead, R. 2006. "Olympic Morality isn't Cost Effective." *Toronto Star*, October 17.
- White, P. 2010. "Province to Pick up Majority Cost on New $115-Million Stadium." *The Globe and Mail*, April 1.

# Olympic Sweat

## By Bruce Kidd

**51.**

*The Games' founders wanted a better world—not one where Olympic-logo sportswear is often made in sweatshops, says ex-Olympian Bruce Kidd*

■ ■ ■ ■ ■ ■

For Pierre de Coubertin and those who helped him establish the modern Olympics in Athens in 1896, the Games were to be not simply an athletic event, but the focal point of a broadly based social movement that, through the activity of sport and culture, was to enhance human development and generally make the world a better place.

In the intervening years, the modern Olympic movement has not only raised the standard of sporting excellence far beyond anything Mr. de Coubertin dreamed about and taken sport all over the world, but intervened on some of the most difficult social issues. The Olympic movement is justly proud of its moral leadership against racism and apartheid, sexism and gender discrimination, and doping and other forms of unethical competition. During the nineties, the International Olympic Committee accepted responsibility for sustaining the natural environment in which the Games are staged.

Today, the Olympic movement is faced with an ethical challenge that affects the social environment in which training, competition, and revenue generation occur. At issue are the business practices of the world's largest sportswear companies. The expansion of international trade in sportswear goods under the auspices of such corporate giants as Nike, Adidas, Puma, Fila, and Roots Canada has drawn millions of people, mostly women, into the global economy.

As a former Olympic athlete, I can attest to the intense pride athletes feel when they don our national colours to represent Canada on the world stage. But how difficult it is to take pride in a uniform made under sweatshop conditions, while wondering whether our garments were sewn by a woman paid pennies for working fourteen-hour shifts in a badly ventilated warehouse.

A new report by Oxfam Canada, the Canadian Labour Congress, and the Maquila Solidarity Network titled "Play Fair at the Olympics" asks fundamental questions about the global sportswear industry, questions that go to the heart of debates on poverty, workers' rights, trade, and globalization. The sportswear business model is based on ruthless pressure on prices, a demand for fast and flexible delivery of goods, and a constant shift in manufacturing location in search of cheaper wages and more lax enforcement of labour regulations.

Many sportswear companies have attempted to address these concerns by establishing purchasing codes of conduct. However, the Play Fair report found that these ethical commitments were all too often contradicted by aggressive purchasing practices, and the lack of independent monitoring and enforcement. As one factory owner explained, "Higher labour standards in Cambodia do not tie a buyer to a factory. Only a good price can do that."

Employment in the sportswear industry is often precarious, involving unreasonably long working hours, low wages (usually paid by piece rate), dangerous working conditions, temporary or seasonal work, and no sick leave, maternity leave, or benefits. Yet the Olympic movement has long been silent about these issues.

The movement seeks to create a way of life based on "respect for universal fundamental ethical principles." It is time to extend this aspiration to the workers who produce the uniforms and equipment on which the movement depends and which it advertises. As the primary holder of the rights to use the Olympic logo, the international Olympic movement can and should enforce changes by building into sportswear licensing and sponsorship contracts commitments to respect internationally recognized labour standards. The IOC should be using its influence to ensure that workers in the sportswear industry are employed under fair, dignified, and safe conditions.

A growing number of North American universities have accepted such obligations. In 2000, the University of Toronto became one of the first Canadian universities to develop a code of conduct for trademark licensees to ensure that manufacturers and suppliers of trademarked merchandise meet minimum employment standards regarding wages and benefits, working hours, and overtime compensation. The code also has specific prohibitions on child labour, forced labour, and harassment, and requires licensees and their contractors to recognize and respect the right of employees to freedom of association and collective bargaining.

On Sunday, the Canadian Olympic Committee will be holding its annual general meeting in Montreal. Delegates will celebrate the hundredth anniversary of the Olympic movement in Canada. This weekend, my colleagues could demonstrate leadership on this issue by calling upon the IOC to protect the right of workers who produce Olympic clothing and equipment. The leaders of the Canadian Olympic movement, including the newly formed Vancouver 2010 organizing committee, can show the world that the movement will again place sport at the service of human development and justice.

Just as you will not see the Olympic movement signing sponsorship deals with tobacco firms, similarly, no deals should be made with companies who are ready to ignore and abuse the rights of workers. After all, if the values of the Olympic movement stopped at the stadium wall, it would be only a shadow of Pierre de Coubertin's dream.

◀◀ **Source:** Bruce Kidd, an Olympian at the 1964 Summer Games in Tokyo, is now an honorary member of the Canadian Olympic Committee and a professor in the faculty of physical education and health at the University of Toronto. This article was originally published in *The Globe and Mail* on April 16, 2004. Reprinted with permission.

# 52. Pink Ribbons Go Corporate
## By Samantha King

The book *Pink Ribbons, Inc.*, by Samantha King, associate professor in the school of kinesiology and health studies at Queen's University, is the first critical study of the breast cancer industry and what she terms "the corporatization" of charitable causes in our consumer-driven society. King traces how breast cancer has been transformed from a stigmatized disease and individual tragedy into a market-driven industry of survivorship.

In an unprecedented outpouring of philanthropy, more and more corporations have been focusing their efforts on raising money and awareness toward finding a cure for the disease. Rates of incidence continue to rise, yet research into public health prevention of breast cancer and its root causes is being overshadowed and neglected.

"Fundraising for breast cancer has developed into a highly competitive market in which large foundations and corporations compete with one another to attract the loyalty of consumers—in this case, well-intentioned members of the public wanting to do their part in the fight against the disease," says King.

What's more, she concludes that only about two-thirds of the money being raised by some corporate campaigns actually goes to fund breast cancer research. The rest gets eaten up in overhead or finds its way to the bottom lines of corporate sponsors.

Not surprisingly, King's views have attracted widespread media attention across North America, and her book has caused people in the philanthropic and medical communities to think again about the value and the direction of the pink ribbon campaign and of the rainbow collection of similar initiatives out there.

Review editor Ken Cuthbertson recently talked with King about *Pink Ribbons, Inc.*, and the reaction to it.

**Q. Your book has come out at a time when a lot of people are talking about breast cancer research and the whole phenomenon of various diseases as corporate-sponsored "causes." Your timing in writing this book was impeccable.**

A. Yes. My timing was very fortunate in that respect. I became interested back in the mid-nineties in the trend towards shopping as a way to show one's support for a particular cause and it soon became clear to me that breast cancer was at the centre of that trend. Since I'd been teaching and researching the politics of women's health for quite some time, I thought that looking at breast cancer fundraising would be a good way for me to investigate that broader phenomenon. I started tracking information about breast cancer-related marketing in 1996, and I began researching in earnest in 1998. One of the things that's really amazed me is that today, ten years later, breast cancer is an even bigger charitable cause than it was back then.

**Q. Did you know at the time that your research findings would turn into a book or did you start doing research because you felt the topic was important?**

A. The work was going to be part of my PhD dissertation initially. In fact, at first, it was going to form just one chapter of a broader project on health philanthropy. But it soon became clear that there was so much going on around breast cancer and that the cultural preoccupation with pink ribbons was worthy of extended study. After completing my dissertation in 2000, and at the urging of my doctoral committee, I decided to try to make it into a book.

**Q. How long did it take to do your dissertation research, and how did you do it?**

A. Well, the first thing I did was to attend the National Race for the Cure, in Washington, D.C., in June 1999, which is part of the Susan G. Komen Breast Cancer Foundation's series of five-kilometre runs. It was the tenth anniversary event that year. Al and Tipper Gore were there, so were numerous representatives from large corporations, and ten thousand runners and walkers. That experience started me on the trail of attending similar fundraising events throughout the United States. I attended other Races for the Cure as well as an Avon Walk for Breast Cancer, where I worked as a volunteer. The Avon walk is similar in format to the Weekend to End Breast Cancer events in Canada.

These events last for two days, and the organizers provide participants with tents, showers, and hot meals. So a major part of the research for my book involved going to these events to do observational research, interviewing participants, and writing about my experiences as a volunteer. I was particularly interested in the messages about breast cancer awareness, survivorship, and physical activity that they promoted, as well their effectiveness as fundraising tools.

There were three other main parts to my research. I spent from 1998 until 2005, when I finished the final draft of my book, tracking corporate involvement in funding for breast cancer research. My focus was on breast cancer-related marketing campaigns that used the pink ribbon symbol to attract well-meaning consumers. Given that this was a relatively recent phenomenon, I wanted to understand how it emerged and why. I did this by reading business management literature, marketing research, and work in non-profit studies. I also wanted to explore how governments were encouraging the public to participate in philanthropic activities during this period. For this, I analyzed government documents related to the breast cancer research stamp, the first fundraising stamp in the history of the United States, which was issued in 1998.

The final step in the process was a textual analysis of breast cancer survivor narratives, with a particular focus on how they've shifted over time. While personal narratives of women with breast cancer in the early eighties tended to highlight political concerns about issues like carcinogens in our environment, I found that recent narratives tend to focus more heavily on the importance of individual strength and optimism in battling the disease.

**Q. In a nutshell, what did you discover in the course of your research?**

A. The conclusion I came to is that in spite of all of the money that's been raised for breast cancer research and all the attention that's been paid to the cause, relatively little improvement has been made in terms of breast cancer incidence or mortality rates. My argument is that this failure is partly due to the corporatization of the disease and how that has limited how we conceptualize the problem of breast cancer and how we spend the money that is raised in the struggle against the disease.

**Q. Has corporatization been entirely a bad thing?**

A. Not entirely. But I think the answer to your question is a bit complicated. My argument is that corporatization has raised substantial funds. That's a big positive ...

**Q. Are we talking about billions of dollars?**

A. Well, certainly tens of millions. But that money comprises only a very small a part of overall spending on research. Most breast cancer research is funded by the government or by large foundations. Of course, corporate contributions are going to those large foundations, but the dollar amounts usually comprise less than 10% of any foundation's income. In addition, because of lack of transparency in breast cancer marketing, it's unclear how much corporations spend on advertising for these campaigns versus how much money they actually generate. The other positive thing to come out of all of the public attention devoted to the disease, I think, is that it's helped to destigmatize it. It would have been unimaginable thirty years ago for any corporation to tie its name to breast cancer. For a variety of reasons, breast cancer has come out of the closet, and I think that the corporatization has assisted in that in process some ways.

**Q. You make the point in your book that to a certain extent, corporations don't want to talk about the death element of cancer, and so they've "sanitized" it, for lack of a better term.**

A. Yes. That's one of the main critiques that I make about the corporate interest in the disease: death doesn't sell. So in order for corporations to market products through a connection to breast cancer, they've had to make the disease less frightening ... more "sexy." What that's done is present the public with an unrealistic picture of where we're at in the fight against the disease. There's a general lack of acknowledgement and awareness that thousands of women—and some men—still die every year from breast cancer.

**Q. Did the corporatization of breast cancer that you talk about follow the cultural shift in how we view breast cancer, or did things happen the other way around?**

A. They happened together. The history that I trace in my book examines the work of the women's health movement and activism around breast cancer, in particular, in destigmatizing the disease. At the same time, in the eighties, we saw the spread of mammography as a diagnostic tool among asymptomatic populations so that it became part of everyday health care for women. These changes placed breast cancer squarely in the public eye. In the early nineties, as breast cancer activism aimed at winning greater government support for research was developing strength, we saw corporations starting to think about ways to tie their philanthropic practices to their bottom lines. Cause-related marketing was one of the tools that emerged from this new way of approaching philanthropy. Since women make most of the purchasing decisions in a typical household, and corporations are constantly struggling to win their share of female consumers, breast cancer came to be seen as a "marketer's dream."

**Q. In recent years, we've come to look at a variety of social welfare issues in our society—health care, education, social services, etc.—in terms of the bottom line, dollars and cents, and social utility. Have we turned breast cancer into just another product?**

A. I think so. Corporations and large foundations are now competing with one another for the loyalty of consumers who are concerned about breast cancer. This is part of a broader commodification of everyday life that makes it hard for us to think about civic participation outside the realm of consumption. And because commercial interests are driving interest in breast cancer, we don't tend to ask certain vital questions about the disease.

**Q. What sort of questions?**

A. Questions about the social inequalities in terms of who gets the disease or who dies from it. Questions about why the vast majority of funds raised go to research on screening and treatment rather than primary prevention.

**Q. Has the fight against breast cancer been affected by the fact it is primarily a women's disease?**

A. In terms of the corporate interest in breast cancer, yes I think so. There are a number of reasons why there is so much interest in breast cancer as opposed to other diseases, and these stem partly from the fact that it affects more women than men. I've already mentioned the purchasing power of women, but why breast cancer as opposed to other illnesses? Lung and heart disease kill many more women every year in North America than breast cancer, but breast cancer became the disease of choice for corporate marketers because, rightly or wrongly, we connect those other conditions with bad lifestyle choices. That's not the case with breast cancer. The disease is also associated with motherhood, nurturance, and sex, all of which are highly valued in our culture.

**Q. What impact has the "F word"— feminism—had on this whole discussion and on interest in breast cancer as a cause?**

A. The breast cancer cause drew on the personnel and resources of the women's health movement in its early years, particularly in the eighties. That's when we saw campaigns against one-step mastectomies and in favour of more research funding. More recently, the mainstream of the breast-cancer movement has explicitly tried to distance itself from feminist principles and to create a movement that's pro-women without being feminist. In other words, politics has been taken out of the equation for the large foundations and mainstream breast cancer organizations.

**Q. That's interesting because you mentioned this earlier and you said in your book that social inequalities are reflected in the campaign against breast cancer. What do you mean by that?**

A. In the United States, the primary focus of my research, the leaders in the campaign to fight breast cancer have historically come from the middle and upper classes and they have not been concerned with access to care. Indeed, the Susan G. Komen Breast Cancer Foundation, the most prominent organization in the United States, has never taken a position in favor of universal health care. This might be one of the reasons for the big difference in mortality rates between, for example, African-American women and white women.

**Q. How much of a difference are we talking about?**

A. African-American women are 2.2 times more likely to die from the disease than white women, even though the incidence rate for African-American women is lower.

**Q. Is there a difference in death rates in Canada and the United States?**

A. There is a difference in terms of the incidence rate. It's a little lower in Canada, where the figure is approximately a one-in-nine lifetime risk, as opposed to a one-in-seven lifetime risk in the United States. According to the Canadian Cancer Society, the mortality rate in Canada in 2006 will be approximately 23.4 deaths per 100,000, which equals about 5,300 total deaths from the disease. In the United States, those figures are 26.4 and 40,970 respectively. The other way that social inequalities are reflected in the campaign against breast cancer, both in Canada and the United States, is that people only get to participate in most aspects of the movement if they have the resources to buy pink ribbon consumer products, pay an entry fee for the Run for the Cure, or raise the $2,000 minimum to walk in the Weekend To End Breast Cancer.

**Q. What's been the reaction to your book and to your ideas?**

A. So far, the reaction has been really positive. The way I'm gauging that is through emails and phone calls I've received, and from the people I've talked with on radio call-in shows. So far, I've only received one negative email, which was from an official at a small breast cancer organization in Ontario who was concerned about how my research would affect their corporate contributions. The media has also shown a great

deal of interest in the findings, and the book has been the subject of a *Maclean's* magazine interview, a *Globe and Mail* review—which was positive, thankfully!—and a piece in *Time* magazine. So far, I've seen only one letter to the editor that took issue with my position. In fact, I've been really surprised by the extent to which breast cancer survivors and people working within cancer organizations have expressed their agreement with the analysis. I knew from the research I did for the book that there was widespread discomfort with the exploitation of breast cancer survivors through marketing campaigns, for example. But I think I may even have underestimated the level of disillusionment out there.

**Q. Do you think you've articulated ideas that a lot of people have been thinking about?**

A. Yes, I think so. I've received numerous phone calls and emails in recent weeks from breast cancer survivors thanking me for articulating what they've been feeling for sometime, but have felt uneasy about stating publicly for fear of seeming untactful or ungrateful.

**Q. How do you respond to those critics who argue that you're hurting the cause of breast cancer research funding, that you're doing something that's negative in the long term?**

A. I'm a strong supporter of a well-funded breast cancer research program, but I think we really need to consider whether we are spending the money we're raising in the most appropriate way. Some organizations in the breast cancer movement who are critical of the commercialization of the disease, and I'm thinking particularly of groups like Breast Cancer Action in San Francisco, are even suggesting that we might actually have enough money coming in to the cause and that what we need to address now is how to spend that money more judiciously.

**Q. How do you feel we should do that?**

A. We need more research on primary prevention. By that, I mean research that considers the environmental causes of breast cancer and the carcinogens in the food we eat, the water we drink, and the air we breathe. We also need to start looking more carefully at the health effects of household toxins and workplace hazards. This is an area of inquiry that has been incredibly underfunded, although that is beginning to shift a little. Environmental causes of disease affect large numbers of people. These causes can also be dealt with at the societal level through a public-health approach. Until now, the focus on prevention has been minimal and too focused on individual lifestyle choices. Individual behaviours have been found to have a very modest effect on risk for breast cancer and are, in any case, very difficult to change.

**Q. Should people continue to support pink ribbon campaigns and products?**

A. I usually suggest to people who want to buy a pink ribbon product that they ask three questions:

First, how much money is the product actually raising for breast cancer research? If they can't find that out from reading the small print on the merchandise or from asking a person in store, they shouldn't buy it.

Second, where is the money raised going and how will it be spent? If that information is unclear, or if it's clear but consumers find that it's not going to be spent in ways that are actually going to make a difference in the number of people who are being diagnosed with breast cancer, then I'd recommend giving directly to organizations whose work does just that.

Finally, what are the ingredients of the product being purchased? Some corporations that have been most active in breast cancer marketing are also those whose products include ingredients that have been linked to breast cancer. In particular, I'm thinking here of cosmetics companies and automobile manufacturers. I recommend staying away from goods produced by what Breast Cancer Action calls "pinkwashers."

**Q. After writing your book, how optimistic are you about the prospects for medical science to ever find a cure or at least an effective treatment for breast cancer?**

A. One of the things we need to do is ask ourselves why we are so focused on cure and not on prevention. Finding a cure would be fantastic, clearly, for the five thousand Canadian women and men who die from the disease each year. And we certainly need more effective, less toxic treatments. But what about the twenty-two thousand people who will be diagnosed with breast cancer in 2006?

So, overall, I have mixed feelings about the direction of breast cancer research and about the pink ribbon industry that helps to fund it. I've realized, based in part on responses to my book, that there's increasing awareness of the problems with the current approach to breast cancer, and that's a really good thing. At the same time, during October, which was Breast Cancer Awareness Month, we saw even more corporations jumping on the breast cancer bandwagon. Until we start to ask difficult questions about how the money raised is being spent and whether corporations who do not have the pursuit of public health as a primary interest should be helping to set research priorities, I'm not sure we will win the battle against the disease.

◀◀ **Source:** This article was originally published in the *Queen's Alumni Review*, 4 in 2006.

# 53.

## The Economic Significance of Amateur Sport in the City of Edmonton in 2000 - Executive Summary

### By Tim Berrett

The Edmonton Sport Council (ESC), as part of its efforts to promote the value of sport in the city of Edmonton, retained Caminata Consulting to determine the economic contribution that amateur sport and active recreation make to the local economy. The study provides an analysis of the economic significance and impact of the "amateur sport and active recreation" sector in Edmonton in the year 2000

The definition of amateur sport and active recreation used in this investigation was as follows:

> Sport and active recreation involves participants who execute skills that require practice or preparation; it involves competition with other participants, oneself, or nature; and it occurs in a structured environment.

For the initial expenditure figures, the definition of Edmonton was the "city of Edmonton" as outlined by municipal boundaries. The economic model employed to determine the output effects of this spending reported the impacts on the Census Metropolitan Area (CMA) of Edmonton.

### ■■■ Edmonton's Gross Municipal Amateur Sport and Active Recreation Product[1]

Adopting the expenditure approach to measuring economic output levels, the first phase of the investigation measured the gross municipal amateur sport and active recreation product of the city of Edmonton for the year 2000. The results are summarized as follows:

- Total gross private household consumption was $346.97 million (or $1454.80 per household),

which was spent by Edmonton residents on various elements of amateur sport and active recreation.

- Government (and related) expenditures in this sector in 2000 amounted to $93.78 million. This included $32 million in spending associated with preparations for the 2001 World Championships in Athletics and World Triathlon Championships (one-time event(s) spending), $21.28 million in provincial expenditures, $14.1 million in net municipal spending, and $20.19 million in spending by public educational institutions.

- Private investment in major projects totalled $6.65 million.

- The "balance of trade" showed an excess of exports over imports of $93.27 million.

- The "gross municipal amateur sport and active recreation product" was estimated to be the sum of these initial expenditures, or $540.67 million.

### ■■■ Economic Impact of Amateur Sport and Active Recreation in Edmonton

Having determined the initial expenditures associated with amateur sport and active recreation in Edmonton in 2000, the second phase of the study provides an assessment of the estimated impact that this spending has on economic output, wages, and employment for both the Edmonton (CMA) and Alberta economies. The results are summarized as follows:

- The overall gross domestic product (GDP) (value added) impact on the greater Edmonton economy of the initial expenditures in the city of Edmonton was $319.59 million.

- The GDP impact on the Alberta economy of the initial expenditures in the city of Edmonton was $424.01 million.

- The total impact on wages and salaries in the greater Edmonton economy resulting from the initial expenditures in the city was $213.23 million.

- The total impact on wages and salaries in the Alberta economy resulting from the initial expenditures in the city was $261.61 million.

- The effect that the initial amateur sport and active recreation spending had on employment in greater Edmonton was 7,360.3 person years of employment.

- The effect that the initial amateur sport and active recreation had on employment in Alberta was 8,619.5 person years of employment.

## ■ ■ ■ Other Key Findings

In addition to the major finding of the study outlined above, the following key results were obtained.

- Based on the economic impact statement, amateur sport and active recreation in the city of Edmonton contributed 0.98% to greater Edmonton's gross domestic product and 1.5% to employment.

- A selected sample of 101 Edmonton amateur sport groups reported that 369,831 sport tourist visitor nights resulted from their hosting events in 2000. These visitors spent an estimated $27.99 million.

- Volunteers contributing to amateur sport and active recreation in the city of Edmonton provided an estimated 4.4 million hours of time in 2000. Although not included in the formal economic analysis, at market wages, the value of this contribution was estimated to have been $73.16 million.

- The City of Edmonton's expenditures on amateur sport and active recreation in the year 2000 are estimated to have contributed to a total economic output for the region of approximately 22.67 times the municipal government expenditure. Net municipal government spending in amateur sport and active recreation was $14.10 million; total economic impact for this sector of the economy amounted to $319.59 million.

It should be noted that these figures do not account for any value associated with various non-economic benefits associated with participation in amateur sport and active recreation, such as health benefits, social or community development, and reductions in crime rates for participants. Nor do these figures account for the impact of professional sport on Edmonton's economy. Amateur sport and active recreation in Edmonton is therefore a significant contributor to the city, regional, and indeed the provincial economies.

**Notes**

1. All findings presented in this executive summary are inextricably linked to a variety of assumptions that are outlined in the main body of the report.

◀◀ **Source:** This article was prepared by Caminata Consulting and reprinted with the permission of the Edmonton Sport Council.

# 54. The Economic Significance of Amateur Sport in the City of Calgary in 2002 - Executive Summary

By Tim Berrett and Russell Reimer

The City of Calgary Sport Policy Steering Committee (CCSPSC), as part of its efforts to develop a long term plan and policy for amateur sport in Calgary, sought to determine the economic benefits associated with amateur sport in the city. To this end, the CCSPSC retained Caminata Consulting to provide an estimate of the economic significance and impact of amateur sport in the local economy. This study provides an analysis of the economic significance and impact of the "Amateur Sport" sector in Calgary in the year 2002. Since numerous sources were used in compiling the various expenditure categories, this is the most recent year for which all data are available.

The definition of amateur sport used in this investigation is as follows:

> Amateur sport involves participants who execute skills that require practice or preparation; it involves competition with other participants, oneself, or nature; and it occurs in a structured environment. Amateur sport does not include professional sports teams, or spectator spending associated with these teams.

The definition of Calgary in this study is the "City of Calgary" as outlined by municipal boundaries.

## ■■■ Calgary's Gross Municipal Amateur Sport Product[1]

Adopting the "expenditure" approach to measuring economic output levels, the first phase of the investigation measured the gross municipal amateur sport product of the city of Calgary for the year 2002. The results are summarized as follows:

- Total gross private household consumption was $484.8 million (or $1,388 per household), which was spent by Calgary residents on various elements of amateur sport.

- Government expenditures in this sector in 2002 amounted to $56.4 million. This included $5.0 million in federal spending, $20.9 million in provincial expenditures, $7.9 million in net (after deducting revenues from user-fees) municipal spending, and $22.6 million in net spending by public educational institutions.

- Private investment totalled $37.8 million, of which corporate sponsorship of amateur sport organizations and events accounted for $3.7 million.

- The balance of trade showed an excess of exports over imports of $150 million, of which sport tourists accounted for $47.6 million.

- The "Gross Municipal Amateur Sport Product" for Calgary in 2002 is $728.9[2] million (the sum of these initial expenditures).

## ■■■ Economic Impact of Amateur Sport in Calgary

Having determined the initial expenditures associated with amateur sport in Calgary in 2002, the second phase of the study provides an assessment of the estimated impact that this spending has on economic output, wages, and employment for both the Calgary and Alberta economies. The results are summarized as follows:

- The overall GDP (value added) impact on the Calgary economy of the $728.9 million in amateur sport initial expenditures in 2002 was $477.8 million.

- The GDP impact on the Alberta economy of the initial expenditures in Calgary was $634.8 million.

- The total impact on wages and salaries in the Calgary economy resulting from the initial expenditures in the city was $309.9 million.

- The total impact on wages and salaries in the Alberta economy resulting from the initial expenditures in Calgary was $381.5 million.

- The effect that the initial sport spending had on employment in Calgary was 11,537 jobs.

- The effect that the initial sport spending had on employment in Alberta was 13,729 jobs.

- The overall local impact of the initial sport spending on taxation revenues in Calgary was $189.2 million. Of this amount, $123.0 million was directed to federal taxation, $47.5 million to provincial taxation, and $18.7 million to municipal taxation.

## ■ ■ ■ Other Key Findings

In addition to the major finding of the study outlined above, the following key results were obtained:

- Based on the economic impact statement, amateur sport in Calgary contributed 1.2% to the city's gross domestic product and 1.8% to employment in 2002.

- A selected sample of 59 Calgary sport groups and event organizers reported that 728,322 sport tourist visitor nights resulted from their hosting events in 2002. These visitors spent an estimated $47.6 million in the Calgary economy. Since there are approximately 250 amateur sport groups in the city, this figure represents only a portion of the total sport tourism in Calgary in 2002.

- Volunteers contributing to amateur sport and active recreation in Calgary provided an estimated 4.3 million hours of time in 2002. Although not included in the formal economic analysis, at market wages, the value of this contribution was estimated to have been $73.7 million.

It should be noted that these figures do not account for any value associated with various non-economic benefits associated with participation in amateur sport, such as health benefits, social or community development, and reductions in crime rates for participants. Furthermore, it should be reiterated that these figures do not include the significant contribution made to the city's economy by its professional sports franchises.

**Notes**

1. All findings presented in this executive summary are inextricably linked to a variety of assumptions that are outlined in the main body of the report.

2. Totals may not add, since all figures are rounded to the nearest $0.1 million.

◀◀ **Source:** This article was prepared by Caminata Consulting and reprinted with the permission of the Calgary Sport Council.

# 55. New Stadium as "Urban Renewal" is More Fantasy than Fact

By Jesse Hajer

David Asper and Sam Katz seem to have finally convinced Vic Toews, the senior Manitoba Tory MP, that a new football stadium is something that the federal government should be investing in. Toews was recently quoted in the *Winnipeg Free Press* as saying that the project "is something to be excited about," citing the "urban renewal" aspects of the new proposal to justify his change of heart. Although nothing official has been announced, it appears that Premier Doer and the provincial government are also onside with the project.

The latest proposal by Asper calls for a $150 million stadium and asks for $25 million from the provincial government and $15 million from the federal government. In exchange, Asper would gain ownership of the now community-owned team and the right to purchase the existing stadium site. A key selling point of the stadium proposal is Asper's commitment to develop retail facilities and a "world-class" resort facility along with an indoor water park.

However, it is unclear to what extent the above estimates include the infrastructure costs required to make room for the facilities and divert existing traffic flows. Asper and Katz have suggested that major traffic infrastructure construction would be required to make the site workable, such as a new connection between the Louise Bridge and the Disraeli Freeway and the elevation or relocation of Higgins Avenue.

Although detailed information on the project is scarce, given the cost estimates of similar projects being considered for Winnipeg, it is not unrealistic to expect such costs to be in the $50 million–$80 million range, just to relocate Higgins Avenue. Asper's proposal also references a $400 million

public-private partnership redevelopment of Waterfront Drive and proposes the city be responsible for assembling the land for the project—another potentially costly endeavor. All of this should be a serious concern for Winnipeggers who are currently facing a significant infrastructure deficit, a projected city-operating deficit of $93 million over the next two years, and a mayor who has committed to repeal the business tax, one of the city's main sources of revenue.

Federal and provincial government support for the project appears to be based on the project's claimed ability to generate "urban renewal." Urban redevelopment is a worthy goal, particularly in Winnipeg, which suffers from low downtown residential rates and significant urban sprawl problems due to poorly planned development. However, it is questionable whether spending millions of public dollars on a new stadium will renew the area in which it is located.

Building new professional sports facilities with public money to revitalize urban centres is not a new strategy. Those in favour of public funding for such projects argue that the positive economic spinoffs and new development that occur around the new facilities benefit all community members, therefore the government should contribute financially to the projects.

Unfortunately, research shows little evidence that new sports facilities generate any significant economic benefits beyond the initial construction project. Money that is spent at these new facilities generally comes at the expense of other entertainment options in a city, resulting in little or no net increase in jobs or economic activity after being built. Despite developers' claims, large arenas and stadia have consistently failed to generate any meaningful sort of urban revitalization. Studies of the two best-case scenarios that have used stadia for neighbourhood revitalization (Baltimore's Camden Yards and the Gateway in Cleveland) show that the cost per job created is very high and that these neighbourhoods did not grow any faster than surrounding areas. Overall, there is very little evidence to support the argument that a new stadium would result in any meaningful long-term economic benefits for Winnipeg or revitalization of the neighbourhood of South Point Douglas. Similar arguments could be made for Asper's private leisure facility and retail complex, which will likely do all they can to capture the dollars of its visitors, leaving little to no external benefits for existing downtown businesses.

This redevelopment project is being marketed as urban renewal and comes affixed with many bells and whistles to gain public support. Winnipeggers need to question the credibility of our various levels of government when it comes to these claims and following up on these popular additions that are often added on to these mega projects to make them more palatable to a skeptical public. Waverley West, for example, was sold to the public by including several environmentally friendly features, many of which are now defunct, and the MTS centre has fallen well short of the claims that it would revitalize Portage Avenue, which continues to be beset by business closures and vacancies.

The real key to generating urban revitalization is increasing urban density, which, for Winnipeg, means getting more people to live downtown and in the surrounding neighbourhoods. The original Point Douglas stadium proposal included reference to a residential component, but it is questionable whether this aspect of the proposal is feasible. There is no mention of residential facilities in the latest released proposal. Chances are a new stadium would actually deter rather than promote urban density and increased residential development: Heavy inflows of traffic, noise, and rowdy football fans on evenings and weekends are unlikely to induce people to purchase a home in the surrounding neighbourhoods. A new stadium puts at risk the progress that has been made in South Point Douglas and on Waterfront Drive, and may end up hurting real urban revitalization in the long run.

The citizens of Manitoba need to ask whether spending millions of their tax dollars on a new stadium and private retail and leisure facilities will deliver the greatest good to the greatest number of people. The figure quoted by Asper is likely only the beginning, and seemingly ignores the infrastructure redevelopment costs that will be required in the vicinity, which will likely be many times more than the quoted $40 million. If our three levels of government are truly interested in urban revitalization, they would be better off investing these funds in projects that have been shown to generate urban revitalization, such as downtown residential redevelopment or a desperately needed rapid transit system.

◀◀**Source:** Jesse Hajer is an economist and research associate with the Canadian Centre for Policy Alternatives Manitoba. This article was originally published in CCPA Fast Facts in June 2008. Reprinted with permission.

# 56. Mathletics

## By Kim Hart-MacNeill and Jasmine Rezaee

*Vancouver 2010's official budget leaves out some big numbers. Here's the real breakdown*

■ ■ ■ ■ ■ ■

Quebec spent thirty years paying off the debt it racked up for the 1976 Montreal Summer Games. There's no reason so far to expect that Vancouver will be any different. British Columbian and Canadian taxpayers have already incurred hundreds of millions of dollars in rampant budget overruns—the Athlete's Village and security budget are only two prime examples.

The problem with the official budget is that it excludes Olympics-related infrastructure costs, like the Sea-to-Sky Highway, despite the fact that the Games are the only reason that money's being spent.

If we include infrastructure and other Olympics-related costs, the total bill for the 2010 Vancouver Olympics is at least $8.1 billion—although no one will know the final bill, realistically, until the games are long past. VANOC intends to recoup some of their costs selling off the Athlete's Village after the Games end—but the recession and subsequent taking of Vancouver's real estate market makes that plan increasingly dubious.

Here's our independent tally of the real cost of Vancouver 2010.

| | |
|---|---|
| Bid Budget | $34,000,000 |
| Security | $900,000,000 |
| Sea-to-Sky Highway expansion | $1,980,000,000 |
| Canada Line construction | $1,900,000,000 |
| Venue construction | $580,000,000 |
| Cypress Bowl ski facility upgrade | $16,600,000 |
| Athlete's Village construction | $1,080,000,000 |
| Opening ceremonies | $58,500,000 |
| VANOC operating budget | $1,750,000,000 |
| Hillcrest/Nat Baily Stadium Park | $40,000,000 |
| Vancouver Convention Centre expansion | $883,000,000 |
| Event tickets for provincial MLAs and cabinet ministers | $1,000,000 |
| **TOTAL** | **$9,223,100,000** |

◀◀**Source:** This article was originally published in *This Magazine* in January/February 2010. Reprinted with permission

# Boosters' Millions: Better Ways Than the Olympics to Spend $6.1 Billion

## By Dawn Paley and Isaac Oommen

**57.**

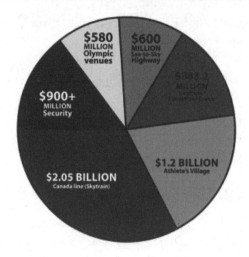

$580 MILLION Olympic venues

$600 MILLION Sea-to-Sky Highway

$883.2 MILLION Vancouver Convention Centre

$900+ MILLION Security

$1.2 BILLION Athlete's Village

$2.05 BILLION Canada line (Skytrain)

**T**he latest estimate of the cost of the Olympics to be borne by the public is $6.1 billion. This figure includes the expansion of the Sea-to-Sky Highway, the construction of the Richmond-Airport-Vancouver rail link, the expansion of the Vancouver Convention Centre, the construction of an athletes' village and various venues, and a ballooning security budget. The two-week sporting event is set to be the most expensive entertainment spectacle in British Columbia's history.

As the tab continues to grow, costs that were at first unquestioned are coming under increased scrutiny by journalists, critics, and boosters of the Games alike. To give an idea how the money may have been better spent, Isaac Oommen and Dawn Paley looked into what $6.1 billion would buy in five key areas of public policy.

## ■ ■ ■ 1. Education

Since 2001, the B.C. Liberals have made substantial cuts to education. Class sizes have grown, rural schools have shut down, children and teens get less support, and hot lunch programs and after-school activities have been scrapped. University students have seen their tuition spike while debt forgiveness initiatives have been cancelled.

"Educators don't have enough money to do proper assessments, class sizes are huge, school sports programs have been cut," said Marla Renn, a high school teacher active with the Olympic Resistance Network. "If there's ever an earthquake, many schools don't have properly engineered structures to ensure they won't fall down on top of everyone inside."

For the cost of the Vancouver-Richmond-Airport rail link ($2.05 billion), the province could:

■ Carry out complete seismic upgrades to all B.C. schools. To date, $400 million of the total $1.5-billion investment necessary to carry out seismic upgrades has been allocated. ($1.1 billion)

■ Operate a community college the size of Vancouver Community College, offering 140 programs and serving 25,000 students, for one year. ($100 million)

■ Fund the annual operating budget for B.C. School Sports, an organization that coordinates extracurricular sporting activities for B.C. students. The government cancelled an annual $130,000 in funding to the group last fall. ($390,000)

■ Build five new, one thousand-student secondary schools in B.C. ($250 million)

- Provide every student enrolled in B.C. public schools with a hot lunch every day for one school year. ($421.6 million)

### ■■■ 2. Family Services

"We need more family programs," and less foster care, said Samantha Sam, an active member of the Power of Women group in Vancouver's Downtown Eastside. There would be fewer children leaving reserves for Vancouver, says Sam, if there were better recreation facilities and programs on reserves.

A Canadian Centre for Policy Alternatives (CCPA) study released in September 2009 found that one in four single mothers in Canada live in poverty, as do 14% of single, elderly women and almost one out of every ten children. The statistics are much worse for Indigenous women and families. A full 25% of Indigenous children in Canada are growing up below the poverty line and a staggering 30% are in foster care, according to the Native Women's Association of Canada.

For a bit more than the cost of the expansion of the Vancouver Convention Centre ($883 million) and the construction of the Athletes' Village ($1.2 billion), the Canadian government could:

- Provide for one year the minimum amount of additional funding First Nations communities across Canada need to safely care for their children in their homes and communities, according to CCPA calculations. ($130 million)

- Introduce a universal child-care system across Canada. According to the CCPA's Alternative Federal Budget, funding towards child care provides at least a two-to-one economic return on investment. ($2.2 billion)

### ■■■ 3. Housing

"When they give homes to people, that's when I'll be happy," said Beatrice Starr, a member of the Power of Women group. "Not shelters but homes, where they can have their privacy and live like real human beings." The 2008 Metro Vancouver homeless count tallied 2,660 individuals sleeping on the street, representing an increase of over 137% since 2002. "If we spent one billion dollars on housing in Vancouver, we could end street homelessness and make significant upgrades to many of the city's aging and decrepit single-room-occupancy hotels," said Laura Track, Pivot Legal's housing campaign lawyer.

For a little more than the cost of the Sea-to-Sky Highway expansion ($600 million), the city or province could:

- Build 3,200 units of housing in Vancouver, according to the Inner Cities Inclusiveness report prepared in 2002. ($647 million)

### ■■■ 4. Community Welfare and the Arts

Raising welfare rates from their unjustifiably low levels is a requirement for creating a more equitable society. In addition, programs that improve the lives of all members of our communities have faced serious funding cuts. Arts programs in British Columbia are slated to lose 88% of their funding over the next two years. Libraries are facing further cuts, and some city parks are on the verge of being shut down.

For less than the cost of building the various Olympic venues ($580 million), the province could:

- Raise welfare rates by 50% in British Columbia (2007 data) for one year ($500 million). Eliminating barriers to accessing welfare would cost an additional $200 million.

- Restore core funding for British Columbia artists ($17.3 million).

- Restore city funding to the Vancouver Public Library and keep the Riley Park Branch of the Vancouver Public Library open ($1.4 million). The Riley Park Branch is marked for closure due to budgeting constraints. Restore funding for Literacy BC's online programs and coordinators ($1.7 million). "In 2005, the province of British Columbia announced the golden goal of becoming the most literate jurisdiction on the continent," said Judy Cavanagh, executive director of Literacy BC, in a press release. "Just four years later, key literacy funding is being cut."

### ■■■ 5. Transportation

Thousands of transit riders in Vancouver can attest to the system's underfunding. Pass-ups are common because buses are too full to pick up passengers, many areas lack night service, and travel from the suburbs can be difficult. "Metro Vancouver is five hundred buses short of what we need today," said Ian Bruce of the David Suzuki Foundation. "Buses are the workhorses of the public transit system, where 80% of the riders take one bus during their commute."

For the minimum cost of the security budget ($900 million), Metro Vancouver's regional transportation authority could:

■ Acquire, operate and maintain 698 new buses, trolleys and community shuttles ($880 million). Such a purchase would bring the city in line with regional plans and greatly improve the quality of bus service in British Columbia.

The social issues that exist in Canada won't be solved with money alone, but the examples above give an idea of just what could be bought for the cost of the 2010 Olympics. And as all levels of government continue to scale back social programs while generously funding wars and a two-week circus, anti-capitalist and anti-colonial resistance to the Games continues to grow.

◀◀**Source:** This article was originally published in *Briarpatch* magazine in January/February 2010. Reprinted with permission.

# Section 10

## Media and Sports

This section, like the previous one, opens with an article expressing concern about sweatshop labour in sport ("My Nike Media Adventure"). Two media—advertising and the Internet—clashed in an interesting way in 2001 after Jonah Peretti ordered a pair of personalized shoes from Nike. Peretti's article reports on what happened when Nike refused to personalize his shoes with the word "sweatshop," and how his email exchange with Nike went viral. Although there are various media campaigns against the use of sweatshop labour for sporting goods (noted in the introduction to Section 9), this article is a reminder that even individual initiatives can have a significant impact.

Stephen Brunt notes how much sports media have changed in the last decade, and argues that this rapid period of change will continue since "Sports Consumption will Undergo Revolution in the Decade Ahead." And Søren Schultz Jørgensen, reporting on the results of the International Sports Press Survey, notes that the sports press is "The World's Best Advertising Agency," because "money interests determine the agenda of sports journalism." Jørgensen also points out that sports "journalists overlook the political and economic aspects of the sports industry" (worth $213 billion in 2004 in the United States alone, seven times the size of the film industry).

The theme of sports journalism is carried on in the next two articles. Robert Gilbert affirms the points raised by Jørgensen in his critical examination of the uncritical relationship between journalists and the sports industry, arguing that they are "Playing on the Same Page." Gilbert provides insights into the working conditions of sports journalists, indicating that their employers expect them to be boosters for teams, rather than reporters who, in the best traditions of journalism, are there to "comfort the afflicted, and afflict the comfortable." Andrew Jennings, an investigative journalist who has exposed corruption in the International Olympic Committee (IOC) and the Federation of International Football Associations (FIFA), claims that he has never heard a sports reporter ask a difficult question at an IOC or FIFA media conference.

William Houston takes a different look at sports journalism, examining the new sports television hiring practices in his article, "Women on TV: Looks First, Knowledge Later." Sports journalism was once an almost all-male endeavour, and even fifteen or twenty years ago female reporters were being harassed when they tried to join their male colleagues to carry out post-game interviews (Kane and Disch, 1993). However, in the business of sports television, where TSN once claimed to advertisers that, "We deliver the male" (Sparks, 1992), Houston argues that women are being hired for their looks rather than their journalistic skills or knowledge of sports because they appeal to the young male viewers that are so crucial to sports television advertising revenue.

In a different view of women in sports media, Alina Bernstein asks if it is "Time for a Victory Lap?" She points out that the amount of media coverage of women's sports has certainly increased in recent years, but that there are few corresponding improvements in the ways that female athletes are being portrayed in the media. In an argument that echoes the one made by Houston in the previous article, she provides examples to show that female athletes are still often shown more for their sex appeal than their sports performance. Although Bernstein's examples may be dated, the case that she makes is still timely.

### Additional Suggested Readings and References

- Black, S. 2007. "Don Cherry for Prime Minister?" *Canadian Dimension*, January/February.

- Davies, R. 2002. "Media Power and Responsibility in Sport and Globalization." Address presented at the third International Conference for Media Professionals in a Globalized Sports World, Copenhagen. (www.iblf.org).

- Dowbiggin, B. 2009. "New Media Redefines Old Sports Landscape." *The Globe and Mail*, December 26.

- Doyle, J. 2008. "Mad Men, Olympic Athletes." *The Globe and Mail*, August 22.

- Houston, W. 2008. "Internet Makes It a Whole New Game." *The Globe and Mail*, November 12.

- Jennings, A. 2006. *Foul!: The Secret World of FIFA*. Toronto: Harper Collins.

- Jennings, A. 2000. *The Great Olympic Swindle*. New York: Simon & Schuster.

- Kane, M. J. and L. Disch 1993. "Sexual Violence and the Reproduction of Male Power in the Locker Room: A Case Study of the Lisa Olson Incident." *Sociology of Sport Journal*, 10(4): 331–352.

- Play the Game for Open Journalism—An International Federation of Journalists and Play the Game Project. (www.playthegameforopenjournalism.org; www.ifj.org; www.playthegame.org).

- Pound, R. 2004. "The Olympics of Television Rights: Building a Billion Dollar Bonanza." *Policy Options*, August.

- Rowe, D. 2006. "Media Sport Culture: An Education in the Politics of Acquisition." Play the Game/Knowledge Bank. (www.playthegame.org).

- Sparks, R. 1992. " 'Delivering the Male': Sports, Canadian Television, and the Making of TSN." *Canadian Journal of Communication*, 17(3): 319–342.

- Sparre, K. 2007. "Promises and Reality in Foreign Reporting from the Olympics. "June 26. (www.playthegame.org).

## 58. My Nike Media Adventure
### By Jonah Peretti

Nike's website allows visitors to create custom shoes bearing a word or slogan—a service Nike trumpets as being about freedom to choose and freedom to express who you are. Confronted with Nike's celebration of freedom and their statement that if you want it done right, build it yourself, I could not help but think of the people in crowded factories in Asia and South America who actually build Nike shoes. As a challenge to Nike, I ordered a pair of shoes customized with the word "sweatshop." Nike rejected my request, marking the beginning of a correspondence between me and the company. None of Nike's messages addressed the company's legendary labour abuses, and their avoidance of the issue created an impression even worse than an admission of guilt. In mid-January I forwarded the whole email correspondence to a dozen friends, and since that time it has raced around the Internet, reaching millions of people, even though I did not participate at all in its further proliferation. The email began to spread widely thanks to a collection of strangers, scattered around the world, who took up my battle with Nike. Nike's adversary was an amorphous group of disgruntled consumers connected by a decentralized network of email addresses. Although the press has presented my battle with Nike as a David versus Goliath parable, the real story is the battle between a company like Nike, with access to the mass media, and a network of citizens on the Internet who have only micromedia at their disposal.

Everyone knows about the power of mass media, especially Nike. Nike is primarily a brand; its main product is advertisements rather than shoes or clothing. By spending nearly a billion dollars a year, Nike gains access to all major media outlets. Nike broadcasts a message that equates its famous swoosh with freedom, revolution, and personal exuberance. Of course, this image is sharply at odds with the oppressive conditions faced by Nike factory workers. Nike's celebration of freedom never reached the ears of the Indonesian woman who had to trade sexual favours to get her job or the Mexican worker who was struck with a hammer by his angry manager. Both of these violations were reported earlier this year, and similarly graphic episodes have been discovered regularly over the past ten years. However, even with the benefit of these reports, activists have had trouble counteracting the lure of Nike's slick TV ads and high-profile endorsements.

Micromedia has the potential to reach just as many people as mass media, especially in the emerging networked economy. Most email forwards die before they are widely distributed, but if critical mass is attained, it is possible to reach millions of people without spending any money at all. Another benefit is that each person receives the email from a friend, often with a personal recommendation such as "I thought you would like this," or "This is really funny." So the audience is pre-selected for its receptivity to the message. When a recipient does enjoy the message, he or she can begin the process again by reforwarding it. It takes so little effort for each person to pass the message to multiple recipients that an idea can almost seem to be spreading on its own, like a self-replicating virus.

Nike has the advantage when it comes to mass media, but activists may have the advantage with micromedia. I discovered this accidentally when I sent my Nike emails to a few friends. My small group of friends may be divided from everyone else in the world by only six degrees of separation, but until the large-scale adoption of the Internet, this did not have such dramatic consequences. I never expected my conversation with Nike to be so widely distributed; the email began to proliferate without my participation. The only force propelling the message was the collective action of those who thought it was worth forwarding. Unions, church groups, activists, teachers, mothers, schoolchildren, and members of the U.S. armed forces sent me letters of support. This contradicts Nike's claim that only fringe groups identify with anti-Nike sentiment. Rather, an expansive group of people from all walks of life are concerned about sweatshop labour and are dismayed by Nike's brand hegemony.

But the Nike emails did not reach these people all at once. Like all micromedia, the Nike emails jumped haphazardly around a network defined by personal relationships. The first people to get the message were friends or friends of friends who tended to be left-leaning and interested in technology. At this point, I received responses from people like Johana Shull, a college student in California, who informed me that she posted the Nike emails to her sociology class discussion list to support their discussion of freedom of expression as it relates to pop culture. As the message spread, it began circulating among diehard activists who saw it as supporting their life's mission. The tone changed the day I got an urgent message from someone who called himself Biker-X. His query: "Please confirm if the entire Nike exchange took place for me. Inquiring activists want to know." In the coming days the message would race through the anti-Nike, culture-jamming, activist community. At this point, I was getting twenty or thirty emails a day, mostly from the United States and Britain, and I assumed that the circulation had peaked.

Then, something interesting happened. The micromedia message began to work its way into the mass media. This transformation was helped along by postings on media startups Plastic.com and Slashdot.org, two sites that use an innovative publishing technique somewhere between micro-

and mass media. These democratic sites blur the line between editors and readers, so that Internet buzz can be transformed into a hotly debated news item seen by thousands of people. Reporters from traditional media outlets noticed posts on these sites or received the email forward directly from friends, with notes saying things like, "You should really do a story about this." At first articles appeared in technology-focused and left-leaning publications like the *San Jose Mercury News*, Shey. net, Salon.com, the *Village Voice*, and *In These Times*. But soon mainstays like *Time*, the BBC, the *Los Angeles Times*, *USA Today*, the *Wall Street Journal*, and *Business Week* were covering the story. NBC's *Today* show flew me to New York for an appearance on national television. In almost every case, the reporters noted that they discovered the story online or heard about it from a close friend. Fatigued by PR-driven pitches, journalists saw the Nike emails as an opportunity to discover a story for themselves.

As the mass-media attention grew, so did the circulation of the email. I began receiving five hundred messages a day, sent from Australia, Asia, Africa, and South America. The majority were letters of support or messages, like the one from Katy Joyce, to verify whether I was a real person or just an urban myth. Those who assumed I was real started to request advice about politics, economics, and the kind of shoes they should buy. I knew the message had spread well beyond my circle of friends when I was cc'd this message from a man named George Walden: "I get a kick out of these elitist, eggheads and their self-serving, self-righteous 'rain forest' ethics and contrived secular pieties. Somebody should burn 'sweatshop' into this foolish c**ksucking fa**ot's forehead with a cigarette." On the other extreme, I also began to receive marriage proposals and correspondence that could be described as fan mail.

Thankfully, my email volume is finally back down to fewer than a hundred messages a day, and the media blitz is tapering off. The exchange is working its way into sociology textbooks, viral marketing seminars, business-school cases, and doctoral dissertations. My guess is that in the long run this episode will have a larger impact on how people think about media than how they think about Nike and sweatshop labour. This larger lesson suggests an exciting opportunity for activists. The dynamics of decentralized distribution systems and peer-to-peer networks are as counterintuitive as they are powerful. By understanding these dynamics, new forms of social protest become possible, with the potential to challenge some of the constellations of power traditionally supported by the mass media.

■■■■■■

Below is an abridged version of the correspondence between Nike and Jonah Peretti that appeared in *The Guardian* on February 16, 2001. The full email exchange can be found on www. shey.net.

**From: Personalize, NIKE iD** <nikeid_personalize@nike.com>

**To: Jonah H. Peretti** <peretti@media.mit.edu>

**Re**: Your NIKE iD order o16468000

Your NIKE iD order was cancelled for one or more of the following reasons.

1) Your Personal iD contains another party's trademark or other intellectual property.

2) Your Personal iD contains the name of an athlete or team we do not have the legal right to use.

3) Your Personal iD was left blank. Did you not want any personalization?

4) Your Personal iD contains profanity or inappropriate slang, and besides, your mother would slap us.

**From: Jonah H. Peretti**

Sweatshop is not: 1) another's party's trademark; 2) the name of an athlete; 3) blank; or 4) profanity. I chose the iD because I wanted to remember the toil and labour of the children that made my shoes. Could you please ship them to me immediately.

**From: Personalize, NIKE iD**

... The iD you have chosen contains, as stated in the previous email correspondence, "inappropriate slang"...

**From: Jonah H. Peretti**

After consulting Webster's Dictionary, I discovered that "sweatshop" is in fact part of standard English, and not slang. The word means: "a shop or factory in which workers are employed for long hours at low wages and under unhealthy conditions" and its origin dates from 1892. So my personal iD does meet the criteria ... Your website advertises that the NIKE iD program is "about freedom to choose and freedom to express who you are." I share Nike's love of freedom and personal expression ... My personal iD was offered as a small token of appreciation for the sweatshop workers poised to help me realize my vision. I hope that you will value my freedom of expression and reconsider your decision to reject my order.

**From: Personalize, NIKE iD**

Regarding the rules for personalization it also states on the NIKE iD website that "Nike reserves the right to cancel any Personal iD up to twenty-four hours after it has been submitted" ... If you wish to reorder ... with a new personalization please visit us again at www.nike.com

**From: Jonah H. Peretti**

Thank you for the time and energy you have spent on my request. I have decided to order the shoes with a different iD, but I would like to make one small request Could you please send me a colour snapshot of the ten-year-old Vietnamese girl who makes my shoes?

◀◀ **Source:** Reprinted with permission from the April 9, 2001 issue of *The Nation*. For subscription information, call 1-800-333-8536. Portions of each week's Nation magazine can be accessed at http://www.thenation.com

## Sports Consumption Will Undergo Revolution in the Decade Ahead

### By Stephen Brunt

**59.**

A decade doesn't pass the way it once did. That perception is not merely a reflection of advancing age—though perhaps it's part of it—but of the lightning-fast transformations experienced now, the seismic shifts that seem to take place in an instant.

In the first ten years of the twenty-first century, the way we consumed sport, its delivery mechanisms, its culture and form, changed remarkably. High-definition television, still an experimental medium in 1999, is now in many ways the standard. Direct streaming of events via high-speed Internet—remember dial-up?—has gone from wild notion to shaky, stop/start pictures to something equal to or better than broadcast quality. In 1999, the Ultimate Fighting Championship was a glorified tough-man contest targeting the lowest-brow crowd; today, cleaned up and codified, mixed martial arts under the same brand name is a mainstream sport that hits a young, sweet-spot demographic.

Conversations this week with sports and television executives and academics suggest that we ain't seen nothing yet, that ten years from now the landscape will be recognizable, but also profoundly transformed. Those changes will have less to do with the games and athletes themselves (though we will still be talking about performance-enhancing drugs at the end of this decade), but in the way we consume them as entertainment.

Begin with who watches, and why. Sport is part spectacle, part escape, part religion, part communal experience. Without a rooting interest, it doesn't mean much, and a rooting interest detached from hearth and home and life experience isn't the same as one with organic roots. The foundation of the business is that people care, that they attach themselves to a city, to a uniform, to a history, and often hang on to it for their entire lives, through championship dynasties and long, long walks in the desert.

There is still appeal and value in that, in immersion in something larger, in simply being part of a crowd in an arena or stadium, caring about the same thing at the same time, an increasingly rare opportunity in the modern world. But the magical experience that once came automatically with walking through the doors of a hallowed arena, or emerging into the stands to see a green field and brightly coloured uniforms means more to those raised in a game-of-the week world than those coming of age in a time of perpetual availability. The boomers and their buying power are heading toward the sunset, and the talk in the sports business now is about how to attract and hold a different generation, with a different, diminished attention span, accustomed to having the whole world laid out for them, every minute of every day, literally at their fingertips.

Getting them out of their homes and into the building or into the ballpark, getting their eyes to linger for more than a few seconds as a game flickers across a screen—not to mention the advertising that pays the freight—has become the core challenge.

Those who run North American professional sport will be trying to find fresh sources of revenue. Most everyone seems to believe that at least one of the leagues (most likely the NBA or the NHL) will establish franchises in Europe by the end of this decade, and with David Stern having recently opened the door a crack, it's not hard to imagine at least one sport in partnership with cash-hungry governments exploiting the massive possibilities of legalized sports gambling. (That would be extraordinary only in a North American context. In many other places, you have long been able to bet games on site.)

But the primary economic engines will remain the two traditional revenue streams in professional sport: ticket sales, in all of their variations, and broadcasting, both in a traditional network/rights fees/advertising structure, and increasingly through new media and direct delivery.

Network television as we've known it may be in trouble, perhaps even in its death throes, but live sports programming could remain a lifeline, because unlike every other form of programming, it is nearly PVR-proof. You can record a game and watch it whenever, skipping happily past the commercials, but its greatest value is in the here and now, in the unpredictability of the outcome, in needing to know who won and who lost when it happens. So for the time being, networks will continue to pay significant money for the right to televise sporting events, and for teams and leagues, that will continue to outweigh the attraction of cutting out the middleman entirely, of taking control not just of the content, but of the pipeline. Not that they won't continue to move in that direction, with their own television channels holding exclusive rights to a portion of their inventory, coupled with an endless stream of exclusive, insider information (the middlemen who get cut out in that case aren't just the television networks, but, to some degree, conventional sports journalists).

Whether those games are broadcast or streamed is a distinction that by the end of the decade will be all but meaningless: There will be a screen in your house, it will be attached to a box, and through it will come everything. The picture, sooner rather than later, will be in 3D. Though the announcement this week that ESPN will broadcast the opening game of the World Cup in that form might have caught many by surprise, the technology is already sufficiently advanced that it is only a question (as it was with HD) of *when* broadcasters believe its worthwhile taking on the extra production costs—or alternately, when hardware prices drop sufficiently that consumer demand creates the need for more content. By 2011, 3D-ready sets will be widely available, at a price only slightly higher than HD-ready televisions fetch right now, and 3D channels will be providing coverage of the biggest sports events.

Those games, and all games, will soon be presented in such a way that viewers at home can choose their own replays, choose what they hear and what they see, and also dip into a continuous stream of game-related information at the same time. Simply sitting back and watching for two or three hours at a time is no longer an option—as anyone with even a passing knowledge of teenagers could already tell you.

The irony is that with the evolution of 3D home theatre/computer, it will become ever more difficult to turn couch potatoes into ticket buyers. There have been plenty of empty seats visible in all sports this past year, which is in part a reflection of the shattered economy, and in part of the reality that enduring a snowstorm to watch a lousy team play out the string, when the alternative at home is pretty darned good, can become an option only for the true diehard. Long gone are the days of sitting in a drafty rink with only the game, the public address announcer, and the odd flourish of organ music as a distraction. The in-game experience, which has grown ever louder and more frenetic over the past quarter century, is about to enter territory that for some will seem like sensory overload.

Thus we have the new Texas Stadium, Jerry Jones's $1-billion vision of the future, a place where attending a game includes all of the high-tech conveniences of home, and then some (watching a game broadcast from there brings the so far unique experience of hearing the crowd react not just to what's going on the field, but to what they're seeing on the world's biggest video screen). Right now, the consensus seems to be that super-stadiums, because of the cost, won't become the norm, nor will individual in-seat monitors, except in private boxes and club sections. Instead, the means to enhancing the live game experience—with those in the know, the concept comes up in conversation again and again—is the telephone, or at least the next generation of smart-phones: Imagine the crowd at the Rogers Centre watching a Blue Jays game while being fed replays and statistics and unique content through their Rogers phones via Rogers wireless (one reason why the communications giant might still have an appetite for the professional sports business despite its rocky ride as an owner in Major League Baseball and part-time host of the Buffalo Bills). A nineteen-year-old will tell you that's how they already live their lives, that surfing and texting and television viewing are meant to be done concurrently, that minus multitasking, sports—and just about anything else—is boring.

The parent of a nineteen-year-old might think that sounds sort of like sitting in Exhibition Stadium with a transistor plugged into your ear, tuned to *Tom and Jerry*, but of course, they'd be dead wrong.

◀◀ **Source:** Stephen Brunt is a lead columnist for *The Globe and Mail*. This article was originally published in *The Globe and Mail*, December 20, 2008. Reprinted with permission.

# 60.

# The World's Best Advertising Agency: The Sports Press

By Søren Schultz Jørgensen

*Home Ground. Money interests determine the agenda of sports journalism—journalists overlook the economic and political aspects of the sports industry—dominating types of sport and sports stars get preferential treatment. Academics: Give up the dream of critical journalism in the sports pages - The most wide ranging survey of the international sports press undertaken so far.*

■■■■■■

Here is the potent formula behind the booming sports economy: a global business partnership between the sports industry and the sports press. Together they have created an industry that excites and involves young and old all over the world and in Europe has an estimated turnover of 165 billion Euro (1.6% of Europe's total GNP) and a turnover of 213 billion dollars in the United States—annually.

But the most extensive survey of the global sports press so far, the International Sports Press Survey 2005, now documents that the powerful cooperation has some deeply problematic consequences for sports journalism. Sports editors of daily newspapers allow the sports industry to set the agenda and the priorities for coverage of sports events.

The survey conducted by the House of Monday Morning and academic research institutions in ten countries on three continents shows that fundamental journalistic ideals are routinely abandoned. The survey comprises ten thousand articles about sport which were published in thirty-seven newspapers in the first six months of 2005. The survey is financed by the Danish Institute for Sports Studies and the world communication conference on sport and society, Play the Game, which takes place in Copenhagen next week (see text box).

The survey shows that the sports pages in daily newspapers are dominated by the particular types of sport, sports stars and international events which create the biggest turnovers on parameters such as advertising, sponsorship, numbers of television viewers, and spectators in the stadium. Conversely, the sports press has great difficulties reporting anything that takes place outside the angle of television cameras and after the stadium spotlights have been turned off.

A new European Union report estimates that the sports industry now make up at least 1.6% of the collective GNP for the Western world. According to industry analysts, the sports industry in the United States is twice as big as the car industry—and seven times the size of the film industry. Sport is one of the fastest growing branches of all industry. Yet, only 6% of the articles about sport in daily newspapers are looking at the economic and financial aspects of sport. Only 0.5% of the stories in the sports pages zoom in on the massive interests in bookmaking and betting. And only 1% of newspaper coverage of sport deals with amateur and recreational sports despite the millions of people globally who practice it.

That the UN has designated 2005 the "International Year of Sport and Physical Education" is only mentioned in three articles of the ten thousand articles in the survey—and they were all published in Swiss newspapers. Obviously, the political statements of Kofi Annan do not sell as many tickets—or newspapers—as David Beckham's haircuts.

This is not the first time that the blind angles of sports journalism have been exposed. Three years ago, Monday Morning conducted a survey of the

About the International Sports Press Survey

The International Sports Press Survey is designed by the House of Monday Morning and the collection of data has been undertaken in cooperation with Play the Game, the world communication conference on sport and society which from November 6–10 will gather three hundred journalists, academics, and sports leaders in Copenhagen to discuss issues such as corruption in sport, match fixing, doping, and the media.

The survey was financed by the Danish Institute for Sports Studies and Play the Game. It has been implemented in cooperation with universities and researchers in the United States, Britain, Scotland, Norway, Germany, Romania, Austria, Switzerland, and Australia. The survey is based on articles about sport published in three to five major newspapers in each country—with a least one tabloid newspaper, a broadsheet paper, and a local newspaper. A total of thirty-seven newspapers are included in the survey that covers fourteen days of publication in the period from April 11 to July 24, 2005.

All articles on the sports pages of the newspapers have been analyzed—apart from brief notes. A total of 10,007 articles have been registered in a database with information about 14 different parameters including the article's journalistic format, the gender of the journalist, the type of sport, the theme of the article, geographical focus, the gender of the athletes, and the number and types of sources.

sports press in Norway, Denmark, and Sweden, reaching similar conclusions. According to Danish sports researcher Knud Larsen from University of Southern Denmark, it could be an indication that it is time to give up the ambition of critical and investigative sports journalism. Knud Larsen says to Monday Morning: "Maybe we will just have to accept that critical and independent sports journalism is never going to find its way into the sports sections of newspapers. Instead of being frustrated about the inadequacy of sports journalism we could hope that business and political journalism will answer the questions that sports journalism leave untouched. That way we can continue to enjoy the fascination in the sports pages."

Dante Chinni is senior researcher with the Center for Excellence in Journalism and recently completed a survey of sports journalism in newspapers in the United States. He says that sport journalism is largely reactive and allows others to set the agenda. "Functionally speaking there is little doubt that sports journalists act as PR agents. The sports press is one of society's biggest myth makers and it leaves a lot of questions unanswered. Unfortunately I see little evidence that these questions are answered elsewhere."

## ■ ■ ■ Similar Priorities Anywhere in the World

There are remarkably few differences in the way that newspapers in different countries cover sport—when you exclude sports with a specific national interest. Baseball, basketball, and American football dominate media coverage in the United States. Skiing is more important in Norway than anywhere else, and cricket fills up the columns of sports pages in England and Australia where Australian football also receives massive exposure. Denmark is home to the best female handball team in the world and also has the most intense media exposure of handball in the world.

But apart from such differences determined by history and culture, the International Sports Press Survey clearly documents that sports journalism is a global culture—just like sport itself. The priorities in sports journalism are more or less the same and it does not matter whether the newspaper is based in Washington, Bergen, Vienna, or Bucharest.

■ **Match reports, results and previews dominate:** 58% of the articles on the sports pages deal with current events—the match yesterday or the expected line-up this evening.

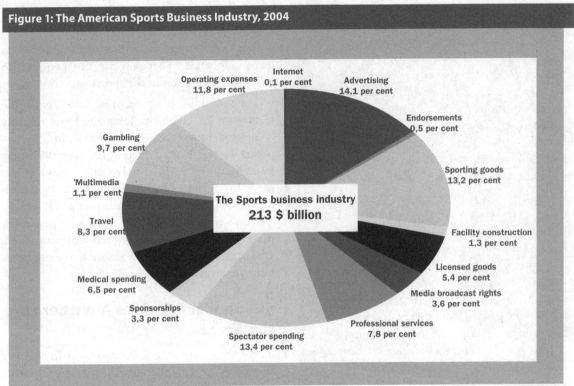

**Figure 1: The American Sports Business Industry, 2004**

Internet 0,1 per cent

Operating expenses 11,8 per cent

Advertising 14,1 per cent

Endorsements 0,5 per cent

Gambling 9,7 per cent

Sporting goods 13,2 per cent

Multimedia 1,1 per cent

The Sports business industry 213 $ billion

Travel 8,3 per cent

Facility construction 1,3 per cent

Licensed goods 5,4 per cent

Medical spending 6,5 per cent

Media broadcast rights 3,6 per cent

Sponsorships 3,3 per cent

Professional services 7,8 per cent

Spectator spending 13,4 per cent

The sports business industry is one of the largest and fastest growing industries in the United States. Our annual survey of the size of the industry estimated the sports business industry last year at $213 billion. It is far more than twice the size of the U.S. auto industry and seven times the size of the movie industry. (Source: *SportsBusiness Journal*, 2005)

- **Stories about money and politics can only be located with a magnifying glass:** Approximately one article in thirty includes political aspects of sport. Only one article in one hundred deals with public funding of sport, and only one article in twenty deals with the commercial aspects of sport.

- **The focus on doping is waning:** On average 1.5% of the sports articles deal with one of the biggest challenges in recent years to sport—the use of illegal drugs by athletes. Compared to Monday Morning's analysis of the Scandinavian sports press in 2002, there is a strong indication that the media has become less preoccupied with the fight against doping.

- **Marginal exposure of social aspects of sport:** Adding all the data from categories dealing with the social impact of sport—recreational and amateur sports, the importance of sport for children, the elderly, and immigrants—the figure barely reaches 2.5% of all sports coverage.

- **Women are invisible:** Men are the focus of 86% of all sports coverage. The explanation may be found in recruitment patterns in sports journalism: Only one in twenty sports articles is written by a female journalist. Norway is also in this area the best in the world with women as subjects in one out of five articles and a female byline over one out of eight articles.

- **Journalism without sources:** 40% of all sports articles refer to only one source in the text. 20% of the articles do not refer to any sources at all. And only 16% of all articles have three or more sources.

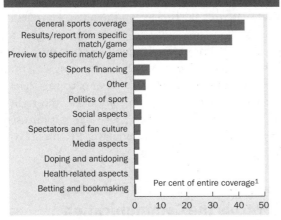

**Figure 2: Main Themes of Sports Coverage**

General sports coverage
Results/report from specific match/game
Preview to specific match/game
Sports financing
Other
Politics of sport
Social aspects
Spectators and fan culture
Media aspects
Doping and antidoping
Health-related aspects
Betting and bookmaking

Per cent of entire coverage[1]

0  10  20  30  40  50

Sports journalism concerns itself overwhelmingly with the stadium spectacle of sport. Little attention is paid to what happens after the floodlights turn off and the camera crews leave.
**Note[1]:** Articles can reside in up to two categories, which brings the sum to above 100%.
**Note:** N=10.007 articles
**Source:** International Sports Press Survey, 2005

- **The sources come from within the sports world:** Athletes, coaches, and representatives of clubs dominate completely as sources for sports journalists—and in only one out of twenty-five articles have journalists included quotes or comments from people outside the sports world such as academics or politicians.

- **Increasing globalization of sport:** Compared to previous studies, this survey indicates that sports coverage is becoming less focused on national interests. In several of the continental European countries, stories with an international focus make up more than half of the coverage. The international focus is less pronounced in the British and American sports press where sport events outside the respective countries only take up one-fifth of the total coverage.

### ▪▪▪ The "Pornographic Amounts of Money in Sport"

The new survey is not only discouraging reading for women, amateurs, media critics, and the professed humanists in the UN system. In a spectacular comment in the *Financial Times*, one of the most prominent figures in world sport, FIFA president Sepp Blatter, struck out at the "pornographic amounts of money" and the "wild-west style of capitalism" that has turned football into a "multi-billion dollar global industry." "FIFA cannot sit by and see greed rule the football world. Nor shall we," he wrote. FIFA will now set up a taskforce to examine and combat the excesses.

Sepp Blatter did not ask for help from sports journalists. And for very good reasons according to media and sports academics. Their assessment is that sports journalists are unable to rise to the challenge.

"To a very large extent the sports press is in the same boat as the money interests in the sport industry. Both parties earn their living from selling the entertainment product that sport has become today. In that way a complex but also extremely dynamic business partnership has developed between the sports press on the one hand and the clubs, sponsors, TV stations, and license holders to big events on the other hand. It goes without saying that in such a structure there is little room for critical and independent journalism. Today sports journalism is characterised by the mechanisms of marketing," says Dr. Thomas Horky, a former sports journalists with the German Press Agency and today a researcher with Hamburg Institute for Sports Journalism.

According to Norway's leading academic in the field, professor Knut Helland from University of Bergen, the majority of the sports press has de facto given up on the ideal of enlightening the public. "Most sports journalism today is editorial advertising," he says. But the explanation is not that sports journalists lack professionalism, a critical mind, or the desire to cover sport from other angles or in other ways, says Helland.

"Sports journalists are amongst the most professional in modern journalism. In general they are extremely good at delivering news and features in highly specialized formats, and they have the high

| Table 1: Most Covered Sports in the National Sports Pages | | |
|---|---|---|
| **Europe** | | |
| **Rank** | **Sport** | **% of coverage** |
| 1 | Soccer | 50.9 |
| 2 | Cycling | 6.3 |
| 3 | Tennis | 5.8 |
| 4 | Formula One | 3.4 |
| 5 | Golf | 3.4 |
| **The United Kingdom** | | |
| **Rank** | **Sport** | **% of coverage** |
| 1 | Soccer | 53.8 |
| 2 | Golf | 8.1 |
| 3 | Rugby | 8.0 |
| 4 | Cricket | 7.1 |
| 5 | Tennis | 5.7 |
| **United States of America** | | |
| **Rank** | **Sport** | **% of coverage** |
| 1 | Baseball | 28.5 |
| 2 | Basketball | 14.2 |
| 3 | Golf | 11.5 |
| 4 | American Football | 9.9 |
| 5 | Other Motor Sports | 8.1 |
| **Australia** | | |
| **Rank** | **Sport** | **% of coverage** |
| 1 | Australian Football | 27.7 |
| 2 | Rugby | 22.2 |
| 3 | Soccer | 8.8 |
| 4 | Cricket | 6.8 |
| 5 | Equestrian Sports | 6.7 |

National culture still holds sway in the sports pages. In a few aspects, this culture remains untouched by globalization.
**Note:** N=10.007 articles
**Source:** International Sports Press Survey, 2005

The media game is about billions of kroner, Euro, and dollars. But the plot of the game is as simple as what takes place on the pitch. For televisions stations the aim is to get exclusive rights to broadcast the most star-studded sports events. This is where the viewers and the advertising revenue are. And in order to attract viewers to the transmissions that the television station has the rights to—and can sell advertising for—the station uses its day-to-day sports coverage as a PR tool. Exit journalistic independence.

### ■ ■ ■ How the Sports Industry Controls the Communication

The survey shows that the newspapers are following the lead of television stations when it comes to selecting which types of sport, matches, and personal profiles to focus on. "Sports journalism is no longer done in the stadiums. It is done in front of the television back in the office. It is quicker, easier and cheaper—and you get to watch details in slow motion," says Thomas Horky.

This is the reason why the electronic and printed media flock to the same few types of sport and events, the same few clubs and sports stars. Obviously this gives the much-courted main actors incredible opportunities for controlling the communication flow. Which they do to an increasing degree in order to get the right form of PR and public exposure.

The sports editors that Monday Morning has talked to all have the same stories about their problems with systematic attempts by clubs and sports stars to exclude critical journalists from getting interviews. At the moment, only a handful of journalists are allowed to talk to the German Formula One champion, Michael Schumacher. The Danish football legend Michael Laudrup used the same strategy for many years—and in that way a few lucky journalists were eating out of his hand. For a long time the Washington Redskins football team refused to talk to journalists from the *Washington Post* because the newspaper had

working pace of journalism generally. But the commercial game of sports is exerting such pressure on journalism itself that it has become almost impossible to work according to classic ideals of journalism," says Knut Helland.

**Figure 3: Gender Distribution of Athletes Featured in Sports Coverage**

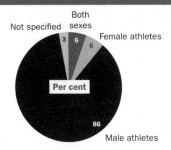

A male reserve is maintained within sports coverage. Male preferences dominate the coverage, the articles being in fact largely both written by and consumed by men.
**Note:** N=10.007 articles
**Source:** International Sports Press Survey, 2005

**Figure 4: Number of Sources Cited in Sports Articles**

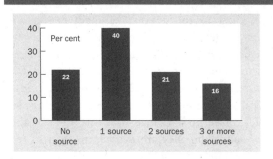

A journalist needs no source in order to relay the action on the pitch. The huge bias of sports journalism towards play-by-play sports coverage means that sourced material is scarce.
**Note:** N=10.007 articles
**Source:** International Sports Press Survey, 2005

published critical articles about the club's new stadium. In a similar way, the Danish top football team, Brøndby, has tried to convince the sports editor of the daily newspaper *B.T.* that a certain journalist should not be allowed to cover the affairs of the club. The journalist's sin was to have written a number of critical articles about affairs in the club's management.

"There are hundreds of such examples in the sports business. Hundreds. It is the fate of sports journalism. There is little doubt that we have to fight that much harder against the dominating organisations and companies to do critical stories than journalists covering other beats. But we do take those fights. I simply do not agree with the contention that sports journalists are less critical than other journalists. I receive angry letters to the editor every day and therefore I know that we fully live up to our responsibilities as watchdogs," said sports editor at *Washington Post*, Emilio Garcia- Ruiz to Monday Morning.

Sports editor of the Danish daily newspaper *B.T.*, Peter Brüchmann, shares the analysis: "The clubs feed the friendly journalists and exclude the critical journalists. That is the way it is. We just have to fight it, and we do," he says. He does admit, however, that the sports pages to a large extent are edited based on simple calculations about what celebrities and clubs might lead to greater sales on the newsstands.

"I constantly update my lists of who are the best people to expose in different clubs and types of sport. I will be honest about that. It is a question of looking after consumer interests and taking the business side into account at the same time. But the fact that we allow ourselves to be directed by demand and readers, does not mean that we have given up on our ambitions to do critical investigative sports journalism On the contrary. I have a clear ambition to influence the strategic agendas in the board rooms of sports clubs. And I believe that we quite often do just that," says Peter Brüchmann.

"Compared to the situation ten years ago, sports journalism definitely functions at a completely different level. We cover far more economic and political aspects of sport—and we do it in a far more critical and independent manner. We have a lot to be proud of if you compare to what you can see in the cultural sections of the newspapers. It is easy to say that we should celebrate less and criticise more, be a little less good guys and a little more bad guys. But that is not necessarily what the readers want," says Peter Brüchmann.

## ■■■ The Readers Hold the Key to Change

According to the editors the main reason why sports pages look and contain what they do can be directly ascribed to the readers of sports articles. The sports editor of Europe's biggest daily newspaper, *Bild*, with 10 million readers, finds it easy to pinpoint causes and effects: "The readers prefer to see how football stars live, the cars they drive, and who they are married to than to read about doping, sponsors, and political power games in the sports federations. So we make our priorities accordingly. It is logical," says sports editor Achim Stecker to Monday Morning.

In its choices of stories and angles, the *Washington Post* is a long way from *Bild*. But the newspaper's sports editor share the conviction that it is the readers who are holding back development in sports journalism—not sports journalists themselves.

"In our professional organization, Associated Press Sports Editors, we have spent the last ten years discussing how we could change the way we report matches and general sports news. But each time we try something new we are inundated with complaints. Right now I have a letter to the editor in front of me which says: "Please explain to your reporters that they do not need to write the big American contemporary novel each time they cover a baseball-game. It is too much. We need facts, not great artistic writing." That is very typical. The sports readers have a very dedicated and fanatical relationship with our sports pages," says Emilio Garcia-Ruiz.

That readers of sports pages are conservative is by all accounts correct. The most inveterate of the kind are both old and male, according to a readers' survey from the Danish newspaper association. But the numbers also indicate that newspapers might be losing their grip on younger readers and that they still fail to attract women who otherwise are major consumers of fitness and health magazines. According to the International Sports Press Survey fitness and health are almost uncultivated in current newspaper coverage of sport.

According to professor Raymond Boyle from University of Stirling in Scotland, the key to renewal of sports journalism lies in accommodating those segments of the population who have a more nuanced relationship with sport. During the past few years, a number of Britain's serious newspapers such as the *Guardian*, *Daily Telegraph*, the *Scotsman*, and *The Times* have developed a far more enterprising and multi-faceted approach to sports journalism, he says.

"These are newspapers that ten years ago would look down on sport. Today they shape the market through their focus on sport. To me it is a clear sign that the market of sports journalism is going through a phase of differentiation. The classic tabloid newspapers will probably continue their one-sided focus on stars, heroes, successes and failures. But the younger generations of readers and journalists are in the process of developing a new form of sports journalism in the so-called serious end the newspaper market," says Raymond Boyle.

### The International Sports Press Survey

The following participating universities and researchers have been responsible for entering data into the database:

**Australia:** The Australian, Herald Sun (Melbourne), Sebastian Hassett and Jane Worthington, Walkley Foundation of Journalism Media, Entertainment and Arts Alliance; Sydney Morning Herald, David Rowe and Nathaniel Bavinton, Cultural Industries and Practices Research Centre (CIPS), School of Social Sciences, The University of Newcastle; The West Australian, Rachel Payne, School of Communications and Multimedia, Edith Cowan University

**Austria:** Kleine Zeitung, Kronen Zeitung, Salzburger Nachrichten, Minas Dimitriou, Sport- und Bewegungswissenschaft / USI, Universität Salzburg

**Denmark:** B.T., Politiken, Berlingske Tidende, Jyllands Posten and Fyens Stiftstidende, Søren Schultz Jørgensen for The House of Monday Morning

**England:** The Daily Telegraph, The Sun, The Daily Mail, John Doyle, Chelsea School, University of Brighton

**Germany:** Frankfurter Allgemeine Zeitung, Bild Zeitung, Hannoversche, Allgemeine Zeitung, Süddeutsche Zeitung, Westdeutsche, Allgemeine Zeitung, Hamburger Abendblatt: Thomas Horky, Hamburg Institut of Sport Journalism, University of Hamburg

**Norway:** Aftenposten, VG, Nordlys, Sigmund Loland, Norges Idrettshøgskole

**Romania:** Evenimentul Zilei, Libertatea, Adevarul, Horia Moraru, School of Journalism and Mass Communication Studies, University of Bucharest; Florian Petrica, Romanian National TV/National Academy of Sports

**Scotland:** The Herald, The Daily Record, The Scottish Sun, Professor Raymond Boyle, Dr. Richard Haynes and Adam Behr, Stirling Media Research Institute, University of Stirling

**Switzerland:** Der Tagesanzeiger, Blick, Neue Zürcher Zeitung, Mirko Marr, IPMZ - Department of Mass Communication and Media Research, University of Zürich

**USA:** USA Today, The New York Times, Kim Schimmel and Theresa Walton, School of Exercise, Leisure and Sport, Kent State University; The Cleveland Plain Dealer, Jae-won Lee, School of Communication, Cleveland State University; Atlanta Journal Constitution, Rob Hardin, Department of Sport and Leisure Studies, University of Tennessee; Nashville Tennessean, Roger Heinrich, Department of Electronic Media Communication, Middle Tennessee State University

# Playing on the Same Page
## By Robert Gilbert

**61.**

*Publicity, 1. Journalism, 0. Why sports writers shouldn't be another member of the home team*

■■■■■■

It's mid-afternoon, about the only downtime in a sportswriter's long working day. Damien Cox, the *Toronto Star*'s hockey columnist, is sitting in the paper's cafeteria, talking about what's wrong with the sports pages. At thirty-nine, Cox looks in good enough shape to skate with the athletes he covers, but his concern at the moment isn't about fitness but about what's fitting in his line of work. "It's easy," he's saying, "to become a booster of a sports franchise. It's something you have to fight against all the time." Cox is as good as his word. He resists the daily pressure to plug the Maple Leafs and the NHL. Even among his outspoken colleagues in the *Star*'s sports department, he stands out for his critical reporting. He despises consensus and thrives on the contrary view. How is it, then, that Damien Cox, along with the best of his sportswriting colleagues, can still be considered a shill for commercial, professional sports? The answer lies not so much in what Cox and company have to say, but where they say it.

"Ever see a team advertise?" asks Roy MacGregor of the *National Post*, and one of Canada's most respected hockey writers. "Why would you advertise when you have a daily advertisement called the newspaper?" Though pro teams do occasionally buy ads, MacGregor's point is well taken: the sports pages are just another cog in the publicity machine of professional sports. The machine itself is greased by a symbiotic relationship in which the sports pages need the pro franchises as much as the franchises need the sports pages. "I'm thankful for newspapers getting the message out to the public," says Howard Starkman, media relations director for the Toronto Blue Jays. "If we weren't covered by the media, there would be no need to be in business."

It's a quid pro quo, of course. The newspapers, in turn, use their coverage of big-league sports to attract the demographically desirable readers (eighteen to forty-nine-year-old men) they need to sell to their advertisers. This audience wants to read all about the latest Leafs' game, not what's happening in amateur rowing or cycling. So that's what they get—in abundance. And when they don't, as *The Globe and Mail* found out in 1990, reader rage is sure to follow. The *Globe*'s editor at the time, William Thorsell, a culture maven who's now head of the Royal Ontario Museum, decided to slash the paper's sports coverage from four pages a day to two. Readership survey after readership survey showed he'd made a serious miscalculation. By the fall of 1997, the missing pages were back and *The Globe and Mail* was heralding its revamped sports section.

"Sports journalism is an oxymoron." So says Mark Lowes, a communications professor at the University of Ottawa. In his view, its underlying purpose is not so much to inform and entertain as to market pro franchises. It doesn't matter how much criticism Damien Cox heaps on the Leafs and the NHL or how troubled the *Globe*'s Stephen Brunt gets about everything from the fate of baseball to the fall of boxing; they and their colleagues are still in the business of keeping pro sports on the lips of fans across the continent.

This public buzz, or, as Professor Lowes would have it, this discourse, is indispensable to the franchise owners whose profits depend on filling their stands with paying customers and selling the whole spectacle to television. "The sports section is a finely tuned, high-performance promotional vehicle for the North American (and increasingly global) sports entertainment industry," writes Lowes in his book *Inside the Sports Pages*. "As long as the sports press continues to deliver such effective service to the relatively concentrated group of corporations and individuals who own and control the major-league sports industry, its profitable synergy with the industry will continue apace. And that means the continued saturation of the sports pages with news about the big-time sports."

"As a newspaper trying to do business," asks Damien Cox, "should we then go cover amateur rowing because it's 'the right thing to do' and ignore the Leafs?" That's not really the choice. There's a big difference between ignoring the Leafs—or any other commercial sports franchise—and showering them with space. A glance through the sports sections of Toronto's four dailies shows that the amount of ink devoted to pro sports, especially the NHL, the NBA, the NFL, and major-league baseball, could easily be cut back. The endless number of game stories, previews of coming games, player articles and columns make for repetitive, and often boring, reading.

At times, this stuff amounts to little more than cheerleading. When a team loses or ties, the excuses start flowing. The *Toronto Sun*'s account of the Leafs against New Jersey last January 14 is typical. "If they could have overcome a few earlier brain cramps, they might have tamed their playoff nemesis, the New Jersey Devils. But the Leafs contented themselves with a 4–4 draw last night." When the home team does well, the tone can get downright celebratory. "Start spreadin' the news," wrote the *Star*'s baseball columnist, Richard Griffin, after David Wells won his twentieth game. "The Jays are alive. They're alive. The race to be the best second-place team in the AL is alive and well."

There's a lot of ambivalence among sportswriters and editors about this kind of rah-rah writing. "If a team's going well, the columnist can say that and it's not cheerleading," says Pat Grier, associate sports editor at the *Sun*. But if the columnist were to write, "Let's all get behind the Jays," and "Go Jays Go," Grier adds, it would be. That's too fine a line for the *Star*'s Cox. "I can't stand the *Sun*," he says. "Once upon a time they did a great job in sports and now they're still trying to believe that they still do when, in fact, they don't. I think whether it's the Leafs or the Raptors or the Blue Jays, the way that the paper approaches coverage is that they're behind the home team." But, in the end, these differences scarcely matter. In the ambivalent world of the sports pages, Cox gets to keep his integrity, Grier gets to keep his hype and big-league sports get to keep on reaping the benefits of all that attention.

"Sure, it's about winning and losing, plus how you market your product," Grant Kerr of the *Globe* wrote in early 2001. Sports journalists give practically the same answer when asked if their pages have a marketing function. Most agree they do, but insist it's unintended. The sports pages themselves, however, provide a different answer. When zealous coaches, including the Leafs' Pat Quinn, decide to protect their players from the pestering press by dictating who can talk after games, the press protests—loudly. Not so much because the fans are being deprived of their right to absorb still more locker-room clichés, but because the teams are hurting their chances to promote their product. "What's odd is that the management types seem to be oblivious to the practical side of this," wrote the *Globe*'s David Shoalts for Fox Sports' website. "By denying the media access to their players, they're denying themselves millions of dollars of free publicity."

In fact, there is almost as much marketing news in the sports pages these days as in the business section. Writers unabashedly comment on putting a quality product on the ice or the field or the court. When Mario Lemieux returned to the NHL last December, ecstatic press response rivalled the second coming of Michael Jordan—and for the same reason: such superstars make it easier to sell the game. "The financial and business elements of his return are obvious, especially to a man whose future security is tied up in the Penguins' franchise," wrote the *Sun*'s Ken Fidlin. "So what? Isn't just about everything in modern pro sport rooted in the almighty buck?" More often than not, then, Lemieux's heroics were gauged not by the fans' delight but by his contribution to the private profit of professional franchise owners, including himself.

"What is cast in stone, though, is the obligation for reporters to write something about their beat every day. This is not negotiable—the newspaper has too much invested in its sports beats for them to sit idle." Mark Lowes made that observation in a chapter of *Inside the Sports Pages* on beat reporters. They're the rank and file, file, file of sports departments, forever under the gun to come up with any morsel of information that might be remotely interesting, while making sure the competition doesn't scoop them. They spend thirteen- to fifteen-hour days trying to reconcile the irreconcilable: struggling to be balanced and fair when their mainstream sources want them to be anything but. Team management and the athletes themselves expect a positive spin—and if they don't get it, they're prepared to make it very difficult for writers to do their job.

To combat this kind of bullying, beat reporters develop an arsenal of inside sources, who provide juicy tidbits that the team's PR department would never give out. Cultivating confidential relationships with general managers, lesser bureaucrats, and player agents allows them to break stories that go beyond the company line. But these relationships are tricky; sources can swiftly clam up if a reporter writes something they don't appreciate. Since beat reporters without inside sources are sunk, they constantly have to weigh the importance of a story against the chance of losing a key contact if they go ahead and write it. Sometimes they write the piece, sometimes they censor themselves—and the reader's the loser.

Operating under such a demanding system can make cynics of the best reporters. "The more you see behind the scenes," says the *Globe*'s Stephen Brunt, "the less majestic it gets." The beat reporter's daily ritual of trying to make the often mundane events of pro sports fresh and absorbing can lead some writers to question the value of what they're doing.

In the *Columbia Journalism Review* last year, Gene Collier, a columnist for the *Pittsburgh Post-Gazette*, explained why he left the sports beat after twenty-two years. He found himself hanging around in a locker room, waiting to interview a young quarterback who was as uninterested in talking to Collier as Collier was in talking to him. They both had ritual roles to play, which would result in placing a hero's mantle on still another pampered athlete. "The joke," Collier wrote, "is this: an actual living hero is ten times as likely to walk down your street, sit next to you on a bus, or hold the door for you at the library than to appear on your television between the never-varying pre-game yammer and the post-game lament."

"It's not fun and games for the sports journalist anymore," says former *Globe* columnist Marty York, "and anyone who tells you otherwise is woefully mistaken or lying." York's right: before televised sports and all-sports television, a reporter's job consisted mainly of finding out who won and who scored. Those were the days of myth making when the florid prose of sportswriters turned Babe Ruth or Joe DiMaggio into cultural icons. "The Ruth is mighty and shall prevail," wrote Heywood Broun in 1923. "You built up the hockey players," says Trent Frayne whose remarkable sportswriting career began in 1938. "They were brave, tall, and tremendous. They were ten feet tall. Later on in my career I found out they were guys who spit."

Nowadays, when readers already know who won and who scored and what the highlights were, the premium is on analysis and opinion. What's news has spilled over into business (management and marketing), labour (strikes, threats of strikes, peripatetic players, and stratospheric salaries), and cops and courts (out-of-control athletes). You can't tell the players without an annual report—or a police blotter.

Back when Trent Frayne was starting out in the thirties and forties, the relationship with pro athletes was easygoing. All a reporter had to do was stroll over to a player and ask, "What do you think about this?" Writers and players would play cards in the clubhouse and hang out together in bars. They weren't all that far apart in status and salary. Now the young millionaires of pro sports disdain the working press. "They're so rich they don't have much time to talk to a lowly scribe," says Frayne. Mitch Albom, of the *Detroit Free Press*, puts it much more specifically: "Baseball players are the biggest assholes on the planet," he once told a *GQ* magazine writer.

By consensus among Albom's peers, he could have added football players, basketball players and, to a lesser extent, hockey players. These role models have been known to grab reporters and oust them from the dressing room, fart in reply to an innocent question, and curse out any writer who crosses them—or simply makes them cross. "F★★k you, you f★★king jerk. Get the f★★k out of here," the Leafs' designated hitter, Tie Domi, demurred to Damien Cox in front of a dressing room full of players and media during the 1999 Eastern Conference Finals. It seems Cox's reporting was too accurate for Domi's tastes.

The mistreatment of Marty York is legendary. He defines what it is to be a despised writer. Over his twenty-eight years in the business, players have visited upon him "everything from threatening to murder me, literally, to throwing things at me on team flights or just deciding to give me the cold shoulder." That's what he gets for sticking his neck out to gather, without fear or favour, anything he feels will be of interest to his readers. He lists among his career highlights a 1985 confrontation with former Blue Jays slugger Cliff Johnson in the Jays' dressing room. York had written that Johnson had been caught having a beer in the team's clubhouse during a game when he was with the Texas Rangers. "Hey [expletive]," yelled

Johnson. "Where do you come off writing that bull about me?" When York tried to walk away, Johnson wrapped his arm around him and had to be restrained by his teammates.

That kind of intimidation is rare, but scorn for sportswriters is the order of the day. It makes it hard for the writers to do their job, which is, among other things, to help make these guys even wealthier.

"Any person with half a brain should know if they should get rid of a coach," says Laura Robinson, a former national team cyclist and now a crusading author. "Anyone can be an armchair athlete." She thinks most sportswriting is that superficial; it also supports the violent nature of male professional sports. In her book *Crossing the Line: Violence and Sexual Assault in Canada's National Sport*, Robinson paints a picture of the dark side of junior hockey, the breeding ground for the NHL, that the sports pages wouldn't show—until they had to. It's a picture of institutionalized abuse in which it's common for the players to sexually assault female fans. So much for the apprenticeship of tomorrow's stars.

The papers sometimes come close to this kind of reporting. For instance, while all others were losing their heads over the last days of Maple Leaf Gardens—Stanley Cups! legendary players!— Damien Cox was keeping his. In a column entitled "Why I Won't Miss the Joint," he wrote of the "hockey shrine" where, among other scandals, nearly ninety kids were sexually abused: "The Gardens, then, to me represents failure, greed, mistakes, selfishness and a near total absence of class and consideration for the past. It is a powerful symbol of waste and sadness and, above all, the vicious exploitation of Toronto hockey fans."

No one should be surprised that there's so little of this kind of work being done. It isn't in the interests of the Toronto papers or the city's three major-league teams. In fact, as Lowes points out, the prevailing ideology of the sports pages is really "a means not to know." He writes, "The routine work practices and professional ideologies that constitute sports newswork—while eminently successful in capturing the goings-on of the major-league commercial sports world with precision and in admirable detail—are principally 'a means not to know' about another, more expansive world: the world of noncommercial spectator sports." Laura Robinson would applaud that notion. She passionately believes that the papers should give much more space to amateur sports, particularly women's sports. "Why do they run five articles on why the Leafs lost a game?" she asks. "Why is that space devoted to men who lose?"

Because others, mostly men, stand to gain: owners, management, players, players' agents, union leaders, sports equipment companies, ad agencies—everything that's integral to the professional sports behemoth, including the sports press. Seen that way, it didn't much matter if, say, Eric Lindros did or didn't come to Toronto; his big play in the papers was much more vital to the NHL than any he'll ever make on the ice.

◄◄ **Source:** © R. C. Gilbert, 2001. This article was originally published in the *Ryerson Review of Journamlism*, Spring 2001. Reprinted with permission.

# 62. Women on TV: Looks First, Knowledge Later

## By William Houston

*It's a basic requirement that women on TV have to be attractive. What's interesting is that younger, female journalists aren't afraid to use this to their advantage, while older ones prefer to be known for brains more than beauty. Is the fight for credibility losing ground? And don't even ask what the men want.*

■ ■ ■ ■ ■ ■

Norma Wick had worked as a broadcaster for sixteen years, most of it in sports, when she sent her résumé and tapes to a sports network in Toronto.

She was forty years old and had been employed by Global Television in Vancouver as well as Orca Bay Sports and Entertainment covering the Vancouver Grizzlies.

But when turned down for a job at the sports network, she was told she lacked experience.

"I said, 'It's interesting that experience is high on your list, because you're hiring people who have none,'" Wick recalled. "And I was told, 'That's because they have magic and you don't.'"

Women have made huge advances in TV sports broadcasting over the past ten years. There are more working in the business. They hold jobs as reporters, anchors and, in the United States, even play-by-play announcers.

But as the numbers have grown, the importance of their physical appearance has increased. More than ever, networks place an emphasis on youth and beauty, and, by no surprise, *Playboy* is now publishing an annual list of the sexiest sportscasters. Within that environment, women continue to struggle for credibility as sports journalists.

Linda Cohn, an ESPN anchor and play-by-play voice, says the good news is that women are getting more opportunities to prove themselves.

"That's the positive," she said. "The negative, and it's out there, is a current trend, which is to go for looks first and then knowledge. And that's disconcerting."

The "magic" cited in Wick's job interview is code for women in their twenties or early thirties. They're attractive. The guys call them sports babes. On the Internet, they are referred to as sideline hotties.

This week, The Score sports network has blatantly advertised on its website for a "hottie" to be the host of a forthcoming TV show. Seductive pictures of the finalists are posted. David Errington, The Score's senior vice-president and general manager, described the ad as a promotion in partnership with a magazine.

For their part, women are hardly oblivious to the attention paid to their appearance.

Jody Vance said a few years ago that her desk at Rogers Sportsnet had a glass top to show off her legs.

Vance, former Sportsnet colleague Hazel Mae, and Kathryn Humphreys of CITY-TV in Toronto once posed for a magazine photo spread in which Humphreys wore leather, appearing as a sort of dominatrix; Mae showed some of her underwear; and Vance was portrayed reclining, glasses off and holding her hair.

Last summer, Erin Andrews, ESPN's "it girl," was reported to have been flaunting her sexuality in the Chicago Cubs' locker room.

Her low-cut top, according to Mike Nadel of GateHouse News Service, incited lewd comments and giggles from the players.

Andrews said she didn't feel that she had dressed provocatively.

"I don't look at myself as a sex object," she told a Minneapolis sports columnist. "I've never carried myself in that way. I'm a girl that loves sports. ... I think my overall reaction is that it's really sad that in 2008 I have people watching every single move I make."

But why wouldn't men watch her? She has movie-star good looks. For the male audience that makes up about 70% of ESPN's viewership, the fact she was voted "America's sexiest sportscaster" by a *Playboy* magazine poll was probably more relevant than her interviewing skills.

"Television is a visual medium," said Scott Moore, who hired Vance and also Mae when he worked as the vice-president of production for Sportsnet. He's now the head of CBC Sports. "You could make the same point about men. There aren't many ugly men on television. It's just a part of the basic requirement."

Still, Moore agrees that things are different now compared with a decade ago.

"Social mores have changed a lot," he said. "Both women and men aren't afraid to use their looks."

Wick, who teaches broadcast journalism in Toronto, says a woman's attractiveness often takes precedence over an ability to do the job.

"I think it would be to a woman's advantage if she were qualified," Wick said. "But given the climate we're in now, I don't think it's necessary.

"Some people are always going to view you as a skirt. Now, it's almost a prerequisite."

After being rejected by the sports network, Wick found work with Raptors NBA TV, where she thrived, according to her boss, John Shannon.

"She was nominated for a Gemini," said Shannon, now the senior vice-president of broadcasting for the NHL. "She had credibility as a basketball reporter. And she was an excellent storyteller."

A change maker for women in sports broadcasting has been the growth of the Internet, where websites are dedicated to celebrating the hottest sports babes.

The digital age has played a big role in raising the profile of female broadcasters, but it also has gone a long way toward diminishing their image. A poll on one website last year asked: Who is Canada's hottest female sportscaster? It received more than two thousand votes (Sportsnet's Martine Gaillard ranked first).

Online discussion ranges from debates about whether women broadcasters are worth "doing" to cackles about their choice of clothing. On an outfit worn by ESPN morning show host Hannah Storm, a deadspin.com poster wrote, "I can't decide whether [Storm] is going for the Pretty Woman Julia Roberts here or more for the Erin Brockovich."

Also on deadspin, this was the lead to a note about Hazel Mae moving to MLB TV, alongside a picture of her in a tight, low-cut dress perched on a television studio desk: "The sultry NESN lead anchor temptress will have to find a new sports desk to prop her stair-mastered caboose on top of next year."

And complementing a picture of Erin Andrews on hogwild: "For the most part, these women are articulate and knowledgeable about sports. But for the most part, us men don't care. Boobies!"

It was suggested on a blog that a reporter should be taken "into the woods" and assaulted.

"Frightening," is the way NBC's Andrea Kremer describes some of the commentary posted on websites.

"The vitriol that is spewed out is unbelievable," she said.

Wick said the violent, misogynistic tone of the online commentary shocked her.

"It's really disturbing stuff," she said. "I found that the more analytical I was as a reporter, the more vicious the commentary."

"The feeling was, if some woman wants to tell me about cooking, fine. But I don't need her telling me about sports."

Will Leitch, the founder of deadspin.com, a popular U.S. sports website that carries this sort of commentary, declined a request to be interviewed.

Internet commentary is an extreme example of the objectifying of women sports broadcasters, but prejudices still exist.

One is the perception that women get into the business to meet athletes. Incidents, such as the one involving Andrews, reinforce an image of women as flirts.

Another reporter, Carolyn Hughes of Fox Sports Net in Los Angeles and a former Miss Texas, was pulled off the baseball beat in 2005 when it was revealed she was having an affair with Los Angeles Dodgers pitcher Derek Lowe.

Mae, who joined the New England Sports Network after leaving Sportsnet, reportedly dated Ricky Davis, formerly of the Boston Celtics and now with the Los Angeles Clippers.

The Hughes story didn't change Mae's attitude toward athletes.

Mae told the Boston media that she would not work for a sports network that prohibited employees from having relationships with athletes.

But most female broadcasters say they make a point of not becoming involved with people they're covering.

"It's never been brought up by my bosses," TSN's Sara Orlesky said. "But, in my mind, it's a very clear-cut, no-go idea. For me, it's never been something I would look at."

Gaillard, who has worked in sports television for ten years, describes the objectifying of women as a reality of the business.

"Our demographics are obviously male driven, eighteen to thirty-five," she said. "So, I guess it's human nature for males to be attracted. But I'm sure there's a hottie website for news anchors, too. It's television. I can only speak for myself, but I work very hard to be recognized for my work."

Twenty-eight-year-old Orlesky, is among the top young female sports broadcasters in Canada. After earning a degree at Simon Fraser University, she worked for The Score in Vancouver before joining TSN. She says she was a sports fan growing up and participated as a volleyball player and coach.

She says she doesn't want her sex to be factor in any aspect of her job.

"I want to be thought of as one of the guys," she said. "There's no doubt you're in an industry that's testosterone-filled. So, you try to present yourself in a way that will minimize incidents, comments, and that sort of thing."

The Score's Nikki Reyes, also twenty-eight, took a different route to sports television. After high school, she moved to the Philippines to work as an actress before returning to Toronto and completing a radio and television course at Centennial College. After working a year at The Score, Reyes is the co-host of its morning show.

Like Orlesky, Reyes says she is a long-time sports fan, but had no experience in sports journalism.

She described her physical appeal as a "fact of television."

"Obviously, people like eye candy," she said. "But I think that only goes so far. What you have to say matters the most."

On her posted biography, she lists her career highlight as "being the only reporter who spoke to Michael Jordan at his red carpet birthday party in Houston for all-star weekend 2006. ... Yeah sure I only said eight words to him, and he responded with 'I don't know' ... but WOW. That moment was paramount for me."

Certainly, the job is less intimidating now than it was twenty years ago when women were barred from dressing rooms and also harassed.

Orlesky says she has experienced no incidents.

"When I walk into a football locker room, I'll hear somebody say 'towel up' or 'lady in the house,' that sort of thing," she said. "You're not faced with what they were faced with before."

But the question that lingers concerns the future. What happens when a woman reaches a certain age? What happens when the magic disappears?

At forty-nine, Kremer is at the top of her game. She works as a sideline reporter on *Sunday Night Football* and had arguably the most important reporting job for NBC at the Beijing Olympics, at the pool covering U.S. star Michael Phelps.

But she's aware that few women past the age of fifty continue to work in her business.

"I'm realistic," she said. "You can't compete with people who are twenty years younger. What you do hope is that the value of your experience does resonate with a potential employer and the audience."

Wick says women face plenty of challenges, age being one of them.

"It's an arbitrary business and fairness doesn't enter into it," she said. "But I have a motto. You don't join the circus and then complain about the clowns."

## ■■■ Those Who Know: And Those Who Don't

NBC reporter Andrea Kremer slots female sports broadcasters into two groups.

"There are women who grew up loving sports, and, by the way, they do television, or they write about it or talk about it on radio," said Kremer, who started in print journalism in 1982.

"And then there are women who think they want to be on TV, and sports is a cool thing. And I do think the audience knows the difference between the two. So I just hope people are getting into it for the right reason."

Lack of sports knowledge is often revealed when reporters ask weak and superficial questions, such as "How do you feel?" or "How important was that interception?" or "Talk about that goal."

Linda Cohn, an ESPN anchor and play-by-play announcer, says a female reporter without adequate knowledge will sometimes be instructed by a producer or director through the audio device in her ear.

"When people who just have looks going for them are told what to say, that sets women in the industry back decades," she said.

Women or, for that matter, men without a strong grasp of the subject may feel safer in a studio environment reading the sports news. But CBC Sports president Scott Moore says the nature of the assignment doesn't matter. If you don't know your stuff, you're vulnerable.

"It gets magnified whether you're in the studio or on the sidelines," he said. "When you're in the studio doing a live show with highlights and you're ad libbing, you'd better know sports."

Everyone makes mistakes, but a glaring gaffe may demonstrate a lack of requisite sports knowledge. For instance, in a live interview this season, Fox Sports sideline reporter Danyelle Sargent told San Francisco 49ers football coach Mike Singletary, "I heard that your mentor, Bill Walsh, was one of the first phone calls that you made when you found out that you had the job." Walsh died in July of 2007.

Because women are perceived to be less qualified than men, they feel they are held to a higher standard. Kremer says that if ESPN anchor Chris Berman makes a mistake, it's just a slip. If SportsCenter anchor Cohn gets something wrong, she doesn't know what she's talking about.

NHL senior vice-president of broadcasting John Shannon says women broadcasters need to be "20% better" than their male counterparts to be accepted as credible journalists by a largely male audience.

"If they make one mistake, they're going to get hammered [by sports fans and the media]," Shannon said.

Cohn cites an example of how men and women are judged differently.

"Let's just say I'm hosting SportsCenter on ESPN and a baseball score comes in and it's 14–7," she said. "And I'm kidding around and I say the Red Sox beat the Yankees by a touchdown, just for a joke, which is done all the time. You can bet there would be phone calls and email. 'Doesn't she know sports? What is she talking about?' I've been at ESPN for sixteen years and been in the business for over twenty. But even at this stage in my career, I can't say that."

In her biography, released in September, Cohn, forty-nine, recounts the story of being screamed at by an NFL player who accused her of being in the locker room to hang out with the men.

"That shocked me," Cohn said. "He never would have yelled at a guy. The only thing I was guilty of was being a woman."

◀◀ **Source:** This article was originally published in *The Globe and Mail*, December 20, 2008. Reprinted with permission.

# 63. Women in Sports Media: Time for a Victory Lap?
## By Alina Bernstein

*Anna Kournikova*
*Girl I want to know ya*
*Anna Kournikova with the eyes so blue*
*If it wasn't for tennis I would never know you*

*You can stay at my place if you want to crash*
*Backhand, forehand, overhead smash*

*Anna Kournikova with the legs so long*
*Please don't hate me when I sing this song to you*

*Let me be your ball boy now*
*Anna Kournikova with the real short hemline*
*Will you take my hand and let's go to the Krem-O-Line*

■ ■ ■ ■ ■ ■

These are most of the lyrics of a song by the pop band Binge titled "Anna Kournikova"—the music video that accompanies it was ranked number one on Lycos' search engine Top Ten Videos at the end of 2002. Following an email worm that was named after her this was yet another testimony to Kournikova's icon status on the Internet (and beyond) at the time.

These are some aspects that define the "Kournikova Syndrome," the definition of syndrome—according to Webster's dictionary—is a pattern of symptoms indicative of some disease. So what, in fact, is the disease?

From a feminist perspective, sport has been viewed for a long time as a sexist institution, male dominated and masculine in orientation. However, it is a fact that over the years women have truly advanced in organized, competitive sport.

Why should the media be discussed in relation to this? Mainly because the mass media—which are an essential feature of modern social life—preserve, transmit, and create important cultural information. Indeed, one central assumption within media studies is that media representations, to a great extent, determine how members of society see themselves, how they are viewed, and even treated by others.

When it comes to sport, the media assume an even greater importance since nowadays the overwhelming majority of spectators experience sporting events in their mediated form.

To date, a substantial body of work examining the role of the media in relation to women and sport has accumulated and, broadly speaking, it tends to focus on two main issues: the amount of coverage and the portrayal of women's sports and female athletes by the media.

## ■ ■ ■ The Amount of Coverage of Female Sport

During the eighties and most of the nineties, a consistent finding—well documented in the literature—is the under-reporting (and thus under-representation) of female athletes and their sporting events throughout all media.

Since the media is seen as reflecting on what is important and has prestige, this severe under-representation is seen as creating the impression that women athletes are nonexistent in the sporting world or of little value when they do exist. Which, in turn, creates a false impression of women's athleticism by denying the reality of the modern female athlete.

This under-representation is also viewed as creating a vicious circle since the growth of women's sport is hindered by the lack of funds which nowadays come primarily from sponsorship and sponsors, who are interested in sports and teams featured regularly on television.

Even towards the end of the nineties and beyond, the research findings of the routine, day-to-day amount of coverage of women in sport, remain that female athletes are still, in many cases, symbolically annihilated.

However, certain changes in the amount of coverage can certainly be traced, especially when it comes to major sporting events. The Olympic Games are a revealing example in this context.

In a study of the 1996 Games, Eastman and Billings (1999) found that NBC succeeded in equalizing coverage for men's and women's sports in two respects: in the number of different events and in the total quantity of minutes devoted to sports of each gender group.

And yet, many buts emerge from such studies. For instance, Tuggle and Owen (1999) in their study of the same Olympics—and in a similar vein to previous studies—found that female competitors at the Games were more likely to receive attention if they competed in what some have called "socially acceptable" individual sports.

Eastman and Billings (1999) argue that their results support the conclusion that the NBC network executives were very concerned about the appearance of gender equity in 1996, and that this concern had a powerful impact on some aspects of the telecast.

They emphasize that a network can dictate the philosophy of coverage, but the professional talent within the organization carries it out, and a policy of gender parity does not necessarily alleviate bias in coverage.

Indeed, as both sets of writers point out, the predominantly male gender of hosts, reporters, and producers might be a primary cause of unknowing or knowing bias. As Eastman and Billings (1999) put it, what the highest executives at NBC wanted and what they actually received may not have been the same.

Overall, nowadays women's tennis might be the only clear example of a sport to which television dedicates much airtime in Western countries on a regular basis. Moreover, according to a recent *Sports Illustrated* article, this is the only sport in which the U.S. television ratings for women's matches routinely surpass the men's. At the 2002 Wimbledon tournament, for example, the women's doubles final outdrew the men's singles final. (Tennis will be further addressed below.)

## ■ ■ ■ Is the Amount of Coverage Important?

It can be argued then that women have gained some ground as far as media visibility is concerned, especially in major sporting events. Moreover, it seems that media organizations—at least in Western societies are nowadays far more aware of, and sensitive to, the need for gender equality in the coverage of sport.

However, the question has to be asked: Does size matter? Does more coverage necessarily bring about a truly equal representation of women in sport? Or are we simply getting more, which is in fact of the same? I would even go as far as to speculate that more of certain types of portrayals, which I discuss below, are even worse, since they may well fixate views of women in sport by repeating them in more volume.

Visibility is certainly important, but a closer look is required at the type coverage women get from the media.

## ■■■ The Media Portrayal of Women's Sports and Female Athletes

The question of whether sports reports of female athletes are not only fewer but also different from those of their male counterparts has been answered in the literature—including that from the nineties and beyond—with a clear yes, although explanations as to how exactly this takes place and what should be done to change it, differ.

In 1992, Sabo and Curry Jansen, for example, argued that while male athletes are "valorized, lionized, and put on cultural pedestals," female athletes are infantilized by sport commentators who refer to them as "girls" or "young ladies" whereas male athletes are "men" or "young men."

Another practice—much referred to in the literature—is the use of names in commentary. In an article published in 1990, Messner, Duncan, and Jensen found that commentators referred to female tennis players by their first names about 53% of the time and to men only 8% of the time. Various writers perceive this as a linguistic practice that reinforces the existing gender-based status differences.

Studies found a variety of practices by which the media trivialize, and therefore undermine, women's athletic achievements, thus constructing female athleticism not only as "other than" but as "lesser than" the males.

Studies from the end of the nineties reveal that some changes did take place in this respect too. For instance, in their study of the 1996 Olympics Jones, Murrell, and Jackson (1999) write regarding female athletes playing female-appropriate sports,

> It is promising to see a trend toward print media accounts that focus more on describing their performance—providing details of what a gymnast does—as opposed to simply describing how graceful she looked or how she has the personality to make her America's next sweetheart.

However, the buts in this case outweigh the positive findings. For example, Koivula (1999) in her study of the Swedish media, still found that the language commentators used for referring to women sometimes included cases of infantilism. She also found that women athletes were referred to by their first names about four times as often as the men.

In concluding his study of the representation of women in football-related stories during the course of the 1996 European Championships in the British popular press, Harris (1999) writes that the message that is being portrayed to women and young girls is that sport is still an essentially male activity in which women are afforded only subordinate and/or highly sexualized roles.

## ■■■ Appearance and Attractiveness

Researchers analyzing the portrayal of female athletes found the coverage to be often framed within stereotypes which emphasize appearance and attractiveness rather than athletic skill. Moreover, scholars found that the media tend to focus on the female athletes as sexual beings rather than serious performers. According to this argument, the sexualization of female athletes trivializes them and in fact robs them of athletic legitimacy, thus preserving hegemonic masculinity.

As I am attempting to assess change, it is worth noting that Eastman and Billings (1999) found that although instances of gender stereotyping were located, their presence was not as overwhelming as expected, but as traditional gender stereotyping suggests, the descriptors applied to women athletes contained more commentary about physical appearance than the descriptors applied to male athletes.

This is the issue the rest of this discussion relates to—considering the amount and type of coverage in a couple of specific cases which provide examples of the ways in which the media persist in emphasizing appearance and attractiveness when it comes to female athletes.

Importantly, the analysis here focuses on popular newspapers, magazines, and websites rather than television, the medium that is at the centre of most of the above mentioned studies. The reason for doing this is that, as mentioned, that television organizations, particularly the American ones, are far more sensitive to gender related issues than ever before. Thus I find it more fruitful to look at the broader media world in order to reveal the existence of deeply embedded perceptions of female athletes beyond the reach of television executives.

## ■ ■ ■ Marion Jones

Clearly, no under-reporting can be argued when it comes to Marion Jones. However, it is worth considering her coverage in the American media prior to the 2000 Sydney Games in which she planned on winning five gold medals. As the British journalist Sharon Krum put it, from the beginning, Jones did not dare to suggest, wish, or hope she might win five medals. She declared it a certainty. According to Krum, writing prior to the Games, especially for the media,

> Jones is too much. She is too boastful, too assertive, too cocksure she will bring home the gold. In short, she is displaying character

traits Americans ascribe to male athletes. But in men the chest-thumping is admired. In women, it is shocking and has led to Jones being called arrogant, pretentious, and a certain word that rhymes with rich.

Moreover, physically, Jones is not frail or model-like-thin, she is visibly strong and muscular which has long been viewed as being unfeminine. Combined with her strong statements, she certainly does not confirm with stereotypes of femininity.

Thus, it should come as no surprise to realize that in the U.S. media build-up towards the Sydney Games the most photographed female athlete was not Marion Jones but Amy Acuff, a six-foot-two blonde, part-time model high jumper whose ambition, as it was reported, was not to win an Olympic gold medal but to work on the *Sports Illustrated* swimsuit edition: "Because people get a lot of attention for that."

Although Jones certainly attracted much media attention prior to, and during the Sydney Games, this pre-Games bias is yet another example of the fact that female athletes tend to gain media attention at least as far as photographs are concerned—for what they look like and not necessarily for their sporting achievements.

More recently Acuff, one of the most photographed female athletes in the world at the time, infuriated some feminist writers when she said in an interview (*Rolling Stone*) following provocative photographs of her in magazines like *Esquire*: "I wanted to show that a woman athlete can be extremely competitive and driven and successful and still retain feminine qualities." Thus implying that competitive, driven, and successful are not feminine qualities whereas posing nude in magazines is. In 2002, Acuff was voted the sexiest athlete in the world by ESPN.

This can be linked into the compliment bestowed on some female athletes: "she plays like a man" which reflects the continuing cultural contradictions between femininity and athleticism.

The athlete is being complimented, yet at the same time the implication is that in being such a strong athlete she is somehow not a "real" woman.

### ■■■ Anna Kournikova

Since the late nineties, women's tennis gets no less and sometimes even more media coverage than the men's, and the ratings are higher too. But this is not the case only because women's tennis seems more interesting in sporting terms but also, as many have noticed, due to the beauty of the some of the players, most notably, at the time, Anna Kournikova.

Despite the much mentioned fact that she is yet to win her first singles title, it is important to recall that she was ranked as high as eight in the 2000/01 season and has won two Grand Slam tournament doubles titles. It is true that in the singles she is now ranked thirty-sixth (in doubles she is ninth) but in 1997, as a sixteen-year-old, she became only the second woman in the Open Era to reach the semifinals in her Wimbledon debut. In 1998, she was the first Russian woman to be seeded at the U.S. Open in twenty-two years. Also in 1998, she beat Steffi Graf in the quarter-finals at Eastbourne. At that point, she became one of only eight players ever to have defeated Martina Hingis and Graf.

And yet, the amount and type of coverage she gains does not correlate with her tennis achievements. As a point of illustration: During Wimbledon 2000 there were twenty pictures of Kournikova in British newspapers for every one of the singles finalist Lindsay Davenport.

The extensive media attention to the blonde, model-looking Kournikova—also dubbed tennis's pinup girl—clearly shows the importance that at least certain branches of the media ascribe to looks and image over tennis skills. As one web-based writer put it, the Anna Kournikova phenomenon proves you don't need to win tournaments to get your name—and photo—in the media.

Moreover, as the introduction to an eight-page spread of *Hello! Magazine* featuring Kournikova put it, "[...] the waist-length flaxen hair, endless legs, smooth tan and metallic silver-blue eyes [...]" have undoubtedly helped her into the celebrity stratosphere.

In a 2001 issue of the same magazine paparazzi photos of the sun-bathing Kournikova were accompanied by statements like: "Tennis heart-throb Anna Kournikova, whose stunning looks have launched thousands of websites and sold millions of bras and Adidas trainers, was topping up her tan recently at her 3 million pounds Miami mansion."

To the point about websites, it is worth mentioning that a search for "Anna Kournikova" at the end of 2002 came up with over 320,000 results,[1] including sites boasting they have sexy pictures of the hottest tennis babe (a search for Marion Jones came up with 35,000 mentions). Although many of the Internet sites are constructed by fans, and not by media organizations, I believe this does reflect on society's attitude towards this tennis player.

It is worth emphasizing that the views of this phenomenon and its implications vary considerably. Within sport itself, some view this trend as highly problematic. In her book *The Underside of Women's Tennis*, the French player Nathalie Tauziat claims that aesthetics and charisma are winning out over sporting performance. She uses Kournikova as the clearest example of how the tennis circuit is now fixated on the style, and not substance, of the women's tour and the media certainly play an important role in promoting this.

Testimony to this is also the fact that in the summer of 2002, as Kournikova's play became consistently disappointing, the media tried to promote other players as tennis babes. Daniela Hantuchova being a prime example (see *TIME*, July 8, 2002).

Although the media tried to push the tall, blonde, nineteen-year-old Hantuchova, who at the time was ranked eighth in the world, into what some have referred to as the "Anna vacuum," she herself did not cooperate in becoming the Bratislava Babe, explaining in an interview: "I'm concentrating on my tennis I don't need the other things."

### ■ ■ ■ Simonya Popova

A further interesting case in this context is that of Simonya Popova.

In September 2002, *Sports Illustrated* ran a story about this tennis player who combined the looks of Kournikova with the playing ability of the Williams sisters. Only the last sentence of the straight-face written article revealed it was a hoax. But apparently, not a lot of people noticed. Lycos (search engine) reported she became the third most popular searched for athlete during that week. It all came about as a play on the film *Simone*, about a computer-generated actress.

And yet, some believe there is an upside to this phenomena. Chris Evert, three-time Wimbledon champion and commentator for NBC, said in an interview: "Girls now want to grow up and be athletes [...] there are attractive, appealing girls out there and now they realize that it is okay to run around and sweat and be tough. Twenty years ago it was frowned upon and wasn't feminine."

Furthermore, according to Sports Sponsorship Advisory Service, women should "play the sex appeal card to attract more media coverage and, therefore, more sponsorship." This suggestion infuriated Yvonne Barker, director of Women in Sport, who said:

> We believe that women's sport should be sponsored for exactly the same reason as men—because they appeal to their audience for their achievement and intrinsic value.

In this context, it is important to recall that some male tennis players ride the sex and sex appeal card on their way to media exposure and lucrative sponsorship contracts. For instance, one can easily find websites dedicated to sexy male tennis players such as, in 2002, Patrick Rafter.

And yet, overall, there are much less sexy images of male tennis players than those of their female counterparts. Furthermore, it can be argued that men are more easily allowed to be sex symbols and serious tennis players while women have to make a choice.

Having said all that, it is also important to stress that Kournikova is not necessarily a victim of the media. She herself and the people surrounding her, as Tauziat claims, orchestrate the type of media coverage and hype she in generating. She clearly poses for many of the photographs and in general doesn't shy away from the "tennis Madonna" label. Thus, her case also shows how much cooperation from the athlete's part is required to create the syndrome discussed here, Hantuchova's non-cooperation is clear illustration of this point. But then, as the paparazzi photos and the serious sports pages show, it can get out of the athlete's control.

As a result of this cooperation, Kournikova has made millions from endorsements; in 2002 she was one of the five female athletes on the Forbes Celebrity 100, list along with four other pro tennis players. This is especially noteworthy when only one male pro (Andre Agassi) made the list. In fact, the short statement explaining her ranking on the list declared:

> So what if she has more cover stories than championship trophies? Her popularity makes her the game's top endorser. Annamania stretches well beyond the hard courts: Her image remains one of the most popular on the Internet.

Generally speaking, a certain ambivalence emerges every time a female athlete is framed as a sexual being or is in fact covered by the media not for her sport performance but because she is attractive and conveys sex appeal.

Although it can be argued that the media cannot change the world, I believe it can help—along with other societal forces—change attitudes about women in sports. But for now, with all the improvements that have been made, they still don't do enough.

### ■ ■ ■ Wonderful Stories to be Told— The Test is How

To conclude, Anita DeFrantz—the first woman to reach the International Olympic Committee vice-presidency said in 2001: "The good news is, finally journalists have realized that we're here to stay. There are wonderful stories to be told."

Based on recent studies, this statement seems correct, at least to some extent. Overall, many steps have been taken in the right direction especially in relation to the amount of coverage in major sporting events but also in the type of coverage women's sports and female athletes get.

And yet, there is still some bad news, which is revealed when looking more closely at some of those wonderful stories told—particularly by certain branches of the media—about female athletes.

There are questions that beg to be asked: If more media coverage means more sexualized images, is more necessarily better? Or is more even worse? If the moment one steps a little bit away from the more aware—and politically correct—television coverage much emphasis on female athletes appearance and attractiveness can still be found, to what extent did the media's views of them, and by extension society's, truly change? Is any media story good news as far as female athletes are concerned—as long as they spell their name right?

---

◀◀ **Source:** This article is based on an invited lecture presented at the Play the Game conference, Copenhagen, 2002. It is also available on the Play the Game website and was reprinted with permission.

### Notes

1. It is worth mentioning that years after Kournikova retired from tennis, a Google search of her name came up with over 4 million results.

### References

- Eastman, S. T. and Billings, A. C. 1999. "Gender Parity in the Olympics—Hyping Women Athletes, Favoring Men Athletes" *Journal of Sport and Social Issues*, 23(2): 140–170.
- Harris, J. 1999. "Lie Back and Think of England: The Women of Euro 96" *Journal of Sport and Social Issues*, 23(1): 96–110.
- Jones, R., Murrell, A. J. and Jackson, J. 1999. "Pretty Versus Powerful in the Sports Pages" *Journal of Sport and Social Issues*, 23(2): 183–192.
- Koivula, N. 1999. "Gender Stereotyping in Televised Media Sport Coverage" *Sex Roles*, 41(7/8): 589–603.
- Messner, M.A., Duncan, M. C., and Jensen, K. 1990. "Separating the Men from the Girls: The Gendering of Televised Sports" Paper presented at the meeting of the North American Society for the Sociology of Sport, Denver, CO.
- Sabo, D. and Curry Jansen, S. 1992. "Images of Men in Sport Media—The Social Reproduction of Gender Order" in Craig, S. (Ed.) *Men, Masculinity, and the Media*. London: Sage.
- Tuggle, C. A. and Owen, A. 1999. "A Descriptive Analysis of NBC's Coverage of the Centennial Olympics—The 'Games of the Women'?" *Journal of Sport and Social Issues*, 23(2): 171–182.

### Further Reading (added in 2010)

- Billings, A. C. and Hundley, H. L. (Eds.) 2009 *Examining Identity in Sports Media*. London: Sage.
- Creedon, P. J. (Ed.) 1994. *Women, Media and Sport - Challenging Gender Values*. London: Sage.
- Fuller, L. K. (Ed.) 2009. *Sport, Rhetoric, and Gender: Historical Perspectives and Media Representations*. Hampshire: Palgrave Macmillan.
- Markula, P. (Ed) 2009. *Olympic Women and the Media: International Perspectives (Global Culture and Sport)*. Hampshire: Palgrave Macmillan.

# Section 11

## Politics and Sports

**P**olitics refers to "the processes and procedures of making decisions that affect collections of people from small groups to societies" (Coakley and Donnelly, 2009, p. 419). Thus, politics involves the power to make decisions, and those decisions may take the form of laws, or policies.

In this section, Jean Harvey considers the relationship between "Sport and Citizenship Policy," looking at some of the ways in which sport may be involved in public policy to promote active citizenship and social cohesion. In particular, Harvey argues that ensuring Canadian citizens the right to participate in sports is an important step towards enhancing citizenship.

Ian Bird, a former Olympic athlete and leader of the Sport Matters Group (www.sportmatters.ca) argues that sport should become an even more important part of politics, and an election issue, in his article "Politicians Can Score by Making Sport an Issue." He outlines a number of ways this could be done, including the long-standing call in the sport community to devote 1% of Canada's health budget (roughly $300 million per year) to the development of sports and sport infrastructure.

Jeff Blair writes about the political involvement of athletes in his article, "Athletes Urged to Voice Concerns." This issue is also examined in Doug Brown's articles in Sections 2 and 4. Brown criticizes athletes for failing to stand up for their own rights, and for failing to speak out on behalf of the rights of others at the Beijing Olympics. Brown also points out that athletes are not even involved in the development of important policies, rules, and decisions that directly concern them (e.g., doping). Blair reports on peace activism (against the Iraq War) by Athletes United for Peace, but also notes the lack of involvement in such activism by professional athletes. As cited in the introduction to Section 2, "governing bodies [and advertisers] seek stars without opinions."

Prior to the Vancouver Olympics in 2010, it had been twenty-two years since Canada had previously hosted an Olympic games (Calgary, 1988). It seems likely that it will be at least that long again before Canada hosts another Olympics and, since the Olympics is an event that brings sport and politics together like no other, the remaining articles in this section deal with politics and the Olympics.

Kevin Wamsley gives us "The Rules of the Games" with regard to becoming the host of an Olympics. He proposes that it's naïve to think "that choosing a host city was an apolitical decision" and advises us to "check the Olympic record," before going on to outline the politics of Olympic host city selection. The article was written shortly after the IOC had selected Beijing (rather than Toronto or other candidate cities) to host the 2008 Summer Olympics.

Jakob Staun and Kirsten Sparre follow Wamsley's argument that the selection of Olympic cities is political by noting the limited capacity of the

Olympics themselves to effect social change. The IOC claimed to have selected Beijing because of the Games' previous success in, for example, Korea, bringing about democracy. Furthermore, Beijing's selection was apparently based on the hope that China's record on human rights would improve as a result of hosting the Olympics. However, in the final analysis the IOC was powerless in a powerful nation such as China to insist on any social and political changes. Thus, although the IOC successfully fought the Canadian Charter of Rights and Freedoms and female ski jumpers to keep them out of competition at the Vancouver Olympics, its moral sway with an emerging superpower is clearly limited.

Bruce Kidd argues that "Canada Needs a Two-Track Strategy for Hosting International Games." He points out that the only way that Canada has developed new sport infrastructure in the last forty years is by hosting major international sports events. Those facilities, built at pubic expense, are then often reserved for professional sports or for a few high-performance athletes. He argues that hosting is a wasteful and inefficient way to obtain sports facilities, and that if we consider such facilities to be important we should develop them anyway for the benefit of all Canadians. The "bids for major games [could be] based upon facilities we already have rather than those we dream about building."

The exorbitant costs of modern Olympic security usually lead to its discussion as an economic issue. After all, the final costs for security at the two previous Winter Olympics were: $1.3 billion (Salt Lake City, 2002) and $1.4 billion (Torino, 2006). We know that Vancouver security cost over $1 billion, and we await the final figures. However, Chris Shaw and Alissa Westergard-Thorpe also address security as a political issue in their article, "Class-War Games: The Financial and Social Cost of Securing the 2010 Olympics." They argue that political freedom was under attack in terms of the heavy-handed treatment of protesters, massively increased surveillance, and the removal of "undesirables" from the city; and they predict that one legacy of the Games will be reduced political freedom.

The section concludes with two articles addressing the Own the Podium program—a politically driven, and mostly politically funded, program intended to ensure that Canadian athletes won the most medals at the Vancouver Games. The first article, written before the Games, considers the absurdity of the name Own the Podium ("*Own the Podium* or Rent it?") and the consequences of "Canada's involvement in the global sporting arms race." The second article, written after the Games, ("Rent the Podium Revisited: Reflections on Vancouver 2010") considers the way in which the program was both a success (Canadian athletes won the most gold medals) and a failure (Canada finished third in the medal table, just as they had in Torino in 2006), and the need for a sport policy that combines funding for high-performance sport with support for grassroots participation.

## Additional Suggested Readings and References

- Bain L. H. 2007. "No Olympics on Stolen Native Land." *The Dominion*, April 4.
- Campbell, M. 2007. "To Score Big, Ontario Athletes Need New Facilities." *The Globe and Mail*, April 10.
- Christie, J. 2001. "Turning Sport Vision into Real Action." *The Globe and Mail*, May 1.
- Christie, J. 2006. "Sport Ministers Call for $10 Billion." *The Globe and Mail*, September 29.
- Coakley, J. and P. Donnelly 2009. *Sports in Society: Issues and Controversies* (2nd Canadian edition). Toronto: McGraw-Hill Ryerson.
- Mayenknecht, T. 2005. "2010 Reasons for a Federal Sport Ministry." *The Globe and Mail*, November 4.
- Sandborn, T. 2007. "Can Vancouver Fend off Olympics Sweatshops?: China's Abuses 'a Warning Bell' for 2010." TheTyee.ca, June 20.
- Sandborn, T. 2008. "Worst Sports Injury: Worker Abuse: VANOC, Nike, Labour Reps to Confer at Olympics Sweatshop Forum." TheTyee.ca, June 11.
- Shepley, B. 2004. "Want More Medals? Get Kids Active Again." *The Globe and Mail*, August 24.
- Wamsley, K. 2002. "The Bad Taste Lingers." *London Free Press*, February 19.

# Sport and Citizenship Policy

By Jean Harvey

**64.**

*A shift toward a new normative framework for evaluating sport policy in Canada?*

∎ ∎ ∎ ∎ ∎ ∎

The mass media, obsessed with the phenomenal performances of certain individuals and the sensationalism of professional sports, spontaneously measures the value of policies for high-performance sports by the number of medals won by Canadian athletes at major international meets. To that effect, some are questioning the efficiency of Canadian policies against the disappointing performance of Canadian athletes at the Sydney Games or, on the contrary, against the recent success of Salt Lake City, where Canadians won the two gold medals in ice hockey, a great contribution to Canadian nationalism.

In terms of Canadians' participation in physical activity, the most recent surveys indicate that after more than twenty years of promotional campaigns on the importance of good health through exercise, Canadians have indeed changed their behaviour—for the worse. Since 1995, physical activity among Canadians has been declining.

In light of these observations—which, while superficial, still shape popular opinion to such an extent that they appeal directly to political leaders—the impulse is to conclude that sport policy has not always achieved its objectives. Yet, research in the social sciences of sports has revealed that the political functions and roles of sport policy are potentially many, given its highly symbolic, metaphoric, and polysemous nature.

Employing a socio-historical analysis, this study sheds light on the potential contribution of sport policy in strengthening citizenship and social cohesion. This analysis explores how "active citizenship" and "social cohesion" offer some of the elements of a normative framework for shaping and evaluating the success of sport policy, while emphasizing the urgent need for research into this issue, which has unfortunately remained unexplored until now.

Citizenship, a thematic rooted in Ancient Greece, has enjoyed a renaissance in the last ten years in the social sciences and in the priorities set by public policy. In broad terms, the rebirth of this thematic can partly be attributed to mounting social exclusion in developed societies, problems in integrating large numbers of immigrants, growing disinterest among citizens in political life, and, lastly, to issues of identity raised by rapid globalization, which has brought back to the fore the question of how individuals live together in local and even national communities.

But what is citizenship? Citizenship means much more than holding a passport that proves that we belong to a political community. Amidst the multitude of definitions that exist today, those put forward by Fred Constant have the virtue of clarity.

> On the one hand, citizenship is a legal, political, and social reality; a distinct way to organize and experience membership in a social and political community. On the other hand, it is both an idea, and an ideal: the particular way in which we reflect upon and evaluate this membership [...] there are at least four dimensions to the idea of citizenship: citizenship as an expression of national identity; citizenship as conferring rights and obligations with regard to a political community; citizenship as a set of specific social roles associated with active

**Figure 1**

The four dimensions of citizenship

1. Promotion of national identity
2. Set of rights and obligations
3. Set of roles for participating in the life of the political community
4. Set of moral qualities (civic virtues)

Source: F. Constant, La citoyenneté (Paris: Montchrestien, 1998), p. 26.

participation in the life of the political community; and citizenship as a set of moral qualities.[1]

Theoretically, it is possible to consider that sport policy may contribute to at least three of the dimensions of citizenship identified by Fred Constant.

Sports contribute to the promotion of national identity. This is the most obvious and well-known facet. National delegations symbolically represent a nation, and their victories, and sometimes their failures, help to forge a sense of belonging to the imagined community, to use the well-known expression coined by Benedict Anderson.[2] This equation, however, is not as accurate as it may first appear. In reality, several identities, sometimes conflicting, can be reinforced by sports. Social tensions can even be exacerbated when minority groups are not included or recognized in the collective "we" represented by a national delegation.

Sports also contribute to the development of local identities. It is here that citizenship and social cohesion intersect. As Judith Maxwell aptly states:

Social cohesion is built on shared values and a common discourse, the narrowing of gaps in wealth and income. Generally speaking, people must feel that they are participating in a common enterprise, that they face the same challenges and belong to the same community.[3]

This quotation by Maxwell brings us to a second facet of citizenship that pertains to rights, namely social rights and cultural rights. As noted by Thériault, "modern citizens are constantly being called upon in the establishment of a certain correspondence between the values that constitute their citizenship and the realities of their individual and social lives."[4] These rights constitute, in effect, citizen entitlements, that is to say the rights enjoyed by those who belong to the political community. Yet, as we will see further on, in the development of modern states, everything occurs as if these rights encompass an ever-growing and more sharply contrasted universe supported by very weak policies, particularly with regard to the right to access sports.

Sport policy may also have an impact on participation in the life of the political community, the third dimension of citizenship. This is evidenced by the intense volunteer participation spurred by the growing number of sports leagues, competitions and tournaments of all kinds. This has prompted several authors, including Laker,[5] to conclude that sports can be an ideal place for learning how to participate actively in the life of the political community.

The last dimension of citizenship in which sport policy may play a role is in the development of moral qualities. In fact, common sense dictates that sports develop a sense of fair play and solidarity, to give only two examples. In this respect, as is the case for the other facets presented here, it must be stressed that sports can contribute just as easily to the erosion of citizenship. Take, for example, the disturbing conclusions presented in the Commissioner of Official Languages' report on services offered to Francophone athletes by national sports associations.[6]

Concretely, we must ask ourselves the following question: Have Canadian sport policies contributed to the development of citizenship? Due to time constraints, this paper will focus only on the process involved in recognizing the right for all to access sports as a public benefit or as an element of

## Figure 2

Contribution of sport policy to citizenship

1. Promotion of national identity and minority identities

2. Attainment of social rights and cultural rights; sport as a common good

3. Participation in the life of the political community (volunteer involvement)

4. Set of moral qualities (civic virtues)

well-being to which each citizen is entitled. The context for this analysis will be the evolution of the Canadian welfare state.

### ■ ■ ■ Sport and Recreation Policy and the Evolution of the Canadian Welfare State[7]

At each stage in the evolution of the Canadian welfare state, we can identify a particular citizenship regime, an expression coined by Jenson and Phillips,[8] that is to say a specific form of recognition of certain rights, to which is associated a dominant form of legitimate state action and the state's relationships with civil society. Each citizenship regime corresponds to a specific type of rights (D) and a legitimate form of state action (A).

The first forms of Canadian state intervention in sports focussed on the obligations of citizens toward the state. The economic crisis of the 1930s shook up accepted ideas about the role of the Canadian state, particularly with regard to the destitute, that is to say the masses of unemployed workers who streamed into major Canadian cities. The Pro-Rec program launched in British Columbia in 1934 was one of the first "sport" policies adopted to eradicate this "scourge." The program's initial objective was to offer physical fitness sessions to the unemployed in an effort to increase their employability.

Fighting "inactivity," the source of "moral degradation," was at the core of this program, which served as an example for future agreements in the context of the Dominion-Provincial Youth Training Program, set up in 1937 after the adoption of the *Unemployment and Farm Relief Act*. The point here is that these initiatives remained essentially liberal in the sense that they took the form of specific state interventions to support citizens, specifically youth, to enable them to take control of their lives and become responsible and productive citizens. In other words, these interventions were based on a citizenship regime that assigned few obligations to the state and few rights to the citizen. In the vast majority of Canadian cities, a similar logic prevailed. In essence, the principle of charity underpinned municipal support for charitable associations, YMCAs, YWCAs, Boys and Girls Clubs, and recreation committees, which organized "good" activities for the most disadvantaged citizens.[9]

World War II brought the whole issue of Canadians' physical fitness to the fore as great numbers of young Canadians called into active service failed the army's health exams. The *National Physical Fitness Act* ensued in 1943 (revoked ten years later) to enable Canadian youth to fulfill their civic duties. The war also sounded the knell of the liberal form of governance of the Canadian state. In the area of recreation and sport, municipalities rose to the call of citizens' demands for a right to recreation by setting up municipal recreation services committed to the direct provision of a growing range of recreational and sport services, taking on a task previously assumed by non-profit organizations (YMCA, YWCA, Boys and Girls Clubs, recreation committees), while not entirely eclipsing the need for these bodies.

The *Fitness and Amateur Sport Act*, adopted in 1961 and still in force, was not—at least as per its objectives—simply about boosting Canadian nationalism. A core component of this act was the desire to increase access for all to participate in sports. The provinces participated in this drive, offering subsidies so they could also implement recreation and sport services. Beginning in the 1960s, a citizenship regime recognizing the right to sports prevailed, prompting various state levels to augment the number of programs that fostered greater access to sports for all citizens. The provinces and municipalities, however, led the charge.

The early 1980s ushered in an era of financial crisis and a fundamental questioning of the welfare state, opening the door to systematic attacks on the concept of social rights. The universality of public services was targeted as the cause of excessive state intervention and bureaucratization as well as loss of freedom. Access to certain services was gradually restricted to the poorest in society, based on ever-narrowing criteria. A new regime of social citizenship was born in which the poor, the sick, and single mothers were viewed as largely responsible for their own situations. Many qualified this new hegemonic discourse as an ideology of victim blaming. In other words, individuals were increasingly seen as responsible for their own health and physical fitness. Government-sponsored public education programs that promote regular physical activities were launched with the explicit goal

of modifying high-risk behaviour, namely physical inactivity and a poor diet. Any recognition of biological, social, or environmental determinants was shelved to shine the spotlight on individual responsibility.

Canada is in a transition period. The renewed interest in citizenship and social cohesion as guidelines for rethinking the role of the state can be explained by a number of factors, including government "victories" over fiscal deficits that have opened up a "margin of manoeuvre," social transformations resulting from the development of the new economy and globalization, increasing indicators of growing exclusion, debates on expanding poverty in Canada, and evidence showing the importance of socio-economic determinants of health put forth by organizations such as the National Forum on Health. In this sense, at least up until the events of September 11, 2001, an observer of the Canadian scene could well have thought that in Canada a new post-welfare state citizenship regime—in which the recognition of social and cultural rights and the implementation of an inclusive governance—could have led to policies promoting full public access to sports. Let's

## Figure 3
Evolution of the Canadian Welfare State and Sport Policy

| Period | Role of the state | Citizenship regime | Policy objectives |
|---|---|---|---|
| 1930–1945 | Emergence of the welfare state | **Liberal** <br> D = Civic rights <br> A = Responsibility for self | • Specific intervention <br> • Moral reform <br> • Employability |
| 1945–1975 | Consolidated welfare state | **Social** <br> D = Social rights <br> A = Social justice | • Right to sports <br> • Disease prevention |
| 1980–2000 | Restructured welfare state | **Neo-liberal** <br> D = Rights based on proven needs <br> A = Citizen responsibility | • Promotion of a healthy lifestyle |
| 2000–? | Post-welfare state | **Inclusive state** <br> D = Social and cultural rights <br> A = Inclusive governance | • Access to sports |

hope that these dramatic events do not spell the end of this emerging model.

## ■■■ Promotion of Cultural Rights

The development of the Canadian welfare state clearly does not in and of itself explain various state initiatives regarding the promotion of citizens' rights. Constant pressure from new social movements, such as the women's movement, has kept the question of equality front and centre in political debates. Furthermore, the evolution of relations between the Canadian majority and the First Nations, as well as the evolution of the multicultural character of Canadian society has led to the recognition, albeit partial, of the right to differences, particularly with respect to cultural diversity.

**Figure 4** provides examples of programs that have recognized, in concrete terms, the cultural rights of minority groups. It shows that these initiatives arose to address certain fundamental inequalities. Initiatives in favour of the First Nations offer

---

## Figure 4

### Initiatives that Promote Minority Cultural Identities

**First Nations**

- North American Indigenous Games
- Arctic Games

- These games also involve organizing committees. The main role of the federal government is to finance these games, which are designed to provide youths from these communities with the opportunity to participate in competitions in both "Western" and traditional Aboriginal sports. These games also serve to strengthen the identities of the members of these nations.

---

a degree of access to sports and promote the identities, beliefs and pride of belonging to these communities, particularly for young people. For First Nations, access to sports is also a means to counter idleness among youths in their communities, as well as to enable these young people to express themselves and realize their potential while engaging in activities they enjoy. In other words, it is a prevention tool well-suited to the problems faced by youths. Too few Aboriginal communities have the means to offer these services to their young people. This is particularly the case for those living in cities where community ties are the weakest and racism and exclusion are the most acute. The work of Paraschak,[10] among others, shows that unequal relations of power between the majority and the First Nations have sometimes led to initiatives perceived to be a strategy of acculturation by the First Nations, rather than as strategies to promote community identities. It is, therefore, crucial that First Nations hold the decision-making power when it comes to the provision of recreational and sport services, a principle that should apply to any group of citizens suffering from some form of exclusion.

## ■■■ Conclusion

The objective of this brief essay was to offer an overview of links that exist between sport policy, citizenship policy, and an approach to public policy aimed at fostering social cohesion. These links were established by looking at the history of certain federal government initiatives in the area of sports. We have shown that the concepts of "citizenship" and "social cohesion" offer a normative framework suitable for informing the development and evaluation of innovative public sport policy.

When proposing this topic as an important theme for policy research, we had also hoped to review the literature on sports, citizenship, and social cohesion. We were stopped in our tracks, however, by the dearth of information. Consultation of the major bibliographic data banks turned up fewer than ten titles. Clearly, there is an urgent need for research on these issues, an undertaking that is salient to the development and evaluation of public policy.

### Notes

1. F. Constant. *La citoyenneté*. Paris: Montchrestien, 1998, p. 26.

2. B. Anderson. *Imagined Communities: Reflections on the Origins and the Spread of Nationalism*. London: New Left Books, 1983.

3. Maxwell cited in P. Bernard, "La cohésion sociale: critique dialectique d'un quasi-concept," in *Lien social et politiques*, no. 41 (1999), pp. 47–59.

4. J.-Y. Thériault, "La citoyenneté: entre normativité et factualité," in *Sociologie et Sociétés*, Vol. 31, no. 2 (1999), pp. 5–13.

5. A. Laker, *Beyond the Boundaries of Physical Education: Educating Young People for Citizenship and Social Responsibility*. London: Routledge/Falmer, 2000.

6. Commissioner of Official Languages, *Official Languages in the Canadian Sport System*. Ottawa: Office of the Commissioner of Official Languages, 2000.

7. This section is a reworked translation of J. Harvey, "The Role of Sport and Recreation Policy in Fostering Citizenship: The Canadian Experience," in Building Citizenship: Governance and Service Provision in Canada CPRN /Rcrpp Discussion Paper No. F|17. Ottawa: Canadian Policy Research Networks, Inc., 2001, pp. 23–45.

8. J. Jenson and S. D. Phillips, "Regime Shift: New Citizenship Practices in Canada," *International Journal of Canadian Studies*, Vol. 14 (Fall 1996), pp. 111–136.

9. See M. Bellefleur. *L'évolution du loisir au Québec : essai socio-historique*. Sainte-Foy: Presses de l'Université du Québec, 1997.

10. V. Paraschak, "Legacy and New Directions: The NWT Sport and Recreation System," Conference Proceedings, 10–11 May 2000. Hay River NT, Yellowknife: Government of the NWT, 2000; "Knowing Ourselves Through the Other: Indigenous Peoples in Sport in Canada," in R. Jones and K. Armour (eds.), *Sociology of Sport: Theory and Practice*. Essex, UK: Longman, 2001, pp. 153-166; "Sport Festivals and Race Relations in the Northwest Territories of Canada," in G. Jarvie (ed.), *Sport, Racism and Ethnicity*. England: Falmer Press, 2001, pp. 74-93.

◀◀ **Source**: Jean Harvey is a professor at the Research Centre for Sport in Canadian Society, University of Ottawa. This article was first presented at the National Conference on Policy Research, Ottawa, December 7, 2001. This article was first published in *ISUMA*, Vol. 3, No. 1, Spring 2002. Reprinted with permission.

## 65. Politicians Can Score by Making Sport an Issue

By Ian Bird

*If all these people are running for office, why don't they talk about sport?*

■ ■ ■ ■ ■ ■

The contenders in the federal election are jockeying madly to be seen as the trustees of our publicly funded health-care system. But it is clear that simply throwing more money at the treatment of illness and disease is the sick part of the health debate.

More than three years ago, Roy Romanow's commission on health care pointed out that government investment in disease prevention and health promotion is just a small fraction of spending on health. Mr. Romanow recommended making prevention a more significant part of the health game plan, with a specific strategy to turn on Canadians to a physically active life. What kind of game plan are our political leaders working on in this campaign?

As a father and former Olympic athlete, I find the state of fitness among our young people both tragic and frightening. More than one-third of Canadian kids under twelve are overweight or obese—and the numbers are increasing. As the rates continue to rise, researchers are warning Canadians that today's children may well be the first generation with a lower life expectancy than their parents.

The economics of the situation are alarming, too, given that a lack of physical activity and access to quality sport programs is a major contributor to obesity and numerous other health problems, costing the health-care system more than $2-billion a year.

This is something that should scare the living daylights out of our leaders; it sure paints a picture that makes me sit up straight and take notice.

What do the national political parties have to say about this, and about the role that sport and physical activity can play as blue-chip prospects for a healthy Canada?

The Liberals and NDP have yet to say anything on the issue. The Bloc Québécois has a broad-based platform that includes a strategy to promote lifelong participation in sport and physical activity, a program to support developing athletes, and greater financial assistance for elite athletes, although most of the public noise has been about its call for separate national teams.

Conservative Leader Stephen Harper promises a tax credit of $500 a child—about $80 in a parent's pocket—to help defray the cost of enrolling children in organized physical activity and sport. Since this was first recommended in a 1998 parliamentary subcommittee report (Sport in Canada: Everybody's Business), Canadian sport organizations have been calling on the federal government to use the tax system to promote greater participation in sport and physical activity, and getting zero response. The Tory promise is at least a flicker of awareness out there somewhere.

No party has come forward with a comprehensive game plan that maximizes the potential of sport and physical activity to promote health and well-being. Sport organizations and individual Canadians across the country are calling on all political parties to endorse a strategy that includes innovative tax measures to promote greater participation, dedicated investments in sport and recreation infrastructure and facilities, and an annual investment in sport and physical activity equal to a mere 1% of the health budget, or about $300-million.

With this kind of investment, we could expect the provinces and territories to reach their stated goal of a 10% increase in physical activity by 2010. We could expect new and upgraded sport facilities in communities where they are needed most. We could expect more affordable and accessible sport programs for our children. We could expect more medals at the 2010 Olympic and Paralympic Games in Vancouver/Whistler to inspire a new generation of kids.

Survey after survey, including the one released this fall by the Strategic Counsel for the True Sport Foundation, shows that Canadians place a high value on sport—because cheering for our Olympic athletes boosts our national pride, because volunteering for a local team increases our sense of community, because having our children participate in sport enhances their physical and social development, and because being active ourselves keeps us healthier.

It's time our politicians show real support for this fundamental Canadian value, by committing to a comprehensive investment in sport and physical activity. Let's get behind the sport and physical activity game plan this election, and give our kids a chance to win at life.

---

**◀◀ Source**: Ian Bird is a two-time Olympic athlete, father of three young children, and senior leader of the Sport Matters Group. This article was first published in *The Globe and Mail* on December 28, 2005. Reprinted with permission.

# 66. Athletes Urged to Voice Concerns

## By Jeff Blair

*Internet petition strongly opposed to invasion of Iraq seeks sport support*

■■■■■

The world has heard protests from actors and authors and songwriters. Now, athletes are giving voice to concerns about U.S. President George W. Bush's intentions in Iraq.

A group called Athletes United For Peace, which includes Dr. Bruce Kidd, Dean of the University of Toronto's Faculty of Physical Education and Health, is working on an Internet petition urging the United States and its allies not to invade Iraq.

Toni Smith, a women's basketball player at Manhattanville College, a small liberal arts school outside New York City, has made headlines by turning her back on the Stars and Stripes during the playing of "The Star-Spangled Banner" before games. Smith has been roundly criticized by opponents, and play was stopped during a recent game when a Vietnam veteran ran on the court holding a U.S. flag to confront her.

At the National Basketball Association all-star game last month in Atlanta, Dallas Mavericks guard Steve Nash, a native of Vancouver, wore a T-shirt that read: No War, Shoot For Peace. He said he was "educating himself" on the matter and said he wore the shirt at the request of friends involved in the anti-war movement at the University of British Columbia.

Nash, who along with agent Bill Duffy did not return phone calls, was criticized by letter writers to Dallas newspapers. But his T-shirt was simply a footnote to the all-star weekend.

"On a personal level, yeah, I wish some of the athletes who were visible and had more public clout would raise serious questions," said Dave Meggyesy, whose anti-Vietnam War stance cost him his career as a National Football League player in the late 1960s.

Meggyesy is one of the driving forces behind the petition.

"But that's something that is always an individual decision and I don't think you can put the onus on athletes any more than entertainers or corporate executives," he said in an interview from San Francisco.

"It comes down to having a certain amount of moral courage, but it was easier for athletes back then, I think, because there were a lot of young people against the war. Hell, there were a lot of people against the war, period.

"Part of it is that to a lot of people right now, war is a freaking video game," added Meggyesy, who now runs the West Coast regional office of the NFL Players' Association and whose memoir, *Out of Their League*, remains a staple of sports sociology classes.

History has rightfully accorded special social status to the courage shown by Muhammad Ali, Jesse Owens, and Jackie Robinson. And there was that symbolic moment when U.S. sprinters Tommie Smith and John Carlos stood on the medal podium at the 1968 Olympics in Mexico City—black-gloved fists raised, heads bowed, as "The Star-Spangled Banner" was played and the Stars and Stripes raised.

During the Persian Gulf War in 1991, Detroit Tigers teammates Chet Lemon and Lou Whittaker taped over U.S. flags that the commissioner's office mandated on all batting helmets, citing their pacifist beliefs as Jehovah's Witnesses.

Professional athletes have remained largely silent, although in some spring-training sites in Arizona and Florida, the proximity of U.S. Air Force bases drives home the possibility of war on a daily basis. The new spring-training site shared by the Texas Rangers and Kansas City Royals in Surprise, Arizona, is located only 16 kilometres north of Luke AFB, home to 220 F-16 fighters.

One by one, two by two, the jets race over the practice fields, banking before heading toward the distant brown hills and the Barry M. Goldwater Air Force Range. Players, driving to their morning workouts, are now used to tapping the breaks on their SUVs and luxury cars as fighters roar into the air, only a few feet above them. There are days, Texas manager Buck Showalter said, when he feels like saluting.

In 1969, Meggyesy, then a St. Louis Cardinals linebacker, intentionally stood with his head bowed and spit repeatedly during the playing of the national anthem as a protest against the Vietnam War. His coach had instituted a code of conduct during the playing of the anthem. As the outcry over his actions grew, so did Meggyesy's resolve and notoriety. His career ended at age twenty-eight.

Kidd is a two-time winner of the Canadian Press male athlete of the year as a middle-distance runner and a former director of the International Campaign Against Apartheid Sport. There are grounds, he feels, for holding professional athletes to a higher standard, while acknowledging the economic ramifications that can result. NBA player Mahmoud Abdul-Rauf, for example, ended his boycott of the anthem in the 1990s when he was threatened with suspension without pay, which worked out to $32,000 a game.

"I don't believe it's unfair to hold them to a higher standard, because [pro athletes] are, in fact, often held to a lower standard around such issues as performance-enhancing drugs and fair play," Kidd said.

"Athletes aspire to and take advantage of representational status. The really top athletes are symbolic representatives of a lot of things, especially considering the way they commercialize themselves.

"They're part of the entire sports-media system ... that socializes against critical commentary," Kidd said. "The international sports community is much more aware of the complexity and seriousness of these issues."

Kidd points out that beyond anti-war sentiment, most of the autobiographies that skewered professional sports, such as Meggyesy's and Jim Bouton's *Ball Four*, were written three decades ago. Now, the sports world eagerly awaits books from such deep thinkers as Jose Canseco.

"If you think about all the autobiographical books that were critiques of athletics and athletic systems, 90% of it came out of that period," Kidd said.

"There was a wave of youth radicalization back then, and the context for it was provided by the women's rights movement and the civil rights movement. I'm not certain the context exists for it today, compared to the '60s and '70s."

◀◀ **Source:** This article was first published in *The Globe and Mail* on March 3, 2003. Reprinted with permission.

# 67. The Rules of the Games

## By Kevin Wamsley

*Surely you didn't think that choosing a host city was an apolitical decision? Check the Olympic record.*

■ ■ ■ ■ ■ ■

For more than one hundred years, the decision to bestow the grandest of international sports festivals upon a chosen host city has been politically motivated. Some Olympic Games boosters, who consider yesterday's naming of China as host of the 2008 Games to be a crushing defeat—those with economic, political, and ideological interests in hosting the Games in their own countries—may still question the decision. They may demand to know how an organization that lays claim to promoting international peace, goodwill, and social betterment came to award the Games to a country understood by Western nations as oppressive and brutal—the very antithesis of the so-called Olympic ideal. But yesterday's decision by International Olympic Committee members was entirely in keeping with tradition.

From the first modern Games in 1896 held in Athens, founder Baron Pierre de Coubertin understood the importance of reading contemporary political currents to secure the future of the Olympic Games. In the following decades, in their quest to fashion the Olympic Games as the most important sport competition in the world, IOC presidents and Olympics supporters cared little about the domestic policies, social climates, or human rights in host countries.

The most blatant example of the IOC's organizational complicity in a regime's brutal treatment of citizens occurred during the 1936 Olympics, which were held in Nazi Germany. Without the participation of the traditionally strong United States team and the influential American press corps, Hitler's Olympics would have been a failure.

But there are other examples too. The Games were held in Mexico in 1968 despite the slaughter of Mexican citizens protesting conditions of poverty. The Games continued in Munich in 1972 after commandos massacred athletes from the Israeli team. The self-proclaimed apolitical credo for Avery Brundage, president of the IOC from 1952–1972 was simply: "The Games must go on."

Political relationships have always been a fundamental element of modern sport. To suggest that sport and politics do not mix—or that there ever was an era when sport did not pit people with different identities and values in competition with one another—is simply naïve.

The decision to award the Games of 2008 to Beijing represents a triumph for outgoing IOC President Juan Antonio Samaranch, a tribute to his leadership, and final compensation for co-opting many current IOC members. Successful, elaborate marketing programs have permitted Mr. Samaranch to spread the Olympic message to all corners of the Earth, to provide opportunities for spectators to view the best athletes, professionals included, and to secure the financial stability of an event that appeared to be precariously teetering after the financial debacle in Montreal and the boycotts of Moscow and Los Angeles. One might soon anticipate whispers of a long-sought Nobel Peace Prize for the retiring president.

On the darker side of a movement that has admittedly given joy to thousands of athletes and spectators around the world is the well-funded promotional campaign to spread the Olympic message internationally—particularly to the young—through Olympic "education" and advertising. We recognize this as news or information, but often it is fashioned as Orwellian Newspeak, espousing the virtues of Olympic ideals, fair play, and the message called "Olympism" during sporting events, on prime time television, emblazoned on our highway signs, and even in our school textbooks. The campaign's message of hope for humankind may be inspiring, but too often the story is sanitized and decontextualized.

Problematic, fundamentally, is the empty glass of Olympism, which can be filled by the dominant social current of the day. In the earliest days of the Games, Baron Coubertin's Olympism and that of his likeminded contemporaries had no place for women or the working classes. Adolf Hitler's Olympism invoked a master race of athletic Aryan superiority, untainted by Jewish blood. Now the Olympism of the late twentieth and early twenty-first century embraces unequivocal ideas about human progress embodied in the motto "Swifter, higher, stronger"—in pushing the quantitative sports such as sprinting into realms riddled with drug abuse, and the qualitative sports such as gymnastics into a legacy of eating disorders and child labour.

Evidence of the politicization of the 2008 Olympic Games, in particular the bid process, has been ample in the past few weeks. For a movement that is supposed to promote world peace, brotherhood, and sisterhood, the actions of bid teams and politicians have been shameful. Never have average Canadians spoken so much about human rights abuses in China—and for all of the wrong reasons (if only we could mobilize such widespread, focused enthusiasm to support social justice in our own country ... evidently, Canadians are most enthusiastic about celebrating multiculturalism and their country's relations with Aboriginal peoples and minority groups when it is politically expedient).

That Canadians thought Toronto had a sporting chance of winning host-city status only demonstrates the seductive, pervasive power of the Olympic message. It is difficult to see beyond the table that has been set for us. It is becoming increasingly difficult for us to perceive the Games to be an international sport competition—nothing more, nothing less.

**Source**: Kevin Wamsley is director of the International Centre for Olympic Studies at the University of Western Ontario. He is an expert on issues of gender in the Olympic Games, Olympic history, and the politics of hosting the Olympic Games. This article was originally published in *The Globe and Mail* on July 16, 2001. Reprinted with permission.

## The Olympic Games as a Force for Social Change  68.
By Jakob Staun and Kirsten Sparre

*Since China was awarded the Olympic Games in 2008, human rights organizations and politicians have applied pressure on the International Olympic Committee to use the Games as a lever to improve China's human rights record. But what is the rationale for regarding the Olympics as a source for political and social change?*

■ ■ ■ ■ ■

Susan Brownell, a professor at the University of Missouri and expert on Olympic politics in China, points out that we still lack a good scientific understanding of the Olympic movement as a movement that is capable of effecting social change.

In the article "The Beijing Effect" she predicts that the greatest legacy of the Beijing Games will be human and cultural. Hosting the Olympic

Games will require China to link up to international standards and accelerate a process that began over one hundred years ago.

Crucial, however, for Brownell is that "the changes that occur will not be forced upon China by others but it will be those that China voluntarily seeks out so that it may play a key role in the global society of the twenty-first century."

Russell Leigh Moses, an American scholar teaching future diplomats at the People's University in Beijing, is also quite sceptical that the Olympic Games will lead to sweeping political and social changes in China. If anything, China has wanted to use the Olympics to show that its one-party state and ancient civilization deserve, at long last, some respect, he believes.

"Beijing is spending as much effort on controlling the environment for the Olympics as it is on construction. For the sports authority this is about gaining as much gold as possible. For the party, it is about the greatness of their rule. For the construction team, it is about image and showcase," he told the *Christian Science Monitor* in an interview.

### ■■■ The World-Is-Watching Effect

But the Olympic Games is much more than sixteen days of elite sports competitions. It is the celebration of a set of fundamental and universal values in the practice of sport, but it is also a billion-dollar industry that ensures that the host city and host nation will be the focus of the entire media world.

And precisely the media attention is a pivotal point in the belief that Beijing's hosting of the Olympic Games will have a positive impact on the human rights situation in China and the social standard in general.

In an email discussion under the auspices of the organization Human Rights In China, Gao Zhan, a researcher at American University specializing in Chinese politics, was asked about her view on the possible impact of the 2008 Olympics on the human rights situation in China.

Gao Zhan said that China has politicized its hosting of the Olympics to such an extent that it will use every possible means to ensure success. In Zhan's view this will force China to loosen its grip on some media outlets.

"Merely for the sake of showing the world that the Chinese do enjoy some basic freedoms, China will gradually lift some website blocks, allow in more foreign press, and tolerate to a certain extent the flow of information from outside of China as it prepares for the event," she wrote.

As a consequence the Chinese people will enlighten themselves with information from the Western media, and a process of furthering the self-reflection of the Chinese individual will be initiated. And as Gao Zhan concluded: "A well-informed and enlightened nation will not be suppressed for too long."

Other critics also support the expected "the world-will-be-watching effect" that the International Olympic Committee (IOC) has put its faith in from the moment Beijing was awarded the games. When twenty to twenty-five thousand international journalists are let out in Beijing and other local regions in China it will be difficult for the government to keep control of dissidents and critics of the state apparatus.

### ■■■ The Role of the IOC

In theory, the International Olympic Committee could also play a role in promoting social change in a host nation during the preparatory phases.

When the IOC awards the Olympic Games to a host city, both parties enter into a certain Host City Contract with mutual demands and obligations. According to Susan Brownell, the IOC does not impose any political requests in the Host City Contract. It concentrates solely on technical matters directly concerning the infrastructure and the Olympic venues.

In the above-mentioned email discussion it was suggested by Andrew McLaughlin, senior adviser to the Internet Corporation for Assigned Names and Numbers, that the IOC could establish an office responsible for monitoring China's human rights environment. As he states: "A quarterly report from a monitoring office would help to maintain steady pressure on the Chinese authorities to keep their promises."

The suggestion never came to fruition. The IOC maintains that it is a sports organization and that it does not have the knowledge or expertise the keep the Chinese political system under surveillance. Immediately after the decision to award the Olympic Games to Beijing in 2008, IOC executive director Francois Carrard told reporters that the Olympic movement was "taking the bet" that China would reform in the lead-up to the Games.

The bet assumes that the task of organizing the Games will make China consider changes on its own, not because it experiences direct pressure from the IOC. Representatives of the IOC have repeatedly stated that the IOC will not pressure China on human rights or other political issues in the lead-up to the 2008 Beijing Olympics.

"We are not in a position that we can give instructions to governments as to how they ought to behave," Hein Verbruggen, head of the IOC's coordination commission for the Beijing Games, said in April 2007 when he was asked specifically about calls for a boycott to pressure China to do more to stop the violence in the Sudanese region of Darfur.

"We don't want to be, as the IOC, involved in any political issues," he said. "It's not our task. We are here for organizing the Games."

---

◀◀ **Source**: This article was first published on playthegame.org. Reprinted with permission.

## Canada Needs a Two-Track Strategy for Hosting International Games
### By Bruce Kidd

**69.**

Canada has mastered the art of staging multi-sport international festivals. In addition to the forthcoming Winter Olympic and Paralympic Games in Vancouver, we have held two Olympics, two Pan American Games, two Commonwealth Games, and similar events such as the World Student Games, the World Masters Games, the Gay Games, and the World Outgames in the last four decades. We've consistently won kudos for our facilities, organization, and hospitality. It's a record that few other countries, let alone middle powers with a population of just thirty-three million, can match.

Each of these games has served as a major vehicle for branding, community building, and investment, not only in sport and physical activity but in housing, transportation, communication, and technology. While none of the actual competitions lasted longer than sixteen days, preparing for them steered urban planning and budgets for many years.

Major games are "multiple narratives." In almost every case, there have been white elephants and scandals alongside concrete benefits and the highs of the events themselves. Benefits have rarely been shared equally across the population. But overall, international games have brought significant improvements to the communities involved, accelerating long-developed plans for infrastructural renewal. Vancouver 2010 will be another exemplary case. Even the 1976 Olympics in Montreal, much maligned because of extravagant stadium and cost overruns, gave a transformative stimulus to sport participation and sport tourism. Today,

Quebec is one of the leading jurisdictions for sport and physical activity, an important accomplishment given the escalating social costs of physical inactivity, especially among the young. The strategy of seeking major games has been so effective that Toronto recently sought and won the right to stage the 2015 Pan American and Parapan American Games. I worked on that bid and am confident that those Games will bring otherwise elusive upgrades to the region.

But even with such a track record, it is time to review the priority Canadians place on major games. Despite Toronto's success, it is becoming much harder for Canada to win the prize, as more countries and regions that have never had the chance seek to host them, and the international selectors are pressured to recognize the rising economies in the global south. The success of South Africa in landing the 2010 World Cup and Brazil, the 2014 World Cup and the 2016 Olympics may well be a trend. India, the world's largest democracy, wants the Olympics; populous, oil-rich Nigeria, the Commonwealth Games. It is unlikely that they will be repeatedly denied.

Secondly, staging games is an inefficient, costly way to improve sports infrastructure, because they invariably require some facilities that are not needed (do we really need two world-class bob runs in western Canada?), and the resulting seating capacity, the most expensive part of construction, is rarely used after the games. Moreover, the costs of security and the difficult challenges they raise for public policy in a democratic society are bound to increase.

Thirdly, the strategy leaves those cities, regions, and sports that cannot manage successful bids vulnerable to long droughts in public investment, as Ontario and the summer sports have recently experienced.

Canada thus needs a two-track strategy for seeking international games. The first track should be developing and implementing a comprehensive, pan-Canadian plan for creating the opportunities we need. If we need "a big idea to do a big thing," as Ken Dryden once argued, then let's tie the next round of major facility and program renewal to Canada's sesquicentennial in 2017, as the provincial and territorial sports ministers have proposed, recalling that the last time many parts of the country got new facilities was the Centennial in 1967. Moreover, it's not just facilities that are needed but training and employment of physical educators and coaches, investment in science and innovation, and reduction of the economic barriers to participation.

The second track should be making bids for major games based upon facilities and programs we already have rather than those we dream about building. Increasingly, as one senior IOC member told me in explaining why he would not vote for Toronto's bid for the 2008 Olympics, the international community will go only to First World countries that show an exemplary commitment to the provision of opportunity for their own citizens, and no longer to those that want to use the leverage of international games to build what they do not have. Even if we lose those bids, Canadians will have the opportunities we need.

The current "action plan" for the federal-provincial-territorial Canadian Sport Policy comes to an end in 2012. What lies ahead will be much discussed when decision-makers gather in Vancouver. If Canadians are to benefit from our rich history of major games, we must commit ourselves to doing the right thing for sport whether we get another games or not.

◀◀ **Source**: Former middle-distance runner Bruce Kidd is dean of the Faculty of Physical Education and Health at the University of Toronto and an honourary member of the Canadian Olympic Committee. This article was first published in *Policy Options* in December/January 2009/2010. Reprinted with permission.

# Class-War Games: The Financial and Social Cost of "Securing" the 2010 Olympics

By Christopher A. Shaw and Alissa Westergard-Thorpe

**70.**

On February 12, 2009, exactly one year before the opening of the 2010 Winter Olympics in Vancouver and Whistler, the grim future of political freedom in British Columbia was on full display. Military and police flanked by helicopters rehearsed manoeuvres in Vancouver, where escalating harassment, intimidation, and surveillance of activists had already begun. Those celebrating the event put aside concerns about the costly preparations for the Games. As the orchestrated magic took hold in Whistler Village, celebrants and athletes were swept up in the moment. They, like most of the mainstream media and all levels of government, were simply not going to think about the elephant on the slopes: security. Security has emerged as one of the largest single costs associated with the 2010 Olympics, and will carry significant costs for civil liberties as well.

To Olympic supporters it may seem churlish, even unpatriotic, to speak of this billion-dollar elephant, question how it got there, or ask how we can remove it before it trashes the place. Olympic boosterism has worked to exclude critical voices and suppress important public policy questions. For critics of the Games, the security apparatus currently being assembled is a major concern.

## ■■■ Challenging the Olympic Mythology

Concerns about the Olympic Games extend beyond the billion dollars taxpayers will pay to provide security for the seventeen-day event or the lasting damage to civil liberties for people in Canada. The 2010 Olympic events are using the resources of Indigenous land which has never been legally ceded to the Canadian government,

while neglecting the outstanding issues of Native communities. The environmental impacts of clear-cuts, destruction of bluffs and mountain ecosystems, road construction, gravel mining, massive consumption of resources, threats to fish and animal populations, and accelerated approval processes for mining, logging, oil, gas, and tourist infrastructure belie claims that these will be "the Green Games." Growing numbers of people oppose the host of issues that accompany the modern Olympic Games: the commercialization of sport, lack of transparency in government, backroom deals for real estate and development interests, exploitative labour standards for migrant workers, promotion of corporate sponsors with appalling human rights and ecological records (including Nike, Shell, Royal Bank, Petro-Canada, Dow Chemical, Teck Cominco, General Electric, General Motors, and Coca-Cola), and appropriation of public space.

Massive public debt (often billions of dollars) plagues host cities: Montreal has only recently paid off its 1976 Games and Vancouver's share of the $6-billion cost of the 2010 Games continues to grow. As British Columbia faces a poverty and housing crisis, efforts to forcibly remove visible homelessness from Vancouver and broken promises of social housing clash with the Olympic claims of social sustainability. Since the 1980s, the Games and related development have displaced over 3.5 million people worldwide.

The issues that unite Olympic critics are those that most threaten the carefully crafted Olympic image. Many groups are critical of the Games, some regarding specific aspects and others opposed to the entire scheme of the Olympics. Community groups in the Downtown Eastside, anti-poverty and Indigenous activists, environmentalists and civil libertarians have been exposing the negative impacts of hosting the Games to a local and international audience. One group that has united some of these elements is the Olympic Resistance Network, whose organizing slogan "No Olympics on Stolen Native Land" accents the fact that the Olympics will occur on unceded territories. That group and others are responding to a call to boycott and oppose the Games from the 2007 Indigenous Peoples Gathering in Sonora, Mexico. The Olympic Resistance Network holds public education forums, rallies, and marches and has called for a public convergence to protest and disrupt the Games in 2010.

## ■ ■ ■ The High Price of Policing Dissent

Vancouver's bid book, submitted in 2002, projected a cost of $175 million for providing security for the proposed Vancouver/Whistler Olympic Games—a substantial sum, but still small by the standards of recent Games and other major events. The Group of Eight meeting held in Kananaskis, Alberta, in 2002 had a security tab of over $300 million for a three-day event that was vastly simpler in scope and geography. The Bid Corporation and the successor organization, the Vancouver Organizing Committee for the Olympic Games (VANOC), have stuck with the projected number, both claiming that security "experts," including the RCMP, had approved the $175-million estimate.

RCMP documents obtained through access to information refute this claim. A 2005 letter by the head of the Vancouver 2010 Integrated Security Unit (VISU) called the VANOC security budget "conceptual." RCMP briefing notes from 2003 noted that the Mounties had never been consulted prior to the bid-book numbers. Other RCMP documents showed that the force was more interested in managing public perceptions about Olympic security costs than in informing the public that they had been deliberately misled.

During this period, the true costs for security from other Olympic cities were revealed: $1.3 billion in Salt Lake City, 2002; $1.7 billion in Athens, 2004; $1.4 billion in Torino, 2006; and a projected $3 billion in London, 2012.

Finally, in October 2008, then–Public Safety Minister Stockwell Day stated that security costs would be vastly higher than the $175 million projection—the new estimate ranging from $400 million to $1 billion. Over time the numbers drifted toward the high-end estimate. Security agencies led by VISU continued to refuse to clarify the final numbers. *Briarpatch* has learned from one journalist with VISU contacts that the agency had no real idea of the cost: "They simply don't know what it will all cost by 2010. There appears to be no bottom line."

By the end of February 2009, it was finally acknowledged that the security bill would be over a billion dollars and could go even higher if potential threats emerged. These figures are only those projected for the provincial and federal governments, and don't include the substantial costs to the City of Vancouver itself, including the Vancouver Police Department.

The publicized numbers for security forces for the B.C. Games are similarly underplayed. The Sydney Olympics in 2000 featured thirty-five thousand police and other security personnel (four security personnel for each athlete), including four thousand troops. The 2004 Olympics in Athens deployed seventy thousand police and troops in addition to NATO's Mediterranean naval fleet. For 2010, the estimates of the various security forces amount to thirteen thousand police officers and troops, plus four thousand private security guards and U.S. military participation. In an era in which extraordinary security operations have become the norm, the official numbers for 2010 are incongruously low compared to recent Olympics and can be expected to go much higher.

### ■ ■ ■ Identifying the True "Threat": Embarrassment

Much of the security planning appears driven by threat assessments conducted by the Integrated Threat Assessment Centre, a branch of the Canadian Security Intelligence Service. The Integrated Threat Assessment Centre initially evaluated three main concerns for 2010 security. In order of severity, these were: foreign-based terrorism, crime, and domestic protests. By the end of 2008, a document released through access to information had narrowed the scope. The concerns now were foreign terrorism, listed as a "low" level threat, and anti-Olympic demonstrations, now considered a primary threat, with a listing of "medium." How demonstrations constituted a security threat or why they were considered more threatening than foreign terrorism was not made clear, though the Canadian government has historically placed Indigenous, environmental, and antiglobalization protesters high on its lists of internal security concerns, and those groups figure prominently in the communities planning to protest the Games.

Whatever threat of disruption the protests may constitute, soldiers and F18s are not the proper response to demonstrations, at least not in a functional democracy. All levels of government are spending an inordinate amount on military-style security, and the only likely targets are protesters and those whose glaring poverty threatens Vancouver's public image. Primarily, the rationale seems to be framed by a fear of embarrassment, rather than any realistic concerns about physical security for athletes or the general public.

### ■ ■ ■ Secrecy and Social Cleansing

These concerns about the exposure of embarrassing realities during the 2010 Games underlie attempts to remove the homeless and petty criminals from Vancouver. Such efforts have been stepped up, with the movement of so-called undesirables from British Columbia to other provinces to face minor charges, previously considered not worth the cost

of relocation. An RCMP officer in charge of the Vernon, British Columbia, detachment predicted "quite an aggressive displacement" of criminals and the homeless by Vancouver police, and warned that other municipalities will face increased social problems due to such tactics.

Those Vancouverites who are not targeted for removal will still have to contend with police searches, video surveillance, and major restrictions on their movement and access to homes, workplaces, and community services. Extensive areas surrounding major hotels, sporting venues, and event locations throughout Vancouver and Whistler will have public video monitoring and police checkpoints requiring credentials and searches. There will be no-fly zones over downtown and most boat traffic will be barred from False Creek.

It is apparent who will bear the brunt of the anticipated crackdown. According to Harsha Walia, a Vancouver organizer with No One Is Illegal and the Olympic Resistance Network, these "Orwellian measures are not just an invasion of privacy for all residents of Canada. They will be disproportionately utilized in and beyond 2010 against Indigenous people, poor people, people of colour, and other communities who are repressed and marginalized not only for what they say or do, but simply for who they are."

Most of the preparations for 2010 policing and social cleansing have occurred in secret. VISU claims that this is for "operational security," but this secrecy extends beyond deployment specifics and encompasses potential civil liberties restrictions, limits on the freedom of movement and plans for spending the $1-billion security budget. VANOC itself is not subject to freedom of information and access to information regulations, and has not been forthcoming with details in response to public requests for information.

Despite such secrecy, security operations at previous Olympics give an indication of how such massive budgets and intense security infrastructure may be used. Traditionally, host cities work to socially cleanse their communities of visible poverty as well as dissent. Former Olympic host cities including Athens, Atlanta, and Los Angeles also relocated or isolated members of poor and minority communities, as Vancouver did during Expo 86. At a February 26 forum hosted by advocacy group Pivot Legal Society (the first at which VISU members were available for public questions), senior police officials stated that no such clearances were planned. In response to audience questions, however, it was acknowledged that homeless people living within security perimeters for Olympic events would be relocated.

Social cleansing can be achieved by many methods. David Eby of the B.C. Civil Liberties Association and Pivot Legal Society says to "watch for the Vancouver Police Department's continued use of bylaw enforcement for minor acts like jaywalking, littering, or sleeping in streets or parks against the homeless in an effort to get 'no-go' orders banning them from particular areas of the city and increased use of private security guards in public space to move the homeless along." According to Laura Track of Pivot Legal Society, "People are afraid—I think rightly given the experience in Atlanta—that these tickets will be used as grounds to arrest and imprison people during the Olympics who have been unable to pay the fines." Eby further warns that the B.C. housing minister has proposed allowing police to force the homeless into emergency shelters in inclement weather (such as during the Winter Games). VANOC has budgeted for a temporary shelter open only for the duration of the Olympics, instead of a long-term investment.

### ■■■ A History of Homegrown Political Suppression

Antiglobalization protesters have been a major focus of Canadian security operations and subjected to police abuses and violence in contexts similar to the Olympics. Canadian trade meetings have featured monitoring, intimidation, and infiltration of political opponents by security forces. The 2007

meeting of the Security and Prosperity Partnership in Montebello, Quebec, for instance, saw the on-video exposure of police provocateurs trying to incite violence within demonstrations.

Other events, such as the 2001 Summit of the Americas in Quebec City, the 2001 Pacific Northwest Economic Region meeting in Whistler, and the 2002 Group of Eight meetings in Kananaskis have shown the extent of police interference and violence with groups exercising free expression. The Group of Eight meeting in Kananaskis included the instruction that police and military could "shoot to kill" demonstrators who entered the secured zone, even for peaceful civil disobedience. Indigenous activists, already heavily targeted by VISU, have long faced a greater level of police and military abuses, with violence and death occurring during police sieges against Natives in traditional territories. In separate Indigenous land reclamations in 1995, thousands of rounds of ammunition were fired against activists at Gustafsen Lake, British Columbia (injuring one), and in Ipperwash, Ontario, Dudley George was killed by the Ontario Provincial Police.

A notable local example of restrictions on civil liberties occurred in November 1997, when the University of British Columbia (UBC) campus, adjoining Vancouver, hosted the leaders' summit of the Asia-Pacific Economic Cooperation (APEC) forum. The excessive use of physical force, pepper spray, and police interference against non-violent demonstrators surprised many, but such tactics continue to be utilized by Canadian police. Later legal proceedings revealed an extensive surveillance effort against even mainstream peace and environmental organizations and small non-threatening groups like the Raging Grannies—older women who wear funny hats and shawls to sing protest songs. Photos and descriptions of potential anti-APEC activists were distributed to police for monitoring and eventual pre-emptive arrests of some organizers.

The office of then-Prime Minister Jean Chrétien promised authoritarian leaders such as Indonesia's

General Suharto that they could attend APEC without fear of "embarrassment." To keep this promise, UBC's administration imposed a blanket restriction on any political signs or demonstrations along motorcade routes or anywhere remotely near the leaders' meeting place. The Prime Minister's Office specifically requested that protests be isolated to fenced-off areas of campus where they could not be witnessed by world leaders. Not only were signs seized from individuals, residences, and offices (even those far from the meeting place), but people were arrested for holding signs (one reading simply, "Democracy, Human Rights, Free Speech") that might have been read by a dictator in a passing limousine.

The involvement of politicians in planning security and restrictions on protest was revealed but never fully explored, since the RCMP's Public Complaints Commission focused on bland recommendations and minor reprimands. However, even the flawed report declared that the right to protest must mean the "right to be seen and heard." Nevertheless, the next time Prime Minister Chrétien returned to Vancouver in 1998, dozens of non-violent protesters were attacked by police, whose weapons escalated from pepper spray to batons. Many fear a further escalation in police violence at demonstrations against the 2010 Olympics.

## ■■■ Policing and the "Right to Be Seen and Heard"

The recommendations that came out of the APEC hearing have seemingly been ignored by those planning security for the 2010 Games. Promises to APEC leaders by Canadian officials that there would be controls on signs and public assembly are similar to those given to the International Olympic Committee by the City of Vancouver. UBC has agreed to restrictions on non-Games signs during Olympic events, but the details of this agreement are being kept from students and student government. Garth Mullins, a local organizer involved in the APEC protests and

hearings and a member of the Olympic Resistance Network, notes, "The RCMP has learned little since APEC and the inquiry. Led by the Mounties, VISU seems to be going down that same tired road of intimidating activists, infiltrating and spying on social movements, and criminalizing dissent."

Protest pens (fenced-in areas for demonstrators that are isolated from the public) and control of political displays are already planned for the Games under the guise of "free-speech zones." Once again, Canadian Charter rights to free expression seem to be limited; if a protest pen is a "free-speech zone," then what is the rest of Canada? "The worst thing that could occur is a repetition of all the mistakes from APEC," suggests Eby. "The key difference between then and the potential errors now is that the rights violations at APEC were focused in just one part of Vancouver, UBC, where here Olympic events will be taking place across the city, and for over two full weeks."

The City of Vancouver has already approved expanded bylaw powers to control "illegal" signs (those not authorized by the Olympics), leafleting, public performances (such as street theatre), and access to public areas near Olympic venues. Council's bylaw changes may allow police and city officials to enter private homes, businesses, and cars to remove unapproved advertising and anti-Olympic signs with "limited notice" and levy $10,000-a-day fines. The host city commitments include removing signs that are not part of the Olympics or those of Olympics' sponsor corporations.

Within the same council motions that curtail public freedoms, VANOC and Olympic sponsors were being liberated from current city bylaws. Vancouver plans to relax building, zoning, noise, and sign regulations to facilitate Olympic events and promotions, while restricting those that apply to non-Games activities or messages. Although city council claims that its concern is to reduce "ambush marketing," it has refused to clarify these powers or specify their use in the context of freedom of expression rights. Meanwhile, every inch of outdoor advertising has already been bought by the Games and their sponsors for the duration of the Olympics.

In January 2009, city council met to vote on several Games-related motions, including the political controls outlined above. After many people spoke out against increased Olympic funding and new bylaw powers which would reduce public displays of speech, expression, and assembly, council approved the motions without alteration. A recommendation for a sunset clause failed, as did a proposed amendment which stated that these powers were not to be used to restrict Charter rights.

Meanwhile, intelligence gathering, intimidation of organizers, and attempts to recruit informants is intensifying throughout the Lower Mainland, Vancouver Island, and in First Nations communities. Dozens of activists have already been questioned or approached for information, including people who had spoken out to council against the bylaw changes who were approached by police on the steps of city hall. VISU officers regularly enter reserves to conduct "home visits" and attend community meetings unrelated to the Olympics.

As activists were preparing for an Olympic Resistance Network march on the day of the one-year countdown to the Games, a vehicle with several march participants was stopped by police for a "random ID check," demanding ID from all the vehicle's occupants. Although by law passengers of a vehicle do not have to identify themselves to police, the Vancouver Police Department detained the group for forty minutes and intimidated them into complying. The office that they had left, that of the Anti-Poverty Committee, also involved in anti-Olympic organizing, had its front door dusted for fingerprints by the Vancouver Police Department just a day before.

It would seem that Olympic opponents and Indigenous activists are being monitored in the same way as anti-APEC protesters were, with the potential for police abuses, surveillance, harassment, and pre-emptive arrests.

In response to these tactics, activist groups and the B.C. Civil Liberties Association have urged VISU to stop harassing anti-Olympic activists. The Olympic Resistance Network has announced that their group will not meet privately with security forces, as VISU's object appears to be to intimidate activists and restrict freedoms of assembly, mobility and expression. Even city council has urged VANOC to hold open community consultations (though it is unlikely they would be effectual in altering proposed security) before security plans are finalized, as VANOC had originally pledged to do.

VISU has told the media that they are "consulting" with activists and civil liberties advocates, but members of the B.C. Civil Liberties Association who attempted to discuss the political implications of security planning with VISU "ran into a brick wall," says Eby.

## ■ ■ ■ The 2010 Legacy

The military and police rehearsals of Exercise Silver, which took place in Vancouver in February, included one thousand members of the police and military as well as surveillance aircraft and armoured personnel carriers. An expanded operation, Exercise Gold, planned for the fall of 2009, will see the security forces attempt to impress upon Vancouver their complete control of the city and its population before the Games even arrive.

"I believe the 2010 Games will be our winter of discontent," says Mullins. "Given what we have seen in the past and in the lead-up to the Games, expect a rather draconian crackdown on dissent. We will see the same intimidation, pre-emptive arrests, disinformation, and agents provocateurs, but this time there is a $1-billion security budget, military deployments and a multi-agency police body with a large staff dedicated to controlling political expression. Also, the mainstream media is even more accommodating than usual, since many are actual sponsors of the 2010 Games, with a financial stake in how the Games are perceived.

"If it takes a police state to hold the Olympics, it's just not worth doing in the first place."

Laura Track from Pivot Legal adds, "Protest groups will use the forum of the Games to raise issues around poverty, Aboriginal rights, homelessness, and other concerns. Without consultation beforehand it is far more likely that there will be repression, arrests, and, potentially, violence."

Activists and residents are concerned that the planned security measures and restrictions of political freedoms for Olympic events will be permanent and used as a blueprint for other cities to copy. Expanded bylaw powers approved by the City of Vancouver are described in that motion as a "template for future special events." The increased ability to limit free speech, expression, and assembly will already be in place the next time the city sees fit to do so.

"We have every reason to worry that much of the security infrastructure will remain behind because that is the typical Olympic legacy if you look at other host cities," says Eby. "The B.C. Information and Privacy Commissioner has warned that there will be no free passes for government to keep the surveillance cameras up after the Games, but every indication is that deals are being cut right now to ensure that the cameras are being left behind." In Sydney, Athens, and other host cities, public space restrictions and closed-circuit television cameras that were installed for the Olympics remained long after the Games were over. On March 26, Vancouver approved funding for CCTV during the Games; although it was described as temporary, it included no requirements that the technology ever be removed. By April 3, additional CCTV had been approved on an ongoing basis for Vancouver and other B.C. cities.

On the day of the one-year countdown to the Games, International Olympic Committee President Jacques Rogge spoke in Whistler. "Security investments always leave a good legacy on security for the country," Rogge said. "Whenever the Games are finished, everything that has been built, the expertise that has been acquired, the hardware that has been put in place, is serving the country and the regions for decades to follow."

Such a massive and costly security apparatus does indeed leave a legacy, since Olympics security expansions typically remain after the Games are over, facilitating increased surveillance and expanded powers to suppress political freedoms. As Harsha Walia points out, "This fortification of the security apparatus serves two primary purposes that have little to do with the propaganda of 'our safety.' The first is to normalize a state of fear that can readily be manipulated by the state and corporate security firms. The second is to legitimize the criminalization of resistance." Considering that Canada plans to host another Group of Eight meeting as well as discussions on the Security and Prosperity Partnership in 2010, the Olympic-style policing of expression and control of public space may become the rule rather than the exception.

Professor Helen Lenskyj has documented the social impacts of modern Olympic Games, particularly on civil liberties. In "The Olympic Industry and Civil Liberties: The Threat to Free Speech and Freedom of Assembly" she writes, "The analysis reveals patterns of Olympic industry threats to civil liberties—most notably, to a free press and freedom of assembly—in recent bid and host cities in Europe, Canada, the United States, and Australia. It is particularly alarming to note that the everyday practices of Olympic industry officials—their cynical 'management' of Olympic news, their co-optation of elected representatives, the sense of entitlement with which they conduct their business, and the 'legacies' of harsh law-and-order legislation—prompt relatively little concern or outrage."

A police state seldom starts with tanks in the streets. It can begin with television cameras on every corner or intimidation and abuse of the poor, people of colour, and political activists. Military-style policing, security infrastructure buildups, and suppression of dissent are common features of modern Olympic Games, and not just in places like

Beijing. As British Columbia prepares for the flag-waving spectacle of the 2010 Games, the elephant on the slopes—the massive security apparatus and its political and economic costs—is settling in as a permanent resident.

◀◀ **Source**: This article was first published in *Briarpatch* magazine in May/June 2009. Reprinted with permission.

## 71. Own the Podium or Rent it? Canada's Involvement in the Global Sporting Arms Race
By Peter Donnelly

*Canada has never won a gold medal at the Olympics it has hosted—in Montreal in 1976 and in Calgary in 1988—but that is expected to change in Vancouver in February, partly because of a $110-million investment in the* Own the Podium *program over the last five years. But Peter Donnelly, director of the Centre for Sports Policy Studies at the University of Toronto, suggests there is a downside to a narrow focus on winning, including the creation of two classes of athletes—the elites and the others, not to mention a very un-Canadian attitude about bragging rights. Among other things, the bar of expectations is being set very high.*

■■■■■■

In February a Canadian athlete will probably, for the first time, win an Olympic gold medal on Canadian soil—an event that will be widely and justifiably celebrated. Failure to win gold medals in Montreal (1976) or Calgary (1988) marks Canada as the only country never to have won a gold medal when hosting an Olympics.

Canadians have won plenty of Olympic gold medals in other countries, and failure to win gold medals in Montreal or Calgary was not a concern for most Canadians. In general, Canadians approved of an implicit social contract with Olympic athletes: "We don't give you lots of money, but if you achieve Olympic qualifying standards we will send you to the Games." Under that contract, Canada achieved remarkable results at the Olympics, at a cost per medal far lower than for many other nations.

In 2004, the Canadian Olympic Committee (COC) unilaterally changed that contract. A number of young Canadian athletes who had achieved Olympic qualifying standards and were looking forward to their dream of going to the Games in Athens were denied their places on the team. The COC had increased the qualifying standards following a decision to send only athletes who were believed to have a chance of winning a medal.

The new qualifying standards emerged as governments and sport leaders began to fetishize "the medal," especially "the gold medal." Under a growing climate of businesslike government in Canada and other countries, of objective-led management, performance measures, accountability, monitoring, and evaluation, investments in high-performance sport came to be seen as having only one measurable objective: medals.

Critical comparisons of Canada's Olympic medal totals with those of Australia, the United States, or some European countries began to contribute to a sense that Canada does not do very well at the Olympics. This was especially the case in 2000, during the Sydney Olympics. Australia, a country with many similarities to Canada and a smaller population, did particularly well at its home Olympics, and many in the Canadian sport community pointed to the high levels of government funding enjoyed by Australian athletes.

In some ways the comparison with Australia and the focus on only the Summer Olympics was unfair. Unlike Australia, Canada is a multi-sport nation, sending full teams to both Summer and Winter Olympics. A more accurate comparison of Canada's Olympic success emerges using the combined medal totals, from both Summer and Winter Games, during each four-year Olympiad. Canadian athletes do well at the Olympics, but Australian athletes have been doing better:

| Winter and Summer Olympics | Total Medals | |
|---|---|---|
| | Australia | Canada |
| 1988 | 14 | 15 |
| 1992 | 27 | 25 |
| 1994/96 | 42 | 35 |
| 1998–2000 | 59 | 29 |
| 2002/04 | 51 | 29 |
| 2006/08 | 48 | 42 |

Recent newspaper reports in Canada cite a prediction from an "Olympic guru," Luciano Barra, that Canadian athletes will win the most medals in Vancouver (twenty-nine). The art and science of "medal projections" has grown out of some forty years of academic research attempting to understand why athletes from certain countries win so many medals and, conversely, why athletes from certain countries win so few medals.

Correlations with medal success have been found with, for example, religion (athletes from Protestant countries win more medals), political ideology (accounting for the success of athletes from the former socialist countries), population size (with some obvious exceptions such as India), and GDP (with some obvious exceptions such as Cuba).

More recent research indicates that the best predictive models combine the last two factors. Success is proportional to population—the higher the population of a country, the more medals are won; and the richer a country (as measured by GDP), the more medals are won—richer countries with large populations (e.g., the United States, China, Germany) win the most medals. Hosting an Olympics also has an effect, accounting for approximately 2% more of the medals than would be predicted by population and GDP. Australian success in Sydney (2000), U.S. success in Salt Lake City (2002), and Chinese success in Beijing (2008) may all be related to this home-team advantage.

But these factors do not explain why Australian athletes have consistently outpaced Canadian athletes in medal performance since 1992. In addition to population, GDP and the hosting advantage, it is now apparent from a European comparative study that the best predictor of success in winning medals is the absolute amount of funding allocated to high-performance sport. The nations that have invested the most in high-performance sport achieve the best results.

Given the evidence that more money leads to more Olympic medals, what do they cost? The few figures that are available vary widely in how they were calculated and significantly underestimate the true cost because they measure only national government spending. Not included is funding from provincial/state and municipal sources, corporate/sponsorship funding, free labour provided by sport volunteers, various forms of fundraising, or even the costs borne by athletes and their families.

Given these limitations, conclusions about the cost of medals are problematic. However, it is important to have some sense of the cost per medal in order to have any meaningful high-performance sport policy. Australian studies have provided the most data on medal costs, and their estimates vary widely. For example, in the period before the Sydney Olympics one study suggests that each gold medal cost Australians A$37 million (or about A$8 million for each medal in general). In two studies of the cost of Australian medals at the Sydney Olympics, the first estimated that each of the fifty-eight medals Australia won in Sydney cost C$4.82 million; the second divided the total reported cost of hosting the Olympics by the number of gold medals won, estimating the cost of each gold medal at A$40 million. Finally, two recent calculations of the cost of Australian medals at the Beijing Olympics achieved similar results. The first study estimated that Australia's fourteen gold medals each cost A$15.6 million. The recently published Crawford Report considered only Australian government spending on Olympic sports in the four years leading up to Beijing, and estimated that each medal cost A$4 million, and each gold medal cost A$15 million.

In Britain, the National Audit Office reported that each medal won by British athletes at the Athens Olympics (2004) cost the British government £2.4 million. And an estimate of the most expensive medals ever was reported for China, which spent US$3 billion on high-performance sport in the four years leading up to the Athens Olympics—its thirty-two gold medals each costing some US$100 million.

In two calculations for Canada, one divided the total reported cost of the 1976 Olympics by the number of medals won, estimating that each medal won by a Canadian athlete in Montreal cost C$37 million. The other study estimates that each medal won by a Canadian athlete at the Sydney Olympics cost the federal government C$4.42 million. Craig Mitton, at the University of British Columbia at Okanagan, stated that "on a per capita basis, Australia spent over seven times more on its Sydney Olympic team than Canada, to win four times as many medals."

Regardless of how they were calculated, two things are evident from these figures. First, it costs a great deal of money to win an Olympic medal, and gold medals are especially expensive. Second, when hosting costs are included in the calculation of medal costs, the 2% home advantage is extraordinarily expensive.

Calculations of success vary widely. Luciano Barra predicts that Canada will be both first, and tied for fifth at the Vancouver Olympics. He explains that Canadian athletes will win the most total medals, but will be tied for fifth in the number of all-important gold medals. Under some calculations points are assigned to medals (e.g., gold = 3, silver = 2, bronze = 1) and that can lead to a different ranking of countries. Other calculations of success measure the proportion of medals to the population of a country—countries such as the United States tumble down the rankings in these calculations, while countries such as Jamaica ascend to the top of the medal tables.

While medals and the different ways that they are counted predominate in terms of national rankings, other metrics may be employed. For example, Canada often uses "top-eight finishes" to determine its ranking; and calculations sometimes include the number of athletes who achieved "personal best" performances during an Olympic Games.

The sometimes conflicting aims of national sports policies—to achieve international success in sport and to achieve significant increases in broad-based participation in sports (for reasons of population health, social inclusion and so on)—have resulted in sport participation increases becoming a part of definitions of success in countries such as Canada and Britain. Hosting major sport events such as the Olympic Games is so expensive that further justification is often needed to take on that task. For example, Canada's Federal Policy for Hosting International Sport Events (2004, 2008) mandates various legacies that are expected as a result of hosting the events—these include economic stimulus and "social, cultural, and community benefits, including enhanced voluntarism, active citizenship and civic participation, cultural programs reflecting Canadian diversity, physical activity, and healthy communities."

London won the right to host the 2012 Olympics in part because Tony Blair promised that the event would be connected to substantial increases in sport participation, not only in Britain but also in low-income countries. And there are now signs that countries such as Australia are beginning to reject narrow definitions of success based only on medal counts, and are exploring ways to include the health and well-being of the population in new definitions of sporting success.

In 2001, Ben Oakley and Mick Green in the U.K. coined the term "global sporting arms race."

Just as the global arms race involved superpowers attempting to outspend each other in weapons development, Oakley and Green observed that an increasing number of nations are prepared to invest more and more money to achieve their goals of winning more Olympic medals. Governments are apparently engaged in this "race" in order to make symbolic statements about national identity, pride, and virility.

The funding strategies are often linked to target-setting campaigns—e.g., China's Project 119 (referring to the number of gold medals available in the sports being targeted by sport strategists in China) and Britain's Mission 2012. Canada stepped up its involvement in the global sporting arms race in 2003 when the Own the Podium campaign was planned, shortly after the announcement that Vancouver would host the 2010 Olympic Games. The campaign set a target of thirty-five medals for Canadian athletes in Vancouver, and budgeted $110 million—some $22 million a year in additional funding for Olympic winter sports for the five years leading up to Vancouver. The federal government is contributing $66 million, and the remaining $44 million is from provincial and corporate sources.

There are clear arguments in favour of Own the Podium. Canada claims that its high-performance sport system is athlete-centred. In such a system it is appropriate to support athletes representing Canada (in terms of training, equipment, competition opportunities, and so on) to at least the same level as many of the athletes they will be competing against. Thus, one purpose of the additional funding is to give Canada's athletes a chance to win.

Own the Podium helped to produce positive results at the Torino Olympics, and in international competition since 2006. But there is something about the campaign that makes many Canadians feel a little uncomfortable. It's bragging, for gosh sakes! With reference to Canada's well-established reputation for Olympic hospitality (in Montreal and Calgary), Bruce Kidd wryly suggests that there is something vaguely un-Canadian about inviting the world to British Columbia so that we can kick ass. And there is a nagging sense that we may be setting ourselves up to fail. Isn't it better to manage expectations rather than to set the bar so high?

There have also been complaints about the program. It is expensive, at a time when such additional expenses seem unreasonable. It is divisive: since most additional funding goes to athletes who are expected to win medals, a number of national team athletes feel like second-class citizens. And it may be promoting a win-at-all-costs attitude—an attitude that Canada came to regret in the late 1980s following the Ben Johnson scandal. Reports that international athletes have not been given adequate training time at the new facilities may or may not be true, but it is clear that Canada is pushing its home-team advantage to the limit. For example, Own the Podium helped to fund the installation of thirty-two cameras along the luge track at the Whistler Sliding Centre. The cameras are for safety, but they also help coaches to provide instant feedback to the lugers. Those cameras were turned off recently when international lugers came to train at the track.

In the final analysis, there are no guarantees that Own the Podium will work. This is sport—every athlete knows that on any given day, anything can happen; and we know that Canada's winter sports athletes are about to face an extraordinary pressure of expectations.

Canada has stepped into the global sporting arms race now, and even our nemesis, Australia, is beginning to recognize that it costs more and more money even to stay in the same place in the medal tables. Competitors include countries that seem both willing and able to outspend Canada in order to win medals: wealthy centralized economies such as China; countries that rely primarily on corporate funding such as the United States; or countries that use national lottery funding to sustain their high-performance sport programs such as Germany and Norway.

Own the Podium represents a particularly narrow strategy based on an extraordinarily narrow definition of success. After their unprecedented success at the Sydney Olympics, Australians were left with debt, and a population whose only measurable increase in sport participation involved attending more sports events and watching more sports on television. Better planning and a broader definition of success along the lines now being considered in Australia would link Canadian medals with the possibility of all Canadians being able to participate in the sport of their choice, and with improvements in the health and wellbeing of the population.

Athletes representing Canada should be well funded. May they win lots of medals in February. But, in the global sporting arms race, no one can own the podium. At best, Canada may be able to rent it for a short time.

◀◀ **Source**: This article was first published in *Policy Options* in December/January 2009/2010. Reprinted with permission.

## 72. Rent the Podium Revisited: Reflections on Vancouver 2010
### By Peter Donnelly

*In a follow-up to his article in the December/January issue of* Policy Options, *Peter Donnelly—director of the Centre for Sport Policy Studies at the University of Toronto—provides a post-mortem on the Canadian team performance at the Vancouver Olympics. He argues that, while Own the Podium funding helped Canadian athletes to be more prepared and stimulated more winning performances than any other country has achieved, it failed to change Canada's position in the medal table. Donnelly argues for a revamped high-performance funding program, one that defines success as more than medals and connects funding to increases in sport participation.*

■■■■■■

**W**hat a wonderful party it was. For the third time, Canada proved to be a generous and gracious Olympic host, and demonstrated again our ability to organize major international sports events. The event was crowned by the marvellous achievements of Canadian and visiting athletes, including the medal winners.

The bragging of Own the Podium (OTP) and the entitlement of Vancouver's motto ("It's Our Turn") were overshadowed by those athletic achievements, the widespread celebrations of the event itself, and the record number of Winter Games gold medals won by Canadian athletes (fourteen).

The realities of everyday life returned far too quickly after the closing ceremonies, bringing with them hyperbolic statements about the Games being a defining moment for Canada, and an event that solidified national unity. However, many are still basking in the emotional warmth generated by the Games and reinforced by the Paralympics. It may, therefore, be too early to expose these achievements to the cold light of analysis; but since the Vancouver Olympic results are already affecting budget and policy decisions, some evidence is warranted.

Canada finished in third place in the medals table, behind Germany and the United States. This was exactly the same position where Canada finished in 2006 (Torino), behind the same two countries. The OTP program had spent some $94 million during the four years since Torino to ensure that Canada finished at the top of the medals table at Vancouver. This confirms what Australia has recently realized: for those involved in the global sporting arms race, it costs more and more money even to try to stay at the same place in the medals table.

Canadian athletes won twenty-four medals in Torino and twenty-six in Vancouver. Those two extra medals thus cost some $47 million each of OTP funding. Canadian athletes were rightly celebrated for winning a record-setting fourteen gold medals in Vancouver, seven more than they won in Torino; the cost per extra gold medal in OTP funds was therefore about $13.5 million. It is worth remembering that the Vancouver medals actually cost a great deal more; OTP (mainly public funds) represented additional funding, over and above what is usually provided by Sport Canada and the national winter sport organizations. The total OTP funding package was some $117 million over five years; Canadian athletes at Torino benefited from the first year of OTP funding—approximately $23 millon.

The metrics of success may be calculated in various ways. In population terms Canada's 26 medals represent one medal for each 1.25 million Canadians. This far exceeds the ratios for Germany (1: 2.7 million), the United States (1: 8.3 million), and Russia (1: 9.5 million); but Norway led the way, winning one medal for every 210,000 Norwegians. Canadian women were particularly successful: of the 206 athletes on the Canadian team, 91 (44%) were female but they, for various reasons, won 14.5 of the 26 medals (56%). (The ice dancing medal is shared.) Quebec athletes were even more successful: 50 of the 206 athletes were from Quebec (24%); 24 of those athletes went home with a medal, a "conversion rate" to be envied. And the OTP program declared itself a success, despite failing to meet its stated goal.

OTP suffered a great deal of criticism during the first week of the Olympics: first, for the name of the program; second, for evidently failing to achieve its goals; and third, for apparently placing additional pressure on the home-team athletes by announcing in advance potential medal winners and medal totals. Strategically, at the midpoint

of the Games, OTP and the Canadian Olympic Committee changed the definition of success. When it became apparent that Canadian athletes would not be able to win the most medals, success was redefined as winning the most gold medals. Canadian athletes exceeded expectations, winning more gold medals than any country had previously achieved at a Winter Olympics.

However, just as OTP is assuming its success, it is equally possible to assume that Canadian athletes could have achieved even more medals under a different funding strategy. The striking number of fourth- and fifth-place finishes by Canadian athletes and the reported comments by some athletes—recipients of OTP funding, medal winners and others—critical of OTP's focus on medals as the only definition of success, and of the additional pressure they felt as a result of OTP's announcements, combine to suggest that perhaps something was left in the tank. Perhaps Canadian athletes could actually have achieved first place in the medals table.

What could have been done differently? What might OTP learn for the future? What policies should be in place to guide Canada's high-performance funding strategies?

First, from the athletes' perspectives (at least those who received funding benefits) the OTP program was a great success. Athletes reported that they were much better prepared than in the past, and that this time they did not feel at a disadvantage compared with their formerly better-funded competitors. But the program was also divisive, reportedly creating two classes of athletes—those expected to win medals and receiving funding, and those not. It seems that Canadian sport officials have not learned the lessons from Canada's past Olympics, especially Torino. Several Canadian athletes rise to the occasion at every Olympics, and unexpectedly win a medal. The Canadian Olympic Committee sent a large team to Torino to give young athletes some Olympic experience before Vancouver—and some of them unexpectedly won medals. All of the athletes who won medals in Vancouver were expected to do so; there were no surprises. Failing to spread the wealth, and creating two classes of athletes, may have discouraged some of the team from believing that they could win. A renewed funding program should support as many athletes as possible.

Second, a renewed funding program should change its name, and manage expectations. The name Own the Podium made many uncomfortable from the start. Eventually it came to be used against the Canadian team (German sports officials used it to motivate their athletes to beat Canadians), and during the first week of the Olympics it became a joke. U.S. snowboarder Nate Holland was widely reported as saying to Canadians, "You can own the podium—we'll just rent it for the month." The boastful name, combined with declarations that Canada would lead the medals table and varying reports of the total number of medals that would be won, served to place additional pressures on athletes who already had to cope with the enthusiasm of home-team spectators. Some managed far better than others. Other teams managed expectations more credibly. The United States Olympic Committee never declared that U.S. athletes would lead the medals table or proclaimed the number of medals that would be won. A more neutral name (e.g., "level playing field") that served exactly the same purpose of permitting Canadian athletes to feel that they were as well prepared as their main competitors, and to enter their events with a quiet confidence, might have worked even better than OTP.

Third, a renewed funding program should broaden its definition of success. As Clara Hughes often stated in her low-key criticism of OTP, we should recognize, support, and reward excellence whether or not it comes with a medal. The single-minded focus on medals does a real disservice to athletes who finished out of the medals but have achieved Canadian records, finished higher than Canadian athletes have ever finished in an event, or overcome extraordinary challenges in order to compete in and finish an event. A single-minded focus on medals also produces funding distortions

in a sport system. Just as Australians recently realized that they were spending more government funds on archery (an Olympic sport with a relatively small number of Australian participants, but where a number of medals are awarded) than cricket (a national sport, but not an Olympic sport), Canadian team sports are beginning to realize that they are being starved of funding because Olympic team sports only award gold medals to the winners of men's and women's tournaments; funding is going disproportionately to individual sports that are "medal rich" because there are multiple events (e.g., swimming).

Finally, a broader definition of success should include achieving a legacy of increased sport and physical activity participation. In public policy terms, Olympic success produces relatively intangible benefits such as increased national pride. The vast majority of the world's population will not remember which country won the most medals at a specific Olympics; the United States is probably not a better place to live because its athletes won the most medals in Vancouver; and Austria is probably not a worse place to live because its team did not win as many medals as expected. But Norway is a better and healthier place to live because public policy has found a way to connect the funding of high-performance sport with providing widespread opportunities for citizen participation in sports and physical activities. The Scandinavian countries consistently report the highest levels of participation.

If the well-being of the citizens of a nation is a major goal of public policy, then having an active healthy population goes a long way toward achieving that goal. Such a population realizes significant savings in health care, enjoys enhanced citizen participation (e.g., increased volunteerism), and has a lower incidence of crime and troubled youth. This is an implicit aim of high-performance sport funding policies, and of programs such as OTP. Governments, programs, and even athletes claim that the trickle-down benefit of inspirational Olympic performances is increased sport participation. This is a convenient fiction, promoted by the International Olympic Committee, and echoed by all of those who stand to benefit from increased funding for high-performance sport. Unfortunately, the evidence from Canada and other countries shows that inspiration is not enough.

Many young people in Canada are currently inspired by the Olympic performances that they have recently seen. Unfortunately, most will soon find that the possibilities of realizing that inspiration are quite limited: geographically (Where are the nearest facilities for practising the sport?); economically (Is my family able to support my participation in the sport?); and infrastructurally (Are there available and affordable facilities, instructors, and coaches to enable participation in the sport?). The answer is no in far too many cases, and measurable increases in sport participation following an Olympic Games are extremely rare.

As a consequence, many of the wealthy countries draw their Olympic participants disproportionately from a relatively narrow segment of the population: those whose families are able to afford all of the travel, equipment, instruction, and other costs required to develop a young athlete to the point where she will be eligible for government funding. Private-school students in Britain constitute 7%–8% of the school population, but it is estimated that some 65% of the British Olympic team in 2012 will have gone to private school. Canada is not as restrictive as that, but the data indicate that even Canada's Olympic athletes are disproportionately drawn from a relatively narrow segment of the population.

Thus, a renewed funding program needs to connect support for high-performance athletes with more democratized opportunities to participate. This may be achieved in various ways, and there are good models in some other countries.

Perhaps one place to start would be to connect high-performance sport funding to opportunities to participate in that sport. A consequence of the distortions introduced by a single-minded focus on medals is high levels of funding for sports in which very few people are able to participate. According to OTP, the sliding sports (bobsled, skeleton, and luge) received $2,874,061 in OTP funding (in addition to their usual levels of funding) in the year leading up to Vancouver. There are probably fewer participants in the sliding sports in Canada than there are in archery in Australia; but that level of funding needs to be compared with funding for a mass participation sport. For example, the annual budget for Basketball Canada is approximately $3 million.

The recent federal budget promised more of the same. The government will supply the funds no longer provided by the corporate sector for OTP; and there is $10 million over the next two years for the Canadian Paralympic Committee, and $2 million over the next two years for Special Olympics Canada—in both of these cases the support is most likely to go to the most able/highest-functioning athletes, rather than to the grassroots. ParticipAction will receive $6 million over the next two years for more public service announcements, but are there many Canadians who still do not know that physical activity is good for you?

We need increased opportunities for all Canadians to participate, and creative thinking to imagine ways to connect needed funding for high-performance athletes with more democratized access to sports and physical activity participation. If Vancouver 2010 is to have a real legacy, we need to start developing it now.

---

◀◀ **Source**: This article was first published in *Policy Options* in April 2010. Reprinted with permission.

# Section 12

## Education and Sports

Sport is connected to education in various ways. Learning sport and other physical skills is an important part of education—in fact, physical literacy and health education are increasingly being seen as important parts of a fully rounded education. Schools in Canada provide the most democratized access to sports, encouraging participation among individuals who would not be able to afford to participate in community or private sports leagues or clubs; and colleges and universities recruit students on the basis of their athletic skills.

The first article in this section, Jenn Hardy's "Selling the Olympics in the Schools," continues the discussion of the Olympics from the previous section. Concerns about the commercialization of the Olympic torch relay, and the exposure of numerous schoolchildren (often during the school day) to the commercial caravan that preceded the torch relay, were expressed by a number of educators. Hardy looks at a different aspect of "Olympic education," the half-million-dollar Sharing the Dream curriculum package that was distributed to schools in British Columbia. Educators and parents who opposed the Olympics attempted to balance Sharing the Dream with an alternative curriculum that provided a more critical perspective on the Games. As with many other examples of Olympic protest, the alternative curriculum was quickly banned.

André Picard considers another aspect of school curriculum in his article, "Is it Time for Examinations in Physical Fitness?" Picard notes the advantages

for learning in all subjects that result from having an active, healthy population of children, and suggests that having fitness examinations will encourage schools to become accountable for the health of children. In a similar vein, the Zambian Education Ministry made physical and health education an examinable subject several years ago in order to ensure that schools gave more priority to the subject.

Specialist sport schools have been introduced in a number of provinces in recent years. Richard Young reports on their introduction in Ontario in "A Sporting Chance." Unlike specialist arts or music schools, sports schools can run into problems because of the need for competition—if all of the best athletes from a region in a particular sport are concentrated in one school, it is difficult for them to find challenging competitors, and other schools in the interschool sport system are reluctant to play them. Young looks at how some sports schools are finding innovative ways to deal with these issues.

Although university-age athletes have been leaving Canada for some time to attend U.S. universities on athletic scholarships, that journey is now increasingly being made by high-school age athletes in certain sports. Specialist schools in the United States (usually private schools, sometimes Christian schools), function as sports academies and are now recruiting Canadian students. Michael Grange describes the journey of one such teenager from Canada in his article "Hoop Dreams—Bound for Glory" (see also, Grange, 2010 in "Additional Suggested Readings and References").

The final article deals with a difficult educational decision that has been made by many talented hockey players over the years. Because those who have played major junior hockey in Canada are considered to be professional athletes by the NCAA, they are not allowed to accept U.S. athletic scholarships. James Mirtle explores this difficult decision with some young Canadian players in his article "When a Career Reaches a Crossroads."

**Additional Suggested Readings and References**

- Grange, M. 2010. "Bound for Glory?" *The Globe and Mail*, March 6.
- Kernaghan, J. 2002. "Search for Equity Leads to Unequal Teams." *London Free Press*, May 17.
- McGregor, R. 2010. "New Thrust in U.S. Promotes College Hockey Over Major Junior. *The Globe and Mail*, January 4.
- Picard, A. 2006. "Daily, Compulsory Phys-Ed Urged." *The Globe and Mail*, June 6.

# 73. Selling the Olympics in the Schools
## By Jenn Hardy

In the name of education, British Columbia has spent at least half a million dollars teaching wee ones the awesomeness of the Olympics. In response, Olympics opponents are trying to counteract what they call "pro-Olympic propaganda" by introducing classroom workshops of their own.

The $500,000 Sharing the Dream program provides every school in the province with an Olympics "teachable moments" DVD that includes videos, podcasts, teacher guides, hyperlinks, and brochures for teachers to use in their classes—all designed to build excitement about the Games.

"Olympic and Paralympic themes span across all courses in the B.C. school curriculum—from language arts to science, physical education to mathematics, social studies to fine arts, technology to career planning," reads the Sharing the Dream website. "We urge you to embrace these educational opportunities and bring the excitement of the Games to your classroom."

Olympics opponents dismiss the Sharing the Dream program as a brainwashing tool. "It is a blatant propaganda effort to bolster support for the Games," says anti-Olympic activist and author of *Five Ring Circus: Myths and Realities of the Olympic Games*, Chris Shaw. "The same government is cutting off school sports programs."

The Sharing the Dream program was launched in the wake of massive budget cuts to public education. These same cuts are affecting public school maintenance, staffing, CommunityLINK (a program that supports students in low-income communities), Parent Advisory Council funding and, ironically, $130,000 worth of provincial grants for competitive sports.

Anti-Olympics organizers aren't short on reasons for opposing the Games. According to Shaw, founder of the watchdog group 2010watch, the Olympics are an assault on the poor, the environment, and the public purse. Detractors also point out that the Games are being held on unceded Native land (B.C. territory that was never signed over to European settlers) over the objections of local Native groups.

In response to the Share the Dream program, Shaw and other activists are doing a little educating of their own. In August, the Olympic

Resistance Network introduced Teach2010, a workshop geared to elementary and high school students that aims to restore some balance to the Olympics debate.

The goal of Teach2010 is to provide teachers with resources to do something revolutionary: provide some critical perspectives on a complex and relevant issue.

Unlike Sharing the Dream's well-funded program, Teach2010 has a budget of just $3,000 (all donated), and relies on a great deal of volunteer labour. Through Teach2010, organizers conduct workshops that teach educators about the issues surrounding the Olympics. They also host youth nights where kids do activities like silkscreening T-shirts. "It's an opportunity for youth to get informed about the issues," says organizer Marla Renn. "It gives participants the ability to respond through their creative expression."

For Teach2010's high school workshops, Renn, a schoolteacher, takes her small team into classrooms to facilitate discussions about the Olympics. "We begin to look at the issues surrounding the Olympics and then we step away and look at whether those things translate into reality," she says. "What are the real impacts of the Olympics? If you had an opportunity to participate in the decision-making process, what would you spend $6 billion of public money on?" Students have suggested building hospitals and community centres, or housing everyone on Vancouver's Downtown Eastside without a home. They've even discussed buying an ice cream for everyone in the city.

Renn and the students discuss environmental impacts and dissect organizers' claims that this will be the "greenest Games ever." They talk about the motivations of stakeholders like the Vancouver Organizing Committee (VANOC), as well as sponsors and the mainstream news media.

It's not entirely surprising that the Olympic resistance's move into the classroom has itself been met with resistance.

Myriam Dumont, an elementary school teacher in Vancouver's Downtown Eastside, tried to organize a Teach2010 workshop for teachers at her school in October 2009 to give them ideas for a balanced lesson about the Olympics.

The issue exploded when the *Vancouver Sun* reported that the Vancouver Elementary School Teachers Association (VESTA) was promoting a Teach2010 workshop. The association had simply put a link on their website to inform teachers that the workshop was taking place.

The Sun article caused a minor media frenzy, and a couple of days later, Sun columnist Cam Cole wrote a piece called "It's elementary, my dear children: The Olympics are a sham," in which he sarcastically attacks the Olympic Resistance Network and VESTA, accusing both parties of crushing children's hopes and dreams.

"Nip those dreams in the bud, I say," writes Cole. "Get 'em early. That's the kind of preventive action that makes us all proud to pay your salaries."

VESTA quickly distanced itself from the event, removing the informational link on its website and replacing it with a disclaimer. The media attention resulted in the cancellation of Dumont's workshop and her holding it off school property.

"I saw it as an opportunity for teachers to get kids to start thinking about issues and what they can do, how it affects them, and taking action." She says discussions about the Olympics are especially important in an inner-city Vancouver school, where pro-Olympic propaganda is everywhere.

---

◀◀ **Source:** This article was originally published in *Briarpatch* magazine, January/February 2010. Reprinted with permission.

# 74. Is it Time for Examinations in Physical Fitness?
## By André Picard

*Physical Education is being pushed aside despite growing concerns about childhood obesity*

■■■■■■

It's an hour before the start of classes, but the gymnasium at Oakenwald Elementary School is quickly filling up with boisterous, laughing kids. The ten- and eleven-year-olds from Winnipeg are pumped because this morning they are playing Frogger, a game they invented themselves.

In fact, in a noteworthy turning of the tables, these members of the Xbox generation have taken a 1980s video game and transformed it into a high-intensity retro game of tag.

With the popular Crazy Frog song "I Like To Move It" blaring, half the preteens run, leap obstacles, dodge bad guys, and retrieve tennis balls while the rest of them dash around furiously trying to tag them.

"This is a good way to start the day," says physical education teacher Ian Bailey, watching intently from the sidelines. "Parents like it because their kids are moving; teachers like it because the kids are wide awake and attentive in class; and, most of all, the kids like it because it's fun."

Oakenwald is the happy exception: a grade school where, in addition to the early-morning program (optional but with an 80% participation rate), students get thirty minutes daily of physical education—a school that has received the highest distinction every year since 1990 from the Canadian Association for Health, Physical Education, Recreation, and Dance (CAHPERD).

Unfortunately, *The Globe and Mail* found that only nineteen school boards of the seventy-four surveyed across Canada say they have daily physical education in all their schools. And while physical education is mandatory in most boards up to Grade 9, it becomes less so in higher grades—in Grade 10, the program is optional in 43% of boards, and by Grade 11 it is optional in 78%.

What's more, less than half of school boards nationwide hired physical education instructors with the applicable post-secondary degree to teach the program, the survey found.

And physical education programs vary wildly around the country, offering as little as thirty minutes a week to more than thirty minutes daily of gym time. At least on paper: Research has shown that, in the average half-hour gym class, children spend only about six minutes actually moving.

"Literacy and numeracy will always be the focus of schools—and they should be," says Grant McManes, president of CAHPERD. "But I want kids to be musically and physically literate, too. Education is about educating the whole child. Right now, we're not doing that in many schools."

At a time when childhood obesity has become epidemic, physical education and recess are being pushed aside as schools try to maximize instructional time, particularly in areas where there are provincial exams.

"The attitude is that the three r's are the most important, but that's simply not true," says Graham Fishburne, a professor in the faculty of education at the University of Alberta in Edmonton.

Prof. Fishburne says that, for more than seventy years, research has demonstrated that increasing classroom time does not correlate with better test scores. Rather, the more active children are, the better they learn.

In fact, a landmark study conducted in 1951 in Vauves, France, found that the school day that maximizes learning consists of two-thirds classroom time, one-third physical education—and no homework. That research has been replicated many times, with slight permutations but the same results.

"Children don't become brighter because they're physically active but they are less tired, less agitated, less stressed, and less sick," Prof. Fishburne says. "Physically active kids are in a better condition for learning."

Yet politicians and policy-makers have failed repeatedly to act. "We present the evidence to the ministers of education and they say, 'That's great,' and they do nothing," Prof. Fishburne says.

In the past couple of years, however, the childhood-obesity bulge has become the subject of intense scrutiny—and governments have begun to act.

Ontario and Alberta have promised daily physical activity (twenty and thirty minutes, respectively), British Columbia has launched the ambitious Action Schools B.C., Quebec has extended the school week by fifty minutes for activity, and there are moves afoot in most other provinces.

Yet it is unclear to what extent the changes are actually happening on the ground—or, rather, in the gym. Many governments are promising increased physical activity, which is ill defined and largely unmeasured; it can consist of extending recess, where kids often stand around.

According to *Canada's Physical Activity Guide for Children*, young people should be active—the equivalent of brisk walking—for at least ninety minutes daily.

But a recent study of 277 Montreal schools, published in the journal *Health Education & Behavior*, showed that children are in fact active for as little as fourteen minutes a day (and as much as one hundred). Put another way, at worst they are essentially sedentary for a staggering twenty-three hours and forty-six minutes.

In addition, only half of the boards in the Globe survey reported that all their schools have intramural sports teams. Intramural programs were more prevalent in Manitoba and British Columbia, less so in Nova Scotia and Saskatchewan.

"Schools where the kids get the most exercise not only place an emphasis on play at recess and during free periods, but they also encourage students to join sports teams, and they organize tournaments and Olympics at the end of the year," says the University of Montreal's Tracie Barnett, who conducted the study.

The single most important factor in determining whether kids will be active at school, the researcher found, is leadership by the principal. Another key factor is having a specialized gym teacher, which most children do not. Only in Quebec and French-language schools in New Brunswick is it mandatory to have physical-education experts teach gym.

In education programs, would-be teachers get as little as ten hours of training in physical education and health, and no more than thirty-nine hours.

"It's not that there's poor teaching going on," Prof. Fishburne says. "There's no teaching at all."

So if teachers think physical education is unimportant, what are students to think? After Grade 10, as reflected in the *Globe* survey, physical education is largely optional. Not coincidentally, after the age of fifteen, physical activity drops off sharply, particularly among girls.

Good physical education is more than free play, recess, or sport—it is a planned, purposeful program that is curriculum-driven and delivered in a varied, balanced way by a trained professional.

What Mr. Bailey does in Winnipeg is a case in point. Every thirty-minute class he teaches requires ten to fifteen minutes of preparation. Yet to the children, gym time—skipping, dancing, playing catch, jumping the doughnut, playing Cookie Monster tag—seems like a spontaneous game.

"I don't want students sitting around listening to me," he says. "I like to see them being happy and I want them to leave class feeling they had fun."

Still, there are clear goals to teach basic movement skills, to give kids a sense of physical self-confidence. Mr. Bailey, who has been teaching physical education since 1975, says that, despite frequent criticism, the program today is as good as it has ever been. What has changed, though, is the life of children outside of school. Most no longer bike to school or play freely outside after classes; even participation in organized sports is falling because of the cost.

"I'm not saying there were good old days, but we didn't have structured lives like kids today," Mr. Bailey says. "I think our real challenge in school today is to plant a seed so that physical activity becomes part of lifestyle as children grow up."

Mr. McManes of CAHPERD says most parents don't realize how different physical education is today than in their youth.

"Many of us have bad memories of gym, where the football coach would spend his time yelling at you to do more pushups," Mr. McManes says. "But it's not like that anymore."

Increasingly, schools are abandoning the sport-delivery model -- where students are taught the basics of team sports and those who excel are recruited for elite teams while the rest are left to plod through the course.

"What we strive for now is a health and wellness model," Mr. McManes says.

Richard Way, director of long-term athlete development at Sport Canada, says the old way of teaching gym was an utter failure because it didn't produce physically active kids, other than a select few.

"Every child is an athlete until we beat it out of them, and that's what we've done," he says.

Mr. Way says the key to improving the physical fitness of children is a better integration of activities—individual and team sports, and play—in schools, the community, and organized sporting leagues. Right now, they all operate separately and often at cross-purposes.

School gyms—sometimes even playgrounds—are locked up tight after hours, and participation in community events can make students ineligible for school sports, intramural or competitive.

Mark Tremblay, president of Active Healthy Kids Canada, is a believer in kinesthetic learning—incorporating physical activity into every aspect of the school day: Teach children to count while they are skipping, go hiking for geography class, learn physics by building snow forts.

Mr. Tremblay also believes that the reason physical activity is neglected in schools is that no one in the education system is accountable for the health of children.

"We isolate certain subjects for examination and that sends a powerful message that they're the only ones that matter," he says. "I think it's time for provincial examinations in physical fitness."

Mr. Tremblay says these exams should not be designed for jocks but, rather, incorporate a number of physical measures—body mass index, blood pressure, girth—as well as measures of physical activity such as skipping, running, and flex tests. But the essential element, he says, would be to rate improvements in personal fitness throughout the school year rather than judge students against one another.

"We don't want kids to be humiliated and embarrassed. We want them to be inspired and keen to be physically active," Mr. Tremblay says.

"I think schools can do it. I think schools have to do it—for the sake of our kids."

◀◀ **Source:** André Picard is a writer with *The Globe and Mail*. This article was originally published in *The Globe and Mail*, January 22, 2007. Reprinted with permission.

## A Sporting Chance

### By Richard Young

**75.**

*Who among us has not been awed by the strength, endurance, grace, and flexibility of athletes—their ability to react, their pursuit of excellence?*

*Ontario teachers, through various specialized sports programs in secondary schools, are finding it easier to recognize students' passions and athletic talents and to build opportunities for leadership, excellence, and learning.*

■ ■ ■ ■ ■ ■

It's 7:35 AM and cold as the twenty or so boys and girls in the Grade 10 Hockey Canada Skills Academy class straggle in for the thrice-weekly seventy-minute on-ice component of the course. The arena sits adjacent to their school, Sir Frederick Banting, in London. Many of them are bleary eyed and complain about how tired they are. But half an hour later they are skating briskly in full hockey regalia, awaiting their teacher's instructions.

This hockey academy course is just one of many specialized sports programs in Ontario schools. There are credit physical education courses that concentrate on a particular sport such as swimming, volleyball, basketball, or hockey; programs for elite students such as the National Elite Development Academy (NEDA) basketball program in the Hamilton-Wentworth Catholic District School Board (DSB); integrated sports academies like those found at Hamilton's Westmount Secondary School (SS) and École secondaire publique Louis-Riel in Ottawa; and a range of high-performance athlete programs. And, since Bill Crothers Secondary School in the York Region DSB opened its doors in August 2008, there is now an entire sports-focused school.

The programs do have critics. Some claim single-sport credit courses like Banting's are too limited. Others suggest that specialized sports programs that are elitist divert resources from other programs and buildings.

Supporters point out that similar criticisms have been aimed at schools for the arts, tech-centred schools, and programs for the academically gifted. They say that Ontario's specialized sports programs strive to engage student athletes, making them feel their athletic pursuits are supported and connected to what they learn in school, while promoting a healthy, active lifestyle for all students.

### ■ ■ ■ Tapping into Something Students Love

Those involved in the hockey academy at Banting bristle at the suggestion that it is limited and elitist.

"You don't have to be rich or athletically gifted to take the course," says teacher Todd Sargeant, who coordinates the academy. "We focus on individual development in a variety of sports, with an emphasis on hockey. The skills that are basic to our program—like hand-eye coordination, strength development, agility, balance, and reacting to environmental clues—are transferable to other sports such as lacrosse, soccer, basketball, and floor ball."

According to Sargeant, the program offers students a great opportunity to earn credits doing something they love. It also provides Banting with a unique course to attract hockey-minded students. The Banting program was the outcome of a sabbatical Sargeant spent in Calgary, where he saw several Hockey Canada academies.

After returning to London, he and then-principal Tony Jones did their research. Sargeant reports,

"Tony gained approval from the board and I applied to Hockey Canada for the course to be accepted as an academy."

The Banting Hockey Academy began in September 2008 with forty-one students in physical education courses for Grades 10 and 12. Sargeant teaches the Grade 10 class, while English teacher Jeff Dundas, who has coached the boys' varsity hockey team for the last ten years, puts the Grade 12s through their paces.

The on-ice part focuses on traditional hockey skills—skating, stickhandling, passing, and shooting. The other component includes fitness and conditioning training and regular physical education requirements like group activities and health units.

"I registered for the course to help improve my skills and be part of a more competitive situation than girls' house league," says Shelby, sixteen. "At first I was a little intimidated by the guys, but I got over it fast. My skating and stickhandling have improved greatly and I feel much more confident."

She hopes that the program will attract others and provide some impetus to the school's fledgling varsity girls' team.

The course taps into and builds on students' love of hockey and their desire to be part of it. Sixteen-year-old Zack likes that Triple A midget players skate side by side with house league players. He says, "We're like one big team of all different levels of players."

### ■■■ Developing our Best

While Banting's hockey academy is open to all interested students, Canada Basketball's NEDA in Hamilton focuses on elite athletes.

On a snowy Saturday morning in December in Barrie, the twelve members of the NEDA girls' developmental team, along with their coaches, are in town for a day-long basketball skills-development clinic at St. Joseph's High School. After putting eighty-six local players through a high-powered workout during the day, the players take

on the Barrie Royals Midget Boys in an exhibition match that night. The clinic and game are just one of several Canada Basketball fundraising events that NEDA teams will participate in during the school year.

NEDA teams compete against a variety of opponents, hold skills clinics, host international competitions, and participate in international tours.

Partnering with schools in Hamilton, the NEDA program brings together the top twelve male and female development athletes from across Canada, aged fifteen to eighteen, to train under the Canada Basketball national team program strategies from September to June. These athletes will compete for Canada.

The students are billeted with families and, depending on language and religious preferences, attend one of three host schools – St. Mary's Catholic SS, Westdale SS, or École secondaire Georges-P.-Vanier. This year, all are attending St. Mary's.

According to Denise Dignard, manager of Canada Basketball's women's elite performance program, NEDA arose from a need. "Over the past twenty years, Canada was not producing enough top world-class athletes in basketball for our senior national teams to consistently qualify for world championships and Olympic Games," she says. "One of the key components of the successful systems was a centralized residential program within a national sport institute for junior-aged athletes, as well as regional feeder sport schools and/or sport academies."

NEDA participants train daily for two to three hours at McMaster University. Other curriculum is delivered by the partner schools.

"In most cases, the daily course schedule at St. Mary's fits NEDA demands," says Mary Cipolla of the Hamilton-Wentworth Catholic DSB and former St. Mary's principal. "Although in some instances we've had to be creative."

The NEDA students have integrated well and proven to be an inspirational addition to the student body. Cipolla says, "They serve as role models for the entire school, consistently maintaining high academic standards and demonstrating what commitment and hard work every day of the entire year is all about."

### ■ ■ ■ Adapt and Diversify

Many schools offer sports academies that appeal to a diverse range of student athletes.

École secondaire publique Louis-Riel in Ottawa, which features a state-of-the-art domed sports facility, is one example. Program coordinator Ken Levesque says the current program is modelled in part on similar highly popular and successful programs in Quebec.

The school offers the program to its Grades 7 and 8 students, and 75% participate. Almost half, 220 of the 500 students in Grades 9 through 12, are enrolled in the program.

"Our program tends to the needs of a vast group of students, from high-performance to recreational athletes. We offer different academic support and specific training depending on the needs of each athlete," says Levesque. The school offers coaching in seven different sports. Other students in individual sports, like speed skating, tennis, martial arts, swimming, and kayaking, train with their club coaches in the afternoon.

"Students take three academic courses in the morning, have lunch and then have a supervised study period to finish homework or take tests before their afternoon training sessions with their coaches," says Levesque. "Our students must maintain a 70% average."

Many Louis-Riel students have received full university sports scholarships or moved on to play their sports at higher levels, including the National Hockey League.

### ■ ■ ■ Building Excellence

The goals and philosophy of Westmount Sport Academy (WSA) at Westmount SS in Hamilton are similar to those of Louis-Riel. The program offers flexible, self-paced learning and customized, fully integrated timetables for high-performing athletes in Grades 9 and 10 from throughout the Hamilton-Wentworth DSB.

More than thirty Grade 9 WSA students are spread out on the gym floor at McMaster University's athletic centre. They are here for their weekly strength and fitness training under the watchful eyes of the centre's fitness and wellness coordinator and their teachers, Sofia Fox and Chris Lychak.

The weekly sessions are an integral component of the program, now in its second year. After training, the students watch intently as the McMaster men's volleyball team goes through its practice in an adjoining gym. Some of the students are, no doubt, dreaming of the day when they will take their place on one of the university's varsity teams.

In addition to year-long health and physical education credits and the use of outside community facilities, WSA students receive additional student-focused support from a dedicated WSA program vice-principal, Jamie Nunn, and program coordinator Greg Ardron.

### ■ ■ ■ Academic Success

"Our students come to us with an athletic gift, talent, or skills set," says Ardron. "Our challenge is to connect our curriculum to those gifts and create academic programming that is attractive to the students, will engage them and let them be successful."

Kevin, a fifteen-year-old basketball and volleyball player, appreciates the self-paced learning format that allows students to complete credit courses at their own pace.

"If you're tired after a tournament, you don't have to stay up all night to get an assignment in for the next morning," he explains. "You can carry it over until the weekend when you have more time—just as long as you get it done so you can move on to the next learning guide. It has really improved my time-management skills."

Twin sisters Maggie and Heather, fifteen, agree that the self-paced format lets students accelerate through units or take additional time, depending on their training and competition demands. Both say that a typical day for them begins around 7:00 AM and ends around 11:00 PM, the time all of their in-school and club training and athletics are done for the day. "I don't think I could manage it all without the support we receive from the WSA program and our teachers," says Maggie.

"It's all about engaging students," says Nunn, noting how important sport can be in reaching out to kids who exhibit at-risk behaviours. "We need to be able to focus these kids and provide them with a program and culture where they feel their athletic pursuits are supported and connected to what they do in school."

### ■■■ Accommodations and Alliances

Other schools meet the needs of student athletes through a variety of programs that offer flexible scheduling, academic monitoring and assistance, and communications networks between school, home, and sports. These programs often partner with local club leagues and community organizations.

For example, the High Performance Athletes Program at John McCrae SS in the Ottawa-Carleton DSB works with the Walter Baker Community Centre to provide its student athletes access to ice rinks, squash courts, pools, and a fitness centre. General Panet High School in Petawawa partners with the Canadian Forces base to share the base's athletic facilities.

Diane Hurska at Eastdale Collegiate Vocational Institute in Oshawa runs her school's program much like a regular co-op program. The Toronto DSB offers programs at Birchmount Park Collegiate Institue (CI), Northview SS, Silverthorn CI and Vaughan Road Academy, ranging in size from seventy-five to more than two-hundred participants, and each has its own unique features.

The Health and Sport Specialty Program at Bawating Collegiate in Sault Ste. Marie takes a two-pronged approach, targeting both elite athletes and students interested in careers in health sciences.

The program, started in 2003, caters to student athletes who compete at the provincial level. Another part of the program provides a focused education in health, physical education, and health sciences. It has nine health-sector-specific courses and ample work-related and reach-ahead experiences that prepare students for post-secondary studies in health.

Coordinator Seth Cond explains: "Our program offers a variety of methods of delivering curriculum to our students, including an extensive independent-study component under which students can complete assignments in a time frame conducive to their training and competition schedule, and a late-school component where classes begin at 11:30 and run until 5:00. Both accommodations are helpful for students who travel to competitions and arrive home late. Rather than having their participation in competitive sports interfere with their schooling, we want to make it an ally to assist in their learning."

What these programs have in common is that they are all integrated into the fabric of a larger educational environment—programs within programs or schools within schools. Unionville's Bill Crothers SS, on the other hand, is Ontario's first purpose-built, sports-focused school.

### ■■■ Breaking New Ground

As you enter the long drive leading to Bill Crothers SS in Unionville, the first thing you notice is the playing fields, one natural grass and two artificial turf. Inside, it's bright, open, spacious, and inviting. To the right, three massive double gyms are visible, thanks to floor-to-ceiling Plexiglas walls. In the office, fruit sits on trays at the reception counter.

Principal Becky Green greets everyone with a "hello" and a friendly smile.

Everything about Crothers—including its outdoor fields, gyms, strength-training area, coaching and wellness centres, e-book-laden library, specialized curriculum, and food—is designed to meet the school's commitment to healthy, active living for all its students.

Having opened its doors in August 2008, the school is still a work in progress. "We get to make a footprint by trying something that nobody else in the province has attempted," says Jacqui Palm, head of physical education. "It's really exciting for the students and staff."

Named for the Olympic silver medalist and long-time chair of the York Region DSB, the school was eight years in the making. Crothers, along with Bruce Kidd, his former Olympic team-mate and University of Toronto dean of health and physical education, and York Region DSB director of education Bill Hogarth, believed that many students competing at a high level did not have the necessary support systems in school to achieve their full academic potential. Crothers and his colleagues wanted to create an accessible, sports-focused school that would value and celebrate the athletic interests of its students, thereby engaging them and increasing their academic achievement.

The school is open to students from across the York Region DSB (and even from outside the region, depending on space and program availability). It admits students who train and compete at school intercollegiate or community competitions and students who have provincial, national, or international athletic aspirations that require training programs of fifteen or more hours a week. Students are selected on the basis of marks, references from teachers and coaches, parental input, and student responses and goals. The school will have 1,500 students from Grades 9 through 12, but in its first year has 225 Grade 9s and 80 Grade 10s.

Crothers features what Green calls a balanced school year. The calendar runs from early August to late June, with shorter breaks throughout the year. The daily schedule consists of five sixty-minute periods, from 8:45 AM to 3:00 PM. All students have a supervised integrated-learning instructional period four days a week to review and complete assignments. In addition, students and staff have a late-start day each Wednesday so they can participate in school brainstorming and planning sessions.

Grade 10 students Ryan and Jacqueline, both fifteen, note that many of their projects and assignments use sports themes. Topics like the Vancouver 2010 Winter Olympics and the Toronto area's bid for the 2015 Pan American Games run throughout the school's curriculum.

Jacqueline's skiing requires her to miss a lot of class time. "I just knew that my grades would probably suffer if I stayed at my old school," she says. "The teachers and administration here understand my commitments and are very supportive. Many of them are competitive athletes themselves. As a result, I've managed to stay ahead with my studies."

Ryan, a volleyball and soccer player, says simply, "I really look forward to coming to school every day."

One of the major challenges of teaching at a school like Bill Crothers SS is the demands it places on staff for individual programming. "Our teachers are also trying to accomplish new structures and methodologies by continually being creative and taking risks," says Green.

"Hearing parents say that their kids really like school, in some cases for the very first time, makes it all worthwhile and much more of a reward than a challenge as a teacher," says head of history Stefano Fornazzari.

"Before we opened, there was criticism from certain quarters that we would be elitist and drain off resources from other buildings and facilities," says Green. "Now that we are in operation, we hope the critics will come to see that Crothers fills a very real and practical need in the education and sports communities. Our system wants to provide choices for student athletes that engage them in learning."

The proliferation of specialized sports programs in Ontario's schools shows no signs of abating. Designed to engage student athletes by accommodating their special needs in curriculum, the variety of programs is likely to continue to expand.

And although critics may persist, the appeal for aspiring student athletes cannot be denied.

As one student mused, "What could be better than taking something kids are passionate about and turning it into curriculum?"

◀◀ Source: This article was originally published in *Professionally Speaking*, March 2009. *Professionally Speaking* is published by the Ontario College of Teachers.

## 76. Hoop Dreams—Bound for Glory
### By Michael Grange

*Hype and big dreams are seducing more and more Canadian teenagers to leave home for mega-money high school basketball programs in the United States*

Hanging in a hallway after practice, sweat-soaked and finishing each other's sentences on cue, Cory Joseph and Tristan Thompson could be any other Canadian high school kids with big dreams, making their way through Shakespeare, but imagining a brighter stage.

The difference? The pair of eighteen-year-olds are already on that stage, starring for one of the best high school basketball teams in the United States, their stories splashed all over the Internet, the hype spilling over.

At the end of this month they will become the first Canadians in more than twenty years to play in the McDonald's High School All-American game, an honour they'll share with everyone from LeBron James to Michael Jordan. Next month they'll lead Number three-ranked Findlay Prep into the ESPN RISE National High School Invitational—the unofficial high school championship of the United States—to defend the title they won last year.

The tournament will be televised across the United States, the high school equivalent of March Madness. Before that they'll be playing in Michael Jordan's own all-star game, sponsored by his Jordan Brand, at Madison Square Garden, no less.

"In Canada, hockey is the first sport, there's more exposure for it," says Joseph, a 6-foot-3 blur of a point guard, explaining how he left Pickering, Ontario, to attend high school on the outskirts of Las Vegas. "In Canada, basketball is on the rise, but here, there's more exposure for it and all that. That's why I think I made the decision to come out here."

Says Thompson, a broad-shouldered 6-foot-10 forward from Brampton, Ontario: "Here it's a lifestyle."

Inspired by their example and others, more and more top Canadian high-schoolers are aspiring to that lifestyle themselves, to the consternation of the Canadian basketball establishment.

It's estimated that as many as one hundred Canadian teenagers—primarily boys from the Toronto area, though there are girls and boys from every region in the country—are chasing their hoop dreams in the United States, often as early as the ninth grade.

"It's growing, it's not going to stop if we don't do something," says Guy Pariseau, technical director for Basketball Quebec, who says nearly all of the province's ten best players have left for the United States. "Everyone is shopping."

At the top of the list is a lucrative scholarship to a top Division I school and dreams of a professional career.

"Ever since I started playing basketball, from the first time I saw it on TV, I was like, 'I want to do that, I want to play there. I want to play for North Carolina or Kentucky or Texas,'" says Thompson, explaining why he left home at sixteen. "I want to play for those programs. It's not like there aren't good programs in Canada, I just wanted more. I wanted the highest competition out there and that's Division I, so I made that my goal."

He's reached it and will play at the University of Texas next season.

Joseph is undecided, but not because of a lack of attention. As the fifth-rated point guard in his graduating class, he's narrowed his list to five teams, but that didn't stop John Calipari, head coach of powerhouse University of Kentucky, from making a special visit to watch Joseph practice in person last month.

But getting to the top hasn't come without sacrifice.

"It's really tough mentally to come down here," says Joseph, who has scholarship offers from Connecticut, Villanova, and Kansas along with a sterling academic record to show for two years spent far from home. "You go through a lot of ups and downs, and the downs are hard because you're alone. [But] my mom told me, if you want, in order to get to your highest level, you have to make sacrifices."

Says Thompson: "It's not for everyone."

It just seems that way as Canadian coaches and sports administrators have become accustomed to their best players leaving before finishing high school.

Among the factors: uneven basketball development opportunities in Canada; National Collegiate Athletic Association requirements that make it difficult to qualify for Division I scholarships from Canadian high schools; and a desire on the part of some players to find safer and more stable places to play and study than they have at home.

"Most of my friends [in Canada] are basketball players," Thompson says. "And they're like, 'I'm out of here too, let's go make it happen.'"

The emigration of Canadian talent—some feel the current cohort of players from Canada is the deepest and richest ever—has become a self-fulfilling prophecy. "Welcome to beautiful Tampa, FL where we hope to see you enroll," is the pitch on one basketball message board by a coach looking to import talent for a start-up program where tuition is $14,000 (all currency U.S.) a year. "WE NEED PLAYERS."

Ro Russell, a fixture on the Toronto basketball scene through his successful club program, Grassroots Canada Elite, took a bold step this year when he moved to Creedmoor, North Carolina, to start an elite team affiliated with Christian Faith Center, an evangelical church.

"I'm the most pro-Canadian guy there is," says Russell, whose roster is nearly entirely made up of kids from the Toronto area. "But for basketball, the proving ground is America."

Many of the kids heading south are from immigrant minorities, from tough neighbourhoods and less-than-ideal home situations.

"There has been a lot of crime in some of those neighbourhoods, no doubt about it," says Mike George, founder of CIA Bounce, another top Toronto-area club that has had several kids head south for high school. "For some parents, they see it like sending their kids to boarding school; it gives them a sense of security. I've had kids get full scholarships to [elite East Coast private schools] Proctor or Brewster. That's worth $45,000 a year. For them it's a no-brainer."

Not all kids are so fortunate. It's estimated about 80% of them have to pay some or all of their tuition, with only the elite getting scholarships to prep schools.

Then there are rumours of kids sleeping three or more to a room, ten to a house, with minimal adult supervision, essentially fending for themselves at schools with dubious academic standing and scant record of developing elite basketball players.

Thompson and Joseph have had the opposite experience. They share a 3,000-square-foot house with their teammates a short walk to the campus of Henderson International, their expenses covered by Cliff Findlay, a wealthy Las Vegas auto dealer who underwrites the entire operation, including the salaries of two full-time coaches.

Both come from good families and neither of them were at risk of remaining undiscovered had they stayed home. Each starred on the summer Amateur Athletic Union circuit, where reputations are made and recruiting relationships often start. They've also represented Canada internationally. And players of Thompson's size, athleticism, and academic chops—he can fill your ear about the role of female characters in Shakespeare almost as well as he can face up, spin baseline and dunk in traffic—don't go under the radar. He's had clips on YouTube since he was fifteen.

Joseph, who carries a 3.2 (out of 4.0) grade point average along with a silky jumper, knows staying home for high school isn't a barrier to entry for Division I basketball. His brother Devoe went from Pickering High School to the University of Minnesota.

But as an elite big man, Thompson wanted to test himself against other top bigs. Joseph needed to upgrade academically. Both have succeeded beyond their expectations.

But it's clear each of them craves something he wasn't getting at home. Like aspiring NHL players from the United States who come to Canada for major junior, there's something to be said about

being in a place where what they care about most is cared about deeply.

"The exposure, the hype, basically the hype," Joseph says. "In Canada, not many reporters come to games, not many D1 coaches. Here the media are at the games, the college coaches, the fans. It's like [the provincial] championship every game."

Thompson nods and finishes his teammate's thought. "If you want to play basketball at the highest level and make basketball part of your lifestyle and take it as far as you can go, then you come down here."

### ■ ■ ■ Tough to Say Goodbye

Connie Joseph admits she had her doubts about having her youngest son leave Canada in Grade 11 to play basketball in the United States, outside Las Vegas, no less: "The plane is flying away and you're looking at the palm trees, I was like, 'I can't believe I'm leaving my kid here,' " said Joseph, a project manager with the Ontario Ministry of Natural Resources. "Honestly, it was going through my head, 'What am I doing?' " But as her son blossomed academically and athletically, her fears were eased. "For every kid, it's different," she said. "But this was the right decision. His academics have improved. He got the marks needed on his ACT [American College Testing], and basketball wise, the exposure that came with winning the national championship was really positive for him."

Andrea Thompson put her faith in her oldest son when it came to allowing him to leave home at sixteen, first for New Jersey, then to Findlay Prep in Las Vegas, where he transferred in the middle of last year. "No, it wasn't a hard decision. Tristan isn't a regular kid. Okay, he [was] sixteen, but he's so mature," said Thompson, a schoolbus driver. "He needed a challenge, he needed to go see the tough ones. In the United States, they play tough. Here, they don't play that hard."

### ■■■ A Basketball Team Like No Other

Findlay Prep is not your average high school basketball program. First of all, it's not named after the school it's attached to—Henderson International—but after Cliff Findlay, a wealthy Las Vegas businessman who established an endowment estimated at $500,000 (all currency U.S.) to fund an elite basketball program in Las Vegas modelled after the tony prep schools in the U.S. Northeast. He funds every aspect of the program, including the 3,000-square-foot house the team lives in with a pair of assistant coaches, each player's $17,000 tuition at Henderson, the salaries of two full-time coaches, and a travel budget that would put most universities to shame. It's unabashedly elitist.

"Everything we do is geared toward preparing them for the next level," says Mike Peck, Findlay's head coach. His record over three seasons is a glittering 94-3, and all his graduating students have qualified academically for Division I. "When they go to college, I'm not saying it's not going to be hard, but they're not going to be surprised by anything. Six a.m. conditioning? Individual workouts? Lifting weights? They've done that. Keeping up with classwork? They've done that. Travelling? They travel more than any college team in the country."

Is there a payoff? Beyond the gratification of placing every graduating senior on a Division I basketball team, those around the program anticipate that with the growing commercialization of high school basketball, Findlay could be in line for considerable sponsorship dollars to offset the cost of running the team. The question now is where. Henderson International will be closing after this year, it was announced last week, but it's believed the Findlay basketball program will affiliate itself with another Las Vegas-area private school next season.

◀◀ **Source:** This article was originally published in *The Globe and Mail*, March 5, 2005. Reprinted with permission.

## When a Career Reaches a Crossroads
### By James Mirtle

**77.**

*The decision looms for every major junior player—whether to keep playing hockey or get on with life. Teams in the Canadian Hockey League (CHL) offer some lucrative scholarships, which makes the decision for young players even harder, and the chosen path can sometimes provide detours of its own.*

■■■■■■

Darryl Boyce's journey through junior hockey is typical for a Canadian kid.

Drafted at sixteen, in the sixth round of the 2001 Ontario Hockey League (OHL) draft, Boyce left his hometown of Summerside and moved to join the St. Michael's Majors in Toronto. It was 1,600 kilometres from home and just the first step in a long road that Boyce—with average size and skill—hoped would end in the NHL.

Four years later, after playing more than three hundred junior games, Boyce attended the Carolina Hurricanes' National Hockey League (NHL) camp as an undrafted free agent, but got cut by that team and again by the American Hockey League's (AHL) Hershey Bears.

At twenty-one, his dream of jumping into professional hockey had taken a detour, a common story for the majority of major junior players.

"I was just playing hockey and thought that's all there was out there," Boyce recalled.

"That's what I thought I was going to do for the rest of my life. It was a reality check, for sure."

Boyce ended up taking a scholarship from the OHL to go to the University of New Brunswick (UNB) and two years later, is with the Toronto Marlies of the AHL. At twenty-four, his pro hockey dream isn't dead.

Between 400 and 450 players finish their Canadian Hockey League junior careers every year, and all but the elite few—those who do not go on to the NHL immediately—reach the same crossroads as Boyce. Do they continue to play wherever they can find a paycheque as a pro, or shift focus and head to college or university?

The CHL's scholarship program has made that choice more difficult. Over the past twenty years, scholarships have evolved from small, inconsistent financial awards from individual teams to standardized, league-sponsored packages.

Now, they are becoming substantial enough to give even high-school aged players with U.S. National Collegiate Athletic Association (NCAA) scholarship potential a reason to consider playing major junior instead.

The scholarships, available to every player, are designed to reward major junior players who likely won't be going to the pros. It's pay-as-you-play: the more years in major junior, the longer the payout for post-secondary education once the junior career is over.

In the Quebec Major Junior Hockey League (QMJHL), where players receive the least amount of funding, they can receive up to $4,000 a year to cover the relatively low post-secondary tuition in Quebec.

Western Hockey League (WHL) graduates receive full tuition and books for every year they play in the league.

The OHL, meanwhile, has made the biggest scholarship funding push of the three leagues within the CHL. After some bad publicity over an unpaid scholarship that resulted in a lawsuit from former player Brody Todd and agent Todd

Christie two years ago, the league adopted the WHL's system of administering scholarships funds centrally.

The OHL has also beefed up its packages, offering a full ride for the first time to players entering the league this season—tuition, books, fees, and room and board for the equivalent number of years played. However, the full ride is available only to first-round selections in the annual midget draft—players who would be of most interest to NCAA schools.

The three leagues estimate they will contribute a combined $2.6 million toward scholarships for major junior graduates this year, an average of more than $40,000 for each of the CHL's sixty teams. Teams also cover their players' education while they're playing.

As a result, more than four hundred major junior grads are playing Canadian university hockey while on some form of a scholarship.

"It's an investment," said Joe Birch, the OHL's director of education services. "That's what our teams are doing, we're investing in young people and either their education or their hockey. It isn't looked upon as a burden. It's business as usual."

Yet, some in the industry question whether increasing scholarship awards are keeping in step with CHL revenues.

Two of junior hockey's marquee events, the world junior championship and the Memorial Cup, contributed $6.9 million to CHL team coffers in the past year, dwarfing the amount currently spent on players' education packages. The CHL also receives millions in player-development fees as part of an agreement with the NHL, and generates profits from more than 2,200 regular-season and playoff games annually—all while paying most players small weekly stipends.

Critics argue that revenues can be shared more fairly with players.

For one, only about 32% of CHL players are tapping into the scholarship program, and those who never pursue college or university receive no financial benefit upon graduation. For those who do entertain the idea of post-secondary education, their window is closed within eighteen months of leaving major junior.

Players may pursue a pro career in the lower minor leagues the first year after major junior, but it's often an either/or proposition. And those who sign a contract in the NHL, AHL, or top European leagues, are ineligible for scholarship funds no matter the length of their career.

"There's certainly an argument to be made that players should be getting a bigger piece of the pie, so to speak," Christie said. "Players are basically receiving the exact same compensation [about $50] now that they were receiving in the early '80s on a weekly allowance basis.

"Now, the league's response to that would be that, 'Well, the education packages have expanded dramatically,' which they have, but I doubt the education packages have expanded even close in proportion to the league's expansion in revenues and the expansion in team values."

Birch, who played for the OHL's Kitchener Rangers and London Knights more than a decade ago, argues that the dollar values associated with players' scholarships will continue to grow. He said the OHL's new full-ride package will begin to affect teams' balance sheets in 2011, when that crop of players begins to attend university.

"People tend to criticize us because our weekly stipend for players is only $50 a week, but never seem to mention that our scholarship program is what it is today," Birch said. "I know exactly how far the program has come because of what I went through and what our scholarship program was when I played. And it wasn't anywhere near where it is today."

Former players say that having the full-ride scholarships in all three leagues would give them more options for their education.

Jean-Philippe Brière, a high-scoring centre for the Rimouski Océanic and Chicoutimi Saguenéens from 1998 to 2003, said his $3,500-

## Where They've Gone

In an analysis of more than three thousand players who finished their major junior careers between 1999 and 2007, an average of 26% played university (CIS) hockey within the first two seasons after graduation. (League totals add up to more than 100% due to players playing in more than one league in this time period.)

|  | WHL | OHL | QMJHL | CHL |
|---|---|---|---|---|
| NHL | 13% | 12% | 6% | 11% |
| AHL/IHL | 35% | 30% | 20% | 28% |
| ECHL | 27% | 23% | 20% | 23% |
| 2nd tier pro | 10% | 11% | 13% | 12% |
| CIS | 23% | 31% | 23% | 26% |
| Top Euro | 6% | 5% | 5% | 5% |
| 2nd tier Euro | 2% | 2% | 2% | 2% |

Source: Gabriel Desjardins / Behindthenet.ca

a-year scholarship paid for a good portion of his industrial relations degree at Laval University while he lived with his parents in Quebec City. He said he had to turn down an admission offer from McGill University in Montreal because of the costs.

"If they were paying my rent, maybe my decision would have been different," said Brière, who was the QMJHL scholastic player of the year in 2001, and now works as a human resources co-ordinator with a large pulp-and-paper mill.

"The program is still very good. But if players can have a little bit more money, for sure, it's going to help because $3,500, it's not that much money for the year."

Regardless of where players end up, they have to begin using their CHL scholarships eighteen months after they leave the league or the funds are no longer available. Those who play more than a half season of pro hockey must also sit out an additional year before they are eligible to play in the university system, an option few players in their early twenties go for.

WHL commissioner Ron Robison says it's necessary for the leagues to set limitations on the scholarship system.

"We believe it's important for a young person to get on with his career goals and make that decision," Robison said. "We have players that play as overagers at twenty and, potentially, they can play a professional year at twenty-one. So we feel by the age of twenty-two, you should be certainly making a decision to get on with your academics and pursue it."

It's a decision that results in the majority of graduates never taking advantage of their scholarship. Even Boyce, who starred for UNB for two seasons, was lured away by the Marlies in 2007, and left half of his OHL scholarship on the table.

About one-third of CHL grads take advantage of the scholarship offer. Most of the other two-thirds go on to various pro leagues, while a small percentage drop out of hockey entirely.

Roughly 35% of CHL players opened their careers in the East Coast Hockey League (ECHL) or other lower minor leagues—where players are paid between $350 and $700 a week over a twenty-four-week season—and few in that group left to play university hockey.

The reasons many don't pursue an education could be related to academics, but coaches in the university system say that, while it can be difficult to get CHL graduates into schools with high academic requirements, most who want to pursue post-secondary education are able to get in through upgrading or as mature students.

For those with the grades, the drive, and the willingness to accept their immediate future lies outside of pro hockey, the scholarship program offers a chance to move on. Some players even double-dip, drawing scholarships from both the CHL and their school.

"In some respects, it is a full ride to a Canadian university," said Blair St. Martin, a former Medicine Hat Tigers defenceman who went on to play hockey and complete medical school at the University of Alberta.

"Between 80 and 90% of my post-secondary education was a direct result of the CHL scholarship fund, so it's been a very big part of me being able to pursue my career."

St. Martin, who finished two years of university while in the WHL and is now a third-year urology resident, says CHL teams stocked with high-school dropouts are a thing of the past. While he has heard the stories from Tigers' alumni about teams that had almost no players attending school, he said the leagues now ensure everyone goes.

"It's unfortunate. It's the best level of hockey in our country, but there's still this idea that you have to sacrifice your education to play there," St. Martin said. "That was the case twenty years ago, but it's not now."

## ▪▪▪ CHL "Contaminating" Kids in Terms of Eligibility, Berenson Says

Red Berenson knows there are fewer and fewer Canadians coming his way through the U.S. National Collegiate Athletic Association ranks every season, but he doesn't chalk it up to improved education packages in major-junior hockey.

The veteran coach of the University of Michigan Wolverines maintains that the shift of young Canadians away from the U.S. system has more to do with recruiting rules than beefed-up scholarships.

"I think what's happened is that the Canadian Hockey League has done a good job of contaminating these kids in terms of their eligibility," said Berenson, a Regina native and former NHLer who has coached in the NCAA for twenty-five years. "They're drafting these kids at fourteen out in Alberta and B.C. and fifteen in Ontario, so they draft them and get them excited about playing in the O [OHL] or the Dub [the WHL] and they bring them up and play them in a game and they're done. Once they've played a game, they've lost their [NCAA] eligibility.

"They can tell the kids they're getting everything they're getting in the U.S., but they rarely do."

Berenson said the Canadian system puts more of a priority on grooming players for pro careers than ensuring everyone gets an education.

"The big difference really between those kids [playing Canadian university hockey] is that, in most cases, their hockey careers are kind of on the down side now," said Berenson, adding that his team will spend upward of $400,000 (U.S.) on scholarships this season. "The kids that are coming down here, their careers are on the upswing. The good players want to get an education, too. It's not just the kids that aren't good enough to play pro.

"I'm a former pro player myself and, for me, there's life after hockey."

◀◀ **Source:** This article was originally published in *The Globe and Mail*, March 18, 2009. Reprinted with permission.

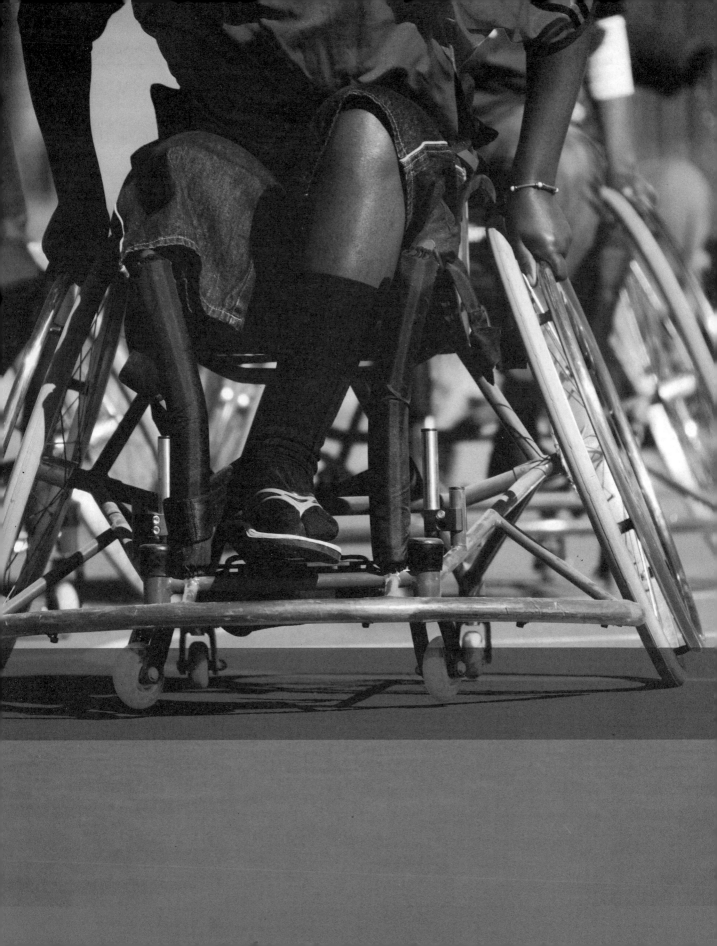

# Section 13

## Disability and Sports

**D**isability studies is a growing area of academic interest, and disability sport is a growing area of research in the sociology of sport. This section begins with an article by Lauren McKeon, whose sister is a Special Olympian. McKeon asks difficult questions such as, "Why won't you let me play?" She argues that the Special Olympics, rather than being inclusive, have begun to mirror the mainstream high-performance system, with the vast majority of funds raised through charitable initiatives and sponsorships going to a few high-functioning athletes who enjoy competitive and travel opportunities. This is not the only critique of the Special Olympics. Keith Storey has authored two articles (see references) that raise a number of concerns about the Special Olympics including, for example, the fact that the individuals who would benefit greatly from integration are presented with segregated opportunities in sport.

In his article "Everyone Deserves the Right to Reach for the Sky" André Picard profiles Canada's leading Paralympian, Chantal Petitclerc. He notes the condescending and patronizing attitudes that are faced by athletes with a disability, and gives examples of the politics of access.

James Mirtle profiles Greg Stewart in "Hoop Dreams at Arm's Length." Stewart is a basketball player with a prosthetic arm who played CIS basketball for Thompson Rivers University in British Columbia. There have been a number of examples in recent years of athletes with disabilities who have fought for the chance to participate in able-bodied sport, perhaps the most famous being sprinter Oscar Pistorius (often referred to as the "Blade Runner" due to the artificial limbs he uses in competition).

Profiles of athletes are a way of coming to understand disability sport, especially when they are placed in the context of barriers that individuals must overcome in order to participate. But Grant Robertson's profile of Earle Connor adds another dimension to the barriers—Connor was described as "the fastest man on one leg," and then failed a drug test. Grant Robertson's article, "His Name is Earle," profiles Connor at the time when he was returning to competition after serving his two-year suspension.

### Additional Suggested Readings and References

- Blatchford, C. 2006. "Stop Noticing the Disability." *The Globe and Mail*, March 4.
- Millar, E. 2010. "The Unsporting Event: Are the Paralympic Games Encouraging Disabled Athletes to Win Big by Aiming Low?" *The Walrus*, March.
- Robinson, L. 2000. "Meet the Real Olympians." *The Globe and Mail*, October 24.
- Storey, K. 2004. "The Case Against the Special Olympics." *Journal of Disability Policy Studies*, 15(1), 35-42.
- Storey, K. 2008. "The More Things Change the More They Stay the Same: Continuing Concerns with the Special Olympics." *Research and Practice for Persons with Severe Disabilities*, 33(3), 134-142.
- Tucker, C. 2005. "No Dissing their Abilities: Canadian Athletes Compete Internationally at the 22nd Défi Sportif." *The Dominion*, May 10.
- Wong, J. 2004. "Nation Builder of 2004: Chantal Petitclerc." *The Globe and Mail*, December 11.

# 78. Why Won't You Let Me Play?
## By Lauren McKeon

*Is the Special Olympics discriminating against the kids it's supposed to help?*

■ ■ ■ ■ ■ ■

When my sister Carol first started soccer at age eight she more closely resembled a pylon than a player. When she did move, it was to sidestep away from the ball. Picture that scene in *Braveheart* where a blue-faced Mel-Gibson-as-William-Wallace leads the onslaught of sword-wielding, battle-crying Scots against the English. I imagine my sister saw something similar whenever the other team came toward her. It wasn't that the kids wearing different coloured pinnies were particularly scary—most were anything but—that's just the way Carol is: different. So were all the kids in her league.

I spent four years as assistant coach of Carol's soccer team for Challenge League Sports—an organization for athletes with special needs in the Durham region of Ontario—and it was there I truly learned that different is not a dirty word. So did Carol. Among those other athletes, Carol found not only acceptance but friendship and a chance to simply be herself. None of her teammates cared that for that first year she was afraid to "get in the game." They also didn't care that some players used walkers or wheelchairs, that two or three always ran the wrong way, or that, inevitably, one player tried to spend the game picking dandelions or doing gymnastics. They were a team and they were having fun.

Not that things were idyllic. There were bullies and more skilled athletes who, at times, could dominate the game. And the other coaches and I did spend a lot of time encouraging players to run the right way, kick the ball, and stop picking

flowers: next to fun, learning the fundamentals of the game and developing those skills were key. But we didn't keep score and what seemed to matter most was that those kids who spent so much time on the outside were finally on the inside.

Challenge League—which, like other grassroots sports groups, is affiliated with, but not fully integrated into, Special Olympics Canada (SOC)—has teams with different skill levels for each of its sports. So too does the better-known Special Olympics. But unlike Special Olympics, affiliates such as Challenge League give as much attention to the worst as to the best players. Carol, who is developmentally handicapped, will likely never be high-skill. (The "developmentally handicapped" label applies to a person whose developmental level is considerably out of synch with his or her age—but the extent and areas of the delay can vary from person to person.) For Carol it means that although she is fifteen, she learns and develops—emotionally, intellectually, socially—at a significantly slower rate. She is not dumb, but would have, years ago, been called "mentally retarded." Since that first summer in 2000 she has become a good soccer player and has added basketball, baseball, bowling, and hockey to her list of sports. But with the exception of bowling, she has never officially worn the Special Olympics crest. And there is a reason for that.

When most people think of the Special Olympics they picture cheery children with Down syndrome or autism, perhaps somewhat befuddled by the life around them. With marketing material full of inspiring images of young athletes waving victory Vs, hugging in camaraderie and "Winning at Life," SOC promotes a specific image of its mission and its athletes. But like so many marketing campaigns, the pictures used to make the sell don't tell the whole story. It is true that SOC is inspiring, enabling, and, well, special, but it is not the organization so many visualize: one that is there for everybody. Contrary to popular perception, the reality is that SOC's highest-ranked athletes—those who go on to provincials, nationals, and worlds—are often adults. Perhaps more troubling, however, is that the hierarchy of competition tends to favour the more able athletes. These are the athletes who, while they may not appear as frequently in promotional materials, receive a disproportionate amount of the revenue the pitches generate.

The Special Olympics movement began gaining momentum in the early 1960s, when some people were beginning to wonder if society had wrongly sidelined those with intellectual disabilities. The most acclaimed of these early disability activists is Eunice Kennedy Shriver, whose siblings included John F., Robert, and Rosemary Kennedy. In June 1962, she opened Camp Shriver in the park-sized backyard of her Rockville, Maryland, estate. Thirty-five boys and girls attended, there to prove that sports wasn't beyond them. Shriver's sister, Rosemary, who had intellectual disabilities exacerbated by a lobotomy in her twenties, is believed to have been Shriver's inspiration. By 1969, through her parents' Kennedy Foundation, Shriver had established thirty-two camps across the country, attended that year by more than ten thousand children with intellectual disabilities.

At the same time, Toronto researcher and professor Frank Hayden was questioning the assumption that lower fitness levels among those with intellectual disabilities—half that of their non-disabled peers—were a direct result of their handicap. His work demonstrated that, given the opportunity, people with special needs could become physically fit and acquire the necessary skills to compete in sports. The low fitness levels, he concluded, were actually a result of study participants' sedentary lifestyles—in turn a result of exclusion from the recreation readily available to other children.

Hayden's work took him across the border to meet with Shriver, and when U.S. educator Anne Burke submitted a proposal to the Kennedy Foundation for a track-and-field-style Olympics competition for those with intellectual disabilities, Hayden was there to make sure Canada was represented. Shriver, not surprisingly, accepted the proposal and Hayden brought in an old pal, Harry "Red" Foster.

The broadcaster had, from early in life, spent much of his time and money working with those with intellectual disabilities. He accompanied a floor hockey team from Toronto to those first games in 1968, and was likely there when Shriver addressed the opening ceremony: "The Chicago Special Olympics prove a very fundamental fact, the fact that exceptional children—children with mental retardation—can be exceptional athletes, the fact that through sports they can realize their potential for growth."

Foster returned to Canada inspired to lay the foundation for a movement in this country, and the first Special Olympics Canada event was held in Toronto the following summer. SOC would continue to grow throughout Foster's life and long past his death in 1985. It was incorporated in 1974 as a national, charitable volunteer organization, to which by 1995 all provinces and territories belonged.

Today, Special Olympics is a worldwide organization, with approximately 2.5 million athletes in more than 180 countries. There are over 31,000 Special Olympics athletes in Canada alone—and many more with special needs who play for other leagues not part of Special Olympics. (The Special Olympics is often confused with the Paralympics, which is geared toward those with physical disabilities, and held in tandem with the Olympic Games.) The last Summer Games were held in 2007 in Shanghai; the next will be the Winter Games in Boise, Idaho, in 2009.

But the push for growth has come at a cost; it is a grassroots movement that has become so large it has adopted a necessary-for-growth system of cash-generation and bureaucracy. And while Special Olympics Canada may be expanding, it's not taking all of its members along with it.

In February, having made the switch from coach to spectator (and now journalist), I travel with Challenge League's basketball group for a tournament. The site for the 2008 Kingston Special Olympics Basketball Classic, the gym at Holy Cross Secondary School, is sliced into two half-courts. A lonely and resigned row of spectator chairs, one for each side, makes up the dividing line—nobody is here to watch except the most dedicated volunteers, the most proud parents. There are no encouraging signs, no giant foam fingers, no flashing cameras. Though there are higher-skilled athletes in attendance, most here, even those in the higher divisions, have never been to the provincial, national, or world games.

Here, the competition is split into four divisions: adapt, D, low-C, and high-C. In the adapt and D divisions there are players who may walk up the court or dribble the wrong direction or miss every time; in low- and high-C, players have the basic skills down, and, in the higher class, are perfecting those skills. Officially, there are technical requirements for each class but this event isn't a qualifier and there are no representatives from Special Olympics here to make the call.

That may be why some teams are so mismatched. The 11:40 AM game in the low-C division pits Oshawa Challenge League against the Oakville Skywalkers. The Challenge League team is made up of mostly younger teenagers. Some have Down syndrome, some are otherwise developmentally delayed, some have behavioural issues. They are short, at least, comparatively. The Oakville team is made up of men, mostly in their mid- to late-twenties, who have muscles that ripple, men who have long hair tied back with bandanas, men with tattoos and baggy NBA-style shorts. It wouldn't be an exaggeration to say most of them top six feet. As they enter the court there is an incredulous chorus from the Challenge League of: "We have to play them?"

The Special Olympics' slogan may be "Winning at Life," but today the Challenge League teens lose at basketball 11–62. There's an oath, evoked at the world level, for Special Olympics: "Let me win, but if I cannot win let me be brave in the attempt." For some, especially the Special Olympics movement at its grassroots, it truly is the brave attempt that matters most—not winning. But for others—like a team of frustrated young basketball players— even the chance at attempt proves cheap and elusive.

While there is an obvious contradiction inherent in introducing a competitive element to something many join for fun and good health—it's hard to know who should advance when you don't keep score—Special Olympics' emphasis on winning means that only an elite few get the most out of the program. An institution that was founded on principles of inclusion has, ironically, come itself to exclude.

The competitive culture has become a strong part of SOC's mandate. As Special Olympics Ontario CEO Glenn MacDonell says, "If you don't have competition, you don't have sport."

The Special Olympics are organized as follows: world, national, provincial, regional, then individual communities within those regions, and clubs within each of those. To make it to the provincial level, an athlete first has to place high enough at a regional qualifier to advance. Triumphing at a regional earns an athlete an invitation to provincials, but victory at provincials does not necessarily mean an invitation to go to nationals. When it comes to teams especially, like floor hockey or baseball, the provincial chapter often has to choose which team will advance, because there are only so many available slots and, with more than one division, more than one team that will have placed first. "The selection of athletes to national games is a carefully controlled process with established parameters," reads the SOC manual. "Chapters should remember that, as in other sport bodies, higher-level competitions are meant for athletes who have, through their performance, proven themselves capable."

mismatched teams

A similar process of selection occurs when those at the national level are chosen to proceed to the world games. Chapter offices are reminded that "it is important that athletes have demonstrated the ability to cope with the pressures involved in travelling, competing, and being removed from their usual environment for up to a two-week period." Arguably, this provision attempts to guarantee a smooth, safe, and rewarding trip for all those involved—but it also tends to favour those placed in the higher-skilled divisions.

As in the big Olympics, many of the athletes who participate at higher levels attend more than one world games and participate in more than one sport, or more than one variation of it—say the 100-metre sprint and the 200-metre sprint. I know one athlete, who is in his late twenties, who returned from the recent Summer Games in Shanghai with three medals. He has been to the 1998, 2002, and 2006 National Summer Games, the 2003 and 2007 World Summer Games, as well as the 2008 National Winter Games. While he is clearly an exceptional and dedicated performer, he is not unique. Many talented athletes participating in SOC are recruited and nurtured once they show potential and a desire to compete at the grassroots level. They may not all have such impressive records, but most do have an ongoing presence at the higher competitive levels.

The Special Olympics doesn't consistently reward lower-functioning athletes, but it does use them to promote the games to volunteers, would-be athletes, and funders. A few years ago, one Special Olympics club member gave the Ontario office a picture of two young girls with Down syndrome gleefully smiling. It's now plastered on banners, awards, and other promotional material. She wonders how much reward those two girls, and others like them, are receiving from all that promotion. "People donate thinking it's going to stay in the community, but once they write that cheque, it's gone," says Theresa Grabowski, co-founder of Challenge League Sports. "I think the intent of it all is good—and nothing runs perfect—

but it's not as evenly distributed as they'd like you to believe it is." She adds, "But, I've got to say, on the other hand, if I were fundraising and marketing for these people, that's the way to do it."

It is true that a more equitable distribution of donations would go a long way toward mitigating the ill effects of the emphasis on competition and winning. Special Olympics Canada has its own operating budget, mainly devoted to the higher levels of competition and the athletes competing in those games. In 2006—the most recent return filed to the Canada Revenue Agency—its revenue was $4.8 million. About $1.3 million of that came from fundraising, both corporate and event based, just under $30,000 from tax-receipted gifts—donations—and about $950,000 from the Canadian government. There is about $2.1 million worth of revenue slotted under the "other" category.

Grabowski does wonder sometimes why those selling Special Olympics cannot receive a greater chunk of the benefits. She founded Challenge League Sports in 1994 with her husband because at the time her local region had no Special Olympics programs for her eight-year-old son. "When we took him to [Special Olympics] swimming they wouldn't take him because he couldn't swim two lengths of the pool. If you can't swim two lengths you're not ready for training, for competition. It was, 'Go learn to swim, because we're not teaching you how to swim,'" she recalls. But, she is careful to add, programs and policies can vary from club to club. "If you go to another town they might have the volunteers and the space and the time. They might teach you how to swim, or develop your swimming so that you can become competitive and swim in a race."

At the time, though, her only choices were to enroll him in a generic club, which she tried to do with baseball—"The parents were not too understanding of why he thought he could go to bat twice, or why he didn't want to stop at first base, or why he was sliding at home—all kinds of whys"—or start her own club, which she also did. In the beginning, it was just a group of people she

Challenge league

St + goal

knew getting together to play baseball, but after an ad in the local paper, Challenge League was officially formed. For the first five years, the organization wasn't even affiliated with Special Olympics and made a go of it on its own, aligning itself with the community-level Oshawa Minor Baseball Association for support.

Grabowski knows as well as anyone how much cash is needed to make the Special Olympics world go round. For SOC, each athlete is expected to set a goal at the beginning of her training, which could range from just learning how to kick a soccer ball, to beating a personal-best time, to making it to the provincials. The greater the goal, the more resources required to support it. Money is needed for everything from the van ride to a regional qualifier potentially hours away, to renting the space to host that qualifier, to paying for the winners' medals. Plus, there are many other things that go into making an athlete's experience complete, like year-end banquets and galas. Organizers, says Chris Ivey, a volunteer ski coach at the community level, always make sure there's that social aspect after any meet or tournament. For some, he says, "it's a bigger deal than actually skiing. That aspect of it is huge." So's the cost.

Fundraising can work on national, provincial, and regional levels. Corporate sponsorship is largely national and provincial, with the majority of the money raised going to sponsor the official games and the athletes who attend them. Hellaina VanErp-Rothenburg, district developer for the Georgian Bay area, admits it is difficult to balance the needs of the few with the needs of the many: "A community may fundraise to send one athlete to a national games, where that amount of money may otherwise cover the budget for two sports addressing the participation needs of up to thirty athletes."

For money to stay in the community, it has to be raised locally, usually through small-scale events like bake sales or golf tournaments, which means teams at the grassroots level can struggle to evenly distribute their funds. Having enough money to spread across all programs to put athletes on an even financial playing field would definitely be beneficial, VanErp-Rothenburg adds. Those at the Ontario provincial office, like MacDonell and Lynn Miller, Special Olympics Ontario's head of marketing, acknowledge that much of the funding is gobbled up by competitive costs—a large focus of Special Olympics energies. They point to new grassroots initiatives, like school programs and community games, as areas where they're seeking to improve fund distribution and opportunity. Even VanErp-Rothenburg doesn't see the competition-based fundraising as a real point of criticism. "Everyone has the equal chance to go on to the games," she says. "By encouraging one athlete, you're still bringing a bit of a dream, or a bit of a goal, to the other athletes by being an ambassador for that town. It's always been a good thing—but it is true it's a lot of money."

She also points out that putting a face on fundraising works both ways. Although it is often the whole club that will fundraise to send one or two athletes on to national games, it is hard sometimes to get individuals or small businesses in the community to donate, say, $500 for field or track time as opposed to something concrete like sending an athlete to the games.

While grassroots fundraising is hard work, on a national level SOC is a relatively easy sell. It's a "feel-good charity," says MacDonell, and as a result, it's a natural place for corporations looking to be community-minded to invest. Special Olympics has partnerships with RBC, TSX, and Air Miles—to name a few. Each sponsor brings its own level of support to SOC, which can include one-time large donations, an ongoing commitment, or unique product-based benefits. For instance, RBC, a sponsor since 1968, has donated money, but also sponsors large fundraising galas and encourages its employees to volunteer and donate; TSX donated $100,000 for the recent National Winter Games in Quebec; and Air Miles allows corporate clients and cardholders to donate their miles to SOC to cover travel to games.

One of Special Olympics' best-known partner-ships is with Staples, with its decade-old Give a Dollar, Share a Dream campaign. The campaign is negotiated with Special Olympics Canada, but the fundraising falls to individual clubs and chap-ters, of which there are hundreds across Canada. Members are "invited" to spend an afternoon at Staples promoting Special Olympics and helping out at the store. They must take pictures to send to the national office to prove they've been there.

The campaign raised about $600,000 in 2007, says Miller. But each of the local clubs that par-ticipated received only $250. The rest of the funds were kept at the provincial and national levels to help send athletes to games.

Special Olympics does state that money raised through the Staples campaign will go to both national athletes and community groups, but donors have no idea just how much of their contri-butions will go toward things like paying the costs of sending an elite-level swimmer to Shanghai.

While cash is much needed for local Special Olympics groups, it's still no cure-all. Even when there's enough money, there's not always enough of a more important commodity: people, some-thing Special Olympics is heartbreakingly short on. The volunteer base is growing, notes VanErp-Rothenburg, but not necessarily at the same rate as potential athlete participation, especially in urban areas. Plus, says a regional developer in Northern Ontario, an elite coach—such as the experienced hockey coach he recruited early this year—is not likely to volunteer at the adapt level, perhaps where he'd be needed most. Volunteers like that, he says, are "really not the type of guys who're going to develop an adapt program, because they've got that competitive, killer instinct. They want to develop the team and take it on competitively."

As SOC's own strategic plan for the years 2006 to 2010 notes, "Public support for people with intel-lectual disabilities is often based on charity rather than empowerment and inclusion." So while SOC receives sizable chunks of money from companies like the TSX Group and Coca-Cola, the challenge is to get corporate support for less money-ori-ented drives. For instance, Glenn MacDonell is encouraging the trend of corporate volunteerism, which asks company employees to donate time to one-day events like Hometown Games.

Canada's immense geography poses another significant obstacle to the success of local Special Olympics affiliates. Northern Ontario—or any area, really, that's distant from its provincial office—faces a new set of challenges. For one, it lacks sponsorships and, as a result, funding for travel to compete in tournaments, says regional coordinator Sean Bryan. "We're just so far apart that competition becomes a big problem. A lot of folks in the south may not realize and recognize that—they're not used to distance and travel cost being a barrier," he says. Also, he adds, it's harder to solicit donations in an area that's in an economic downturn. Plus, the dearth of teams means that even when money is scraped together for a trip, clubs are so spread out that getting to a meet could take a day, leaving few eager or able to make it.

Special Olympics Ontario is currently working on the northern Ontario planning and action strategy with members from the provincial office and representatives from the north, to address the region's unique challenges. Bryan believes it has merit, but the plan has been greeted with distrust by many in his area, who feel the provincial office has not done much for the north in the past and is unlikely to start now. However, he is optimis-tic, and believes in the power of Special Olympics to do good: "Northern Ontario is definitely on the cusp of a great new season. Tomorrow we will look back on the challenges of today as the cata-lyst that brought us into our own, revitalizing and strengthening our SO programming and family."

Yet the north isn't the only region facing chal-lenges. I spoke to one representative from south-western Ontario who was considering shutting down clubs in one community for lack of volun-teers, and she was not alone. "It gets to the point," she says, "where we have the one-to-four, one-to-five ratio for safety purposes for the athletes and if we don't have the volunteers to provide that ratio, we can't really provide that program for them." Things are so stretched, she adds, "I have some of my smaller communities where my community coordinator is actually the head coach for four sports, and they're the treasurer and the secretary and they take all the athletes to ambassador programs."

This is unfortunate, given what grassroots clubs do for their participants. "I don't think we can underestimate the impact Special O has on athletes' lives," says Bryan. "It's easy to forget that when you look at problems." SOC has made a huge impact on the life and health of his brother, who was two hundred pounds overweight before he started. For many athletes, Special Olympics, and sport, is like a lifestyle. Athletes don't realize the challenges of what is going on behind the scenes, Bryan says—or at least they shouldn't.

Chris Ivey, whose brother is also an athlete in Special Olympics, adds, "You can tell if athletes didn't have this opportunity available to them, they'd get very little activity in their lives." The rest of us, he says, take it for granted. "We find ways to get involved with sports and activities—it's fairly easy to do—but when you're a person with disabilities, you need help to participate in an activity. It's great that an organization like Special Olympics exists and provides that opportunity."

Indeed, many I spoke to were hesitant to criticize SOC because not only is it the biggest, most influential—and sometimes only—kid on the block, it's the kid who does a lot of good. After all, Special Olympics is not just about sports, points out Jenn Klaus, an Ontario regional coordinator. Among many benefits, "athletes can enhance their social skills in an environment where they're not being judged. They can excel at things here that in the outside world they really can't."

At least, that's the idea. Special Olympics positions itself on the principle that any person is good enough to compete. But for some, that chance may never come, whether for reasons of skill or, as in many far-flung areas of Canada, lack of opponents.

Special Olympics is trying to fix this, but with varying degrees of both effort and results. That's why it started Hometown Games and why it holds events like the Kingston Invitational, which, in theory, give the experience of competition to lower-skilled athletes.

"We need more competition, not less competition, for all of our athletes and we need it at a local level," says MacDonell. "Hometown Games is a miniature one-day competition that is just like the big games." It may not really be just like the "big games"—the salmon-and-industrial-green interior of Kingston's Holy Cross can attest to that—but for some who may never even make it to regionals, it holds the best approximation.

It's hard to judge whether a trip to Shanghai compares to the "whoop" feeling of scoring one's first goal or winning one's first round robin. And there is no reason why an elite athlete with special needs should want anything less than any other elite athlete: to make it to the very top and win. They deserve our respect and support, but so, too, do the athletes who may not win, or compete, or even have the desire to; those athletes who simply revel in play; and all those who wear the Special Olympics logo and present themselves as the face of the organization. They need the same level of opportunity to do better and to do more—regardless of their chance of winning a medal. As Bryan says, for many who are part of the grassroots movement—athletes, volunteers, and relatives, "It's not about the half of a fraction of athletes that are going to the World Games in Japan. It's about the 99.9 percent of athletes who just need to build this kind of activity into their life." And the uneven levels of opportunity for Special Olympics athletes seem to run counter to their own message: "Losing the game is not defeat. Never competing is."

In 1999, my family took Carol to a figure-skating learn-to-skate session run by Special Olympics. Contrary to what the program description suggested, there were no coaches to assist during hour-long ice times—and it was either sit despondently watching Carol struggle or do the assisting. Luckily, we knew how to skate, but not every parent or sibling did. A fee was charged for the winter, presumably to cover ice costs. After one of those dismal sessions we met the Durham Dragons, who were practising on an adjacent ice pad. The Dragons is a hockey club for players with special needs and is not associated with the Special Olympics. Carol has been playing with the team since 2000.

At first it was both agonizing and thrilling to watch her fulfill her dream of becoming a goalie. But her team and her coaches continued to encour-age her no matter how many—and in the beginning it was definitely many—goals she let in. Last year, at the big tournament, in Arlington, Virginia, Carol had her shining moment. She stoned the opposing team's star player, who'd already scored five goals, when he was sure he would make it six with a penalty shot. Two weeks later, at the year-end banquet, the head coach told the story of "the best save of the tournament." Carol received a standing ovation from the entire league.

◀◀ **Source:** This article was originally published in *This Magazine* in May/June 2008. Reprinted with permission.

# Everyone Deserves the Right to Reach for the Sky      79.
## By André Picard

Chantal Petitclerc is the picture of good health. With sixteen "Olympic" medals, she is one of the most outstanding athletes in Canadian history. No qualifying adjective is required. No asterisk appears beside her world records. The gold on the five medals she collected this summer in Athens—in the 100-, 200-, 400-, 800-, and 1,500-metre races—is no less lustrous than medals belonging to racers who use form-fitted shoes instead of streamlined chairs.

Yet when we speak of Ms. Petitclerc and her stunning athletic accomplishments, the starting point is too often her disability, the fact that she uses a wheelchair.

The same is true of our attitude toward the other 3.6 million Canadians living with disabilities—physical, developmental, and psychiatric.

Individually or collectively, we too often slap "them" with the label "disabled," and we do so dismissively.

This condescending attitude was glaringly evident when Ms. Petitclerc was named co-winner of the prize as the country's top track-and-field athlete, rather than the outright winner.

Athletics Canada has been hammered, and rightly so, for that decision—which clearly implies that a disabled athlete, no matter how dominating, cannot compare to an able-bodied one.

But sport is not the only area where the disabled are treated unjustly. A patronizing approach also pervades public policy.

The health and social welfare systems tend to classify the full range of people with disabilities—the factory worker who loses his legs in an industrial accident, the man with Down syndrome employed by the YMCA, the stockbroker with bipolar disorder, and the retired teacher blinded by macular degeneration - as needy, and relegates them to specific treatment and assistance programs.

While many treatment programs are excellent—though often in short supply—the "assistance" programs are often anything but.

The greatest threat to the health of many people with disabilities is not their underlying medical condition, but poverty—income being one of the most powerful determinants of health.

People with disabilities are systematically marginalized. Children with disabilities are not well integrated into the school system, which results in a lower level of education that translates into lower income later in life. Seniors, the age group where disability rates are highest, find themselves doubly isolated in a society built for speed and uniformity.

Yet many people with disabilities do work—the majority of those of working age toiling away like everyone else. Because most disabilities are invisible, they are hidden in plain sight. What we do know, however, is that most people with disabilities are not reaching their potential.

The 12% of the population living with disabilities, by and large, want the same thing the other 88% want: a good life.

As Al Etmanski, founder of the Planned Lifetime Advocacy Network, points out, a good life can be defined the same way for virtually everyone: "Friends and family, a place of your own, basic wealth, choice, and—this is one that is too often forgotten—the ability to make a contribution to society."

Mr. Etmanski says the key issue for the disabled is citizenship: If our commitment to rights and equality is real, then the disabled need to be full citizens, meaning they have an equal opportunity to participate fully in all aspects of community life.

Equality, of course, does not mean sameness. But it does necessitate flexibility, accommodation, and commitment.

When Ms. Petitclerc was injured—her spine snapped by a barn door that fell on her—the community rallied: An elevator was installed at school and machinery was modified to work with hand controls. In gym class, she swam while others ran.

Nice gestures all, but, as full citizens, the disabled should not have to depend on generosity.

Public buildings and workplaces should be accessible—not as an exception, but as a matter of course. So should parks, ski hills, and beaches.

There will be grumbling that accessibility is costly, but the reality is that the changes that benefit the disabled benefit everyone: the mother pushing a baby carriage, the grandfather with fading eyesight, and the child learning in an environment with his peers—all his peers.

Access cannot be merely be a token gesture. As Rick Hansen is fond of saying: "It's not enough to get in the theatre. You should be able to get on stage."

Which brings us to the real injustice that has befallen Ms. Petitclerc. Nobody in this country—perhaps in the world—better embodies the Olympic credo "faster, higher, stronger." So why was Ms. Petitclerc relegated to competing at the Paralympic Games, a week after the "real" Olympics? There is no place for such segregation in the Olympic movement, or in a just society.

What Ms. Petitclerc has reminded us, through her deeds as well as her words, is that the yearning for belonging and meaning unites us all. The sooner she and other people with disabilities are afforded the full rights of citizenship, the richer we will all be.

---

◀◀ **Source:** This article was originally published in *The Globe and Mail* on December 16, 2004. Reprinted with permission.

# Hoop Dreams at Arm's Length

## 80.

By James Mirtle

*Canadian Interuniversity Sport rookie making an impact with unique prosthetic limb*

■ ■ ■ ■ ■ ■

His motto is "the one-armed man can."

It's something Greg Stewart applies to every facet of his life, and it has guided him to many things in his nineteen years.

The one-armed man can play the piano. Or lacrosse. Or tie his shoes. He can counsel disabled children. Go to university. Win a world disabled volleyball championship.

The one-armed man can even play university basketball at Canada's highest level.

At 7-foot-2, Stewart is obviously built for the game, but with one caveat: He was born without a left arm below the elbow. Still, with the aid of a specially designed prosthetic limb, he's made a big impact—no pun intended—in his first Canadian Interuniversity Sport campaign.

Stewart is a student at Thompson Rivers University, a new school in his hometown of Kamloops, and the university's fledgling men's basketball program, the WolfPack, finished their season last Friday with an 89–79 loss to Simon Fraser.

It may have been a bumpy, 2-18 season for the first-year team, but the gains were there—especially for Stewart.

"I'm really proud of him," WolfPack head coach Nevin Gleddie said. "This year I found, especially after Christmas, he was so consistent that we did move to starting him. I don't know if he had that as a goal, and I don't know if that would have been realistic.

"But it turned out he worked hard enough and he was keen enough. He's constantly coming to me, you know, 'Coach, can you work on this with me?' He does that more than any other player I've ever had."

Stewart struggled in the first half of the season, with a scoring average of slightly more than 6 points while playing sixteen minutes a game. He returned from the Christmas break, however, with renewed vigour and doubled his scoring average to 12.5 points in twenty-one minutes a game in the second half of the season. He finished the season fifth in the country with a field-goal percentage of 63.5.

"It felt great," Stewart said. "Sometimes, in games, I started to feel like a dominating force, like I could control the game. I look at it as being 80% mental and 20% physical, so the arm—it's not a huge factor."

Playing at such a high level of basketball with his disability is far from easy, and Stewart is considered a sort of trailblazer for what he has accomplished so far. His prosthetic arm—worth nearly $10,000 and paid for in part by the War Amps' Champ program—went through an approval process with Canada Basketball, and while it does allow him to play at a high level, it does have its limitations.

The arm's hand is essentially a scoop apparatus, one that Stewart can use to corral—but not hold on to—the basketball, something that makes him the quintessential "one-handed" player.

With his height advantage, it's no surprise Stewart can dunk the ball, but it's often trying to rebound where he runs into problems. Opponents began to key on the prosthetic arm in games, often fouling it without Stewart's knowledge.

He confesses that one of these days he's hoping to detach the arm and leave the culprit holding the evidence, so to speak.

Gleddie has seen the arm's limitations in practice nearly every day throughout the season and says Stewart is often frustrated with what he cannot do on the court.

That's why, Gleddie says, it was upsetting to hear some call the arm's use into question this season.

"Initially, I think there was some resistance. People felt that he was ..." the coach said, pausing. "The word 'club' was thrown out quite a few times. You know: 'He shouldn't be allowed to play with that club.'

"I know one of the teams, I talked to their sports psychologist, who had said their team was talking about it [the arm] and how that wasn't fair. And he said, 'Fine then, next practice, you can hold a Ping Pong paddle in one hand and we'll see how you do,' " Gleddie said.

"They were kind of saying it was an advantage. And he told them, 'How can it be an advantage to play with one arm?' Like seriously."

For Stewart, the remarks were just more adversity to overcome. Currently without a major, he hopes to begin social work courses next year and work toward becoming a high-school counsellor.

In the off-season, Stewart works in a similar role with the War Amps—which he says are "like a second family"—talking to disabled children and acting as a role model.

Gleddie says he has seen Stewart's inspirational side at work in games.

"What I've enjoyed, and particularly this year I've noticed it more, is that people are just genuinely appreciative of what Greg can do," he said. "When he plays, you're in a visiting gym and he scores, he always gets applause—always."

"I just feel [my success] gets the word out," Stewart said. "It lets people know that there's success out there, even though you might have a disability or you might be suffering from something."

While his coach projects Stewart will become an all-Canadian over the next three years, Stewart likes to think even bigger—nearly as big as his own stature. When asked about future goals, he doesn't hesitate in saying he dreams of becoming the first disabled player in the National Basketball Association.

It may sound unbelievable, but, then again, so does everything else Stewart has accomplished so far.

◂◂ **Source:** This article was originally published in *The Globe and Mail* on February 14, 2006. Reprinted with permission.

## 81. His Name is Earle
### By Grant Robertson

*Two years after a drug test destroyed his reputation, champion sprinter Earle Connor is on the brink of recapturing his former glory as the world's fastest man on one leg. But this time, he's chasing more than fame and fortune.*

On a summer day in 2004, a young man steered his black Ford Explorer down the narrow alley behind his home in downtown Calgary. As he coasted to a stop, a truck suddenly pulled up alongside.

"Are you Earle Connor?" the driver asked.

"Who are you?"

"I'm here to do a test."

Mr. Connor felt sick.

Perhaps you have never heard of him, but at that moment, Earle Connor was the world's fastest man on one leg. His victories weren't just impressive. Some were downright cruel, with his opponents only halfway down the track when he crossed the finish line.

He was so good that some people thought that he might become a household name—and make disabled sport famous in the process. The Athens Olympics had just started, with the Paralympics about to follow, and Mr. Connor, who is missing his left leg from the knee down, was favoured to win two gold medals and carry the Maple Leaf.

"Earle was a bit of a golden boy for us," recalls Patrick Jarvis, then head of the Canadian Paralympic Committee. "He made people look differently at the sport."

The first disabled athlete to join national track coach Les Gramantik's training program in Calgary, he travelled in an elite circle, golfing with Tiger Woods, hanging out with Sean Connery, and playing tennis with Boris Becker. Nike had come calling with a sponsorship deal.

In fact, he so dominated disabled sport that he had begun to outgrow it. In recent years, he had managed to sprint into the realm of able-bodied athletes, nearing a mark few thought possible: 100 metres in less than twelve seconds, on one leg and a titanium prosthetic engineered for speed. At that pace, he could have competed in the 2000 Olympics and not finished last; in 1896, the first year the modern Games were held, he could have won gold.

Clearly, he was on the brink of perhaps the biggest achievement of his life. But as the man in the truck followed him inside, everything began to fall apart.

The next morning, he called Mr. Gramantik, who was already in Athens. "I think I just failed a drug test," he said.

In truth, he knew perfectly well he had failed. His career was ruined. But one question loomed: Why would someone who could win so handily be caught cheating?

Two years later, with the good life just a memory, Earle Connor is sitting in a Starbucks in Calgary, ignoring patrons who can't help but stare at the robotic-looking prosthetic that pokes out from his knee-length shorts.

It is August 2006, and he is attempting a comeback. Despite having spent two years in exile and giving up most of his training—instead of the gym, he went to work at 7 AM—he believes that he can recapture his past glory, that he hasn't ruined his life.

"I have to do this," he says. "I have to know if I can do this."

He is looking ahead. In a few days, his two-year suspension from Canadian athletics will officially end. Then he will board a plane for Germany and compete for the first time. And he has vowed that, if he doesn't cross the line first, he will never race again.

But while he was banned from competition, he was also banned from having a coach, and so has been training on his own. "I don't feel fast," he says over the coffee-shop din. "Not like I was."

On a rainy afternoon one week later, he lowers himself into the starting blocks at a sparsely populated stadium in Leverkusen, on the Rhine just north of Cologne.

He knows the track well. It was here, in 2003, that he set three world records in one day—the last after he'd broken his prosthetic leg.

When the limb suddenly buckled near the end of a 400-metre sprint, he was so far in front that he was still able to get back on his feet and limp across the finish line first.

But as he begins to warm up, his eyes fill with tears. His return is more emotional than he had expected. He tries to stay focused. He needs to win, which means he needs to beat Wojtek Czyz.

In the two years he has been away, Mr. Czyz—the pride of Germany—has assumed the throne as the world's top amputee sprinter. He took gold in Athens, and now holds one of Mr. Connor's former records. He also has the Nike contract.

Kneeling in Lane 3, Mr. Connor listens intently for the sound of the starter's pistol. But something is wrong. Lane 5 is empty. Where is Wojtek Czyz?

To understand Earle Connor's story, it helps to go back to the beginning, when he had two legs, if only for a little while. He was born on July 30, 1976, in Castlegar, British Columbia, to first-time parents Dave and Diane Connor.

She was a teacher, and he was a disc jockey, spinning vinyl for a local AM radio station. However, when the baby arrived, there were complications: His left leg had somehow developed without a fibula, the smaller of the two lower bones used for bearing weight.

It was a rare condition with no known cause. Only two other babies were born without fibulas in North America that year, one in Mexico, one in the United States. Curiously, they were also on the West Coast.

All three families had the same choice to make: Insert a steel rod into the leg, which might not work and would require surgery every six to eight months as the children grew, as well as confine them to a wheelchair for much of their youth. Or the leg could be amputated.

"Like any parent, you have to look at all the options. And of course you always think in the back of your mind that something could be done," Dave Connor now says. "We went down to see doctors in the U.S. and the answer was no, there was no reconstructive surgery they could do."

After three months of agony and consultation, the Connors made their choice. In the fall of 1976, Earle was bundled up and taken to B.C. Children's Hospital in Vancouver, where the left leg was severed through the knee.

"The doctors said the easiest way to get us to adjust as parents was to change the bandages

ourselves," Mrs. Connor says. "But changing the bandages was the most traumatic. Here is a little baby, and all of a sudden there's no limb where there was one before."

The baby cried for days. His father remembers taking the bus home after the surgery and feeling helpless.

"Earle was screaming, and the bus driver wanted to kick us off. But I told him what happened, and I told him not to do it."

Although new to fatherhood, the deejay was no stranger to a microphone, so he got on the bus's public-address system and explained the situation to the annoyed passengers. Another sound interrupted the screams.

"People started clapping," he says. It wouldn't be for the last time.

When Earle was still quite young, the Connors moved to Saskatchewan, where his mother had been hired to teach on a Native reserve. The money was good and the family had relatives near Saskatoon, so the relocation made sense.

Small-town life on the Prairies had a profound impact on young Earle. He was the only kid with a rubber limb, and the only one on the reserve with blond hair—which, even more than the leg, made him feel like an outsider. His mother remembers the Halloween that he took her mascara and tried to colour his hair black. "He was worried he wouldn't get any candy."

Even then, he could run, and he soon realized that sports was currency he could use to buy acceptance and respect. But in rural Saskatchewan, there were few disabled sports. So Earle learned to play with the rest of the kids, or sit on the sidelines. It made him more focused than your average nine-year-old.

"I've never, ever said this to Earle," Diane Connor says on the phone from Moose Jaw. "But I don't necessarily know if Earle would have concentrated as much on sports if he had been able-bodied. Who knows if he would have had the same determination?"

He tried minor hockey, and when skating proved cumbersome, he strapped on the goalie pads. His cousin Chuck Tersky played against him in a neighbouring town and remembers the dressing-room chatter when the two teams met.

"It was a lot of 'Guess who we're playing? The team with the goalie that has one leg. We're gonna kill him,' " Mr. Tersky says. "Then, maybe after the game, they'd be talking about how he stopped them on a breakaway. He faced a lot of prejudices."

Mr. Connor's desire to compete against able-bodied kids drove him away from disabled sports. When the family moved near Saskatoon and the opportunity to join Paralympics came up, he wanted nothing to do with it.

Stan Holcomb, a prosthetist in Saskatoon and himself a disabled athlete, remembers trying to persuade the boy to take part, but he always refused.

Mr. Holcomb had competed in the 1976 Paralympics for Canada and raced against the legendary Terry Fox at meets in which the best they could hope for in the 100-metre sprint was a twenty-second performance, because the prosthetics made back then were so clunky.

Recognizing that young Earle showed promise, Mr. Holcomb handed him a brochure whenever he came to have his limb adjusted. Finally, at fourteen, he agreed to give it a try, and the family drove to Calgary for a national disabled meet. But when the boy beat the adults to win gold in the long jump, he was told he was too young to compete at the real Paralympics.

"I was like, 'Okay, that's it, then. I'm done,' " Mr. Connor now recalls. " 'I'm not doing it.' "

It wasn't until years later, after he had graduated from high school, that he finally changed his mind.

One afternoon in 1996, he was lounging on the couch watching TV and happened upon the 100-metre final at the Atlanta Paralympics. He watched unimpressed as Swiss sprinter Lukas Christen took gold with a world-record time of 13.54 seconds.

"I'm faster than those guys," he remembers thinking. "And they're on TV."

It was no idle boast. Fast-forward a few years, and Earle Connor is tearing the sport apart.

When Lukas Christen set that record, skeptics figured that no amputee sprinter would ever break the thirteen-second barrier. Technology had taken the sport a long way - prosthetics were now marvels of modern engineering - but there were certain physical limitations that simply could not be overcome.

For example, losing a leg, even if just from the knee down, means that key muscles don't function as they should. "There's a lot of things, biomechanically, that are different," says Mr. Gramantik, the track coach who had to rewrite his training program when he agreed to work with Mr. Connor. Whenever an amputee runner strides, "it's a huge challenge to bring that one leg forward," he says.

In 1998, two years after strapping on a real running leg for the first time, Mr. Connor broke the Christen record, clocking a time of 13.18 as a relative unknown.

After seeing him race, veteran amputee sprinter Rob Snoek pulled some strings to help him enter a race for cash in San Diego. "I called them up and said, 'You've got to let this guy in.' "

Mr. Connor walked away with $25,000 (U.S.)—most of the money that was up for grabs.

Over the next few years, his times fell like a thermometer on a cold day: 13.38, 12.81, 12.61, and 12.36.

"The stories were apocryphal," Mr. Jarvis says of the Paralympic Committee. "Here's this guy who just shows up one day and says, 'I want to be a sprinter.' "

Soon, just running fast wasn't enough. Winning became paramount. At the 2000 Paralympics in Sydney, he took gold in the 100-metre final, but finished second in the 200 metres when a misstep on the first corner cost him a few seconds.

He was livid, and the next day had "Silver Hurts" tattooed on his right foot. A day after that, he took the medal to a beach outside Sydney and hurled it into the ocean.

At the coffee shop in Calgary, as he tells this story for the first time to someone outside his immediate circle, Mr. Connor speaks softly but insists he has no misgivings. "I said, 'This isn't going to happen again. I'm not taking the silver home with me.' "

The frustration also made him decide to drop the 200 event and focus on 100 metres. Winning became so automatic that it soon was clear he needed a new challenge. "Nobody was even close to him," Mr. Gramantik says. "He could toy with the opposition, he was just that much better. So we needed to set our own objectives."

They decided upon a new barrier: under 12 seconds. It was a delicious number – faster than Jean Randriamamitiana, an Olympian from Madagascar who clocked a leisurely 12.5 seconds, on two legs, at the Sydney Games, and within reach of elite women sprinters.

If he could break 12 seconds and move beyond disabled sprinting, "the controversy alone would raise the sport to another level," Mr. Jarvis says.

Looking back, Mr. Connor acknowledges that he became obsessed with the target. "That's all I wanted. I knew I was going to win gold medals. I knew I was going to set world records in Athens, but I wanted 11.99."

It began to look possible. In 2003, he broke his own world record with a time of 12.14. Then, in early 2004, Mr. Gramantik took his squad to Texas to train against U.S. college sprinters.

On a desert night at the University of Texas at El Paso, Mr. Connor lined up against seven young women. He beat six of them, feeling that he could have gone faster, and then his time flickered across the digital scoreboard: 12.01. The numbers were seared into his memory—his best time ever.

Having come so close to his goal, he says, "I was mad. It pushed me even more. I'd train constantly. I'd have to be in bed at 9 o'clock. I'd have to get twelve hours of sleep. I'd have to do this, I'd have to do that."

But something was troubling him. In early 2001, he complained to his doctor about swelling in one of his testicles. Fearing cancer down the road, the doctor ordered it removed. The surgery went fine, but Mr. Connor's testosterone level plummeted.

Most men don't notice a minor fluctuation, but when testosterone drops sharply, the impact is felt throughout the body. Lethargy, loss of strength, a depleted immune system, and an inability to perform in bed are all possible consequences.

"If you read through that list, you're reading the story of an eighty-year-old man," says Mike Nolan, a Canadian decathlete who battled low testosterone throughout his career. "Not only is it embarrassing, but if you're trying to be an elite athlete, you pretty much feel like shooting yourself in the head."

He sought medical clearance to take testosterone supplements, and was ridiculed in athletic circles. Some accused him of lacking machismo. Others noted that testosterone is a favourite of cheaters. It helps the body build muscle and can allow athletes to recover more rapidly after training.

Having seen what Mr. Nolan went through physically, Mr. Connor began wearing a prescription testosterone patch to boost his hormone levels. And knowing what he had gone through emotionally, he told few people about his surgery and no one about the patch. Women and athletes had no business knowing, he figured.

At that point, he also made a cataclysmic error in judgment: Obsessed with his training and fixated on breaking through twelve seconds, he neglected to seek permission from Canadian athletic authorities that would allow him to use the patch legally.

When Mr. Gramantik asked about his testosterone levels after the surgery, he said the papers were at home and he planned to fill them out.

"He would never go too deep," the coach recalls. "But he was under medical supervision, so I didn't get too much into it. He wasn't totally willing to explain all the details of his health life."

Mr. Connor had figured out that, once he took off the patch, the synthetic testosterone could be flushed from his body in a matter of days. For three years, he used this system, halting the treatment several weeks before a meet. He never failed a drug test.

But in June 2004, the Canadian Centre for Ethics in Sport (CCES), which administers Canada's anti-doping policies, brought in a new system for testing athletes. It didn't want any embarrassments at the Olympics. Random exams were being stepped up. A list of three thousand amateur athletes was compiled, and officials were sent out to collect urine samples from hundreds of them.

One of those agents showed up at Mr. Connor's home and waited. As soon as the man identified himself, he knew his life as a sprinter was over. Athens was still weeks away and stuck to his backside, with two days left on the prescription, was a testosterone patch he shouldn't be wearing.

"Testing outside of competition is important for us," says Paul Melia, president of the CCES. "We often say that it's only the stupid athlete that gets caught in competition."

The testosterone patch is known to be a favourite of athletes searching for an edge because the hormone spike it delivers dissipates so soon after the square is discarded. "It's more difficult to detect ..." says Christiane Ayotte, director of the Montreal lab that tests for the World Anti-Doping Agency. "It's causing us a major problem."

To make matters even worse, Mr. Connor's urine sample also turned up signs of nandrolone. This was especially troubling. Surgery or not, if testosterone made an appeal to Canadian doping authorities difficult, the evidence of a second performance-enhancing substance made it nearly impossible.

Nandrolone is a curious steroid. It has been known to arrive in the body through tainted supplements taken by tennis players. It's also one of the easiest steroids to detect, since evidence of its use lingers for weeks. It can be masked to some degree, but athletes who use it are inviting a positive doping test.

Mr. Connor remains steadfast that he has no idea how nandrolone got into his system. The CCES finds this hard to believe, but doesn't press the point, since he accepted the two-year suspension for the testosterone patch and served the penalty without raising a fuss.

"I have asked him," his father says, "and he has said he doesn't know. So I take his word and leave it at that. The bottom line is, whatever goes into a person's body is their own responsibility. If he did try to cheat, he got caught. If he didn't, and something was in there, it happened. I just told him that I was behind him."

Cheating isn't unknown in the Paralympics. For example, wheelchair athletes have been known to use a tactic called "pinning," in which they poke needles into unfeeling limbs to produce adrenaline before a competition. "A lot of times, when people talk about 'cutting corners' in disabled sports," Mr. Connor says, "they're talking about pinning."

But breaking the rules is not widely talked about, so when it becomes public, the sport is shaken even more than mainstream athletics.

Everybody was talking about Mr. Connor. Word of the suspension sparked more media coverage than he had ever received as an athlete. He made the CBC National. His cousin Chuck Tersky was travelling in Europe on his way to Athens at the time, and he remembers watching Mr. Connor's name flash across a TV set in Holland.

Patrick Jarvis remembers that he was walking through a park in New Brunswick when his cellphone rang. He stopped in his tracks the moment he heard a colleague say: "We've had an incident with testing, but you're not going to believe who it is."

It was a devastating blow. "I know everybody likes to talk about the feel-good stuff in our sport," Mr. Jarvis explains. "But for us, when it comes to our legitimacy, results matter. And Earle was breaking those misconceptions."

The man he had seen as the next great ambassador for the disabled sport was now its biggest pariah.

This spring, Mr. Connor decided he had had enough despair. He had lost friends and his sponsors, except for Ossur, a prosthetic manufacturer who fixes his leg. Nike, which had signed him just a month before the doping test, exercised a clause to cancel the deal.

But a month after his suspension he had been introduced to Stephanie Sterne, who knew about him only from a newspaper article about the day he set the three world records that had been posted at the Calgary gym where she worked.

On their first date, they went to a movie. But the second one was unusual, to say the least. Over dinner, he told her everything—the surgery, the suspension, and the life he no longer lived.

As time went by, she realized that he was not ready to move on. "He just used to dwell on it all the time." Sometimes she would console him, and sometimes "I would just say, 'It's over. Enough is enough.' "

By then, the world of disabled sprinting had crowned a new king. Wojtek Czyz was four years younger, had a website, six figures' worth of endorsements and one of Mr. Connor's records.

None of this sat well with his predecessor, whose racing leg sat buried in the back of a closet. He decided it was time to rescue it from purgatory.

Mounting an assault on Mr. Czyz would not be easy. The rules of his suspension prevented Mr. Connor from training with a coach and from running alongside other top-ranked athletes—the key ingredient, he says, that had brought him to the cusp of breaking the twelve-second barrier.

In April, when the snow melted in Calgary, he took a tape measure to a lonely schoolyard near his house and began pacing off 100 metres. He didn't own starting blocks—he had never had to buy them—so he just crouched on the grass, day after day.

Every so often, softball players from a nearby diamond would wander over and strike up a conversation. "They would get a few beers into them and say, 'What's that thing on your leg?' "

He always obliged those who stopped to talk, but he never told them who he was. He wanted solitude.

To simulate the sound of a starter's pistol, he had Stephanie smack two small blocks of wood together. Every night before going to sleep, they would do ten practice starts, with him crouching on the bedroom floor.

He set only one rule while training: no clock. The risk was too high. Stop the watch too quickly and his times would be spectacular, wait a fraction too long and it would crush his confidence. As a result, when he boarded the plane for Germany, he had no idea what he was capable of running.

Leverkusen was exactly as he remembered it. John McFall, the British amputee who had been there the day he set all those world records, was in Lane 2. And over on the sidelines was the hometown favourite: Mr. Czyz.

But five minutes before the race, the champ—primed and ready to go—suddenly gathered his things and left. He and his coach had been watching intently as Mr. Connor warmed up, doing a sprinter's typical mock starts: crouching in the blocks, imagining the sound of the gun and charging forward for 15 or 20 metres.

Without a coach to calm his nerves, however, the comeback kid was tense and emotional, trying too hard and running too fast. Had Mr. Gramantik been there, he would have spotted the problem immediately and told him to save it for the race.

Sitting in a Calgary pub months later, Mr. Connor admits that "I was showing off, trying to show everybody I was still fast."

But would that alone be enough to make the German bolt?

Mr. Czyz did not respond to requests for an interview, but Mr. Gramantik says that sprinting is much like boxing. If the champ doesn't get in the ring, he can't be dethroned. Had Mr. Czyz somehow lost to Mr. Connor in Leverkusen, he risked losing his sponsorships as well. There aren't many dollars to go around in amputee sprinting, so it's usually winner take all.

"These guys, more so than anybody else, live and die by their endorsements," Mr. Gramantik explains. "And sometimes the smartest thing to do is not race, if you don't think that you can win."

Also, the world championships were just around the corner, and everybody knew that Mr. Connor wouldn't be there because his suspension had kept him off Canada's roster. So this race wasn't crucial.

When the gun went off, sounding remarkably like two blocks of wood being smacked together, Mr. Connor leaped forward and, at the 10-metre mark, couldn't stop himself from taking a slight glance to either side.

Mr. McFall was slightly behind. By 60 metres, he could no longer be seen or heard—which was important, since prosthetics make a thundering racket on the track. At 95 metres, Ms. Sterne nearly jumped from the bleachers as Mr. Connor crossed the finish line in 12.67 seconds—a time he later dismissed as "pedestrian" even though he was well out in front.

Track officials quickly approached, and said: "Mr. Connor, please come with us." He was led to a small room where Ms. Sterne, as his witness, watched him suck back water and then urinate into a cup.

The tests would came back clean—as did a second random test back in Calgary three months later. Mr. Connor says he has sworn off the testosterone patch until he and Stephanie decide to have children, which he hopes will be after the 2008 Paralympics in China. He wants another chance to run for his country—for redemption. And maybe respect.

A few weeks after Leverkusen, Mr. Connor is back in Calgary, living in anonymity.

Late one night, he gets out of bed and walks to his computer. There, in the glow of the screen, he waits for the results from the world championships in Holland to be posted.

When they finally appear, Wojtek Czyz has won. But the time is a mere 12.79.

Mr. Connor picks up the phone and starts leaving messages for people he knows.

"I feel great," he says. "I'm back. I'm ready for Beijing."

◀◀ **Source:** Grant Robertson is the media writer with *The Globe and Mail*'s "Report on Business." This article was originally published in *The Globe and Mail* on February 14, 2006. Reprinted with permission.

# Section 14

## Future and Sports

Predicting the future is clearly hazardous; it is much easier to examine the sociological process of social change with regard to changes that have already occurred than with those that may occur. Thus, this section really deals with some issues that are relatively new in the area of sociology of sport, but which seem likely to continue to be important in the future.

As athletes have become bigger, stronger, and faster, and performance enhancements of various types have become the norm, injuries and other forms of wear and tear on athletes' bodies are increasingly becoming an issue. In his article "The Killing Field," Randy Turner provides an in-depth examination of the phenomenon of former professional football players dying at a relatively young age. Research is at an early stage on this issue, and has focused mainly on head injuries; but serious epidemiological research is likely to be necessary as gymnasts, figure skaters, football, and hockey players, and athletes in various other sports from the recent era of high performance begin to age.

The next two articles deal with the burgeoning movement of sport for development and peace. Bruce Kidd provides an insightful overview of the movement ("The Power of Sport for Development") from an insider's position as chair of the Commonwealth Advisory Board on Sport (CABOS). And Grant Shilling's article ("Hunting Waves—and Peace—with the Gaza Surf Club") provides a specific example of the use of sport (in this case surfing) in a peace-building initiative.

Alex Hutchinson deals with the issue of new technologies and performance enhancement in sports in "Faster, Higher, Sneakier," which asks in the subtitle: "Does Canada's top secret sports technology program undermine the Olympic spirit?" Hutchinson argues that programs such as Own the Podium's Top Secret are deliberate attempts to move athletes away from a level playing field—to tilt the playing field in their favour by employing technologies not available to all athletes. This thought-provoking article raises all kinds of questions about the advantages enjoyed by athletes from wealthy nations, who win the vast majority of Olympic medals.

The section concludes by returning to "the Canadian specific," hockey. Brandon Hicks addresses the concern that "we're not developing as many kids as we used to," noting how changing demographics in Canada are leading to a decline in the number of hockey players.

### Additional Suggested Readings and References

- Dryden, K. 2004. "The Game of Our Lives: Reflections on Money, Fans and the Future of Sports." *Maisonneuve* 7, February/March.
- Peritz, I. 2010. "Moroccan Hockey Team Brings Muslims and Jews Together to Make Peace on Ice." *The Globe and Mail*, 14 April.

# 82.

# The Killing Field

## By Randy Turner

Nick Benjamin's kids used to make fun of the way he ate his fried chicken.

In lighter moments around the family dinner table, they would mimic how the big man's two ring fingers would be sticking straight out. You see, Benjamin couldn't bend those fingers anymore, the collateral damage of nine seasons playing a game so punishing that the former Winnipeg Blue Bombers offensive lineman had a ridge of hardened tissue form at the back of his neck from the thousands of jarring helmet-to-helmet collisions.

Turns out, those knobby digits were the least of Benjamin's problems. He was suffering from diabetes discovered during a Bombers training camp in the early '90s—where Benjamin lost fifty pounds in ten days. Without, it should be ominously noted, missing one of the gruelling two-a-day practices.

That was a year after Benjamin—before diagnosis and low on sugar during one game—accidentally walked into the wrong huddle during a game. Recalled his widow, Debbie: "He didn't even know where he was."

But it was the final year of his life that was the hardest. Benjamin was in kidney failure, taking dialysis treatments four times a week. The soft-spoken giant who played with the Bombers and Ottawa Rough Riders from 1985 to 1993 was deteriorating in front of his family's eyes.

And only his family's eyes. After all, the fans don't see what happens after the final whistle blows and they turn off the lights. Too often, it's not very pretty.

"They don't know," Debbie Benjamin said, of the anonymity of pain and struggle. "They just watch the game. But when you live with somebody, you see it. Because I saw how long it took him (Nick) to get out of bed in the morning. Even after he stopped playing. It was ridiculous how many times we replaced the banister on the stairway because without that banister he hardly could get up and down the stairs. The aches and pains he had were ridiculous."

That's the thing about professional football. They can put cameras in helmets, inside the locker room, on cable lines over the field. They put cameras in blimps, for heaven's sake.

But how often do you see a camera around after the cheering stops, and the only action is a grown, broken-down man crawling to the bathroom in the dark of the night?

Debbie met Nick Benjamin at a nightspot called Strawberries almost twenty years ago. She was smitten by the quiet, brawny football player. She had no idea how, so few years later, Benjamin's body would betray him.

"Near the end, it killed me," Debbie Benjamin said, "He was absolutely depressed. To see somebody that was a big, burly football player crawling on his hands and knees up the stairs, or getting up to go to the bathroom in the middle of the night and falling down and crawling to the toilet, it was heart-wrenching. It was very sad to watch."

Last August, at age forty-six, Nick Benjamin died of kidney failure. But Debbie ruefully believes it was an occupational homicide, and points her finger directly at football.

"I think that Nick deteriorated as quickly as he did because his body was already beaten up," she insisted. "I do believe (football) added to it. I think he felt he was cheated out of his life long before it was his time."

For Debbie, her husband's demise isn't all that complicated. She asks, "What's the first thing the doctor tells you? Don't be stressed. Well, he (Nick) went out there every week and stressed the shit out of his body.

"I think that beating your body up the way you do contributes to it for sure," she added. "No matter what you catch later on, your body is so beat up and stressed ..."

How stressed was Benjamin's war-torn body? It was so misaligned, so in disrepair, that one of his buttocks was higher than the other.

"He walked with a limp," Debbie said. "His hips were crooked. His whole body was out of alignment. He had a twelve-inch scar all the way down his spine where he had surgery."

That's what Debbie Benjamin saw. It's what must have also moved playwright and humourist Merle Kessler to acidly observe: "Football players, like prostitutes, are in the business of ruining their bodies for the pleasure of strangers."

Nick Benjamin died too young. And his wife swears football pulled the trigger, dropped the gun and ran.

Nick Benjamin isn't the only former Bomber to die young recently. Cancer took the colourful and bombastic linebacker Tyrone Jones, a linchpin of the Bombers glory years of the 1980s, last June at age forty-six. Just four months later, Steve Rodehutskors, an offensive lineman who also played in the 1980s, died of cancer at age forty-three. Offensive lineman Bobby Thompson, whose Bombers career lasted from 1979 to 1983, died of a massive heart attack at age forty-six in the spring of 2006. Then came word that offensive lineman Orlando Bobo, who suited up for Winnipeg in 2004, died on May 14, 2007, of heart failure. He was just thirty-three.

That's five deaths in just two years with an average age of forty-two years and ten months.

Bombers president and CEO Lyle Bauer, who was diagnosed and treated for throat cancer in 2004–05, isn't unaware of the funereal tolls. Far from it. Over the course of Bauer's decade-long career—glittered with Grey Cup victories in 1984, 1988, and 1990—he was teammates with Jones, Rodehutskors, Benjamin, and Thompson. Bobo was recruited under Bauer's watch and lined up at the CEO's old position at centre.

"It seems like we're losing more guys from the '80s forward now than we're losing from the days before that," said Bauer, who in 1998 was inducted into the Bombers Hall of Fame. "For every one that hits their sixties and seventies, you seem to lose one in their forties. And I don't know what that's all about. You expect guys in their seventies, eighties, and nineties, that's going to be a normal occurrence. But when it happens to guys in their twenties, thirties, forties, fifties, that's a little abnormal."

"And who knows how many others there are that we aren't aware of," added Bauer's former teammate, Hall of Fame receiver Joe Poplawski. "Sure, it's frightful."

And it isn't just the Bombers. The Hamilton Tiger-Cats had lost two promising young players; defensive back Jamacia Jackson, twenty-six, died suddenly of heart failure last April, on the heels of the death of offensive lineman Travis Claridge, who at twenty-seven died mysteriously in Las Vegas of "acute pneumonia, exacerbated by respiratory depression brought on by intoxication with the painkiller oxycodone," according to a CBC report. This past summer, former Tiger-Cat receiver Leif Pettersen died of a heart attack. He was fifty-seven.

Average age of the Ti-Cat trio: thirty-six years, seven months.

The Edmonton Eskimos haven't been immune from grief, either. Former offensive lineman Bill Stevenson, a seven-time Grey Cup winner, died at age fifty-five last year, ravaged by chronic alcohol abuse. Former defensive lineman David Boone was found dead on the deck of his home in Washington state of an apparent suicide in March 2005. Boone, who won five Grey Cup rings, had reportedly suffered from chronic pain and depression from haunting football injuries. York Hentschel, who along with Boone formed a defensive front dubbed "Alberta Crude" in the mid-to-late 1970s, died of organ failure at age fifty-two. Hentschel finished his illustrious career, which included three Grey Cups, with the Bombers in 1981.

A third member of that formidable "Alberta Crude" line, Ron Estay, was diagnosed with cancer last summer. Estay, fifty-nine, an assistant coach with the Saskatchewan Roughriders, is battling non-Hodgkin's lymphoma.

Of course, this is not a phenomenon isolated to professional football north of the border. National Football League (NFL) players are also going to their graves at alarming rates.

According to a 2006 survey by the Scripps-Howard news agency of 3,850 professional football players born in the last century:

- 130 players born since 1955 had died.

- Of that total, the ones who weighed the most were likely to be deceased prior to their fiftieth birthday.

- 28% of all pro football players born in the last century who qualified as obese died before their fiftieth birthday, compared with 13% who were less overweight.

- One of every 69 players born since 1955 is now dead.

- 22% of those players died of heart diseases; 19% died from homicides or suicides.

- 77% of those who died of heart diseases qualified as obese, even during their playing days, and they were two and a half times more likely to die of coronaries than their trimmer teammates.

- Only 10 per cent of deceased players whose birthdates were from 1905 through 1914 were obese while active. Today, 56% of all players on NFL rosters are categorized as obese.

- The average weight in the NFL has grown by 10% since 1985 to a current average of 248 pounds. The heaviest position, offensive tackle, went from 281 pounds two decades ago to 318 pounds.

But when it comes to the Grim Reaper, nothing compares to the dire plight of the Pittsburgh Steelers, a venerable organization whose zenith was reached during four consecutive Super Bowl victories in the mid-to-late 1970s (much like the Eskimos of the CFL).

Consider this fact: The Steelers have lost eighteen former players, age thirty-five to fifty-eight, since 2000.

Seven died of heart failure, most of them offensive or defensive linemen. But the range of causes of death are as wide as they are disturbing.

Offensive lineman Terry Long, forty-five, committed suicide by drinking antifreeze. Centre Justin Strezelcyk was just thirty-six years old when he perished during a high-speed chase with police that ended with a fiery crash into a tanker-trailer. Quarterback Joe Gilliam, who suffered from drug abuse much of his post-playing career and was periodically homeless, died at age forty-nine.

But the most tragic case involved former centre Mike Webster, long considered a cornerstone of the Steelers' dynasty years. Webster's trademark was short sleeves, regardless of the weather. He was considered fearless. Indestructible. They called him "Iron Mike."

Well, not long after retiring, Iron Mike was living in a car, suffering from dementia, which doctors believe was caused by the trauma to the frontal lobe of Webster's brain, the equivalent of "25,000 automobile crashes" over fifty years. Webster also suffered from post-career depression and was once living out of his pickup truck. When he was inducted into the NFL Hall of Fame in 1997, Webster's speech was often incoherent. He died of a heart attack in September 2002.

In fact, all three of the regular Steelers centres from their Super Bowl days of the 1970s are dead: Webster; Jim Clack, who died of heart failure at age fifty-eight in 2006 after a four-year battle with cancer; and Ray Mansfield, who died of a heart attack at age fifty-five in 1996.

When asked once about the disturbing number of deaths, longtime Steelers executive Joe Gordon replied: "Maybe it was something in the water."

Oh, really? Or maybe it was something in the steroids. Pittsburgh Steelers offensive lineman Steve Courson, the first NFL player to openly admit using steroids, died at age fifty after being crushed by a fallen tree. Webster was long suspected of steroid use, as was defensive lineman Steve Furness, who died of a heart attack in 2000 at age forty-nine.

Regardless, the cause of deaths among the Steelers—along with admittedly anecdotal cases in the Canadian Football League (CFL)—run the gamut from accidental to deliberate to simple destruction both during and after football: cancer, liver disease, suicide, heart failure, dementia.

What's more curious, if you ask a lot of former and current CFL players what they think is the life expectancy for a member of their occupation, many don't hesitate to answer.

In fact, this project began not long after the death of Jones to cancer in June. Three days later, a former Buffalo Bills backup offensive lineman named Mitch Frerotte died of a heart attack. He was just forty-three.

I phoned Bauer and simply asked, "Can you explain all this death to me?"

"Well," the former all-star replied, "I've always known that the lifespan of a professional football player is around fifty-five. You know that going in."

"That can't be right," I protested.

"Sure it is," Bauer replied.

Bauer wasn't alone. A quick email to Bombers' current defensive MVP Doug Brown came back, "I think it's fifty-six."

Bombers centre Matt Sheridan, who missed much of the 2008 season due to injury, came up with the fifty-five figure immediately.

So did Hall of Fame receiver Joe Poplawski, a staple with the Bombers from the mid-1970s to the mid-1980s, who nonetheless doesn't believe the life-expectancy figure is universally known.

"The number of people knowing the average age is fifty-five, if you polled people, I think it would be a great surprise," offered Poplawski, fifty-one. "It is a surprise that maybe it hasn't been written about in greater detail."

But maybe it's not more well known because it simply isn't true, that football players don't have a life expectancy some twenty years below the average for a North American male.

"This is not publicized anywhere," offered former Canadian Football League Players Association (CFLPA) president Stu Laird, forty-eight, a former defensive lineman with the Calgary Stampeders. "It's one of those urban legends that may or may not be true. Most players have heard about it, but they don't know if it's true or not."

Without question, the data are too slim and sketchy to determine a firm number for life expectancy, according to most experts and players contacted by the Free Press. That, in itself, is rather unsettling.

After all, professional football is the perfect storm of occupational hazards. Think about it: What other occupation involves prolonged and repeated head trauma; the need to carry up to 150 extra pounds for several years; coping with a post-career in the civilized world and aging with the battle wounds that turn joints into sworn enemies and body organs into weakened hosts of disease? Oh, and it's a profession that in one study ranked in stress behind only surgeon, astronaut, Indianapolis race car driver, firefighter, and president of the United States.

Throw in artificial turf and possible steroid use and you've got yourself a cocktail for an early grave.

Statistics are woefully sparse, but anecdotal evidence abounds in deaths mainly in four categories. One, from carrying too much weight that taxes the heart, such as perennial Pro Bowler Reggie White, dead at forty-three. Two, from crushing blows to the head leading to depression or dementia, such as Pittsburgh's Long. Three, the inability to cope with the loss of celebrity and familiarity in retirement, such as Edmonton's Stevenson. And, four, the general abuse and stress on the body that could impair its ability to fight off disease, which could have been the case with former Steelers receiver Theo Bell, who died at age fifty-two from scleroderma, a disorder that causes hardening of the skin and damage to internal organs and blood vessels.

The direct relationship to football is impossible to prove, largely because not much systematic information has been collected. But at the very least, the deaths cry out for more study.

Still, while football players toss around the fifty-five-year life expectancy as casually as a pigskin during warm-up, other experts are skeptical.

"I don't know the factual basis," said Dr. Arthur "Archie" Roberts, a heart surgeon who now oversees the Living Heart Foundation, based in Little Silver, New Jersey "I would not hold that out as an objective and true statement. Unless you're very careful and have a scientific approach and access to good data, it's hard to be accurate in these predictions."

At least, that's what Roberts, a former NFL quarterback who played with the Cleveland Browns and expansion Miami Dolphins said initially. Because lack of empirical data doesn't make a theory wrong, either.

And it didn't stop several retired NFL players from cashing their pensions out at forty-five, rather than wait until the dreaded fifty-fifth birthday. "You know that tennis shoe commercial?" said one player, responding to a questionnaire in the *Atlanta Journal-Constitution*. "The one about, 'Life is short, play hard'? Well, with the way we're [dying], our motto should be: 'Play hard, die young.'"

It's a credo particularly understood in the trenches. As former Los Angeles Rams offensive lineman Bill Bain once observed: "The actuarial tables show that linemen in this game die at the age of fifty-three. I start collecting my pension at fifty-five. Nice."

Actually, there don't appear to be any such tables. A physician who works for several life insurance companies told the Free Press that premiums are based on industry standards such as height, weight, and family history. Occupation is not a factor, he said.

Old football players don't need an actuary number for life expectancy. Or an actual number, for that matter. They just have to keep going to the funerals for fallen comrades like Jones, Rodehustkors, Stevenson, Boone, Thompson ...

"It can be quite thought-provoking," offered former Bomber and Winnipeg product Leo Ezerins, now a businessman in British Columbia. "It really does hit home, and I start thinking about it a little bit more. There's not dwelling on it, but it's just thinking how quickly the time can come."

When they played, the fate of football players lived and died by a clock that is forever counting down to zero. You can send in the plays faster. You can do a two-minute drill. Or perhaps the best strategy is to simply run the clock out. Take the snap and kneel.

But in this case, the speed of the clock has already been set in motion. The risks manifest themselves.

"I don't know that the numbers say, 'Here's what football players are dying of' that's so specific that you can relate it back," Laird said. "But something is going on in the lives of football players that makes it (life expectancy) so dramatically different than the rest of the population."

Five, four, three, two, one ...

■■■■■■

Let's begin with the meat of the issue. Or rather the fat.

Hector Pothier won six Grey Cups during a sterling twelve-year career on the Edmonton Eskimos offensive line. These days, however, Pothier is all about losing.

Now fifty-four, Pothier has lost about 130 pounds from his playing weight of between 275 and 300 pounds, which ballooned to 375 after retirement in 1989.

"I'm going for the whole kebang," Pothier vowed. "I'm going to lose it all and fight like hell to keep it. I figure this is my last kick at the cat. If I can't do it, I can't do it and I'll have to live with being an overweight guy.

"That'll give me a better shot at being eighty or ninety, which is where I want to be."

Bombers offensive lineman Matt Sheridan arrived at training camp for the 2008 season after shedding some sixty pounds.

Prior to this season, cut short by injury, Sheridan was a poster boy for excess weight. The stress on his body and heart was beginning to take an ominous turn.

Sheridan promised himself to get rid of the excess baggage.

"One of the realities is there's life after football and it's inevitably going to come sooner than expected," the thirty-one-year-old said. "You have to think about those things. No matter how much our coaches strive to live in the moment and you have to keep your focus on, 'How am I going to best do the job I'm being paid to do on the football field?' I also have to do it being conscious of my health long-term, as well."

This would be chamber music to the ears of the aforementioned Dr. Roberts, who grew up in rural Massachusetts dreaming of being a professional athlete and a heart surgeon. He became both.

As a football player, Roberts was once recruited to play for the Montreal Alouettes, who coaxed him to also attend medical school at McGill University. Instead, Roberts wound up backing up Hall of Fame quarterback Bob Griese in Miami before ending his two-year NFL career to pursue medicine.

At the turn of the century, Roberts founded the Living Heart Foundation, which has since tested the beating hearts of more than 1,400 former and current NFL players—and 38 Toronto Argonauts last summer.

Roberts said the data on the risk of professional football to athletes' hearts are only now beginning to be studied seriously. "We don't really have an answer," Roberts said. "We can have our opinions. But for doctors to really determine if the cardiovascular risk has really increased, or the risk and the consequence of concussion ... you'd have to study the data. And those types of studies weren't available and generally aren't available now. So we're left with anecdotal stories."

Still, Roberts is quick to acknowledge the obvious: Linemen on both sides of the border are getting increasingly more massive, and it's an accepted fact that excessive weight leads to greater risk to the cardiovascular system.

"That's true," he allowed. "Now that players are much bigger. What is to come in the future we don't know, but we'd be concerned about it."

Players need to be evaluated, tested, and followed "so we can learn if players are at high risk, who is at high risk, and if we can develop strategies so these guys live healthy. That's the bottom line. That would be a good thing to do in the CFL, as well."

Hence the tests, which Roberts hopes to also continue to conduct in the CFL, which recruited the heart surgeon to Toronto last June.

But the question could be asked: Why hasn't a program like Roberts' been developed sooner league-wide? Wouldn't the death of Reggie White, who died in his sleep of cardiac arrhythmia at age forty-three in 2004 set off some alarm bells?

Of course it did—but only specifically for overweight players with cardiovascular risks.

That seems to be the multi-headed monster facing any investigation into health risks from exposure to professional football. Really, where do you begin? Especially in the CFL, a more transient league made up mostly of Americans who return home after their playing days are over. How can you have accurate data on their lives after football? The long-term ramifications of head trauma are only now being taken seriously. What about all those players from the 1970s with their stories about playing through excruciating pain and concussions?

And how do you determine the impact of steroids when it's impossible to determine who took what and when?

"That's something everybody would be concerned about, but the evidence is lacking," said Dr. Neil Craton, a Bombers physician. "Nobody says, 'Listen, I've been using growth hormone for the past ten years and my buddy hasn't been using it. Which one of us has more health problems?' It's all done under the cloak of darkness and secrecy. Nobody knows."

Craton does know this much, however: "In terms of big athletes ... folks that carry around excessive body weight—whether it's muscle or fat—their life expectancy is notoriously short."

So what's up, doc? If a patient is one hundred pounds overweight, you'd tell them to lose it because statistics show it will reduce life expectancy. Is your patient smoking cigarettes? You tell him he has to quit, right?

Then why not tell a three hundred-pound man with two knee surgeries, who uses his head for a jackhammer, to quit? Isn't he reducing his life expectancy and risking his health, too?

"It's a fabulous question that cuts right to the heart of the sports-medicine world," Craton conceded, with surprising candor. "It's one that's not asked enough and even as you ask it I'm on the other end of the phone here blushing. Because there's a bit of a nudge and a wink when it comes to recommending health behaviours.

"These folks know the risks," Craton added. "You won't find a kid who comes to football who thinks it's going to make him live longer. Most folks know intuitively that smoking and being overweight is bad for their health, yet they still engage in those health behaviours.

"It's a very, very important question. It definitely is a weak spot—and I'll point at myself—in my own professional ethic. Because I don't routinely have that conversation with offensive linemen. I know Matt Sheridan. I'd call him a friend. But I don't sit down and say, 'Matt, you have to stop playing football. It's a risk to your health.'

"It's like saying, 'I'd have a better influence from the inside out than the outside in. If I was to say, 'You know what, I'll decry professional football and say this is hazardous to your health and we should shut the whole thing down. You might not be called a lunatic. But this is a potent community thing and in the United States it's a potent business thing. Everybody is chasing that brass ring."

Craton was being brutally honest about the role of medicine in general, and team doctors in particular, in professional football. Football is here to stay. In fact, just like the participants themselves, the game is getting bigger, especially in the United States. It's not going anywhere and neither are the dreams instilled in so many young men of someday playing professionally.

Besides, telling a twenty-five-year-old athlete who's finally achieved his lifelong goal to walk away from the game because it's not healthy? What are you, an idiot?

"I think if you spoke to 99% of them (young players), I think they'd say they're having the time of their lives," Poplawski said. "If a twenty-year veteran would have come and spoken to me when I was in the midst of my career, I probably would have said, 'You know, at this certain time I'm good and I'm having too much fun to leave the game.'"

That's the response, to a man.

"Absolutely," Laird agreed. "You don't think that far ahead when you're in your early twenties.

We were having such a good time, I wouldn't give it up for the world."

Former Bombers defensive lineman Glen Scrivener would walk around the stadium in Winnipeg as a boy with his father, the late Harvey Scrivener, a long-time Bombers executive. Scrivener was in awe of both, and as a child would envision playing someday in the CFL.

Scrivener would grow—and grow, and grow—to eventually play twelve seasons in the league, including three with the Bombers (1997–99).

"That's all I ever wanted to do," Scrivener recalled, in a recent interview. "It was my refuge. It made me feel good about myself."

Quit? Sorry, wrong animal.

You see, how can you tell a professional football player he should quit because of long-term impact on his health when he's already staring the immediate impacts—broken bones, torn ligaments, concussions—straight in the face every single week?

"You have to understand the beast you're dealing with," Bauer concluded. "These are people who, one, don't want to show fear and, two, don't want to show injury when they play. It's ingrained in them, the culture of it. And you feel you're invincible. You're playing games when you shouldn't be playing. You're doing things to your body you shouldn't be doing. We've all played games when we can barely walk, do you know what I mean?"

Did Bauer feel invincible when he played?

"Definitely," he said.

Does he feel invincible now?

"Hell, no," came the reply of a fifty-year-old man.

■ ■ ■ ■ ■ ■

Glen Scrivener sells propane and propane-related products for a living now.

So how often does Scrivener hear *King of the Hill* jokes?

"All the time," the big man deadpans. He's not laughing.

Scrivener is forty-one years old now and in the midst of starting over. Most of his contemporaries are in middle management, driving company cars, and pulling out corporate credit cards at power lunches.

Scrivener, meanwhile, is hauling himself all over the province by car, getting his start in the spectacularly unglamorous world of propane distribution. On the day we caught up with him, he had started first thing in the morning. If he was lucky, he would get home to his young kids by 8 PM.

No supper at the family table. Just grab a drive-through burger and go to the next job.

Ah, livin' the life.

Yet it wasn't so long ago that Scrivener, who always brandished his trademark Maple Leaf bandana, was larger than life and on television once a week. Over twelve seasons, Scrivener carved out a solid CFL career.

The rest of the time, doctors carved Scrivener.

Funny, these days Scrivener will be talking to some peer, perhaps a young executive at a party, who will express envy at being denied the life of a professional athlete.

Scrivener will reply, sardonically: "I've had eighteen orthopedic surgeries. How many have you had?"

And to those who press him to be a ringer in their flag football games: "What do you want me to do? Come out and throw up on everybody? Give me a break. Chase a twenty-year-old kid around who has good knees. I'm not doing that."

This is Scrivener's life now; an honest, Joe-the-Propane-Salesman existence where—after more than a decade of grappling with equally large mammals in an attempt to identify and tackle the one carrying the inflated skin of a dead pig—now everything is about making some modest money for the wife and kids. Scrivener entered the "real world" just after the turn of the century and like so many football players, it was a world with which he was not familiar.

For starters, he said, "Truth be told, unless your parents have a business, you're starting out at the bottom of the totem pole."

And, furthermore, all those hours in the weight room preparing that fleshy armour for battle become afterthoughts. "In the real world, nobody cares about that," the old lineman conceded. "You don't need to bench 400 pounds and you don't need to be 285 (pounds). You just pay more for your food."

You don't have to remind Scrivener of the physical toll of his football career, either.

"There are mornings when I get out of bed (and feel pain) and I'll say, 'Yeah, I remember that. That was B.C. Place. I remember getting hit by (former Lions offensive lineman) Jamie Taras when he shortened my neck,' " Scrivener recalled. "Or you've got turf toe on one foot so you can only wear certain types of shoes now. No more cowboy boots.

"There's constant reminders of when you used to play," he added. "Some of them are really positive, when people come up and say, 'Hey, I used to be a season-ticket holder and sat behind the bench. I thought I recognized you.' That's a good thing.

"But I can't remember the last time I ran because I wanted to. Having eight knee operations and a couple shin surgeries and the turf toe and two ankle operations ... running is something that's not on my radar. So I've got to find something else to keep active."

When football players are younger, when they don't even know how to spell orthopedic, their bodies are often compared to finely tuned automobiles or race cars. But there's also an axiom that every human body is good for only so many miles. Eventually, the warranty expires on all of them.

"You put more miles on your body and sometimes way more," Scrivener said, with a rueful chuckle. "I feel like a high-mileage demonstrator quite often."

Hence yet another potential risk for old football players, especially those who carried all that excess baggage over the years. Scrivener now weighs about 290 pounds, would like to shed about 25, but both his past and future occupations are conspiring against him. "I'm working so much and I've got one son and another one due (in September) and I'm doing my damnedest to provide for my family," he said. "There's not enough of me to go around. That's my excuse."

It's not uncommon for a professional lineman to retire, and within a few years shrink back to his natural weight. These are the lucky ones. They are probably the healthy ones, too. Others are far more susceptible to being prisoners of the ailments they developed on the field.

"Many of these guys develop significant lower extremity problems. Hip injuries. Knee arthritis. Foot and ankle arthritis," Craton noted. "And they can't exercise much going into their late adult years. So they lose the protective effect of aerobic exercise."

Scrivener, for one, is well aware of his own circumstances.

"I knew that our life expectancy would be shorter than that of the average Joe," he acknowledged. "There are several contributing factors to that. The constant pounding, especially as an interior lineman. The standard joke is, 'I used to be 6-foot-5. Now I'm only 6-foot-4.'

"I would agree that your life expectancy would be shorter. But I would also say that it doesn't have to be, if the individual would use the same amount of vigour that they used to get ready for a season, to use that same type of drive to get back to a normal weight and a healthy lifestyle."

But like his old Eskimos foe, Hec Pothier, Scrivener can't run anymore. Not unless he's being chased.

Unfortunately, many football players who step away from the game must face more than attempting to enter the mainstream about ten to fifteen years behind the curve. They must do so cold turkey—and, almost to a man, against their strong will.

"In the thirteen years I played," Laird recounted. "I can probably count on one hand how many players that left because, 'You know what? I don't want to play the game anymore. I'm done.' It just doesn't happen that way. The game leaves you before you leave the game."

Poplawski was one of the few to walk away young, retiring from the Bombers before his thirtieth birthday, largely due to chronic back pain. The increased use of muscle relaxers "convinced me I wasn't going in the right direction," he said. Today, Poplawski is a successful player in the Winnipeg insurance industry.

Yet the irony is that many of the players are addicted to the game, the moments, more than to any man-made chemical.

"A lot of people use the term—I probably shouldn't say this—but when they first use drugs there's such a high and after that you're always chasing the dragon trying to reach that high again," Scrivener said. "I think there's something similar with our guys who stop playing football.

"I made the mistake one day telling my new boss that nothing in the field I am now will ever give me the same high as having sixty-five thousand fans in Edmonton telling you that you suck, then you sack the quarterback and turn around and say, 'How do you like me now?' No matter how many propane tanks I sell, it's never going to be like that.

"So part of problem with guys is depression," Scrivener continued. "After they play, they don't get the same high, that same recognition. If we're all being truthful, a lot of guys aren't prepared for life after sports. Because you've played your whole life giving up things and reprioritizing things to make yourself the best you can be to get on the field and perform. When that's over, a lot of guys don't have any other skills.

"And I've talked to friends of mine that are hockey players and in other sports and they all agree with me on that. And it's not like you can make the average person understand. There will always be a void for us. If we're being truthful with you, there's nothing like walking out of that tunnel ... and the place is rocking and the hair on the back of your neck stands up. And they say your name, there's nothing that will ever replace that."

Not alcohol. Not drugs. Not painkillers.

Overnight, the person-as-an-athlete dies. So what's left for so many who are woefully unprepared for such a monumental life transition?

"These guys, it's like a bomb goes off in their heads," one financial planner, who has worked with professional athletes, told the Free Press, requesting anonymity. "These guys can't adapt. Financial is only one part of it. It's emotional, too. You look at all the divorces that go on in sports. When the guy is a hero, the girls are down in the lounges waiting. But when he becomes a washed-out hockey player or football player, the wife's thinking, 'This isn't who I married.'"

A life once so suddenly cemented in celebrity, discipline, and supervised routine becomes unglued.

Remember that Scripps-Howard study of football deaths? How the second-leading cause of death, behind heart disease (22%), was homicides and suicides?

After the deaths of Stevenson, Hentschel, and Boone, the Edmonton Eskimos have become the first CFL team to begin an alumni program to deal specifically with players who are having difficulty making the transition from the locker room to the workplace. Pothier hopes it will prove a model for other CFL alumni.

In fact, at this weekend's Grey Cup in Montreal, the first annual meeting of the Canadian Football League Alumni Association (CFLAA) will officially be held to address coping and health issues, along with establishing a player support/dire straits fund. It would be a first for the CFL, with Pothier as the inaugural president.

"The reality is we're new," noted Ezerins, a member of the CFLAA executive. "What we'd like to do and what we can do (at the start) are two different things."

A few issues top the agenda, including medical screening tests for former players, such as Roberts offers to NFL alumni.

"That's something we'd want to look into, absolutely," Ezerins said. "Also all sort of neck and head injuries as well."

And given many of the tragic deaths that have befallen their numbers, perhaps such an organization is long overdue.

Said Bauer: "Maybe some of the old dogs are starting to stand up."

If only because they're not young pups anymore.

One final point: Does it really matter if there is—one that could be mathematically and medically proven—an average age for a professional football player to die?

After all, the majority of current and former players thought it was fifty-five, give or take, but did it stop one of them? Hardly.

If anything, professional football is as close to armed combat as non-military personnel can get. Go figure their analogies are littered with references to soldiers on the front lines, who cannot afford the luxury of focusing, even for a fleeting moment, on the risks involved in the enterprise.

Charge. Entrench. Retreat. Resist. And if a comrade falls, call the medic and push forward.

"In football you do that," Ezerins said. "Until the last play, you gotta move on. So you have that mindset just playing the game. If you keep dwelling on what has happened, then you can't be successful moving forward. You analyze the film and see what you did wrong and what you did right and, boom, you move forward."

On the field. Even at the cemetery.

More than a dozen former teammates attended Rodehutskors' funeral, for example. "We talked about some of those things, about some of the other young players who've passed away," Laird recalled. "You start to think about it more as you get to that point (late forties, mid-fifties) when some of the guys who [you] knew or played with or against,

when some of [them] start passing away it becomes part of the reality. When you're twenty-two or twenty-four ... you don't really think about that. You don't know those players."

But the denial is strong in these ones. Just as when Lyle Bauer ignored the danger warnings in his youth. "You know it, you hear it. Do you believe it? Not a chance. It's not going to happen to me." The old lineman has no time for second-guessing now.

"It is what it is," he said. "You move forward. It's inevitable for anyone, no matter what. It's just a matter of time frame."

As for the analogy of comrades falling, Bauer added, introspectively, "Lately, it's kind of like that. You have to move on. But that doesn't mean you don't appreciate, respect, or celebrate the lives of the people who created so many memories with you. It goes with the territory. It's unfortunate ... but it does. The things that we've heard when we were younger and probably didn't believe are coming true."

Hector Pothier has a response to the inevitable toll that, once dismissed as the future of others, eventually comes to drop off the bill: Suck it up, boys. You knew the drill. You knew the potential consequences. Yet you held on tight as long as you possibly could.

These are big boys in more ways than one.

"I mean, we know we're pushing our bodies above and beyond what they were created for," Pothier said. "It's part of what we do and what we like to do. It comes down to people's choice, right? No one's choosing to die. We've got lots of old football players here in their seventies who come to every game. So it's not everybody."

Pothier then points to his wife's home in St. Catharines, Ontario, where almost every man on her street toiled for years at the local paper mill. "I swear to God, three-quarters of the men on that street died of cancer from working at that company. So why do we let people work at those factories? There's all sorts of professions and occupations that are higher risk, and it's not like anybody doesn't know. The bottom line is you make a choice about what you want to do for a living and you accept or don't accept.

"It's not like most of us didn't know those numbers when we started playing football. We knew those numbers and we didn't like them. But it's like anything else; it's thirty years away and you're twenty. Let's face it, when you're in your twenties you're invincible. It's when you get into your thirties that you go, 'Hmmm. Maybe we aren't so infallible.'"

Added Trevor Kennerd, a long-serving placekicker with the Bombers in the 1980s: "That does give you pause. It's normal to think, is there a connection with the occupation they were involved with? Likely not. But what you're telling me makes me think potentially professional football players should be given more information for sure about these risks. This will be groundbreaking in Canada. I have never read anything like what you've been talking about."

Indeed, there's no end of anecdotal evidence that professional football could be linked as a cause to no end of health risks, some fatal. Former Montreal Alouettes defensive back Tony Proudfoot, suffering from ALS, believes strongly that his disease—which also took the life of his former teammate Larry Utech—is partially the result of repeated head trauma.

A handful of football players, from high school to college to the pros, die of heat stroke almost every year. So precautions are made to increase water intake, and practices during searing heat are limited.

But no one stops playing football. That's just not an option.

Meanwhile, there doesn't seem to be any movement to look at the risks incorporated into football's DNA in order to get a grasp on the impact of the dangers as a whole. Studies related to head trauma are ongoing, as are efforts to increase cardiovascular screenings. Organizations such as the newly minted CFLAA, hopefully, will be better able to tend to the needs of ailing, elder veterans in the near future.

Still, just looking at the fate of the Pittsburgh Steelers of the last half-century, one wonders why the phenomenon of football players dying young isn't put further under the microscope, regardless of the potential findings.

Remember the skeptic, Roberts, who balked at a life expectancy for football players of fifty-five years old? When asked to consider the issue from a far more wide-ranging viewpoint—the steroids, the cement-hard turf, the stress, the potential for abuse, the skull-pounding drudgery—the doctor wasn't so skeptical anymore.

"That's a good point," the old quarterback eventually acknowledged. "There's a lot of components to the life of a professional athlete, NFL players included. (They) are unique, stressful, and can put you at risk for ill health as you age.

"Our study is chiefly cardiovascular. But the body is a whole system. And the concussion problems, the emotional aspects, the stress and strain, the lifestyle—all of these things are reflected in your outcomes over years following the active-player period. So it's hard to say it's just cardiovascular that influences your life after football. In fact, that would be false.

"As you pointed out, you have emotional problems and the dementias and the head-trauma relationships. When you throw all of those in the mix, one wonders what the long-term outcomes are."

At least, Roberts cites, those larger, irregular hearts are being found quicker. Concussion symptoms are being diagnosed sooner. Steroids have been banned. That's progress, undoubtedly to benefit the next generation of professional football players.

"Finally, we're getting to the point where we're making the players aware of the problems and we're hedging our bets in terms of treating the players when we find the abnormalities in cardiovascular," he concluded. "I'm sure they're doing the same thing now with head trauma. They're receiving treatments.

"So the right process is being followed for these players. But we don't have all the answers. And, certainly, early death is alarming. When we see athletes that are in good health and the epitome of fitness dying at young ages, it's a tragedy."

Of course, you don't have to tell that to Debbie Benjamin.

It took a while for Nick Benjamin to die. The diabetes had ravaged his body, and last August his brain started to bleed. Still, there was time to look back.

"It's when you're lying in the hospital four days a week on dialysis," Debbie recalled, "that you lay there and think about things that you've done in your life that you should have maybe done differently. I know that happened with Nick. He had way to much time to sit and think."

Nick's eyes were failing, too. But looking back didn't require vision, in the worldly sense.

Only one regret.

"If you asked Nick would he change anything, he'd say not at all," she noted. "He loved football. But he never thought he'd die at forty-six, either."

They buried Nick Benjamin at Glen Eden Cemetery. On the day he died, Debbie said, he hadn't had anything to eat or drink for ten days.

"He looked," she said, "like he was twenty years old again."

But to be twenty again, without all the accumulated scars, broken fingers, and battered knees. That's how almost all young football players enter the professional domain of their sport.

Today, on a football field in Montreal, the 2008 Grey Cup will be played between the Montreal Alouettes and the Calgary Stampeders before a crowd of more than sixty thousand roaring spectators, and millions more watching on television. Youth at its most virile will be on full display. Even aging veterans are only in their mid-thirties.

The players will be at their peak, in terms of their athletic careers. Not unlike Benjamin himself, who was a member of the 1990 Bombers who captured the Grey Cup in Vancouver by destroying the Edmonton Eskimos 50–11.

On that day, eighteen years ago, Benjamin was a champion.

And today another group of young champions will be crowned, and they'll hold the Grey Cup towards the confetti-filled skies. But what will be the future for many of them? What price are they paying to hold that trophy?

Glen Scrivener has a saying about the physical and emotional toll of chasing that invisible dragon: Is the juice worth the squeeze?

Ultimately, that's for every player in pads to decide, even though he won't know the true answer for years. Indeed, maybe the player wouldn't want to know at all.

"Having said everything I've said," Debbie said, "I know Nick wouldn't have wanted to live his life any other way. He just would have preferred not to die as young as he did. I mean, he didn't get to see any of the children marry. [Nick and Debbie's marriage was the second for both of them. They each brought three children to the marriage and they added one more]. No grandchildren. None of that stuff that you're supposed to enjoy later on in life. That was taken away too soon.

"He had a good life, though. He did what he wanted to do."

Then Debbie Benjamin sighed a heavy sigh. Sometimes, there's only so much juice.

"He left us a lot of memories and there's memorabilia around the house to prove it," she said.

"We just don't have him."

Debbie Benjamin believes football killed her husband, and others.

The suspect is still at large.

◀◀ **Source:** This article was originally published in *The Winnipeg Free Press*, November 23, 2008. Reprinted with permission.

## The Power of Sport for Development

### By Bruce Kidd

**83.**

While the dramas of test cricket, test rugby, and the Commonwealth Games provide the Commonwealth with its most visible face, sport at the community level is becoming another shared Commonwealth resource as a vehicle for broad social development and the realization of the Millennium Development Goals in education and health. The Commonwealth is an innovative site for the emerging movement of sport for development and peace. This article discusses the contributions of sport to development across the Commonwealth, some of the challenges, and the efforts of the Commonwealth Advisory Board on Sport (CABOS) to strengthen those contributions further.

Sport is arguably the most visible face of today's Commonwealth. As former Pakistan cricket captain Imran Khan has said, "Cricket has been a big unifier in the Commonwealth. Commonwealth countries know each other much more than the countries that are outside the Commonwealth through cricket." Much the same could be said about test rugby and the Commonwealth Games. The successes of Kuala Lumpur (1998), Manchester (2002), and Melbourne (2006) have raised the Commonwealth Games to the first tier of sporting events in the world, with their vast media coverage. The 2010 Games in Delhi will be India's biggest sporting event ever. When the expected 8,500 athletes and officials march into the Nehru Sport Complex for the opening ceremonies next October, they will affirm the identities and symbols of their sixty-one countries and the ties of history, language, and culture that bind the Commonwealth together.

Well below the radar of the mass media, sport also plays a vital role across the Commonwealth as a vehicle of individual and social development. While the power of sport to instruct and empower is age-old, increasingly it is being planned, carried out, and evaluated as an explicit strategy to realise the Millennium Development Goals. In Rwanda and Sierra Leone, for example, sport has been used to restore "normalcy" in communities torn apart by war and violence. In Ghana, its popularity is used to extend basic education; in Kenya, to keep adolescent boys and girls in school and teach them community responsibility; and in Botswana and Namibia, to give youth outside the school system the skills and self-discipline of leadership, organization, and entrepreneurship. Everywhere in Africa, it is used as preventive education about HIV/AIDS.

Similar interventions are under way in other parts of the Commonwealth. In Pakistan, sport is used to enrich the lives of children and youth in refugee camps; in Oceania, to improve the lives of girls and women and affirm them as leaders in community life. In the Caribbean, it delivers a skill-based curriculum around physical activity and healthy lifestyles. It is not only in the global South. In Australia, Canada, and the United Kingdom, sport is used to empower Aboriginal and other marginal youth, and combat the spread of drugs, guns, and gangs in blighted cities. It is clear that where these interventions have been sustained, and linked to other programs of development, sport has transformed the lives of participants in remarkable ways.

### ■ ■ ■ A New Social Movement

The use of sport to contribute to education, health, equity, and community safety is the ambition of a new social movement known as "sport for development and peace" (SDP) that began to take shape in the 1990s. SDP can be distinguished from "sport development" in that it takes little interest in the recruitment and training of athletes and coaches for competition, but focuses on the inclusion, education, health, and safety of participants and their communities, whether or not they are involved in organized competition. It can be distinguished from earlier forms of social intervention through sport, such as the North American and European "playground movements" of the early twentieth century, in that it is global and involves a myriad of different organizations, including international and national governments, corporations and non-governmental organizations (NGOs). It enjoys the full support of the United Nations, through resolutions of the General Assembly and the creation of an Office of Sport for Development and Peace reporting to the Secretary General.

SDP is also very much a youth movement, with many of the most important initiatives and NGOs having been started by young people, moved by their own beneficial experiences to pass on the benefits of sport to the most disadvantaged, impoverished, and marginalized peoples of the world. The Toronto-based NGO Right to Play, founded and led by Olympic athletes from several countries, is the best known example. Today it has programs in twenty-three countries, including nine in the Commonwealth. But there are many other youth-initiated and led NGOs and programs. This is an inspiring case of the determination of young people today to use their own knowledge to bring about social justice.

## ■■■ SDP in the Commonwealth

The Commonwealth has always been an important site for this growing movement.

In 1993, Commonwealth Games Canada (CGC), with the financial support of the Canadian government, launched the Commonwealth Sport Development Program to contribute to coaching, youth development, the inclusion of girls and women, and the fight against HIV/AIDS in Africa and the Caribbean. In 2001, it added the Canadian Sports Leadership Corps to give active and recently retired athletes and recent graduates from Canadian universities in physical education and kinesiology the opportunity to serve as development leaders. By 2003, there were so many other programs under way that CGC changed the name of its program to International Development through Sport (IDS CGC). Today, there are important undertakings in virtually every Commonwealth country. Both the United Kingdom and Australia are major contributors. When London was awarded the 2012 Olympic Games, the organizing committee, drawing upon the experience of UK Sport, the British Council, the UK Sport Trust, and other agencies, created the International Inspirations Programme to transform the lives of twelve million children of all abilities in twenty countries, including the UK, during the build-up to the Games, and employ older youth in the provision of those opportunities. Programs are now under way in schools and communities in fourteen countries, including ten in the Commonwealth. This is a breathtaking commitment that challenges the entire international sports community to do more to enable the youth of the world to experience the "fundamental right" to participate in healthy sport.

There are other inspiring examples of multi-country and multi-agency cooperation. In Africa, the successful Mathare Youth Sports Association of Nairobi, Kenya, which uses sports to enhance school retention and environmental clean-up, and to fight HIV/AIDS and violence against girls and women, lends leaders to other programs in southern Africa. The South Africa-based SCORE recruits and trains volunteers from all over the world. Eighteen Commonwealth governments contribute to the International Working Group on Sport for Development and Peace. A side benefit of these partnerships and relationships is a strengthened understanding of the Commonwealth.

### ■ ■ ■ Sport for Development and Peace

SDP draws its allure from the worldwide fascination for sports and its passion from the engrossing experiences youth leaders have had themselves. But it is also grounded in the international community's recognition of sport and physical education as a basic human right in such documents as the UNESCO Charter on Physical Education and Sport, and the International Convention on the Rights of the Child, and the growing evidence from monitoring, evaluation, and research that under the right circumstances, sport can make a difference. In 2007, this author was commissioned by the International Working Group on Sport for Development and Peace to coordinate literature reviews on the effectiveness of sport as an intervention in five aspects of social policy—sport for girls and women, sport for children and youth, sport for people with disabilities, sport for health, and sport for reconciliation and peace. In the first three areas, my colleagues and I found that where there was qualified leadership, a supportive social context, and sustained activity, there was clear evidence that sport has been effective as a strategy of social change. In one of our most encouraging findings, sport has been shown to enhance school retention and academic achievement, especially among girls and young women. In health, physical activity (but not always sport) significantly reduces the risk of non-communicable diseases such as cardiovascular illness, some forms of cancer, and diabetes. It was only in the area of sport for reconciliation and peace that we found insufficient evidence to draw confident conclusions.

### ■ ■ ■ Growing Pains

Despite these encouraging results, only a minority of children and youth across the Commonwealth enjoys the benefits of sport and physical activity. In part, this is a consequence of the cutbacks in school-based sport and physical education in many countries, and the broader social changes that contribute to more sedentary societies across the globe. But SDP is too poorly funded to change this picture significantly. Many programs amount to small pilot projects, operating far below the scale necessary to touch large numbers of participants. Moreover, while the best organizations work closely with each other, many small NGOs compete fiercely for resources and photo opportunities, with the unfortunate result that in some cities, volunteers fight with each other to train the same youngsters—while 20 kilometres away there is nothing. Some NGOs send such poorly trained youngsters, for such short periods of time, that they create more problems than they solve. In those cases, first-world volunteers return with rewarding experiences while underfunded, overstressed community leaders in the recipient countries wonder why they are training first-world youth with so little in return. Moreover, the justifiable expectation of accountability often steers activity away from locally defined needs and places onerous reporting requirements upon understaffed organizations. To be sure, these issues can be found in any area of development, but they must be addressed by SDP in the Commonwealth as well.

### ■ ■ ■ CABOS

In 2005, following the meeting of the Commonwealth sports ministers in Athens, the Commonwealth Advisory Body on Sport (CABOS) was established to promote the value of sport as a tool for social and economic development, and to advise Commonwealth governments and the Commonwealth Secretariat on sports policy. During its first four years, CABOS took the evidence-based message of sport for development to meetings of Commonwealth education, health, sport, and youth ministers. Working with the World Anti-Doping Agency (WADA), it helped fund the creation of regional anti-doping organizations in Africa, the Caribbean, and Oceania where governments and national Olympic committees did not have the resources to create them alone, and lobbied for the adoption of the UNESCO Convention Against Doping in Sport. It established links with the Commonwealth Youth Secretariat and the Commonwealth Youth Caucus.

During the next four years, CABOS will continue its advocacy with Commonwealth ministers, documenting best practices in policy and programs. It will strengthen its links with the Commonwealth Youth Secretariat, so that SDP can be effectively integrated with the youth development work of the regional Commonwealth youth offices. Staffing is being provided by a secondment from the Indian government. The collaboration with the Commonwealth Youth Programme (CYP) is already paying dividends. In September,

the regional CYP office in Zambia collaborated with the Ministry of Sport, Youth, and Child Development in the organization of the Yotham Muleya sports festival in the village of Siasikabole.

Sport brought the eight hundred participants together, and while they were there they talked about the challenges they faced with respect to education and HIV/AIDS and what could be done to address their challenges. The day started a process of constructive planning and engagement. It provides one small example of the power of sport to connect people and contribute to important social development.

◀◀ **Source:** Bruce Kidd is chair of the Commonwealth Advisory Body on Sport (CABOS). He is professor and dean, Faculty of Physical Education and Health, University of Toronto. This article was reprinted with permission.

# 84. Hunting Waves—and Peace—with the Gaza Surf Club
## By Grant Shilling

*Could surfing really help bring Israelis and Palestinians together? Grant Shilling meets the beach bums, peace activists, and ex-soldiers who believe it's possible.*

■ ■ ■ ■ ■ ■

Surf's up in Ashkelon. So I hop on the train in Tel Aviv bound for the southern Israeli city with my surfboard bag in tow. The bag, stencilled with Boards Not Bombs, attracts more than a few stares and the interest of Israeli state security at the train station. The bag is scanned, the board is tapped up and down its length, and the question has to be asked:

"You came here to surf in Israel?"

Well, yes.

"And what does this mean," says the security soldier, "Boards Not Bombs? You know we take bombs very seriously here in Israel."

Don't I know. I went to Israel in February 2009, during the biggest military operation in Gaza in more than a decade. Israel had launched an enormous offensive reply to years of Hamas bombs on southern Israeli towns like Ashdod, Sderot, and Ashkelon. On January 2, foreigners were ushered out of Gaza. On January 3, Israeli tanks rolled into Gaza to begin a ground offensive. A month later the death toll in Gaza was estimated to be close to one thousand civilians.

So you can be forgiven if surfing is not the first thing you think of when Israel, Gaza, or the Middle East is mentioned. Neither is peace. But there is a thriving surf scene in Israel and an emerging one in Gaza, and both are part of the global brother-

and sisterhood of surfers united by the waves that connect us all.

I'm a Jew—but my true religion is surfing. I had come to Israel because I was increasingly disturbed by the conflict between Israel and the Palestinians, and it was precisely because the situation had become so bad that I felt it necessary to see it myself. I believe surfing and peace are related; surfers everywhere know the peace that can come from riding a perfect wave. So I went to Israel in the hopes of delivering wetsuits to members of a loose-knit group of surfers known as the Gaza Surf Club, along with the T-shirts I made with the (now-notorious) Boards Not Bombs phrase printed on them. Call it fun over fundamentalism.

The security guard is still waiting for an answer to his Boards Not Bombs question.

"Ever hear of the Beach Boys?" I ask him.

"Of course," he says.

"Well, it's true," I tell him, breaking into song. "Catch a wave, and you'll be sitting on top of the world."

He shakes his head like I'm *meshuga* and sends me through, anyway.

Once on board the train we travel south for an hour through a jumble of expressways extending out of Tel Aviv, lined by orange groves, the occasional camel, Arab and Jewish villages, and the faint blue line of the Mediterranean and its fickle waves.

On the train I meet Avram, a young Israeli soldier in uniform who is curious about my board. I tell him of my plans to surf in Ashkelon and then, hopefully, Gaza.

"I surfed Gaza," says Avram, to my surprise. He served there during the second intifada and smuggled his board in on a troop vehicle.

"There were a few soldiers in the water and a few Gazans. Some of us lent them our boards."

You see? I think, there it is—the aloha spirit! Not so fast. "In Gaza they said we were stealing

the waves," says Avram. "We told them, 'learn how to surf.'"

For all the laid-back spirit of surfing, there is also a testy localism, a result of limited carrying capacity: too many surfers, not enough waves. Territorial conflict, already abundant in the Middle East, apparently extends to the beach, too. Sometimes I think the Middle East is a case of localism gone crazy—spiralling out from the Old City of Jerusalem divided into its quarters of Muslim, Jewish, Christian, and Armenian. Jerusalem is more carved up than Bobby Orr's knee.

In 1956, eight years after the formation of the State of Israel, surfing arrived with the American surfer and physician Dorian "Doc" Paskowitz, the undisputed father of Israeli surfing. He brought his 10-foot Hobie surfboard with him. Four years later he returned with six surfboards, each emblazoned with the Star of David. Aiming to repopulate the world with Jews, he raised nine kids out of a 1949 Studebaker and then later in an RV, while chasing waves; his life was recently vividly captured in the feature documentary *Surfwise*. Paskowitz was like Moses carrying the Ten Commandments down from Mount Sinai: Thou shalt surf.

The first surfer Paskowitz taught on a Haifa beach happened to be an Arab boy. He's been trying to bring Arabs and Israelis together to surf ever since.

The sport grew slow and steady in Israel: in the late '70s, a group of hard-core surfers were centred in Tel Aviv. In the early '80s, Shaun Thomson, a Jew and world champion surfer, came to Israel to teach a surf clinic. He was treated like a rock star and thousands of Israelis watched Thomson from the beach. The next year Tel Aviv played host to a stop on the World Surfing Tour.

Today there are close to thirty thousand surfers in Israel. In Gaza, the scene is much smaller, with perhaps fifty or sixty surfers— equipment being one limiting factor. For instance, Salah Abu Khamil is considered the first Palestinian surfer in Gaza: now in his forties and working in Israel, he first saw surfing on Israeli TV in the early '80s and started out on a homemade board he painted himself. Lacking anything else suitable, he used knives for stabilizing fins.

The train station in Ashkelon has a quiet, eerie quality. The city does not see many tourists these days. In early March 2008, rockets fired by Hamas from the Gaza Strip hit Ashkelon, wounding six and causing property damage, marking the first time that Hamas had been able to reliably strike the town. In May 2008, a rocket fired from the northern Gazan city of Beit Lahiya hit this shopping mall in southern Ashkelon, causing significant structural damage and a number of injuries, but amazingly, no deaths. Outside the train station is a big-box discount store. Though it's open, the parking lot is almost empty.

Pulling up to meet me in his Toyota Corolla with a short board strapped to the roof is Chico Maayan. Maayan, now forty-two, a diminutive former Israeli surfing champ, has lived here in Ashkelon, a coastal community of 120,000, for thirty years. We are off to Delilah's to check the waves there. Delilah's is a popular beach named after the legend of Samson and Delilah, which played itself out here on the shores of Ashkelon and Gaza 15 kilometres to the south. We drive through a maze of modern white three- and four-storey apartments with red-tiled roofs separated by patches of green, the building style typical of much of Israel.

Ashkelon's current slow pace means the waves are not crowded today. That suits Maayan fine for now, but he runs a surf school in Ashkelon, and since the bombing, business has been in the toilet. He tells me about a surf lesson he was teaching a while ago that ended abruptly.

"I was in the army, so okay, I know combat," says Maayan. "I hear this whistling. I know it's a rocket. I tell the kids, 'Get down! Get down!' The bomb landed 100 metres from us, a mushroom of smoke. We were shocked; this is the middle of summer. All the parents call me and tell me to bring the kids home. Since then it has been a

problem." (In surf lingo, catching a big wave is called "riding a bomb." So you can imagine that Maayan's experience brings a whole new meaning to the idea.)

This year the celebration of Purim—the festive holiday where children and adults dress in costumes that commemorate the deliverance of the Jewish people of the ancient Persian Empire from Haman's plot to annihilate them—was cancelled in Ashkelon. "No one comes here," says Maayan. "It's a ghost town."

Maayan's parents are from Chile and came to Israel around 1960. They are proud Zionists. "My mother will kill anyone if they say anything bad about Israel," he chuckles. Maayan served in the army during the first intifada. He describes himself as a patriotic Israeli. "Israel didn't do enough in its recent war in Gaza," says Maayan. "Not until we see a white flag from Hamas should we stop."

And yet Maayan believes in a two-state solution and that Israel should support the more moderate Fatah party in Palestine. I ask Maayan how he feels about the Gazan civilians during the operation going on not far from here. "Really it didn't bother me very much," he says. "Sometimes I get a clinch in my heart; it's a pity, but really, the Israeli army dropped flyers warning people to clear the area. We did our best. Hamas has got a policy that they hide behind their citizens … Fatah is more reasonable; they recognize Israel. They are more suitable to rule. If not, then it's like having Iran next door."

And yet, Maayan is optimistic. "Things will get better. I love Ashkelon, I love the place, the people; I know the beaches, and this is my home." I tell Maayan that tomorrow I plan to go to Gaza in hopes of hooking up with the surfers there and delivering some equipment. He looks at me and says, vaguely, "So you are like that, I see."

The next day I plan to enter Gaza. Mohammed Alwayn is my surfing contact there. Alwayn is an agronomist who works for Care International. "When you surf, you don't think about the situation," he tells me over the phone. "When surfing, we feel free." Alwayn and I made plans to meet up and he'd introduce me to some of his surfing friends. All I had to do was get across the border.

My friend Arthur Rashkovan is to drive me to the Gaza border. Now thirty, Rashkovan grew up two blocks from Israel's famed Hilton Beach, home to some of the best surf in the country, and has lived there his whole life. A former Israeli skateboard champion, he's a first-generation Israeli whose parents are from Moldova in Eastern Europe. I asked him what brought his parents to Israel and he told me, "The usual: anti-Semitism."

Rashkovan grew up in what he calls a "mini-California, a surfer's paradise." Despite the conflicts, life continues as normal in Tel Aviv. It's an extremely safe city. With a population of 400,000, street crime and homelessness are virtually non-existent, children are free to play in the streets and parks by themselves, and women can safely walk the streets late at night in a city that never sleeps.

"Tel Aviv is in a bu-ah, a bubble," says former Israeli surf pro Maya Dauber, thirty-six. "For me, the last war with Gaza was like a reality TV show. You feel removed.

"You have to understand. This is not the first war we ever had," says Dauber, who served in the military while being allowed to compete as a surfer in the World Qualifying Series. "Every few years we have a war. Every few years I know a soldier who died or was hurt because of a war. You start to develop a thick skin. You start to protect yourself more and more. You don't want to hear about it. That's why Tel Aviv is one of the best cities to hang out in in the world. Because people want to forget. They want to go out and have fun, to drink to clear their minds. Surfing," she says, "is an extension of that."

During his youth Rashkovan would "surf my brains out. I lived like a true beach bum. Nothing else mattered." When he turned eighteen, Arthur had to serve in the military. "I realized I need to serve my country, and I didn't want to get out of the army. So I had a goal of getting the best job I could have and keep on skating and surfing." So he took a desk job not far from home. "My experience in the military was a lot of skate injuries," laughs Rashkovan. "I broke my arm twice and my ankle from skateboarding. Luckily you get a very long leave to heal up, so I went on two surf trips to San Diego. The third time I got injured the army had no use for me, and they released me."

After Rashkovan left the army he gradually became one of the prime movers and shakers in the burgeoning Israeli surf industry. In 2004, Doc Paskowitz came to Israel looking to meet some Arab-Israeli surfers. Rashkovan was in a position to help him out. Paskowitz and Rashkovan gave impromptu lessons to Arab kids on the beach between Tel Aviv and Jaffa, a spot where Israelis and Arabs surf together. "At that moment, I realized, hey, why not organize the first surf event for Arabs and Israelis?" says Rashovan. "I thought it would be a good opportunity to show that surfers can overcome barriers such as religion and politics."

The 2004 Arab-Israeli surf contest was just the beginning. Last year, as part of something he describes as beginning as a "lark," Rashkovan got together with Doc Paskowitz and surfing god Kelly Slater (who is of Syrian descent) to teach surfing clinics to Arabs and Israelis. They dubbed it Surfing for Peace. Young Arab girls in hijabs and young Israelis with yarmulkes caught waves with Slater looking on. Fun versus fundamentalism.

Then, pushing his luck, Doc Paskowitz, along with his sons David, Josh, and Jonathan, headed for the border to deliver some surfboards to Gaza. Despite there being a total blockade on entry, Doc managed to cajole some border guards into letting him exchange the boards with some waiting Gazans. "Kissing was the secret to getting across the border," says Doc. "All the guys that want to shoot me, I grab them and kiss them."

Nobody believes that you can actually bring peace simply through the act of surfing. But you can create moments of peacefulness, create some friendships, and demystify your so-called enemy.

Or, as Doc says, "God will surf with the devil if the waves are good enough."

"That day when we delivered the boards was a very magical day," recalls Rashkovan. "We were swamped by the media. Everybody was calling me: the *New York Times*, the *L.A. Times*. I had newspapers call from Germany, South Africa, Indonesia, Brazil—really everywhere. The funniest part is we had maybe one or two minutes on Israeli TV. People are turning cynical here and indifferent. Because on one side we have war all around and we have gotten a bit insular. You get used to what's going on around and just get on with it. The whole world was excited and Israel was like, 'Whatever.'"

Friends asked Rashkovan why he was bothering with Surfing for Peace. "I want to prove that there are large populations on both sides who want to live their lives peacefully," he says. "The problem is they are controlled by politicians who have other interests. Peace is a political process, but luckily friendship isn't. Initiating actions on the grassroots level between common people is a much faster way to move things. Surfing as a peaceful way of living is just perfect for this goal. Why not just go out and forget about our worries for a moment? This is what the Arabs in Israel do when they go surf, this is what the Israeli surfers do when they go out, and it's the same for the guys in Gaza."

Rashkovan is determined to keep Surfing for Peace grassroots and out of politics. "We know there is a huge population in Gaza that wants to live its life quietly, but it's controlled by extremists," he says. "I wanted to show the Gazans on the other side that there are a group of people here who want to have the same life. And maybe through the common ground of surfing show the world something else. We just want to make friends with a few guys on the other side."

As you get closer to Gaza the highway winnows down to two narrow lanes surrounded by farm fields and overhung by orange groves. There is a sweet perfume of orange blossoms in the air. The pastoral landscape is abruptly interrupted by a clearing covered in asphalt and a big sign that reads "Welcome to the Erez Crossing." The Gaza crossing looks like a hangar in a mid-size airfield with plenty of parking spaces. There are many people milling about their cars—simply waiting.

The crossing has a parkade shed with a gate. At the gate Lior, a friendly, engaging young Israeli soldier, greets me. The surfboard makes him smile. I tell him surf's up in Gaza and I want to join my Palestinian brothers on the waves.

"Not today."

"Come on, I heard it's as big as Indo in Gaza." He laughs at my reference to the surf mecca of Indonesia. I spend about a half-hour trying to charm and disarm the young soldier, but there will be no getting into Gaza today—or on several other attempts I make. Hamas and Israel are still lobbing bombs at each other and things are just too hot.

Having come all this way from Tel Aviv, we stop at the Arab port of Jaffa instead to visit Rashkovan's friend Abdallah Seri. An Arab-Israeli, Seri lives with his family in a simple flat with a patio garden. His father, a fisherman, joins us over strong Arabic coffee while a soccer game plays on the TV.

Seri, now twenty-eight, learned to surf at the age of twelve and is part of the Surfing for Peace project. He talks about his love for Doc Paskowitz and for surfing and how it can bring people together. But then he turns serious. "The people in Gaza are not an autonomous people," he says. "They don't know how to think for themselves anymore, and they can't tell right from wrong anymore. They're victims of both the Israelis and their own Arab brothers and sisters."

Seri's father points to the soccer players on the screen: "Look at these guys. They're from all over the world, playing together as a team. That is what sport can do. That is what surfing can do."

Using surfing as an approach to solving an intractable problem like the Middle East conflict involves a leap of faith. In fact, many writers have questioned whether surfing itself is a faith. Does God reside in a double-overhead wall of blue?

(The ancient Polynesians prayed over tree trunks to their god of surfing before shaping them into surfboards and built temples dedicated to the sport.)

Rabbi Nachum "Shifty" Shifren, a.k.a. the Surfing Rabbi (he wrote a book of the same title), is a deep believer in the divine peace that surfing can bestow. "I think if there is anything that can bring about peace, it's surfing," Shifren, a former lifeguard and triathlete, tells me by phone from Santa Monica, California. "What I am advocating is a synthesis between the physical and the spiritual. I believe that surfing is the answer to modern man's dilemma of stress, of lack of security, of lack of self-esteem, and even in the search for peace. Surfing is a spiritual connector. It's like a conduit where one could appreciate God and the forces of the world."

Divine conduit or not, surfing does seem to help individuals overcome barriers to understanding. Despite his self-described hard-core rightwing views, Chico Maayan also took part in the Surfing for Peace operation. "We started Surfing for Peace because we thought of it as not connected to politics—it is connected to the ocean," he says. "We're surfing. The Gazans are surfing. We should surf together. It won't bring peace, but we will see the enemy differently."

Back in Tel Aviv, I call Alwayn in Gaza to tell him I hadn't been able to get past the border. He was hardly surprised. "Have faith," he says.

A week after I got back to Vancouver Island, Arthur Rashkovan emailed to tell me that a German-based journalist had received permission to get into Gaza and took along four of the wetsuits I had left behind. He also took some photos of the surfers unpacking the suits in delight.

So I keep the faith. Searching for waves and peace in Israel and Gaza may be an act of faith, but this is a region, after all, that hosts three of the world's major religions. Faith is all we've got, and surfing is my religion. I do believe that hope resides in a double-overhead wall of blue. Or as Chico Maayan told me, "As long as there are waves, there will be a type of peace."

◀◀ **Source:** This article was originally published in *This Magazine*, October 13, 2009. Reprinted with permission from the author.

## Faster, Higher, Sneakier
### By Alex Hutchinson

**85.**

*Does Canada's Top Secret sports technology program undermine the Olympic spirit?*

■ ■ ■ ■ ■ ■

The cold war was over, they'd told him. Soviet equipment factories converted to Benz dealerships. East German labs switching from steroids to solar panels. But a new world meant new threats.

He paused to button his collar to the top, then wound a scarf carefully around his neck, covering most of his face. Out the back door he went, into the biting wind. Twenty-one, maybe twenty-two kilometres per hour, minus 26, for a wind chill of minus 38.5 ... no, 38.6.

No time! he muttered to himself, quickening his pace through the night.

The Olympics were coming, and Ottawa had sent word to every scientist in the land: Canada would be bullied no more. Montreal in '76. Calgary in '88. Not a single gold medal. The only nation ever shut out at its own Olympics, and we'd done it twice. It was time to start fighting back. Against the Americans and their speed suits. The Dutch and their clap skates. And the Aussies. How he loathed the Aussies.

He strode toward the pay phone at the end of the block, slipped the receiver off the hook, and dialed the number *he'd memorized when he enlisted in the program four years earlier.*

*"Gaëtan?" the familiar voice said.*

*"Boucher," he responded.*

*"Barbara Ann?"*

*"Scott."*

*"Excellent, you're clear. What have you got for me, Cranston?*

*"It's the new bobsled cowl, sir," he said. Then paused, shifting his gaze warily. The man walking down the other side of the street seemed to be lingering, and he looked vaguely Swiss. Cranston waited until the man passed, then resumed speaking.*

*"We've got the drag down by nearly 2%. Another day in the wind tunnel, and it should be ready for field testing."*

*"Excellent." The voice was smooth and reassuring. "You've done well. Very well. Your country is proud of you."*

*The line went dead. Cranston hurried along the frozen street back to the lab. Two months left until the opening ceremonies. There would be no shutout this time. Top Secret had come too far.*

■■■■■■

On July 2, 2003, the natural cycle of debate about Canada's Olympic ineptitude—a month of anguish followed by two years of indifference—was disrupted. By a vote of fifty-six to fifty-three, the 2010 Winter Games were awarded to Vancouver and Whistler over Pyeongchang, South Korea. With that, taking part and fighting well were no longer enough. We wanted to win, we decided, and launched the Own the Podium program to that end a year and a half later. The initiative has since disbursed $117 million, with the aim of propelling Canada to the top of the medals table in 2010. For our elite athletes, the money has translated into better coaching, more training camps, extra massages, and, just as crucial, access to a shadowy cadre of scientists.

Vancouver-Whistler will mark the first time Canadian athletes will benefit from the single-minded, government-funded pursuit of the technological upper hand. The vehicle for this drive is Own the Podium's Top Secret wing, which has funnelled $7.5 million toward applied research into air, snow, and ice friction, as well as sophisticated physiological testing and performance monitoring. Partners including Bell Canada, the National Research Council, and universities across the country have chipped in by loaning scientists and research facilities. In keeping with its cloak-and-dagger moniker, Top Secret's officials and researchers have stayed mum amid rumours of wired ski helmets and ultra-sleek speed-skating suits. Own the Podium head Roger Jackson told me last fall that fans (and competing teams) will see the new technologies in action "either in the last World Cup events or in the opening rounds of the Olympics."

The decision to create a program specifically devoted to technology has its roots in the bitter experiences reported by Canadian Olympians in debriefings after the 2002 Salt Lake City Games. "They were being beaten by athletes who had better suits, or better runners on their bobsleds, or better skis, because the manufacturers were giving the best ones to other countries," Jackson says. In some cases, the technologies in question were demonstrably superior—but even if they weren't, perception led to reality.

"Canadian speed skaters were sitting in the grandstand, watching the American speed skaters in their fancy new suits and saying, 'wow,'" Jackson recalls. The Americans gained confidence from the suits, while the Canadians lost their nerve before the races began. Australian researchers sought a similar edge in a series of "precooling" techniques designed to condition their endurance athletes for hot weather, starting with ice vests at the 1996 Atlanta Games, then advancing to ice baths in 2004, and slushies in 2008. Whether drinking slushies is actually better than dunking in an ice bath is debatable, Australian researcher

Louise Burke admitted at a post-Olympic conference in 2008. "In Beijing, we wanted something new," she said. "You always have to have something new for athletes, for that placebo effect."

Jackson cites (without divulging any details) several potential innovations with genuinely quantifiable benefits. Among them is a more aerodynamic bobsled cowl—the technical term for a sled's fibreglass-on-steel body—designed in a wind tunnel, then tested on the track. The measurable success of such advances has changed how athletes view science: "It seems to take a long time for people to really appreciate how good some of these improvements are," he says. "But once they see it, everybody jumps on the bandwagon."

Soon after the 2010 Games, Canada will have to decide whether to extend the Top Secret mission for another four years. Jackson hopes we'll build a centralized sports technology institute like those in Australia and Germany, with staff scientists to lead the country's research program. Such a move would undoubtedly boost medal counts. But it also conjures visions of an athletic arms race, dominated by a nouveau-Soviet approach in which duelling sports institutes pit scientist against scientist. The implications of such a shift would reach well beyond the lofty realm of elite sport.

Under the bright sun of an antipodal spring day, Sharni Layton guides a few dozen school kids and their parents to the large windows overlooking the new swimming pool at the Australian Institute of Sport (AIS), near Canberra. She begins to rhyme off its high-tech amenities. Around the entire pool, underwater windows allow coaches to track their athletes from different angles. Force plates built into the starting blocks and walls measure reaction times with infinitesimal precision. Cameras zip along tracks on the pool bottom to follow the swimmers during their laps. And when the athletes pop their heads out of the water, their training efforts are instantly replayed on plasma screens at the edge of the pool, alongside graphs and vectors analyzing their performance.

Layton is a promising twenty-one-year-old netball player, one of some 150 funded athletes living at the institute. She trains twice a day with the AIS team for a total of about four hours, which leaves time to pick up extra cash leading tours of the sprawling sixty-five-hectare campus. The new pool, which opened in 2007 at a cost of $17 million, is the site's current crown jewel, though Layton points out that the old fifty-metre pool, just a few buildings away, is still pretty good. Once, when six-time Olympic medallist Michael Klim was struggling with his turns, they drained it and installed mirrors on the bottom so he could adjust his technique as he swam. "The better the sport does, the more money you get," she says a bit wistfully. "And swimming wins the most medals."

Set in the rather nondescript Canberra suburb of Bruce, the AIS was born of Australia's failure to win a single gold medal at the 1976 Olympics in Montreal. It is funded out of the $164 million the country dedicated to elite athlete development in its most recent annual budget. The results of this level of investment have been fairly clear: Since the institute was created in 1981, the athletes receiving its direct support have brought home 142 Olympic medals. Naturally, other countries have taken note. A week after my visit in October, a delegation headed by Alex Baumann, the former champion swimmer who now heads Canada's Summer Olympics medal initiative, toured the AIS and other Australian sports facilities.

One distinguishing feature of the AIS is its sports science and sports medicine unit, which employs about one hundred full-time staff, ranging from doctors and physiotherapists to physiologists and biomechanics experts. Among that group is a core of a dozen people who, as AIS director Peter Fricker puts it, "drive the sharp end of our performance research focus." He continues: "As much as we'd like to think we've got really talented athletes and really good coaches, how does a country like ours succeed internationally against big populations with lots of money? I think it's by being clever." Relative to its population, Australia earned four times as many medals in Beijing as Canada, and six times as many as the United States.

That dominance was made possible by innovations like the techno-pool—"the ultimate wet lab," Fricker says with evident pride—and their spinoffs. It was from the AIS's wet labs that Speedo's super-buoyant, corsetlike polyurethane LZR swimsuit emerged in 2008, triggering an avalanche of new world records. Working with AIS scientists, the company's Aqualab development team had tested streamlining with a motorized pulley that hauled swimmers along Lane 1 of the old pool at greater-than-world-record speeds. (They also carried out drag tests in an open-water flume in New Zealand, and air resistance trials of more than one hundred fabrics at a NASA facility.)

A display on the wall of the AIS visitor centre touts the LZR as "the most successful suit ever," but it ultimately became a victim of its own success when companies like Jaked and Arena developed imitations that outdid the original. Heading into last summer's world championships in Rome, more than 130 world records had been broken in the year since the LZR's introduction. The Canadian team, preparing for the worlds at a holding camp in Italy, decided almost en masse to forsake the free suits provided by team sponsor Speedo and order the latest Jaked suits at around 500 euros each, though they could be worn just two or three times before becoming stretched beyond usefulness. "It was the first time we'd had to pay for suits ourselves," says breaststroker Martha McCabe. But the differences in performance were too great to ignore.

On the eve of the championships, FINA, swimming's international governing body, announced that the new super-buoyant suits would be banned in 2010. This set the stage for a final orgy of polyurethane-fuelled speed, as forty-three world records fell during the world championships, leaving the 1,500-metre freestyle marks as the only ones predating 2008. American phenom Michael Phelps suffered a rare loss after sticking to the slower Speedo suit out of loyalty to his sponsor; other members of the well-funded U.S. team were

reportedly running around the hallways between races begging for better gear. With the new restrictions, says McCabe, "we're taking a step back. But we're all on the same playing field, and that's all that matters."

A finalist in her first world championship appearance at just nineteen years of age, McCabe now faces a career in which—barring a decision by FINA to wipe the slate of polyurethane-aided times—she may never swim another personal best time, let alone approach a world record. Yet it's difficult to pinpoint the moment when swimming officials should have stepped in. Should they have banned the first skimpy nylon-spandex suits, donned by the likes of Mark Spitz in the '70s? Or the full-body suits that first appeared in 2000? The aim in each case was to reduce drag resistance; the only difference is that the newest suits are so much better at it. "It seems to me that what they did is the worst option, because they allowed them for a year and now all these records are broken," McCabe says. "If they were going to allow them in the first place, they might as well just accept that technology is going to continue enhancing sport forever."

That technology enhances sport for everyone is undeniable. "Look at what's happened in the fitness industry," says Roger Jackson. "Twenty-five years ago, no one was cycling. Now you can't get on the roads on a weekend without seeing bands of people on really lovely, efficient bikes with good gear systems and tires." Regardless of skill level, consumers benefit from high-performance gear developed for elite athletes, whether it's light-weight kayaks, faster skis, or warm, dry clothing. And of course the companies whose sponsorship dollars are the lifeblood of sport benefit as well. The challenge is managing innovation in a way that doesn't compromise fairness.

Problems arise most obviously during times of transition, when some competitors have new technology and others don't. Jackson, a three-time Olympic rower who earned gold in the coxless pairs event at the 1964 Games in Tokyo, experienced this first-hand. "The rowing shells we used in my first Olympic Games were quite heavy and clumsy and not very adjustable," he recalls. But in the '60s and '70s, some countries began developing lighter, stronger, more manoeuvrable boats. "If a shell was 250 pounds, the Germans were building them at 200 pounds," he says. "They used new materials like Kevlar and carbon fibre well before others did." The international rowing federation decided to allow the boats, reasoning that such advances would be widely available to anyone who could pay.

The point of programs like Top Secret, by contrast, is to produce technology that isn't available to everybody, thereby tilting the playing field, however slightly. And that raises some thorny questions. We would encourage a neurosurgeon to take a pill that steadies his hands before surgery, notes ethicist Thomas Murray of the Hastings Center in Garrison, New York, but would condemn an archer who popped the same pill before an event. The difference, Murray argues, is that in sports we value the "virtuous perfection of natural talent"—the ideal of contestants competing on the basis of the genetic cards they were dealt, supplemented only by perseverance, sacrifice, dedication to training, tactical acumen, and other routes to improvement we deem "virtuous." If a new technology is to be introduced into a sport, he writes, it should satisfy two criteria: continuity and equal opportunity. The advent of fibreglass poles for pole vaulters in track and field, for example, met that threshold: "Continuity was assured because the poles still required the same skills from pole vaulters, such as speed down the runway, strength, and agility. Equal opportunity meant that all athletes had to have access to fibreglass poles."

Super-buoyant swimsuits seem to meet the basic criteria of continuity and access, but their virtue is more difficult to judge. Technologies used in training rather than directly in competition present an even stickier dilemma. The hyper-instrumented $17-million AIS swimming pool, for instance, tilts the playing field for Australian swimmers no matter what they wear during the race.

Elsewhere on the AIS site is an altitude house with adjustable oxygen levels, which allows athletes to live and sleep in conditions simulating elevations favourable to the production of red blood cells. This kind of altitude training has created controversy in recent years, leading to accusations of "technological doping." The proliferation of portable altitude tents, worth between $5,000 and $10,000, in the run-up to the 2002 Winter Games led the International Olympic Committee to ban them from the Olympic Village in Salt Lake City. It was a token gesture, since the benefits obtained from the tents are achieved long before the actual competition. In 2006, the World Anti-Doping Agency ruled that the practice violated "the spirit of the sport," but a proposed ban was dropped after a backlash from athletes and scientists. It's hard to see how such a prohibition could have held up anyway. Would they also ban moving to Banff?

The University of Calgary's Human Performance Lab occupies a cavernous, gymnasium-sized space in the Roger Jackson Centre for Health and Wellness Research. Along one wall, a researcher encourages a cyclist pedalling furiously on a stationary bike plugged into at least five different machines. In a corner, nine motion capture cameras focus on a patch of artificial green next to a large black curtain, creating a virtual golf swing analysis system. A runner outfitted with reflective markers at each joint prepares to run back and forth across the force-sensing floor. In a smaller room next door, a glass-walled altitude chamber sits next to an enormous treadmill built into the floor. The buzz of activity and the assortment of bizarre machines recall James Bond's visits to the R & D wing of MI6.

The lab's gear guy—its Q, if you will—is a young kinesiology professor named Darren Stefanyshyn. In the wake of the Canadian team's disheartening experience in Salt Lake City, he helped develop the new speed suit—an ultra-tight superhero outfit criss-crossed by stretchy silver bands—worn by Nordic skiers and others at the 2006 Turin Olympics. He is also one of the world's leading footwear researchers, and he proudly shows off an enormous pneumatic shoe-testing robot that accurately simulates what happens when a foot makes contact with the ground under various conditions. The machine also performs three-point bend tests on skis, and break-point tests on composite hockey sticks.

The projects Stefanyshyn is working on for Own the Podium are, needless to say, top secret. His research for speed skaters encompasses everything from apparel to footwear, he says, and he's also working with the sledge hockey and luge teams. Once again, speed suits will be a crucial theme. "People are now using their apparel as a piece of equipment," he says. He expects other countries to be developing similar ideas, which is why, even though the suits rely on the same technologies swimming just banned, he doesn't feel they confer an unfair advantage.

Down the hall from the Human Performance Lab is another hub of Top Secret guile, the Sports Technology Research Lab run by kinesiology professor Larry Katz. He and his colleagues are developing a database to help monitor the performance of Canada's Winter Olympic athletes, and they've also done research into virtual reality training simulators for sports like bobsledding. To demonstrate the analytical tools they've created, biomechanics consultant Pro Stergiou pulls up training footage of the national luge team. Video tracking measures every aspect of the force exerted and acceleration produced in each push-off. And as with the Australian pool, the data can be accessed in real time, allowing for rapid analysis and adjustment.

Even the most hidebound traditionalist would be hard-pressed to find anything unethical or contrary to the spirit of sport in Katz's efforts to help athletes monitor their training. This suggests that we have no fundamental objection to pouring cash into the pursuit of an edge that the luge team from, say, Slovakia can only envy from afar. Perhaps we draw the line only at having our athletes wear something so advanced that the unevenness of

the field is too obvious—or so advanced that we wonder how many batteries it takes.

The first skates, as far as we know, were fashioned about four thousand years ago by Finnish hunters who strapped horse ankle bones to their feet in order to traverse their frozen, lake-dotted landscape. By pushing themselves forward with a stick, hardy Finns could reach speeds of about 5 kilometres an hour ("quite good fun," reported one of the British researchers who figured this out in 2008). It wasn't until the thirteenth century that wooden skates with iron blades appeared, likely in the Netherlands, enabling a more conventional skating motion. The pace of innovation quickened thereafter, with longer steel blades in the eighteenth century and one-piece boot-and-blade combinations in the nineteenth.

Dutch biomechanics researchers built the first prototypes of what are now known as "clap skates" in 1985. They feature a hinge near the toe, allowing the skater to twist his or her foot and push off while the blade continues to glide along the ice. Elite speed skaters were initially hesitant to try the new contraptions, but in 1996 three women on the Dutch national team agreed to test them out. When one, Tonny de Jong, won gold at the European championships in 1997, word that the skates delivered a 3 to 5% performance boost spread quickly. Just one year later, every single competitor at the Nagano Olympics used clap skates, leading to the evisceration of every world record in the books.

The newest frontier in skate technology also traces its origins to 1985. That's when Calgary inventor Tory Weber, then a college student, pulled on a pair of sneakers left to warm on a heating vent, headed outside, and slipped on his icy front walk. Twenty-two years and $17 million in venture capital later, he unveiled the Thermablade at a press conference at the Hockey Hall of Fame in Toronto. None other than Wayne Gretzky touted the skate's heated runner as "the most significant advance in skate blade design in at least thirty years." Tests showed that the blades reduced sliding friction by more than 50%, upping speed and reducing fatigue. And yet, after making some encouraging noises, the National Hockey League hesitated, eventually demoting Thermablades to the minors for an additional year of testing.

As of October, Weber was in discussions with two "non-English-speaking" teams about the possibility of outfitting them with heated blades for the 2010 Winter Games. (Canada, to his great dismay, had yet to call.) But it's the NHL that sets the standard for hockey players in most of the world, and Weber's strategy is geared primarily toward getting the league on board. He has a few gambits in mind, notably a simpler recharging process and studies on whether heated blades reduce injuries. He's also hoping to contain costs. With sales of the $400 skates stalled and credit scarce, his company filed for bankruptcy in July—a sign, perhaps, that people believe battery power, and its attendant expense, would be taking things one step too far. Millionaire pro hockey players might not balk at the extra few hundred dollars, but as any hockey parent will attest, the cost of gear is already high, with younger and younger players shelling out for such high-tech equipment as composite sticks to remain competitive. And it's here that the collateral damage from the sports technology arms race becomes clear.

In the early '80s, sociologist Roger Barnsley was attending a Lethbridge Broncos game when his wife, perusing the program, noticed that nearly all the players were born in the first few months of the year. The observation led to the first study of the "relative age effect," which revealed that NHL players were four times as likely to have been born in the first three months of the year as in the last. The phenomenon, which has subsequently been identified in a wide range of other sports and activities, stems from the differences in physical maturity among children in a given cohort. At an early age, an extra six months of growth confers a slight size and speed advantage, making it more likely that kids with birthdays in January will be selected for elite teams than those with birthdays in July. As a consequence, January children are better coached and more motivated to succeed. By adolescence, when the size deficit has been erased, coaches' early assessments of which kids would make the best players have become self-fulfilling prophecies.

Barnsley's work demonstrates how seemingly trifling barriers can limit later success. This isn't just a question of fairness. It's also in Canada's interest, if we want to win medals, to maximize the talent pool we're drawing from, and not to thin it unwittingly on the basis of birth month—or access to the latest equipment. Limiting the effects of the latter barrier will require a shift in the way we think about sports technology.

In 1997, the winner of the Lou Marsh Trophy as Canada's top athlete was Jacques Villeneuve. The young race car driver, himself the son of a famous driver, was honoured that year for capturing the Formula 1 world championship for the Williams-Renault team. The next season, though, Villeneuve failed to win any races and slipped to fifth overall in the standings. He then changed to a new team, then another and another, never once taking the checkered flag before he bounced out of F1 entirely in 2006. It was a strange fate for a man who'd won seven times in 1997 alone. At least, it was strange if you didn't understand F1 racing. To followers of the sport, who knew it to be a battle among engineers as much as between drivers, Villeneuve's decline made perfect sense: after the 1997 season, Renault had stopped making engines for the Williams team.

Compare the F1 approach with that of Florida-based NASCAR. As its full name, the National Association for Stock Car Auto Racing, suggests, NASCAR originated as a form of stock car racing, which is based on as-sold production models of cars. If everyone was driving a 1949 Oldsmobile Rocket, the thinking went, then the best driver would win rather than the best engineer. NASCAR rules have evolved considerably since the circuit's early days, so the current cars bear only a superficial resemblance to street legal vehicles, but the sport's basic philosophy remains focused on equalizing the cars. It's not that the technology doesn't improve—far from it—but that the association allows only slow, incremental changes.

Both F1 and NASCAR have millions of fans around the world, but their fans have different expectations about what they're watching. That Villeneuve should be at the mercy of his engine maker is acceptable to F1 followers; that Michael Phelps should be betrayed by his swimsuit isn't. The unspoken covenant we have with most of the sports we watch at the Olympics, and many professional sports, too, is that they will be regulated like NASCAR rather than like F1. Had FINA officials operated on that basis, its regulations on swimming gear would have been enacted in 2000, not 2010.

Some sports are already moving along this path. In Olympic sailing, Roger Jackson points out, the host organizing committee provides identical boats for competitors. That's NASCAR. The F1 equivalent is America's Cup racing, where anything goes if it makes the sailboat faster. Similarly, in modern pentathlon, participants receive a horse from a common pool. "You have a draw to see which nag you get," Jackson says, "and then you compete with the good, the bad, or the ugly."

Almost every sport, in fact, has some set of rules intended to keep equipment relatively uniform and safe. A simple litmus test of their effectiveness might be to ask whether the top countries and teams are nevertheless spending millions of dollars in pursuit of technological advantages. If so, that sport's rules might be allowing too much leeway.

Not every sport can follow sailing's lead and issue identical, interchangeable gear—skiers, for instance, really do need skis that fit them. The goal in a NASCAR-oriented sporting world would simply be to reverse the default status of new technologies and equipment modifications so that they're banned unless expressly permitted instead of the other way around. Innovation would hardly grind to a halt, because sports equipment makers still want to sell lighter, safer, more comfortable gear to the masses. Aluminum baseball bats, for example, have flourished despite Major League Baseball's decision not to accept them. As for more esoteric advances without mass-market appeal—polyurethane swim corsets, for example—would anyone really miss them?

For now, the realpolitik of global sport dictates that countries with golden aspirations deploy their operatives in programs like Top Secret, ethereal concepts of virtuous perfection be damned. Canada grew tired of having snow kicked in its face by the powers of sport, so we've committed ourselves to developing some tech-enhanced brawn. And with the rules as they stand, that's fair game: few laud the integrity of the committed ninety-seven-pound weakling. A couple of tweaks to those rules and stronger stewardship from international sports federations, though, and we might nudge the Olympics back toward its ideals — and bring our sports scientists in from the cold.

◀◀ **Source:** This article was originally published in *The Walrus*, January/February 2010. Reprinted with permission.

# "We're Not Developing as Many Kids as We Used To"
## By Brandon Hicks

**86.**

*Minor hockey will suffer as Canada's child population keeps shrinking*

In the next few years it will be wishful thinking for the folks who hire referees and book ice time in the world of minor hockey to plan for expansion. Success will be defined as keeping the status quo.

It's not that the kids don't want to play. It's just that there aren't as many of them.

The under-fifteen population is shrinking in the country, and the trend is only going to continue.

"What we're seeing is that simply, that age group from four to fifteen, the population is decreasing," said Glen McCurdie, senior director of membership services for Hockey Canada. "We're not developing as many kids as we used to."

In 1995, the country had nearly 6 million kids aged fourteen years and younger, according to Statistics Canada. In 2005, that number had dropped by almost 300,000, to less than 5.7 million.

"Hockey's share of that group of kids is a reasonably consistent percentage of what's available, but the number that's available is decreasing. And that decrease is only going to continue," said McCurdie.

Statistics Canada projects that over the next six years, the number of Canadian children under the age of fifteen will continue to decrease.

## ■■■ Taking the Initiative

The population in Newfoundland and Labrador is expected to be the oldest in the country in a

| Table 1: National under-15 population | | | |
|---|---|---|---|
| | **1995** | **2000** | **2005** |
| Population 0–14 (millions) | 5.973 | 5.884 | 5.686 |

| Table 2: Projections for under-15 population by year | |
|---|---|
| 2010 | 5,450,800 |
| 2011 | 5,421,900 |
| 2012 | 5,409,000 |
| 2013 | 5,408,800 |

| Table 3: Newfoundland population statistics | | |
|---|---|---|
| | **2001** | **2006** |
| Provincial under-15 population | 88,760 | 78,235 |

Source: Statistics Canada

few years. But Hockey Newfoundland executive director Craig Tulk said the province hasn't seen a drop in hockey registration yet.

"We're fairly stable with our registration numbers," he said. "A lot of our associations are offering programs that are keeping players in the game, which is great."

Instead of letting the population numbers dictate where registration will go, Tulk says Hockey Newfoundland is taking the initiative to attract players to the game.

"We understand that there are fewer children available to play hockey," Tulk said. "So we do things with local communities to ensure players that are in the community have an aptitude to play the game of hockey."

But if the province starts to have trouble holding its numbers, Tulk knows exactly where it's going to hit hardest—outside the cities.

### ■■■ Rural Areas in Tough

"Our biggest challenge is going to be the rural areas," Tulk said. "And whether or not they are going to be able to keep their arenas open, if you don't have enough children in that area.

"In the urban areas, even if numbers decline, there will be enough players there to maintain programs," he said.

McCurdie agrees.

"We're going to have a tough time in certain rural areas continuing to be able to put together hockey programs," he said.

Tulk says that one possible option is to combine struggling rural associations to keep things afloat.

It's an opinion seconded by Bryce Kulik, president of the Northern Ontario Hockey Association (NOHA), which has the same problem among its smaller communities.

"We do what we can to help, because it's the really small communities that are being devastated," he said. "(But) a lot of them don't want to lose their identity, and that's the problem.

"But it's time to put your pride in your pocket and save your minor hockey association," he said.

### ■■■ "People are Heading into the Cities"

Kulik says NOHA numbers have fluctuated around 1,500 kids for the past sixteen years, and he doesn't see a kid shortage being the big challenge for northern Ontario.

"Our winters are cold," he said, laughing.

Instead, a different trend could make things difficult for the NOHA.

"Our population is dropping up here. People don't like to admit to it, but it is," Kulik said.

"People are heading into the cities."

From 1981 to 2001, the national rural population hovered around 6 million people, according to Statistics Canada. In that time, Canada's urban population jumped from 18.5 million to 24 million.

"There's no question there's a little bit of a migration as a whole, from rural centres to more urban centres, and that puts a strain on urban facilities," said McCurdie.

"You can only shoehorn so many kids into those facilities," he said.

"Most cities in this country have waiting lists to play hockey. Most rural areas have all kinds of ice," he said.

### ■■■ More Recruitment Efforts Needed

Canada's demographic shifts are going to make it harder for some associations to keep their registration numbers steady.

That is why McCurdie thinks that a bigger recruitment effort needs to happen, from Hockey Canada all the way through to the local associations.

"Without a commitment to recruitment efforts, I think our registrations are going to be going down across the board," said McCurdie.

"Unless we change our thinking, accommodate the changing demographics in this country, we're going to be getting what we've always got, which is kids choosing to come to registration that day and that's it," he said.

"And in certain areas of the country, that's not going to be much."

◀◀ **Source:** This is part 2 of a series on the number of kids playing our national game, and why some are opting out. This article was originally published on "Our Game" on CBC News Online. Reprinted with permission.

RECYCLED
Paper made from
recycled material
FSC® C021757

Marquis Book Printing Inc.

Québec, Canada
2011

Printed on Silva Enviro 100% post-consumer EcoLogo certified paper,
processed chlorine free and manufactured using biogas energy.